Ancient Egypt

ANATOMY OF A CIVILIZATION

Second edition

Barry J. Kemp

 Routledge
Taylor & Francis Group

LONDON AND NEW YORK

First published 2006
by Routledge
2 Park Square, Milton Park, Abingdon, Oxon OX14 4RN

Simultaneously published in the USA and Canada
by Routledge
711 Third Avenue, New York, NY 10017 (8th Floor)

Routledge is an imprint of the Taylor & Francis Group, an informa business

© 2006 Barry J. Kemp

Typeset in Baskerville by The Running Head Limited, Cambridge

British Library Cataloguing in Publication Data
A catalogue record for this book is available from the British Library

Library of Congress Cataloging in Publication Data
Kemp, Barry J.
    Ancient Egypt: anatomy of a civilization / Barry J. Kemp.—2nd ed.
        p.   cm.
    Includes bibliographical references and index.
    1. Egypt—Civilization—to 332 BC I Title
DT61.K44 2005
932—dc22   2005007843

ISBN 10: 0–415–23549–9 (hbk)
ISBN 10: 0–415–23550–2 (pbk)
ISBN 13: 978–0–415–23549–5 (hbk)
ISBN 13: 978–0–415–23550–1 (pbk)

Printed and bound by CPI Group (UK) Ltd, Croydon, CR0 4YY

Ancient Egypt

This fully revised and updated edition of the bestselling *Ancient Egypt* seeks to identify what gave ancient Egypt its distinctive and enduring characteristics, ranging across material culture, the mindset of its people, and social and economic factors. It identifies the ideas by which the Egyptians organized their experience of the world and explains how they maintained a uniform style in their art and architecture across three thousand years, whilst accommodating substantial changes in outlook. The underlying aim is to relate ancient Egypt to the broader mainstream of our understanding of how all human societies function. This comprehensive survey of Egyptian society and history transforms our understanding of this remarkable civilization.

Ancient written documents often provide the essential information and these are used where necessary. However, the book highlights the contribution that archaeology makes, seeking an integration of sources. It uses numerous case studies, illustrating them with artwork expressly prepared for the book from specialist sources.

This revised edition adds new chapters on who, in ethnic terms, the ancient Egyptians were, and on the final ten centuries of ancient Egyptian civilization. Barry Kemp's book is an indispensable text for all students of ancient Egypt and for the general reader.

Barry Kemp is Professor of Egyptology at the University of Cambridge. He is the Field Director of the Egypt Exploration Society's excavations at El-Amarna.

Contents

Acknowledgements

I am indebted to the editorial staff at Routledge for urging on me a revised edition, and for patience in waiting for me to complete it long after I should have. Jerry Rose has saved me from several errors and inappropriate expressions in Chapter 1.

For illustrations thanks are due to the following for permission to reproduce photographs: Philipp von Zabern: Plate 4; The Egypt Exploration Society: Plate 10.

The drawings for Figures 2, 20, 59 and 96 were made by B. Garfi.

List of abbreviations

AEL   M. Lichtheim, *Ancient Egyptian literature: a book of readings*, 3 vols, Berkeley, Los Angeles, London, 1973–80

AfO   *Archiv für Orientforschung*

AJA   *American Journal of Archaeology*

AJSL   *American Journal of Semitic Languages*

ANET   J.B. Pritchard, ed., *Ancient Near Eastern texts, relating to the Old Testament*, third edition (with supplement), Princeton, NJ, 1969

ASAE   *Annales du Service des Antiquités de l'Égypte*

BAR   J.H. Breasted, *Ancient records of Egypt: historical documents*, 5 vols, Chicago, 1906–7

Bard, *Encyclopedia*   K.A. Bard, ed., *Encyclopedia of the archaeology of ancient Egypt*, London and New York, 1999

BIFAO   *Bulletin de l'Institut français d'archéologie orientale*

CAJ   *Cambridge Archaeological Journal*

CdE   *Chronique d'Égypte*

EA   *Egyptian Archaeology*

GM   *Göttinger Miszellen*

JAOS   *Journal of the American Oriental Society*

JARCE   *Journal of the American Research Center in Egypt*

JEA   *Journal of Egyptian Archaeology*

JEOL   *Jaarbericht van het Vooraziatisch-Egyptisch Genootschap 'Ex Oriente Lux'*

JESHO   *Journal of the Economic and Social History of the Orient*

JHS   *Journal of Hellenic Studies*

JNES   *Journal of Near Eastern Studies*

JSSEA   *Journal of the Society for the Study of Egyptian Antiquities*, Toronto

KRI   K.A. Kitchen, *Ramesside inscriptions: historical and biographical*, 7 vols, Oxford, 1968– in progress

KRI (trans.)   K.A. Kitchen, *Ramesside inscriptions, translated and annotated*. Oxford 1993– in progress

LAAA   (Liverpool) *Annals of Archaeology and Anthropology*

LD   C.R. Lepsius, ed., *Denkmaeler aus Aegypten und Aethiopien*, 6 vols in 12, Berlin, 1849–58

Lexikon   W. Helck and E. Otto (later W. Helck and W. Westendorf), eds, *Lexikon der Ägyptologie*, 7 vols, Wiesbaden, 1975–92

MDAIK   *Mitteilungen des Deutschen Archäologischen Instituts, Abteilung Kairo*

MDIAAK   *Mitteilungen des Deutschen Instituts für Ägyptische Altertumskunde in Kairo*

MDOG   *Mitteilungen der Deutschen Orient-Gesellschaft zu Berlin*

NARCE   *Newsletter, American Research Center in Egypt*

NSSEA   *Newsletter of the Society for the Study of Egyptian Antiquities*, Toronto

OMRO   *Oudheidkundige Mededelingen uit het Rijksmuseum van Oudheden te Leiden*

PM   B. Porter and R.L.B. Moss, *Topographical bibliography of ancient Egyptian hieroglyphic texts, reliefs, and paintings*, 8 vols, Oxford, 1927– second edition in progress

RdE   *Revue d'Égyptologie*

RdT   *Recueil de travaux relatifs à la philologie et à l'archéologie égyptiennes et assyriennes*

SAK   *Studien zur Altägyptischen Kultur*

Urk. IV   K. Sethe, *Urkunden der 18. Dynastie*, Leipzig, 1905–9

VA   *Varia Aegyptiaca*

ZÄS   *Zeitschrift für Ägyptische Sprache*

Introduction

In the mid-1980s the then history commissioning editor of Routledge, Andrew Wheatcroft, asked me to write a general book about ancient Egypt, which I duly did. I recall a wish somehow to convey an angry feeling that the story of ancient Egypt is simultaneously a record of human achievement in the distant past and a pointer to a future failure of humanity – which is with us now – to face the terrible destructive consequences of many of those achievements. I would like history to be a record of the struggle to be free of the craving for power already evident in the Bronze Age and subsequently twisted into even more awful shapes by fierce creeds and strict ideologies. Progress is there, to be sure, but it is painfully slow, fitful and subject to reversal. Rightness of cause as seen across the us-versus-them divide still ensnares too many minds. Since, however, I had not been asked to write a political polemic, my wish broke the surface only occasionally, and the same remains true of this revised edition. None the less, the longer view which archaeology and ancient history afford does invite one to take stock of how humanity has been faring for the last five thousand years. Remote though one's studies might appear to be, they are of events and processes which are parts of the continuum of which the current world is a product. Many deep-seated aspects of ancient societies have proved to be remarkably enduring, changing their clothes as fashions have moved on so that they ever seem a natural part of the contemporary landscape. They are mostly to do with collective identity and sources of authority, and especially deserve to be held up to critical scrutiny, for they are often the least benign parts of our inheritance.

In producing a revised edition I have tried to accomplish several things at once. One is simply an update on discoveries and newer publications, though with the latter I have been less thorough than I should like. I have responded to a suggestion that the later centuries be included as well, although this is not my speciality and has led to some of the earlier material being cut out. But part of the revision is also another stage in personal exploration, an attempt to clarify the meaning of the studies upon which I have been engaged for almost half a century. I have found myself returning time and again to ask myself the question of just what, whether we study ancient Egypt or our own present society, we are really looking at. I find a beginning in the most obvious fact of all. Past and present, we are all – readers of this text and ancient Egyptians alike – members of the same species, *Homo sapiens*, equipped with a brain that physically has remained unchanged since our species emerged. Abundant written sources from ancient Egypt confirm the conclusion that we all share, and have in the past shared, a common consciousness and substratum of unconscious behaviour. We all face the same basic experience, that of existing as a uniquely important individual, looking out into a world that recedes away from the circle of daily life to a wider society of common culture, to more distant and 'foreign' societies lying beyond, all within the context of earth and heavens and the powers of luck, fate, destiny, the will of supernatural beings and now the immutable forces of scientific laws. They come mixed up together, jostling for attention, and in thought and conversation we flit easily from one to another. We live and keep our reason by virtue of the way that our minds select from the ceaseless flood of experiences that crowd around and flow past us from birth to death and arrange what appears significant into patterns. Those patterns, and the responses that we make – fleetingly in speech and more permanently in the shape of institutions and monuments – are our culture. Culture begins as a mental therapy to protect us from being overwhelmed by the information that our senses collect, and through it we make sense of the world. On the one hand, therefore, I am trying to be an objective observer, examining evidence from ancient Egypt as if I were a botanist looking at species of ferns. Yet I can only make sense of the evidence by accepting that I myself am part of it, and how I join up the fragments depends upon the fact that I am human, too. There is no clear and absolute answer as to where the line should be drawn between too much empathy and too little.

One could argue that, since differences in personality and in local and temporal setting combine to ensure that no two people are ever quite the same, there have been as many cultures as there have been human beings. But in practice culture is a collective phenomenon. A characteristic of being human is a wish to be part of a broader group with a distinctive identity, founded in language, religion, citizenship, guild, local society and so on. Moreover, through hearsay and some of the written and visual signals of culture people imagine that they belong not only to the community which surrounds them but also to a broader 'people' or 'nation' which defines itself, at least in part, by how different it appears to be from others. Shared identity is one of the most powerful and alluring sources of mental order. It provides a ready-made answer to the question: who am I? It also provides a basis for separating myself as observer from the people who are the object of my study. The first chapter explores for ancient Egypt what that collective identity was, attempting to separate culture from ethnicity.

Creative minds within the community strengthen the bonds of identity by means of myth and symbol, fashioning ideologies. Ambitious individuals create from the framework a basis of power, establishing systems of conduct which direct the energies and resources of others. The history of the world is not an account of the development of innumerable pools of merging cultures and points of consciousness. It is the record of the slow subjugation of people to polities of increasing size, ambition and complexity, sometimes with and sometimes without their consent. When they are small and 'primitive' we are accustomed to call them chiefdoms. When large, hierarchical and incorporating many specialist groups they become states. The state provides both the most practical framework within which we can study culture, and, at the same time, one of the most conspicuous aspects of culture. The nature of the ancient Egyptian state and its wealth of devices – myth, symbol and institution – to manipulate minds and to direct the lives of its people are at the centre of this book.

By these means the lives and views of a whole population are reduced to a singularity. This serves as a great convenience to all, including ourselves when looking at ancient Egypt. In treating them as a bloc we can say 'the ancient Egyptians did this', or we can move to a personification of the kind: 'Egypt in the New Kingdom expanded her empire'. The process extends beyond convenience. Extreme generalizing feeds our natural taste for story-telling and gossip which is helped along if we can also identify named leaders, Pharaohs in our case. They, their people treated as if a single individual, and enemies amongst their neighbours presented in the same way provide the ingredients for little dramas, in which dynasties rise and fall and battle honours are exchanged. Through journalism we perceive much of the contemporary world in the same way. I imagine that readers will mostly see this as a harmless form of shorthand. But it carries us at the same time into the realm of myth.

We live by myth and should not regard it as standing in opposition to rational knowledge. Myth and rational knowledge overlap when we use phrases like 'I am generally aware of', 'I have a smattering of knowledge of', and try to explain to others how genes and chromosomes work or what is the nature of electricity. Many of the facts are likely to be wrong, some of the elements misunderstood, and the general picture woefully incomplete. What matters is that it has the shape of a story and that is what myth really is. Myth is the more obviously story-telling form of what is otherwise called metaphor. It pervades the sciences although its presence in a particular form is often not wholly apparent until it has been discarded. The history of the sciences demonstrates how explanatory models are developed to meet the expectations of researchers for a time, but later are seen to be false when replaced by new models which are based upon better knowledge. What are those discarded explanations but myths? Much of what we think we know is provisional and relies upon our remarkable capacity to join up fragments and turn them into stories. Lack of observational knowledge is no hindrance, for invention and myth-making seamlessly fill the gaps.

If I am truthful with myself, much (perhaps all) of my knowledge of my special field – Egyptology – is of this kind. The sources that I work with are tangible things, 'facts'. They are tombstones in museums, pictures on temple walls, drawings of excavated pots. How they fit into a sensible set of explanations, however, requires a huge amount of creative infilling now embodied in traditions of understanding, nurtured in university departments which have been growing for more than two centuries. My ancient Egypt remains, none the less, very much an imagined world, though I hope that it is, like a marquee in a wind, pegged to the ground at many points. The pegs in the case of this book are the endnotes which relate my statements to a large body of literature which stores factual information and often instructions as to where, in a museum or at an archaeological site, the original source is to be found. This is the crucial difference between what we might term 'rational myth' – my ludicrously inadequate working-knowledge of nuclear physics, or my better informed but still largely speculative account of, say, the workings of the ancient Egyptian economy – and myth based wholly in the mind, on thought experiments. The history of thought has been of an increasing multiplication of myths, mostly of the former kind, allowing us to choose amongst them, and so giving us the power to discard those that we find inappropriate.

When looking at human societies, behind our imagined views of them, our extreme generalizations and the stories that historians compose, there lies a reality that is altogether very hard to come to terms with. A society is a system composed of all of its people, in the case of ancient Egypt somewhere between one and three million of them. As people they are individuals and within the system they are agents, each and every one, living within a matrix of opportunities for interaction. Yet no two are exactly the same, they are not equal performers. If we take one of the simplest physical attributes, body height, and plot a graph for how it varies in a population, we will find that most people's heights will group together towards the centre of the graph, but that increasingly fewer people will have heights which register further and further towards the taller and shorter extremes. The graph will shape itself like the profile of a bell. What is true for height is true for every-thing else, from assertiveness to resistance to illness, from intelligence to athletic prowess. Each person is situated at a particular point on an innumerable array of curves which describe different human characteristics. Moreover, from population to population the norms themselves vary, whether they concern body height or willingness to die in a cause, and within the same population some degree of variation is to be expected over time and as circumstances change.

With each possessed of a unique set of attributes, people act out their lives within their opportunity space, at the very least with the purpose of survival and often of improve-ment to their lot. They unwittingly exchange illnesses, they communicate information, from gossip to revelations, they seek to emerge with satisfaction from a transaction, even if that transaction consists only of getting across a point of view. It is something one cannot avoid: lying low and attempting to do nothing is itself an act with repercussions, espe-cially if many people choose that course. Yet that matrix of opportunities for interaction – normal human life for a population – is far from being an even field. People are born into family groups which are themselves lesser systems and which, over the years, waver between increasing their standing and their property as a unit and subdividing again into new families sometimes through disputes. The process tends to be self-cancelling. One family's promotion is likely to be at the expense of another's decline so that a general degree of equilibrium maintains itself, but sets of circumstances arise – good fortune for those involved – which propel one family beyond normal expectations to a longer-lasting prominence, perhaps even, in traditional societies, to the founding of a ruling house. Those few individuals in whom, say, the urge to excel and dominate is unusually strong (Ram-eses II perhaps) will have a measurable effect on the system as a whole and might, for a brief time, drive it in a new direction or beyond its previous boundaries. But the system remains, albeit in an altered state, preserved through memory and cultural tradition. Fam-ilies are only one kind of lesser system, and perhaps more influential in the past than now. Institutions are another kind, and ancient Egypt possessed many, principally the court, the many temples and, in the later centuries, the army.

As the full population of the country constantly interacts, the system which they inhabit does not remain stable, as if it were a pot of water endlessly simmering on a low heat. It develops complex swirls of activity that, described at an instant of time, form the profile of that society. When followed over time, changes in the system's configuration are seen to feed back and become in turn influential, to tiny or to large extents, producing self-reinforcing trends. Certain patterns recur, but not in a way that is wholly predictable. Collective behaviour, which becomes history as the years pass, takes a non-linear course. If we keep to the metaphor of the simmering pot and substitute oil for the water, and turn up the heat, we will see the oil develop structure, in the form of visible hexagon-shaped flows which disperse the heat more rapidly. Those structures have their human counterparts in changes in belief and behaviour that usually come to our attention only by the time that they are fully formed and their genesis is lost.

How a mass of individuals interacts within a system in a way that becomes a fragment of history is apparent in modern stock markets in which, day by day, many thousands of transactions are made, each involving an element of judgement by the human actors or agents. Moods of confidence and uncertainty are the self-reinforcing factors. On seeing that many others are buying or are selling in a determined way, an individual is very likely to join them. In consequence of such herding behaviour, broad movements in favour of expansion alternate with broad movements in favour of contraction, the oddly named 'bull' and 'bear' markets. The stock market is measured daily in a single way, through the value of the individual stocks and of the companies whose credibility they represent, so it is possible to model and to simulate it with computer programs which incorporate the mathematics of complex non-linear systems.

Why is this not done for contemporary society as a whole? To have an adequate working model, constantly updated, ought to be hugely useful to social scientists, to politicians and to people who sell things. But think of what one would need: sample populations whose lives would be constantly documented, and ways and means of measuring their daily actions and changes of mood and state of health that were not crudely simplistic and took into account that dark submerged current of perversity which is bound to react against any system. If such a scheme existed, after it had been running for some years historians might, at last, be in control of their subject. For the moment, however, in the study of the past we are spared from having even to contemplate such a fantastic world, because information at that level of completeness and intrusiveness is lost for ever. The study of the past cannot, therefore, be anything other than an approximation, a fairly crude puppet-show. This does not prevent it from being both instructive and enjoyable, but it is important not to lose sight of the fact that the more we choose a narrative style of history, locate heroes and villains and tell a good story, the more we veer towards soap-opera and away from contemplating the infinitely complex human biomass that is a society and that is, in reality, almost beyond our reach.

Embedded within the myriad points of consciousness which lie at the heart of a population is the one factor which makes any study of human behaviour, whether it is ancient history or the modern stock market, so resistant to precise modelling and prediction even if we are armed with adequate data. That factor is perversity. Whilst one direction of human endeavour is towards inhabiting a stable system – a cosy home in a harmonious community under a benign government, at every level a triumph of order over chaos – it stands constantly in a tension with jagged moments or long-nurtured schemes of rejection. In most parts of the world the last five thousand years are a documented record of perversity and conflict. It has not been just the clash of armies. Fears of disorder and of alienation in a hostile world were a theme of thoughtful ancient Egyptian literature as far back as the early third millennium BC, and from time to time Egyptian society took on a more fragmented mode which promoted internal conflict. These are the so-called Intermediate Periods of ancient Egyptian history, and I will touch on them in Chapter 8. In the end, Egyptian culture was not destroyed by conquerors but from within. In the early centuries AD, enthusiastic Egyptian adherents of Christianity rejected altogether their cultural inheritance (by that time a mix of the Pharaonic and the Greek) and celebrated, in tales to encourage the faithful, the smashing up and burning of what survived of the old religion. Indeed, what mostly characterizes the history of humanity as a whole since the Neolithic is the conscious search for improved systems, and their simultaneous or subsequent compromise and even rejection. People are forever seeking to wreck and dismantle what others have built up or even what they themselves, in another mood, will approve of. Triumphs bring mockery, the tragedies of others provoke relish, iconoclasm destroys what others revere. It is not a simple cleavage into good and evil, for it is perversity which equally undermines inhumane and unpleasant systems. And it is through dissatisfaction that innovation arises.

What long-term function does contrary behaviour serve? Why are people so perverse? The creation of orderly regimes has been a regular aim of government since very early times, and it is very noticeable in ancient Egyptian sources. Why then are we not more ant-like than ants themselves? That many people evidently find the idea unwholesome only underlines the puzzle: why do we not *like* the idea of living an ordered and perhaps very comfortable hive-like existence?[1] In the long run, it seems, complacency is an unsustainable condition, hard-won stability an abhorrence. One answer comes from within the scientific community. There is a view that the 'purpose' of all activity including that of life itself is to disperse the universe's energy towards a state of final inertia, and that complex ways do this ever more effectively. Hence the paradox that progress towards total equilibrium in which all energy has been dispersed involves an increasing use of energy. Life steers itself towards ever more ambitious combinations of turbulence and complexity which yet require at the same time the constraints of order against which to react. This is the great paradox of existence. Everything provokes its opposite; everything needs its opposite in order to survive.

What is meant by energy when spoken of in the context of human societies and their history? We might think first of the more intensive production of food than would happen in nature and the use of natural resources generally; the creation of societies in which material expectations rise and population numbers increase so that the levels of exploitation also rise in turn; the picking on weaker neighbours, especially when, from the ashes of war, societies are renewed. But underlying them all is perversity itself, the wish for change born from dissatisfaction with the old and the attraction of something new. Over the last two thousand years the most powerful releasers of energy have been ideas which are simultaneously destructive and creative, which wreck an old order and seek to build a new one in its place.

Thoughtful Egyptians, very early on in their history, seem to have appreciated this endemic tension in the world as they saw it. The theme of order versus chaos is embedded within Egyptian thinking and produced some startling written portrayals of chaos let loose in the world. Their factual knowledge was vastly smaller than our own but they still wanted the grand stories to explain what existence really was. They expressed their explanations of the underlying forces at work in myth, and this makes it hard for us to grasp its essence, but if one can overcome the strangeness of having impersonal forces represented by gods and goddesses, sometimes with animal heads, in spirit the Egyptian universe was much closer to that of modern science than that created in the Middle Ages by Christian theology. I claim this because it was essentially an impersonal mechanistic universe. It did not give much place to the spatial relationships of sun, planets and stars. It concentrated on the essences of existence, free from the demeaning vagaries (and gross unfairnesses) of a god whose approval had to be sought. Within this universe order and chaos faced each other. And even though chaos had its myriad demons, everything was constrained towards an underlying harmony which affected mankind (mostly Egyptian 'mankind') through an acceptance that social ordering was part of the scheme, an aspect which was transferable to daily life and involved the role of the king. In the end, order – the Egyptian concept *maat* – prevails and stands in the place of unrule and so the outlook is optimistic. The phrase that the philosophy of science has made popular in recent times, 'systems standing on the edge of chaos', describes the Egyptian world-view quite well. Again, emphasizing the need to separate the symbolic language (which we are bound to find strange) from content, this seems to be a reasonable working model to have at the back of one's mind in contemplating what goes on in the world. More reasonable than that of the Judaeo-Christian tradition.

Reduced to this absolute level history becomes a tale of increasingly flamboyant ways by means of which energy is dispersed. If the outcome were to be wholly destructive then that end would be thwarted. Sufficient of what has evolved and developed must survive to allow the play – gaming is a powerful metaphor here – to move on and to rise to levels of ever greater complexity. A positive outcome of some sort is inherent in the process. It is thus entirely normal that society as a whole should experience progress, and equally normal that disruption and setback should be an inescapable accompaniment. The problem for the historian is that the preliminaries to times of change – they are not really 'causes' – lie almost wholly unrecorded within populations whose societies serve as the playing-field on which moods and ideas, opportunities and reactions to external factors endlessly compete for winning energy-consuming outcomes. We, as observers, arrive after each particular game has reached its end and know only the result and the names of a few players but not the myriad details of the play itself. One can sometimes pick out what seem to be causes for moments of drama – the ending of the Old Kingdom in Egypt is an example – but these can only be simplifications of quickening alterations in the patterns in which energy is being dispersed by the population as a whole. In this case perhaps a long stability was moving towards inertia and, in a reaction spontaneously taking shape, in the minds of sufficient people a preference developed for a more dynamic kind of society, in this case one which replaced a single central government with local centres of power, so bringing about armed conflict. No matter how elegant our construction of how this manifested itself in the fine details of who did what, the underlying reason why history took its particular course is that the background mood was in a state to respond in a particular way. Fantasies of violent change are wired into the human mind, yet most calls to arms fall flat because the time is not right, and most prophets and would-be rulers of the world pass their lives unheeded. A complete history would be one which explains why an infinite number of possible outcomes did not happen.

From this viewpoint how can one write a book about ancient Egypt? The honest answer is that one cannot. Most of the desirable evidence has irretrievably gone, ruling out any serious kind of quantification or deep exploration of what brought about changes. What remain are the conventional tools of metaphor and the tradition of arts-and-humanities essay writing on the broad themes that pervade the study of human thought and behaviour, as well as some control over the evidence selected. And a realization of the scale of our approximations and a generosity towards alternative interpretations. This latter is how the Egyptians themselves approached serious knowledge. For them complicated subjects were best expressed through parallel alternative explanations that did not require to be unified. Our own culture has grown not to like this, although in practice we acknowledge it every day.

In the scheme I have chosen, the first part, Chapters 1 to 3, serves to introduce the ancient Egyptians and the processes by which their culture and their state came into being. In essence it is a narrative of conflict resolution. The second part, Chapters 4 and 5, examines the processes at work which expressed an urge towards refining the degree of order that had already been achieved within society. It is about conscious efforts to improve the means of control. I have postponed a discussion of the contrary tendency, dissolution towards disorder when local identities provided a kind of safety net to limit the consequences, to the final chapter, in part because it serves as an introduction to the last thousand years of Egyptian history. In between are two chapters, 6 and 7, which, drawing largely on evidence from the New Kingdom, explore the complex balance that could be achieved when energies were directed peacefully towards refashioning the state and violently towards the conquest of neighbours.

I have wanted to convey the scope that frequently is there for more than one interpretation of the evidence, and what the limits are to the inferences that we can draw. And, in seeing myself as more an archaeologist than any other kind of enquirer, I have tried to make archaeological sources speak a little louder than they often do in books about ancient Egypt. Some will find the result idiosyncratic. But all should bear in mind the likelihood that survey and excavation in Egypt will continue indefinitely to bring in new archaeological evidence, especially evidence for the histories of local communities. By contrast, seeing how the rate of discovery of new written sources declined sharply during the last century, the current stock might well represent most of what we will ever have.

The Egyptian setting in space and time

Egypt's civilization developed in one of the largest arid desert areas in the world, larger than the whole of Europe. It was possible only because of the River Nile, which crosses an almost rainless desert from south to north carrying the waters of Lake Victoria more than 3,000 miles to the Mediterranean Sea. In ancient times Egypt was just the last 700 miles of this waterway, the stretch that begins at modern Aswan and the set of rapids known as the First Cataract. Along most of this course the Nile has scoured a deep and wide gorge in the desert plateau, and then built on its floor a thick layer of rich dark silt. It is this deep carpet of silt which has given the valley its astonishing fertility and transformed what might have been a geological curiosity into a densely populated agricultural country.

The Nile valley proper ends in the vicinity of Cairo, capital of Egypt since the Arab invasion of 641 AD. To the north the river flows out from the valley into a large bay in the coastline, now entirely choked with the same rich silt, to form a wide, flat delta over which the river meanders in two branches, the Damietta on the east and the Rosetta on the west. Anciently the branches numbered more than two. The delta now represents about two-thirds of the total arable land in Egypt. The striking two-fold division into valley and delta creates a natural boundary for administration particularly when viewed from Cairo or its ancient forebear, the city of Memphis. The ancient Egyptians recognized this by giving to each part a distinctive name and treating them as if they had once been independent

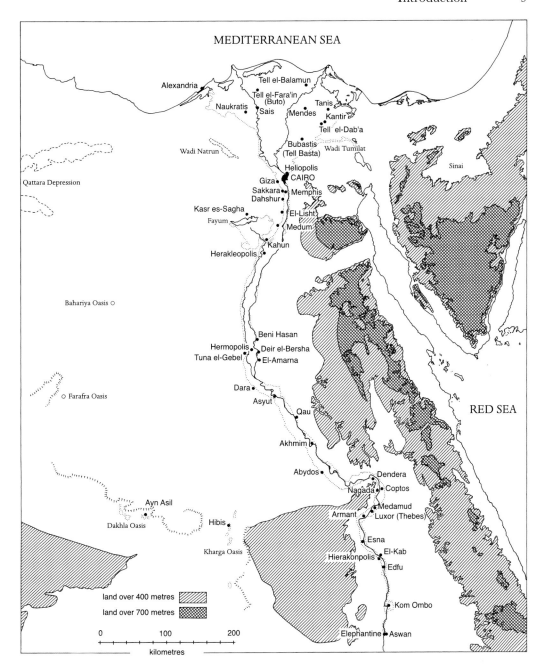

MEDITERRANEAN SEA

Alexandria

Tell el-Balamun

Tell el-Fara'in
(Buto)

Naukratis

Tanis

Sais

Mendes

Kantir

Tell el-Dab'a

Wadi Natrun

Bubastis
(Tell Basta)

Wadi Tumilat

Sinai

Qattara Depression

Heliopolis

CAIRO

Giza

Sakkara

Memphis

Dahshur

Kasr es-Sagha

El-Lisht

Fayum

Medum

Kahun

Herakleopolis

Bahariya Oasis

RED SEA

Beni Hasan

Hermopolis

Deir el-Bersha

Tuna el-Gebel

El-Amarna

Farafra Oasis

Dara

Asyut

Qau

Akhmim

Abydos

Dendera

Nagada

Coptos

Ayn Asil

Medamud

Armant

Luxor (Thebes)

Dakhla Oasis

Hibis

Esna

Kharga Oasis

El-Kab

Hierakonpolis

Edfu

Kom Ombo

land over 400 metres

land over 700 metres

Elephantine

Aswan

0   100   200

kilometres

Figure 1 Map of the northern Nile valley showing ancient Egyptian sites.

kingdoms. These names are conventionally translated as 'Upper Egypt' for the valley, and 'Lower Egypt' for the delta.

This is, however, something of an over-simplification. Upper Egypt has its own internal division in the vicinity of Asyut. This is apparent partly from observing the course of history, which has tended to reveal this division at times of internal weakness, and partly from topography. North of Asyut the west bank becomes broader, the western cliffs fade into a low escarpment, and the land is watered not only by the main course of the river but also by a winding parallel offshoot, the Bahr Yusef (Figure 1). Because of its distinctive character the term Middle Egypt is often used for the valley north of Asyut. The delta is topographically much more of a unity, but nevertheless tends to be seen by its inhabitants as having an eastern and a western side, the former joining the vital land-bridge to Asia across the Sinai Peninsula.

The arable lands of valley and delta today present a flat, unvarying landscape of intensively cultivated fields, crossed by irrigation and drainage canals, and studded with towns and villages half-hidden by groves of palm trees, and increasingly displaying signs of rapid growth and modernization. The transition from fields to desert is abrupt and striking. Civilization visibly ends along a clear line. On the east the desert plateau above the valley gradually rises to a distant range of jagged hills and mountains bordering the Red Sea, while on the west it stretches for a distance of more than three thousand miles to the Atlantic Ocean, an empty, silent, windswept land of gravel and sand.

The Nile receives two tributaries, the Blue Nile and the Atbara, both rising in the high, mountainous plateau of Ethiopia. The heavy summer rains in Ethiopia swell enormously the volume of these tributaries, and sweep down them a heavy load of sediment, rich in minerals. Since the middle of the nineteenth century AD this annual surge has increasingly been held back and controlled by a series of dams. Before that it was sufficient to flood the Egyptian valley and delta, transforming the country into a long shallow lake, towns and villages remaining on low islands linked by causeways (Plate 1).

As the current was checked some of the silt settled on to the land and was left behind when the waters receded in October and November. If crops were then sown in the thick wet mud, the moderate sunshine of autumn and winter would have ripened them by March or April with little or no need for further watering. Then, after the harvest in summer, the ground dried and cracked, enabling aeration to take place, which prevented water-logging and the excessive accumulation of salt. These three seasons formed the basic divisions of the ancient Egyptian calendar: *Akhet* (inundation), *Peret* (growing), and *Shemu* (drought).

It was an ideal natural cycle but one that human ingenuity could still do much to improve. Earthen banks could be raised to enclose large basins where the farmer could allow the waters to remain for a period before releasing them back into the river. Water could be raised mechanically to irrigate areas above the normal reach of the flood, or in summer, when the river was at its lowest, to irrigate the fields for a second crop or to maintain kitchen gardens through the year. Beyond this the waters of the Nile could be spread further and more efficiently by the creation of a system of irrigation and drainage canals, controlled by locks, and ultimately, as has been the case since the opening of the High Dam at Aswan in 1970, by damming back the flood and letting it out gradually so that the river level remains almost constant and never overflows its banks. In building up a picture of ancient society it is necessary to consider how far along this path of improvement the Egyptians went.

Plate 1   View of the city of Asyut at the height of the inundation, photographed early in the twentieth century. From L. Borchardt and H. Ricke, *Egypt: architecture, landscape, life of the people*, London, 1930, 120.

The answer appears to be: not very far at all. The need was not there. The idea of using the fertile land to grow cash-crops to be sold for profit abroad (as has happened in modern times with cotton and sugar) was far from the ancient way of thinking. Population grew only slowly and by the time of the late New Kingdom had probably not exceeded three million, a very modest total by today's standards. When we examine the ancient sources they suggest a very elementary picture of land management. The state remained very interested in the annual yield of the land for the purpose of collecting rents and taxes: this much is clear from ample written sources. But the same sources say little or nothing about irrigation. The implication is that this was a local matter outside government control. It suited everyone concerned to maintain the banks around the basins, and the annual filling of these by the flood left sufficient moisture in the soil for a single grain crop. There was a professional interest in the maximum height of each year's inundation. Records of this were carved on suitable markers: Nilometers or temple quays. But there is no evidence that the figures were used in calculations to assess crop yields, although people must have been very well aware of the consequences of flood levels either much higher or much lower than the average.

Modern irrigation in Egypt involves not only regulating the flow and availability of water from the Nile via networks of canals, but also the use of machines for lifting it up to ground level. Nowadays a range of machines is to be seen. Anciently there was only one: the *shaduf*, a device of simple construction, a pivoted, horizontal pole with a counterweight

Figure 2 Cultivating perennial gardens: the original method. Water is carried to the square growing-beds in pairs of pottery jars suspended on wooden yokes. On the right a man kneels planting a lettuce in a hole made with a stick. Tomb of Mereruka, Sakkara, *c.* 2300 BC, after P. Duell, *The mastaba of Mereruka* I, Chicago, 1938, Pl. 21 (redrawn by B. Garfi).

at one end and a bucket or its equivalent suspended at the other (Figure 3). It occurs in tomb scenes from the late 18th Dynasty (*c.* 1350 BC) onwards, but even then only in scenes of men watering gardens. In earlier versions, before the 18th Dynasty, the method was even cruder. We see water brought to gardens in pairs of pottery jars slung from yokes on the shoulders of men (Figure 2). In such scenes we are clearly dealing not with the irrigation of farmland for the production of a main crop of cereal or flax, but with the watering of only a limited amount of land out of reach of the flood, and confined to vegetable- and flower-beds and orchards maintained all the year round. This evidence serves to reinforce the argument that main-crop cereal agriculture was a matter of a single annual crop dependent upon moisture left in the soil after the inundation.

The importance of appreciating this is not just that it provides the background picture to life in ancient Egypt. It has sometimes been thought that organized society – civilization – in Egypt and elsewhere arose from the need for collective effort to control rivers to allow agriculture to develop. In the case of ancient Egypt one can state that this was not so. The origin of civilization is not to be sought in something so simple. It is true that modern Egypt is maintained by an elaborate irrigation system. This is necessary, however, only because of the development of agriculture as a business, and on account of the massive increase in population that has occurred in the last two centuries.

Modern Egypt is an Arabic-speaking country, predominantly Islamic in religion, and secular in laws and institutions, the product of thirteen hundred years of Arab and Ottoman rule and influence since the first Arab invasion of 641 AD, modified by the country's Mediterranean position. Even by the time of the Arab conquest, however, the ancient Egypt of the Pharaohs lay far in the past. We can formally recognize its end with the conquest of Egypt by Alexander the Great in 332 BC, which initiated three centuries of rule by Macedonian kings (the Ptolemies) who managed to live in Greek style in Alexandria whilst still posing as Pharaohs for the benefit of the more traditionally-minded parts

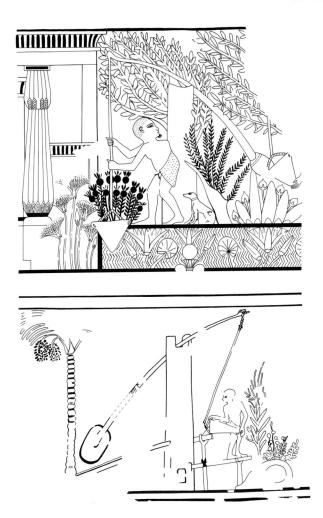

Figure 3 Cultivating perennial gardens and orchards: the improved New Kingdom method, using a *shaduf*. The top scene shows a simple *shaduf* being used to irrigate a garden beside a shrine. The man (his dog behind him) stands on the bank of a canal and pulls down the vertical pole to dip the suspended bucket into the water. The long pivoting beam of the *shaduf* rests on a tall brick pillar, and has a rounded counterweight of mud at its opposite end. The bucket of a second *shaduf* is being emptied at the right-hand edge of the picture. Tomb of Ipy, Thebes, *c.* 1250 BC, after N. de G. Davies, *Two Ramesside tombs at Thebes*, New York, 1927, Pl. XXIX. In the bottom scene a more complicated *shaduf* is shown in operation. It stands beside a well, at the right-hand edge of the picture, over which projects a platform for the operator. This man is emptying the bucket into a raised trough which passes through the brick *shaduf*-pillar and runs down to irrigate an orchard. Tomb of Neferhetep, Thebes, *c.* 1325 BC, after N. de G. Davies, *The tomb of Nefer-hotep at Thebes*, New York, 1933, Pl. XLVI.

of the country. The last of the line was Queen Cleopatra VII (*the* Cleopatra). Subsequently, as a province first of the Roman and later of the Byzantine Empire, Egypt became a fervently Christian country. The Christian legacy in modern Egypt is the Coptic church. Its language, no longer spoken but preserved in liturgy and in scriptural translations, is the language of ancient Egypt shorn of hieroglyphic writing.

These three great infusions of outside culture – Hellenistic Greek, Christian, Arab – effectively destroyed the indigenous Nile valley culture of ancient times, sometimes by a process of gradual modification, sometimes by deliberate attack. Modern knowledge of ancient Egypt is, therefore, the result of reconstruction by scholars. It has two main sources: study of ancient evidence revealed by archaeology, and careful reading of the accounts of Classical times, some made by Greek visitors during the last centuries of Pharaonic rule, some written from within the country. In the early days of Egyptology one of the latter provided a ready-made framework of history and chronology, which is still universally accepted. It is a set of summaries of a now-lost History of Egypt written in Greek in the third century BC by an Egyptian priest, Manetho. Despite inaccuracies introduced by copyists, Manetho's access to temple archives gave his work a degree of detail and authority which has stood the test of time. In particular, his division of Egyptian history into thirty dynasties, or ruling families (to which a thirty-first was subsequently added), still provides the basic framework of history. For convenience, however, modern scholars have grouped Manetho's dynasties into broader units, as follows:

Predynastic Periods (Neolithic)	*c.* 5300–3000 BC
Early Dynastic Period (Dynasties 1–2)	*c.* 3000–2686 BC (or Archaic Period)
Old Kingdom (Dynasties 3–8)	2686–2160 BC
First Intermediate Period (Dynasties 9–mid-11)	2160–2055 BC
Middle Kingdom (Dynasties mid-11–13/14)	2055–1650 BC
Second Intermediate Period (Dynasties 15–17)	1650–1550 BC (includes the Palestinian 'Hyksos' Dynasty in the north of Egypt)
New Kingdom (Dynasties 18–20)	1550–1069 BC
Third Intermediate Period (Dynasties 21–24)	1069–715 BC
Late Period	715–332 BC
Kushite (Sudanese)/Assyrian rule (Dynasty 25)	747–656 BC
Saite Period (Dynasty 26)	664–525 BC
First Persian Period (Dynasty 27)	525–359 BC
Local dynasties (Dynasties 28–30)	359–343 BC
Second Persian Period ('Dynasty 31')	343–332 BC
Conquest by Alexander the Great	332 BC
Ptolemaic Period	332–30 BC
Death of Queen Cleopatra VII	30 BC
Roman Period	30 BC–AD 395
Egypt ruled from Byzantium (Constantinople or Istanbul)	AD 395–641
Arab conquest of Egypt	AD 641

Before the 1st Dynasty came a period of advanced Neolithic culture often called the 'Predynastic'. This lasted for somewhat less than a millennium although its roots in earlier Neolithic cultures extend back to the sixth millennium BC. For the Predynastic of Upper Egypt more than one set of terms is currently in use for the succession of individual cultural phases. The older scheme ran from the Badarian, through the Amratian to the Gerzean and then, via a somewhat ambiguous transition, to the 1st Dynasty. Subsequently Amratian and Gerzean were often replaced by the terms Nagada I and Nagada II, which still left the transitional period undefined. A re-division was proposed some years ago, which recognized three Nagada phases: I, II and III, and this has found much favour amongst scholars. Nagada III, it should be noted, overlaps with most of the 1st Dynasty.[2] They are, however, phases of culture, defined by styles of pottery and so on. Politically it is clear that with the last century or two of the Predynastic we are dealing with 'kings', and a useful general term for them is 'Dynasty 0'.

For absolute dates I have used the chronological table in I. Shaw, ed., *The Oxford History of Ancient Egypt*, Oxford, 2000, 479–83.

Part I
Establishing identity

1
Who were the ancient Egyptians?

Books about ancient Egypt take for granted that the ancient Egyptians were already, in essence, a nation. It is natural to say that the Egyptians believed in such and such a thing and acted in a certain way. Modern historians, however, might not altogether agree and ask: 'Are you sure? Are you not being naive?' For they tend to see the concept of nationhood and national consciousness as having begun in western Europe in the eighteenth century, and as having been somehow linked to the decline in the power of religion. Nationhood is, from this point of view, to be contrasted with large cultural systems that preceded it, in particular the 'religious community' and the 'dynastic realm'. Mediaeval Europe supplies the pre-modern norm. Its Christian religion and Latin language, and the transfers of rulership of huge swathes of territory through dynastic marriages and conquests, created loyalties and enmities that transcended boundaries of shared inheritance and common language. Henry II, King of England (and Wales) spoke French as his first language and owned and ruled almost the same amount of territory in France. This seems the antithesis of circumstances in which nationhood exists. Another example, very relevant to Egypt, is the Ottoman Empire which, in its heyday, extended from Budapest to Baghdad, from Cairo to the Caspian Sea, and held within its embrace many diverse societies, separated by language and local history. What unified them was Islam, the Arabic language (and to a lesser extent the Ottoman language of state business) and loyalty to the Sultan and to his representatives. Only in the wake of its collapse came the assertion of local identities which either transformed themselves into nations (as with Greece and Egypt, and the Ottoman heartland of Turkey) or, primarily in the Balkans, have struggled to do so through more than a century of communal violence which is still not at an end.[1]

Collective identity is an ancient, deeply felt, and sometimes rather murky attribute of humanity. It begins on the very local scale, and much of human history is concerned with its evolution. Early anthropologists recognized that human groups have passed through a series of stages of development, starting with the tiny band of hunters and progressing to the tribe, then to the chiefdom, and on finally to the state. This evolutionary scheme has to be broadly true because, at one end, the state has emerged as the dominant form of society in the modern world, and at the other end the hunter-gatherer bands which survived in the more remote regions of the world into modern times provide the best (in fact, the only) guide to interpreting the archaeological evidence from the Palaeolithic Period. But the route from one end to the other is not necessarily straightforward and in a single line. Each stage has a working stability, amounting to what is appropriate for its time and place. A society can progress to the next stage as circumstances change, or it can dissolve back into what we, if we have tidy minds, can see as a previous rung on the evolutionary ladder.[2]

Nor is the nation-state necessarily the final and topmost rung. Beyond it lies the potential of trans-national or trans-regional groupings which have been achieved in the past (often in the form of empires). India, the United States of America and China are examples that have managed to become 'natural' units; the voluntary union of European states aspires to something like this status; and in the 1960s the short-lived political union of Egypt, Syria and Libya as the United Arab Republic had the same aim. We still live in a politically transitional time.

The imagined community

Central to the concept of the nation:

> is an imagined political community . . . It is *imagined* because the members of even the smallest nation will never know most of their fellow-members, meet them, or even hear of them, yet in the minds of each lives the image of their communion.[3]

By this definition ancient Egypt passes the test reasonably well. The ancient Egyptians, speaking and writing a common language, occupying a territory with a well catalogued geography centred on the Nile valley and subscribing to a distinctive culture, imagined themselves as a single community. Central to that imagined community – and it is here that we meet the principal difference from modern nationhood – is that it was presided over by a dynasty of divine kings. Yet we should not emphasize this difference too much, for Egypt had an existence separate from Pharaoh and rulers were heavily obligated to maintain the integrity of 'Egypt'. They served it and were 'the herdsmen of mankind', the latter term meaning, of course, Egyptians (just one version of the conceit that anthropologists have found widely spread in the world of tribal societies, that 'we' alone are synonymous with true humanity). Moreover, kings owed their own unique position to the continuing existence of the country called Egypt that they ruled and of its wealth of traditions. The line of the Pharaohs and all the marks of their legitimacy to rule continued through the first millennium BC, even though by then the holders of the office were mostly of foreign origin.

Ancient Egypt provides an example of national consciousness which is sufficiently clear to create the impression that it was perhaps exceptional. Yet the careful study of modern smaller-scale societies reveals just how widespread is the sense of cultural identity amongst groups of people, frequently joined by a common language, and reinforced by a feeling of exclusiveness with respect to outsiders. They possess 'all the characteristics by which political scientists and philosophers habitually define "nations"'.[4] The growth of political structure from hunting band to state keeps in step with an evolution of the sense of identity. Even though the scale might be small the sense of group identity might be just as strong. To see them arising for the first time in conjunction with one another only in modern Europe is to take a very parochial view of the past.

The imagined community of the nation contrasts itself with the world outside. 'We' are special, 'they' are inferior and do strange things. The sense of community in the modern world is developed and maintained by diverse means, including the reading of newspapers the editorial policies of which promote national identity, most strongly by disparaging foreign peoples and nations. The Egyptians took pleasure in this kind of thinking. We meet it well developed in a piece of ancient Egyptian fiction, the Story of Sinuhe, a tale of temporary exile in Palestine endured by a courtier of the early 12th Dynasty who feels the need to flee as a result of accidental implication in a conspiracy to thwart the royal succession. The assumed readership is the Egyptian literate class and, although seemingly composed around 1950 BC, the story was still being copied as a school exercise seven centuries later.[5]

To leave his country, Sinuhe has to creep by night past the frontier fortress named 'The Walls of the Prince' which, he states, 'was made to repel the Asiatic and to crush the Sand-farers' (i.e. the Bedouin). Close to death in the desert he is rescued by one of these very same people, a passing cattle nomad who offers hospitality. In his subsequent exile in Palestine he exchanges his persona as an Egyptian courtier clad in fine linen for that of the head of a tribe, and is eventually forced to adopt the role most antithetical to that of the Egyptian scribal elite, the warrior who becomes the hero of personal combat. Despite his local success, there is no mistaking the sense of longing for the distant homeland, which is both a place and a community, namely Egypt. 'Come back to Egypt!' are the very words of the king's subsequent personal advice. At the heart of this longing is the thought that Egypt is the only proper place in which an Egyptian can be buried. Much emphasis is placed on this. To ease the pain of exile, the Palestinian ruler who befriends Sinuhe tellingly remarks on the linguistic aspect of community: 'You will be happy with me; you will hear the language of Egypt', evidently from other Egyptians who, he states, were already with him. Eventually, pardoned by a benign king, Sinuhe returns to Egypt, to an enthusiastic welcome and to an almost ritualistic shedding of the taint of foreignness: 'Years were removed from my body. I was shaved; my hair was combed. Thus was my squalor returned to the foreign land, my dress to the Sand-farers. I was clothed in fine linen; I was anointed with fine oil. I slept on a bed.' And a magnificent tomb with a gilded statue in its chapel was made for him at the king's expense.

It is all there: geographical frontiers, language, dress, bodily cleanliness, even sleeping on proper beds; and were not Egyptians lucky to be ruled by so powerful yet kindly and generous a king? By these marks Egypt was defined as a nation, which could still be imagined in these terms centuries later as the text was copied and read. It should be noted, none the less, that Sinuhe's picture of the 'Asiatics' is essentially a kindly one. They might be uncouth, but they behave with honour and kindness. They do not commit acts of savagery. Sinuhe inhabits a world, or at least a literary dimension, of civilized manners.

The term which Sinuhe uses throughout for 'Egypt' (*Kmt*) means literally the 'black land'. In other sources it is often contrasted with the 'red land', as in the reference to a mythical partitioning between the gods Horus and Seth: 'The whole of the Black Land is given to Horus, and all of the Red Land to Seth'.[6] It is thus reasonable to understand the pairing of the two terms as a contrast in basic soil colour: the black soil of the alluvial plain of the Nile and the sands and rocks of the desert which Egyptians included within

Figure 4   Foreigners in the Memphite tomb of Horemheb (*c.* 1330 BC). From left to right, in three groups, Asiatics, Nubians and Libyans. After G.T. Martin, *The Memphite Tomb of Horemheb, Commander-in-Chief of Tutʿankhamūn* I, London, 1989, Pls 116, 117.

a colour term which we conventionally translate as 'red' but which really embraced a wider palette. As for themselves the Egyptians often used a term which is sometimes to be appropriately translated 'the people' (as in 'people of Egypt' in Sinuhe) or more broadly as 'mankind'. It made them the centre of the universe; they were the norm. In a myth recorded in several royal tombs of the New Kingdom 'mankind' rebels against the aging sun-god Ra, who is in one place called 'the King of Upper and Lower Egypt'.[7] From his wrath they flee into the desert and are there pursued to destruction by an avenging goddess whose lust for blood is assuaged by red-pigmented beer being poured over the fields as if it were an inundation of the river Nile. The imagined location is clearly Egypt and 'mankind' are the Egyptian people. As the norm of humanity Egyptians as 'mankind' were to be contrasted with specific groups who lived in the other parts of the world known to them. At the furthest limits were the inhabitants of Punt (modern Eritrea) who were said to 'know nothing of mankind'.[8]

Egyptians delighted in type-casting their subdivisions of foreigners, and did so with deft caricatures (Figure 4). By means of clear conventions of classification, using facial shape, skin colour and dress, they identified particular groups: Nubians, Asiatics, Libyans, peoples from the Aegean, and from the eastern Sudanese/Eritrean land of Punt. These stereotypes came to life again in the nineteenth century AD as western scholars began to record the ancient monuments and thus to explore the ancient Egyptians' world through their eyes. It produced, for a while, a mood of over-confidence, in which the Egyptians' portrayals of foreigners were regarded as almost photographic representations of 'racial types', a subject then high on anthropologists' research agenda. 'The same form of head is characteristic of the Armenian to-day, though with a larger nose' was one such comment on a relief at the temple of Abu Simbel.[9] We have become more cautious with the evidence since then.

To complement racial stereotyping the Egyptians from time to time expressed demeaning opinions. 'The Asiatic is a crocodile on his bank. He snatches from a lonely road. He cannot seize from a populous town' is part of the advice of one king to his successor.[10]

> A coward is he [any Egyptian king] who is driven from his border, for the Nubian responds to the tone of voice. To answer him back is to make him retreat. Attack him, and he will turn his back. Retreat, and he will start attacking. They are not people to respect. They are wretches, craven-hearted

announces King Senusret III on his southern boundary stela.[11] Libyans who, in the time of Rameses III, threatened Egypt, are made to admit their folly in another Egyptian text:

> We have heard it said of Egypt from the time of our father's father: 'She is the one who breaks our back'. We have begged our own death by our own choice. Our very own legs have carried us to the fire.[12]

More often, the foreigner, when in the position of a foe, is simply designated by an adjective which seems most appropriately translated as 'vile'.

From pictures and words of this kind – and the examples are very numerous – we might paint a picture of the ancient Egyptians as racially exclusive. By the first millennium BC outsiders were already claiming this to be so. The Greek travel-writer and historian Herodotus, observing that 'no Egyptian, man or woman, will kiss a Greek, or use a Greek knife, cooking-spit, or cauldron, or even eat the flesh of a bull known to be clean, if it has been cut with a Greek knife', put this down to Egyptian distaste of any people who were prepared to sacrifice cows, sacred to the goddess Isis.[13] In a similar tone, the Jewish historians who put together the Old Testament around this time or even later, in compiling their parable-like tale of Egypt and Israel, explained the seating arrangements for a meal

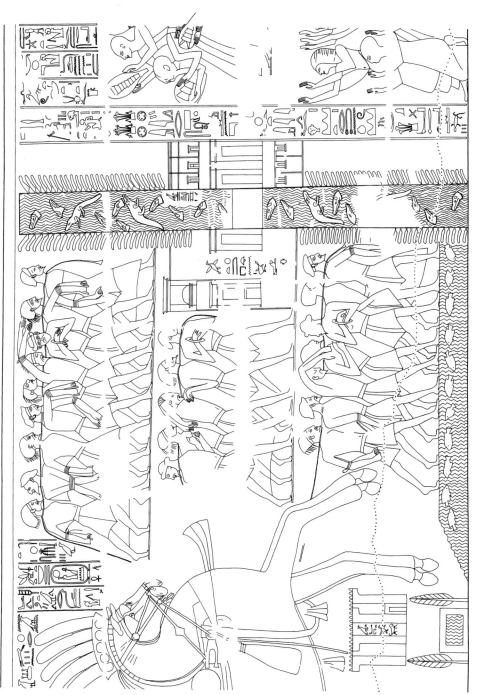

Egypt

frontier canal

north Sinai land route

at Joseph's house by saying: 'for the Egyptians cannot eat with the Hebrews, for that is detestable to the Egyptians'.[14] To what extent these are themselves caricatures made to pander to the intended home audiences is now hard to tell. For by contrast, sources from within Egypt point to a much greater variety of Egyptian response to foreigners in day-to-day affairs.

Building frontiers

The Egyptians attempted, by means of border controls at the corners of the delta and across the Nile in the south, to check the immigration of the Asiatics, Libyans and Nubians. The 'Walls of the Prince' which Sinuhe had to avoid was one such control. It has yet to be identified with an archaeological site, but its probable successor in the New Kingdom, by then named Tjaru (Sile), has been tentatively located at Tell el-Habwe not far from Kantara on the east side of the modern Suez Canal (Figure 5; also the map, Figure 13, p. 43).[15] Dating from a few reigns later than Sinuhe, the massive fortifications which the Egyptians erected to mark their southern frontier at Semna in Nubia survived to a remarkable degree until the 1960s (for notes and a plan see pp. 236–9 and Figure 88). A short text inscribed upon a stone tablet by the king who built them (1862 BC) makes their purpose explicit:

> The southern boundary which was created in the 8th year under the Majesty of King Senusret III to prevent any Nubian from passing it when faring northwards, whether on foot or by boat, as well as any cattle of the Nubians. An exception is a Nubian who shall come to barter at Iken [a fortified trading-post], or one with an official message.[16]

This is an echo of an even earlier text (an entry on the Palermo Stone, c. 2590 BC) which records the 'building the wall of the south and north-land (called) "the mansions of Sneferu"'.[17]

When immigrant pressure in the west, from Libyan tribes, became acute in the 19th Dynasty and was supported by landings of raiders from across the Mediterranean, a line of fortified settlements was constructed along the Mediterranean coast westwards from the Nile delta.[18] On the other side of the delta, in the reign of Merenptah a fortress controlled the eastern end of the Wadi Tumilat which offered an entry point from a more southerly crossing of the Sinai Peninsula (the text is translated below).

Figure 5   The frontier defences in the north-eastern Nile delta, depicted in part of the battle reliefs of Seti I at Karnak, 19th Dynasty, c. 1290 BC. The scene captures the ambiguity of such defences. The fortress and the crocodile-filled canal are to keep out foreigners who wish to enter Egypt of their own accord, but when captured and under Egyptian control the same foreigners are herded across to be forcibly settled in Egypt. The hieroglyphic label within the fortress in the bottom left corner reads: 'The lion's den'; that within the buildings on the left side of the canal: 'The fortress of Tjaru [Sile]'; that actually within the borders of the canal: 'The dividing canal'. Waiting to greet the returning king are the 'chief priests and mayors of Upper and Lower Egypt'. After The Epigraphic Survey, *The battle reliefs of King Sety I*, Chicago, 1986, Pl. 6, with additions (including all below the dotted line) from nineteenth-century AD copies provided by A.H. Gardiner, *JEA* 6 (1920), 100, Pl. XI.

None the less, it was not feasible to surround the whole country with a wall. There were innumerable entry points from the deserts to east and west and, of course, it was also possible (as Sinuhe did) to sneak past the border posts which did exist and which lay across commonly used routes of access. Their effectiveness depended to some extent upon patrolling the desert around them. One ancient witness to this practice is a papyrus roll of neat copies of letters sent to a central office (perhaps at Thebes) from Semna and from other fortresses which were spaced along the Nile in Nubia. One topic concerns a people whom the Egyptians called the Medjay and who lived in the valleys of the eastern desert. The Egyptians employed some as desert trackers as they sought to collect intelligence about the movements and intentions of strangers. One letter reports that a little group of other Medjay had been brought in for questioning; another that a different group of two men and three women had approached one of the forts asking for employment but had been sent away again.[19] Surveillance is the subject of a model letter included in a scribe's set of practice pieces which deals with the fortress mentioned above at the eastern end of the Wadi Tumilat (Tjeku: perhaps the archaeological site of Tell el-Maskhuta, see the map, Figure 13, p. 43):

> We have finished letting the Shasu tribes of Edom pass the fortress of Merenptah which is in Tjeku en route to the pools of Pi-Tum of Merenptah which are in the province of Tjeku, in order to sustain them and sustain their flocks through the good pleasure of Pharaoh . . . I have sent details to the place where my lord is, as well as other dates when the fortress of Merenptah in Tjeku was passed . . .[20]

It was acceptable to let them in for a while, but then to keep watch over them.

Opening the gates

These measures reflected a wish to control those who might enter and pose a threat to the lives and property of Egyptians. They did not aim to keep the country racially separate. Demeaning generalizations about foreigners and attempts to bar them from entering did not express absolute values but were heavily dependent upon context. Whatever their sense of superiority, Egyptians did not translate it into exclusion laws or into customs and behaviour which formed an effective barrier. Throughout its history Egypt took in and absorbed outsiders. For one thing, they could be useful. Through the recruitment of soldiers, and through the capture of prisoners on foreign campaigns, the numbers of those brought to the Nile valley who were available for the (to the scribal elite) distasteful tasks of fighting and labouring were swelled. Transferred to the Egyptian side, the cowardly foreigner became a valued warrior.

In the direction of Nubia, to the south, and towards the adjacent deserts, the practice of recruitment to serve in Egypt began at least as early as the Old Kingdom. Commissioned to raise a national army to counter a threat in Palestine, the high official Weni (a classic 'scribe' who bore civil and not military titles) extended his demand for soldiers beyond the provinces of Egypt to the peoples of five named Nubian homelands (one of them, Medja, the homeland of the Medjay, probably in the eastern desert) and of 'Libya', a conventional modern translation of a vague term for the western desert. Whether, when released from

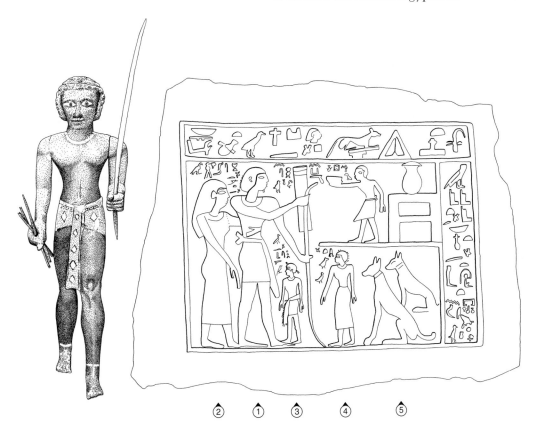

Figure 6   Nubian bowmen locally employed in Egypt in the First Intermediate Period. *Left.* One of the figures (35 cm high) in a wooden model of a Nubian troop, from the tomb of Mesehet, Asyut (Egyptian Museum, Cairo, CG 257). His skin colour is a darker red than that of Egyptian spearmen in a companion model from the same tomb. Whilst the latter wear a white undecorated loincloth, most of the Nubian garments consist of a red loincloth held in place with a green-blue waistband over which is tied a broad red sash, the ends of which hang down the front. Both the loincloth and the sash are decorated with large diamonds. There is sound archaeological evidence for interpreting the colour and decoration of the loincloth and sash as deriving from a myriad tiny coloured beads stitched to a cloth backing. After M. Bietak, *Mélanges Gamal Eddin Mokhtar* I, Cairo, 1985, Taf. IIIa. *Right.* Limestone tomb stela from Gebelein (Museum of Fine Arts, Boston 03.1848), 37 cm high. The hieroglyphs identify the owner (1) as a Nubian (Nehesy). He carries a bow and a bunch of arrows; dots around the edge of his hair distinguish it as tightly curled (as with figure no. 4), and he has a long sash over his loincloth. His wife (2) stands behind, and a son (3) in front, whose sash is shown as with a fringe. Behind him is a Nubian woman (4), perhaps a daughter, and two dogs; above (5) a 'butler' presents a drinking-bowl. The skin colour of (1) and (3) is a darker red than that of the butler (5), who is presumably an Egyptian. Both women are given a yellow skin colour. The hieroglyphic names are not easy to read but seem to be, in part, Egyptian. After H.G. Fischer, *Kush* 9 (1961), 57.

military service, they returned to their homes or settled in Egypt the source does not tell us. But the continuing presence of Nubians in Egypt as a recognizable group who could, in a reversal of roles, actually force Egyptians to work for them was recognized by a royal decree of the same period which gave protection against them (they are called 'friendly Nubians') as well as against a wide range of others who might prey on the property belonging to certain old religious endowments.[21]

Perhaps a century and a half later still, a group of Nubian bowmen were settled upstream from Thebes, in the vicinity of Gebelein, where a number of them were buried. Our only means of identification are small gravestones, the idiosyncratic hieroglyphs of which point to a date in the First Intermediate Period (Figure 6, *right*). They identify themselves as Nubians by sometimes using for themselves the clear Egyptian ethnic term for those who lived in the Nile valley south of Aswan, 'Nehesy' (which gave rise to the personal name Panehsy/Pinehas). They are shown with bushy hair, darker skin colour, and a distinctive sash which hangs down the front of their kilts. They carry bows and arrows and sometimes are attended by dogs. As riverine Nubians their cultural background is well known from excavations in Nubia itself and is quite distinctive. So far few traces of it have been found much to the north of Elephantine (Kubbaniya and Hierakonpolis are two sites, perhaps Gebelein is a third). In most of the material necessities of their lives they must have used things of Egyptian style, including the carved and inscribed gravestones furnished with the standard Egyptian offering-formula. Even further to the north, an Egyptian nobleman of the time, named Mesehet, included within his tomb at Asyut wooden models of a troop of Nubian archers and another of Egyptian spearmen (Figure 6, *left*). We identify them as Nubians on account of the darker paint used for their skin and their costume, but nothing from local archaeology identifies the presence of a Nubian population.[22]

These are examples, and they occur repeatedly, of a basic aspect of the archaeology of ancient Egypt. Even if immigrants retained for a time their own style of dress and other habits, and perhaps their own language, they tended rapidly to abandon the kind of cultural markers which survive best on archaeological sites, most particularly their own pottery. (This is true even for the Jewish colony of Elephantine of the fifth century BC, see pp. 364–6.) The history of the important subject of immigration has to be written largely from texts and from artistic representations, neither of which provide anything like a continuous and representative record.

From periods prior to the New Kingdom come sporadic records of Palestinians ('Asiatics') in Egypt, too. Some were brought as prisoners-of-war. A granite slab from the temple of Memphis (the Mit Rahina stela), in recording court events of the reign of Amenemhat II (*c.* 1900 BC), states that one campaign netted 1,554 'Asiatics'; another reference (to the same group?) deals with the dispersal of 'Asiatic women'.[23] One consequence of such dispersals is to be found in a papyrus (now in the Brooklyn Museum, USA) of the 13th Dynasty (*c.* 1745 BC) which includes a list of slaves in a large household, probably that of the vizier Resseneb son of the vizier Ankhu. There were originally ninety-five of them, for whom the slightly damaged text preserves the names and/or 'titles' of seventy-nine, two-thirds of them women. More than half of the names are preceded by the masculine and feminine variations of the word 'Asiatic' (i.e. 'Asiatic man'/'Asiatic woman'). In the remaining cases the term used is either 'king's servant' (male) or 'servant' (female), an indication that they are Egyptians. Already some of the Asiatics had taken the first steps towards assimilation. Eight of the Asiatic women are listed as having with them a son or daughter who all bear Egyptian names. One of the boys, whose Asiatic mother also bore an Egyptian name, is stated to have been the son of a 'skipper' whose non-ethnic designation and Egyptian name probably identify him as an Egyptian, too.[24] A later part of this book (in Chapter 5, pp. 211–21) describes the large planned Middle Kingdom town of Kahun, a royal foundation. That, too, supported contingents of Asiatics, male and female. This is known from papyri, but their presence is not to be deduced independently from archaeology.[25]

In the New Kingdom foreign campaigns were pursued with greater vigour and probably on a larger scale. The battle texts gloat over the massacre of enemies and of the terror they feel when Pharaoh attacks. Those who were captured, however, immediately became assets, were carefully counted and were sent back to Egypt to become part of the property of Pharaoh, or of the temples (virtually the same thing), or of men rewarded for their bravery by the king with gifts of prisoners. A temple text describes Rameses II as the king 'who carries off the land of Nubia to the delta, and the Asiatics to Nubia. He has placed the Bedouin (Shasu) in the land of the west and has settled the Libyans (Tjemehu) in the hill country (the east).'[26] Something similar is said of Rameses III concerning the Libyans, who, once captured, were 'made to cross the Nile, transported into Egypt and turned into garrisons of the victorious king'.[27]

Initially, at least, they could be kept together in ethnically distinct camps. Two stelae from the mortuary temple of Tuthmosis IV record the foundation of settlements for prisoners captured by the king, one group from the Palestinian city of Gezer and another from the Nubian lands of Kush. His son, Amenhetep III, surrounded his mortuary temple with settlements of Hurrians (Palestinians?), whilst a place name at Memphis, 'field of the Hittites', perhaps derived from another such camp.[28] Rameses III, in summarizing his achievements, adds telling details about the fate of captured groups: 'I established their leaders in strongholds bearing my name. I appointed among them chiefs of bowmen, leaders of the tribes, [they being] branded – made as slaves – with the cartouche of my name; their wives and children were treated similarly.'[29]

To assess the impact which this process had on the overall population of Egypt we need some indication of scale, although numbers from ancient texts are notoriously difficult to use with confidence. We have already encountered 1,554 as the number of 'Asiatics' captured on a Middle Kingdom expedition. Papyrus Harris I lists the following donations made by Rameses III to the temple of Amun: Syrian and Nubian settlements containing 2,607 persons; to the temple of Ra: 2,093 chariot-warriors and others (including Aperu, a Palestinian people); to the temple of Ptah: 205 Syrians and Nubians; and also a general donation of 971 Libyans (Meshwesh) for looking after herds.[30] We cannot, of course, check the reliability of these numbers. They are, however, hardly likely to be underestimates given that the purpose of the text was to record the achievements of the recently deceased king. Yet although hardly overwhelming they have to be set against the relatively small population of Egypt in antiquity. On a larger scale, Merenptah's Libyan war claims to have netted, as its principal batch of captives, an apparent total (the text is damaged) of 9,376 persons.[31] Far larger figures are given for Amenhetep II's second Palestinian campaign (Memphis stela), totalling around 100,000, including 36,300 Hurrians. Although they are said to be 'plunder which his majesty carried off', the numbers are sufficiently disproportionate to raise the suspicion that they are guesses at the total numbers of the populations involved. For one thing, if all were brought back and settled in Egypt the problems of dispersal and support would have been huge, given that this figure is around one-thirtieth of the total population (of around three million) which has been estimated

Figure 7 Brickmakers (left) and bricklayers and carriers (centre and right) as depicted in the tomb of Rekhmira, mid-18th Dynasty. The text on the right reads: 'The captives which His Majesty brought back for the projects of the temple of [Amun]'; the text to the left of the middle reads: 'Making bricks to rebuild the workshops [of Amun] in Karnak'. The modern copyist of the scene commented: 'Fair-skinned Syrians with blue or red (for brown) eyes mingle with darker Nubians, whose hair is dyed (?) red or blue and whose loincloths are of leather, and with others who are scarcely distinguishable from Egyptians', adding that the blue eye colour could stand for grey. After N. de G. Davies, *The tomb of Rekh-mi-reʿ at Thebes*, New York, 1943, 54–5, Pls LVIII, LIX; colour Pl. XVII.

for Egypt at this time.[32] A rare example with numbers from an even earlier period is the result of a Nubian campaign of Sneferu of the 4th Dynasty recorded on the Palermo Stone: 7,000 captives (as well as 200,000 sheep and goats).[33] If one chooses to accept the figure then one can make the case that this was a move to boost the labour force needed for the exceptional building programme of Sneferu, which embraced two major pyramids at Dahshur as well as possibly the completion of the pyramid at Medum.

One can form the impression that at times, and in places where large groups of people were gathered to work on great projects, especially monumental building, foreigners would have predominated (Figure 7). One witness document is a work record scribbled on a flake of limestone, which tells us that a gang labouring with stone blocks for a temple in western Thebes in the reign of Tuthmosis III comprised sixty Palestinians and only twenty 'men' (i.e. Egyptians).[34]

Where the battles were in Palestine and Syria, the captured places and defeated armies belonged, as was the case in Egypt, to slave-owning societies. For some of the prisoners, therefore, capture will have meant only an exchange of owners. The process continued in times of peace, when people from the same areas were sold into captivity in Egypt, although when numbers are cited they are relatively small. The annual tribute of 'Syrian slaves' listed in the annals of Tuthmosis III at Karnak varies between fifty-one and 702.[35] Some of the El-Amarna Letters of the late 18th Dynasty, which are likely to be more realistic than temple texts, occasionally mention slaves either as gifts to Pharaoh or given in exchange for gold or silver, and these numbers are also not large. The prince of Jerusalem, for example, sends ten slaves, twenty-one girls and eighty prisoners.[36] By contrast, when we read of 2,093 chariot-warriors assigned to the temple of Amun by Rameses III (the implication is that they are the king's captives from his battles), we are clearly dealing with men, probably mostly young men, from among the local elites now experiencing a great change of fortune.[37] The same social stratum is depicted in the tomb of Rekhmira, vizier to Tuthmosis III:

> Leading in the children of the princes of the southern lands, together with the children of the princes of the northern lands, carried off as the pick of the booty ... to fill the labour camps and to be the serfs of the temple estate of his father Amun.[38]

This treatment by the Egyptians of the defeated sounds somewhat less harsh than that meted out later during warfare amongst the slave-owning city-states of Greece and the Aegean in the fifth century BC, when the men of military age were put to death and the women passed into slavery.[39]

Once within Egypt they were turned into useful Egyptianized subjects. 'They hear the speech of mankind while following the king. He made their speech disappear, changing their tongues; and they travelled upon the road which [they] had not taken [before].' Captives from Nubia were 'turned into shield-bearers, charioteers, retainers and fanbearers attending the king'.[40] The Sherden allies of the Libyans, whose homeland lay across the Mediterranean (they probably gave their name to Sardinia), were particularly prized in the late New Kingdom as warriors, and they came to form separate contingents in the Egyptian army, keeping their distinctive headdress (Figure 8). They are worth singling out for we know something of their longer-term fate. A land-register from the fourth year of the reign of Rameses V (1143 BC) which covers a part of Middle Egypt lists Sherden amongst various categories of people who were cultivating farmland (probably under a lease). Also mentioned are a 'Village of the Soldiers' and a 'Village of the Army'. Together they suggest a policy of rewarding veteran soldiers with grants of land. We catch a glimpse of Sherden as normal members of local society in this same part of Egypt acting as witnesses to a legal document concerning family inheritance around the same time. The various processes of dispersal probably meant that no part of Egypt would have remained untouched by foreign settlement and that, for the long-settled local populations, encounters with foreigners would have been part of normal life.[41]

The ideal of peace achieved through the king's victories was, by the time of the Rameside kings, an ancient one. By this time, however, it was also officially recognized that select groups of loyal foreigners were essential to the process. A hymn of thanksgiving for Merenptah's having released Egypt from the fear of a Libyan invasion singles them out:

> Fortresses are left to themselves,
> Wells are open for the messengers' use.
> Bastioned ramparts are becalmed,
> Only sunlight wakens the watchmen;
> Medjay are stretched out asleep,
> Nau and Tekten are in the fields they love.[42]

Rameses III claims credit of the same kind:

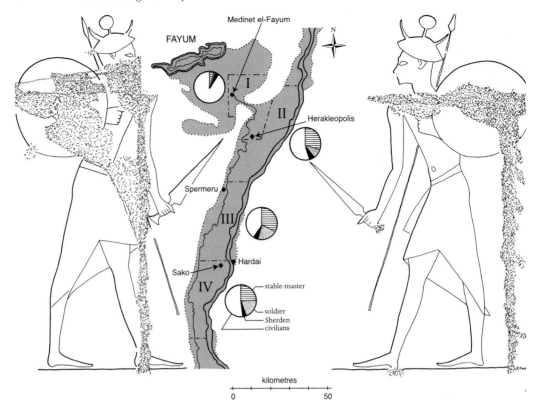

Figure 8 Military settlement in a portion of the Nile valley in Middle Egypt in the 20th Dynasty. The agricultural land is divided into four sections or zones, and against each one a pie-chart shows the relative proportions of four different categories of person renting land from institutions. The three shaded portions of each chart represent people connected with the military: stable-masters, soldiers and Sherden; the unshaded portion represents several groups who can broadly be regarded as civilians. The source of the information is not a full census but a large register of land rents (Papyrus Wilbour) which probably excludes much land in private ownership. To this extent the figures might be misleading. The four charts combined represent 1,571 individuals. After D. O'Connor, 'The geography of settlement in ancient Egypt', in P.J. Ucko, R. Tringham, and G.W. Dimbleby, eds, *Man, settlement and urbanism*, London, 1972, 691, Fig. 3 and p. 694, Table 5. The flanking figures are Sherden warriors, wearing their distinctive helmets and forming a bodyguard for Rameses II. After N.K. Sandars, *The Sea Peoples: warriors of the ancient Mediterranean*, revised edn, London, 1985, 109, Fig. 66.

I caused the infantry and the chariotry to rest in my time;
the Sherden and the Kehek were in their towns, laid out on their backs.
They had no fear, no enemy from Kush or foe from Syria.
Their bows and their weapons remained in their stores . . .
I sustained the entire land, the foreigners, the common folk, the citizens, the
general populace, men and women.[43]

The named groups in both of these passages are foreign soldiers, wholly at home in the landscape of a peaceful Egypt. With these admissions we can perhaps see the overt beginnings of the process by which the Egyptian identity was deconstructed, and Egypt eventually became a part of the trans-regional cultural systems that are so marked a feature of the Middle East as well as of Europe in the Classical and mediaeval periods. Chapter 8, the last in the book, takes a closer look at this process.

Becoming Egyptian

The bureaucractic side to ancient Egyptian society offered scope for maintaining official knowledge of every person's personal history. Thus a model letter:

> I have investigated [the matter of] the Syrian of the House of Thoth about whom you wrote to me. I have found that he was put as a field-labourer of the House of Thoth under your authority in year 3, second month of summer, day 10, from among the slaves of the ship's cargo brought back by the commander of the fortress. Note that his Syrian name is Nakady, son of Seleretjy, his mother being Kedy of the land of Arwad, a slave of the ship's cargo of this Temple in the ship of the captain Kel.[44]

But for how long would such records be maintained? We are still poorly informed about routes out of slavery but they clearly existed. Military service seems to have brought freedom to the Sherden. In a civilian example from the New Kingdom a slave has become so integral a part of the owner's family as not only to be given freedom but also a leading place in the family through marriage. The person making the declaration is a childless widow:

> We purchased the female slave Diniheteri and she gave birth to these three children, one male and two female, three in all. And I took them and nourished them and brought them up, and I have reached this day with them without them behaving badly towards me, but they dealt well with me, I having no son or daughter except them. And the stable-master Padiu entered my house and took Taamenne their elder sister to wife, he being related to me as my younger brother. And I accepted him for her and he is with her at this day. Now behold, I have made her a freewoman of the land of Pharaoh, and if she bear either son or daughter, they shall be freemen of the land of Pharaoh in exactly the same way.[45]

When the slave-owner was a temple a cosy relationship of this kind is less likely. Slave camps, however, must have created their own demographic pressure. They appear not to have been single-sex prisons but to have accommodated normal family structures. When first brought in, slaves will often have been at their reproductive peak and likely, therefore, to have reproduced at above their rate of replacement. We are more or less bound to accept that 'leakage' out of these camps happened all the time. Eventually, perhaps several generations onwards and as the circumstances of society changed, whole groups would have transferred into the general population. Moreover, from the point of view of the composition of the population of ancient Egypt, the degree of freedom which people had is of small importance. Although some doubtless fled back to their homeland, many immigrants must have remained resident for long enough to form part of the reproducing population.

Many lines of evidence leave the impression that the barriers which the Egyptians thought kept them separate from foreigners were, in practice, very permeable. We have no evidence that the Egyptians developed a concept of citizenship. If you were a slave you were registered and your life was controlled, but that was true for Egyptians and foreigners alike. Otherwise, birthplace and lineage seem to have had no clear standing in law. What was probably generally needed to stay on and avoid expulsion was to occupy a recognized niche – that of a foreign soldier was one – or to have the protection of an Egyptian patron, or in the end just the hope which immigrants have that they will not be noticed. From then on, an informal process of 'naturalization' and absorption into the Egyptian population was open. To be an Egyptian one simply acted the part. It was all a matter of style, of cultural statement.

Most important, it seems, was speaking Egyptian and, for a man of ambition, reading and writing it, too. Language must have come close to being the qualifying test for Egyptianness. It was a subject that required self-conscious study. As time passed, the spoken language changed, in grammar and in vocabulary. But by the New Kingdom the form of the written language of the Middle Kingdom (which in its time had presumably reflected the vernacular) was being carefully preserved through scribal schools. It gave access to old literature that was regarded as instructive and improving, and allowed an archaic feel to be maintained in texts which required an extra stamp of authority, usually those carved on temple walls. To join the elite, therefore, required a degree of dedicated language study. A close second to language was dress. From numberless artistic representations, from clear written statements, and from the many finds of textiles, the Egyptians reveal a deep attachment to white linen dress. Recall Sinuhe. Foreigners are, in part, distinguished by dressing differently, usually in the use of colour and probably by a greater use of wool.

Some immigrants went on to become members of the Egyptian scribal elite. These people are perhaps more likely to have come to Egypt as captives or hostages drawn from the aristocratic families of conquered places and allowed to retain their status at the Egyptian court. This was politically useful to the Egyptians, for as one text explains, 'if any one of these rulers [i.e. of a conquered city] died, His Majesty would send his son to stand in his place', the son having been an enforced resident at the Egyptian court.[46] In the New Kingdom such men often took an Egyptian 'loyalist' name built around the name of the king or the word for 'ruler', *heka*. An example is Ben-Ia (a Semitic name) called Pahekamen ('the ruler endures'), page and architect at the court of Tuthmosis III.[47] He shows his parents as a purely Egyptian couple (Figure 9). Does this mean that he was the son of immigrants or could this be a statement of cultured politeness on his part? Another example is Ben-Isina called Ramessu-emperre ('Rameses in the house of Ra'), who was fanbearer to Rameses II.[48] A class of courtiers of the Ramesside Period bore a title which, for convenience, we translate as 'royal butler'. A study of sixty-five of them reveals that fourteen (22 per cent) were definitely foreign and another sixteen (25 per cent) bore 'loyalist' names and so might have been foreign.[49] This is part of the background to the development of an 'international' court culture in Egypt about which more will be said in Chapter 6.

Figure 9 Just another ancient Egyptian couple? In his tomb at Thebes (no. 343) the Asiatic page at the court of Tuthmosis III, Ben-Ia called Pahekamen, honours his parents, shown here. The text above the couple reads: 'his beloved father Irtenna, justified before the great god; his beloved mother Tirkak, justified'. Their names are foreign, presumably Semitic, and the father has no title. Did they really move to Egypt following their son and become Egyptians, or did they remain behind in Syria or Palestine and their Egyptian appearance here is in deference to the son's aspirations? After *LAAA* 14 (1927), Pls 20, 23; *MDIAAK* 4 (1933), Taf. Vb.

A vivid example of the progress of transition, almost of pilgrimage, to the court circle of Egypt concerns members of aristocratic families from northern Nubia in the New Kingdom (Figure 10), an area firmly under Egyptian control by this time. In the tomb of the Egyptian viceroy of Kush, of the time of Tutankhamun, named Huy (*c.* 1330 BC), a group of them are painted with great skill. They are dark-skinned but dressed in the loose white robes of the Egyptian official class. The scene informs us by hieroglyphic label as to who they are. In front of (2) are the words 'Princes of Lower Nubia (Wawat)', whilst between (4) and (5) is the label 'Children of the princes of all the foreign lands'. The discretely placed label in front of the chest of (2) adds an unusual element of familiarity in naming the individual: 'Prince of Miam, Hekanefer'. We know from archaeological survey

Figure 10 The Nubian elite as seen by their Egyptian counterparts. A scene from the tomb of Huy. After N. de G. Davies and A.H. Gardiner, *The Tomb of Huy, Viceroy of Nubia in the reign of Tutᶜankhamūn (No. 40)*, London, 1926, 23–4, Pls XXIII, XXVII, XXVIII.

and excavation that Miam was simultaneously the name for an Egyptian colonial town in the vicinity of the modern village of Aniba, and a more extensive strip of the Nubian Nile valley. The actual tomb of Hekanefer is known, cut into an isolated hill of rock 25 kilometres upstream from the Egyptian town that had, in practice, taken over control of the Prince's territory.[50] Hekanefer is not likely to have been the name given to him at birth. This is not recorded. Hekanefer is a loyalist name which is likely to have been chosen by him or perhaps bestowed as an honour upon him through contact with the Egyptian court. It means 'The good ruler', in reference to Pharaoh. The fact that he is named in the viceroy's tomb suggests that he had accommodated himself well to his Egyptian masters, that he had made himself very useful or had established himself as the viceroy's personal friend. His fellow princes are not named (and the fact that the whole group numbers three need only be an indication of plurality), but we can make an informed guess as to who one of them was, at least. A little further upstream lay the Nubian territory called Tehkhet (in the vicinity of the modern village of Debeira) wherein were situated tombs of New Kingdom 'princes' of this territory.

The whole group in the painting is a careful study of cultural integration. Egyptian artists of the time exercised a degree of stylistic choice, between naturalism and stylization. In every aspect the artist has decided what effect he wants to convey. In the case of foreigners stylization normally meant ethnic caricature. Huy's artist, however, has followed a middle way. The skin colours are dark, alternately black and brown, a standard technique to help the viewer more easily distinguish individual figures. The facial profiles, however, lack the 'Negroid' features that artists commonly used for southerners and which Huy's artist himself used for other Nubians in the same scene (but not included in Figure 10). This group is special. With all his Nubians the artist has painted their hair with a yellow or reddish ground and then added thick black strokes to give it texture. This is in contrast to his Egyptians whose hair, as is normal, is rendered as an undifferentiated black area. Is this a sign of a Nubian custom of working clay into the hair? Whatever the reason, it has aided the artist in showing the hair of individuals (4) to (8) arranged in the manner of a fashionably dressed Egyptian. Indeed, these figures could be wearing Egyptian-style wigs. Most striking of all is that persons (4) to (8) are dressed wholly in white linen, in the billowing drapes which had become the height of fashion in the late 18th Dynasty. Individual (4), in dress and slim build, could pass as an Egyptian princess, except that on her and on the children the artist has added pairs of animal tails suspended from their elbows and, on the woman herself, a superabundance of armlets. These are people who are aspiring to be Egyptian courtiers but who have not yet quite made it. The standing woman (4) holds the attention, in part by an added degree of separation from the other figures. Is she Hekanefer's wife, or a daughter now resident at court? The four who stand behind her seem to be juveniles. Two of them, (5) and (7), have plaited sidelocks in their hair which in Egypt was a symbol of childhood. They are dressed as males but shown with body fat on the chest. What is their home ground? Are they now being brought up at court and preparing to adopt Egyptian names?

Huy's tomb scene is not the last word on Hekanefer and his family. The latter's tomb at Toshka was modelled on that of the viceroy Huy at Thebes, was decorated with Egyptian-style paintings (as were the tombs of his neighbours at Teh-Khet, see Figure 11), and accommodated burials which had also followed Egyptian practice. To Egyptians he remained a Nubian, but to his local community he presented himself as if he were an Egyptian. If his children had joined the court in Egypt, and had been fed, clothed and kept in some degree of luxury at the state's expense, they might have chosen to make their tomb in one of the court cemeteries, perhaps at Thebes or Memphis (Sakkara). Here, in their monument for posterity, they might well have chosen to appear wholly Egyptian and we probably would not be able to recognize their foreign birth.

The archaeology of immigration

Where archaeologists study prehistoric societies (for example, those of pre-Roman Europe) they confront a problem of explanation when the material culture of one region undergoes widespread change linked to the culture of another region. Does it represent a migration, perhaps even an invasion, or the fruits of more intensive trading? Preferring one explanation to another – trade or invasion – is often a matter of academic taste and fashion. For much of the time for ancient Egypt the situation is reversed. We know of foreign immigration and settlement not from archaeology at all but only from Egyptian texts and artistic representations. This is noteworthy in itself, for it suggests that immigrants very quickly abandoned the use of those things which tend to survive as part of the archaeological record: distinctive pottery, or jewellery, or burial customs. No one has yet recognized,

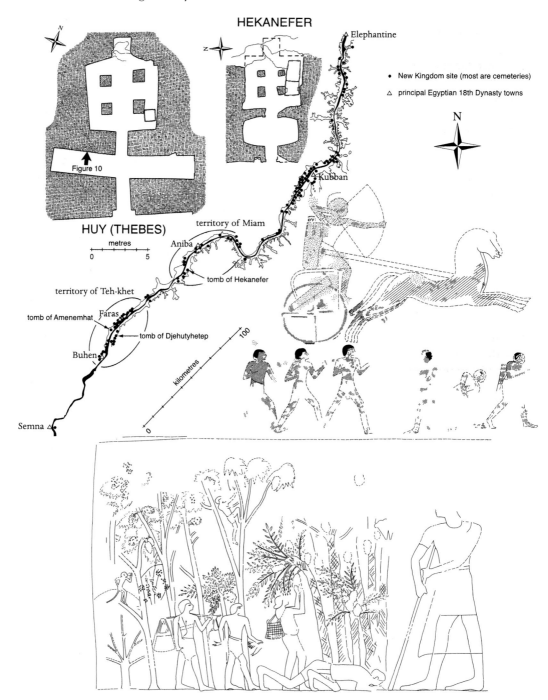

HEKANEFER

HUY (THEBES)

Figure 10

metres
0   5

△ Elephantine

● New Kingdom site (most are cemeteries)

△ principal Egyptian 18th Dynasty towns

N

Kubban

territory of Miam

Aniba △

tomb of Hekanefer

territory of Teh-khet

tomb of Amenemhat   Faras

tomb of Djehutyhetep

Buhen

100

kilometres

0

Semna △

for example, a cemetery of the Sherden people in Middle Egypt, or tombs or houses of Libyans from the Third Intermediate Period in the same area and across the western delta.[51] Yet we know they were living there from written sources. If these people retained their own language for use amongst themselves, they did not seek to write it down.

There are two notable exceptions. The first concerns a span of time that seems to have begun in the latter part of the Middle Kingdom and was brought to an end at the beginning of the New Kingdom. Two quite separate groups of people were involved, and this alone suggests the workings of factors that were not exclusive to one region.

In 1898/9 the archaeologist Flinders Petrie and his assistants, working along a series of desert-edge cemeteries in the vicinity of Dendera in Upper Egypt, encountered a category of 'shallow pan-shaped graves' in which the dead had been buried with objects which were a mix of pieces from a culture which bore resemblances to that of the prehistoric Egyptians, and of Egyptian objects which seemed to post-date the 12th Dynasty. In the ensuing years other sites of the same 'pan-grave' culture, a few of them desert-edge settlements, came to light, spread along the edge of the Nile valley in Upper Egypt as far north as the vicinity of Asyut (Figure 12). For a time a neat explanation applied. Pan-grave culture belonged to groups of warriors from the mountainous eastern desert, the Medjay (of the land of Medja), who were mentioned in a key text as having been employed by the Theban king Kamose in his battle against the occupying Hyksos Dynasty in the north of Egypt. Further investigation has shown, however, that the features that make up pan-grave culture occur far more extensively. They are to be found along the banks of the Nile through Lower Nubia, and their distinctive hand-made pottery occurs in the rubbish layers of Egyptian towns at least as far north as Memphis. It also seems to appear during the 13th Dynasty, thus some time before the civil war that ended the Second Intermediate Period.[52]

When pan-grave sites occur on their own they give the impression of having belonged to small groups of people, perhaps a single extended family. The inclusion in and around their tombs of the horns of goats, sheep, gazelle and oxen suggests that herding was part of their original way of life. They might indeed be the Medjay population from which Kamose drew special troops of warriors; but it was a population that had descended to settle in the Nile valley well before his time. The numbers in individual groups might have been small, but their geographical spread suggests that a significant episode of immigration

Figure 11 The Nubian elite as seen by themselves. The map shows the distribution of population in Lower Nubia during the New Kingdom (and mainly the 18th Dynasty) according to the results of archaeological survey. The approximate boundaries of two native princedoms, Miam and Teh-khet, are marked. One of the princes of Miam, Hekanefer, was the very same one identified by name in the tomb at Thebes of the Egyptian viceroy Huy (Figure 10, p. 36). The plan of Huy's tomb is shown in the top-left corner, the arrow marking the position of Hekanefer in the wall paintings. Hekanefer's own rock tomb within Miam is shown alongside at the same scale. It was clearly designed to have the same plan. The tombs of two of the princes of Teh-khet, Amenemhat and Djehutyhetep, lay on opposite banks of the Nile. Two of the paintings from Djehutyhetep's tomb are shown. In the upper scene the prince hunts in his chariot, a skill he is likely to have learnt at the Egyptian court. In the lower scene he inspects men who work in a plantation. Not only is he himself shown as if an Egyptian, so too are all of the men except for the one picking dates, who looks as if intended to be a Nubian. Map after B.G. Trigger, *History and settlement in Lower Nubia*, New Haven, Conn., 1965, 100, Fig. 3. Plan of Hekanefer's tomb after W.K. Simpson, *Heka-nefer and the dynastic material from Toshka and Arminna*, New Haven, Conn. and Philadelphia, Pa., 1963, 7, Fig. 4. Scenes from Djehutyhetep's tomb after T. Säve-Söderbergh, *Kush* 8 (1960), 32, Fig. 5; 39, Fig. 10.

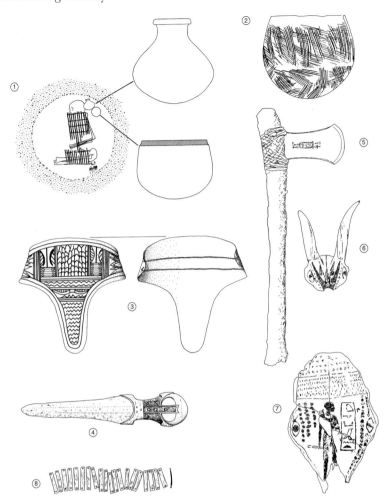

Figure 12 Immigrant culture: eastern desert settlers of the so-called pan-grave culture. (1) Grave, 1.65 m deep, for a single tightly contracted burial. It contained numerous small beads in addition to the two pots. The storage jar is of Egyptian style, the bowl (hand-made, with black top) is of a type favoured by these people. (2) A second example of a hand-made bowl, with a characteristic pattern of incised lines. (3) Decorated leather object worn by archers on the inside of their wrist and palm to protect them from the bow-string. (4) Composite dagger, the blade and handle-frame of copper alloy/bronze inlaid with wood and topped with an ivory pommel, the copper rivets fitted with silver washers. (5) An axe with a bronze blade lashed with leather thongs to its wooden handle, the blade incised with the name of a king Nebmaatra of the Second Intermediate Period. (6) Skull plate and horns of a goat, painted red and black with a pattern of eyes and lotus leaves. (7) Skull plate of an ox painted red and black with a pattern of eyes, dots, and a warrior with axe, club and shield which bears what is perhaps his name, Qeskanet, in hieroglyphs. (8) A favoured form of body decoration: small pierced strips of mother-of-pearl intended to be strung together. (1) and (3) are from Balabish. After G.A. Wainwright, *Balabish*, London, 1920, Pls XII, XIV, XV. (2) and (4)–(7) are from Mostagedda. After G. Brunton, *Mostagedda and the Tasian culture*, London, 1937, Pls LXXIV–LXXVII; W.V. Davies, *Catalogue of Egyptian antiquities in the British Museum* VII. *Tools and weapons* I. *Axes*, London, 1987, Pl. 18, no. 102. (8) is from Sayala in Nubia. After M. Bietak, *Ausgrabungen in Sayala-Nubien 1961–1965. Denkmäler der C-Gruppe und der Pan-Gräber-Kultur*, Vienna, 1966, Taf. 32.

had occurred, probably originating in the huge zone of the Sudanese Red Sea hills. Nor might it have been a quiet trickling in. A text at El-Kab, to the south of Thebes, records an attempted invasion by a coalition of southern peoples amongst whom the Medjay are mentioned.[53] The people of pan-grave sites could have been the terror of their Egyptian neighbours. By the end of the Second Intermediate Period some of the cemeteries show increasing Egyptianization in grave goods and burial customs, pointing to the absorption of these small communities into the local population. In the early New Kingdom the archaeological signs by which we identify them vanish altogether.

In the north of Egypt the same period saw immigration and settlement from Palestine, probably by the descendants of the people who had befriended Sinuhe. Elements of their culture, including pottery, metalwork and the distinctive practice of burying equids (donkeys) and sometimes sheep beside their graves, have been found in sites along the eastern side of the Nile delta and along the Wadi Tumulat, which extends a fertile finger eastwards towards the Gulf of Suez (Figure 13). Their presence is most famously documented at Tell el-Dab'a, a huge town site in the north-east delta. Called Avaris in ancient times, it became the fortified centre for the line of Palestinian kings, the Hyksos, who at this time ruled northern Egypt for just over a century and, for a short time, might even have ruled the whole country.[54]

The Egyptian texts that refer to this time express outrage directed against the 'Asiatic' character of the intruders in the north. It is not just their rulers. The Theban war against the Hyksos began with an attack on the town of Nefrusi (near Asyut), which is styled 'a nest of Asiatics'. What psychology is at work here? Does it represent a broadly based ethnic hatred or the language of dynastic advancement against an internal political challenge? In the initial war council, the Theban king Kamose alone is of this view. His courtiers express acceptance of the situation. But is this just a literary cliché intended to highlight Kamose's qualities of incisive leadership? Since we lack sources that cover the consequences of the Theban pacification of the north we are in a poor position to make a balanced judgement. From modern experience we can recognize the basis for purification, for ethnic cleansing, but was it seen in this way and executed? We do not know what attitude the Egyptian population of the north had towards the Palestinians amongst them, nor how they felt about being 'liberated' by an aggressive Theban family from the south. The war against the Hyksos started by King Kamose of Thebes could equally be seen as a civil war for the advantage of Thebes rather than as a war of 'national' liberation. The Theban texts express a combination of dynastic righteousness and a rejection of foreignness, but they are the only written sources we have.[55]

The second major exception to the normal rapid loss of identifying archaeological characteristics by immigrants takes us to a much later period of history. It is the settlement of Greeks in Egypt from the seventh century BC onwards, expressed in archaeological terms most strikingly at the Greek-Egyptian city of Naukratis in the western delta. I have reserved this for Chapter 8 (pp. 366–8, Figure 129).

These two episodes had very different consequences. Following the reassertion of Egyptian national culture at the hands of the kings of Thebes, who created the powerful state that we call the New Kingdom, almost overnight (as it seems from our distant perspective) the immigrant cultures of the Second Intermediate Period vanished. Their bearers, the Palestinians and eastern desert peoples, either left the country or were absorbed. The founding of Naukratis, however, was simply a first step in a widening spread of Greek culture which culminated in the development of Alexandria as one of the centres of Greek learning and as the capital of the ruling dynasty of the Ptolemies, whose culture was so thoroughly Greek that, so we are told, the last of the line (Queen Cleopatra VII) was actually the first to have spoken Egyptian.[56]

The difference in consequences reflects whether or not the content of immigrant culture attracted wider interest. Pan-grave pots and burial customs belonged to small bands of people whose unwritten culture might have been (for all that we can tell) intricately structured but evidently aroused no interest in outsiders and could not be transmitted further. The Greek pots of Naukratis, however, are only a tiny fragment of a culture whose scope and transmissability were so great that, in the end, elements of Egyptian culture were able to survive only by blending with it. Even the Egyptian language was gradually pushed to one side by Greek and, in the end, lived on in written form through the replacement of the hieroglyphic system by Greek letters (the script known as Coptic).

Land of promise

Many of the foreigners who ended up in Egypt were torn from their homes. But for some, the country's prosperity and opportunities were a lure. As far as we can tell, the desert people and the Palestinians who migrated to Upper Egypt and to the eastern delta respectively in the late Middle Kingdom and Second Intermediate Period, and who for a time retained their own culture, did so of their own choosing. They would have been distant forerunners of the Arabs and Bedouin who, after the Arab conquest of Egypt in 641 AD and in a process which was still active in the nineteenth century, set up their camps in Egypt and eventually merged with the existing population.

Migrancy in the modern world is a major political topic, made more urgent by the universal adoption by states of fixed frontiers and legal rules of residence. For the benefit of the established property-owning citizens, the whole world has become a police state. People still move, and in ever-increasing numbers, through fear and in response to hopes of a better life. But since the mid-twentieth century countries of migrant destination have had sufficiently robust systems of government to control the place in society that migrants occupy. Following the huge European migrations to the Americas, Australasia, parts of Africa and (in the case of Israel) the Middle East there seems no longer scope for migration by whole groups who keep their own hierarchies intact and seek to re-establish them either in unoccupied territory or within the confines of someone else's.

A relatively well documented case of this kind of transfer, of a complete society from one region to another, concerns the Libyans during the first millennium BC who feature so

Figure 13 Immigrant culture: Palestinian settlers of the Middle Bronze Age in the eastern delta. The grave is from their main site at Tell el-Dabʿa. (1) A supplementary pit containing the carcasses of sacrificed donkeys. (2) A narrow-bladed bronze battle-axe. (3) The blade of a bronze dagger. (4) and (5) Black polished Tell el-Yahudiya-style juglets in vogue at this time. (6) Scarab-shaped seal bearing the name of the 'Deputy treasurer, Aamu (Asiatic)'. The door jamb (*top left*), from the same site, bears the name of one their Egyptianized kings, 'the foreign prince, Seker-her (or Sikri-Haddu)'. After M. Bietak, *Avaris: the capital of the Hyksos: recent excavations at Tell el-Dabʿa*, London, 1996, 39, Fig. 34 (map); 66, Fig. 52 (door jamb); M. Bietak, *Tell el-Dabʿa* V, Vienna 1991, 51–60, grave A/II-l/12-Nr. 5, objects 4 (pot), 809 (scarab), 810 (dagger), 811 (axe); also 183, Abb. 140, object 8 (pot) from a different grave.

TELL EL-DAB'A

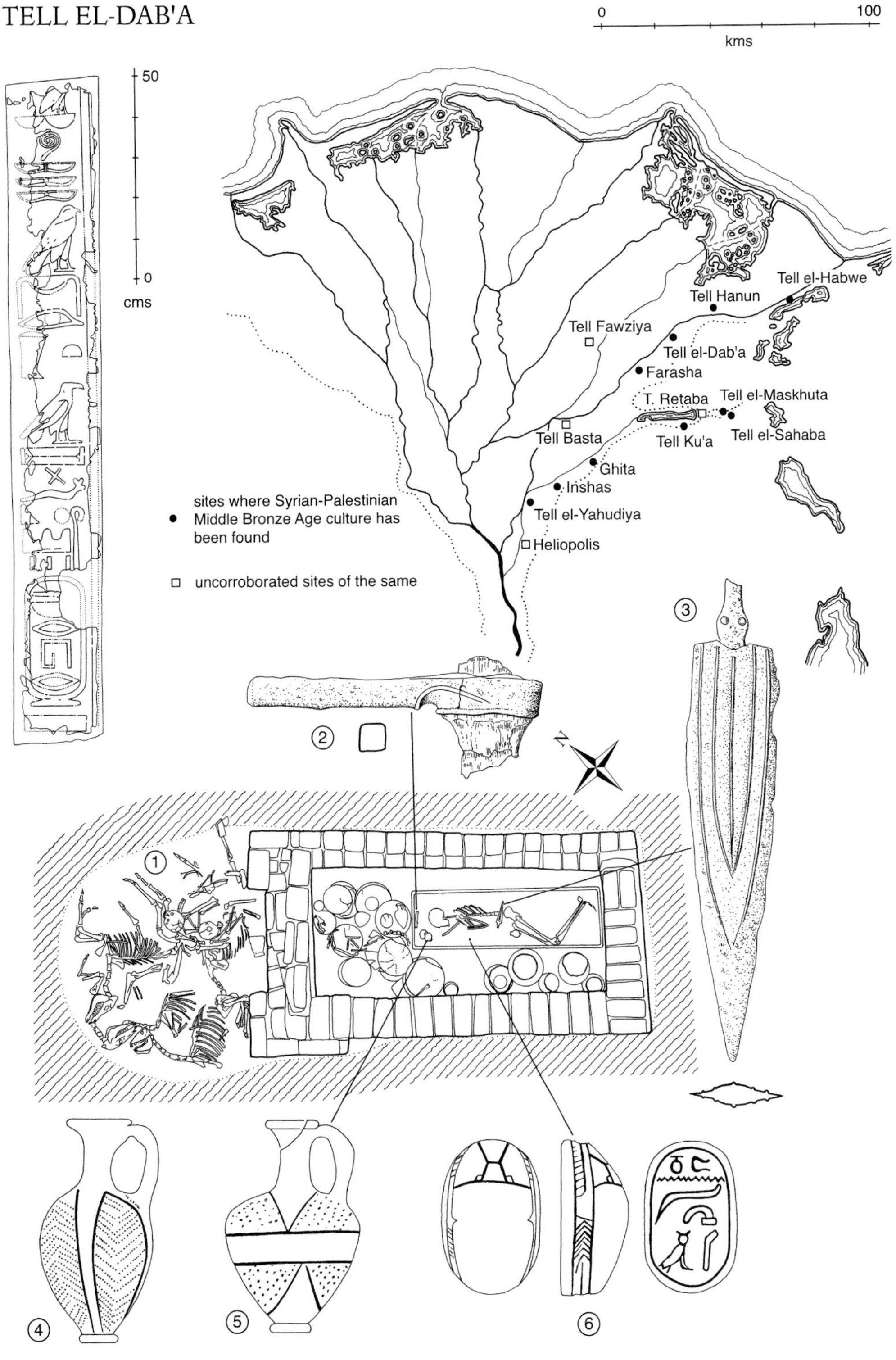

0
100
kms
50
0
cms
Tell el-Habwe
Tell Hanun
Tell Fawziya
Tell el-Dab'a
Farasha
T. Retaba
Tell el-Maskhuta
Tell Basta
Tell Ku'a
Tell el-Sahaba
Ghita
Inshas
Tell el-Yahudiya
Heliopolis
sites where Syrian-Palestinian Middle Bronze Age culture has been found
uncorroborated sites of the same
N
①
②
③
④
⑤
⑥

prominently as the enemy in Egyptian battle records of two to three centuries earlier. In a kind of reverse exodus, and despite the earlier defeats at the hands of the Egyptians, they successfully moved as a series of complete societies from homelands that must have lain along the Mediterranean coastal zone to the Nile valley. There they set themselves up in positions of authority, eventually becoming the rulers of large parts of the country. Early in this historical process the Egyptians began to identify them by more specific tribal names, primarily the 'Libu' (from which the modern name Libya derives) and the Meshwesh, who became the dominant group, as well as tribes called Isbet, Qayqasha, Shaytep, Hasa and Baqana. First in the reign of Merenptah and then in the reign of Rameses III the Egyptians fought battles against them that were recorded as overwhelming victories.[57]

Interspersed amidst the language of triumph are short passages of description. We learn from these that they had named leaders, Mariy son of Didi in the time of Merenptah, and Meshesher son of Keper in the time of Rameses III. They travelled with their wives, children, other leaders, a large number of followers, and with herds of animals, including cattle. They had tented camps (which the Egyptians burnt). As a pastoral people, however, they had undergone a transformation, for they came armed and otherwise equipped with the trappings of the military societies of the Mediterranean Bronze Age: with swords, horses and chariots, vessels of bronze and silver. Someone, it seems, had been supplying them with up-to-date weapons and the means to acquire real wealth. They were politically organized, too, for they had formed some sort of league with raiders from across the other side of the Mediterranean, people whom the Egyptians identified as Aqawasha, Turshu, Luku, Sherden, Shekelesh 'and the northerners who came from every land'. The background to this transformation of 'Libyan' societies is unknown, for so far there is remarkably little archaeological material (even from their presumed homelands) with which to supplement the Egyptian written and pictorial sources.[58]

The triumphalism of Egyptian battle texts was in vain. Over the next two centuries a large part of Egypt fell under the control of Libyan families whose men sometimes bore non-Egyptian names such as Sheshonk, Osorkon and Nemlut, and the title 'Great Chief of the Ma', an abbreviation for the Libyan tribal name Meshwesh. Some of them created local dynasties of kings. To judge from the scale of Libyan penetration it is entirely reasonable to conclude that, perhaps on more than one occasion and spread over a period of time, Egyptian armies were actually defeated and Libyan groups entered as victors and took over the government of many major cities by force (even though written sources do not document this). Although they kept something of their non-Egyptian identity (did they continue to speak their own language amongst themselves?), they ruled within the existing system and seem to have been particularly attracted to some of the most prestigious of the cults and priesthoods of Egypt. Two examples will suffice to illustrate this. One is a memorial stone set up in the Serapeum at Sakkara, which records the piety and generosity of the donor in arranging for the burial of a sacred Apis bull at a time close to the end of the Libyan political ascendancy of the 22nd Dynasty (Figure 14). The donor, Pasenhor, was both commander of an army and high priest of the cult of the god Heryshef at the provincial city of Herakleopolis in Middle Egypt. He added his genealogy, ascending back through fifteen generations. Some of his male ancestors were previous Libyan kings of Egypt, but most had been, like him, in charge of the temple of Heryshef. The earliest are also termed 'great chief', and the very first in the list is simply called 'the Libyan, Buyuwawa', presumably the patriarchal leader of a tribe before the descent into Egypt.[59]

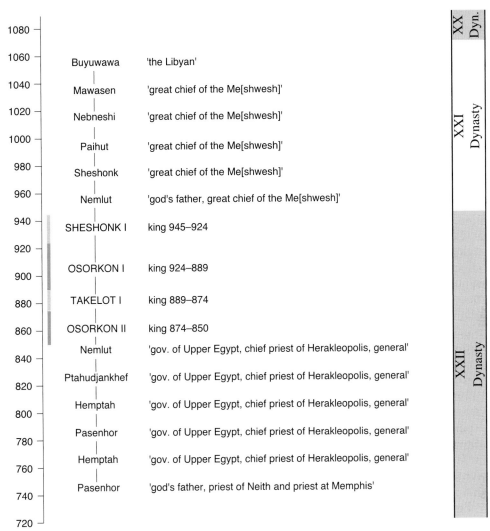

Figure 14 The genealogy of the priest Pasenhor who lived in the reign of Sheshonk V of the 22nd Dynasty. On a commemorative stela he lists fifteen generations of ancestors who included four kings and, before them, Libyan chiefs probably settled in Egypt (Nebneshi and Paihut are Egyptian names). The first ancestor he recognises, Buyuwawa, was perhaps the leader who brought the tribe into Egypt. If all the generations represent roughly the same length of time, Buyuwawa would have lived shortly after the end of the New Kingdom. The last of the ancestors to have a Libyan name was Nemlut. After K.A. Kitchen, *The Third Intermediate Period in Egypt (1100–650 BC)*, third edn, Warminster, 1995, 105–6, 488, Table 19.

The second example also concerns a high priest, of Amun at Karnak (Thebes). It has long been known that, at the end of the New Kingdom, southern Egypt came under the effective rule of the high priests. This should not be seen as a triumph of the clergy, however, since these men also possessed their own armies. The first, Herihor, bore an

Egyptian name, as did his wife, Nedjmet. As part of the decoration which he added to one of the Theban temples, dedicated to the god Khonsu, were pictures of his sons and daughters. Five of the nineteen sons have Libyan names: Masaharta, Maskaharta, Nawasun, Osorkon and probably Madenen. It seems likely that Herihor was either another of these successful Libyan soldier-settlers, or descended from one. The high priesthood of Amun remained under their control for three centuries, until the establishment of the Sudanese 25th Dynasty (see Chapter 8, pp. 343–6).[60]

As is so often the case with pre-modern history, it has been necessary so far to rely upon evidence that is hard to quantify and is often anecdotal. The tomb of 'Ben-Ia called Pahekamen' might be a nice illustration of a process of naturalization but how typical was it? At different periods what was the rate of immigration and absorption? The only possibility of quantification of population change lies in the study of actual human remains from ancient cemeteries, and the attempt to identify the ethnic origin of individuals or groups. This, however, leads to an altogether more controversial subject. For one thing, we need to have a baseline of comparison, thus an agreed view of what the early indigenous population of Egypt looked like, and to whom they were most closely related, even perhaps from where they came.

The peopling of Egypt

'White (Caucasian) male, in his mid-sixties, height 5 feet 9 inches (1.75 metres), weight 150 pounds (68 kilos) . . .' So a police file might describe me. The broadly phrased racial categorization is normal and is an aid to recognition, at least in my own country and the USA. It extends back into the skeleton where it becomes a means of helping to establish the identity of decayed human remains in police cases. As long as one keeps to very broad categories, groups of certain skeletal traits turn out to offer a highly reliable guide to placing the bones of an individual within one category or another. Since these methods and categories become evidence to be tested in law courts they can be said to possess a reasonable degree of objectivity. The racial categories which are defined in forensic manuals are three: Mongoloids, Blacks or Negroids, and Whites or Caucasoids. An example of the criteria is the shape of the nasal aperture: very broad and lacking a sharp lower border in Blacks, and very narrow and with a prominent sharp lower border in Whites. Its exact breadth, when combined with other measurements in a carefully constructed scoring system and definitions of scope, provides an arithmetical basis for identifying race based on modern reference populations of the USA. At the skeletal level, defined in this broadest of fashions, I share my 'whiteness' with peoples of North Africa and India.[61]

The reason for making this point is that conventionally the boundary between Caucasoids and Negroids runs through North Africa, passing across the Nile valley well to the south of Egypt, in the northern Sudan. Egyptians are thus classed as Caucasoids, along with the peoples of the Middle East, India and Europe. What is a broad classification of convenience becomes politically contentious when the ancient Egyptians are also put into this group, and by implication a truly 'African' origin for ancient Egyptian civilization – to which black Africans of all parts of the continent, as well as Afro-Caribbeans, can look with pride as part of their heritage – seems to be questioned.[62] Although the modern practice of racial identification is intended to be neutral and descriptive, it easily slides, in the case of ancient Egypt, into a concept of ancestral homelands. Might not the evidence show that the Egyptians, as Caucasoids, ultimately came from the eastern Mediterranean and Middle East? Discussions took this course even into the 1950s, most notably on the theme that the development of Egyptian civilization was given a vigorous push by the immigration around the beginning of the 1st Dynasty of a forceful and intelligent people from the east, the 'dynastic race', who came to dominate the existing population of predominantly Negroid type. Today these are troubled waters which most people who write about ancient Egypt from within the mainstream of scholarship avoid.[63]

Groupings as broad as this do not correspond with most people's conceptions of 'race', which recognize more finely divided stereotypes. The 'whiteness' which I share with people from the Maghreb and the Punjab is obviously far from 'street' experience. Although skin colour and other superficial aspects play an important part, it has long been apparent that genetic distances between populations (the modern euphemistic phrasing for 'race') are reflected in sets of precise measurements taken at agreed points or along agreed lines on the skull. Much thought has been given to ways of pooling sets of skull measurements to produce a convenient and statistically valid single summary measure, an 'index', by which a given ancient population, from say an Early Dynastic cemetery from Abydos, can be compared with an index similarly derived for other groups. But there are many reasons to be cautious in evaluating the results of such studies.

Unless a population has been isolated to an unusual extent (in a way that did not happen in ancient Egypt), the physical, including facial, features of individuals within a population can be expected to display a degree of variation which can be quite wide and which may overlap with that present in a different population. One of the aims of modern studies by anthropologists is to determine whether a particular set of people resembled one another closely or not. Did the population in question tend towards homogeneity or heterogeneity? The general reader wanting a clear picture of what a particular ancient people looked like hopes for the former, whereas the latter tends to rule. At first sight it might seem that we already know what the ancient Egyptians looked like from the innumerable pictures and statues that they made of themselves. The skeletal evidence, as well as our own general experience of living in large communities, however, warns us that this must disguise a range of variation by time and locality which art did not reflect, the reason being that absolute likeness was not generally its purpose. Egyptian artists turned the same ability by which they stereotyped foreigners on to themselves as well. They created an Egyptian stereotype.

Archaeological samples tend to be quite small, those from Egypt being no exception. The statistical pooling process is naturally influenced by the degree of variation from one individual to another, and with small samples – perhaps twenty individuals – there is a danger that the presence of a very few people who were a little unusual in their own day will have a disproportionate effect on how the averages appear. Moreover, time and again it emerges that sets of measurements taken on male skulls differ from those taken on females even allowing for the general natural difference related to stature. This reduces sample sizes still further, more or less by half. Heterogeneity can then be quite marked. Then again, over the kind of long periods of time that archaeologists deal with there is a chance that a degree of genetic drift has taken place, an accumulation of tiny modifications which in the end make later representatives of the same population look a little different from their ancestors. This is especially likely if the way of life has changed, particularly if this involves diet.[64] One result of heterogeneity is that the diagrams which are often used to illustrate the statistical pooling process will place one population in respect to others – for example, an early Predynastic group from El-Badari (near the modern village of Qau) compared to a mediaeval group from Edfu – in a significantly different part of the chart depending on the exact procedures of the individual researcher.[65]

If we are looking for changes to an indigenous population we must first define what that indigenous population was. For Egypt this has meant, in practice, the people represented by burials in Predynastic cemeteries, for these are the earliest human remains which have been found in significant quantities. Of these the very earliest belong to the Badarian culture of Upper Egypt, dated to around 4400–4000 BC (possibly a little earlier). Yet in terms of the history of human presence in the Nile valley, otherwise represented only by stone tools, the Badarians and other Predynastic groups are actually quite recent. How can we know if Predynastic Egyptians were not themselves a population already modified by immigration, and so on, ever further back in time? It could well be that the concept of an indigenous population of the Nile valley has to remain only a theoretical possibility and that it will never be identified owing to the extreme rarity of the survival of human remains from periods prior to the Predynastic (Neolithic) periods. Many tens of thousands of years of human presence had preceded the Predynastic groups but smallness of numbers and a simpler style of life have not left us conveniently dense cemeteries to excavate.[66] A rare exception is a Late Stone Age cemetery at Gebel Sahaba, in the northern Sudan. It contained the skeletons of about sixty persons (men, women and children) buried over a period of time somewhere around 12,000 to 10,000 years ago, a remarkably early date for such a find.[67] Primarily a hunting population, from time to time they engaged in conflict with other groups, for almost half those buried had died violently, mostly from flint-tipped weapons. In appearance, these people would not have fallen into an easily identifiable modern category and certainly would not have looked like Predynastic Egyptians or Nubians. Instead they shared features with a population of early *Homo sapiens* which is found spread across North Africa and into Europe (Cro-Magnon). Their physical difference from Predynastic Egyptians implies that the latter were the product of further genetic modification, primarily in the direction of slenderness of features (gracilization). Whether this took place in a stable population all the time occupying the same part of Egypt or within groups elsewhere who later migrated to the valley, or a combination of the two, we simply cannot tell for lack of evidence. We are also obliged to see these past populations only as shapes. The history of colour (of skin and eyes and usually of hair, too) remains completely unknown and, at present, unknowable.

The importance of appreciating that the ancient Egyptians, even those from the early periods, were the result of tens of thousands of years of micro-evolution and of movement is that it prepares one for the difficulties of drawing clear conclusions from the many detailed studies of human skeletal material (often just the skulls) which have been recovered from ancient cemeteries. The subject is, for one thing, dominated by sampling bias. Partly this is natural, for bones are much better preserved in the dry deserts of the south than in the damper soils of the north. This means that it is much easier to compare Upper Egyptians with Nubians and Sudanese than it is to compare Lower Egyptians with the peoples of Palestine and the Near East, another huge area where preservation is usually poor. Partly the bias has been created by archaeologists. Most of the thousands of bodies and bone groups discovered in the nineteenth and over much of the twentieth centuries they threw away or reburied without record, mistakenly regarding human remains as far less important than the objects found with them. When they did collect they tended to do so from earlier periods at the expense of later periods. The result is that the samples available for study are only a tiny, sad and unrepresentative remnant. A notable low point in available data is the New Kingdom, a time when, from its general air of prosperity, it is tempting to think of a peak in population numbers. Since this also appears, from historic sources, to have been a time of considerable immigration, partly enforced, the small amount of skeletal evidence available for study is particularly disappointing.

As a way of putting the subject into perspective, consider one recent comparative study of Egyptian skulls that uses data taken from thirty-one cemeteries spread across roughly four thousand years, from the Badarian period to the beginning of the Christian era.[68] The skulls total 4,058, but many were not sufficiently well preserved for all the necessary measurements to be taken and so the working total is less (2,886). It might still seem like a reasonable number to work with, except that it represents a span of four thousand years. That might be 130 generations with a mean age at death of thirty in a population for ancient Egypt of, let us say conservatively, a million and a half on average. So during that four thousand years at least two hundred million people will have died.[69] The 2,886 selected skulls are thus a tiny fraction of 1 per cent. Moreover, over 40 per cent of these come from a single cemetery (Giza) from the Late Period leaving only 60 per cent to represent thirty sites over four thousand years. In living societies social scientists and opinion-poll analysts are content to work with small samples, but go to great lengths to achieve representative selections. We cannot do that with archaeological data. We have to work with what has accidentally and haphazardly survived. With microscopically small samples and often poor knowledge of who they represent it is not surprising that progress in writing a population history of ancient Egypt is slow.

Then there is the question of methods. Those that are accepted with confidence in modern forensic investigations compare an unknown individual with data derived from modern reference collections. The ethnic affiliations of the individuals who make up these collections (mainly poor whites and blacks from the cities of the USA) are known from the full range of their characteristics, including the colour of their skin. With ancient remains there are naturally no equivalent reference collections where more is known about the people than what is preserved on their skeletons. Reference collections are the very thing that the anthropologist is attempting to create. Consequently it cannot be assumed that the refined method of calculation used in modern police cases works to the same degree with ancient populations. A recurrent and disconcerting tendency for the characteristics used for ethnic grouping to differ noticeably between males and females in ancient Egyptian sets of skulls, as if each half of the population had a different origin, should also be taken as grounds for great caution in interpreting the evidence.

Three thousand years of pooling

There is a general acceptance, in part intuitively based, that the size of human populations everywhere gradually increased during prehistoric and early historic periods. The best attempt at reconstructing a curve of increase for ancient Egypt probably remains Karl Butzer's.[70] It is based upon an assessment of archaeological and geographical factors and pays

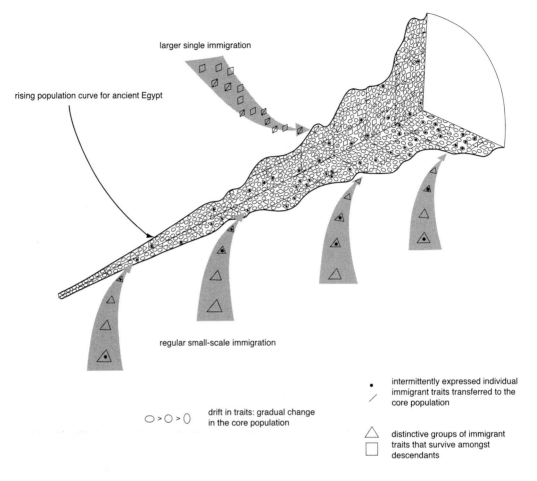

larger single immigration

rising population curve for ancient Egypt

regular small-scale immigration

○ > ○ > ○   drift in traits: gradual change
in the core population

•   intermittently expressed individual
immigrant traits transferred to the
/   core population

△   distinctive groups of immigrant
▢   traits that survive amongst
descendants

Figure 15   Model of population growth and change in ancient Egypt. The hypothetical rising
population curve is that of K.W. Butzer, *Early hydraulic civilization in Egypt*, Chicago, 1976, 85, Fig. 13.
As time passes immigrants introduce to the population traits of their own, which I have indicated
as a single marker for each one, becoming pooled to differing extents. This takes place against a
background of slow 'drift' in overall traits. To the scientist the traits are genetic since only these are
properly measurable. But for the peoples themselves cultural traits and markers will have been equally
important. Scientists have to ignore them because they are not properly measurable.

heed to the broad 'feel' of the historical periods. It displays an overall rise across three
millennia though with dips. From a base population for the late Predynastic of slightly
less than one million, it peaked at around five million in Roman times, with the delta
population gradually outstripping that of the valley. In many modern countries, whether
the population remains stable or increases or dwindles depends in part upon the natural
rate of replacement through births and deaths, and in part upon the balance between
immigration and emigration. How much of the upward curve in Butzer's graph represents
one rather than the other? A four million increase over three thousand years represents a
net increase of around 1,300 per year. If we imagine immigration (voluntary and forced)

running at a broad average of 200 per year, which does not seem unreasonable in the light of the various sources, it would represent 15 per cent of that increase, year on year. The cumulative effect on the gene pool as a whole would have been, over several centuries, quite significant, not least because immigrants tend to be at their reproductive peak.

When populations come together and interbreed, the physiological consequences are not predictable in a simple fashion. Some traits give an adaptive advantage and survive, others are lost. Moreover, the characteristics that are thrown together through intermarriage are not just the physiological, the aspects that we see, like skin colour or waviness of hair or relative lengths of limbs. They can, for example, be differing degrees of resistance to a particular disease. In the unlikely event that some of the immigrants shared characteristics with some of the modern populations of East Africa, excellence in endurance running (now famous from athletic events) might have been another. This leads one to ask of the fighting characteristics that the Egyptians saw in the Medjay: did these derive wholly from culture or was there a genetic component? Since any functioning body of people is a composite of genes and culture the question is to some extent academic. If the fighting traditions of the Medjay were wholly a matter of culture, that, too, will have had some influence on the aggregation of traits that made up the totality of the ancient Egyptian population and its culture.

In Figure 15 I have taken Butzer's population curve and tried to imagine it made up of countless individuals, each marked in a particular way, by traits that could be genetic or could be cultural. The point of the exercise is to make it seem natural and unexceptional to find the variation that does, in reality, show up from sample to sample (represented by individual cemeteries), both over time and from place to place. There is no single ancient Egyptian population to study, but a diversity of local populations. That does not negate the existence of trends, though as yet it is hazardous to identify any particular one. There is, for example, a suggestion of a geographical cline, or chain of variation, running along the Nile valley.[71] It is to be expected simply on the grounds that people tend to marry those from their neighbourhood. In the south of Egypt the population would have been close to, and would have ultimately merged with, that of northern Nubia. One trait was presumably a darkening of skin colour. As one moved north so local populations should, in general, have diverged more from those further south. This ought to mean if all factors worked equally (and they might not have done) that the population of the north-eastern Nile delta merged with that of southern Palestine.

I conclude this review with notes on six studies or groups of studies of skeletal datasets that help to define the subject and its inherent complexity.

1   A major collection of human remains covering a long period of ancient Egypt's history and excavated by modern methods comes from the island of Elephantine and an adjacent cemetery on the west bank, Qubbet el-Hawa.[72] Both represent part of the population of the frontier town of Elephantine that will feature often in later chapters. The total sample comprises 1,487 individuals (but with only 683 skulls preserved) unevenly spread between the 6th and 26th Dynasties, with a major gap in the later New Kingdom and Third Intermediate Period. A welcome feature is the division of the material into social levels according to the architectural types of the tombs. A thorough analysis points to substantial continuity in the physical characteristics of the population through the whole period studied, although this omits the Predynastic and

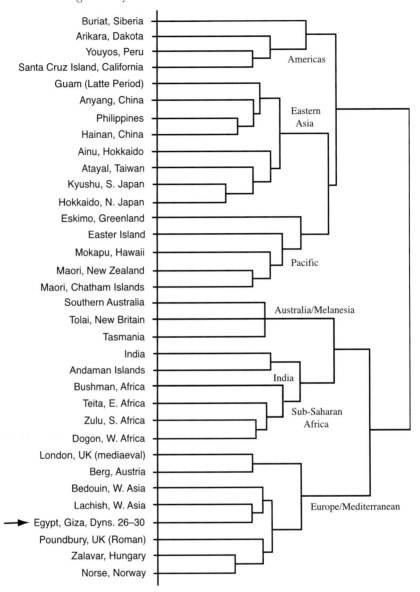

Figure 16a and b Two dendrograms which show by means of a two-dimensional diagram how similar or dissimilar groups of skulls are to each other. Each skull group represents a pooling of a series of measurements. The computer program arranges the groups in a sequence which is a best attempt at placing as neighbours groups which are most like each other. The branching lines of linkage attempt to show at what level of similarity, or with what degree of confidence, the neighbours really resemble one another. If one starts from the lowest level of grouping (on the right-hand side in these diagrams) then the first branch which encompasses all the entries is simply saying, these are all skulls. As one moves to the left one is looking at the material with increasing levels of discrimination until one's focus is so close and precise that each group or entry becomes a separate branch. By this time the basis of discrimination is usually so finely tuned that very minor alterations

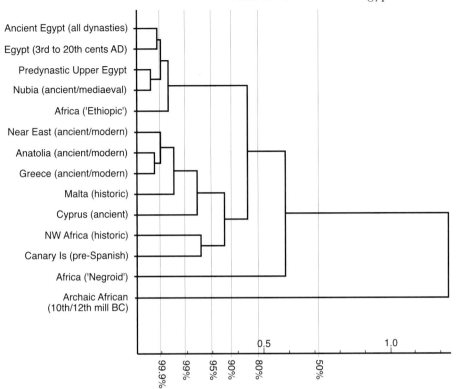

to the basic data, say by the addition of new specimens, can change the relative positions of the individual groups. There is thus, at this finer end, a degree of instability in the arrangement. Another way of looking at such diagrams is to say that the more one's conclusions are based towards the left-hand end of the diagram, the less is the degree of confidence with which those conclusions should be expressed. By contrast, the conclusion based on the far right end of the diagram, that all the entries are indeed skulls, is not likely to be challenged!

Above (b). Dendrogram which shows the relative closeness to or distance from one another of four-teen human populations from Africa and the Mediterranean region. The 'ancient Egyptian' group is a pooling of data from twenty-one cemeteries including those at Elephantine and the Late Period cemetery at Giza. The Egypt, Nubia and Africa ('Ethiopic') groups form a cluster at some distance from others. But although the 'Africa ("Negroid")' group is placed next to the 'Canary Islands (pre-Spanish)' group, the substantial difference between them is indicated by how far one has to travel to the right along the branches of the dendrogram before meeting a linkage line. Indeed, the bottom two 'Africa' groups could more reasonably (and without violating the overall arrangement) be rotated to the top of the diagram. If a three-dimensional display were to be adopted this oddity would be lost. After F.W. Rösing, *Qubbet el Hawa und Elephantine; zur Bevölkerungsgeschichte von Ägypten,* Stuttgart and New York, 1990, 209, Abb. 134.

Left (a). Similar dendrogram (from the CRANID program) which places Egypt amidst popula-tions from the main world regions. In contrast to the previous diagram, Egypt is represented by only a single cemetery, that of the Late Period at Giza. The other dendrograms (especially those of Figure 17, pp. 56, 57) question how representative of ancient Egypt the Giza group is. After *New Scientist,* 23 February 2002, 23.

Early Dynastic Periods. When the Elephantine results are added to a broader pooling of the physical characteristics of populations drawn from a wide geographic region which includes Africa, the Mediterranean and the Near East quite strong affinities emerge between Elephantine and populations from Nubia, supporting the idea of a south–north cline (Figure 16b, p. 53).

2   Moving to the opposite geographical extremity, the very small sample populations available from northern Egypt from before the 1st Dynasty (Merimda, Maadi and Wadi Digla) turn out to be significantly different from sample populations from early Palestine and Byblos, suggesting a lack of common ancestors over a long time. If there was a south–north cline of variation along the Nile valley it did not, from this limited evidence, continue smoothly on into southern Palestine.[73] The limb-length proportions of males from the Egyptian sites group them with Africans rather than with Europeans.

3   By contrast, an excavated set of around 300 burials from Tell el-Dab'a in the northeast delta belonging to a group considered to be Palestinian immigrants living in the late Middle Kingdom/Second Intermediate Period (c. 1750–1550 BC) have physical characteristics which group them more closely with ancient populations from the Near East and at a greater distance from those from Elephantine, although male and female characteristics also show differences.[74] The Levantine association matches expectations from archaeology, and the general result encourages confidence that skeletal measurement can produce believable results. What is unfortunate is that the poor conditions of preservation in the delta mean that no other delta populations of the historic period of significant size are yet available for comparison. One might wonder if, by this stage in history, the distinction between the peoples of the eastern delta and those of Palestine apparent in the Predynastic Period (and the subject of the last paragraph) was beginning to break down generally.

4   The most debated studies are those based on groups of early skulls collected during the late nineteenth and early twentieth centuries. Predynastic skulls, all from Upper Egypt, appear to be noticeably different in their measurements from an Old Kingdom group from tombs around the pyramids of Giza. This finding prompted one investigator to claim that 'the pyramid builders were a different race from the people whose descendants they had hitherto been supposed to be'.[75] The change, he explained, was the result of immigration from the east of people who came to form Egypt's elite who ruled an indigenous population akin to African peoples living further south. But might this not be a distinction of geography within Egypt, between populations actually separated by 500 kilometres? More recent studies based on many of the same skull collections have taken this view. Taking measurements is not the only way to describe skulls. There are other characteristics to note (non-metrical variations) that might be sensitive genetic markers. Non-metric studies of these very same collections have not substantiated this population divide but have instead found continuity rather than discontinuity across this period of time.[76]

5   Wadi Halfa in the northern Sudan provides a rare case of a clearly formulated historical problem that could be directly addressed by new and major excavations.[77] The early New Kingdom saw the wholesale replacement of indigenous Nubian culture (the C-group phase) with purely Egyptian culture, in this case in a part of the Nubian Nile valley not directly adjacent to an Egyptian colonial town (probably part of the terri-

tory of Teh-Khet, see Figure 11, p. 38). The historical problem asks: are we witnessing the old population adopting the styles of its conquerors or the results of population replacement in which Egyptian immigrant colonists pushed out the local people? Excavations in the 1960s provided substantial comparative collections of skeletons of both periods (although those of the New Kingdom were badly preserved). Detailed analysis determined that the two series were not identical, but the later one, instead of looking more 'Egyptian', resembled most closely the male population of a Sudanese site (Kerma) from even further south. The anthropologist responsible concluded that none of the hypotheses put forward fully explained the data. The lack of a clear answer in a better-than-normal situation underlines the intrinsic difficulties of matching skeletal populations to the cultural groups that we construct from other kinds of evidence.

6   In a database of human cranial variation worldwide (CRANID) based on standardized sets of measurements, the population that is used to characterize ancient Egypt lies firmly within a Europe/Mediterranean bloc (Figure 16a, p. 52).[78] The original source is the largest series of skulls from Egypt (1,500), collected by Petrie in 1907 from a cemetery on a desert ridge to the south of Giza and dating from the 26th to the 30th Dynasties. Some of the skulls bear weapon injuries. The cultural material found with them is wholly Egyptian, but was small in quantity. Conceivably the community was immigrant, perhaps mercenaries and their families. Or it could be that, by this period, northern Egyptians, so long exposed to population mixing, were tending towards a greater similarity with European populations than had been the case earlier. If, on the other hand, CRANID had used one of the Elephantine populations of the same period, the geographic association would be much more with African groups to the south. It is dangerous to take one set of skeletons and use them to characterize the population of the whole of Egypt.

Imagining Egyptians

Television has popularized one way of partially answering the question – what did the peoples of the past look like – by demonstrating the technique of facial reconstruction. Trained medical artists reconstruct in modelling-clay (or sometimes on computer screen) the features that originally existed in fleshy tissue over a skull. Pioneered for police work, it has been 'successfully' tried on ancient skulls, including a few from Egypt. In a uniquely rich combination of ancient sources Roman Egypt (mid-first to mid-third centuries AD) has supplied many astonishingly life-like painted portrayals of the dead that accompanied their mummified remains.[79] Many of these people lived in towns in the Fayum, a fertile oasis-like region on the western edge of the Nile valley, that had by this time been settled by Greek immigrants. Whilst they retained for a long time much of their Greek culture, as people they were in the position of other immigrant groups who settled over the centuries, and so it would be wrong to say that they were not proper Egyptians. The painted images appear to be portraits, in that family groups share facial characteristics, such as a cleft chin, whilst examination of cases where the mummy has also survived reveal correspondences between the two of age and sex. Facial reconstruction has been carried out on the skulls of four of the portrait owners. Two of the reconstructions closely resemble

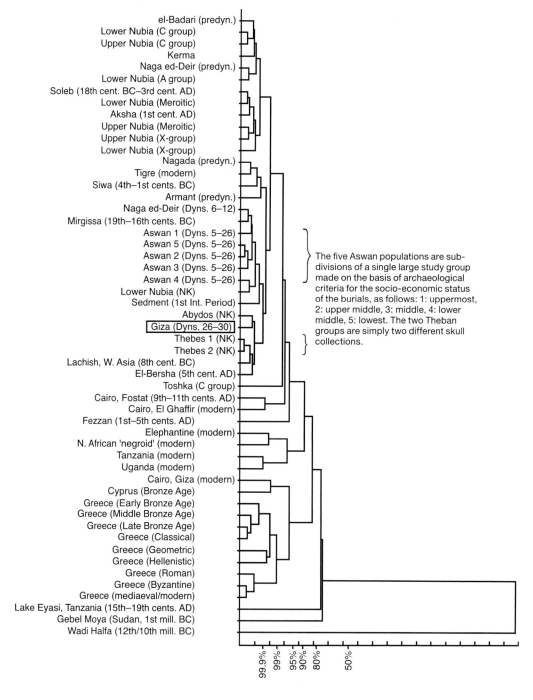

The five Aswan populations are sub-divisions of a single large study group made on the basis of archaeological criteria for the socio-economic status of the burials, as follows: 1: uppermost, 2: upper middle, 3: middle, 4: lower middle, 5: lowest. The two Theban groups are simply two different skull collections.

Figure 17 Male and female skulls tend to differ not only in size but also in other less obvious ways. These differences become entangled with differences which derive from ethnic origins. This results in different relative placings in dendrograms depending on whether the skulls are male (right) or female (above). One should be very cautious in reading historical significance into such differences.

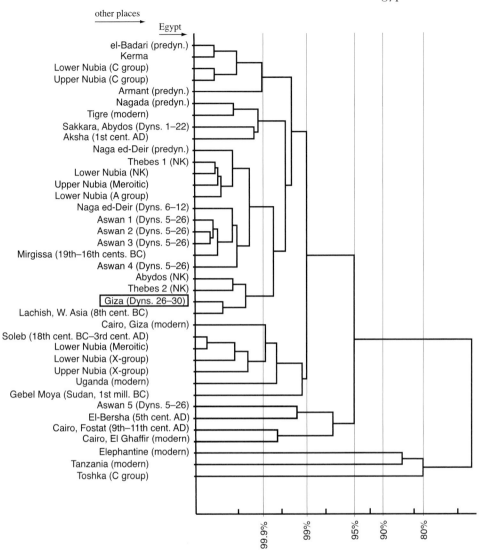

other places

Egypt

el-Badari (predyn.)
Kerma
Lower Nubia (C group)
Upper Nubia (C group)
Armant (predyn.)
Nagada (predyn.)
Tigre (modern)
Sakkara, Abydos (Dyns. 1–22)
Aksha (1st cent. AD)
Naga ed-Deir (predyn.)
Thebes 1 (NK)
Lower Nubia (NK)
Upper Nubia (Meroitic)
Lower Nubia (A group)
Naga ed-Deir (Dyns. 6–12)
Aswan 1 (Dyns. 5–26)
Aswan 2 (Dyns. 5–26)
Aswan 3 (Dyns. 5–26)
Mirgissa (19th–16th cents. BC)
Aswan 4 (Dyns. 5–26)
Abydos (NK)
Thebes 2 (NK)
Giza (Dyns. 26–30)
Lachish, W. Asia (8th cent. BC)
Cairo, Giza (modern)
Soleb (18th cent. BC–3rd cent. AD)
Lower Nubia (Meroitic)
Lower Nubia (X-group)
Upper Nubia (X-group)
Uganda (modern)
Gebel Moya (Sudan, 1st mill. BC)
Aswan 5 (Dyns. 5–26)
El-Bersha (5th cent. AD)
Cairo, Fostat (9th–11th cent. AD)
Cairo, El Ghaffir (modern)
Elephantine (modern)
Tanzania (modern)
Toshka (C group)

99.9%   99%   95%   90%   80%

Left. Dendrogram which shows the relative closeness to or distance from one another of *males* in fifty-three human populations from Africa and the Mediterranean region. The program has no geographical or chronological intuition. It is thus reassuring to find expected groups actually coming together, sometimes with a degree of chronological ordering, which suggests evolutionary change. The extent to which the Late Period Giza cemetery is not representative of Egypt as a whole but only of one stage in population change is made clear. Note how the extreme difference of the Wadi Halfa archaic population from all of the rest has had the effect of compressing to the left the rest of the dendrogram in comparison to the dendrogram for females. After F.W. Rösing, *Qubbet el Hawa und Elephantine; zur Bevölkerungsgeschichte von Ägypten*, Stuttgart and New York, 1990, 202, Abb. 132.

Above. Similar dendrogram for *females* in thirty-eight of the same populations. Although there is an overall similarity with the male dendrogram, individual groups can be given significantly different placings in comparison to their male counterparts. In general, female skulls being less robust preserve less well and so samples are often smaller. After Rösing, op. cit., 203, Abb. 133.

the portraits, two are rather different, being perhaps more 'African'. With such a small sample it is hard to judge what is going on, and this illustrates the principal limitation of this approach. Facial reconstruction requires not only the presence of the skull itself but also much time of a skilled specialist. It is not feasible to devote this level of intensity to, say, a couple of hundred skulls excavated from a cemetery, and skull measurements which are now routinely taken in the field are not an adequate substitute for the skull itself (or a good cast of it). So, apart from occasional and virtually random examples, this technique plays no part in assessing the physical similarities and differences in ancient populations. Moreover, it has so far not proved possible to determine original skin colour even when the original tissue survives. Yet this, in the end, is the knowledge that is the most potent in a debate on ancient Egyptian ethnicity. The building up of the face also requires prior decisions on broad ethnic grouping since facial tissue, for example the configuration of the lips, does not cover the skull in quite the same way worldwide. The technique is not wholly objective.

Does DNA research have something to offer? It certainly should have, given its astonishing powers to identify the genetic background of living individuals. It offers the prospect of identifying successive sources of immigration in a way that is independent of other kinds of evidence. It has proved possible to isolate small fragments of DNA from the tissue and bone of ancient Egyptians and to amplify them into sequences large enough for serious study.[80] The procedures, which entail careful screening to identify modern contaminants that readily arise from the handling of the samples, are time-consuming and therefore costly. As with all such research, believable conclusions require results from a significant number of individuals, who represent a good geographical and chronological spread. At the time of writing those believable conclusions still seem to be a long way off.

If one is obliged to reconstruct an ancient Egyptian scene, even to engage modern people to act parts in it, the most honest course is to use the modern population of Egypt as a guide. It will not be exactly right, for the processes responsible for change and variation in the population had another two thousand years to run before today, much more if one's drama is set when the pyramids were being built. But any other course is likely to be more wrong. The exact mix of characteristics, at its simplest the range of facial types and skin shades, is a piece of micro-genetic history that is now beyond recovery. This does not make the ancient Egyptians any less a people of Africa, for 'black' Africans – by which term is generally meant the descendants of the Bantu – represent only a part of the population of the African continent. The Negroid/Caucasoid dividing line is a textbook abstraction, justified perhaps for the broadest of generalizations but for little more. Likewise, the 'black/white' argument is understandable as a symptom of modern political expression, and has certainly had a healthy sharpening effect on how the subject is discussed and presented. The over-simplified choice that it offers, however, does not lead to an appropriate evaluation of such evidence and understanding as we have.

In the end one is entitled to ask: so what? Does our genetic inheritance contribute all that much to who we are, individually and collectively, beyond the fact that we are humans whose biological characteristics vary slightly from person to person? Where we think we have come from easily becomes part of our culture and therefore helps to define us, but that is not the same thing. After all, in the past, Britons have variously believed that their ancestors were a tribe from Israel or the descendants of Aeneas and a band of refugees from Troy (claims which, if they were ever taken seriously, could have startling political consequences). That culture is influenced by genes is not wholly impossible. But to identify any aspect of such a process lies far beyond current knowledge. For working purposes our identities are created by culture and its history. The ancient Egyptians as a physical people are of interest to specialists who study population history, but the Egyptians whom most of us study are, to all intents and purposes, the bearers of a culture. It was a culture subject to processes of change which eventually deleted from the script the elements which initially had served to define it, and substituted instead new ideas and forms of expression which seemed more attractive at successive times, including those pertaining to Greece, and then to Christianity and then to Islam.

For the ancient Egyptians themselves, of course, these avenues of research and speculation were closed. They could peer into their own early origins only via their imaginations, which were shaped by the culture that they had created in historic times. They began from certain assumptions, and these form the basis of the next chapter.

2

The intellectual foundations of the early state

With the imagined community – the nation – people feel that they share bonds of common interest and inherited values with others, most of whom they will never see. It is a vision of people. By contrast, the state is a vision of power, a mixture of myth and procedure that twines itself amidst the sense of community, giving it political structure. In the modern world the state has become the universal unit of supreme organization. No part of the land of planet Earth does not belong to one. Like it or not most people are born members of a state, even if they live in remote and isolated communities. The stateless are the disadvantaged of the world, anachronistic. Its powers have grown so inescapable that, at least in the English language, the word 'state' has taken on a sinister overtone.

What are the roots of this condition, this vast surrender by the many and presumption by the few? People have recognized the state as an abstract entity only since the time of the Classical Greeks. But the real history of the state is much longer. If we move further back in time to the early civilizations – of which Egypt was one – we can observe the basic elements of modern states already present and functioning vigorously, yet doing so in the absence of objective awareness of what was involved. The existence of the state was either simply taken for granted or presented in terms which do not belong to the vocabulary of reason and philosophy which is part of our inheritance from the Classical world. We must accordingly make allowances if we are not to miss important truths. Essentially we must not confuse substance with language. The growth in the mechanisms of the state, as with other products of the mind, has been a process of addition. The ideas and practices that we associate with more modern times have been grafted on to a core which has remained fixed and basic since the appearance of the first states in the ancient world. The study of ancient history exposes this core and thus the bedrock of modern life.

Fundamental to the state is an idealized image of itself, an ideology, a unique identity. It sets itself goals and pursues them by projecting irresistible images of power. These aid the mobilization of the resources and energies of the people, characteristically achieved by bureaucracy. We can speak of it as an organism because although made by people it takes on a life of its own. Ideology, images of earthly power, the enabling force of bureaucracy, these are some of the fundamental elements of states both ancient and modern. They contain and reinforce the roles of the state's leaders as effectively as they do those of its people, and bear it onwards in times of weak leadership. They are themes that will recur throughout this book.

Ideology has become one of the shaping processes of modern times. It is the distinctive filter through which a society sees itself and the rest of the world, a body of thought and symbol which explains the nature of society, defines its ideal form, and justifies action to achieve that ideal. We might consider using the word with strictest regard to its origin only to refer to the political philosophies of the nineteenth and twentieth centuries AD, of which Marxism supplies the paradigmatic example. Because of their immediate earthly concerns ideologies might also appear to contrast with religions, with their appeal primarily to the spiritual condition of individuals and their redemption. But this convenient contrast between ideology and religion reflects the viewpoint of modern western culture. Islam and Judaism, for example, are concerned equally with personal righteousness and with the form that human society should take on earth. Both prescribe a complete way of life, including a code of law. With ancient speculative thought we move to a state of mind that could envisage the forces behind the visible world in terms only of divine beings and their complex interactions. For the Egyptians the ideal society on earth, although not formulated in the manner of a modern treatise, was a fundamental reflection of a divine order. It was, however, liable to disturbance by incautious kings and so required constant care and attention through ritual and pageant, as well as through occasional more forceful reminders. It seems entirely appropriate to use the term ideology to cover their vision of the state, embedded within theology yet politically valid and constantly stated in powerful symbolic terms. It was a consciously created framework within which the Pharaonic state functioned.

Yet it was not the sole source of order. Egyptian bureaucracy came to express an implicit ideology of social ordering that was never raised to the level of a fully formulated conscious scheme. This implicit ideology of social order (as distinct from the explicit ideology discussed in this chapter) will be explored in Chapters 4 and 5.

Egyptian ideology stressed three themes: continuity with the past, a mystic territorial claim of unity over geographical and political subdivisions, and stability and prosperity through the wise and pious government of kings. It also took for granted, as did the ancient Egyptians as a whole, the notion that those who lived in the Nile valley under the rule of Pharaoh formed the imagined community of 'Egyptians'.

The Egyptians' view of the past

Ideology requires a past, a history. For a dynamic ideology of change, such as Marxism, the past has to be unsatisfactory, an imperfect time whose shortcomings are the spur for action, for revolution. The past exists in order to be rejected. More commonly, however, societies embrace the past, or some parts of it, with respect. History makes the detailed tracery of a myth of the past that provides a model for the present. Ancient Egypt belongs firmly in this category. It knew its own past, and fitted the images so derived within the myth-world of ideology.

The past for the ancient Egyptians had a straightforward and rather prosaic course. No epic narrative of events spanned past generations, no great theme or tale of destiny urged a moral on the living. The Egyptians and their neighbours had always, so it seemed, lived in their respective homelands. The past was a model of order, a continuous and almost exclusively peaceful succession of reigns of previous kings, each one handing the throne on to his successor in a single direct linear sequence. This mirrored how things really were during the 'great' periods of peace and stability. It also reflects, incidentally, an elementary view of what history is about – namely the succession of rulers – that still has wide popular currency in the modern world.

Continuity emerges most explicitly from the lists of dead kings that the Egyptians themselves compiled. The majority derive from the New Kingdom, by which period the Egyptians had accumulated a millennium and a half of history.[1] The best known is to be found carved in fine low relief on one of the inner walls of the temple of King Seti I at Abydos (c. 1290 BC; Figure 18). At the left end of the scene stands Seti I himself, accompanied by his eldest son Rameses (later Rameses II), in the act of making offerings. The beneficiaries of the offerings, as the accompanying text makes clear, are seventy-five royal ancestors, each represented by a single cartouche, together with King Seti I himself, owner of the seventy-sixth cartouche, and whose own twin cartouches are then repeated nineteen times to fill the bottom row completely. The order of the cartouches appears to be more or less correct historically, but numerous kings are omitted, primarily those from periods of internal weakness and division. As Figure 18 shows, the largest group (thirty-nine of them) covers the earliest kings, whilst the next seventeen cartouches belong to the immediately ensuing kings who were weak in power but legitimate in status and were perhaps represented by a mini-list or set of statues in the old Osiris temple at Abydos which lay not far away. The whole scene represents a particularly generous version of a common temple cult of royal ancestors. Normally the cult focused on individual statues placed in a temple by individual kings. At Abydos a list of names achieved the same end, more comprehensively but also more economically. Correct chronological order was not essential, however (or was not always achieved). Another king list, in the temple of Amun-Ra at Karnak, and of the reign of Tuthmosis III (c. 1479–1425 BC), represents each of a list of sixty-one kings by a picture of a statue rather than by a simple cartouche.[2] But with this list the kings appear not to be in correct chronological order.

An interesting extension to the scope of this royal ancestor cult occurs in the tomb of a high official at Sakkara of the reign of Rameses II, an overseer of works named Tenroy.[3] At the centre of the scene is a list of fifty-seven cartouches of earlier kings, in correct order. Tenroy asks them in a prayer to grant him a share of the daily offerings that were made to them in the temple of Ptah at Memphis. A similar mixture of expectation and reverence

Figure 18 *Above.* Legitimizing the present by revering an edited version of the past: King Seti I (and Prince Rameses) present offerings to the names of kings made up into a single continuous sequence which connected Seti I to Meni (Menes), the earliest king of whom the Egyptians had a firm record. In the accompanying diagram the names have been divided into blocks representing periods of legitimate rule as interpreted by the priests of Abydos. The gaps in 'real' time and history, visible to ourselves, were periods to which a stigma was attached. The weighting of the list towards kings of earlier periods is striking, presumably because this gave a more intense feeling of antiquity. The weighting has been partly achieved by including the kings of the 8th Dynasty, whose ephemeral reigns continued the rule of the great Memphite kings of the Old Kingdom, but in reduced circumstances. Temple of Seti I at Abydos (c. 1280 BC). *Below.* Private reverence of the ruling house and its ancestors, by Amenmes, the chief priest of an image of the cult of the long-dead king Amenhetep I called 'Amenhetep of the Forecourt'. Amenmes lived in the time of Rameses I, Seti I's father. From his tomb at Western Thebes, after G. Foucart, *Le Tombeau d'Amonmos*, Cairo, 1935, Pl. XIIB, itself a copy made in the nineteenth century by Thomas Hay.

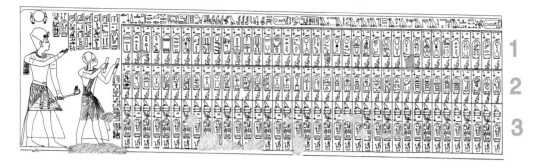

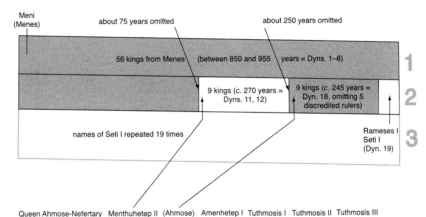

Meni
(Menes)

about 75 years omitted

about 250 years omitted

56 kings from Menes   (between 850 and 955   years = Dyns. 1–8)

9 kings (*c.* 270 years = Dyns. 11, 12)

9 kings (*c.* 245 years = Dyn. 18, omitting 5 discredited rulers)

Rameses I
Seti I
(Dyn. 19)

names of Seti I repeated 19 times

Queen Ahmose-Nefertary   Menthuhetep II   (Ahmose)   Amenhetep I   Tuthmosis I   Tuthmosis II   Tuthmosis III

Amenhetep II   Tuthmosis IV   Amenhetep III   Horemheb   Rameses I   Seti I

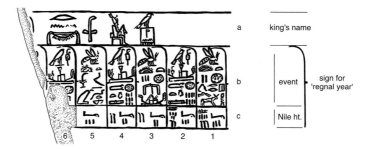

Figure 19 An extract from the Palermo Stone recording events in six years of King Nynetjer of the 2nd Dynasty (the extract begins with his fifteenth year). His name is written in line 'a'. The compartments in lines 'b' and 'c' are divided by vertical lines, curved at the top and with a small projection to the right placed half-way down. Each of these lines is in fact the hieroglyph used to write the word for 'year' (see also Figure 37F, p. 106). Row 'b' summarizes in hieroglyphs the main events of the years: (1) Appearance of the king, second running of the Apis-bull. (2) Processional tour of Horus (i.e. the king), eighth time of the enumeration. (3) Appearance of the king, third time of the Festival of Seker. (4) Processional tour of Horus, ninth time of the enumeration. (5) Appearance of the king, offering to (?) the goddess Nekhbet; the Djet-festival. (6) Processional tour of Horus, tenth time [of the enumeration]. The biennial rhythm of the king's official life, built around an enumeration of the country's wealth every second year (probably an early kind of Domesday record), is striking. The lowest row of compartments (c) contains an exact measurement of the height of the Nile flood above a fixed point: (1) 3 cubits, 4 hands, 3 fingers (1.92 m); (2) 3 cubits, 5 hands, 2 fingers (1.98 m); (3) 2 cubits, 2 fingers (1.20 m); (4) 2 cubits, 2 fingers (1.20 m); (5) 3 cubits (1.57 m); (6) destroyed. The variation in height, in this five-year span amounting to 0.78 m, would affect crop yields in higher-lying fields. See T.A.H. Wilkinson, *Royal annals of ancient Egypt: the Palermo Stone and its associated fragments*, London and New York, 2000, 126–8.

doubtless underlies other New Kingdom tomb scenes where offerings and prayers are made to deceased kings. The tomb at Thebes of the priest Amenmes (Figure 18, *below*), for example, shows him worshipping the statues of twelve New Kingdom Pharaohs regarded as legitimate, plus the founder of the Middle Kingdom, Nebhepetra Menthuhetep II. Again the chronological ordering is correct.

Although these lists are relatively late, the practice of honouring named royal ancestors was an old one. The pious regard shown by kings of the 12th Dynasty towards members of the preceding 11th Dynasty, whose power they had usurped, also reveals that the search for continuity in kingship could transcend the political details of dynastic succession.[4] The fact that most lists put their selection of kings into correct chronological order reflects a natural Egyptian inclination towards the keeping and archiving of administrative records. The archival element is very evident in the lists of the Palermo Stone (Figure 19). This name is given to a group of fragments of a black basalt slab, evidently carved during the latter part of the 5th Dynasty (*c.* 2350 BC). Most of the design consists of horizontal rows of compartments, each one separated by a vertical line with curving top, which is, in fact, the hieroglyphic sign for 'year'. Each of the compartments contains a summary of the principal events in a single year of kings whose names run across the top of the appropriate block of compartments. The events tell us what things the Egyptians of the time thought were important. They are a mixture of religious festivals, creation of statues of the gods, occasional warfare, regular taxation, and, in a separate subdivision, the precise height of that year's Nile flood. The Palermo Stone portrays an interest in the deeds of the past, adding an intellectual cladding to the bare lists of names, yet one which still remained in harmony with the ideal. We can assume that this kind of chronicle provided the basis for the later summary lists of kings. It must itself have been compiled from several different sources, since there is only limited consistency in the kind of things recorded line by line, and in the length of the entries.[5]

Administration and piety towards royal ancestors do not provide a complete explanation for this interest, however. The records at their disposal enabled the Egyptians to measure past time, and offered them the prospect of an intellectual journey to the point where time met the cosmos. The most vivid expression of this is found in another king list, again from the New Kingdom, but this time written on papyrus and now in the Turin Museum.[6] Originally it listed around 300 names of kings, and the aim of its compiler was completeness. No king seems to have been too minor or short-reigned for inclusion. The Palestinian kings who formed the Hyksos Dynasty were included, even though they did not merit having their names written in cartouches. This, in fact, was a remarkable concession to reality: tacitly admitting a break in the succession of legitimate kings just for the purpose of attaining completeness. Against each king in the Turin list was written the precise length of his reign, sometimes to the exact day. At certain points a summary of numbers of kings and total length of reigns was inserted. Thus at the end of what we now call the 8th Dynasty, a summary of 958 years from the reign of King Menes, the first name of the lists, was provided.

If this was all the Turin king list did, it could be classed as an elaborate administrative device. The compiler of the list attempted, however, to continue back in time beyond the reign of Menes. It is here that the modern and the ancient mind part company. Beyond history we place prehistory: the record of human society in a world without writing, an anonymous place where names and deeds are unknown. Such a state of affairs was inconceivable to the ancients. But this did not prevent curiosity about what had gone before the first recorded king. The Turin list devoted more than one column of its text to this. Immediately before Menes came several lines which summarize the collective reigns of 'spirits', not given individual names, and before these, and heading the whole compilation, a list of deities. The name of each is written in a cartouche, as if a king, and followed by a precise length of reign. In the case of the god Thoth, for example, this is 7,726 years.[7]

From the whole Turin list one could trace in direct line the royal succession from a period when the gods had ruled as kings, and from the completeness of the data gain the added satisfaction of calculating exactly the entire period involved. On consulting it, the ancient scribe could have known the age of the world since the time of the first creator god and he would have seen how the kings of the past and their great monuments fitted within this majestic scheme. The rigid linearity of this view of time is brought out in detail from the way that overlaps of whole dynasties at times of internal division are ignored, and the reigns simply placed end to end, and all figures added together for grand totals.

Sources of this kind tell us what the Egyptians themselves found interesting about their own past and how they preferred to organize it. If it was chronologically incorrect and pervaded with invention it did not matter, because they had no knowledge of the past independently derived with which it could conflict, and this was, anyway, the past they wanted to have. We have largely though not wholly lost that innocence. We know how to 'deconstruct' texts that purport to record the past objectively. We know that they are bound to be complex products of far-from-mechanical minds, reflecting the ideas and biases of their time, and malleable by later editing even if they are dryly administrative. Knowledge of the past is never 'true', it represents a set of interpretations in a constant state of change and is bound to be, to some extent, what we choose it to be. Through archaeology and social history, moreover, we have developed an altogether broader view of what the past is about, and a multiplicity of tools for studying it. Yet ancient annals still exert their power. There remains within Egyptology a strong literalist tradition that cannot bear to let go of the thought that king lists and other similar documents are fundamentally true. By this view the onus rests upon scholars to find ingenious and sometimes tortuous ways of explaining discrepancies. When learning about ancient Egypt for the first time it is helpful to work with clear schemes of history and chronology, but it is also important not to put them beyond the reach of scepticism.

Continuity of orderly kingship was the principal image that the Egyptians wanted the past to project. It was something satisfactory to contemplate by itself, and failed to provoke an interest in the writing of narrative history that explained people and events in terms appropriate to their times and that posterity would understand. Occasionally one encounters a more varied reaction. A few reigns had a certain 'flavour'. Sneferu of the 4th Dynasty, for example, was later regarded as the archetypal good king from the distant past.[8] Rameses II was likewise a model for his successors. 'You shall double for me the long duration, the great kingship of King Rameses II, the great god' prayed Rameses IV some sixty years later (the prayer failed: he died in his seventh regnal year).[9] Khufu (Cheops), builder of the Great Pyramid, on the other hand, acquired a reputation for cruelty and arrogance, which appears in a collection of stories (Papyrus Westcar) apparently written in the late Middle Kingdom.[10] It reappears in Manetho's *History* and in the narrative of Herodotus.[11] Whether this was a true reflection of Khufu's character, or an imagined consequence of having been the builder of the largest of all the pyramids, is something we can no longer tell. Papyrus Westcar tells the story as a prelude to introducing the ultra-pious kings of the succeeding 5th Dynasty, the point evidently being that by arrogant and offensive behaviour Khufu brought doom to his house. The reigns of other kings from the distant past who were thought not to have maintained the standards of kingship that the Egyptians regarded as proper were likewise made the settings for didactic discourses. King Pepi II, last king of the 6th Dynasty was one: he is apparently credited with homosexuality in a later tale.[12] A king with an unsavoury reputation probably provided the setting, now lost, for the lengthy set of lamentations on disorder composed by a Middle Kingdom scribe named Ipuwer.[13]

At this point we must draw a distinction in our sources. Texts of this nature, recorded only on papyrus, were the speculative literary products of the scribal elite, part didactic, part entertaining, not meant as statements of theology. It was from the same educated elite that the 'theologians' were drawn. But we should not imagine two sets of people, one with a less respectful view of the past. An attitude that looks disrespectful to us can be found in papyri narrating events in the lives of the gods. In one such story the goddess Isis ('a clever woman. Her heart was craftier than a million men') schemes to discover the secret name of the sun-god Ra, depicted as an old man who succumbs to the pain of a snake bite and reveals his hidden name to her.[14] The text is complete and its purpose is clear. It provides 'historical' authority for using the story itself as a cure for scorpion sting. Another story, beautifully written out and part of a private library that also contained conventional ritual and theological material, narrates the quarrel between the gods Horus and Seth. Their confrontation was one of the cornerstones of the myth of the state. It took the optimistic view that the forces of good and evil, of order and chaos, of truth and falsehood, as symbolized by these two beings who were embodied in kingship, were not in the end symmetrically balanced. Horus, and what he stood for, would ultimately triumph. But this version presents it as a burlesque, in which the gods – amongst them Isis and Osiris – are quarrelsome, vulgar and open to ridicule.[15] What was permissible in literary scribblings and what was proper to formal theological texts would have been a matter of clearly understood taste. Systems of authoritatively stated belief need channels for release and are not necessarily damaged thereby. Instinct for survival tells most people how far to go and when to stop. The reputations of Khufu and Pepi II did not exclude them from the formal king lists, nor were the images of the gods Horus and Osiris made any less majestic by their prototypes being made the subject of mirth. Moreover, this limited 'licence' or intellectual freedom created settings in which the lessons of bad kingship could be expounded. The acknowledgement of periods of disorder and injustice served as a warning and gave credence to the role of the king as maintainer of order and justice.

There was, however, a limit, perhaps self-imposed through deference to decorum, or perhaps derived from a blindness to perceiving that the affairs of the state can be presented as a narrative on a larger scale than that of simple story-telling built around a few characters. We know, from modern researches, of a period of internal unrest culminating in civil war between two contemporaneous ruling families, the 9th and 11th Dynasties, of Herakleopolis and Thebes respectively. This was the First Intermediate Period. Later Egyptians treated it circumspectly. The founder of the principal breakaway group, King Khety of the 9th Dynasty, later became, like Khufu, the object of unfavourable anecdote, preserved in the copies of Manetho. The entry for this king, in fact, summarizes neatly the anecdotal, moralistic view of history: 'King Achthoes [the Greek form of Khety], behaving more cruelly than his predecessors, wrought woes for the people of all Egypt, but afterwards he was smitten with madness, and was killed by a crocodile.'[16] There is no hint here of the political opportunism which must have given Khety and his family temporary control of the Egyptian throne, soon disputed by a rival dynasty based at Thebes (the 11th). No later text that we know of used the setting of provincial breakaway or warring dynasties directly. In the immediately ensuing period (the Middle Kingdom) thoughtful men composed literary texts which dwelt on the nature of a disorderly society, but within them they kept recent historical reality at a distance. The First Intermediate Period was not used directly to point to a moral. One device put the description of disorder into a prophecy uttered by a priest (named Neferty) at the court of the long-dead but highly regarded king Sneferu, of the early 4th Dynasty.[17]

All happiness has vanished;
The land is ruined, its fate decreed,
Deprived of produce, lacking in crops.
What was made has been unmade.

The disorders of this unspecified future time are terminated by the saviour-like arrival of a King Ameny, whose historical model was probably Amenemhat I, first king of the 12th

Dynasty. The lamentations of the scribe Ipuwer were another product of the same mood, but their dramatic pictures of social upheaval likewise lack historical names and events.

By the time of the New Kingdom a second period of internal disorder had occurred, again culminating in a civil war: the Hyksos Period (see the previous chapter, pp. 41). But here the circumstances were very different.[18] The Hyksos were Palestinian kings who had taken over the delta. Since this was a period of rule by foreign kings eventually ejected by military force from Egypt it was legitimate to see it as an unfortunate aberration from the ideal picture of the past. Even the Turin list accepted this. The Hyksos kings appear, but shorn of royal titulary and cartouches, and labelled instead with a hieroglyphic sign which categorized them as foreigners. In one remarkable temple text, Queen Hatshepsut, herself a successful usurper of the early 18th Dynasty, used the Hyksos Period as the scenario of disorder from which she had saved Egypt, ignoring the half-century of peaceful and prosperous rule of her 18th Dynasty predecessors. Here the theme of royal responsibility for deliverance from chaos was used with a vengeance. It was permissible in a formal text because the Hyksos Period could be explained away, unlike the First Intermediate Period.

Departures from the picture of the ideal past were few, and (the Hyksos Period excepted) confined to individuals. More typically the past was the fount of authority and authenticity. A characteristic image is provided by King Neferhetep of the 13th Dynasty (c. 1740 BC), piously visiting 'the house of writings', examining the 'ancient writings of (the creator-god) Atum' in order to discover the correct form for a new statue of Osiris, laid down by the gods themselves at the beginning of time.[19] With a similar reverence for ancient forms Egyptian artists retained the original shapes of hieroglyphs with scarcely any modification for 3,000 years. The general continuity of style in art and architecture owes itself to the careful reproduction of codified styles created in the Early Dynastic Period and Old Kingdom. But there was an element of self-deception in this. Changes of ideals and forms did occur, and these must reflect intellectual development, something directly apparent from written sources also. The whole modern scholarly apparatus of art history in Egyptology is based upon the premise that style did change from period to period. Thus the brooding, careworn images of kings in Middle Kingdom statuary conveyed a very different message from their idealized youthful counterparts of the Old Kingdom.[20] King Neferhetep's new statue of Osiris would have been recognizably a product of the craftsmanship of its time. Indeed, the 'writings' that the king examined can have specified the nature of the ancient image in only general terms, such as the precious materials of which it was composed. The Egyptians could not have put into the words of their language a description of the style of a statue in the way that we can do now. The same was true of architecture. The New Kingdom saw a major reappraisal of temple architecture in which, at least as it relates to the royal mortuary cult, we must recognize significant shifts in meaning. Change did occur, but on the whole tastefully and reverently through retention of the basic vocabulary of traditional forms, sometimes reinforced by appeals to the past. More will be said on this in later chapters.

On occasions the exploitation of the past could be quite elaborate. In the next section of this chapter an extract from an important mythological text will be quoted, known as the Shabaka Stone.[21] In its preamble King Shabaka of the 25th Dynasty (716–702 BC) claims to have copied the text from an ancient worm-eaten document, and it is, indeed, written in a very archaic style. For a long time scholars accepted Shabaka's claim at its face-value, and set the original composition of the text as far back as the 3rd Dynasty. It has now become generally accepted that, although the themes of the myth belong to the mainstream of Egyptian thought, this particular composition is relatively late, perhaps even of Shabaka's time. As for its archaic style, there is good evidence to show that in the Late Period scribes had a working knowledge of an archaic form of the language, and could compose in it (pp. 372–3). An appeal to antiquity, and sometimes a cloaking in antique forms, made new ideas or new interpretations of old ideas, more acceptable. The past was a cultural womb.

The myth of the state

The kings of the lists shared one title in common: all were Kings of Upper and Lower Egypt, the two archetypal geopolitical divisions of valley and delta. In this title lay a powerful expression of unity. Again, however, we find the Egyptians shying away from the unpleasant realities of politics. Order versus chaos is a theme that occurs in various guises in Egyptian thought. It was a theme of kingship. Several of the reflective texts of the Middle Kingdom mentioned above (including the lamentations of the scribe Ipuwer) dwell on the nature of a disordered world, making the king responsible for its cure, but these, as noted above, belong to a tradition of limited free speculation at court. At the level of formal ideology division and disunity were seen not in terms of potential fragmentation into multiple territories, or into the topsy-turvy chaos of the lamentations of Ipuwer. That would have given too much weight to a disturbing possibility. Instead a symbolic dualistic division was proposed. This appealed to the Egyptian love of symmetry, as reflected throughout their art and architecture. Moreover, the idea of two originally separate kingdoms provided a basis for the king's unique unifying role that was safer and more respectable than a greater number of lesser units, or a wider condition of anarchy. It also matched the general geographical division of the country into two halves, although real political history shows up internal divisions along different lines.

The elaboration of this aspect of kingship was as much pictorial as written. The Egyptians excelled in strong and direct visual symbolism. In this they were helped by the nature of hieroglyphic writing. Most hieroglyphic signs stood for groups of consonants, so that pictures of things could be used to write other words that had the same sequence of consonants even if pronounced differently. It is as if, in modern English, we chose the picture of a leaf to write all words with the sequence of consonants *l* and *f*: thus, *leaf*, *life*, *loaf*, *laugh*, and *aloof*. (Context and additional signs when necessary prevented ambiguity.) This dissociation between sign and meaning was boldly exploited by artists. And it remained a characteristic of the writing system that, although at an early date a cursive form of writing (hieratic) was developed, for use with pen, ink and papyrus, in formal contexts artists lovingly retained all the detail and natural form of the originals so that the roots were never lost. Artists could thus take hieroglyphic signs standing for abstract concepts and work them as tangible objects into artistic compositions whilst retaining congruity of style. This emblematic use of hieroglyphs contributed a visual element to a theological language-game. It is an important characteristic of the Egyptian art style, as is the restraint with which it was exploited. In any one composition only a very few signs would be treated in this way, giving a clear and immediate message

A good set of examples which summarizes the basic ideology of the Egyptian state is

Figure 20   The source of political order and stability: the reconciliation of conflicting powers epit-omized by the gods Horus (left) and Seth (right), in whose reconciliation is subsumed the political divisions of Egypt (see Figure 34, p. 97). The reconciliation is symbolized by the tying together of the heraldic plants of Upper and Lower Egypt around the hieroglyphic sign for 'unification'. Throne base of Senusret I (1956–1911 BC) from his pyramid temple at El-Lisht. J.-E. Gautier and G. Jéquier, *Mémoire sur les fouilles de Licht*, Cairo, 1902, 36, Fig. 35; K. Lange and M. Hirmer, *Egypt: architecture, sculpture, painting in three thousand years*, third edition, London, 1961, 86 (prepared by B. Garfi).

carved in low relief on the sides of ten limestone statues of King Senusret I of the early 12th Dynasty (*c.* 1956–1911 BC) from his mortuary temple at El-Lisht (Figure 20).[22] Down the centre runs a segmented vertical sign that is actually a stylized picture of a windpipe and lungs, but which was used to write not only the word for 'lungs' but also the verb 'to unite', which possessed the same sequence of consonants: *s*, *m*, and a strongly aspirated *a*. The word and its hieroglyph were the key components whenever the theme of the unifi-cation of the kingdom was presented. On top of this emblematic sign for 'unity' rests the oval cartouche containing one of the names of the king. Around the sign two plants are being tied in a reef-knot: on the left a clump of papyrus stalks, the heraldic plant of Lower Egypt; on the right a clump of reeds similarly characteristic of Upper Egypt. The act of tying is being performed by two gods: on the left the hawk-headed Horus, and on the right Seth, whose animal was a mythological creature.[23] The hieroglyphs above each god refer to two localities. Seth is 'The Ombite', that is, from the city of Ombos (Nubt, near the modern village of Nagada) in Upper Egypt. Horus is 'Lord of Mesen', a town name used for places in both Upper and Lower Egypt (for reasons explained shortly), but here meaning one in Lower Egypt. On some of the throne bases Seth is called 'Lord of Su', a place lying just within the northern border of Upper Egypt, whilst Horus is several times called 'The Behdetite', that is, the one from Behdet, another toponym used for more than one place, but here clearly referring to somewhere in the north.

The artists who carved these statue bases were masters of elegant variation. Other dualistic themes were also woven into the same basic design. On five of the bases Horus and Seth were replaced by figures of plump Nile gods identified by symbols as Upper and Lower Egypt, whilst the hieroglyphic captions at the top refer to the 'Greater' and 'Lesser Ennead' (Company of Nine Gods), 'offerings' and ideas of fertility using paired synonyms in both cases. There is also another variation of the Horus–Seth theme. In this case the pairing is between, on the one side, 'The united portion of the two lords', with a little picture of Horus and Seth to identify who the two lords were, and on the other, 'The thrones of Geb', an earth-god who, in longer texts on the theme, presided over the reconciliation of Horus and Seth. The dualism could thus be extended beyond the pairing of two contrasting entities to the pairing of synonyms, each one of which contained a reference to some aspect of the balanced pairs.

Within this rearrangement of entities to illustrate the concept of harmony through the balancing of pairs we can glimpse a simple example of one form of the Egyptians' thought processes: the manipulation of words, especially names, as if they were discrete units of knowledge (which in a way they were). Ancient knowledge, when not of a practical nature (of the kind: how to build a pyramid and how to behave at table), was essentially the accumulation of names of things, beings and places, together with their associations. 'Research' lay in extending the range of associations in areas which we would now term 'theology'. Meaning or significance was left in the mind and remained largely unformulated. Mythological scenes such as this one provided a kind of cross-tabulation of concepts.

The esteem in which names of things were held is nicely brought out by a class of text that scholars call by a Greek term 'onomastica' (singular, 'onomasticon').[24] The best known, compiled in the late New Kingdom (*c.* 1100 BC) by a 'scribe of sacred books' named Amenemope, and much copied in ancient schools, has the promising heading: 'Beginning of the teaching for clearing the mind, for the instruction of the ignorant, and for learning all things that exist.' But without a single word of commentary or explanation it runs on as a list of names of things: the elements of the universe, types of human beings, the towns and villages of Egypt in great detail, parts of an ox, and so on. To the modern mind this form of learning appears like the most stifling kind of pedagogy. But to the ancients knowing the name of a thing made it familiar, gave it a place in one's mind, reduced it to something that was manageable and could be fitted into one's mental universe. We can, in fact, still recognize some validity in this: the study of the natural world, whether bird-watching or classifying plants, begins with knowing names, and with arranging the names in groups (the science of taxonomy), just as was done intuitively in the onomastica, which served as memory aids for the range of knowledge which was absorbed simply as a result of being a reasonably well educated Egyptian.

This view of names led to a prominent characteristic of Egyptian religion. The names of gods became the building-blocks for expanded definitions of divinity which at the same time directed the attention towards an underlying unity. Thus in one version of the Book of the Dead, Osiris is defined as: 'Lord of eternity, Wenen-nefer, Horus of the Horizon, with many forms and manifestations, Ptah-Sokar, Atum in Heliopolis, Lord of the Mysterious Region'. The names of no fewer than five 'gods' are used here to enrich the imagery by which Osiris is to be understood.[25] A very explicit revelation of this phenomenon is contained in a short speech by the sun-god: 'I am Khepri in the morning, Ra at mid-day, Atum in the evening.'[26] Fascination with the 'names of god' produced Chapter 142 of the Book of the Dead, which carries the heading 'Knowing the Names of Osiris in his every seat where he wishes to be', and which is an extensive list of geographically local versions of Osiris, as well as of versions of several other divinities finally summarized as 'the gods and goddesses in the sky in all their names'.[27]

An appreciation of the Egyptian mode of thinking is essential to the correct evaluation of texts which may seem to have a more direct bearing on the real, material world; texts which can become sources for history. Place names were just as open to manipulation, giving rise to a form of symbolic geography. It was a kind of word game which sought an idealized and symmetrical layout of places which were handled primarily as place names given mythological associations. Often, perhaps always, there was something there on the ground, a huddled mud-brick town or a nondescript little locality. But although symbolic geography articulated a myth of territorial supremacy on the part of the state, it is a mistake to take the geographical references in religious sources as guides to ancient real geography. To do that is to miss the abstracting powers of the Egyptian mind which created an ordered and harmonious myth-world from common and often probably rather humble experience. The result was full of familiar names yet belonged to a higher plane. It hovered tantalizingly between reality and abstraction.

It also, however, sets a trap for the unwary. Modern scholarship inclines towards the approach of lawyers: documented facts are assembled, they are discussed point by point, and a verdict is reached which satisfies modern logic and the 'weight of the evidence'. But ancient texts and scenes reflect their own intellectual aesthetic. They were composed from within the minds of their creators, and reflected an inner world which was not a straightforward projection of the material world, the world which, for example, archaeology uncovers. Symbolic geography was a product of an imaginative people. We should not think of using it as a straightforward basis for historical reconstruction.

We are now in a slightly better position to pursue the imagery on the throne bases of Senusret I. A written version of the myth occurs as part of the Memphite Theology, or Shabaka Stone, mentioned earlier.[28] Outwardly it has narrative form:

> [Geb, lord of the gods, commanded] that the Ennead gather to him. He judged between Horus and Seth; he ended their quarrel. He made Seth king of Upper Egypt in the land of Upper Egypt, up to the place where he was born, which is Su. And Geb made Horus king of Lower Egypt in the land of Lower Egypt, up to the place where his father [Osiris] was drowned, which is 'Division of the Two

Lands' [a mythical place name although an Egyptian would probably instinctively think of Memphis]. Thus Horus stood over one region, and Seth stood over one region. They made peace over the Two Lands at Ayan. That was the division of the Two Lands . . . Then it seemed wrong to Geb that the portion of Horus was like the portion of Seth. So Geb gave to Horus his inheritance, for he is the son of his firstborn son. Geb's words to the Ennead: 'I have appointed Horus, the first-born' . . . He is Horus who arose as King of Upper and Lower Egypt, who united the Two Lands in the Nome of the Wall [i.e. Memphis], the place in which the Two Lands were united. Reed and papyrus were placed on the double door of the House of Ptah [the temple of Ptah at Memphis]. That means Horus and Seth, pacified and united. They fraternized so as to cease quarrelling in whatever place they might be, being united in the House of Ptah, the 'Balance of the Two Lands' in which Upper and Lower Egypt had been weighed.

On the El-Lisht thrones Horus and Seth are representatives of Upper and Lower Egypt of equal status. On the Shabaka Stone Seth's place is diminished. From an initial equal-ity with Horus he is subsequently disinherited, though acquiescing in his new role. An archetypal tension has been created which each king must resolve by ensuring the triumph of the sense of legitimacy and orderly rule that Horus stood for. This text, and a mass of further ancient allusions on the same theme which can be found spread over a good part of Pharaonic history, pose a fundamental question. Does the myth reflect a formative historical phase in the history of the Egyptian state? Or was it devised as a piece of intel-lectual aesthetic to provide a philosophical basis for the Egyptian state which had, in fact, developed along a different historical path?

Past generations of scholars were frequently attracted to the first of these hypotheses, that the myth somehow reflected a formative historical phase. Before the 1st Dynasty they saw two kingdoms, each with a 'national god': Lower Egypt under Horus, Upper Egypt under Seth. A turning point had come when Lower Egypt defeated the south and estab-lished a unified kingship, even though this might have been short-lived in view of other evidence which suggested that the 1st Dynasty began with unification imposed from the south. That there is an alternative explanation owes much to archaeology. Indeed, the synthesis of sources, of archaeology with ancient myth, provides a case history of how ideology is created.[29]

The formation of the state: a model for early Egypt

Ideology emerges with the state: a body of thought to complement a political entity. How states arose in the first place has been the object of much study by archaeologists and anthropologists. Individual cases vary a great deal in their particular circumstances, and we should not look for a checklist of universally valid causes or a single cause which out-weighed all others. Egypt is particularly interesting because, apart from being one of the earliest examples, state formation seems to have taken place in the absence of some of the more obvious factors.[30] It is hard to imagine, for example, that in a land where popula-tion was relatively small and natural resources so abundant, competition for resources from sheer necessity was a major factor in the emergence of political domination.[31] It also strains the evidence needlessly to promote trade into a major force. Nor was there an external military threat, and the conflicts that developed within the Nile valley in the period leading up to the 1st Dynasty seem to have been amongst communities already well advanced along the path to statehood. Some evidence points to long-distance external connections in the Nagada II Period, reaching as far as southern Mesopotamia and Elam.[32] But these connections are far more likely to be signs of local success than to be pointers to a determining influence in local affairs.

The dynamic for the growth of the state seems in many instances to lie inherent within the very fact of settled agriculture and the population increase which this allows. To this extent it is as justifiable to look for 'causes' that slowed down the process in some parts of the world as it is to search for those which allowed it a rapid passage in others, such as Egypt. The essential factor is psychological. Permanent occupation and working of the same tract of land give rise to a powerful sense of territorial rights which come to be expressed in mystic, symbolic terms which in turn create a peculiar sense of self-confidence within the community concerned. The legacy of this in the modern world is the magic word 'sovereignty'. It awakens in some a competitive urge, and they see the possibility of obtaining an agricultural surplus for a more satisfactory life not through extra agricultural work on their own part, but by purchasing it or coercing it from others. It need not be perceived or presented as crudely as this. Placating the gods through the development of shrines and the donation of produce under the supervision of a priestly elite achieves the same end. Into modern times it remains particularly difficult to separate piety from worldly ambition. Whatever the rationale, the combination of ambition and mystic sense of identity puts individuals and communities into potential competition with one another. It wrought a once-and-for-all-times change in the nature of society. From essentially leaderless aggregations of farmers, communities arose in which a few were leaders, and the majority were led.

The course which this competition took in a landscape of almost unlimited agricultural potential, of the kind supplied by ancient Egypt, we can envisage through the analogy of game playing (see Figures 21, 22, 23). We can begin simply by imagining a board game of the 'Monopoly' kind. At the start we have a number of players of roughly equal potential. They compete (to some extent unconsciously) by exchanges of different commodities, and later more openly by conflict. The game proceeds by means of a combination of chances (e.g. environmental or locational factors) and personal decisions. The game unfolds slowly at first, in an egalitarian atmosphere and with the element of competition only latent, the advantage swinging first to one player and then to another. This can last for so long that the players can abandon the game from boredom or fatigue (perhaps the fate of many incipient states). But one outcome is that the initial equality amongst the players does not last indefinitely. An advantage that at the time may escape notice upsets the equilibrium enough to distort the whole subsequent progress of the game. It has a 'knock-on' effect out of all proportion to its original importance. A person on a winning streak finds that his advantageous position continues to reinforce itself. And so the game inexorably follows a trajectory towards a critical point where one player has accumulated sufficient assets to outweigh the threats posed by the other players and so that player becomes unstoppable. It becomes only a matter of time before he wins by monopolizing the assets of all, although the inevitability of his win belongs only to a late stage in the game.

We can move closer to historical reality by imagining thousands of games proceeding

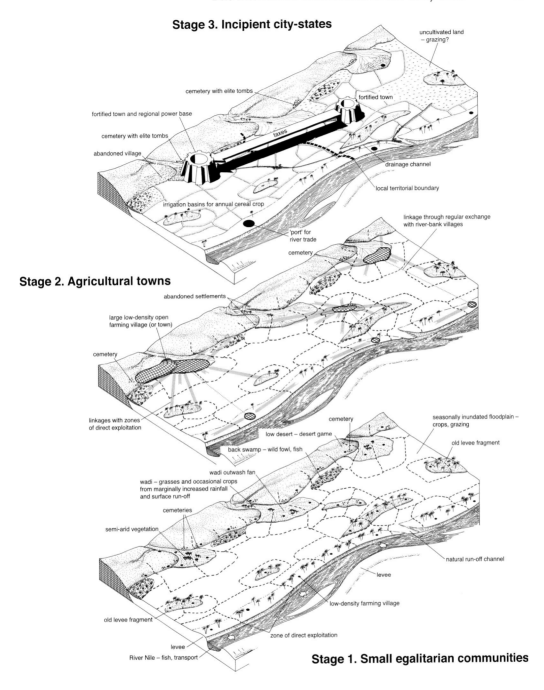

Stage 3. Incipient city-states

uncultivated land
– grazing?

cemetery with elite tombs

fortified town

fortified town and regional power base

cemetery with elite tombs

abandoned village

taxes

drainage channel

local territorial boundary

irrigation basins for annual cereal crop

'port' for
river trade

cemetery

linkage through regular exchange
with river-bank villages

Stage 2. Agricultural towns

abandoned settlements

large low-density open
farming village (or town)

cemetery

linkages with zones
of direct exploitation

cemetery

low desert – desert game

back swamp – wild fowl, fish

wadi outwash fan

wadi – grasses and occasional crops
from marginally increased rainfall
and surface run-off

cemeteries

semi-arid vegetation

seasonally inundated floodplain –
crops, grazing

old levee fragment

natural run-off channel

levee

low-density farming village

old levee fragment

levee

zone of direct exploitation

River Nile – fish, transport

Stage 1. Small egalitarian communities

Figure 21 Model landscape of Upper Egypt in the late Predynastic Period showing the likely environmental factors and local pattern of territorial and political expansion during the crucial phase of state formation.

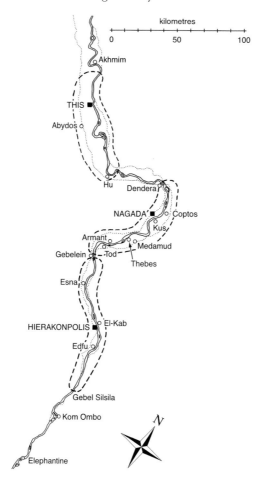

Figure 22   State formation: hypothetical map of the most important proto-states of Upper Egypt as they developed in the late Predynastic Period (see Figure 23, p. 77).

simultaneously, with winners promoted to join a progression of increasingly select games, where they dress in strange costumes and perform the acts of play with exaggerated formal gestures, the successful amongst them playing for ever higher stakes. We need also to correct the timescale, our view of who the 'players' really are. For the most part, so few significant changes of circumstance occur in any one real lifetime that each player is actually many generations treated as a unity. And in real life the games continue beyond the point of winning. Processes of decay and fission set in and the games go on with different outcomes likely. This point will be developed further in Chapter 8.

The attraction of this analogy is that it sets up in our imaginations a simple system with feedback loops.[33] It concentrates attention on the essence of a basic process at work in history and draws one away from the temptation to explain events through single causes. Human societies large and small are made up of individuals whose behaviour is not com-

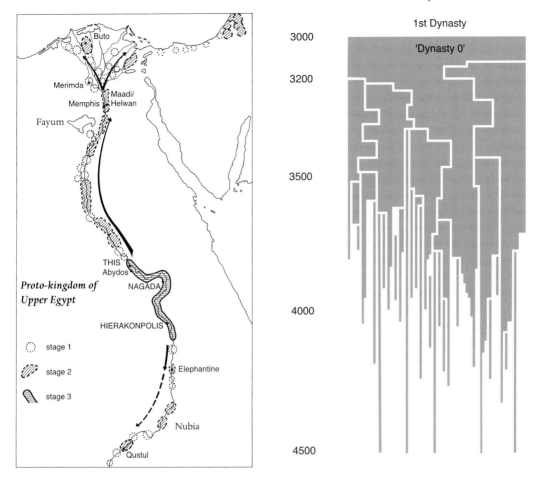

Figure 23 State formation. *Left*. A simple linear view. The processes of centralization are at work throughout the area but at different rates, so that different stages of development (arbitrarily reduced to three) had been reached by the time that the politically most developed centre, a proto-kingdom of Upper Egypt based at Hierakonpolis (Figure 22, p. 76), embarked on a military expansion (marked by arrows) which engulfed the whole of Egypt. Early in the 1st Dynasty the expansion continued into Nubia. *Right*. A more likely process, of complicated but now unrecoverable micro-history involving an ebb and flow of success for individual places, not necessarily based upon violence. In the diagram the boundaries are those of local autonomy.

pletely predictable. The result is not wholly randomized 'background noise'. As with any complex adaptive system that allows a degree of free association and interaction of its constituent parts – the molecules of air in weather formations, for example – tiny variations can set up self-reinforcing consequences that grow in power out of all proportion to the starting conditions. Hurricanes suddenly appear. The process can also lead away from a level of integration already achieved. The rapid collapse of communist states in eastern Europe in the 1980s and 1990s and the equally rapid collapse of the market economy of the west in 1929 are striking modern examples of human social and economic systems running temporarily in reverse, towards dispersal of the energy that has gathered into centres of power, where the prime factor has been the accumulation of innumerable personal acts, borne of disillusion, frustration or greed.

Analogies have drawbacks. A misleading aspect of my imagined board game concerns the notion of rules. They stand for the limits which most people place on their behaviour and for the various restraints which systems impose. The study of history, however, including cases of recorded state formation, reveals that striking transformations often happen through the agency of unusually dominant individuals who flout the rules, kill their rivals and seize everything. Charismatic leadership is, in a way, another 'chance' factor, but to make good progress it has to come at the right point in the game. The interaction between system and individual lies at the heart of much modern historical (and archaeological) study.[34]

We can draw the implication that all parts of Egypt where settled farming communities were early established should have advanced some way along the trajectory of play before its final and more theatrical stages, simply as a result of local internal processes. There was thus a receptive background to the last phase of political unification. The final expansion of the winning kingdom was into a social and economic landscape in which the processes of state formation were already under way, although at different rates.

Foundations of ideology (1): local tradition

It is very difficult to penetrate in a specific way the minds and the dealings of people during the Predynastic Period, before writing had appeared. But archaeology gives us two signals to inform us when the process of state formation was in progress. One is the physical drawing together of communities into larger settlements that become towns. This is the process of urbanization, which increases the scope for interaction amongst individuals in whom the great change in outlook is taking place, involving an expanding sense of imagined community and mystic association with a defined tract of land. The other is the appearance of the rewards of successful competitive interaction in the form of evidence for conspicuous consumption and display. The familiar picture of social stratification, of a society of haves, have-nots and many in between, has arrived. In Egypt this reveals itself in more richly equipped tombs for a minority, and signs of an emerging ideology of power. Two sites in Upper Egypt, Nagada and Hierakonpolis, exemplify both aspects.

The modern village of Nagada, 26 kilometres downstream from Luxor, on the west bank, has given its name to a site more properly known as Ombos (Nubt).[35] In Pharaonic times this was an important centre for the cult of Seth. Excavation and survey have revealed that a town had stood here from the Nagada II phase of Predynastic culture (from *c.* 3500 BC, thus around 500 years before the beginning of the 1st Dynasty), and that from the 18th Dynasty or earlier it had possessed a small stone temple dedicated to Seth. The extent and importance of the town in historical times seem to have been far less than during the Predynastic Period when it is, in fact, one of the largest known sites in the Nile valley (Figure 24). This applies both to the area covered by a deposit of Predynastic settlement debris, which included part of a walled town (the South Town) built of brick, and to a series of cemeteries. One of them, cemetery T, small and lying on a ridge just behind the town, has the hallmarks of a rulers' cemetery. Some of the graves had been

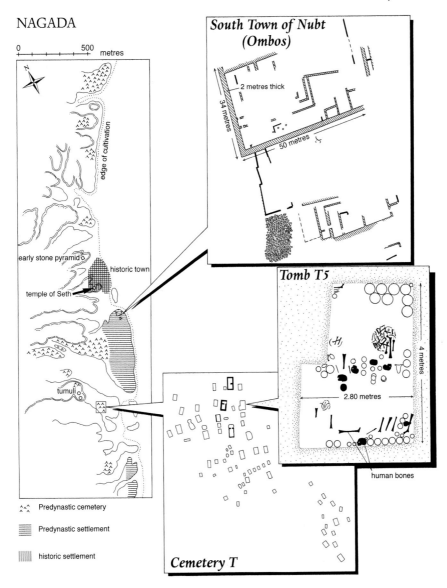

Figure 24 Nagada: centre of one of the first proto-states in the Nile valley. Note the extent of the Predynastic town, with its substantial mud-brick enclosure and other buildings at the northern end. The town of the historic period occupied much less space, but probably made up for this in increased density of occupation. The temple of Seth, however, remained a building of modest size throughout ancient times. The huge Predynastic cemetery behind the Predynastic town is the largest to have survived from this period. Cemetery T, although small, contained unusually well-constructed tombs for rich burials, probably those for a ruling house of Nagada. The basic map is after W. Kaiser, *MDAIK* 17 (1961), 16, Abb. 3 (see W.M.F. Petrie and J.E. Quibell, *Naqada and Ballas*, London, 1896, Pl. IA); the inset map of the South Town is after Petrie and Quibell, op. cit., Pl. LXXXV, and that of tomb T5, ibid., Pl. LXXXII; the inset map of cemetery T itself is after B.J. Kemp, *JEA* 59 (1973), 39, Fig. 1, itself after Petrie and Quibell, op. cit., Pl. LXXXVI.

HIERAKONPOLIS

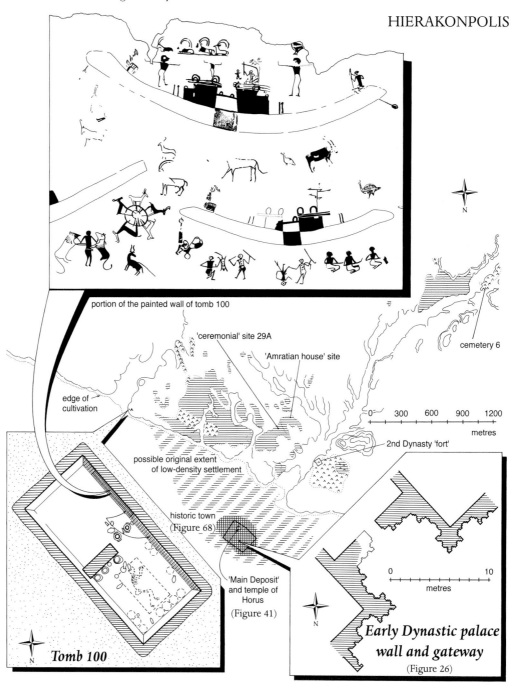

portion of the painted wall of tomb 100

'ceremonial' site 29A

'Amratian house' site

cemetery 6

edge of
cultivation

possible original extent
of low-density settlement

2nd Dynasty 'fort'

0   300   600   900   1200

metres

historic town
(Figure 68)

'Main Deposit'
and temple of
Horus
(Figure 41)

Tomb 100

0   10

metres

*Early Dynastic palace
wall and gateway*
(Figure 26)

unusually large and well furnished and, most unusually for the Predynastic Period, had been lined with brick. If we combine the archaeological picture of Nagada with the later position of Seth, we have a reasonably firm basis for claiming that at some time in the later Predynastic Period Nagada had been the capital of a chiefdom or small state.

The association between a major early archaeological site (Nagada) and the cult of one of the gods most closely associated with kingship (Seth) is encouragingly neat. The second site, Hierakonpolis, also contains the essence of a similar association, this time with Horus, but of an altogether more complex kind. The site itself lies in the most southerly region of Upper Egypt (Figure 25).[36] Its importance is visible from two aspects of its archaeology. One is the sheer size of the spread of settlement debris of the Predynastic Period (7 hectares on the desert, and more now buried beneath modern fields). It includes an enigmatic set of structures (locality 29A) that might be the remains of a ceremonial area (see below, pp. 147–9). The second aspect comprises a number of unusually rich and well constructed tombs divided between at least two widely separated cemeteries (cemetery 6 and the other unnumbered). One tomb at the latter, no. 100, lined with mud brick and painted with a series of scenes, must have been the tomb of a late Predynastic king.[37] Although in style the painting appears alien in comparison with the formalized art of the Dynastic Period, we can recognize at least two motifs which survived into historic times: the victor smiting bound enemies with an upraised mace (Figure 33, lower, p. 96), and the ruler standing beneath a simple awning, reminiscent of later scenes of the king seated during the jubilee or *Sed*-festival (see below).

In its general aspect Hierakonpolis resembles Nagada. Both sites also exhibit a pronounced shrinkage towards the end of the Predynastic Period. This marks a fundamental change in the nature of settlement, bound up with the appearance of true urbanism in Egypt: the shift from sprawling low-density settlements to walled brick-built towns of far higher population density. The city on the floodplain into which the low-density occupation of Hierakonpolis eventually coalesced has fared much better than Nagada. Destruction has been less intense, and much of the archaeological digging has been reasonably careful. One discovery has been a fragment of a sector of the Early Dynastic town, kept separate

Figure 25 Hierakonpolis: cradle of Egyptian kingship. The base map shows the areas of low-density Predynastic settlement together with the cemeteries on the low desert, and the possible continuation of settlement beneath the present floodplain, on an ancient wadi outwash fan now buried beneath alluvium. In the midst of the latter area stands the walled town of Hierakonpolis of the Dynastic Period (see Figures 41, p. 122, 68, p. 196), which represents, as at Nagada, a smaller but much denser settlement than its Predynastic predecessor. The map is after W. Kaiser, *MDAIK* 17 (1961), 6, Abb. 1 and M. Hoffman, *The Predynastic of Hierakonpolis*, Giza and Macomb, Ill., 1982, end map. Towards the beginning of the developmental sequence of kingship is tomb 100 (the 'Decorated Tomb'), probably the tomb of an early king of Hierakonpolis of the Nagada II period (*c.* 3300 BC), and the enigmatic 'ceremonial' site 29A (Figure 53, p. 149); at the other end is the fragment of Early Dynastic palace wall (*c.* 3000/2700 BC) and the huge mud-brick 'fort' of the end of the 2nd Dynasty, both monuments of the aristocratic family which continued to occupy Hierakonpolis for several generations after the beginning of the 1st Dynasty. The Early Dynastic palace gateway and wall are a simplified version of Figure 26, p. 82. The 'Main Deposit' is an anciently buried cache of temple votive equipment of the late Predynastic/Early Dynastic Period and somewhat later, found in the early temple enclosure of Horus. A detailed plan of the temple remains is given in Figure 41, p. 122. Amongst the material in the deposit were the Narmer Palette (Figure 27, p. 84) and Smaller Hierakonpolis (or Two-dog) Palette illustrated in Figure 31, p. 94.

HIERAKONPOLIS

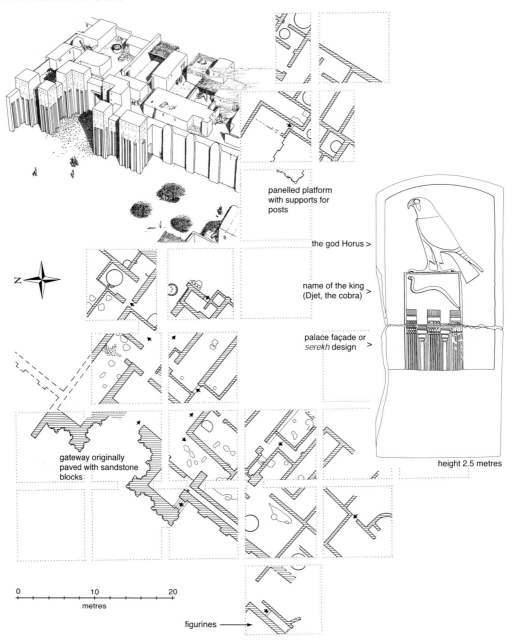

panelled platform
with supports for
posts

the god Horus >

name of the king >
(Djet, the cobra)

palace façade or
serekh design >

height 2.5 metres

N

gateway originally
paved with sandstone
blocks

0   10   20

metres

figurines →

from the rest of the town by a distinctive, whitewashed enclosure wall marked at regular intervals with buttresses (Figure 26). Part of the way along it was broken by a projecting gateway decorated with a more elaborate style of panels and niches that seems to have been a symbol of rule (the heraldic device knows as a *serekh*, meaning something like an 'announcement', which was used as a frame around the king's Horus name, the first of the set of names that each king bore, is derived from it, Figure 26, inset). It is an example of the way that architects sometimes use the scale and design of gateways to summarize the function and interior of the building as a whole. The gateway gave access to a maze-like settlement that seems to have surrounded a central space into which protruded a small brick platform, also with panelled sides provided with supports for wooden poles, perhaps for a canopy. The complex as a whole is our best candidate anywhere in Egypt for an early palace, which turns out to have been a mud-brick compound, seemingly modest in the scale of its individual parts, and providing only limited separation between the huts of the king's followers and the needs of ceremonial. It was in these surroundings that the products of high craftsmanship that we so admire were made and used, and the power of the early state was wielded.[38]

Another portion of the early town to have survived is the principal temple (described below, pp. 121–4 and Figure 41), within which priests of later centuries had piously buried deposits of votive offerings from the late Predynastic/Early Dynastic periods. Once again the royal associations are plain. The deposits include statues, stone vases and other fragmentary inscribed pieces of one or more kings of the late 2nd Dynasty and, above all, the Narmer Palette (Figure 27). This remarkable object, carved in low relief on both sides of a palette of mudstone (or 'slate'), commemorates a victory over a northern enemy by a King Narmer from the very beginning of the 1st Dynasty. He wears the crowns of Upper and of Lower Egypt, and is faced on one side by a figure of the god Horus. The whole is decorated according to the full artistic canon of Pharaonic Egypt, displays certain of the key distinguishing marks of kings in its depictions of Narmer, and contains small groups of hieroglyphs. The Narmer Palette encapsulates certain of the essential elements of Pharaonic culture, and announces their presence at the very beginning of the dynastic sequence.

In later times Hierakonpolis was the seat of one form of the god Horus, called Horus of Nekhen (Hierakonpolis). Aside from his connection with kingship, Horus (and to a

Figure 26 Hierakonpolis: a mud-brick ruler's compound (or 'palace') of the Early Dynastic Period. The niched 'palace wall and gateway' appear also in Figures 25, p. 80 and 68, p. 196. From front to back the ground level rose, so that the panelled platform was higher than the entrance. The small arrows mark upward slope. Omitted are various walls, mainly in the central open space, which seem to belong to an Old Kingdom town-phase which followed, although much of the rear was also buried in sand, whether naturally blown in or deliberately dumped is not clear. After W.A. Fairservis, *The Hierakonpolis Project, season January to May 1981. Excavation on the Kom el Gemuwia*, Vassar College, Poughkeepsie, N.Y., 1986, Figures 7A and 7B; also K. Weeks, *JARCE* 9 (1971–2), unnumbered fig.

Inset. The substance of early monarchy: the name of King Djet of the 1st Dynasty (*c.* 2900 BC), written with the hieroglyphic sign of the cobra, appears above a stylized rendering of the distinctive architecture of the royal palace. This the Egyptians called a *serekh*, and a common modern term for the style is 'palace façade'. Standing above is a figure of the falcon-god Horus, of whom each king was an embodiment. Funerary stela of King Djet, from his tomb at Abydos. After A. Vigneau, *Encyclopédie photographique de l'art: Les antiquités égyptiennes du Musée du Louvre*, Paris, 1935, 4.

Figure 27 The Narmer Palette, 63 cm high, is a slab of 'slate' carved on both sides with scenes commemorating the reign of a king with the Horus name of Narmer (written at the top in the 'palace façade' rectangles), who must have lived immediately prior to the beginning of the 1st Dynasty and may well have been the last and greatest of the kings of Dynasty 0 of Hierakonpolis. On the *left side*, Narmer, wearing the white crown of Upper Egypt and other insignia of early monarchy, stands with upraised mace about to smite a kneeling captive. Beside the captive's head a group of hieroglyphs gives his name as Wash. The design above probably conveys the supplementary message that the Horus-king (the falcon) has won a victory over an enemy based in the delta, of whom Wash was presumably the ruler. Behind Narmer is a high-ranking figure who carries the king's sandals. On the *right side* the images of conquest in the top and bottom registers are balanced by the central design which expresses harmony, in the form of the intertwined and captive mythical animals. In the top register Narmer, now wearing the red crown of Lower Egypt and accompanied by two men of high rank, walks to inspect two rows of bound and decapitated enemies. The party is preceded by four bearers of standards of distinctive shape. These standards were later called the 'Followers of Horus', or 'The gods who follow Horus'. Whatever their origin, by the time of Narmer they were clearly part of the array of symbols which contributed to the unique aura of kingship. The symbols above the decapitated enemies cannot be interpreted with confidence. In the lowest register the conquering power of the king, symbolized by a bull, is directed against a walled and fortified town. The drawings of the palette are after J.E. Quibell, *ZÄS* 36, 1898, Taf. XII, XIII; J.E. Quibell, *Hierakonpolis* I, London, 1900, Pl. XXIX; W.M.F. Petrie, *Ceremonial slate palettes and corpus of protodynastic pottery*, London, 1953, Pls J, K; V. Davies, *Nekhen News* 10 (1998), 22.

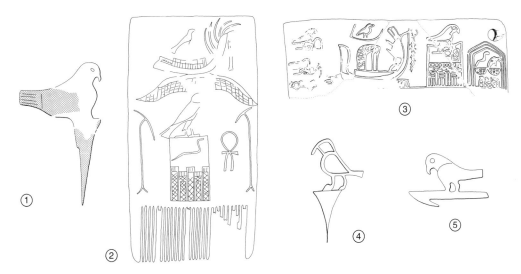

Figure 28   The dual aspects of Horus: as heavenly power, wielding instruments of destruction, and as earthly ruler. (1), (4) and (5) are figures of Horus wielding a spike or harpoon. On (3) (*left*) he also wields a mixture of mace, shield and hoe. Towards the right side of (3) the Horus name of the king, Aha ('the fighter'), written with a mace-and-shield hieroglyph, is borne as an emblem by the figure of Horus. In (2) and (3) the ubiquitous nature of Horus as heavenly power is symbolized by a boat which, in (2), is also borne aloft by a pair of wings. The Horus name of the king commemorated on (2), Djet, is the same as that depicted in Figure 26, *inset*. (1) is a reconstructed figure on the side of one of the Coptos colossi (see Figure 45, p. 130). (2) is an ivory comb, length 8 cm, from Abydos. After R. Engelbach, *ZÄS* 65 (1930), 115–16; F. Tiradritti, *The Cairo Museum; masterpieces of Egyptian art*, London, 1999, 44. (3) is the top register of one of a pair of ivory year-labels from Nagada, width 5.6 cm, after V. Vikentiev *ASAE* 33 (1933), Pl. II; F. Tiradritti, op. cit., 42. A companion piece fills in the missing area of water beneath the central boat, J. Garstang, *ZÄS* 42 (1905), 62, Fig. 3.

lesser extent his female counterpart, the goddess Hathor) was, in historic times, a god of widespread immanence in specific local forms. He was thus, at one and the same time, universal and local, although how far his universality was recognized in Predynastic times is difficult to judge. The name Horus means 'The One on High', and as such he appears in a boat astride a pair of wings in the sky, above a second Horus figure surmounting a king's name (Figure 28.2). Later thinking located Horus more particularly at the horizon, and associated him with the sun-god Ra at the time of sunrise, in the combination Ra-Horakhty ('Ra-Horus of the horizon'). Early representations (Figure 28) also stress a violent aspect and show him wielding weapons – a spike, a harpoon, a mace-and-shield or a hoe (for hacking down walls) – an aspect which survived into much later times as 'Horus, avenger of his father' (Osiris) and 'Min-Horus, the victorious', the object of a cult at Abydos.[39]

In historic times local forms of Horus (and Hathor) appear both within Egypt and in certain foreign territories under Egyptian control. 'Horus Lord of Hebenu' was, for example, the presiding divinity at the town of Hebenu in Middle Egypt; 'Horus Lord of Buhen' and 'Horus Lord of Miam' were cults set up by the Egyptians at two of their fortresses in Nubia, Buhen and Miam (modern Aniba). Two more of these topographically defined Horus-gods appear on the El-Lisht throne bases: 'Horus, Lord of Mesen', and 'Horus, the Behdetite', but here, as we have seen, they stand for Lower Egypt. Yet the first time that 'Horus of Behdet' appears, on a carved stone panel beneath the Step Pyramid (c. 2650 BC), the symbolic connections are actually with Upper Egypt.[40] There has to be the strong suspicion that the Lower Egyptian association of Horus is the product of rationalization, taking place during the Dynastic Period and reflecting the need to create a geographically comprehensive myth. The celestial Horus, who also embodied each king, was perfectly fitted to this mobile role.

Hierakonpolis remained important during the Old Kingdom, becoming a walled town of densely packed buildings. Thereafter it seems to have declined as a centre of settlement, although its temple remained in use and was rebuilt in both the Middle and New Kingdoms though not on a grand scale. Its place as a major focus of urban life on the west bank in this part of Egypt was taken by Edfu, 15 kilometres upstream. The archaeological record here reveals a place of negligible significance in the early periods.[41] Only with the Old Kingdom, perhaps the 4th Dynasty, does a walled town seem to have appeared, which then grew, reaching a maximum extent in the First Intermediate Period. The rise of Edfu as a regional centre at the expense of Hierakonpolis led to one of several outbreaks of local internal warfare in the early part of the First Intermediate Period. In the course of this, Edfu was for a time taken over by the governor of the Hierakonpolis region, a man named Ankhtif who, to judge from the location of his tomb at Mo'alla, lived not at Hierakonpolis itself but 50 kilometres downstream, near the northern border of his territory. By the early Middle Kingdom a Horus cult at Edfu had become prominent, remaining so until Ptolemaic and Roman times and attracting the resources for the monumental sandstone temple of that late era that still stands almost wholly intact. The place names Behdet and Mesen, primarily Lower Egyptian names, came to be used as synonyms for Edfu, a recognition of its symbolic status. The changing mythical role of Horus exemplifies how traditions are moulded and reshaped as history moves on.

Parallel to the symbolic geography of Horus and Seth is that for a pair of goddesses who stood for the duality of kingship. They are the vulture-goddess Nekhbet of the ancient city of Nekheb (modern El-Kab; her name means simply 'She of Nekheb') and the cobra-goddess Wadjit of the delta city of Buto. El-Kab lay across the river from Hierakonpolis. Its archaeological record appears to be that of a Predynastic settlement of only modest size, growing to a walled town during the Old Kingdom.[42] It is not a counterpart to Nagada and Hierakonpolis. The inclusion of its goddess within the basic symbols of kingship must reflect some local interest, perhaps a family connection, on the part of the late Predynastic kingdom of Hierakonpolis not apparent from the general archaeological picture.

Buto in the north has been the object of a modern archaeological quest, and serves to introduce the early archaeology of the Nile delta. Aside from the association with Wadjit, other sources of the historic period paired it with Hierakonpolis through the mythological entity 'the souls of Pe [Buto] and Nekhen [Hierakonpolis]' (Figure 29, *above*), an interesting abstraction in itself. Is this a way of referring to ancestral founding figures from the most distant past that the Egyptians could imagine? This ancient mythological claim has been sufficient to create the modern expectation that, buried beneath the mud of the delta, there lie the remains of the Predynastic capital of Lower Egypt. Textual sources locate Buto at Tell el-Fara'in, very close to the likely ancient shoreline of the Mediterranean. A huge archaeological site exists here, but all that is visible dates to the later

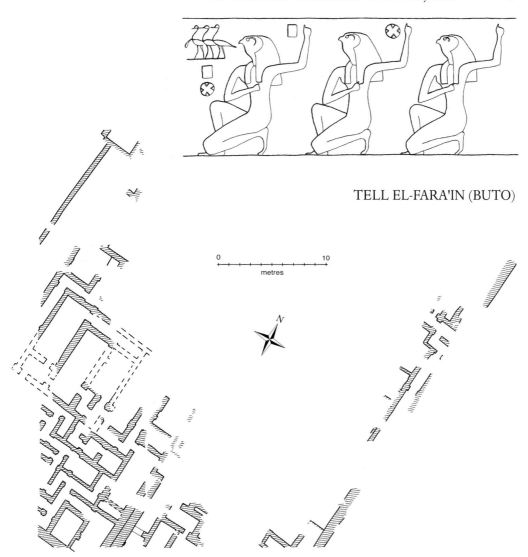

TELL EL-FARA'IN (BUTO)

Figure 29 Plan of Level V at Tell el-Fara'in (Buto) in the north-western delta. It dates to the Early Dynastic Period. The interlocking pattern of rooms and corridors might be compared with the small building inside the Shunet ez-Zebib at Abydos (Figure 35A, p. 102) or even the Hierakonpolis palace (Figure 26, p. 82). After M. Ziermann, *MDAIK* 58 (2002), 480, Abb. 8. *Above.* In later centuries Buto (as well as Hierakonpolis) was thought to be the home of 'souls' (spiritual royal ancestors), here shown as hawk-headed beings. After E. Naville, *The Festival-Hall of Osorkon II in the Great Temple of Bubastis (1887–1889)*, London, 1892, Pl. IX.6.

periods of Egyptian culture. It took a methodical programme of hand-drilling into the surrounding fields to locate the lost early settlement, which had stood on a now wholly buried sandy mound located to one side of the later city. So far only limited exposures have been possible but they reveal an oddly unprepossessing beginning for a place of later legend.[43] The first settlement (stratum I), 4–5 metres below the present ground level, appeared in the first quarter of the fourth millennium BC. Its remains display no recognizable architecture and its inhabitants had made for themselves copies of pottery that was at home in Palestine during the contemporary Chalcolithic Period. Were they themselves immigrants? In the subsequent phase (stratum II) the pottery seems to be largely derived from northern Egyptian styles, and the remains of a simple architecture of wooden posts and wattle-and-daub screens can be recognized. Then, towards the end of the Predynastic Period (beginning Nagada IId), came a substantial change in the local way of life (stratum III, continuing into IV). Mud-brick buildings appeared, along with pottery of the Upper Egyptian (Nagada) tradition and a major change in the types of flint tools. With stratum V and the Early Dynastic Period the excavated area is filled with a fragment of an extensive mud-brick building of small interlocking spaces (Figure 29). Is it a palace? A closely similar sequence (but without a 'palace') has been found at Tell Ibrahim Awad in the north-eastern delta, and is probably represented at other delta sites.[44] At Minshat Abu Omar, also towards the north-east, a Nagada-style cemetery appeared in the late Nagada II period and served a settlement into the Early Dynastic Period, but as yet insufficient is known of the settlement to visualize what kind of place it had been previously.[45]

The culture of the lower, pre-brick building phases at Buto is sufficiently distinctive to merit the use of a separate term to distinguish it from the Nagada cultures of Upper Egypt. The term that has come to be accepted derives not from Buto but from the previously excavated site of Maadi, now within a southern suburb of Cairo of this name.[46] This was an extensive settlement (130,000 square metres) that did contain houses, but made from wooden posts which must have supported screens of reeds. Mud bricks were used hardly at all. Its material culture is similar to that of Buto stratum II, and neither by structures nor by artefacts can we detect any significant accumulations of wealth or prestige. Copper was present, not only as the material for a limited number of objects, but also as a poor-quality ore. Yet the extent to which a copper industry had been developed remains unclear. The occupation of Maadi began in mid-Nagada I and came to an end in the latter part of Nagada II, but whether as a consequence of political and social change or of environmental deterioration (it stood on the desert edge) is also not clear. Its place as a local centre of population was taken by a community whose extensive cemetery was long ago excavated at the site of Tura, only one kilometre away, where the material culture buried with the dead was of the Upper Egyptian Nagada tradition.

Throughout the Dynastic Period, with only isolated exceptions (of which the most conspicuous occur in the Second Intermediate Period, see above, pp. 39–41), the visible culture of Egypt was more or less uniform from Elephantine to the Mediterranean. But Maadi culture represents a period of perhaps four centuries (based on radiocarbon dates) when this had not yet come about, and the way of life at Buto and elsewhere in the north seems to have been different. From our standpoint it was less advanced in terms of buildings and artefacts and the technology that the latter required. Uniformity came about through the northward expansion of the Nagada culture of which the towns of Nagada and Hierakonpolis were important centres. Nagada culture had roots even earlier in Upper Egypt, some of them visible in the traces of tiny communities of the fifth millennium BC found in the region of the modern village of El-Badari (hence the archaeologists' term Badarian). Cultural difference notwithstanding, a settled farming way of life seems to have developed in the north at least as early as it did in the south. The same competitive processes must have begun to come into play there as well, losing out only in the later stages of disequilibrium.

The significance of this difference is hard to evaluate. So much that makes up culture and identity is not expressed directly through material remains and so leaves the archaeologist with little that is firm to grasp. The ability to organize and to fight is not, for example, wholly to be measured in how well villages are constructed and how ornate are the pots. Thucydides in the fifth century BC made the point tellingly in a contrast between Athens and Sparta, both great powers yet the latter 'simply a collection of villages, in the ancient Hellenic way'. He invites the reader to imagine Sparta reduced to ruins: 'I think that future generations would, as time passed, find it very difficult to believe that the place had really been as powerful as it was represented to be.'[47] The archaeological evidence from Buto suggests that palace culture, if such it was, arrived only with the 1st Dynasty, but that does not answer the Thucydides paradox: that power and display are not wholly dependent upon one another.

This brings us back to the topic of identity. In the south, the material culture of Nagada had much more in common with that of northern Nubia, its neighbour, and the peoples of the two areas were closely similar at the skeletal level, as we saw in the last chapter. Yet we know, because the difference persisted into historic times, that the two societies were divided by language and that Egyptians saw Nubians as a different people. To the north the distinction, at the level of archaeology, between the Nagada and Maadi cultures seems to be larger. What other differences might there have been, which are now invisible to us? Those who write about this period tend to take for granted an ethnic and linguistic homogeneity for all Egypt, leaving a greater burden of proof on those who would argue otherwise. Experience over the last few centuries of the expansion of cultures that have become dominant, however, is that language is a ready victim in the reduction of cultural diversity. There is, I would have thought, an equal justification for holding that the north had, until Early Dynastic times, an identity of its own, expressed in its own language. The conspicuous 'Egyptianness' of the historic periods, which was later so easily able to absorb outsiders, might itself have been the result of the northward expansion of an Upper Egyptian identity in which language played a key role. We are unlikely ever to be able to explore this possibility further, but should retain it as an option.

Late in the Predynastic Period a third major player emerged in Upper Egypt, represented in the archaeological record at the site of Abydos (Figure 30).[48] Throughout the Pharaonic period Abydos remained a town on the edge of the desert, one of those places that coalesced from several tiny settlements at the end of the Predynastic Period. From the Middle Kingdom onwards it was nationally famous for its cult of the god Osiris, whose tomb was thought to be in the desert behind Abydos and was a place of pilgrimage for any who wished to enhance the prospects of resurrection after death. It seems never to have served, however, as a regional centre. That position, in historic times, was held by the city of This, which seems to have lain close to the river, probably in the vicinity of the modern town of Girga. The local inhabitants of Predynastic times used a number of cemeteries on the desert edge. But further out across the sand, at the very place which was later seen as containing the tomb of Osiris, a separate cemetery developed (in modern times named the Umm el-Qaʿab, 'mother of pots', on account of the vessels left by pilgrims of later periods), beginning in the Nagada I period and culminating with the actual tombs of the kings of

ABYDOS

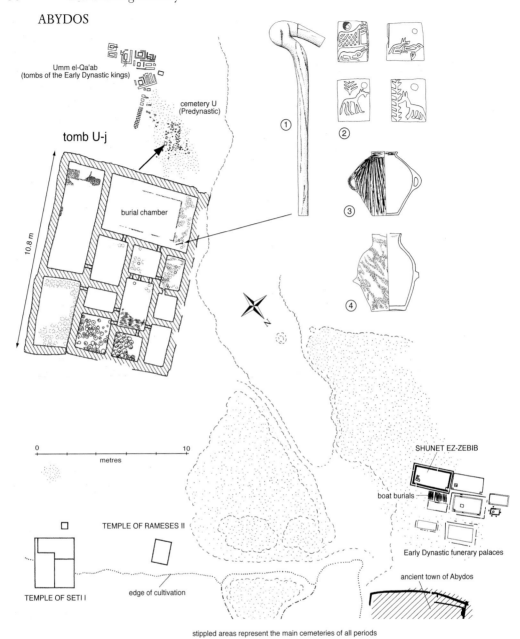

Figure 30 Abydos and Egypt's early kings. Superimposed on the sketch map of Abydos is the plan of tomb U-j of Dynasty 0 and of some of its contents. (1) Ivory sceptre of office (originally painted red). Height 33.5 cm. (2) Four ivory labels incised with early hieroglyphic signs. (3) and (4) Two examples of the approximately 200 imported Palestinian pottery storage jars (decorated with red-brown lines) found in position in the tomb. After G. Dreyer, *Umm El-Qaab* I, *Das prädynastische Königsgrab U-j und seine frühen Schriftzeugnisse*, Mainz, 1998, after p. 4, Abb. 2 (plan), 147, Abb. 85 (sceptre); 122, Abb. 77 (labels); and 103, Abb. 66 (pots).

the 1st Dynasty. As revealed by excavations in the late 1980s and 1990s, it is a classic demonstration both of long continuity and of the emergence of social and economic disparity, in this case the emergence of the people who would become the rulers of all Egypt and the founders of the Dynastic state. I will return to the architecture of the funerary monuments of the Early Dynastic kings at Abydos later in the chapter. For the moment we will concentrate on the area where the tombs of their immediate predecessors were located.

Mostly it had been badly disturbed by the time it was investigated by archaeologists, and the contents of the individual tombs were to some extent scattered. But the earliest of the recognizable names of kings come from here, and they form a short sequence which extends a little way – a few generations – before the start of the later king lists and our own sense that Egyptian history had begun. The custom has grown up of referring to these rulers collectively as forming 'Dynasty 0', as a way of marking their kingly status in relation to the unassailable numbered list of dynasties given to us by Manetho. One tomb (its modern designation U-j), better preserved than most, provides a particularly valuable point of reference (Figure 30).[49] Its twelve brick-lined chambers were intended to house a richer burial than its predecessors, one of the chambers still containing over four hundred wine jars imported from Palestine. Left over from the debris of robbery were the remains of an ivory ceremonial sceptre and 173 small bone and ivory labels originally attached to other commodities to identify them by means of groups of signs. Though hard to read with confidence they must count as the earliest use of hieroglyphic writing that we can recognize. The owner of the tomb lived at a time when Nagada culture had spread across the delta. Did his own rule spread that far as well?

Further intriguing questions arise. Where did he and his family live at this time and what would he have counted as his home territory? Was he from a long-resident line of local leaders who were in the process of enlarging their territory, or was he one of the rulers of Hierakonpolis who, having extended their territory northwards to include an existing cemetery on already sacred ground, were now taking advantage of the opportunity to locate their own tombs there, too? Related to this is the equally difficult question as to whether there is any real historic connection between the choice of this piece of desert for a cemetery by a royal family, and the selection by later generations of one of the tombs (of King Djer) as supposedly the tomb of Osiris.[50] For our present concerns it should simply be noted that yet another fundamental aspect of Egyptian myth, intertwined about kingship and the tension between Horus and Seth, has a strong connection with an archaeological site in Upper Egypt central to the emergence of the Egyptian state.

In the principal king lists (Sakkara excepted) the earliest name is Menes and his should be one of the tombs on the Umm el-Qaʿab.[51] As first king of the lists Menes has tended to attract more attention in modern times than he did anciently. For there appears to have been no special body of legend attached to him. In the Ramesseum (the mortuary temple of Rameses II) a short list of all the kings of the New Kingdom down to Rameses II is prefaced first by King Menthuhetep II of the 11th Dynasty, victor of the civil war of the First Intermediate Period, and before him by Menes. But we cannot be sure if this reflects any special knowledge of Menes as the first unifier, or is a deduction from the simple fact that his was the first name in other lists. The Sakkara king list actually omits him, starting its enumeration a few reigns further on. This is particularly surprising in view of the fact that Herodotus records a story that Min (as he calls him) founded the city of Memphis, to which Sakkara belonged as the principal cemetery. Manetho has nothing special to say at all. The entry for Menes reads: 'He made a foreign expedition and won renown, but was carried off by a hippopotamus.'[52]

Menes belongs to the final stage in state formation. One new aspect of the dynastic state was the keeping of written annals: brief hieroglyphic notes on the most significant events in a royal year. The Palermo Stone was compiled from such documents. Specifically these records commenced with the period of Manetho's 1st Dynasty (the earliest belonging to the reign of Narmer himself). This may have been sufficient reason for later generations to start their lists with Menes (Narmer or Aha): he was simply the first of the kings to have a reign properly documented by annals.[53] I mentioned earlier that the Turin king list ventured beyond Menes, with groups of unnamed 'spirits' placed between Menes and the gods. The Palermo Stone provides us with a clue as to the origin of this tradition. Along the very top of the stone ran a line of little rectangular boxes which contained not the events of the passing years but simply names plus little pictures of seated kings. On the main fragment they wear the crown that, in historic times, had come to signify the kingship of Lower Egypt. On another, in the Cairo Museum, they wear the double crown. These names must belong to prehistoric kings about whom nothing more was known by the 5th Dynasty. When grouped as 'spirits' by the even later Turin compiler they made a suitable transition between gods and real kings with recorded reigns. For us there is the temptation to take them as the kings of Dynasty 0, in charge of several territories – the incipient city-states – throughout Egypt. The noteworthy fact that on the Cairo fragment some of these little figures wear the double crown means also that the Egyptians themselves did not, at least in the 5th Dynasty, see Menes as the very first unifier. If it is a reliable tradition (and it is a big 'if'), it fits in with a more protracted political history of formation of a unified state, such as the archaeological and artistic record implies.[54]

Foundations of ideology (2): the containment of unrule

State formation seems often, perhaps normally, to involve violence, although violence against other human beings was not something that only appeared at this stage. As already noted (p. 48), many of the people buried in the late Palaeolithic cemetery at Gebel Sahaba several millennia earlier had suffered weapon injuries.[55] Violent conflict is one of the themes of a range of delicately carved low relief scenes in soft stone and ivory which must have originated from the courts or elite households of Predynastic Upper Egypt.[56] They contain their own symbolism. Some elements survived into the iconography of historic times, but we cannot be sure if the values and meaning were modified in the course of transmission. More serious for our chances of correct understanding is the absence altogether of many of the most distinctive features of the iconography of historic times. Thus almost the whole of the later iconography of kingship is missing, at least until the very end of the sequence of the objects in question. The end is represented by the Narmer Palette and a few comparable carvings (most notably the Scorpion mace head, also from Hierakonpolis). As objects – commemorative palettes and mace heads – they belong to the world of the late Predynastic. But in their content and style the last pieces are the products of a great codifying of traditions that took place immediately prior to the beginning of the 1st Dynasty. At this time, and building on the work of the creators of earlier commemorative pieces, creative individuals thought out a remarkably homogeneous intellectual system. It embraced hieroglyphic writing, formal commemorative art of the kind that became one of the hallmarks of Pharaonic Egypt, and a basic iconography of kingship and rule. It was, in total, not quite the Egyptian culture of later centuries. Particularly in formal architecture and its meaning the Early Dynastic Period acquired a tradition of its own which was subsequently, during the early Old Kingdom, subject to a second major re-codification of form and meaning. But despite later re-workings the meaning of Early Dynastic culture is to some extent accessible to us because of the wealth of later material in the same style. This is far less true of Predynastic material. The process of conscious, academic codification that laid down the initial rules by which we now interpret Egyptian culture also acts as a barrier to our understanding the material that had been produced by previous generations, during the late Predynastic. We are obliged to attempt interpretation but this has to involve no small measure of intuition.

One of the most prominent aspects is the use of animals, both real and imagined, as an allegory of the forces of life (Figure 31). The species are primarily of the deserts, not those from which the Egyptians later developed animal cults. Sometimes they occur alone, sometimes they share a scene with human figures. They engage in violence, the predatory strong attacking the weak, or are at rest. Prominent is a harmonious pairing and balancing of particularly fierce beasts: wild dogs, lions and long-necked mythological creatures. They are always quadrupeds, and in no respect do they show a resemblance to the figures of Horus and Seth. One example occurs on the Narmer Palette, and here the context implies that the paired beasts stand for a political harmony. The theme generally conveys powerfully the intention on the part of the artist to depict an ultimate, attainable, harmonious framework to a turbulent world, the framework in the form of reconciled opposites, portrayed in allegorical form. An alternative depiction of order, again using animals to symbolize raw, natural life-forms, was by peaceful processions of animals, arranged in horizontal rows one above another. Sometimes they are accompanied by a more heterogeneous group of 'shepherding' figures that must symbolize a form of control. Sometimes, too, the orderliness was emphasized by using parallel horizontal base lines on which the animals stand. In these cases we can see the beginnings of the division of artistic space into defined horizontal bands (registers) that was to become such a distinctive feature of Pharaonic art. The use of animals as an allegory of untamed chaotic life-force survived into the religious art of historic times, most notably in scenes of king and gods capturing wild birds (and in the Graeco-Roman Period animals as well) in a huge clap-net, where texts and context make it clear that the symbolism is of the containment of disorder (Figure 32, *below*).[57]

The wall painting in tomb 100 at Hierakonpolis (Nagada IIC phase, *c.* 3400/3300 BC; Figure 25) is amenable to the same interpretation. It portrays a symbolic universe in which the central element is a line of boats. This is an early example of the prominent use of the boat as symbol that was to have a long history in Egypt. Some societies (including those of Europe from Roman times onwards) have found in the horse a powerful image of authority, which elevates and almost enshrines the rider. The Egyptians used the boat, often decked out in a distinctive way, to achieve the same effect, sometimes turning it quite literally into a shrine (see below, p. 249). In the Hierakonpolis tomb the boats appear as unassailable points of order and authority, conveying also the sense of passage through time. One of them, with its depiction of a ruler seated beneath an awning and protected by female guardian figures, is specifically associated with rule. On all sides are the threats

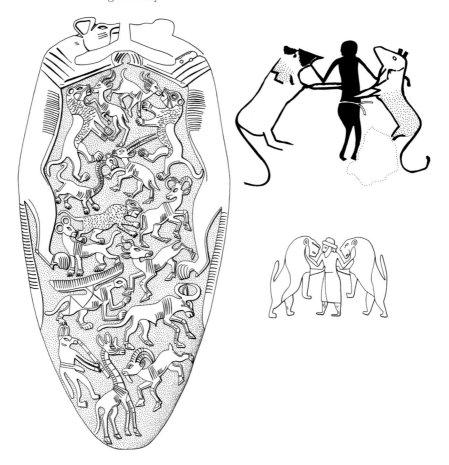

Figure 31   The containment of unrule in the universe. *Left*. The smaller Hierakonpolis (or Two-dog) Palette, reverse side. It portrays life allegorically as an unequal conflict between the strong and the weak, seemingly animated by the flute-playing presence of the Seth-like figure in the bottom left corner. The pre-eminent predators are the facing lions at the top who are, however, not far from a point of equilibrium in which their powers are mutually balancing. This ultimate point of harmony is hinted at by the framing figures of the fierce hunting dogs. *Right*. The actual point of arrested conflict is shown as having been achieved in two other scenes in which the facing lions are now held apart by a male human figure, perhaps a king. The upper example is from tomb 100 at Hierakonpolis (see Figure 25, p. 80); the lower is on the Gebel el-Arak knife handle. Photographs of the palette are in W.M.F. Petrie, *Ceremonial slate palettes and corpus of proto-dynastic pottery*, London, 1953, Pl. F; J.E. Quibell and F.W. Green, *Hierakonpolis* II, London, 1902, Pl. XXVIII; M.J. Mellink and J. Filip, *Frühe Stufen der Kunst* (Propyläen Kunstgeschichte 13), Berlin, 1974, Taf. 208. For the Gebel el-Arak knife handle, see Mellink and Filip, op. cit., Taf. 210; *Ancient Egypt* 1917, 29, Fig. 4.

from manifestations of raw life-force, some as desert animals and others in human form. The threats are countered by vignettes of capture or defeat. The same elemental struggle waged during a perpetual boat-voyage through time lies behind some of the much later scenes painted in the tombs of New Kingdom Pharaohs at Thebes. But by this time, fifteen

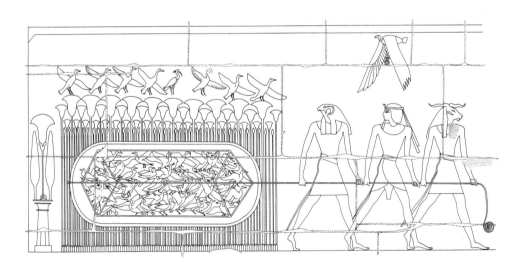

Figure 32 *Above.* The theme (containment of unrule) transferred to a cosmic plane of cyclic rebirth in which the triumphant voyager is the sun-god, here passing in his barque through one of the hours of the night. In the upper register are three beheaded figures identified as 'the enemies of Osiris', and three prostrate figures labelled 'the rebels'. In the lower register the demon of evil, the giant serpent Apopis, is butchered. Part of the Seventh Division of the 'Book of What is in the Otherworld' as painted on the walls of the tomb of King Tuthmosis III in the Valley of Kings at Thebes (*c.* 1430 B.C). The cursive hieroglyphic text has been omitted. After A. Piankoff, *The tomb of Rameses VI* I, New York, 1954, 277, Fig. 80. Coloured photographs are in J. Romer, *Romer's Egypt*, London, 1982, 170, 173. *Below.* The same theme illustrated by simple allegory from nature. Disorder is symbolized by wild fowl of the papyrus marshes. They are trapped and therefore constrained by a fowler's clap-net operated by King Rameses II and the gods Horus (*left*) and Khnum (*right*). Great Hypostyle Hall at Karnak, inner face of the south wall. See H. Frankfort, *Kingship and the gods*, Chicago, 1948, Fig. 14.

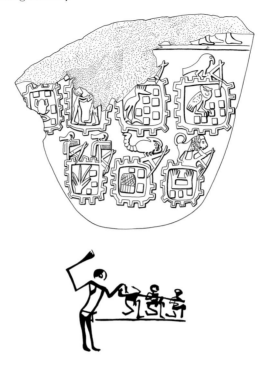

Figure 33 *Above.* One side of the Tjehenu Palette. The main scene, probably of battle, has been lost. The remaining bottom part shows seven fortified towns being attacked by animals symbolizing the monarchy and wielding hoes. The palette presumably celebrated a series of victories in the northward expansion of the kingdom of Hierakonpolis. After W.M.F. Petrie, *Ceremonial slate palettes and corpus of proto-dynastic pottery*, London, 1953, Pl. G; M.J. Mellink and J. Filip, *Frühe Stufen der Kunst* (Propyläen Kunstgeschichte 13), Berlin, 1974, Taf. 214b. *Below.* The scene of a warrior brandishing a mace over a line of bound captives is taken from tomb 100 at Hierakonpolis (Figure 25, p. 80), and probably depicts a Predynastic king in his role of victor in battle.

centuries or more of intellectual and artistic development had transformed the simple real landscape of chaos into an imagined Otherworld of dangers represented by invented demons (Figure 32, *above*). Real wooden boats also came to be an element of the royal and elite tomb constructions of the Early Dynastic Period (see p. 100, and Figure 30, p. 90, the row of boat burials amongst the funerary palaces at Abydos).[58]

We are entitled to ask: what was the source of the disorder that made itself felt at this time? It is a common sensation for the people of a settled society to feel surrounded and threatened by a turbulent and hostile outside world. For the small political units of late Predynastic Egypt the settings were parochial: the alien deserts and neighbouring communities not too far away along the Nile. But the more successful of these communities, the incipient city-states, had become engaged in more organized conflicts over territory, the conflicts which were to lead to the birth of the Egyptian state. The urgent reality of conflict involving attacks on walled settlements and the horrors of the battlefield was sometimes translated into pictorial scenes of actual combat (Figure 33), although the essence of conflict, of disequilibrium, was still viewed in generalized allegorical terms. From the

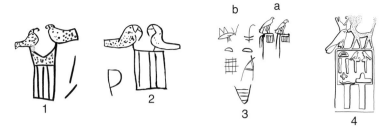

Figure 34   The theme of duality in early royal monograms and names. Nos. 1 and 2 (transition to 1st Dynasty) are monograms which represent in a simple way a section of royal palace façade, without adding the king's name (compare Figure 26, *inset*, p. 82), surmounted in each case by two Horus figures. After J. Clédat, *ASAE* 13 (1914), Pl. XIII; H. Junker, *Turah*, Vienna, 1912, 47, Abb. 58.5. In no. 3 the same two Horus figures (a) accompany the name of King (Adjib) Mer-pu-bia (b) of the 1st Dynasty (after W.M.F. Petrie, *Royal Tombs* I, London, 1900, Pl. V.12). No. 4 is a writing of the name of King Khasekhemui of the 2nd Dynasty in which one of the Horus figures has been replaced by a figure of Seth (compare Figure 20, p. 70). After J. Capart, *Memphis à l'ombre des pyramides*, Brussels, 1930, 119, Fig. 116.

experience of disorder and struggle, the shattering of an earlier equilibrium, arose the perception of a world in conflict, real or potential, between chaos and order. This was to remain a theme of intellectual concern for the rest of Egyptian history. So did the notion that containment (though not ultimate defeat) of disorder and unrule was possible through the rule of kings and the benign presence of a supreme divine force manifested in the powers of heaven, of Horus and of the sun. The intellectual view of the nature of the universe coincided with the structure of political power.

The paired animals are always identical. Even on the Narmer Palette they have no distinguishing marks to suggest a wish to identify each one in a distinctive way with one part of the country or a separate kingdom. Political harmony must be there in the meaning, but only as an urgent aspect of the ideal of general harmony in the world that the Egyptians knew. The paired animals are, none the less, the forerunners of the paired figures of Horus and Seth. The former are the symbols of a general statement; the latter represent a more specific application of the concept and its depiction to the new political circumstances of dynastic Egypt. There is an interesting transitional phase to recognize, too. The earliest depictions of paired figures standing explicitly for the unity of two kingdoms are not figures of Horus and Seth, but two facing figures of Horus, in an archaic form that particularly resembles that of Horus of Hierakonpolis (Figure 34).[59] This is a straightforward adaptation of the paired identical figures on the 'slate' palettes. It recurs occasionally in historical periods, when the two kingdoms can both be represented as an inheritance from Horus.[60]

The cosmic balancing act was not, by itself, enough. Egyptian society of the Dynastic Period was strongly hierarchical. Harmony within the state flowed down from a single source, the king, through loyal officials to the people. The king's role of maintainer of order was paramount. It covered not only responsibility for justice and piety but also the conquest of unrule. The philosophical texts of the Middle Kingdom depict unrule in terms not only of social upheaval, but also of natural and cosmic catastrophe. The final guarantee of harmony in society and in the natural order was not a balancing of opposites. One force had to be superior. We can glimpse this already in one of the vignettes in Hierakon-polis tomb 100 (Figure 31, *top right*). Here the two paired and facing animals (lions in this case) are held apart and balanced by the central figure of a ruler. The introduction of Seth enabled this to be reflected in the eternal verities of theology, and to understand this we must remember that each king was also a particular embodiment of Horus. And so Seth becomes the loser, and the antagonist to Horus. He becomes the antagonist to order on a grand scale: celestial disturbance in the form of storms, the hostile nature of the surround-ing deserts, the exotic character of foreign gods, even red-headed people – these were expressions of Seth. Yet, as the Shabaka Stone tells us, Seth also acquiesces in the divine judgement against him. He retains the power to be a reconciled force in the ideal balance of harmony.

The myth of Horus and Seth is not a reflection of how the Egyptian state emerged politically. The details of the period of internal warfare among the incipient city-states of the Nile valley are unlikely ever to be known, but we can safely assume that it was not a simple epic struggle between two protagonists. The myth of the state in historic times was a clever transformation of an earlier, more generalized statement of an ideal world originating in Upper Egypt. It combined the old concept of an ultimate harmony through balanced opposites with the newly perceived need for a single superior force. It was created as part of the great codification of court culture. It drew upon local mythologies, which in the case of Horus and Seth were both centred in Upper Egypt. It became part of the long active interest that the Egyptians maintained in symbolic geography; in effect, a process of internal colonization at an intellectual level.

There is a broader dimension within which to consider this theme. Much later the Middle East became the home to a philosophical tradition of dualism, which imagined a perpetual conflict between a good and an evil force in the universe, between light and darkness. It saw the material world as evil and urged the individual to struggle to over-come its superficial attractiveness, and to seek a path of separation from worldliness. Through Christianity and various rival 'heresies' the idea rooted itself very firmly in Egypt and it has had a profound influence upon European spirituality. In the material discussed in this section we seem to see the ancient Egyptians facing up to the same philosophi-cal challenge – the source of discord and chaos – but giving it a more optimistic and less personally troublesome resolution. Ultimately the struggle was waged externally by divine proxies on behalf of the people, although in the foreground king and people were obligated to heed the ordering concept of *maat* in their lives. A harmonious outcome was held to be within reach.

One further observation needs to be made. The 1st Dynasty began as a state that was territorially as large as most that were to occupy the lower Nile valley until modern times. There was no long process of growth from a spread of city-states, a common early political form that had a thriving history in, for example, Mesopotamia. We have already used the term 'incipient city-state' for territories in southern Upper Egypt centred on Hierakonpolis and Nagada. 'Incipient' seems an appropriate word since they cannot have matched the complexity of contemporary city-states in other parts of the Near East. We can be fairly sure of two, and we can suspect that there were others either already in existence (e.g. one based on This) or still at an even earlier stage of formation (perhaps at Maadi and Buto in the delta, Abadiya in Upper Egypt, and Qustul and Sayala in Lower Nubia).[61] The inter-nal warfare pursued most vigorously from the south terminated this polycentric period of political growth, but as states everywhere discover sooner or later, regional assertion remains a powerful force even when its centres are submerged within a larger polity. The game goes on. The Pharaonic state was remarkably successful, through the mechanism of symbolic geography, in creating an ideology with numerous provincial ramifications. We can speak of a national framework of myth. Yet submerged local identities remained. The one we see most clearly in the later historic periods (from the 6th Dynasty onwards) is a submerged city-state of Thebes. More will be said on Thebes in Chapter 7, and on the general theme of local identity and assertion in Chapter 8. It would, all the same, be wrong to try to reconstruct the late Predynastic political landscape from the details of later regionalism, for far too many local changes took place after the beginning of the 1st Dynasty. The rise of Thebes at the expense of Nagada, and of Edfu at the expense of Hierakonpolis, are only particularly striking examples.

Foundations of ideology (3): architecture as political statement

The unification myth was but one aspect of what emerges with the 1st Dynasty as the principal focus of effort, both intellectual and organizational: the projection of kingship as the symbol of power supreme over all others. On the late Predynastic 'slate' palettes conquering figures occur in the form of animals (a lion, a bull, a scorpion, a falcon, see Figure 33) that we can take to be symbols of human power, perhaps of a king. But it is only with the Narmer Palette (and Scorpion mace head) that we find figures of human kings to which detailed treatment has been given in order to convey some of their symbolic attributes. When we turn to architecture we find an equivalent process but on a far grander scale. The royal tomb became the principal public statement on the nature of kingship. Changes in royal tomb architecture are thus our most important single guide to the evolution of ancient perceptions of monarchy.

Nagada and Hierakonpolis have provided us with tombs that, by their size, brick linings and, in the case of Hierakonpolis tomb 100, wall paintings, imply royal ownership. They are, none the less, quite small constructions, and it is unlikely that they ever possessed an elaborate superstructure. The 1st Dynasty brought substantial change. Against a background of increased tomb size throughout the country, reflecting the increased wealth and organization of the Early Dynastic state, we find the builders of the royal tombs taking the first steps towards monumental scale and distinctive architectural symbolism.

We must now return to Abydos, and to the tombs of the kings of the 1st Dynasty (and of the last two of the 2nd) who were buried in the part known as the Umm el-Qaʿab.[62] The royal tombs consisted of brick chambers constructed in large pits dug into the desert, covered probably by a simple superstructure in the form of a plain square enclosure filled to the top with sand and gravel. This was a straightforward evolution from the brick 'royal' tombs at Nagada and Hierakonpolis. Their royal ownership was proclaimed by pairs of free-standing stone stelae bearing the Horus name of the king in question (an example is Figure 26, *inset*, p. 82). Each tomb also possessed a second element, a separate building located closer to the edge of the flood plain, and just behind the site of the ancient town of Abydos. The best preserved is one from the end of the 2nd Dynasty, the Shunet ez-Zebib, belonging to King Khasekhemui (Plate 2).[63] The Shunet ez-Zebib is an enclosure

Plate 2   Early royal architecture: the Shunet ez-Zebib at Abydos, mud-brick funerary palace of King Khasekhemui of the 2nd Dynasty (*c.* 2690 BC), looking south-east.

measuring 122 by 65 metres externally, surrounded by a double wall of mud brick, pierced by doorways. The inner wall, still standing in places to a height of 11 metres, is a massive 5.50 metres thick. On its outer surfaces it was decorated with niches to give a panelled effect. The panelled façade on the long side facing the cultivation was emphasized by the insertion at regular intervals of an inner, deeper niche. Along one side a row of twelve wooden boats had been buried, 18 to 21 metres long but only about 50 centimetres high, encased in mud and bricks (Figure 30, p. 90). They have individual counterparts in boats buried alongside the tombs of courtiers of the Early Dynastic Period at Sakkara and

Helwan, and presumably represent a continuation of the theme of the perpetual voyage by the upholder of authority that is so strikingly portrayed in tomb 100 at Hierakonpolis. A small part of the interior of the enclosure was occupied by a free-standing building near the east corner. This contained a suite of rooms in some of which pottery storage jars had been stowed. The outer faces of this building had been decorated in the same panelled style as the great enclosure wall (Figure 35).

Two paths lead us towards the meaning of this building and its companions. One concerns the panelled effect on the outer walls. The most striking examples occur on the façades of large tombs of the Early Dynastic Period (Figure 35.B), mostly in the Memphite area (although one is at Nagada).[64] Some examples preserve the lower part of elaborate painted decoration, which reproduces in great detail a way of further decorating the walls: by draping over them long strips of brightly coloured matting lashed to horizontal poles. These panelled surfaces were broken by deep recesses with similarly panelled sides, and at the back of each recess stood a broader niche, painted red, apparently to signify the wooden leaf of a door. The whole design of panels, recesses and applied matting-patterns became a fixed scheme of decoration on later sarcophagi and offering-places in tomb chapels, and these supply us with the details missing from the upper parts of the Early Dynastic tombs.

The design occurs in another context, too. A narrow section of it formed the basis for the heraldic device in which the Horus name of Early Dynastic kings was written (Figure 26, *inset*, p. 82). From this it was long ago deduced that the architectural style belonged specifically to the royal palace. Scholars coined the term 'palace façade' for the architectural style. It was only in 1969, however, that an actual stretch of wall decorated in this style was found which was not part of a tomb. It lay in the centre of the Early Dynastic town of Hierakonpolis, and formed the gatehouse for what is evidently an Early Dynastic palace, the one briefly described in an earlier section (Figures 25, 26, pp. 80, 82). The Hierakonpolis gatehouse, the Shunet ez-Zebib and the frame around the king's Horus name reveal that the Early Dynastic kings adopted the niched and decorated façade as a symbol of power. It denoted by itself the idea of 'palace' as a ruling entity, and for those who were part of the court – the palace elite surrounding the king and administering his power – it was permissible to use a scaled-down version to decorate their own tombs. By its distinctive and imposing style early monumental architecture in Egypt set up a barrier between king and people.

For the second path we must turn to a monument which in time is only a generation later than the Shunet ez-Zebib, but which belongs to another plane of architectural achievement: the Step Pyramid at Sakkara, tomb of Djoser, the first (or second) king of the 3rd Dynasty (*c*. 2650 BC).[65] It is the first building of truly monumental scale in Egypt, constructed throughout of stone.[66] In its detailing it also contains many of the basic decorative motifs of Pharaonic architecture. It represents, in architecture, a major act of codification of forms such as had occurred in art around the beginning of the 1st Dynasty.

The Step Pyramid confronts us with a major problem of interpretation. It has many distinctive parts, each of which must have held a particular meaning. However, very little of it bore any figured or written decoration to declare its meaning explicitly. For much of it we have to rely upon interpretations derived from far later sources, principally the Pyramid Texts (collections of short theological statements carved inside the burial chambers of pyramids from the end of the 5th Dynasty onwards, and the first surviving religious texts

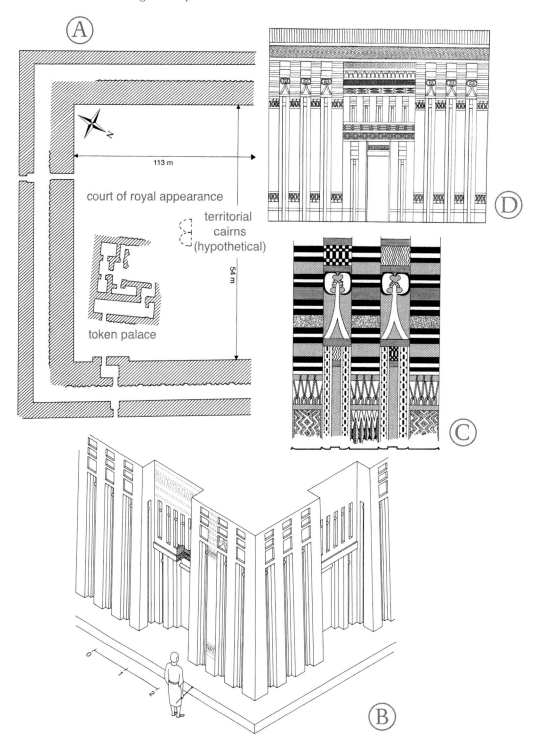

court of royal appearance

113 m

54 m

territorial
cairns
(hypothetical)

token palace

of any significant length). By this time, however, pyramid layouts had changed, and so, too, must have the meanings of the various parts. There is thus, for example, no straight-forward answer to the basic question: why a stepped pyramid? By the time of the Pyramid Texts the true pyramid had long replaced it, and so, presumably, had a different symbolism that made a strong link with the cult of the sun centred at Heliopolis. A common modern explanation finds a link between the plain mounds which stood over early tombs and were, in the Early Dynastic Period, turned into plain brick rectangles, and the square plain block of stone masonry which covered Djoser's tomb and over which the Step Pyramid was then erected. Similar mounds are known to have been incorporated invisibly into the palace-façade superstructures of court tombs at Sakkara. For explanation one can turn to a rich tradition of later times that made earth mounds into symbols of creation and rebirth.[67] Possible playful ways (modern and ancient) of working with this imagery will be explored further in the next chapter.

Fortunately not all of this amazing monument is mute. Djoser's stepped pyramid stands at the centre of a rectangular enclosure, 278 by 545 metres (Figure 36). It was surrounded by a thick stone wall with external towers, the façade carved with a simpler and modified version of the palace-façade style, although each tower was treated as if it were a gateway with closed door-leaves imitated in stone. The one true entrance is at the south-east corner, and in the general design of the whole complex we can still recognize the basic shape of the Shunet ez-Zebib at Abydos. Across the centre of the enclosure extends a huge open inner space, a rectangle measuring 108 by 187 metres, faced by panelled walls. At each end stood originally a pair of stone horseshoe-shaped cairns, and immediately in front of the pyramid a stone platform reached by steps faced the alignment of the cairns. This arrangement of cairns and stepped platform is known from Early Dynastic scenes. In one of them, on a mace head of the reign of Narmer (Figure 37), we can see that the setting appears to be in use for reviewing the livestock and prisoners captured in a battle. In another, a label of the reign of the 1st Dynasty king Den, the king appears twice: once on the stepped throne beneath an awning, and once on the arena running or striding between the groups of cairns. This latter element is one of two subjects of scenes actually carved within the Step Pyramid complex itself, in underground corridors beneath the Southern Tomb and the pyramid proper.[68] Two groups of three carved panels occur at the backs of imitation doorways. Some of the panels show Djoser performing this very ceremony of striding or running between the cairns, accompanied by other symbols. The shape of the

Figure 35   The royal style of architecture in the Early Dynastic Period. (A) South-east sector of the Shunet ez-Zebib at Abydos (Plate 2, p. 100; reign of Khasekhemui, late 2nd Dynasty, *c.* 2690 BC). The position of the territorial cairns is hypothetical. After E.R. Ayrton, C.T. Currelly and A.E.P. Weigall, *Abydos* III, London, 1904, Pl. VI. Note the simplified 'palace façade' niched style of brickwork on external surfaces. For a section of real (as distinct from funerary) palace wall see Figure 26 (p. 82), from Hierakonpolis. (B) Reconstruction of part of the façade of a 1st Dynasty court tomb, reproducing in miniature the 'palace façade' architecture of court buildings. (C) The reconstruction of the elaborate designs – largely painted – on the upper parts is based on later reproductions on sarcophagi and tomb chapel offering-places. This example derives from the 5th Dynasty tomb of Tepemankh at Abusir, after J. Capart, *L'art égyptien* I: *L'architecture*, Brussels and Paris, 1922, Pl. 46, itself derived from L. Borchardt, *Das Grabdenkmal des Königs Ne-user-reʿ*, Leipzig, 1907, Bl. 24. (D) A further example, a carved 4th Dynasty sarcophagus from Giza, tomb of Fefi, after S. Hassan, *Excavations at Gîza (1929–1930)*, Oxford, 1932, Pl. LXV.

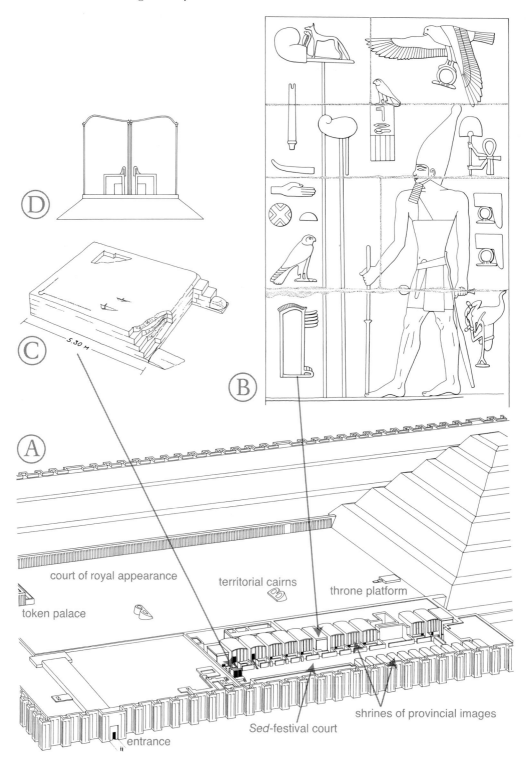

Ⓓ

Ⓒ

5.30 M

Ⓑ

Ⓐ

court of royal appearance

territorial cairns

throne platform

token palace

shrines of provincial images

Sed-festival court

entrance

cairns can be clarified by later references, as can one of the prominent groups of symbols. They are markers of territorial limits.[69] Later sources also tell us that the arena itself was called simply 'the field', and that the ceremony was termed either 'encompassing the field', or 'presenting the field', with the emphasis then on the dedication of the arena to a god, although this element is not apparent from the early depictions.

One of the general needs of monarchy (and of other forms of state leadership) is a formal setting for the display of the leader in person, either to the public at large or to the select representatives who compose the court. In later times the Egyptian sources make much of the 'appearance of the king', and we should anticipate that each age sought a dramatic setting for this moment, built around certain basic elements: an open space for assembly, an elevated place where the king could be seen within a formal framing, and a token palace where robing and resting could comfortably and privately take place. In Chapter 6 the elaborate devices adopted by the New Kingdom Pharaohs for displaying themselves will be described and we shall find settings of just this kind. The early sources, both pictorial and architectural, also combine to satisfy this demand exactly. We have to imagine that an important part of an Early Dynastic king's palace was an enclosed arena or plaza, equipped with cairns which symbolized territorial limits and with an elevated throne dais shaded by a canopy of distinctive shape (this latter element present already in one of the boats in Hierakonpolis tomb 100) at one end, and a token palace at the other. It was used as the setting for major royal occasions, such as the reception of tribute, and for a particular ceremony in which the king laid claim to his territory by striding forcefully around its limits. The Shunet ez-Zebib at Abydos and the great plaza in front of the Step Pyramid are replicas at full, if not exaggerated, scale that provided the king with the necessary setting for his own pageantry for the eternity of death.[70] One might identify a less developed example (with as yet no trace of the cairns) in the courtyard with panelled dais in the Hierakonpolis palace (Figure 26, p. 82).

This is not, however, the end of the story. There is another element to the essential ritual of early kingship, a periodic celebration that the Egyptians termed the *Sed*-festival.[71] Sources from early times onwards make the *Sed*-festival a great jubilee celebration of the king's earthly rule over a period that was ideally thirty years, although second and third celebrations could subsequently take place at shorter intervals. The way that the festival was conducted changed over time, and so, probably, did the meaning. It is tempting with Egyptian religion to combine sources from all periods in order to create a comprehensive explanation for a particular ritual or belief because the pictorial forms tended to remain

Figure 36 Political architecture. (A) Reconstruction of the southern part of the Step Pyramid of King Djoser at Sakkara, eternal plaza of royal display and setting for the *Sed*-festival (see Plate 3, p. 108), after J.-Ph. Lauer, *La Pyramide à degrés*, Cairo, 1936, Pl. IV. (B) Scene of King Djoser proceeding to visit the temporary shrine of Horus of Behdet. The column of hieroglyphs in front of the king reads: 'Halting at the shrine of Horus of Behdet.' The last sign is actually a picture of a temporary shrine of the kind modelled in stone around the *Sed*-festival court at the Step Pyramid. Note that Djoser wears the crown of Upper Egypt. Northern stela beneath the Step Pyramid at Sakkara, after C. Firth and J.E. Quibell, *The Step Pyramid* II, Cairo, 1935, Pl. 17, and A. Gardiner, *JEA* 30 (1944), 26, Pl. III.4. (C) Stone platform with double staircase as found at the southern end of the *Sed*-festival court in the Step Pyramid (see Plate 3, p. 108), after Lauer, op. cit., Pl. LVI.1 and p. 145, Fig. 146. (D) Ancient representation of the double throne dais with canopy as used at the *Sed*-festival, based on a carved lintel of King Senusret III (12th Dynasty), as reproduced in K. Lange and M. Hirmer, *Egypt: architecture, sculpture, painting in three thousand years*, third edn, London 1961, 102–4.

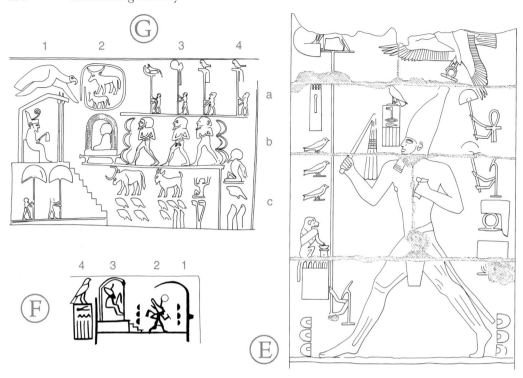

Figure 37   Ritual of territorial claim. (E) Scene of King Djoser running (or striding) across the ceremonial arena between the two sets of territorial marker cairns. In front of the king is the standard of the god Wepwawet, and a vertical column of hieroglyphs, the meaning of which is somewhat obscure. The literal translation is 'The Great White Ones', a plural reference to a baboon-god whose picture forms part of the last hieroglyph. The first element in the name, however, is also a word for a shrine, evidently a 'White Shrine'. It has been suggested that the baboons in question are images of ancestral spirits, though this is only a hypothesis. See *Lexikon* II, 1078–80; H.W. Fairman, *ASAE* 43 (1943), 260–1; A.J. Spencer, *Catalogue of Egyptian antiquities in the British Museum* V, *Early Dynastic objects*, London, 1980, 13; 16, no. 16, Pls 8, 9; G. Dreyer, *Elephantine* VIII. *Der Tempel der Satet. Die Funde der Frühzeit und des Alten Reiches*, Mainz, 1986, 69. Behind the king is a pair of symbols used to write a word (*mdnbw*) meaning 'limits'. Central stela beneath the Step Pyramid at Sakkara, after C. Firth and J.E. Quibell, *The Step Pyramid* II, Cairo, 1935, Pl. 16. (F) Part of a wooden label of King Den of the 1st Dynasty from his tomb at Abydos, to be read from right to left: (1) the sign for 'regnal year' (see Figure 19, p. 64); (2) the king running between the territorial cairns; (3) the king appearing seated beneath a canopy upon a stepped throne dais; (4) Horus name of King Den. After W.M.F. Petrie, *Royal Tombs* I, London, 1900, Pls XI.14, XV.16. (G) Part of a scene from a ceremonial mace head of King Narmer, 1st Dynasty, from Hierakonpolis. It depicts a ceremonial appearance of the king on the stepped and canopied throne dais (1), accompanied by bearers of the 'Followers of Horus' standards (3a, 3b, see Figure 27, p. 84). The occasion is evidently the review of prisoners (2b–4b, 4c) and animals (2a, 3c, 4c) captured in battle. The many small signs in line 'c' are numerals. Note the seated figure (divine image?; 2b) in a portable carrying chair with curved canopy (see Figure 51, p. 145). A particularly significant element is the way that the human captives are paraded between the territorial cairns. After J.E. Quibell, *Hierakonpolis* I, London, 1900, Pl. XXVI.B.

constant. But continuity of forms masked changes in meaning and practice. Inventing traditions was something that the Egyptians were very good at. For each period the sources
should be interpreted within the spirit and for the illumination of that age alone. (In
Chapter 6, pp. 276–81, we shall examine one particular set, those of Amenhetep III of
the 18th Dynasty.) Two aspects seem more than any other to have characterized the *Sed*-
festival. The king, often wearing a distinctive robe, sits on a special dais provided with
two thrones for an appearance as King of Upper Egypt and of Lower Egypt. The thrones
are normally shown back to back, but this may be an artistic device for rendering a pair
which were actually side by side.[72] More elaborate scenes, later than the Early Dynastic
Period, give as the setting for this ceremony a series of shrines pictured as constructions of
wood and matting. The origin and meaning of this style of architecture will be explored
in the next chapter. For the moment it is sufficient to know that it originated as a type of
temporary building. In these scenes one design stood for Lower Egypt and one for Upper
Egypt. Sometimes they were specifically for the cobra-goddess Wadjit of the delta town of
Buto, and for the vulture-goddess Nekhbet of El-Kab. But they were for other deities as
well. This gathering of provincial images of deities in a series of temporary shrines beside
the double throne of the king was a gesture of provincial homage to the person of the king.
The other element specifically associated with the festival after the 3rd Dynasty is the ceremony of laying claim to the 'field' by striding around the cairns. At some time, therefore,
this separate and presumably more frequent ceremony was absorbed into the pageantry of
the *Sed*-festival.

Again the Step Pyramid clarifies the picture. Beside the great arena with cairns is
another but quite separate part of the complex. This runs along the east side of the main
enclosure and consists of a series of mostly solid, dummy buildings arranged along both
sides of a court (Plate 3). They have a very distinctive appearance: a series of small rectangular structures, with exterior detailing which creates in solid, full-scale, three-dimensional
architecture the shapes of the temporary shrines which were envisaged as constructed of
timber and matting. They are, in fact, representations of the very kind of buildings which
later scenes show gathered for the *Sed*-festival. This seems to be their meaning at the Step
Pyramid, too. For at one end of the court is a square throne dais with two flights of steps,
originally covered with a little stone building. It is hard to escape the conclusion that
this was a rendering in stone for eternity of the double-throne dais covered with special
canopy, and that this part of the Step Pyramid complex gave King Djoser the eternal
setting for the periodic *Sed*-festival. Scenes of the king visiting the various shrines form the
other subject of the carved panels in the underground galleries (Figure 36B, p. 104).

We can now better appreciate the meaning of the architecture of early royal tombs,
of which the Step Pyramid is the most complete and elaborate. They provided an arena
for the eternal pageantry of kingship as it was experienced on earth: the king as supreme
territorial claimant, protected within his distinctive palace enclosure, the focus of rituals
centred on his actual person.

With the 4th Dynasty the form of the royal tomb changed dramatically. The stepped
pyramid became a true pyramid, and instead of occupying the middle ground of a great
complex of other buildings, it towered at the end of a linear architectural sequence which
stretched down to the edge of the alluvial plain (Figure 38). The great enclosed arena or
plaza of the royal appearance and the special *Sed*-festival architecture all vanish. In their
place comes a temple intended primarily for an offering-cult for the king's spirit via an

Plate 3 The Step Pyramid of King Djoser, 3rd Dynasty, at Sakkara, looking north-west. In front of the pyramid are the renderings into stone of the tent-shrines erected on pedestals, forming part of the *Sed*-festival court. Note the probable double-throne platform in the foreground.

offering-place on the east side of the pyramid, and via a group of statues. These elements had been present in Djoser's complex, but now they were dominant. *Sed*-festival scenes occur on walls, but alongside other themes. The true pyramid was a symbol of the sun (another aspect of the great codification discussed in the next chapter), and there is other evidence from the 4th, and especially the 5th Dynasties to show that serious intellectual consideration – theology – was paying more attention to the power of the sun as the supreme force. The prominent title of kings, 'Son of Ra', appears first at this time. The 4th Dynasty and later pyramids convey a new image of kingship. Gone is the raw power of a supreme territorial ruler. The king is now sublimated into a manifestation of the sun-god. Architecture conveyed this fundamental reappraisal to the greatest possible effect.

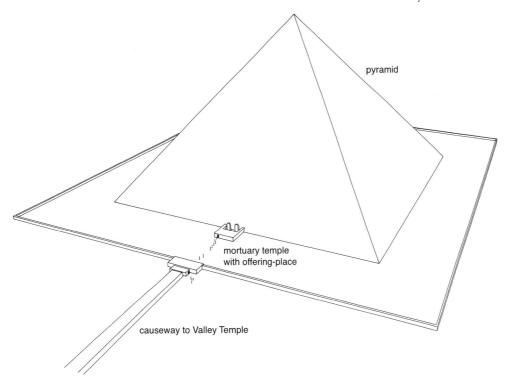

Figure 38 The apotheosis of kingship. The pyramid of Medum (reign of King Huni, end of the 3rd Dynasty, *c*. 2620 BC) was the first of the new generation of pyramid tombs which conveyed a radically different view of the nature of the monarchy. In place of a tomb which celebrated the king as supreme territorial claimant and perpetuated his earthly pageantry (Figure 36) the new-style pyramids proclaimed his absorption into the mystic symbol of the sun. The tiny offering-temple was the principal gesture to his human aspect. Later pyramid complexes softened this stark contrast in scale between pyramid and temples.

The social and economic climate in which the early Egyptian state arose still remains sketchily documented. We can recognize as a general background a relatively egalitarian farming society settled in low-density villages and larger settlement areas spread through the Nile valley and delta during the fourth millennium BC. Local identities and community leaders emerged, but at a pace and on a scale which varied from place to place. Inherent in the nature of the process was that local variations that were initially quite small were amplified on an ever-increasing scale. This became an exponential rate of growth for the most successful, which culminated in a single state by the end of the Predynastic Period. Those involved in this final phase of dynamic growth and terminal competition already perceived the consequences of power on a grand scale and codified its expression in distinctive intellectual form. This cleverly fused together a generalized concept – the superiority of a locally derived order over a universal chaos – and the position of a single king whose power as earthly territorial ruler was expressed in monumental architecture, in ritual and in symbolic art. As a set of ideas and ideals for legitimizing the rule of a king over his subjects it was to survive the ups and downs of political history for three thousand years. It also left the Egyptians incapable of visualizing the polycentric pattern of their own early political growth. Whenever political fragmentation reappeared it seemed to be a fall from the original ideal yet (as we can now see) quite mythical state of things. And as the next chapter will show, a parallel erection of a myth-world shut the Egyptians off from their cultural beginnings.

3
The dynamics of culture

If I visit the pyramids of Giza or the decorated temples and tombs at Luxor I am aware immediately of facing a distinctive human creation. I will feel the same when in the presence of a mediaeval mosque in Cairo or a castle or cathedral in Europe. All are products of great and distinctive traditions of culture. They leave conveniently different images in the mind. When, on the other hand, as an archaeologist I excavate amidst the dwellings of one of ancient Egypt's poorer communities, the distinctiveness is much less. The men from the local village whom I employ to do the digging will see the outlines of human life not too different from their own: here the kitchen, there the cattle byres. The ordinariness and predictability can be discouraging. I have to remind myself that culture and environment are never really the same from place to place and from time to time, and that the search for variation within the broad regularities of human life is an essential part of understanding the complete spectrum of human behaviour. That variation might be less visually arresting than the subject matter of tourist guidebooks, and harder to define, but it is bound to be there and is the prime source for investigating life at grass-roots level.

'Great culture', which in time becomes tourist culture, was not the spontaneous creation of the common person. It is no accident that we meet its manifestations in large religious buildings, in palaces, mansions and castles. Great culture, which requires patronage and the direction of labour, originates in courts. The wealth, size, splendour, craft standards and intellectual novelties are part of the instruments of rule. And the mystique of rule seems to be most effectively expressed through religion. Temple and palace, and in the case of ancient Egypt their extensions into the culture surrounding the dead, often seem to account for much of what is distinctive about past cultures. When well established, a great tradition may have an influence that is felt throughout society. But to reach this stage it has to expand at the expense of other traditions. It has to colonize the minds of the nation. Whatever does not succumb becomes 'folk culture'.

Ancient Egypt is amongst the earliest of the world's great cultural traditions. We are fortunate in being able to observe, through a relative abundance of material, the codification of tradition by which it started at the time of transition to the 1st Dynasty. It had, however, a very restricted scope in the beginning. The objects were themselves small in size, and were probably very limited in numbers. They expressed the pretensions of a new generation of rulers, and the beginnings of an attempt to systematize religion. But should we assume that, from this moment on, all cultural expression in material form took its cue from this source? Did the 1st Dynasty kings throw a cultural switch that instantly lit up the whole country? Was there the will, or the means, or even the interest to convert the whole country to this intellectual outlook?

To answer these questions we must investigate how court culture expanded at the expense of other local traditions, and consider not only early works of art, but also the general archaeological record in which we might find traces of 'folk culture'.

Conventionally art historians ignore this issue. They select the best pieces and find that their material, drawn mainly from cemeteries of the elite, provides a record of continuous development in which geographical homogeneity is also prominent. From this perspective the source material does provide a generally most satisfactory basis for writing a history of Egyptian 'high' culture. From prehistoric times, a single line of progress can be followed from the late Predynastic cultures of Upper Egypt, through the Early Dynastic Period to the full flowering of Pharaonic culture in the Old Kingdom. Late Predynastic artistic achievement comes to us as a series of isolated objects, small in scale, individual in expression. Its culminating product is the Narmer Palette from the very beginning of the 1st Dynasty (c. 3000 BC; Figure 27, p. 84). From this phase of great creativity emerged a carefully composed visual art that successfully moulded the shape of Pharaonic culture to the very end, and just as successfully has influenced modern appreciations of ancient Egypt. Hieroglyphic writing, statuary and two-dimensional art became aspects of a single, rigidly studied mode of visual expression. Religious iconography was an integral part of this process, in which many of the gods were reduced to variants of a single image. This was the achievement of the Early Dynastic Period. Subsequently the Egyptian impetus for innovation turned to monumental architecture, culminating in the pyramids and their temples. In the eyes of the art historian the lights were indeed switched on in the Early Dynastic Period. Later dynasties added to their number and luminosity.

Early shrines as autonomous centres of culture

The simple unilinear model of a national cultural transformation from the tentative products of prehistory to the achievements of a Great Tradition serves the art historian well. Its weakness is that it fails to incorporate adequately the archaeological record of a group of significant sites. All appear to be early temple sites. They introduce features that do not fit comfortably into a simple scheme. They suggest that, in the provinces, the great transformation was a matter of fitful court patronage applied to a scene that was changing only very slowly from the patterns of late prehistoric times. In local religion – in art as well as in architecture – parochial traditions, more diverse, more informal, more intuitive and personal, and generally, to our own eyes, far less sophisticated, developed and persisted. One by one they became subject to court initiatives, and these replaced local diversity with uniformity in the style that we are most familiar with from Egypt. But this process was a slow one, and had not been completed by the beginning of the Middle Kingdom (c. 2050 BC).

For an evaluation of the varying rate of change, the existing nomenclature is something of a hindrance. It is tied strictly to the course of Egyptian dynastic history, transferring to art and archaeology the major division between prehistory and history (Predynastic vis-à-vis Early Dynastic or Archaic), and then the further divisions of political historians. The material in question – early shrines and their contents – lacks, however, the sensitive stylistic points that we can perceive in court art, and so fails to acquire the labels of precise dates. It consequently fails to find its proper place in a historical account of early Egyptian culture. If it is to escape from this limbo and find a status of its own, a term is required which places this material in the cultural sequence of Egypt, without subordinating it to the inflexible progression of kings and dynasties. The term used here is 'Preformal'. It covers the products of the Predynastic Period, together with later material still in this tradition that runs well into the historic period. Some of the material is artistic, some is architectural, and both had their centres in local temples. It should also be noted that Preformal shrines were not replaced immediately by temples in the familiar architectural style of ancient Egypt. Evidence has been slowly accumulating for some time that the 'typical' stone temple of the New Kingdom so favoured by modern textbooks had been preceded by an earlier phase of local temple building, smaller in scale, often employing limited stonework set into an architectural framework of mud brick, and on the whole much simpler in form. The term used here for this phase is 'Early Formal'. With the New Kingdom came the 'Mature Formal' temple, and finally the 'Late Formal' temple absorbed much energy in the period between the 30th Dynasty and the earlier part of the Roman occupation of Egypt.

We need terminology to enable us to handle what we perceive, but it is often more precise than the reality it seeks to organize. The terminology for cloud formations – 'cirrus', 'nimbus', and so on – is an extreme example of a necessary attempt to fit a constantly shifting phenomenon into set categories. In the case of the material under consideration, the lack of a common model, reflecting decisions locally taken, means that the boundaries of the terms Preformal and Early Formal are not distinct. Their purpose is only to deflect the reader from the even greater rigidities of the dynastic system of chronology. Having introduced them, a group of sites will be examined accordingly. Before doing so, however, it is worth taking a little time to consider the question: if earlier shrines do not much resemble the temples of later times, how do we know they are shrines at all? How do we recognize religious cult through purely archaeological remains?

Recognizing religion

Religion is essentially experience. Even if, as is frequently the case, people express it in a special way, this need not require distinctive buildings or leave behind a litter of debris from which, long afterwards, others can reconstruct what was done and thought. For the modern developed world, as for ancient Egypt, religious expression is mostly a self-evident phenomenon, centred on mosques, churches, synagogues and temples. I say 'mostly' to allow for that austere puritan view that piety and worship do not require ostentation or any visible props at all. Ancient Egyptian temples fall into the category of the self-evident. Or almost so, because it is sometimes not clear where the boundary lies between temple and palace. The merging of kingship with state religion, and consequently the merging of palace and temple architecture and decoration, seems to be widespread in complex societies generally.

All such things have a history of development. In the case of religious buildings – the word shrine becomes more suitable than temple – when their designs are followed backwards in time, earlier less developed stages start to lose that quality of being instantly recognizable. The extremity of cases is provided by traditional cultures far to the south of Egypt, in the Upper Nile region (as exemplified by the people of Ingessana on the Sudan–Ethiopian border), where the basic form of settlement remained till modern times the individual farmstead composed of a cluster of circular dwellings surrounded by a fence. The shrine was a hut, in appearance indistinguishable from others and usually empty. Although regarded as dwelling houses for gods, an important part of their purpose was to shelter those outside from what was thought to be inside. Myths explained them as having been 'built as ordinary houses but at an extra-ordinary time, usually at the origin of the world as it is today'.[1] They contained no carved images of divinities; indeed, they have sometimes been described as containing no artefacts at all. If converted to an archaeological site, how could anyone identify which (if any) of a group of huts was a shrine? In looking back at the excavation reports of Egyptian Predynastic villages any one of the little huts could have been a shrine of this kind but we could never know this. Given the prominent place that the image of the hut-shrine had in Egyptian religion of historic times (see below), this is a very real possibility.[2]

It is fortunate, for our ability to get to grips with the history of religious practice, that this modesty in material expression had a limited future.

> From what we know of African societies since their contact with the West, it is quite clear that the nature of people's religious edifices is linked in some way to its social organization. The more a society departs from the simplest forms of social organization – lineages and clans – in the direction of state structure, the more the places of worship tend to take on importance. In other words, political and administrative centralization itself requires a certain concentration of religion into well-defined buildings, while the division of society into lineages and clans favors the scattering of places of worship and diminishes their distinctiveness to the point that certain of them blend into the environment.[3]

By this evolutionary process an archaeology of religion is incidentally born. To help deal with this phase of emergence, which lies between the (for us) anonymity of the simplest sacred places and, at the other end of the spectrum, the defined religiosity of temples, it is possible to draw up a list of criteria which one can apply to specific cases. This has been done in a standard introductory textbook on archaeology to which the following version (influenced by my own regional specialism) is heavily indebted.[4]

- There should be ways of focusing attention, by manipulating various of the channels of sensation, which naturally in the archaeological record tend to be only the visual: the location of the place, perhaps its orientation, and pre-eminently the design of the building. Music, dance, incense and spoken or chanted words, whilst they might have been regarded as essential, are mostly lost with time, or the evidence becomes separated from the original context.
- The same factors simultaneously create a boundary between the material world and the imagined spiritual world, separating profane from sacred space, the latter perhaps

only temporarily created in the open air by means of special behaviour, such as procession or dance.

- Foremost of ways of seizing the attention visually are images of the deity or, when the tradition eschews them (and it is then said to be aniconic), pointers to an invisible presence that do not actually depict it.

- Part of the purpose of creating the special setting is protection: of the sanctity of the sacred space within (and of treasures if there are any) and sometimes also of people who might stray too close and so endanger themselves. The perimeter of the shrine can thus also be a focus of attention.

- Since participation and offering are fundamental in religious practice, even if performed only by specially designated representatives of society (priests), the means of access and where those permitted inside will go and what they will do, are considerations that are likely to affect design.

- Offerings – which are, in a way, a special currency by means of which transactions are possible between humans and the spiritual world – are frequently the key evidence for identifying what can otherwise be the elusive sacred character of the place.

It has to be admitted that, whilst it is helpful to examine specific cases with lists of points like this in mind, in the end one's mind is usually made up in advance of a full analysis, which then serves to demonstrate how right the first impression was. It is hard to increase the level of provability by formal, logical steps in studying a topic like this. The claim that Hierakonpolis site 29A (see below, pp. 147–9 and Figure 53) served ceremony or ritual rests on hunch rather than on step-by-step deduction. But it does create a framework around which discussion can be organized. In the following examples the reader might care to consider how or to what extent each one of the early shrines satisfies the above criteria, and also how far such formal analysis is helpful. I felt it to be too laboured to carry out the exercise with each of my examples. One must also be careful in taking for granted that the Egyptians (or any other people) drew the neat distinction between the sacred and the profane that is required to make such a formal analysis work. An obvious marker, the enclosure wall, exemplifies this. At various points in this book examples will be cited which show that individual temple enclosures seem to have served as urban citadels in which the temple was a leading asset to be protected but which also housed functions which we are inclined to see as secular. This is especially true of the post-New Kingdom periods (see Chapter 8, pp. 351–60).

It should be noted that 'relatively large in size' is not on the list. The question of the relative scale of things in society is a complex one. Ancient Egypt is famous for the large size of some of its monuments: the Great Pyramid, the Colossi of Memnon, the Great Hypostyle Hall at Karnak are examples. We now know enough to see that these were exceptional in their day. Most Egyptian buildings, predominantly of mud brick but the same applies to many in stone, ranged from the exceedingly small to the modest. Even well into the Dynastic Period some temples to major gods did not achieve the gigantism that people often expect of ancient Egypt (e.g. the temples of Seth at Nagada and of Min at Coptos).

I will begin the review of sites with Elephantine, where the degree of preservation and the quality of the modern reporting enable one to speak with a reasonably firm clear voice.

Plate 4 Provincial tradition: Preformal mud-brick temple at Elephantine in its late Old Kingdom phase, looking south-west. From G. Dreyer, *Elephantine VIII. Der Tempel der Satet*, Mainz, 1986, Tafel 2a. By courtesy Philipp von Zabern.

Elephantine[5]

This small town site on the southern tip of Elephantine Island was built directly over natural rounded granite boulders. Its development as a town, with a fortified annexe, occurred during the Early Dynastic Period. In 1972–3 a shrine serving this early town was discovered (Figure 39, Plate 4). It lay in an angle formed by the walls of the town and the fortress, in amidst the boulders themselves. This particular setting has provided archaeology with a so far unique set of circumstances. At other temple sites, on flatter ground, the rebuilding and enlargement of temples in later periods inevitably did much damage, and sometimes wrought havoc, to the earliest shrines. Not so at Elephantine. The builders of later temples, in seeking to escape the space restrictions created by the boulders surrounding the early site, simply filled the site in, and then paved it over, so sealing the early shrine and its associated floors and artefacts. The resulting archaeological record gives us, for the first time, a fairly complete picture of what an early local shrine looked like, and helps to solve more than one problem.

ELEPHANTINE

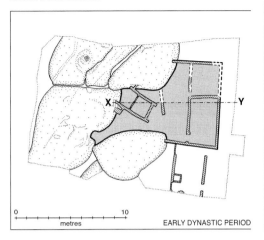

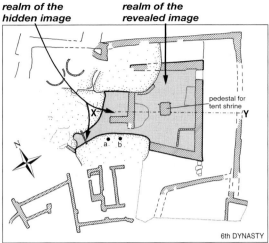

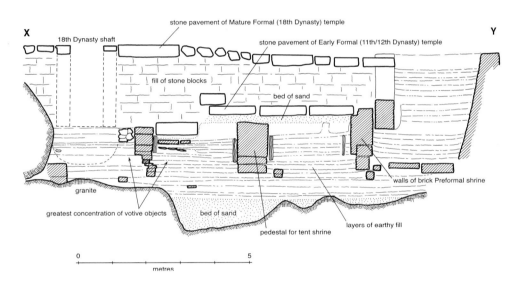

Figure 39   The early shrine at Elephantine, preserved beneath the pavement of the 18th Dynasty temple of the goddess Satet (also Plate 4, p. 116). The two plans at the top record two stages in the architectural evolution of the brick shrine. In the 6th Dynasty plan, 'a' is a cartouche of Pepi II, 'b' is a short inscription of Merenra. Below is the section along the line X–Y. For a reconstruction of the pedestal for the portable image, see Figure 51, p. 145. After G. Dreyer, *Elephantine* VIII, *Der Tempel der Satet*, Mainz, 1986, 13, Abb. 1, 4, 7.

The first sanctuary was set in a corner at the back of a squarish space occupying the natural niche between the boulders. It must have looked like a small cave. The qualities of enclosed spaces that emulate cavities within the earth – the term chthonic is quite useful here – exert a powerful attraction in the search for sacred presences, though, as we shall see at other sites (especially Hierakonpolis and Coptos), there were other directions in which the attention could be drawn. What the object of veneration was is not known. We should not take it for granted that there was one at all. It could be that an aniconic tradition was part of the early diversity of religion in Egypt.[6] Nor did the cult leave any marks on the actual rock faces, which seem to have been left in their natural state. This sacred niche was protected by two small brick rooms. The space in front was enclosed by further brick walls to create a courtyard (or a roofed hall). The date of this earliest phase is within the Early Dynastic Period, although some of the pottery found is Predynastic.

The basic form of the shrine – a niche in the rock served by modest brick shelters – was kept throughout the Old Kingdom, and apparently on until the time of the reunification of Egypt in the 11th Dynasty (c. 2040 BC): a period of six centuries. Over this time the principal changes were to replace the small shrine with a partition wall across the whole rock niche, and to provide a larger forecourt or hall, increasing generally the thickness of the walls. In the centre of the forespace stood a square pedestal, 0.95 x 1.10 metres, constructed from courses of brick separated by layers of matting for extra strength. A wooden pole stood against each corner. As will be argued in a later section of this chapter, this could have been a canopied podium (facing north) to support a portable divine image (Figure 39). The whole little complex was then protected by an outer corridor and second wall.

In the 11th Dynasty an entirely new shrine was laid out, in part built from decorated stone blocks. From what little direct evidence survived, its plan seems to have been a continuation of the existing one. In turn this shrine was replaced at the beginning of the 12th Dynasty by another building using stone. However, to judge from the extent of stone pavement which is all that is left, even the 12th Dynasty temple kept to the same restricted limits as had developed during the Old Kingdom. The appearance of decorated stone blocks marks an application of court patronage, and probably the building of a small temple with stone sections around a mud-brick core in the Early Formal style.

In the 18th Dynasty the site took on a very different aspect. The existing stone shrine was pulled down, the ancient niche and court were filled with blocks of stone to build the level of the ground up to the top of the granite boulders. On this new higher and level surface, a larger stone temple was erected, in the reign of Tuthmosis III (c. 1450 BC). The Mature Formal phase had arrived. Yet even at this time the builders tried to maintain some contact with the original sacred ground that they had so thoroughly buried. The new sanctuary was sited over the old one, and direct communication was made by means of a stone-lined shaft that descended through the foundations to the floor of the early sanctuary. The direct evidence for architectural evolution into a self-evident stone temple, dedicated to a named Egyptian goddess, leaves little scope for doubt that, at all stages, we are dealing with a shrine.

If the simplicity of the early shrine is striking, corresponding to the great age of pyramid building in the north, so also is the relative crudeness of most of the votive objects recovered from the associated floor levels. These seem to relate to a stratum of religious belief and practice separate from the one to which we are accustomed in ancient Egypt. The 'formal' theology that decorates tomb and temple in Egypt does not prepare us for this material, which thus serves in its own right as the main evidence for an aspect of ancient religion. The votive objects were numbered in their hundreds (Figure 40). Many were found scattered in the various levels, but one particular concentration seems to have formed during the 5th Dynasty. Most were made from faience (the shiny blue/green glazed

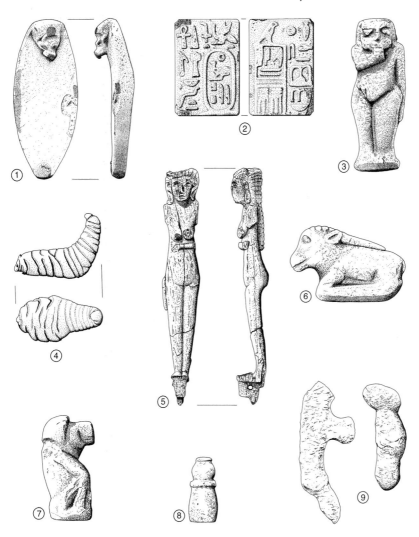

Figure 40 Selection of votive objects from the early temple deposits at Elephantine (*top row*), Hierakonpolis (*middle row*), and Abydos (*bottom row*). (1) Faience plaque with head of hedgehog, height 8.5 cm (after G. Dreyer, *Elephantine* VIII, *Der Tempel der Satet*, Mainz, 1986, Taf. 37.202). (2) Faience plaque commemorating the first *Sed*-festival of King Pepi I, 6th Dynasty, 6.4 by 4.5 by 1.5 cm (after ibid., Abb. 58, Taf. 56.440). (3) Faience figurine of a young girl, height 8.1 cm (after ibid., Taf. 17.42). (4) Faience scorpion with raised tail and sting, length 7.6 cm (after B. Adams, *Ancient Hierakonpolis*, Warminster, 1974, Pl. 13.98). (5) Ivory figurine of woman, height 20.4 cm (ibid., Pl. 44.360). (6) Faience figurine of kneeling ibex, length 9.4 cm (after J.E. Quibell, *Hierakonpolis* I, London, 1900, Pl. XXII.17). (7) Faience baboon, height 18.9 cm (after W.M.F. Petrie *Abydos* II, London, 1903, Pl. VI.51). (8) Faience model of pot on a stand, height 6.8 cm (after ibid., Pl. XI.244). (9) Two natural flint nodules in suggestive shapes, heights 87.6 and 64.8 cm (after ibid., Pl. IX.195, 196). For other early votive objects see Figures 27, p. 84, 31, p. 94, 44, p. 127, 50 (d)–(f), p. 143, 51 (4), p. 145.

synthetic material which was anciently the equivalent to modern plastic), but pottery, ivory, limestone and sandstone were used as well. They can be grouped as follows:

- human figures: both adults and children, the most numerous group being children with fingers at their mouth; a unique figure is the lower part of a seated king, which bears a single sign interpreted as reading the name of the 1st Dynasty King Djer (although from a 6th Dynasty level)
- baboons/apes, a few also with fingers to mouth
- a small number of animals and birds, the former including frogs, crocodiles, lion, pig, hippopotamus, cat and hedgehog
- oval faience plaques bearing at one end the head of an animal, apparently a hedgehog (forty-one examples of this curious design); there is a parallel from Tell Ibrahim Awad (Figure 44.2) where the plaque has a clear boat shape
- faience tiles of the type otherwise used in wall inlays, many with an incised or painted sign on the back
- faience objects of various forms, mainly large beads, necklace spacers and model pots
- natural flint pebbles of curious shapes
- flint knives

In addition to these groups a number of objects were found bearing the names of Kings Pepi I and II of the 6th Dynasty (c. 2250 BC). Some of them, perhaps all, were in celebration of the first *Sed*-festival (jubilee) of these kings. One was a vase in the form of a squatting ape holding its young. The remainder were faience plaques (mostly for Pepi I). The 6th Dynasty provided also the only inscriptions found in position: two graffiti of King Merenra and of King Pepi II scratched on one of the granite walls of the niche, the former commemorating a military campaign into Nubia.[7]

This material comes from a series of stratified layers that range through all of the first six dynasties. Yet vertical position does not automatically assign a date of manufacture to an individual piece; it merely shows when it was discarded, and some pieces may have been very old when finally buried in the floor of the shrine. The traditions involved clearly began in the Early Dynastic Period, and set a tone that lasted for a long time. The detailed study of the material piece by piece, however, shows that whilst the Early Dynastic Period is the date for the origination of the style and repertoire of forms, it is not necessarily the date for the manufacture of every piece. The tradition ran on through the Old Kingdom, and at the end the faience plaques bearing the names of 6th Dynasty kings were being produced in the same crude way. A small group of craftsmen attached to the shrine must have met a demand for temple votive objects, retaining forms and techniques over a long period of time, the entire first six dynasties in fact.

One other conspicuous feature of this group of objects, which applies also to similar groups from Hierakonpolis and Abydos, is the absence of representations that can be associated with the local deity or deities. To judge from the text on a granite offering-place donated by Pepi I and reinscribed under Merenra, in court theology the local royal presence came under the patronage of the goddess Satet, who later appears as one of a group of three Elephantine deities: Khnum, Satet and Anukis.[8] Their forms were distinctive: Khnum was a ram, and the others were ladies with unusual headdresses. Yet nothing relating to these forms occurs amongst the votive material. The explanation probably involves two factors. One is that Early Dynastic Period formal religion had a range of emphases somewhat different from later times, although the early images themselves were preserved by later tradition, sometimes with changed identifications. The cults of baboons and scorpions are two examples.[9] The other is that whilst the shrine came to have a formal dedication recognized by priests and kings, for the local population it served as the focal point for beliefs which had an independent origin and existence of their own. The most likely explanation for the figurines of children, for example, is that they mark an approach to the shrine by a local person before, or after, or in the hopes of, successful childbirth. Beliefs of this kind found no expression in formal theological texts. They are one aspect of the hidden dimension of life and society in ancient Egypt.

Hierakonpolis[10]

During the Old Kingdom a walled town developed over the site of the final nucleus into which the sprawling low-density Predynastic settlement had shrunk (see Figure 25, p. 80). The principal sacred area occupied the southern corner of the town. On the map this is shown within a separate rectangular enclosure (Figures 41 and 68, p. 196), but this is probably much later still, of the 18th Dynasty.[11] Several periods in this part are represented in a compressed stratigraphy that remains ambiguous. The area has been examined twice, first by a British expedition in 1897 and 1898 (J.E. Quibell, W.M.F. Petrie and F.W. Green), and then by an American expedition of the 1970s and 1980s (W.A. Fairservis). One aim of the latter was to clarify the results of the former, but this proved to be difficult, in part because a rise in the water-table has made the lower levels virtually inaccessible.

The contents of the enclosure fall into roughly three parts. That on the north-west is largely blank, because the ground had been denuded down to below the main building levels. That in the middle is occupied by part of a dense arrangement of brick walls laid out on a rectangular plan, and overlying a low artificial mound of sand, measuring 48 x 48 metres and 2.3 metres high, kept in place by a revetment of small roughly cut sandstone blocks. That on the south and south-east contains fewer remains, but amongst them are most of the pieces that derive from a stone temple of the New Kingdom which faced north-eastwards, towards the river, and had initially been built by Tuthmosis III. It includes the remains of a pair of pylons from an entrance, the brick foundations for columns, and a scatter of foundation deposits. As was usually the case, the New Kingdom builders had removed the walls of earlier constructions to make way for their own. The brick walls of the adjacent middle part of the site are at the same level as the 18th Dynasty temple. Are they of the same period? Although their overlap with the 18th Dynasty temple is slight, it does occur, and seems to bear no relationship to it.

A tempting interpretation is that two main periods of temple development at Hierakonpolis lie side by side instead of, as was more often the case, superimposed one over the other. Thus the brick walls of the central part are the remains of a planned Middle Kingdom layout of a temple and its ancillary buildings (representing its Early Formal phase) whilst alongside King Tuthmosis III subsequently added a Mature Formal stone temple. Was the adjacent site so important that it was preferable to leave it visible, the earlier brick buildings perhaps reduced to a mound suggestive of great antiquity? The brick building at its centre may well be the actual shrine, for which the Middle Kingdom supplies the chief parallel (at Kasr es-Sagha in the Fayum).[12] In the central chamber a brick-lined pit lay in

HIERAKONPOLIS

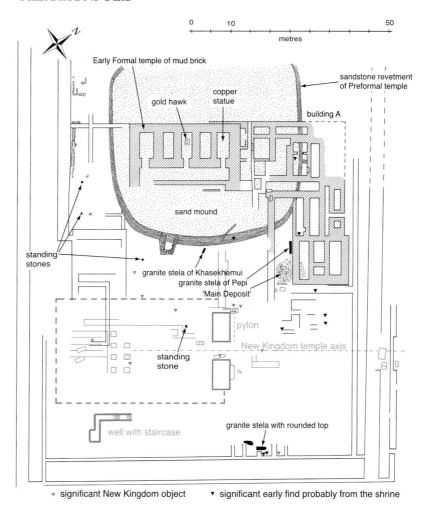

Figure 41 The temple remains at Hierakonpolis (see Figures 25, p. 80, 26, p. 82, and 68, p. 196). The scant remains of the Mature Formal temple (18th Dynasty and later) are in grey. For the earlier brick buildings (cross-hatched) I have preferred the outlines of J.E. Quibell and F.W. Green, *Hierakonpolis* II, London, 1902, Pl. LXXII to those of the later Fairservis expedition, published in W.A Fairservis, *The Hierakonpolis Project, Season January to March 1978. Excavation of the temple area on the Kom el Gemuwia*, Vassar College, Poughkeepsie, N.Y., 1983, Fig. 6. In the former time the buildings were much better preserved, and the latter plan is little more than a sketch. The two are difficult to reconcile. Fairservis was of the opinion that building A was later (and was the foundations for a New Kingdom stone building), whilst B was of the Old Kingdom (on account of abutted settlement walls of this period).

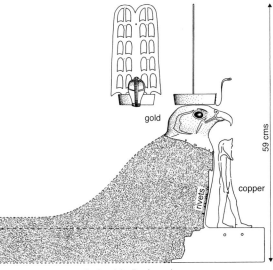

Figure 42   An early divine image: the falcon-god Horus of Hierakonpolis protecting the figure of a king. Originally of wood (now perished), sheathed in copper and with a gold head. Found buried in a pit in the sanctuary of the Early Formal Temple at Hierakonpolis (Figure 41, p. 122). After J.E. Quibell and F.W. Green, *Hierakonpolis* II, London, 1902, Pl. XLVII; J.E. Quibell, *Catalogue général des antiquités égyptiennes du Musée du Caire: Archaic objects*, Cairo, 1904–5, Pl. 65.

the floor, covered with a basalt slab. The pit contained a complete divine image: a hawk of thin copper plate, with head and plumes of gold, exquisitely made yet small in scale (Figure 42).[13] A second deposit was found beneath the floor of the end chamber to the north. This contained two copper statues of Pepi I and of another king of the 6th Dynasty, one of the 'slate' statues of King Khasekhemui of the 2nd, and a fine pottery lion probably of the Early Dynastic Period. These pieces are all in the formal 'classic' Pharaonic style.

Lying not far away in the ground beneath the walls, but in an ill-defined heap instead of in a pit, was the 'Main Deposit'. Part of it consisted of important artistic material: 'slate' palettes (including the Narmer and Two-dog Palettes, Figure 27, p. 84 and Figure 31, p. 94), carved mace heads, ivory statuettes and other ivories with designs in relief, a fragmentary limestone statue of the same King Khasekhemui and stone bowls of his reign. But numerically preponderant were small objects, often crude in execution. The commonest were mace heads, little shallow alabaster bowls, other vessels in stone and faience, including model vessels on tall stands, and animal figurines in various materials: monkeys, including one hugging its young, birds, frogs, hippopotamuses, dogs, a boar, gazelle or ibex, and numerous scorpions or scorpion tails. These latter add a distinctive element to the collection. The parallel with Abydos and Elephantine is very close, and again the material hardly corresponds with the known divine attribution of the temple, to the falcongod Horus of Nekhen, the embodiment of early kingship.

The Main Deposit lay beneath the walls of part of the Early Formal temple. Beneath another part of it lay the greater portion of an earlier structure: a circular mound of clean desert sand encased within a sloping wall of rough sandstone blocks.[14] Its stratigraphic position implies that it was created late in the Predynastic Period. Old Kingdom houses had been built around it, but had not encroached upon it, so that it may well have stood visible and in use for a part of the Old Kingdom at least. The universal interpretation of its function is that it was the base for the early temple at Hierakonpolis.

Around it had been erected a number of free-standing stone pillars, one of which might have been in the form of a tall striding man (it was found re-used in a different part of the site). These introduce a very different idea as to how a sacred space could be laid out. The last chapter illustrated a range of early ideal shapes for shrines, made from timber and matting. In neighbouring regions outside Egypt, to the south, south-west and north-east, however, there is evidence for a widespread interest in marking sacred places by means of standing stones, either individually (where they were themselves the focus of interest) or arranged in circles (where the thinking was more complex). The presence of standing stones around the central mound at Hierakonpolis shows that this tradition had a role in early Egypt as a way of creating a boundary to sacred space that dispensed with a surrounding wall. One of the more 'theological' ways in which such stones were construed will be discussed later in this chapter, in a section on the *benben*-stone of Heliopolis, the principal survival into later times of sacred standing stones. In other contexts (e.g. those beside the simple superstructures of the early kings on the Umm el-Qaʿab) they bore royal names and served as markers of personal identity. When in the form of statues they perhaps acted more as guardians (e.g. those at Coptos, see below, and the one from Hierakonpolis). Certain slabs found in the vicinity of the Hierakonpolis mound may well represent further variations from dynastic times. One was a plain, round-topped granite stela, 2.60 metres high, similar to the free-standing stelae which stood in open courts in the mortuary temples attached to certain of the Old Kingdom pyramids (see Figure 48 (3), p. 139; cf. Figure 38, p. 109).[15] A second was a granite 'door jamb' of King Khasekhemui on which was carved a scene of the temple foundation ceremony,[16] and a third belonged to one of the Kings Pepi of the 6th Dynasty.[17] Did anything originally stand on top of the mound? This question, so important to understanding how such a structure was viewed and used, is impossible to answer from direct evidence because the later building occupied the same ground. The options are: nothing at all, a single post or tall stone, a small shrine of timber and matting,[18] or a small building of mud brick. The fact that most of the votive objects and one royal statue that formed the Main Deposit were found to one side of the mound could be a sign that an enclosed 'shrine', supposing it existed, originally lay to one side of the mound.

Abydos[19]

As already mentioned (p. 89), the provincial town of Abydos probably came into existence close to the beginning of the 1st Dynasty. Late in the Old Kingdom the temple site which lay adjacent to the town saw a major phase of rebuilding which represented a step towards formality (Figure 43). The main emphasis was on creating a new enclosure with a thick girdle wall. On the north-east side, towards the north corner, lay a stone-lined gateway bearing traces of the cartouche of one of the Kings Pepi of the 6th Dynasty. A number of mud-brick buildings of modest size stood within the enclosure, none of them, by size or layout, self-evidently a temple. For one of them, none the less, some of the associated finds do lead to this identification. Most explicit are limestone stelae concerned with the temple

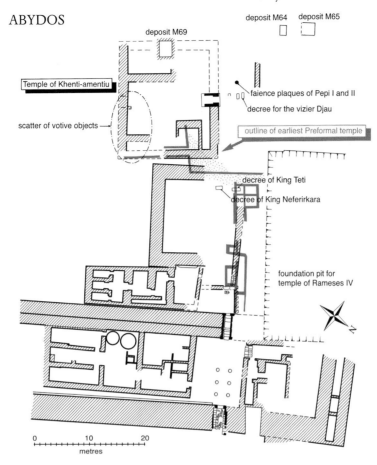

ABYDOS

deposit M69

deposit M64   deposit M65

Temple of Khenti-amentiu

faience plaques of Pepi I and II

decree for the vizier Djau

scatter of votive objects

outline of earliest Preformal temple

decree of King Teti

decree of King Neferirkara

foundation pit for
temple of Rameses IV

N

0   10   20
metres

Figure 43 Remains of the early temple of the god Khenti-amentiu at Abydos. The temple stood close to the corner of a heavily walled enclosure, surrounded by storerooms and other buildings. After W.M.F. Petrie, *Abydos* II, London, 1903, Pls L–LIV.

administration that seem to direct one's attention to this building. But the building also lay at the centre of the distribution of objects to which the term 'votive' is naturally applied. Some were found inside, and included faience tablets and alabaster vases bearing the names of Pepi I and II. At a depth of 50 centimetres beneath the floor was a large deposit of ash and burnt earth containing hundreds of little twists of burnt clay. Similar objects were found in an apparently Early Dynastic deposit beneath the New Kingdom temple at Armant.[20] Other votives had been buried in nearby pits, one of them (pit M69) actually beneath the line of the wall of this late Old Kingdom temple. They consisted of human figurines, made mostly of ivory and faience, a large group of animal figurines mostly of faience, limestone and ivory, and models of pots, boats, portable shrines, fruits and flowers, practically all of faience (see Figure 40, p. 119). One of the human figurines was a beautiful ivory statuette of a king in jubilee-festival robe.[21] This material shares the same dating problem with the deposits from Hierakonpolis. It became separated from its context when the temple was rebuilt, and its Preformal style creates an impression of extreme age. It has, however, a close parallel with the material from Elephantine. Some is undoubtedly Early Dynastic, but other pieces probably extend the range through the Old Kingdom. By the time that the temple came to be rebuilt late in the Old Kingdom they were no longer actively required in the temple, so they were carefully buried in the foundations.[22]

The building that lay at the centre of this spread of material was rectangular, measuring 18 by 21 metres, with internal subdivisions. It had been built of brick, but its doorway had been lined with stone. The structural remains that could be traced beneath the floor consisted of only patches of sand and lengths of thin brick walls that do not join up to form a single coherent building. One part seems to consist of a rectangular courtyard from which a narrow brick-lined corridor leads off, recalling in a general way the basic ground plan of the Preformal temple at Medamud (see below).[23] In the late 11th Dynasty and the reign of Senusret I the temple was rebuilt, employing limited amounts of stonework, presumably set into walls of mud brick. All trace of this building had been destroyed in the rebuilding of the New Kingdom. The Old Kingdom temple was one of many buildings, some of them houses, which seemingly filled the large walled enclosure, so turning it into an early example of an urban citadel that protected the community's main assets, the temple being one of them.[24] Another of its buildings, which lay closer to the gateway, contained the remains of many statues of wood, and a tiny statuette of Khufu, builder of the Great Pyramid. Whether it was acting as a storeroom for statues or was a supplementary cult place for statues, is now hard to judge.

One consequence of court patronage and the involvement of the formalizing approach at Abydos was the change in the identity of the god to whom the temple was principally dedicated in the Old Kingdom: from Khenti-amentiu, a local jackal-god, to Osiris, whose cult was to take on national significance. This aspect of the cult at Abydos, which exemplifies the re-codification of tradition, will be taken up a little later. However, as at Elephantine and Hierakonpolis, the range of votive figures in no way reflects either of these deities that the formal sources of the later Old Kingdom tell us were principally associated with the temple. One model of a portable divine image shows a figure without any of the characteristics of either Khenti-amentiu or Osiris (Figure 51, no. A31, p. 145).

Tell Ibrahim Awad[25]

Most of the evidence considered in this chapter, and, indeed, in the book as a whole, derives from Upper Egypt. The intensification of archaeological research in the delta during the final decades of the twentieth century has, however, brought to this, as to other topics, discoveries which help to increase the geographical spread of evidence and give a more even and representative coverage. Tell Ibrahim Awad, in the north-eastern delta (Figure 82, no. 16, pp. 226–7), is the worn-down stump of an archaeological mound which preserves the remains of a provincial town whose name has been lost but whose beginnings extended back into the Predynastic Period. An excavation begun in 1988 exposed the deep foundations of a Middle Kingdom brick building at a level below that of the original floor and surrounding ground (Figure 44). As is characteristic of the Middle Kingdom, the walls are thick (up to 2.90 metres) and enclose relatively small spaces. They define a rectangular building that seems to have stood within an enclosure wall. The Middle

TELL IBRAHIM AWAD

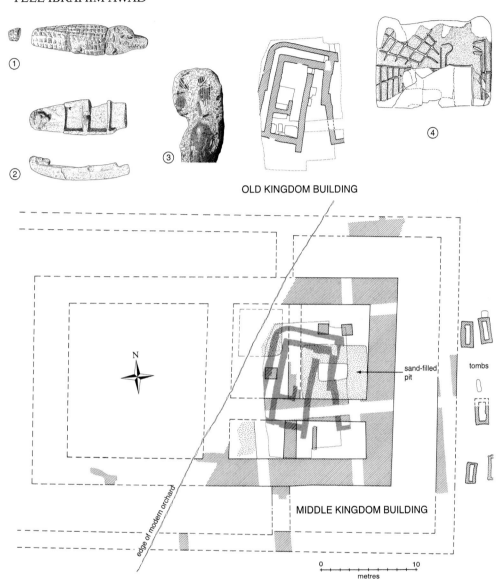

Figure 44 Superimposed Old Kingdom and Middle Kingdom brick buildings at Tell Ibrahim Awad in the eastern delta. They have been identified as temples mostly on account of the votive objects found in the fill of soil. After D. Eigner, 'A temple of the early Middle Kingdom at Tell Ibrahim Awad', in E.C.M. van den Brink, ed., *The Nile Delta in transition: 4th–3rd millennium BC*, Tel Aviv, 1992, 70–1, Figs 1, 2; W.M. van Haarlem, *EA* 18 (2001), plan on p. 33. (1) Faience crocodile, length *c.* 19 cm. (2) Pottery hedgehog-ship, length *c.* 10 cm. (3) Ivory female figurine. (4) Faience model of a shrine, its door flanked by a pair of poles with streamers (?) at the top, the later sign for divinity. (1) and (3) after photographs in Haarlem, op. cit., p. 33; (2) after W.M. van Haarlem, *JEA* 82 (1996), Pl. XX.1 and 2; (4) after W.M. van Haarlem, *MDAIK* 54 (1998), 184, Fig. 3.

Kingdom layer seems not to survive over other parts of the site so it is not possible to judge to what extent, if any, this building fitted within a larger planned town of the period. The fact that a cemetery lay against one side does, however, point to the likelihood that it stood towards the edge of the town.

The excavators discerned, both in the fragmentary plan and in certain associated features, sufficient reason for identifying the building as a temple. The features were a bed of sand beneath the main walls, and, almost straddling the east–west axis, a rectangular sand-filled pit (c. 7 x 5.60 metres) over and around which were numerous limestone chippings assumed to be from the destruction of a small structure built of limestone blocks. Deeper excavation then revealed walls from a far more modest building, on a different alignment, and with a far less formal plan. This, too, has been interpreted as a temple, of the Old Kingdom. Within a rectangular chamber (8 x 3 metres) a partition wall defines a tiny space (2 x 1.5 metres) that, according to a religious interpretation, becomes the niche for the cult statue.

From the architecture alone the temple identifications of both levels seem fairly weak, in part because we still have an insufficient basis for defining what the range of options is for these periods. The starting criteria for recognizing shrines seem hardly to be met. Can we properly eliminate other possibilities?[26] It is the associated artefacts that provide the principal support. Scattered within the surrounding soil, buried in pits, and left within some of the rooms were objects that, collectively, appear to represent another version of the votive deposits known from Elephantine, Hierakonpolis and Abydos. They include figures of humans and a variety of faience and ivory animals (largely from hippopotamus tusks), such as baboons, crocodiles and hippopotamuses; also mace heads, gaming pieces, jewellery, faience wall tiles, natural stones in curious forms and vessels deemed to be 'cultic'. Particularly striking are a hedgehog-shaped boat in pottery of a type known primarily from Elephantine, and models in faience of wood-and-matting shrines, buildings quite unlike the shrine in which they were found.[27]

It is possible that, in addition to the figurines from these excavated sites, a group can be identified from a fifth shrine. It is dispersed amongst several collections of antiquities and derives from an illicit find evidently made in the late 1940s or 1950s.[28] Although the core of the collection has been confidently ascribed to Abydos, other sites remain a possibility. This uncertainty, which may never be resolved, illustrates the general character of all of this material: on its own it provides few if any points of reference to local cults as they are known from later sources. Some of the pieces are particularly interesting, being models of tent-shrines, and in one case of a portable divine image (see below, and Figure 51).

If the votive material from Tell Ibrahim Awad, so far to the north of the other sites, suggests a greater degree of national uniformity in this respect, material from the next site to be considered, Coptos, illustrates how differently a local tradition could develop.

Coptos[29]

Once again the main source for this site, 38 kilometres north-east of Thebes, is an early excavation report, by Flinders Petrie who dug out the temple area in 1894. Even by that time most of the temple masonry had disappeared. The remaining traces suggest a familiar combination: a Ptolemaic portico on the front of a stone temple of Tuthmosis III of the 18th Dynasty – thus 'Late Formal' added to 'Mature Formal'. Despite the importance of the cult of Min, the temple was never developed to be particularly large. Petrie encountered no earlier architecture at all, but it is not clear what weight should be given to this fact. Within the soil he did discover a range of figurines, made from stone or poorly baked clay. They must be seen as products of another local Preformal tradition of votive offerings, and therefore equivalent to the material from Elephantine, Abydos, Hierakonpolis and Tell Ibrahim Awad, but different in their style. Faience was not part of this tradition. The clay figurines included humans, some of them carefully modelled statues, others 'roughly pinched into form with the fingers, and have details marked with scored lines'. Crocodiles were also modelled. A distinctive class was ring-stands with relief designs. On one the design included hunting dogs and a pair of lotus flowers tied together.[30]

The most remarkable objects found were torsos of three colossal limestone male figures, holding a wooden staff or similar object (now missing) in one hand, and erect penis (carved separately in stone and now also missing) in the other (Figure 45). A fourth piece was a broad head, heavily bearded yet bald. Their original height was probably around 4.1 metres, implying a weight of nearly two tons. Their overall shape, of a flattened cylinder, gives to them something of the character of a stela. In their present broken and decayed state they now look crudely fashioned, but where patches of their original surface survive it can be judged that they originally had carefully finished surfaces which bore a good deal of subdued modelling of anatomical detail. The figures wear a broad girdle, and down the right side of each a series of symbols had been carved in relief on a slightly raised panel. They cover a curious range of subjects: a stag's head, *pteroceras* shells, the 'thunderbolt' emblem of the god Min on a pole, long branching trees (probably), an elephant, a hyena and a bull with feet resting on hills. As a group they belong to a vocabulary of symbols in use during the period immediately prior to the 1st Dynasty, the period of 'Dynasty 0', though quite what they represent is hard to establish. Are they, for example, the names of clan-like subdivisions of the society of this part of Upper Egypt?

The figures represent a substantial achievement of organization. They are large masses of stone brought from quarries that lay some distance away, a likely site being el-Dibabiya, 70 kilometres upstream. They remind one of the well-studied case of the colossi on Easter Island in the Pacific Ocean, quarried and erected by people with a technology and organization probably not much different from that of the later Predynastic Period in Egypt. The vital element is the will to do the work: simple technology and communal effort do the rest. There had also been companion pieces of animal sculpture – crouching lions and a bird – rendered in a highly stylized way. On stylistic grounds the lions can be ascribed to most probably the early 1st Dynasty.[31]

Petrie found no evidence for the shape of the early temple to which the colossi belonged. There is thus even more scope for speculation than there is for Hierakonpolis. The disposition of the standing stones at Hierakonpolis does, however, offer a model of how the 'colossi' might have been arranged, not as the centre of attention, but as an arc of guardian figures surrounding a central feature of interest, perhaps a simple hut-shrine on a low natural mound (Figure 45, *below*; Figure 47.3, p. 138, illustrates a tradition of an archaic hut-shrine peculiar to Coptos). Petrie and others observed the remains of the mound, and it was evidently a distinctive feature of the local landscape in the 6th Dynasty, to judge from a mention of it in a text of that time.[32]

Since their discovery the statues have seemed a particularly alien and 'primitive' product of the Nile valley. Yet that is because we ourselves see them with hindsight, our aesthetics

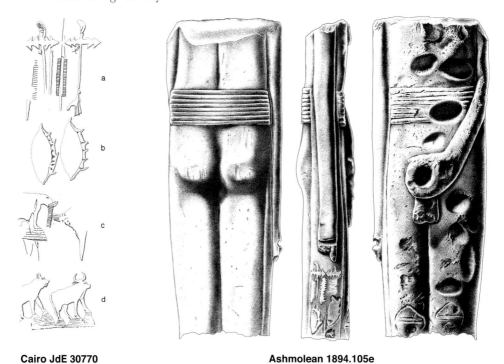

Cairo JdE 30770   **Ashmolean 1894.105e**

Figure 45 Preformal art on colossal scale: the limestone statues from Coptos. *Top left.* Carvings on the side of the colossus in the Egyptian Museum, Cairo (JdE 30770): (a) A pair of standards topped with a 'thunderbolt' emblem and feather alternating with what might be a pair of saw-bones from the Red Sea saw-fish; a small stork or ostrich has been added. (b) A pair of Red Sea shells. (c) An elephant, its feet resting on conical hills, and a bird (rear part only preserved), perhaps Horus above a spike, see Figure 28.1, p. 85. (d) A lion or hyena and a bull, their feet resting on conical hills. *Top right.* The torso and upper legs from one of the pair in the Ashmolean Museum, Oxford (no. 1894.105e). Its height is 1.93 m. Original drawing by A. Boyce. *Below.* Reconstruction of the original setting of the Coptos colossi. Reproduced from B. Kemp, A. Boyce and J. Harrell, *CAJ* 10 (2000), 211–42.

moulded by what, in the end, became the sole significant tradition in Egyptian art. The colossi communicate powerfully in their own way, and represented to their creators and admirers an emotional and aesthetic satisfaction of a different kind, in a style that allowed for the existence of shapes not fully determined by nature, a unique achievement of pre-ferred local traditions. It was a style that could have been maintained or developed further into a tradition of somewhat surreal renderings of forms. Instead, the line of development was subsequently turned towards a far more literal style of art that delineated perfect natural forms and helped to cut the Egyptians off from their own roots.

For how long were the statues accepted as objects of veneration? The conservative atmosphere of local temples in Upper Egypt, to judge from the archaeological record, could have accommodated them until a royal edict came ordering their replacement, which could have been at almost any time in the Old Kingdom. Furthermore, even after they had been formally abandoned they probably remained a source of power to local people. They bear on their bodies many smooth rounded depressions probably from people grinding away to obtain magically efficacious dust. Many of the depressions can have been made only whilst the statues were lying on the ground.

Medamud[33]

Medamud (ancient name Madu) was a provincial town with a temple lying 5 kilometres north-east of Karnak at Thebes. In historic times it was the cult centre for the falcon-god Menthu. Here we can find, from the superimposed layers of architectural foundations, the four main periods of temple building. The 18th Dynasty saw the erection of a new all-stone temple in the Mature Formal style. In the Graeco-Roman Period a broad court-yard in stone in Late Formal style was added to the front, with a double colonnade. A stone wall had extended back from this to embrace the whole sacred precinct. Beneath this stonework and on the south side of the enclosure, excavations in the 1930s revealed a layer of mud-brick foundations. No final report on the last and most vital seasons, those of 1938 and 1939, has been published, but one preliminary report does contain a general plan (Figure 46). It represents a rectangular enclosure with external dimensions of 95.5 by 60 metres. The girdle wall was 5.5 metres thick. One entrance lay through the middle of the east side. The interior was densely built up with rectangular units, carefully pre-planned in the formally rigid style of the Middle Kingdom (see below, Chapter 4). Only the foundations have been preserved, below threshold level, so that the positions of door-ways have been lost. Thus whilst we can distinguish individual units we cannot tell how their individual rooms communicated with one another. In general they seem to be sur-rounded by a more or less continuous street running along the base of the wall, as in the Middle Kingdom fortresses constructed in Lower Nubia (see Chapter 4). On the south a perpendicular street separates two individual blocks. A third, to the north, covers the full width. The streets were provided with limestone drains running along the centre line.

The space to the north is unfortunately the part where the later temple building was concentrated, destroying most of the brickwork of this level. The Middle Kingdom temple at Medamud had evidently stood in this location, but we have no direct evidence for its plan. Many stone architectural elements of this date, reused in later constructions, had been discovered during earlier seasons of excavation. These included columns, Osirid royal statues, door elements, and statues. Many blocks came from two huge portals that might

MEDAMUD

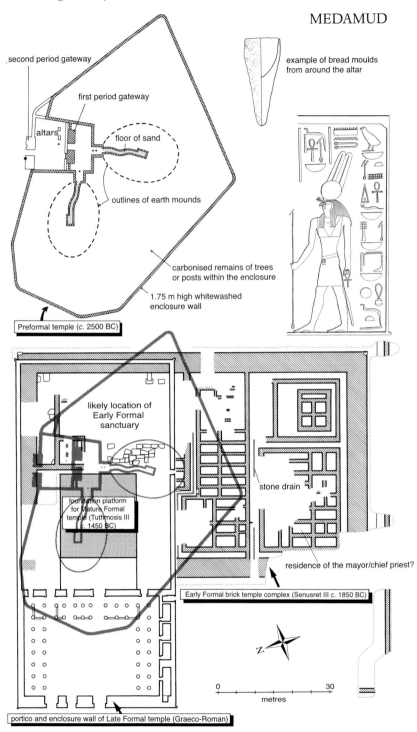

second period gateway

first period gateway

altars

floor of sand

outlines of earth mounds

example of bread moulds
from around the altar

carbonised remains of trees
or posts within the enclosure

1.75 m high whitewashed
enclosure wall

Preformal temple (c. 2500 BC)

likely location of
Early Formal
sanctuary

stone drain

foundation platform
for Mature Formal
temple (Tuthmosis III
c. 1450 BC)

residence of the mayor/chief priest?

Early Formal brick temple complex (Senusret III c. 1850 BC)

0   30
metres

portico and enclosure wall of Late Formal temple (Graeco-Roman) have stood in the brick enclosure wall. As far as one can tell from the reports, however, there is insufficient masonry to account for a Middle Kingdom temple whose walls were of stone-block construction. The walls would have been mostly of mud brick.

The excavators produced a reconstructed plan of the complex, which includes a ground plan of the temple, and this has passed into textbooks. It seems to contain, however, a great deal of personal interpretation, and in Figure 46 the plan of actual remains has been preferred. They recognized, none the less, that the southern part must have consisted of storerooms and houses for the temple community. They also drew attention to its fortress-like appearance, and, indeed, the Nubian forts do supply the closest parallel. Protection is one theme expressed in religious architecture and this would seem to be an excellent early example. But other powers could have taken advantage of this. It is worth considering that the building block in the south-west corner is actually a civil residence, for the local representative of authority, perhaps the mayor of the town. At this time the combination of civil and religious authority in the same person is common, usually to be seen in the paired titles 'mayor' and 'chief priest'. It fits other evidence (summarized in Chapter 8) that in the Middle Kingdom the accommodation for such people could be the dominant building in the town. The powerful bureaucratic building machine of the Middle Kingdom could here have been applied to rendering into concise architectural form the local structure of power. Medamud would then become an example of the temple citadel in the Middle Kingdom. It would imply that the independent rectangular building in the south-west corner was his residence, though at 22 x 27 metres it is only a quarter of the size of one of the large Kahun houses (60 x 40 metres).

This Middle Kingdom intervention had left behind in the underlying ground traces of a yet earlier temple enclosure that challenges our preconceived images of Pharaonic culture, rather as do the Coptos colossi but in a very different way. This was excavated in 1939, and again is the subject of only a preliminary report.[34] A brick wall had enclosed an irregular, polygonal plot of ground, 83 metres at its widest point. The wall and its associated buildings stood on alluvial soil that had evidently not been built on before, although it contained a few prehistoric implements. The wall had enclosed a grove of trees, which had left carbonized remains behind (or were they upright wooden posts, counterparts to standing stones?). Within the 'grove' two oval structures had stood, inferred from negative traces on the ground. It was thought they had been simply mounds of soil. A winding corridor of brick, less than one metre wide, passed to a chamber in the centre of each mound, the floors covered with fine sand. The corridors led from a courtyard by means of a vestibule in each case. Pottery supports for offering-basins or incense-burners stood in these vestibules. The courtyard was closed by a wall containing an entrance flanked by two small brick towers, and there is a strong temptation to restore the towers as pylons, so making them the earliest examples from the Nile valley (though at just over 3 metres wide they are

Figure 46 Two-and-a-half thousand years of temple worship: the temple site at Medamud, showing the superimposed layers of architecture. After C. Robichon and A. Varille, *CdE* 14, no. 27 (1939), 84, Fig. 2; C. Robichon and A. Varille, *Description sommaire du temple primitif de Médamoud*, Cairo, 1940, folding plan at end. The image of the god Menthu comes from a lintel belonging to a monumental stone portal found on the site, made in the reign of Senusret III and taken over by a later king of the 13th Dynasty, one of the Sebekheteps. After F. Bisson de la Roque and J.J. Clère, *Rapport sur les fouilles de Médamoud (1927)*, Cairo, 1928, Pl. VI.

unlikely to have risen much above human height). Subsequently an outer court was added and the towers were replaced by a new pair further to the north. The emplacements for one flagpole were in front of each of the new towers, in one case represented by a circular stone support. This outer court contained two rectangular brick pedestals, covered with ashes. Were they altars or did an image stand on them?

No inscriptions were found relating to this curious building, but pottery seems to date it to the latter part of the Old Kingdom. There has to be, therefore, the strong presumption that some kind of shrine had stood here even earlier, and that the surviving Preformal temple itself represents an act of architectural renewal within the Dynastic Period and made with little reference to court traditions. The reports also make no mention of the finding of votive figurines or of other material comparable to the groups considered so far.

This early temple seems to have been built around the architectural symbol of the mound. It is possible to interpret this in terms of the unifying theology of later times. One element of this took the concept of the primaeval mound that had first appeared above the waters of chaos as a symbolic source of regenerative power, including new life beyond the grave. But no later inscriptions link this particularly to Medamud, and, as always, we should be cautious in making interpretations using sources from much later times. It still remains the most striking example of Preformal architecture from Egypt. Its date, well within the historic period, is an important reference point for other sites. It adds credibility to historic datings for the other material discussed here, and is particularly useful in interpreting the architectural remains at Hierakonpolis.

Much of the Preformal artistic material has been known since the turn of the last century (Elephantine and Tell Ibrahim Awad excepted). Its discovery made a considerable initial impact, and provoked a book that is still a useful introductory study: J. Capart's *Primitive Art in Ancient Egypt*, published in 1905.[35] In Capart's view, the stylistic contrast was to be explained by the widespread survival amongst the population at large of an indigenous 'primitive art', alongside a developing 'official art, the art of the masters', introduced by the small group of invading Pharaonic Egyptians who, it was then thought, brought in with them the essential ideas of ancient Egyptian civilization. Although its invasion aspect is no longer acceptable as an historical explanation, Capart's model did at least give to this material a weight that it subsequently lost. If we replace a superior invading group by an innovative but indigenous court circle then Capart's presentation becomes a reasonable one, although he, too, may have unnecessarily confined too much of the temple votive material to the prehistoric period.

The unilinear model of early cultural development in Egypt – the art history approach – oversimplifies, and in so doing discards evidence that does not fit. The strictly formal approach to design which we identify as quintessentially Pharaonic, and which replaced the more intuitive and less disciplined creations of the Predynastic Period, was slow in coming to certain provincial corners of Dynastic Egypt. The academic court art created during the Early Dynastic Period was not used in a wholesale programme of replacement throughout the country. In provincial temples, buildings and objects either inherited from the past or created in styles of the past, continued to hold interest for a long time. The reasons for the slow and piecemeal progress of transformation may well have included limitations in court resources. For a long time they were concentrated on pyramid building and court cemetery construction. Furthermore, the creation ('birth') of a new divine image was an act imbued with great importance, so much so that individual examples were solemnly recorded in early annals as one of the few significant acts of a given year of a king's reign.[36] Yet the main reason must have remained individual preference for the old.

The time-scale is no mean one. The Dynastic Period must have begun around 3000 BC. The Old Kingdom ended around 2160 BC. Something like a millennium is involved at some of these sites. It means that for about a third of its history, Pharaonic Egypt was a country of two cultures (if not more when the Late Period is considered, see Chapter 8, p. 371).

The roots of culture

The key to understanding formal Egyptian visual culture – architecture as well as art – and its remarkable homogeneity through three thousand years lies in the concept of the ideal type. This is a universal characteristic of the mind. We all have an image in terms of our own cultural experience of what, for example, a traditional king should look like, or a desirable residence, or a proper place of worship. Modernism in art and architecture has been directed towards breaking these ideal types and showing that within the imagination there need be no stereotypes. A different attempt to break visual stereotypes is found in Islam. God is to have no visual image at all, and is to be encountered through a multiplicity of names. The Egyptians were at the other extreme. The ideal type, the image of what constituted a proper form, was elevated to the pinnacle of intellectual and aesthetic desirability. Because it was centred in the art of the court, the prime source of patronage, it was a self-perpetuating ideal, automatically selecting and promoting those artists with a natural aptitude for absorbing the range of ideal types into their artistic consciousness and skilled in the translation of these types into the precise graphic style that was so preferred.

The history of writing in Egypt aptly illustrates the power that visual archetypes had.[37] The first short groups of hieroglyphs used as writing occur at the transition to the 1st Dynasty (examples are Figures 30.2, 34.3, 4, pp. 90, 97). The signs are pictures of objects that conform in style to the developing canon of formal art. Properly drawn hieroglyphs were not, however, very suited to the rapid writing that is needed for letters or administrative documents. By the 4th Dynasty, or perhaps before, the Egyptians had developed a more rapid form of writing which we call hieratic (Figures 58 and 60, pp. 165 and 169, are examples). Individual hieroglyphs were reduced to a few easy strokes of the reed pen, and sometimes run together into groups. Hieratic changed its style over the generations, so that modern scholars can date texts to within certain limits by handwriting. Some good scribes, particularly in the later New Kingdom, developed elegant flourishes in their handwriting. But in no case can we honestly claim that this represents calligraphic art as developed, say, by traditional Islamic or Japanese culture. The reason is simple: the writing that demanded care and attention was hieroglyphic writing. Although more signs were added from time to time the ideal type never changed. It was the accurately delineated natural form as pioneered in the late Predynastic. The artist who wished to lavish his talents on hieroglyphs did so by working harder at the internal details of outlines that it would have been unnatural and improper to change.

The Pharaonic art style is relatively easy to describe,[38] and to judge from the scale of the ancient output, it was relatively easy to acquire, given that there was every incentive to do so. A good artist was amongst the official, scribal class, as the sculptors' workshops in the New Kingdom city of El-Amarna show (see Chapter 7). We can select three essential elements. Whole compositions were given a markedly linear format through subdivision by horizontal lines from which individual figures spring. The resulting bands, or registers, of figures portray themes, but the sequence of registers could contain a more general element of order: of space progressing away from the viewer although no thought was given to diminishing the size of figures with distance; or of time, in a sequence running vertically upwards. The second element, which also relates to overall composition, is the intimate connection between figures and accompanying hieroglyphic writing. Because hieroglyphs retained their original natural forms and were drawn to the same conventions as other elements in a picture, texts and pictures combined harmoniously into a single channel of communication. This is most apparent when signs are worked emblematically into the actions of the scene, as illustrated by the El-Lisht throne bases (Figure 20, p. 70). In the Early Dynastic Period hieroglyphs and pictorial groups tended to mingle more equally than later, when the balance changed and hieroglyphs became more of a commentary upon a dominant pictorial scene.

The third element concerns the conventions of the individual figures, be they humans, animals or pieces of furniture. Each figure or each major component part of a figure is reduced to a characteristic profile, and if necessary recombined to produce a composite image which does not offend common sense too much. For an ox the reduction was into three parts: side profile of the body, front profile of the eye and front profile of the horns. The human body was similarly treated. For birds the shape of tail feathers was profiled as if seen from above.

Because of the limited subject matter and format of Egyptian art, both wall scenes and statues, the reproduction of ideal types was a straightforward matter. Indeed, for certain elements, primarily the proportions of the human figure, a specific canon of proportions was devised which, from the Middle Kingdom onwards, related the parts of the body to a grid consisting of eighteen squares from the soles of the feet to the hairline.

The aim of the artist was to render the elements of his pictures truthfully and informatively. The subject matter itself, however, portrayed reality only within frames of reference taken from a world of myth and ideals. In the case of religious scenes this is self-evident. But Egyptian tomb art also sought to record an eternal environment for the deceased tomb owner. The scenes that were selected created a world of banquets with friends, of hunting parties, and of overseeing the affairs of a country estate that included busy craftsmen. It is easy to conclude from tomb pictures that most ancient Egyptians of all ranks lived in the country, in a society without towns and cities. Yet the archaeological record shows that this was not the case. By the latter part of the Old Kingdom densely settled walled towns had grown up in numerous places, sufficiently so as to suggest that a mature urban framework existed, and that for most educated Egyptians the town provided the basic experience of living. But this had no part in dreams of an ideal world, which was that of a peaceful agrarian living. Such scenes are the staple of the tomb of Ankhtify at Mo'alla, from the early First Intermediate Period, despite the written narrative in the same tomb of civil war and famine which find no reflection at all in the pictorial decoration.[39] Egyptian art (and, as we shall see, architecture also) was a carefully and deliberately constructed style. It was not, however, built upon an empty cultural landscape, but over a pre-existing culture that, if Pharaonic Egypt had advanced no further, we would recognize and study as a viable tradition in its own right. The creation of Pharaonic art and its gradual expansion as a medium of religious communication involved a complex interplay with the Preformal tradition, selecting some elements and rejecting others. Two examples will illustrate this. The first concerns the religious iconography of the god Min.[40]

In formal Pharaonic religion the god Min had a prominent place as a god of procreation, with an important centre at Coptos. In the classic iconography he is depicted as a swathed standing male figure, holding a flail aloft in one hand and grasping the root of his erect penis in the other (Figure 47). His headdress is a pair of tall plumes. Other distinguishing attributes are a strange tall version of the primitive tent-shrine (see below), and a bed of growing lettuces, the milky sap of which was apparently interpreted as the god's semen.[41] He was also given an emblem on a carrying pole, an object still not positively identified but called conveniently a 'thunderbolt'.

This stock set of images had been codified by the late Old Kingdom.[42] Indeed, the basic image of the god Min himself appears as early as the late 2nd Dynasty.[43] The Preformal colossal statues found at Coptos provide us with some of the raw material from which the classic stereotyped image was fashioned. We can see how the court intellectual systematizers went to work. The basic pose was retained, but details and overall style were remodelled to produce a variant of the single standard image of a god that the court style of religious art dictated. Thus, for example, the distinctive appearance of the head and thick long beard were discarded. A number of emblems were associated with the original cult, carved on the sides of the colossi. The religious systematizers from the court circle chose one, the 'thunderbolt', and ignored the rest. The overall result of their work was a collection of attributes pinned, as it were, on to the stock all-purpose model of a god. In this state he became amenable to theological language/image-game. The combination Min-Amun appeared, in which a degree of merging took place with the god Amun from the nearby town of Thebes. At Abydos, in the Middle Kingdom, a cult of 'Min-Horus the Victorious', which brought the cult of Min into association with the cult of Osiris, achieved some popularity.

The second example is the sacred *benben*-stone.[44] It seems to have stood in a shrine at Heliopolis and was presumably an example of the widespread ancient cult of individual stones thought to have peculiar properties. The original is now lost, but pictorial evidence suggests that it was an upright stone with rounded top (Figure 48). The stone became the prototype for a range of architectural symbols, and as such re-appears spasmodically through Egyptian history in its primitive shape. King Akhenaten, for example, set up a round-topped *benben*-stone in one of his sun temples at El-Amarna.[45] An earlier elongated version was erected in the Fayum, at the site of Abgig, by King Senusret III of the 12th Dynasty,[46] and other examples were noted in the section on Hierakonpolis. But the rounded shape more frequently jarred on the aesthetics of the Egyptians. It lacked geometric purity. They preferred to convert the rounded top into a purer geometric shape, a pyramid, and the complete stone into a truncated obelisk. Monumental versions in this form were built as the focal point of solar temples associated with the pyramids of 5th Dynasty kings near the site of Abusir, and the pointed tops of pyramids and obelisks were called by a feminine form of the name: *benbent*. They could even be added (incongruously from our point of view) to the tops of replicas of tent-shrines (Figure 49, and see below).

But why the solar connection? Theologians took up the similarity in consonantal sequence between *benben* and the verb *weben*, 'to shine', 'to rise' (of the sun). Verbal similarity supplied a logical linkage. From the practice of theological language-game the *benben*-stone became

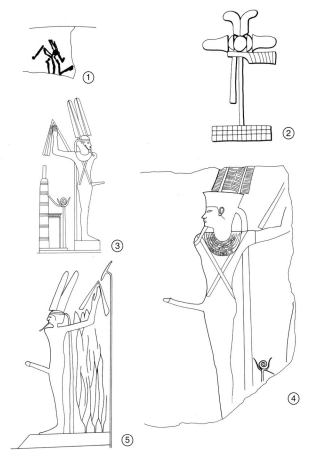

Figure 47   The formalized images of the god Min. Nos. 3–5 exemplify the classic image of Min as fertility god, adding to the ideal anthropomorphic image of god the elements of erect penis and brandished flail derived from the Coptos colossi (Figure 45, p. 130). The tall plumed crown is also common to the image of the god Amun from nearby Thebes. Behind Min in no. 5 is a stylized bed of tall lettuces, their white sap regarded as a symbol of semen; behind no. 3 (and originally behind no. 4) is a depiction of a tent-shrine peculiar to the Min cult: a tall cylindrical tent linked by a rope to a staff topped with bovine horns (the basis for the reconstruction in Figure 45). No. 5 is from a decree from the Coptos temple of the reign of Pepi I of the 6th Dynasty (*c.* 2290 BC), after R. Weill, *Les décrets royaux de l'ancien empire égyptien*, Paris, 1912, Pl. VII; no. 4 is from the same site, but of the reign of Senusret I of the 12th Dynasty (*c.* 1950 BC), after W.M.F. Petrie, *Koptos*, London, 1896, Pl. IX; H.M. Stewart, *Egyptian stelae, reliefs and paintings from the Petrie Collection* II, Warminster, 1979, Pl. 39. No. 3 derives from a kiosk of Senusret I at Karnak, after W.S. Smith, *The art and architecture of ancient Egypt*, third edn, New Haven, Conn., and London, 1998, 92, Fig. 162. The earliest recognizable image of Min in the formalized tradition is no. 1, an ink drawing on a sherd from a stone bowl from the tomb of King Khasekhemui of the 2nd Dynasty (*c.* 2690 BC) at Abydos, after W.M.F. Petrie, *Abydos* I, London, 1902, 4, Pl. III.48. No. 2 is the 'thunderbolt' symbol of Min also used for the name of the Coptos nome. It was the only one of the symbols carved on the Coptos colossi (see Figure 28, p. 85) which was taken into the formal canon of images used for Min. This example is from the Valley Temple of Sneferu at Dahshur (*c.* 2590 BC), after A. Fakhry, *The monuments of Sneferu at Dahshur* II.1, Cairo, 1961, 20, Fig. 9.

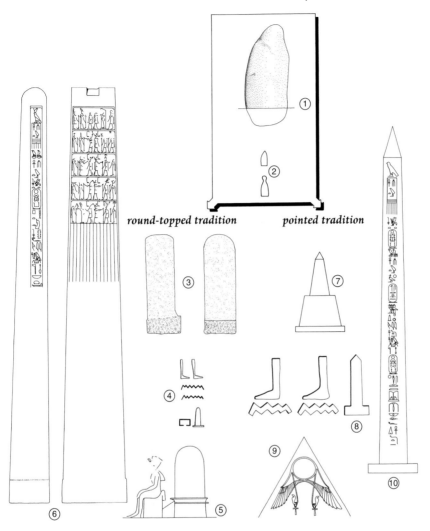

Figure 48 Artistic transformation of a symbol: the sacred *benben*-stone of Heliopolis. (1) Hypothetical original sacred stone. (2) Early depictions as hieroglyphs in the Pyramid Texts (Pyr 1652b, 2069a). Artists preferred to give it a symmetrical, geometric shape, creating two traditions, one of flattened rectangular section with a rounded top (3–6), and another of square section and with a pointed top (7–10). (3) Round-topped stela from Hierakonpolis temple, height 6 m, after J.E. Quibell and F.W. Green, *Hierakonpolis* II, London, 1902, Pl. LXVII. (4) Writing of *benben*-stone in the tomb of Meryra at El-Amarna, 18th Dynasty, after LD III, 97e. (5) Depiction of a *benben*-stone erected in a sun-temple at El-Amarna, tomb of Meryra, after N. de G. Davies, *The rock tombs of El Amarna* I, London, 1903, Pl. XXXIII. (6) Granite standing stone at Abgig, Fayum, erected by Senusret I, 12th Dynasty, height 12.62 m, after LD II, 119. (7) Profile, partially restored from ancient depictions, of the central feature of the 5th Dynasty sun temples at Abu Ghurab. (8) Writing of *benben*-stone on an inscription from El-Amarna, after J.D.S. Pendlebury, *The City of Akhenaten* III, London, 1951, Pl. CIII.48. (9) Top of a pyramidion from the top of the pyramid of King Khendjer of the 13th Dynasty at Sakkara. On it is carved the winged disk of the sun. After G. Jéquier, *Deux pyramides du moyen empire*, Cairo 1933, Fig. 17. (10) Granite obelisk of Senusret I at Heliopolis itself, height 20.4 m, after LD II, 118h.

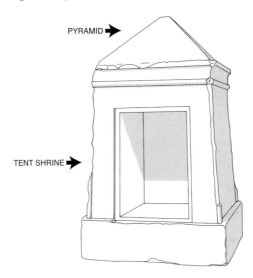

PYRAMID →

TENT SHRINE →

Figure 49   Combining unrelated symbols. A naos (or inner shrine for a divine image) in the form of a tent-shrine with a pyramid placed on top, something structurally incongruous, but aesthetically satisfactory as a combination of symbols. 30th Dynasty, after G. Roeder, *Catalogue général des antiquités égyptiennes du Musée du Caire: Naos*, Leipzig, 1914, Taf. 16b.

a symbol of sunrise and the renewal of life. For the same reason, the heron ('phoenix'), which in ancient Egyptian was called *benu*, was brought into association with the cult of this stone, so that the temple at Heliopolis could be called 'The Mansion of the Phoenix'. The statement which linked them all together and implied that a cogent meaning was there ran as follows: 'O Atum-Kheprer [god of creation], you became elevated on the height, you rose up [*weben*] as the *benben*-stone in the Mansion of the Phoenix [*benu*] in Heliopolis.'[47] By this kind of thinking, more akin to poetry and arousing no further curiosity in the Egyptian mind, order was imposed on a small part of the Egyptians' inheritance from prehistory. Language-game replaced some sacred meaning that that particular stone had once held and is probably permanently lost to us. The ideal type was recast in both shape and meaning. In this instance, as with the history of the god Min, we are witnessing the invention of tradition, something that the Egyptians enthusiastically pursued until the end of their civilization.

We can recall a further example. By the early Middle Kingdom Abydos had become the centre for the cult of Osiris.[48] The theologians who tried to systematize and rationalize the diverse local traditions concerning holy things in Egypt had already, for reasons that we shall probably never know, made a connection between Osiris and Abydos during the late Old Kingdom. We know this from statements in the Pyramid Texts. Yet on the ground, in the temple which actually stood in the town of Abydos, the first known reference to Osiris dates only to the 11th Dynasty. In the Old Kingdom the temple belonged to a local jackal-god associated with the great cemetery nearby, called Khenti-amentiu, 'Foremost amongst the Westerners', the second element a reference to the blessed dead. From the Middle Kingdom onwards this name becomes principally an epithet for Osiris, as 'Osiris,

Foremost amongst the Westerners'. For the earliest period of the Abydos shrine's existence a similar complex relationship seems to have existed between Khenti-amentiu (assuming that his cult was of this antiquity) and popular practice as revealed by the votive objects. They contain no image of this god, although a model shrine depicts a human-headed deity to which we are unable to give a name.

From the range of evidence available it is all too apparent that intellectual intervention shaped Egyptian religion over a long period, stirring the cauldron of tradition and adding new ingredients. The problem for modern scholarship in too ready an acceptance of this, namely a powerful dynamic and creative element in ancient religion, is that it undermines the principal method of research: that of carefully following the sources backwards in time from the better understood later ones to the more fragmentary and elusive earlier ones, and assuming that the meaning always remained the same. We tend to work by trying to identify fossils of early beliefs embedded within later sources. Yet if we take this easy course we run the risk of substituting for ancient language-game a modern scholarly game.

Folk culture?

The urge for purity of form and consistency of style came to have a generally debilitating effect on spontaneity. The modern world recognizes that cultural expression appears at more than one level. Whilst great or high culture originates from centres of established patronage and inevitably makes the greatest general impact, popular culture, which is 'folk culture' when of the past or of agrarian origins, although less intellectual, has a vigour and originality of its own and is a legitimate aspect of the whole culture of a people. It can find its energy through expressing deliberate rebellion against 'high culture'. We should be prepared, in studying ancient societies, to encounter the same plurality of expression.

The problems that arise for the distant past are, however, peculiarly large. Popular culture uses music, oral tale and dance as much as figurative arts. These are lost to archaeology except when caught in rare ancient pictures that cannot, in any case, convey more than the briefest programme note. This is true for ancient Egypt. Tomb pictures and occasionally temple scenes show dances and acrobatics, and singers and musicians performing. But we cannot reconstruct living shows from them. In local shrines the serious business of religion kept local tradition alive. But outside these cultural enclaves the success of court art and the tendency towards mass stereotyped production of artefacts sapped local creativity.

We can apply a simple test. Pottery has survived abundantly from all periods of ancient Egypt and had common use in the households of rich and poor alike.[49] It has also become in other cultures a vehicle for folk-art expression. Predynastic Egyptian pottery contains the beginnings of just such a tradition. A class of Nagada II (Gerzean) pottery, actually called 'Decorated Ware' by early archaeologists, combines a distinctive shape with a range of simple painted designs that belong to the same tradition that created the scenes in the Hierakonpolis Painted Tomb. It is easy to imagine that this type of decorated pottery could have become the archaic phase of a long history of decorated ceramics in which the characteristics of the medium produced distinctive derivatives from the Pharaonic art style with a life of their own, matched in modern times by detailed analysis by art historians. It did not happen. The development, in the late Nagada II period, of the low relief carvings which represent the beginnings of court art and the codification of ideas seems to have undermined any further interest in ceramic art. The decoration on pottery declines into simple squiggles and then vanishes altogether. Henceforth pottery decoration was a rarity, except for a brief interlude in the mid-New Kingdom. Pottery became a utilitarian product. It is sometimes well made, notably in the case of fine orange burnished bowls produced in the Old Kingdom, but nevertheless still falls short of an artistic tradition offering individual expression. There was an element of regionalism in pottery styles. But none of this amounts to a tradition of ceramic folk art. The Early Dynastic and Old Kingdom pottery types of the provincial towns that possessed the local shrine cultures outlined above are regional variants of utilitarian objects ranging from the coarse to the bland.

If we look carefully, however, we can find exceptions. One concerns the art of carving seals. The cylinder seal was a foreign idea early brought to Egypt.[50] The first ones occur in the late Nagada II and are either imports from or copies of imports from the contemporary cultures of Western Asia. From the 1st Dynasty the Egyptians began to carve hieroglyphs on them and to use them as instruments of administration, sealing letters, jars, doors, boxes, and so on with a distinctive official design (Figure 50). Carved cylinders continued to be, however, objects of interest in their own right, with a value that was not straightforwardly administrative. Numerous private seals are known from the Early Dynastic Period bearing designs which use both hieroglyphs and other design elements in a somewhat surreal manner, displaying an interest in developing designs away from the natural models which normally so entranced the Egyptians.[51] By the latter part of the Old Kingdom they had become a minor art form, occurring occasionally in court cemeteries and sometimes accompanying hieroglyphic inscriptions. They then passed through a sudden transformation, abandoning the cylinder shape for a flat disc with a shank or a prism shape, becoming stamp seals bearing designs in the same non-formal tradition on their bases.[52] The centre of this industry seems to have been Middle Egypt. Further steps in design development can be observed through the First Intermediate Period, and by the end the characteristic Egyptian scarab-shaped seal had been born. Moreover, it had also been taken up by the administrative class as a more convenient way of applying seals, and so the scarab replaced the cylinder seals altogether. With official recognition came the application of proper formal designs, and the snuffing out of this minor provincial art tradition.

This particular case illustrates how court culture could, on occasion, continue to take on board new designs of provincial origin. It was part of the success of the Egyptian state that it managed to build local traditions into a national framework of myth and design. The process took time and, as discussed in the first part of this chapter, in provincial shrines local tradition continued to thrive until well into the Old Kingdom. In later periods when new elements appear, such as the popularity of the domestic god Bes from the New Kingdom onwards (see Figure 133, p. 383), or the huge interest of the Late Period in sacred animal burial (Chapter 8), we are entitled to suspect a derivation in popular consciousness and behaviour: folk culture surfacing only when taken up by official patronage and made explicit and visible in sources that we can understand.

Ideal types in architecture

Architectural ideal types were less amenable to mechanical reproduction, and had a more complex evolution. They had a very real existence in the minds of the Egyptians, but gave

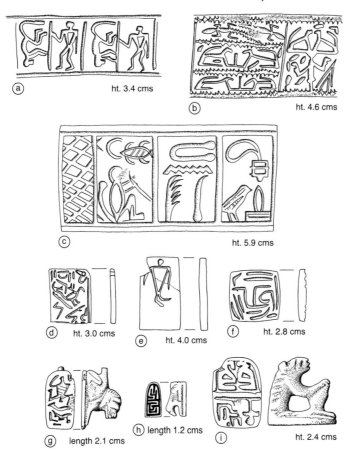

Figure 50 The makings of an alternative art-style which failed to develop, revealed by small carvings on Old Kingdom objects. (a)–(c) Seals from Abusir, Staatliche Museen, Berlin, 15600; Egyptian Museum, Cairo, JdE 72610; Staatliche Museen, Berlin, 16433. After H.G. Fischer, *Metropolitan Museum Journal* 6 (1972), 5–16, Figs 4, 18, 21. (d)–(f) Faience votive plaques from the temple at Elephantine, after G. Dreyer, *Elephantine* VIII. *Der Tempel der Satet*, Mainz, 1986, 151, Abb. 60, Taf. 57. (g)–(i) Button seals from Middle Egypt, after G. Brunton, *Qau and Badari* I, London, 1927, Pl. XXXIII.118, 121, 112.

rise to broader scope in their realization as structures and buildings. Even more than with art, Pharaonic architecture reveals how tradition was invented.

By the Early Dynastic Period the normal material in use for building was mud brick. People used it for houses, for town walls, for the linings of tomb pits, and for the memorials and offering-places built above them. The potential of brick for creating interesting patterns in the method of laying was realized for palaces, and for court tombs, in the palace-façade style of architecture (Figure 35, p. 102). Its most important monumental survivor, copied in stone, is the great plaza and token palace in front of the Step Pyramid at Sakkara (Figure 36, p. 104). It seems not, however, to have been used for temples. It appears suddenly, its details fully developed, at the beginning of the 1st Dynasty. This has led to a theory that it derives from the temple architecture of Mesopotamia where the style was deeply rooted with a long history of evolution behind it. This is not as far-fetched as it might seem at first, for there is other evidence for contacts with southern Mesopotamia during the later Nagada II period, although their nature and significance are now hard to judge.

Alongside the palace-façade style of brick architecture, however, we have to recognize the existence of a second architectural tradition that was to have, in the end, the determining influence on Egyptian stone architecture to the end of Pharaonic Egypt. This was the architecture of temporary structures built of wooden frames covered partially or wholly with plain wooden panels or with sheets of woven matting or bound reeds (Figure 51). To appreciate the technology we can turn to early artistic representations that are inevitably ambiguous in communicating to us their details, but better still, actual examples have survived from the Old Kingdom. The two most famous are the cabins on the funerary boat of Khufu (Cheops) at Giza,[53] and the tent of Queen Hetep-heres, Khufu's mother, from her tomb also at Giza.[54] The various sources agree as to structural form: slender wooden supports often with papyrus-bud finials, wooden roofing-ties to join them together, being equally slender and either flat or evenly (though only gently) curving upwards, or curving asymmetrically. At the front these formal tents could be completely open, or only partially so through the use of a screen covering the lower part. The ancient word for such a structure was *seh*, and one of the hieroglyphic signs used to write it was a simplified picture of the structure itself.

The Hetep-heres tent was made for temporary use and to be portable. The whole structure could be taken apart, packed up in a box and transported. This fact probably explains the widespread use of this type of structure. It was suitable for royal occasions outside the brick palace; for funerals, where the burial equipment could be laid out for display and possibly even for the preparation of the body prior to burial; and for the comfort of the official class when visiting the countryside (Figure 52.3).[55] Their use in private funerals has a striking analogy in modern Egypt, where large portable tents consisting of decorated coverings laid over a rectangular framework of poles can be hired to accommodate mourners paying their last respects and listening to a religious oration. Some representations of what seem to be portable tents mounted on carrying-frames are also known from the Early Dynastic Period, as in the scene on the Narmer mace head (Figure 37.G, p. 106).

By the 1st Dynasty brick architecture was well established in Egypt, and from the material reviewed in the first part of this chapter it seems fairly clear that built temples of various kinds made early appearances in provincial towns. It seems unlikely, therefore, that the image of the tent-shrine reflected the common appearance of provincial temples. Yet some early representations of what appear to be shrines are of tent form (Figure 51.1).[56] One class seems to have been made to look like a horned animal (Figure 51.3). How are we to explain this contradictory evidence?

The answer is provided by some of the votive objects from early shrine deposits (Figure 51).[57] They actually depict little tent-shrines with curving tops, in three cases (P243, A29a on the outside, A31 on the inside) showing the criss-cross pattern on the cover. The same appears also in the early depictions, and is probably a pattern, or a method of binding, in the matting used as covering material. Three examples (P132, P243, A31) seem to rest on frames with legs (A31) or projections representing carrying handles

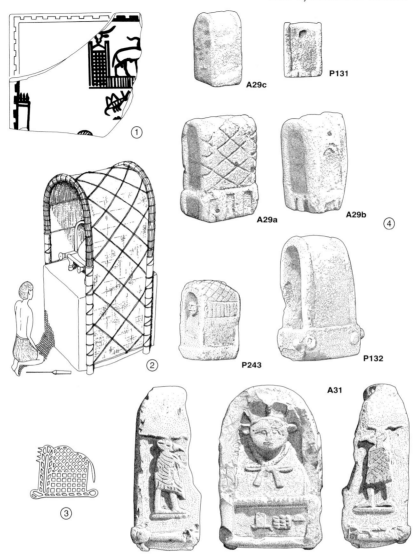

Figure 51   The early tent-shrine: prototype for Pharaonic formal architecture. (1) An early tent-shrine for the cult of a ram statue, set within a panelled brick enclosure. Ivory tablet from the tomb of King Den at Abydos, 1st Dynasty. After W.M.F. Petrie, *The royal tombs of the earliest dynasties* II, London, 1901, 25, Pl. VII.8. (2) Reconstruction of a tent-shrine for the revealed image of a god, based on the brick dais in the Old Kingdom temple at Elephantine, see Figure 39, p. 117, and Plate 4, p. 116. (3) Ancient depiction of tent-shrine with the profile of an animal, perhaps on a carrying frame and thus portable. Part of the design on a mud-seal impression from the tomb of King Aha (Hor-aha), early 1st Dynasty. After W.B. Emery, *Hor-aha*, Cairo, 1939, 27, Fig. 23. (4) Models of early tent-shrines, P131, P132 and P243 in faience from early deposits at Abydos. After W.M.F. Petrie, *Abydos* II, London, 1903, Pl. VII.131, 132; Pl. XI.243; A29a–c in faience and A31 in limestone from an uncertain source, possibly also Abydos, the last after H.W. Müller, *Ägyptische Kunstwerke, Kleinfunde und Glas in der Sammlung E. und M. Kofler-Truniger, Luzern*, Berlin, 1964. They vary in size between 4 and 10 cm.

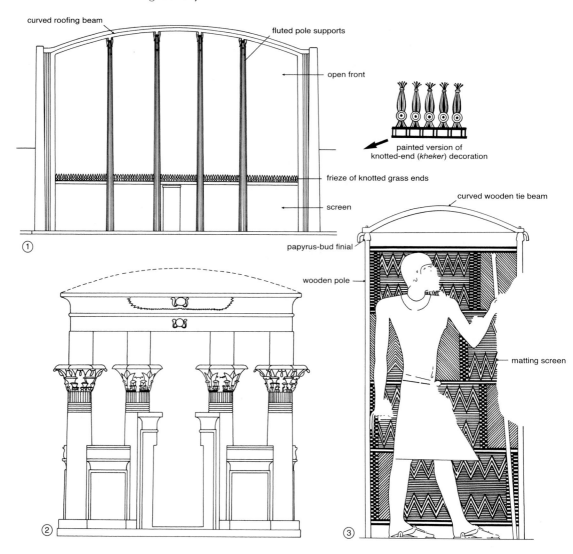

Figure 52 Ideal types in architecture: the open-fronted tent-shrine (see Plate 3, p. 108). (1) Rendered into stone at the Step Pyramid of Djoser at Sakkara. After L. Borchardt, *Ägyptische Tempel mit Umgang*, Cairo, 1938, Bl. 10. (2) Likewise, but in a more developed form, at the Roman kiosk at Philae, the broken roof line representing a now perished curved wooden roof. After ibid., Bl. 5. (3) The same architecture retained for convenience as a portable framed tent for visits to the country-side, from the tomb of Werirni, 5th Dynasty, at Sheikh Saïd (see map, Figure 116, p. 339). After N. de G. Davies, *Rock tombs of Sheikh Saïd*, London, 1901, Pl. XV.

that made them portable. Two of them, however, (A29a and b) rest on pedestals with sides decorated with panelling, making it likely that they are of solid, mud-brick construction.[58] Two of them (P243, A31) contain a human-like figure, in the latter case with a face very similar to those which top the Narmer Palette. It is labelled with the hieroglyphic word *Repit*. Whether this is a proper name for a goddess, or a term for a type of image or essence of a divinity, it is now impossible to decide. Sources from later periods cannot be relied upon; for they might have reinterpreted the word.[59] Occasional hieroglyphic writings of this word use a sign depicting the same small portable shrine, and in so doing imply that portability was of its essence.

Institutions that are basically irrational thrive on an interaction between a hidden and a revealed element. The carefully staged drama of formal appearances of the king illustrates this. In New Kingdom and later times, when the nature and rhythm of temple life are much better known, we can see it reflected in religious architecture and ceremonial. The hidden aspect of divinity required a sanctuary, as cut-off as possible from contact with normal human life, in which resided the most sacred of images. Revelation was achieved by careful theatrical management which brought a tangible symbol of the divine presence into the public, or semi-public domain, yet still behind barriers, both physical and psychological. By the New Kingdom the means of public manifestation was by portable boats borne on carrying poles and supporting, in place of a cabin, a small and partly enclosed shrine (Plate 5 and Figure 90, pp. 249 and 250).[60] The word used for this shrine on a boat was *kariy*. It is reassuring to find that the earliest known writing of the word, in the Pyramid Texts of the late Old Kingdom, uses as its hieroglyphic determinative a picture of a portable tent-shrine of the Early Dynastic type; reassuring because the two are functionally the same.[61] Wherever the later portable images were rested, a special platform or a complete building was constructed. In the New Kingdom they, too, could be called a 'tent of the god', although built of stone. Within them the actual resting-place was marked by a more-or-less cubic pedestal of stone with ornamental top on which the portable boat shrine was placed.

We can therefore look to earlier periods for functional equivalents, and if we do this, some of the key pieces of evidence fall into place. Portable holy images were already widespread, but carried not in boat shrines but in carrying-chairs of the kind used by the nobility, sheltered by a canopy of matting on a curved wooden frame. Wherever they were set down, a pedestal was needed, often built of brick with either plain or panelled sides. This could have its own canopy similarly constructed. The one complete early shrine that we possess, at Elephantine, can be interpreted along these lines. Here, in a simple and modest way, is visible the duality of domain that belongs to a religion in which sacred images play a major part. At the rear, between the granite boulders, we find the enclosed sanctuary for the hidden images; in the courtyard in front is the pedestal for the portable image, complete with poles for the canopy support.[62]

The portability of the revealed images (called generically *Repit*)[63] took them not only on very localized journeys, but also from time to time to the royal court for the *Sed*-festival, where they were likewise housed inside tent-shrines erected on larger brick pedestals. Although the design of these tent-shrines was basically a common one, they were sometimes given a distinctive appearance by varying the shape slightly, or by adding details, including pairs of vertical poles.

The discussion of early shrine architecture has been given more substance by the discovery of a small site in the desert at Hierakonpolis, locality 29A, in use mainly during the Nagada II period (Figure 53).[64] At its centre was an elongated space (measuring 40+ x 12 metres) with a curving end which sloped upwards towards the east and was surfaced with packed mud. It was surrounded by eroded traces of walls, fences and palisades, the product of many alterations. Some of the post holes were large and in one case (belonging to Structure III) still contained the base of a wooden post perhaps 30 centimetres in diameter. The pattern of shallow trenches around the perimeter, which had perhaps anchored the bottom edge of fences of reeds, suggests that some of the posts had in fact formed the front of buildings or enclosures lying behind, to some extent outside the excavated area. At the south-east end of the oval stood an upright object, either a stone slab or a large post. The north-west end had been overbuilt by a thick wall enclosing a polygonal space. Most of the finds consist of flint implements, some of them fine borers for beads, debris from the making of flint implements, many pottery jars, perhaps drinking-vessels, and also numerous animal bones, many from cattle and from wild animals. No groups of identifiable votive objects have been recovered, however. On its own this material could suggest a butchery and perhaps feasting site. The unusual nature of the plan has, however, aroused a very different interpretation. On the (unstated) criterion that if something is odd then it must be sacred or ceremonial, the post holes and trenches around the edge have been taken as the remains of tent-shrines facing a ceremonial area for the use of kings, the focus of attention a tall pole at the end topped with a divine emblem. A reconstruction of the largest shrine (Structure III) actually gives it the animal profile known from early pictures of such buildings (like Figure 51.3). *If* this interpretation is correct it illustrates first how hard it is to predict what things really were like on the basis of artistic evidence alone – no one had considered that a Predynastic ceremonial site with timber shrines would have looked quite like this – and secony on how modest a scale early monarchy in Egypt functioned.

It has generally been thought that in the tent-shrine we have an image of what local temples in the Early Dynastic Period looked like, despite the evidence that mud brick, which lends itself to a different kind of architecture, had been in widespread use for some time. The interpretation offered here, which utilizes the one actual early shrine to have been found and recorded in any degree of completeness (Elephantine), puts the architecture of wood and matting into a very specific setting. It had been abandoned as a way of making a complete shrine. It survived only as a shelter for the revealed image, but at the same time its antiquity and distinctiveness made it an ideal basis for an easily identifiable symbol for shrines and holy places in general. The originality of the Step Pyramid lies in the way that its architect created a style of permanent stone architecture from this vestige of traditional architecture. The vocabulary of forms now rendered into stone became henceforth the ideal type of religious building to which later temple architects almost invariably looked. We can recognize three versions at the Step Pyramid. The most common, with more than twenty examples, depicts a rectangular wooden framed tent with curved roof standing on a pedestal (Figure 36, p. 104, and Plate 3, p. 108). Some are small and with plain fronts; the fronts of the larger ones, however, display carved poles supporting the roof, implying that they are really depicting tents that are open at the front. From this we can guess that the smaller ones were thought to have open fronts as well. In two cases at least, a flight of narrow steps ran up to the top of the pedestal or platform on which the tent stands.

HIERAKONPOLIS 29A

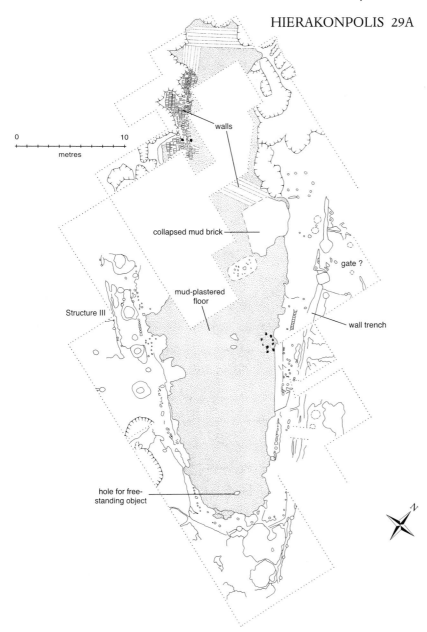

Figure 53   Plan of site H29A at Hierakonpolis: a place for royal ceremonies? Do the post-holes around the edge belong to the façades of tent-shrines? The main contender is Structure III, although the posts seem not to have been equidistant nor the east side wall (represented by a single smaller hole) at right-angles to the front. If not by post holes and traces of trenches, how else in reality would such buildings be recognizable? After R. Friedman, 'The ceremonial centre at Hierakonpolis Locality HK29A', in J. Spencer, ed., *Aspects of early Egypt,*, London, 1996, 19, Fig. 2; *Nekhen News* 15, Fall 2003, plan on p. 4.

In examining the Step Pyramid architecture we must not forget that we are seeing the fruits of modern reconstruction. When excavated, the all-important façades of the buildings inside the complex were found reduced to the lowest courses of stonework. We are fortunate in that the study and partial reconstruction of these buildings has been carried out by a gifted architect, Jean-Philippe Lauer, who based his results on a close examination of loose blocks found in the rubble as well as on ancient depictions of traditional shrines. The honesty of his work has made this particular group of shrines look very similar. But from the evidence of ancient pictures we must hold in our minds the possibility that some or all of them bore some distinguishing mark to make them look individual, since they probably represent the temporary festival shrines to house divine images assembled from provincial towns.

The second type is a larger variant, and directly on the ground instead of on a pedestal. There are two examples, the so-called North and South Houses. Again they depict an open-fronted building displaying the outer row of slender carved roof supports. But privacy of the interior is provided by a screen running between the roof supports and broken only by a doorway (Figure 52.1). The screen was imagined as made from reeds, a message conveyed by carving in stylized form the knots tied in the loose top ends. This general design was a potent one, particularly in the use of the screen wall linking columns, and in the row of stylized knots which, as the *kheker*-frieze, passed into general use as a decorative motif.

The third version of the temporary wooden structure had perhaps four examples. One of them, 'Temple T', is of particular significance since it is one of the very few 'real' buildings of the Step Pyramid, having a complete interior of rooms and corridors. The exterior of Temple T is a severe version of the wood and matting style (Figure 54.1). All four exterior walls look the same: plain rectangular surfaces, topped by a narrow horizontal rolled binding and above this the loose tops of reeds reduced to a plain frieze. All four corners of the building were protected by further bound rolls of reeds. The interior, however, is incompatible with a building of these materials. Its complex internal plan resembles the funerary palaces at Abydos constructed of mud brick. Although pilasters have been added, decorated after the style of bundles of reeds, it is the plan of a building of solid materials, an impression reinforced by the ceilings, which were carved in imitation of closely set logs of wood. This is a type of roof that, from its weight, demands solid walls of brick or stone. Light timber frames and matting screens are structurally unsuited.

Temple T, with its wrap-around application of tent architecture to a building of more solid form, set the style for centuries to come. Externally it shows the essence of the ideal type of later Egyptian temples. This is occasionally made explicit in temple scenes where, in a ceremony of purification of the temple building, the building itself is depicted hieroglyphically in this simple original form (Figure 54.3). It was, however, primarily the model for temple exteriors. The severe rectangular wood and matting building became a façade, the proper wrapping for a building whose interior reflected the practical needs of the occasion.

Just how the reconciliation between form and function was achieved by later architects becomes, in effect, the remaining history of Egyptian temple architecture. Internal plans accommodated needs that changed from time to time and from place to place. In Chapter 6 we shall see how the New Kingdom taste for portable boat shrines, and various aspects of the royal funerary cult, created distinctive plans that were still kept uncompromisingly inside the jacket of the old ideal type. For the moment this point will be illustrated by examples that show just how enduring the imagery created at the Step Pyramid was.

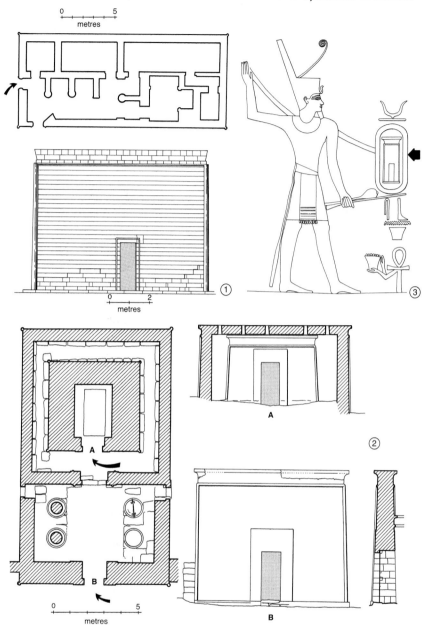

Figure 54 Ideal types in architecture: the enclosed tent-shrine. (1): Temple 'T' at the Step Pyramid of Djoser. After J.-Ph. Lauer, *La pyramide à degrés* I and II, Cairo, 1936, Pl. LV, and Fig. 157. (2) The temple-tomb of the God's Wife of Amun Amenirdis I at Medinet Habu (*c.* 715 BC), in which one tent-shrine is nested within another, a common Egyptian architectural ploy. After U. Höls-cher, *The excavation of Medinet Habu* V. *Post-Ramessid remains*, Chicago, 1954, Fig. 24. (3) Scene of King Tuthmosis III purifying the temple of Amada in Nubia by sprinkling natron over it, before the god Horakhty. The temple itself is symbolized by a picture of a tent-shrine (marked by arrow). After H. Gauthier, *Les temples immergés de la Nubie: le temple d'Amada*, Cairo, 1913, Pl. XVII.

The first is the almost intact temple-tomb of the God's Wife Amenirdis I at Medinet Habu, which dates to the 25th Dynasty (*c.* 750 BC; Figure 54.2; for its context see Figure 122, p. 353). Essentially the building consists of two tent-shrines nested one inside the other. The shrine that covers the entrance to the tomb of Amenirdis is a simple version, a single chamber which approximates to the original form in both interior and exterior. This is set within a larger building that includes a colonnaded courtyard, a favourite element in the design of temple interiors. For the final external impression the architect has returned to the tent-shrine prototype, though emphasizing the front of the building by making the wall taller. This was also a favourite device, though on larger buildings the tall façade was normally, from the New Kingdom onwards, divided in the centre to create the character-istic pair of pylons, a limited gesture of re-interpretation of original form. It is particularly to the kind of inner shrine found here that the Egyptians gave the name 'tent of the god' (*seh-netjer*), although from the New Kingdom onwards it was also used more loosely as a synonym for 'temple' generally.[65] This was not an illogical move since the whole building externally was modelled on the same ideal type.

We can gain the most impressive idea of how strong was the hold of the ideal types from Egypt's beginnings by looking at buildings from the very end of ancient Egyptian civilization, when Egypt was ruled first by the Ptolemies, Greek-speaking inheritors of Alexander the Great's Egyptian province, and then by the Roman emperors following the death of the last of the Ptolemaic line, Queen Cleopatra VII. In the rural hinterland of the Nile valley these alien rulers encouraged the building of traditional temples in which they themselves appeared in the guise of the divine Egyptian kings of old, featuring in similar scenes of divine birth as had occurred in New Kingdom temples.

The finest example of Ptolemaic temple architecture is the temple of the falcon-god Horus at Edfu (237–57 BC).[66] Outwardly the body of Edfu temple faithfully recalls the plain box-like form of the archetypal tent-shrine, the front magnified into two pylons. Inside, the architectural vocabulary continually pays deference to this ideal, from the ornate screen wall and canopy in front of the main columned hall, to the shrine in the sanctuary carved from a single block of black granodiorite which renders this form in miniature, although a pyramidal *benben*-stone has been carved on the top (very similar to the one in Figure 49). The arrangement of the elements of the plan, however, is character-istic of the time and could not be mistaken for a temple of a much earlier period. Equally distinctive of the period is the *mammisi* (a Greek word), or birth-house, outside the front of the temple. Its purpose was to celebrate the divine birth of the king, and for its form the architects returned to the idea of the semi-open tent-shrine with screen walls. Some of these buildings even had curved wooden roofs in closer deference to the ideal type, some-thing apparent from the surviving holes for timber beams (Figure 52.2).

For the Egyptian priests this was a time of threat to traditional culture. The scenes and texts that cover the walls of Edfu as of other Ptolemaic temples reveal an enhanced aware-ness of their own rich inheritance of mythology and ritual. They are far more informative in these areas than are earlier temples. The texts on the walls are not, however, the complete originals. Rather they are extracts from or summaries of several longer 'books', often referred to by their names, which must have been held in the temple library. One set concerns the building itself.[67] These building texts are rich in language-game and symbolic geography, and incapable of resolution into a single scheme of modern logical form. They do reflect, however, a common viewpoint. This was that the new stone temple

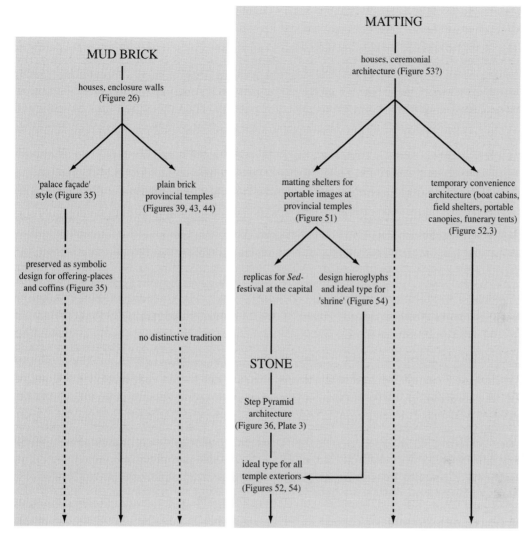

Figure 55   The sources of Egyptian architectural styles.

that was being built, although designed in the style of the times, embodied a range of
ideal types whose existence could be counted on through the descriptions and allusions of
the texts themselves. The texts, which actually contain the dimensions of the ideal buildings expressed in cubits, were capable, with the help of ritual, of holding the essence of
these mythical constructions in place. Their history was set in a mythical time, 'the early
primaeval age of gods', and within a mythical geography wherein the temple site itself was
the 'Seat of the First Occasion', a reference to a creation myth. The term 'reign of Tanen',
an earth-god, is also used, recalling the historical scheme of the Turin king list which

began with a series of reigns by gods. The setting is devoid altogether of human life. In places it recalls instead the time of the creation of the world, which began with the appearance of a mound from the all-covering waters. The mound, or mounds, became the site or sites of the original shrines. One of these contained the perch of the falcon-god to whom the temple was dedicated, Horus the Behdetite, which originated as a slip of reed planted in the primaeval water. For the mythical shrines brief descriptions with dimensions are given (Figure 56). One of the terms used for the sanctuary (*seh*) is the common Egyptian word for the tent-shrine, and helps to reinforce the view that these primaeval buildings were seen as the timber and reed constructions of which the Ptolemaic Edfu temple was a reincarnation in stone.

It is, of course, tempting to take these accounts literally, particularly since dimensions are given, and to regard them as containing something of the real history of Edfu temple. It is, indeed, true that Edfu stood on a mound of natural sand and rock within the alluvial floodplain, and so became at inundation time an island. However, the archaeological record shows that until the Old Kingdom it was not a place of significant settlement. The archaeological record of early temples shows great variety in construction, but also the use of brick and of informal plans in the earliest ones that have survived. The earliest shrine at Edfu, therefore, is likely to have been of brick, and probably along the lines of the Elephantine or Tell Ibrahim Awad shrines, and very small. The precedence of the tent-shrine in the Ptolemaic texts as the exclusively correct and original temple design arose because it fitted exactly the myth-world of the primaeval age of the gods. As to where the measurements in cubits of the primaeval temples came from, we just cannot tell. They could be records of buildings which had been erected on the site at various times since, say, the Middle Kingdom, or they could be the result of a symbolic-numbers game carried out by the Ptolemaic priests themselves.

Egyptian visual culture strove consciously to create the impression of a direct transfer from nature. But it was far from being a spontaneous celebration of natural or inherited primitive forms. It involved a very deliberate process of selection and modification in order to create a set, a vocabulary, of ideal types possessing internal consistency. This latter aspect was sufficiently achieved to produce a degree of interchangeability which gave scope to an endless (and for us bewildering) recombination of elements which lay at the heart of the constant invention of tradition. From this we can expand our understanding of the language-game that underlay Egyptian religion: its vocabulary was also rich in elements of visual culture that could be manipulated just as words were.

Nor were the limits of recombination ever reached. The process is continued, unintentionally, by modern scholars as we try to 'explain' Egyptian religion and its art and architecture. For the relationship between modern study and ancient source is not quite what it appears to be at first sight. We like to think that the sources are inert, and ourselves objective observers. But the interplay is much more complex. Ancient thought is not dead: it lies dormant in the sources and within our own minds, and when we study the former the latter begins to move within us. One example will suffice to illustrate this. Excavations at western Thebes early in the last century led to the discovery of a combined tomb and temple of King Nebhepetra Menthuhetep of the 11th Dynasty (*c.* 2055–2004 BC) at the site called Deir el-Bahari (Figure 57). The centrepiece was a square mass of stone masonry standing on a huge podium and surrounded by a colonnade. The excavator, E. Naville, restored a pyramid on the top of the square base, the reconstruction drawing passed

EDFU

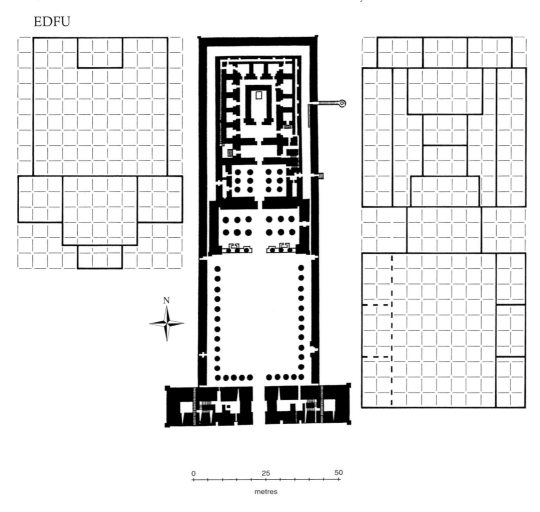

0   25   50
metres

Figure 56   Temples of the mind. In the centre, plan of the temple of Horus of Edfu, Ptolemaic Period, 237–57 BC. To left and right, outlines representing mythical temples invented through speculative processes by the priests, and expressed as written descriptions complete with dimensions in cubits. *Left.* The primitive temple of the sacred falcon (Horus). The opening text reads: 'Laying out the foundation made in the temple of "Uplifter of God" in the reign of [the god] Tanen, in the presence of Ra, according to what is in the book called "Specification of the Sacred Mounds of the Early Primaeval Age".' *Right.* The temple of the sun-god. Although these temples (and others) are set in a mythical primaeval age of gods before mankind existed, in their overall scale and proportions they reflect the architectural perspective of the Ptolemaic priests. They are unlikely to be records of early real buildings. After E.A.E. Reymond, *The mythical origin of the Egyptian temple*, Manchester, 1969. Other Edfu texts which describe the foundation of the real temple provide a description, with cubit dimensions, which is fairly realistic, see S. Cauville and D. Devauchelle, *BIFAO* 84 (1984), 23–34.

into textbooks and for over half a century remained a very familiar element in Egypt's architectural history.[68] It fitted within the general line of architectural development, and could even be seen as echoing the landscape, for a natural pyramidal peak rises above the cliffs and was regarded as a holy place by the Egyptians themselves. The building was later re-examined by a German expedition. Finding that there was no specific evidence for preferring a pyramid on top of the base, the excavator restored it as a flat-topped construction, and linked it, with ample scholarly reference, to the notion of the primaeval mound.[69] Later still came a reconstruction that added an actual tree-covered mound of earth on top.[70] Whichever solution we adopt we can justify it by learned references to specific Egyptian sources. Thus, although only one (or none of them) must be technically correct, all are true to Egyptian cultural roots and were potentially present in ancient times, even if they have had to wait three thousand years before being realized.

There is a parallel of sorts here in the revival of Classical culture in Renaissance Europe, and, limited more to architecture, the later Gothic and Egyptian revivals. Here artists and architects strove to use the spirit and the visual vocabulary of a dead culture in pursuit of a living art, and thus realized the potential latent for further development within a past culture, though producing an overall effect that the ancients would never have thought of. The gifted forger of antique art is doing the same. And sometimes scholars unintentionally pursue the same path in constructing hypotheses to explain a very fragmentary past.

Egyptian temple architecture recalled a lost and largely mythical past of primitive simplicity. What we know and the builders of Edfu temple did not is the relatively late and to a degree artificial nature of the myth behind the ideal type of shrine. The Step Pyramid shows that it arose from the rejection of Early Dynastic brick architecture that had demonstrated, in the palace-façade style, potential for proclaiming places of power. By the 3rd Dynasty this style had been in Egypt for at least three to four centuries and could well have remained the model for all formal architecture, including temples, as it did in Mesopotamia. Instead, after the Step Pyramid, it was retained only in token form in funerary architecture: in the offering-places of tomb chapels, as a way of decorating sarcophagi, and as decoration for a section of wall around the royal burial chamber. Henceforth, formal temple architecture looked for inspiration to what the Egyptians considered to be their roots, a world of tent-shrines and no palaces, blotting out a distinctive aspect of the early state. Just as the political history of ancient Egypt was shaped by a mythical view of the past, so the history of Egyptian formal temple architecture is a record of deference to another myth.

The re-codification of architectural form in the 3rd Dynasty did not, however, provide a model for religious architecture which all desired to follow at once. No general rebuilding programme followed in the provinces, as the first part of this chapter showed. The new style was an intellectual creation of the court. It was confined at first to the royal tomb, and was used as a guide elsewhere only in cases of fitful royal patronage of other temples. The form of the royal tomb itself underwent major re-codification again at the end of the 3rd Dynasty, though this was as much a matter of function and meaning as of style. The eternal palace, which is what much of the Step Pyramid enclosure was intended to be, was replaced by a temple to the king's spirit and to the sun dominated by the true pyramid, a geometrically rendered version of the *benben*-stone in deference to grand and more abstract theology which increasingly made the sun-god into the source of all power. But here and

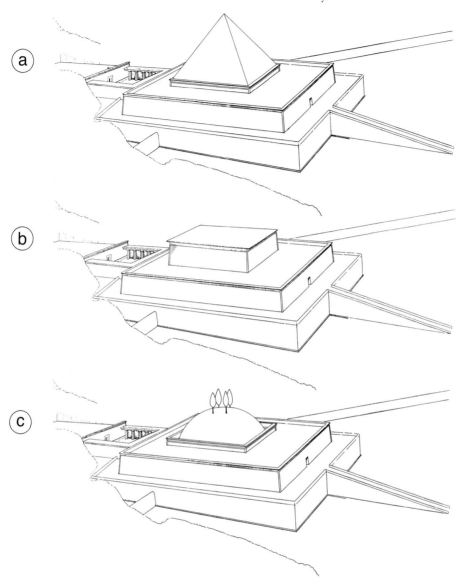

Figure 57 Religious language-game resumed: scholarly manipulation of Egyptian religious symbols for modern didactic ends. Three reconstructions of the mortuary temple of King Nebhep-etra Menthuhetep at Deir el-Bahari, Thebes, 11th Dynasty. Each is 'true' to the spirit of Egyptian religion and can be supported by scholarly argument, and thus they continue the realization of the potential of ancient Egyptian thought. Whether any of them is 'true' in the sense that it was actually built at Deir el-Bahari we shall probably never know. (a) A true pyramid, after E. Naville, *The XIth Dynasty temple at Deir el-Bahari* II, London, 1910, Pl. XXIV. (b) A flat-topped mound made of stone, proposed by D. Arnold, *Der Tempel des Königs Mentuhotep von Deir el-Bahari* I. *Architektur und Deutung*, Mainz, 1974, Frontis. (c) A mound of earth supporting trees, proposed by R. Stadelmann, *Die Ägypt-ischen Pyramiden*, Mainz, 1985, 229, Abb. 74.

later new ideas remained true in forms to the ideal types that we first meet as monumental architecture in the Step Pyramid. Religious architecture well illustrates the Egyptian genius for clothing change in traditional costume.

The role of individual initiative

The instrument of change was personal intervention. We have to think in terms of great artists and architects. But the ancient myth that whatever was new and admirable was in fact true to the past allowed no room for the recognition of individual genius. The initiative in art and architecture was articulated by royal decree. The process is documented in the Berlin Leather Roll.[71] This is a New Kingdom copy of a building text of King Senusret I of the early 12th Dynasty. It begins with a formal 'appearance' of the king in his palace, before his assembled courtiers. He opens with an oration on his own divinely appointed destiny, then announces his plan: the construction of a temple for the god Atum. The motive is not disinterested piety. Piety is mixed with the pragmatic observation that the best means of immortality is a building constructed in one's own name. 'A king who is evoked by his works is not doomed.' His courtiers offer deferential support for the scheme, emphasizing the personal benefit for the king himself: 'When your temple is built, it will provide for the altar. It will give service to your image. It will befriend your statues in all eternity.' Finally comes the action. The king appoints the architect:

> the royal seal-bearer, sole companion, overseer of the two gold-houses and the two silver-houses, and privy-councillor of the two diadems: It is your counsel that carries out all the works that my majesty desires to bring about. You are the one in charge of them, who will act according to my wish . . . Order the workmen to do according to your design.

This is, for an Egyptian text, an unusually frank statement on royal delegation of creativity. But note who the architect was, or rather was not. No name is given, and the man's titles have no specific reference to building at all. We cannot, on the basis of his titles, call him an architect. We know of dozens of officials with titles of this kind from the Middle Kingdom, but if they were great artists or architects we cannot tell. The great architect's skill was perceived as admirable performance of a royal commission, on the same level as organizing a large and difficult quarrying expedition, or clearing navigable channels through the rocky barriers of the First Cataract at Aswan. It was not a deliberate anonymity. Some draftsmen and builders who did little else with their lives used these callings as their official titles, and so we can identify them.[72] It reflects more the Egyptian lack of awareness of or interest in abstract divisions of knowledge. Art and architecture were parts of the stream of directed activity that emanated from the court. The process worked simply because an intuitive appreciation of what was really good ensured that good artists and imaginative architects were promoted at the expense of bad ones. But they were applauded for their success as good officials rather than as good artists or architects.

The case of the builder of the Step Pyramid provides another angle from which to view the question of who the real creators were. We have no ancient account of the building of the Step Pyramid, yet we instinctively recognize in it a work of architectural genius. This remote and poorly documented period has in fact provided us with the name of a great man of Djoser's court, Imhotep.[73] On the base of a statue of Djoser from the Step Pyramid Imhotep's name is carved, together with his titles: 'seal-bearer of the King of Lower Egypt, first one under the king, administrator of the Great Mansion, prince, chief of seers' (a religious title). On the wall of the unfinished step pyramid of Djoser's successor (King Sekhemkhet) his name occurs again, simply as 'Sealbearer of the King of Lower Egypt, Imhotep'. From the discovery of this material Egyptologists have made the not unreasonable assertion that Imhotep was the man behind the Step Pyramid. Now Imhotep was also one of the lucky few who achieved long posthumous fame in ancient Egypt. His name was honoured fifteen hundred years later in the New Kingdom, but not as an architect. He was famous as the author of a set of thoughtful sayings. 'I have heard the words of Imhotep and Hordedef, with whose discourses men speak so much', says one song, pairing him with another famous sage of old, one of the sons of King Khufu. Imhotep's fame did not stop here. By the 26th Dynasty he had become a minor god, son of the god Ptah of Memphis, and healing was to become his speciality so that the Greeks identified him with their god of healing, Asklepios. In some late texts he is given a set of titles, but they are creations of the day: 'vizier, overseer of works, mayor'. He was correctly placed in the reign of King Djoser, but the history of Djoser's reign was recast into more modern shape. A papyrus of the first or second century AD, for example, sends Djoser and his vizier, Imhotep, off on a campaign to Assyria.

We are probably still right to identify Imhotep as the Step Pyramid's architect (though having done that we have simply played the ancient game of elevating names into knowledge. It really tells us nothing about him.) Through this he achieved fame as a great official, and it was as a great official, with the inevitable attribute of being 'wise', that he was remembered. It was the fact of his success that counted, not the means − architectural genius − by which he acquired it. Indeed, it would have been contrary to the myth-world of his architecture if it had been given an historical point of origin.

This raises another conundrum for ourselves. We must accept that from time to time the Egyptians produced figures of great intellectual ability responsible for major changes in traditions. Yet the Egyptians remained without the means to conceptualize this. Past innovators were remembered, but as 'wise men'. How, therefore, can we find out why these people were famous?

In the previous chapter the point was made that with the pyramid of Medum of the reign of King Huni we have the product of a major re-evaluation not only of architectural form but also of the meaning of kingship, amongst the most important intellectual concerns of the day. If we wish to credit the originality of the Step Pyramid to a single outstanding mind, we should be prepared to do the same with the Medum pyramid. By the Middle Kingdom the Egyptians possessed the testimony of a 'wise man' which they believed to belong to just this period, the reign of Huni. It is a set of instructions on good behaviour that urges an abstemious approach to life. The author was a vizier whose name is unfortunately lost (it may have been Kai-irisu, another famous sage). He addressed himself to his children, one of whom may well have been the vizier Kagemni whose name occurs at the end of the text. This vizier Kagemni is a known figure, for his tomb exists at Sakkara. But it dates to the reign of King Teti of the early 6th Dynasty, thus nearly three centuries after the time of Huni. Furthermore, a fair case can be made for dating the actual composition of the text later still. We can comprehend this inconsistent evidence if we see it as part of a more general phenomenon that runs though ancient Egypt (as through other cultures): the invention of tradition, which has in this case involved a process of compression. We have to imagine a sequence like this: a great rationalizer and organizer at the court of Huni responsible for the extraordinary Medum pyramid; the loss in subsequent generations of the reasons which made him famous, leaving him as a 'wise man'; eventual confusion with an official of the late 5th/early 6th Dynasty, famous for some other reason; final crediting of this person with a suitable wise teaching which was composed even later.[74]

Tradition is not wholly a mechanical repetition of ancient forms that thereby provide a key to past times. It is subject to modification as time passes, which sometimes amounts to invention. Traditions can thus obscure the past as well as illuminate it. They answer current needs and are the products of ingenious minds.

When we look at Early Dynastic brick palace architecture and Preformal shrines and their associated objects it is possible to imagine that they could have formed the beginnings of a cultural and artistic tradition very different from the one that actually did develop. Or if, as with the Indus Valley civilization, Early Dynastic Egypt had advanced no further along a straightforward cultural trajectory and the early material was all that we had, our evaluation and interpretation of it would be rather different from the way it actually appears now: as a formative stage to something much richer and greater later on. This is another way of saying that Pharaonic culture was not a naturally evolved tradition. It was invented, but so successfully that it left the Egyptians (and to some extent ourselves) feeling that it was all somehow rooted in the country and in the psychology of the people in a most fundamental way.

At the heart of a cultural tradition is a trade-off between respect for past achievements and the accommodation of fertile and creative minds who look for something new. Ancient Egypt provides an early case history of the dynamics of the Great Tradition of culture: how it arose and was maintained as a living system, how it expanded at the expense of local traditions, and how it achieved this difficult balance between past and present. It also enlarges our understanding of the scope of myth in society. The previous chapter was devoted to showing how the Egyptians wrapped history and political power in myth. This chapter has attempted to do the same with material culture. Myth is not only a narrative form of expression. Myth statements that do not require verbalization can be conveyed powerfully through art and architecture. They provide a distinctive dimension to the assault on the senses that lies at the heart of state ideologies.

Part II
The provider state

4
The bureaucratic mind

The material achievements of ancient states – pyramids, conspicuous wealth, palaces, temples, conquests – all depended on a particular skill: administration of resources. Although its basic purpose was to manipulate the economic environment for the benefit of the elite, in so doing benefit was incidentally spread to a significant sector of the population. This was achieved essentially through taxation to bring in resources and then through their redistribution as rations to an element of the population – probably a large one – engaged temporarily or permanently on work for the state. The first part of this classic resource cycle of early states – taxation – is best illustrated for Egypt by material from the New Kingdom, reserved for Chapters 6 and 7. This chapter is more about bureaucracy as a shaping force in society and the consequences of large-scale ration distribution on the relations between state and population.

A developed bureaucratic system reveals and actively promotes a specific human trait: a deep satisfaction in devising routines for measuring, inspecting, checking, and thus as far as possible controlling other people's activities. This is a passive and orderly exercise of power in contrast to direct coercion. It draws upon a particular aptitude, as distinctive and important for a society as the genius of its artists and architects, or the bravura of its military men. When dealing with ancient Egypt we call a member of this class a 'scribe'. It is a fair translation of an Egyptian word that means simply 'a writing man'. There is a tendency in modern societies where literacy is widespread to denigrate the junior official or clerical worker. But this is a luxury inappropriate to less developed societies. Where most are illiterate the writing man holds the key to the power that administration bestows. In Egypt scribes were not only amongst the elite, they knew it, and said so plainly. 'Be a scribe', ran the advice, 'it saves you from toil, it protects you from all manner of labour.' 'Be a scribe. Your limbs will be sleek, your hands will grow soft. You will go forth in white clothes, honoured, with courtiers saluting you.'[1] And many a senior figure in the state included 'scribe' amongst the accumulated titles of his curriculum vitae. The reader of this chapter should suppress any feeling of disdain associated with words like 'bureaucracy' and 'scribe'. In the Egyptian world both attracted a very different set of values.

name of the	through deliveries sent to the residence						name of the	brought from the palace		the altar of Ra / in the solar temple			in crates		
								ida-bread, *padj*-bread, *hetja*-bread, *pesen*-bread, beer		consignments of *pat*-bread			delicacies		
porter	jars of *sekhpet*-drink	jars of beer	jars of flour	*beset*-bread	*pesen*-bread	*hetja*-bread	place of origin			balance	delivered	amount due	balance	delivered	amount due
									18			14			
temple employees									18			14			
							estate of Kakai	18	18			14			
								18	18			14			
	1	1	1	1	1	1	Iu-Shedefwi	18	18		70	14			
Ni-ankh-Kakai		3		1	1		estate of Kakai	18	18	14		14	10		10
Ni-tawi-Kakai		3		1	1		estate of Kakai	18	18	14		14	10		10
son of Hatu		1		1	1	1	Djed-Sneferu	36	18	14		14			
									18	14	14	14			
								18	18		14	14			
								18	18		14	14			
		3		1	1		estate of Kakai	36	18		14	14			
									18		14	14			
								18	18	(14)	14	14	10		10
Ni-tawi-Kakai	2 haunches of beef			mixed 30	100	(?)	brought from the altar of Ra	18	18	(14)	14	14	(10)		(10)
								18	18	(14)	14	14			
brought by boat	mixed 30	mixed 30					solar temple	18	18	(14)	14	14			
								18	18		14	14			
boat	1	1	1	1	1	1	Iu-Shedefwi	18	18		14	14			
								18	18	14	14	14			

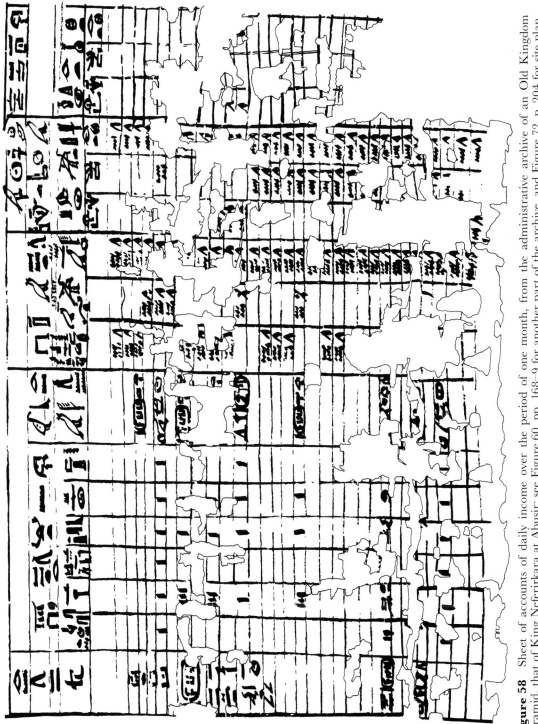

Figure 58 Sheet of accounts of daily income over the period of one month, from the administrative archive of an Old Kingdom pyramid, that of King Neferirkara at Abusir; see Figure 60, pp. 168–9 for another part of the archive, and Figure 72, p. 204 for site plan. After P. Posener-Kriéger and J.L. de Cenival, *Hieratic papyri in the British Museum*, fifth series, *The Abu Sir Papyri*, London, 1968, Pl. XXXIV.

Tidy minds

Large numbers of administrative sources have survived from ancient Egypt, which carry the history of bureaucracy back to the third millennium BC. We will begin with a set of early texts which reveal vividly the bureaucratic scribe's concern with system and detail. It is the papyrus archive from the pyramid temple of King Neferirkara of the 5th Dynasty at Abusir.[2] It dates mostly to the reign of King Isesi, thus to at least fifty years after the death of Neferirkara (in *c.* 2455 BC).

By the beginning of the 4th Dynasty a standard royal tomb layout had developed. Burial was within or beneath a pyramid. The offering-cult for the king's eternal wellbeing was performed in a mortuary temple attached to the pyramid's east face. A causeway linked this temple with a separate one on the valley floor (the Valley Temple) which, so it has often been thought, accommodated the rites over the king's body prior to burial. Central to the cult was the presentation of food and drink offerings. Priests were needed for this, and for other ceremonies, and further staff were required to protect the building and its equipment. All were paid in kind, in commodities, which included a basic ration of bread and beer and grain, and additional items such as meat and cloth. The receipt of income and its subsequent distribution as rations set in motion its own little administrative cycle. Although the income could be supplied by the palace of the living king, a greater security of source was obtained by establishing a pious foundation in perpetuity. This consisted essentially of agricultural estates, the income of which was directed to the support of the staff maintaining cult and fabric at the pyramids.

The papyrus sheet illustrated in Figure 58 is a table of daily income written in an early style of hieratic which still maintained many of the outlines of the original hieroglyphic signs. We can recognize instantly a sensible tabular format, ruled in red and black ink. Each horizontal line is set aside for one day in a thirty-day month, and contains mainly numerical entries in vertical columns. Each column bears a concise two- or three-tier heading, covering the supplying institutions, the kind of foodstuffs involved, and (for the three right-hand columns) the status of the delivery.

The supporting foundation, composed of individual estates, was cleverly incorporated into the formal decorative schemes at pyramid temples, illustrating once again the Egyptian genius for deft symbolic presentation of humdrum reality. Few peoples have turned the collection of rents and gathering of taxes into subject matter for sacred art. Each funerary estate, or domain, appears as an offering-bearer, individually named. The most complete set comes from the Valley Temple of King Sneferu at Dahshur (Figure 59).[3] They occupied a strip at the base of some of the internal walls. Each estate is personified as a woman bearing an offering-table. On the head is a sign-group reading: 'The town: Mansion of Sneferu'. In front of each is the name of the place, compounded from the name of Sneferu in a cartouche, with further signs to designate the administrative district (nome). Altogether thirty-four estates belong to Upper Egypt, distributed amongst ten nomes (with the record of eight nomes missing). In Lower Egypt the record is fully preserved for only a single nome, and numbers four estates. This scattered pattern of landholding is typical for ancient Egypt. No details are given of the size of these holdings, but other and rather rarer statements on size vary from 2 *arouras* (16.4 hectares) to 110 *arouras* (905 hectares).

The temple staff was organized into groups for which the conventional modern term is phyle (a Greek term meaning company, tribe). This was the common form of temple

Figure 59 Part of a list of estates providing the income for the pyramid temple of King Sneferu of the 4th Dynasty at Dahshur. Each estate is personified as a female bearer carrying a tray of food offerings. The name of each estate is written over and in front of each figure, and they are grouped according to nomes (administrative districts). In front of the second figure from the left is the heading 'Oryx nome', the area of Beni Hasan. After A. Fakhry, *The monuments of Sneferu at Dahshur* II.1, Cairo, 1961, Fig. 16 (redrawn by B. Garfi).

organization, with five phyles in the Old Kingdom, each one subdivided into two divisions, which apparently worked at different times. Each subdivision, of around twenty men, served for only one month in ten.[4] Presumably for the extended leave periods they reverted to agricultural or other work in their villages, so that the undoubted benefits of temple service – payments as well as prestige – were widely spread. Whatever ancient reasoning lay behind the system, the practical consequence was a sharing out of jobs by the state. The number of employees required was multiplied by many times, hugely increasing the numbers of people receiving partial support from the state. Because most of the jobs were only part-time the system itself was not clogged by the presence of unnecessary personnel.

In the course of its duty, each phyle undertook a complete inspection of the temple and

haematite	crystalline stone				flint	iron		offering-tables	
bowl: gold-plated	bowls		vases		ritual knife	blade	total of	small	large
	black	white	black	white			silver items		
1	2	1	1	1	1	2	23	2	1
	(?)	various repairs to rim & base (x2) (x2) & to sides	repairs to rim & base	repairs to sides; holed (x2)	handle chipped; repaired	chips missing, having been dropped		badly split; loose joints; corroded	badly split; loose joints; corroded
1	2	1	1	1	1	2	23	2	1
	(?)	ditto	ditto	ditto	handle & blade chipped	ditto		ditto	ditto
1	2	1	1	1	1	2	23	1	1
	ditto	ditto	ditto	ditto	ditto	ditto		ditto	ditto
	(?)	ditto	ditto	ditto	ditto	ditto		badly split; loose joints; holed	badly split; loose joints; holed
1	2	1	1	1	1	2	23	2	1
		(repairs) ditto	ditto	(chipped) ditto	ditto	ditto		ditto	ditto
1	2	1	1	1	1	2	23	2	1

Figure 60 Sheet of equipment inventory, from the same source as Figure 58, p. 165. After P. Posener-Kriéger and J.L. de Cenival, *Hieratic papyri in the British Museum*, fifth series, *The Abu Sir Papyri*, London, 1968, Pl. XX.

its property. From the Neferirkara archive we know that the inspection included the seals on all doors and every item of temple equipment. The sheet illustrated in Figure 60 is an example of an inventory of this kind. Again a sensible tabular format meets the practical requirements. The items are not listed haphazardly. Far from it. They are arranged according to an overall scheme of classification that includes an element of progressive subdivision to create subclasses within broader categories, so displaying a basic grasp of taxonomy of the kind that underlies modern knowledge. By the time of this archive the temple equipment was becoming worn. Exact details of damage are listed underneath each item, together with the numbers present. The fragment of table illustrated also reflects some kind of double-entry procedure which is not properly understood, for the space for each set of inspections is itself subdivided by double lines ruled in red to accommodate two sets of observations if necessary.

One set of sheets covered an activity that the ancient Egyptians rated very highly: sealing. Instead of sealing-wax the Egyptians used a very fine grey clay which took the impression of a seal and then set very hard around a binding of cord. In the Old Kingdom the seals themselves were little stone cylinders bearing incised hieroglyphs that could be rolled across the clay. In the Middle Kingdom they were replaced by stamp seals carved in the shape of scarab beetles, the design or inscription scratched into the flat base. Seals were fixed to rolled-up letters and other documents, around the knobs on wooden chests to secure the lids, around the necks of sacks and jars, and over the wooden bolts which closed doors. The relevant sheet from the Neferirkara archive deals with the seals on doorways of rooms in which sacred boats were stored.[5]

The physical barriers to theft in ancient Egypt were not very strong. No ingenuity was displayed in inventing locks. Breaking and entering would have been quite simple, and the long history of tomb robbery in ancient Egypt shows that some people were strongly motivated towards theft. The great fuss that was made over sealing, including the repeated inspection of seals, was a psychological ploy. It concentrated the minds of those responsible on a specific point of security, laid security open to bureaucratic control, and the link between sealings and the keeper of the seal became a bond of responsibility. The system was probably more effective than one might think at first. It created a little field of symbolic power around storeroom doors.

Much of the Neferirkara archive reflects methodical routines – inspections and duty rosters – where the units recorded were single and indivisible, namely human beings and manufactured objects. But many units of administration (land and commodities), in being divisible, required exact quantification as well. Many texts reveal how arithmetical procedures were developed to facilitate this.[6] At the risk of deterring the general reader, a few examples will be cited simply to convey the flavour of this kind of work, which occupied a significant number of those who ran the ancient Egyptian state. One feature of ancient Egyptian mathematics that is a major obstacle to modern readers should be noted at the outset: with the sole exception of $2/3$, no fraction was ever written which had a numerator greater than one. Thus the fraction $3/4$ was written by them as $1/2 + 1/4$; $6/7$ was written as $1/2 + 1/4 + 1/14 + 1/28$; and so on. Although we find it cumbersome because of its unfamiliarity, it is a mathematically respectable method, and Egyptian scribes used it fluently and to great practical effect.[7] Furthermore, at moments of uncertainty they could refer to arithmetic manuals. These often deal with problems that are quite complex, but it reflects the basic Egyptian mentality that each problem is dealt with as a specific and individual case rather than as an application of general mathematical principles. Practised scribes must have developed a degree of mathematical intuition, but the idea of pursuing this as an end in itself – to create the subject of mathematics – did not occur to them.

Rationing

An important area of arithmetical administration was food supplies: rations. The word 'rations' has a special significance. No one had yet invented money. In the modern world money has become such a basic part of life that it is easy to conclude that a world without it would be a very simple place indeed. Where there is no money people have to barter rather than buy and sell, and the word 'barter' is itself stamped with a colonial image of beads and trinkets changing hands in savage lands. This is one of the comfortable myths by which modern people distance themselves from the past and regard their world as being not only much better but a different kind of place altogether.

Money does, indeed, provide a wonderfully easy way of doing business at every kind of scale. Electronic commerce takes away the need even to carry notes and coins, let alone beads and trinkets. But non-money systems have, in the past, managed remarkably well.[8] They exemplify a general characteristic of cultures: that systems tend to be adequate for the demands placed upon them. People cope. The ancient Egyptian economy supplies a good example. The Egyptians managed large economic operations over long periods of time with a moneyless system that was adequate. They were able to do this partly because in the ancient world in general people remained in far closer handling contact with real material wealth – commodities – than we do, and partly because they had developed an accounting system that was half-way towards the abstraction of 'money'. It was half-way in the sense that its language was that of commodities – loaves of bread, jugs of beer, *hekats* of wheat, and so on – but its procedures allowed for the manipulation of quantities which was not necessarily matched by the movement, or even existence, of the substances themselves. It was a typical ancient compromise: abstraction disguised by concrete terminology. We will meet it again in Chapter 7, in looking at the way that goods were priced and how they were bought and sold (see Figure 113, p. 321). It is also another lost world of the mind. For it is now very difficult to reconstruct the whole system in a way that pays suitable heed to the niceties of the ancient documents and satisfies modern common sense. This will become apparent in the next few paragraphs.

Rations administration lay at the heart of the system. In the absence of money people were paid in kind, in commodities. In effect this was a 'wage', but on account both of the commodity-based nature of the recompense and the modern connotations of personal economic freedom of the word 'wage', the term 'rations' is preferable. But the distinction is somewhat artificial.

The basic cereal food cycle from harvest to ration distribution involved a series of points of scribal intervention. The initial yield of grain was measured at the threshing-floor by means of wooden scoops of a given capacity, which gave quantity in terms of a *hekat*, about 4.78 litres. Transport, frequently by river, to the granary involved scribal checking to ensure no theft took place *en route*. Another group of scribes receiving the delivery at the granary checked it again. They or their superiors would already know the maximum capacity of the individual silos, even if they were circular, by calculation:

A circular container of 10 by 10 cubits.
Take away $^1/_9$ of 10, thus $1^1/_9$; remainder $8^2/_3 + {}^1/_6 + {}^1/_{18}$.
Multiply the $8^2/_3 + {}^1/_6 + {}^1/_{18}$ by $8^2/_3 + {}^1/_6 + {}^1/_{18}$ (i.e. square it); result: $79^1/_{108} + {}^1/_{324}$.
Multiply the $79^1/_{108} + {}^1/_{324}$ by 10; it becomes $790^1/_{18} + {}^1/_{27} + {}^1/_{54}$.
Add a half to it: it becomes 1185.
Multiply the 1185 by $^1/_{20}$, giving $59^1/_4$. This is the amount that will go into it in quadruple-*hekat*s, namely $59^1/_4$ hundreds of quadruple-*hekat*s of grain.[9]

The interest of this model calculation is that the container is circular. The first two steps involve squaring $^8/_9$ of the diameter, which yields a very fair approximation to the correct answer that we would find by using a formula involving the constant, *pi* (π).

The next points of scribal intervention were at the beginning and end of the milling, and at subsequent stages in the production of the staple elements of the Egyptian diet: bread and beer. Ancient beer, readers should note, was not only mildly alcoholic but also nutritious. Its prominence in Egyptian diet reflects its food value as much as the pleasurable sensation that went with drinking it. Its centrality to life is represented by the fact that well constructed breweries provide some of the earliest evidence in Egypt for communal organization within settlements (Figure 61.1). Baking and brewing came near the end of the whole cycle of cereal production. For the scribes who painstakingly followed the progress of cereals from fields to ration payouts the essentially messy and labour-intensive processes of baking and brewing presented a challenge, and it was met by a simple but ingenious solution.

For the background – the realities of brewing and baking – we are very well supplied with evidence, in the form of detailed tomb pictures of the Old and Middle Kingdoms, and wooden models from the latter period. Both brewing and baking began with raw cereals and so had a common origin. It used to be widely thought that an essential part of the brewing process was the soaking and straining of lightly baked loaves rich in yeast, but the study of beer residues by microscopy has shown that this is unlikely. Instead it now seems that Egyptian beer relied upon malting (allowing the grains to begin to sprout and so release their sugar) and, crucially, the mixing and blending of uncooked malt with cooked grain or malt.[10]

The model building illustrated (Figure 61.2, from the tomb of Meketra, a high official of the early 12th Dynasty)[11] exemplifies a common subject of Egyptian art, the making of bread and beer seemingly side by side. It has two major parts, each with a subdivision. The outer door leads to a vestibule, to the right of which is the brewery and straight ahead the bakery. The bakery is subdivided by a low partition wall, reflecting two different methods of baking, one to produce flat loaves, the other to produce cylindrical loaves baked in pottery moulds. On the floor lie several flat circular objects which must represent circular limestone mortars set into the floor, as are sometimes found in excavations. In the brewery part a man wields a long wooden pestle to crush grain in one of them. This is an operation preliminary to grinding, which loosens the husks that tightly encase the grain (modern free-threshing wheat would not require this step). In both the bakery and brewery stand paired grindstones set in quern emplacements. Excavated evidence shows that the normal grindstone was an oval piece of quartzite or granite, rough underneath but with a smooth and slightly curved upper surface. Each stone was set into a mud-brick construction, sometimes built against a wall and then having the plan of a letter 'B'. The

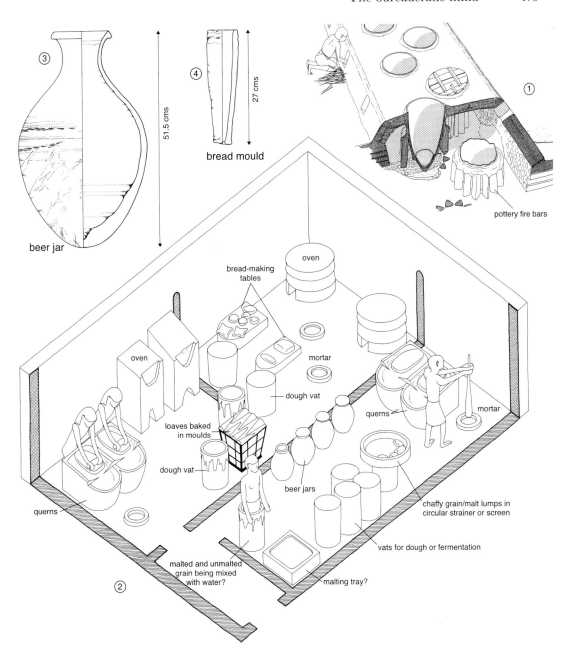

Figure 61 Brewing and baking: an early industry. (1) Reconstruction of a Predynastic brewery, based on an example found well preserved at Abydos. After T.E. Peet and W.L.S. Loat, *The cemeteries of Abydos* III *1912–1913*, London, 1913, 1–2, Figs, 1, 2; Pl. I. (2) The model bakery/brewery from the tomb of Meketra at Thebes, 11th Dynasty. After H.E. Winlock, *Models of daily life in ancient Egypt*, New York, 1955, Figs 22, 23, 64, 65. The two pots (3) and (4) are from the mortuary temple town of Amenemhat III at Dahshur. After Dorothea Arnold, *MDAIK* 38 (1982), 29, Abb. 5, 31, Abb. 7.

stone was set into the top of one half, with sloping surface, and the coarse flour and husks fell into the little trough formed by the mud-brick curb of the other half of the 'B'.[12] The Meketra models lack the collecting trough, but are otherwise of this design. The miller stood behind the higher end and leant forwards over the stone, using a smaller stone for the crushing. The millers were normally women. The ground product would not have been an evenly textured flour, but a crushed mixture of flour and husks which needed to be sieved. In each of the bakery compartments are also two large kneading vats. In the inner compartment they stand next to two low tables on which individual open loaves are made.

Not all bread came in the form of hand-formed loaves, however. A common practice was to bake some bread in pottery moulds. In the Old Kingdom the moulds were large and heavy and designed to produce solid conical loaves (Figure 63, p. 183). By the Middle Kingdom they had evolved into long narrow tubes, still hand-made, rough on the outside, but with a fine smooth inner surface (Figure 61.4).[13] They occur in large numbers on Middle Kingdom sites, and the practice continued into the New Kingdom, during which time it seems to have served primarily religious occasions, to judge from the close association between bread moulds and shrines and temples. Beside the doorway that connects the two compartments stands a square basket filled with loaves of just this shape. Each compartment also contains two ovens, but of a different design in each. In the inner compartment they are of a standard cylindrical type with a hole at the bottom for inserting the fuel. The other two, however, are rectangular. Excavated evidence shows that these were used specifically either for baking the bread in pottery moulds or for the initial firing of the moulds themselves.

The interpretation of the brewery equipment is not quite so certain. Cereal-processing by mortar and querns is catered for at the back of the room, and the large jars in a row against the partition wall are most likely to be for storing the finished beer. In terms of the Middle Kingdom pottery repertoire, the beer jars must have been a well-known type, also illustrated in Figure 61.3. Some of them are shown with a broad low stopper made from mud. Opposite them stand five large cylindrical tubs presumably made of pottery. On one rests a wide tray containing lumps. This is likely to be a sieve or screen through which the mixture of grain and malt, liberally watered, had to be pressed. A cloudy liquid ready for fermentation passed through, leaving behind in the sieve damp chaffy lumps which were themselves edible and, from the malt, might have had a sweet caramel-like taste. Just inside the door of the brewery half of the model is a tall pottery vat. A man stands waist deep in it, holding on to its rim, as if mixing something by treading it with his feet. Could this be the two batches of malt and grain now combined with warm water? And the flat square tray close by: is this for spreading out the grain to allow malting to take place?

Baking and brewing contained elements that unavoidably thwarted a simple control of quantities as they passed from one stage to another. Water was added, dough rose, and a proportion of inedible matter was lost through milling and sieving. Loaves emerged in a variety of shapes, and the strength of beer was affected by the amount of water squeezed through the malt and grain mixture. The scribes' approach was to treat the whole operation as a kind of 'black box': it was possible to measure what went in (either neat cereal grains or already milled flour), and what came out at the other end as quantities of loaves and vessels of beer. Ignoring what went on inside, input and output bore a simple relation to one another: the number of loaves and jugs of beer that came from a given quantity of grain or meal. This scale of values the Egyptians called *pesu* (or *pefsu*), which we can translate as 'baking value', and it represented a stage on the road towards mathematical abstraction. The *pesu* scale was set for the number of loaves or jugs of beer that could be obtained from one *hekat* of grain.[14] The higher the value, the smaller the loaves or the weaker the beer (or the smaller the jugs). *Pesu* enabled the scribe to calculate equivalences between loaves and jugs of different sizes and strengths. '155 loaves of baking-value 20 are equivalent to how many loaves of baking-value 30? You express the 155 loaves of baking-value 20 in terms of meal: thus $7\frac{1}{2} + \frac{1}{4}$ *hekats*. Multiply by 30: result $232\frac{1}{2}$.'[15] In other words, divide 155 by 20 and multiply the result by 30.

Many ration lists have survived. They tend to ignore *pesu* values.[16] They assume standardized jugs of beer, and the various kinds of bread can be grossed together as 'mixed' loaves. This assumes standardization, a reasonable step in thinking in view of the scale and ubiquity of the operations, in which those involved, including potters making beer jugs, would tend naturally to produce standardized shapes from a lifetime's practice. We do actually have an opportunity to check for ourselves. Although very few actual loaves have survived, we have substitutes. The commonest are the pottery moulds in which bread was baked. Thousands have been found on excavations. As already noted, they went through an evolution over time. In the Old Kingdom they turned out loaves that were in the shape of a squat cone, characteristically about 16–20 centimetres across the base. By the Middle Kingdom the cones had evolved into tall thin cylinders (see Figures 61.4, 63, pp. 173, 183). Although so many have been discovered, they have not been examined from the point of view of how the loaves they turned out compare with ancient accounting practices and dietary needs. Photographs of some large finds do give the impression of reasonably standardized capacity within that particular group, which could have been maintained if, as has been suggested, they were themselves formed over reusable moulds (perhaps of wood).[17] Nevertheless, examples from different sites and dates vary by quite a lot. There is no hint that they met a standard officially laid down. The scribe presumably performed his *pesu*-calculations periodically to test whole batches. This was not, however, the end of the story. Not all bread rations were in the form of mould-baked loaves. Soldiers at one of the Middle Kingdom Nubian fortresses (Uronarti) possessed wooden tallies in the shapes of their bread rations, with amounts of wheat and barley carved on them in hieroglyphs (Figure 62).[18] Some represent mould-baked loaves (of barley), but others flat round hand-made loaves (of wheat). These tallies look like the recipient's (a soldier's) own check on the value of his rations, calculated in terms of the grain allocation behind them rather than on the actual number of loaves received. They could have formed the basis of a demand to the scribe to check the *pesu*-value of a batch of mixed loaves issued as rations.

Beer-jug capacity is more difficult for us to check. We know which was the common shape of Middle Kingdom beer jugs, and although most pottery from excavations is too broken to enable capacities to be calculated, many complete ones have been found. As with bread-moulds, however, no serious attempt has been made to measure actual capacities with this question of standardization in mind. However, modern drawings of such vessels found in different tombs in a single cemetery certainly look as though they reflect a range of sizes and only roughly met a standard.

It is typical of the ancient lack of interest in the idea of efficiency that standardization does not seem to have been a conscious goal. Scribes and potters (and bakers) were worlds apart. The gulf of status kept the scribe from breaking out of the limits of his own art, that

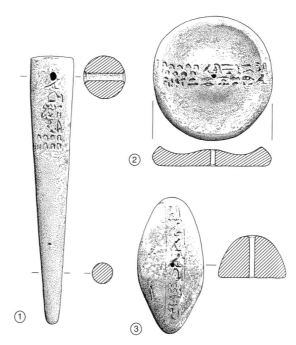

Figure 62 Soldiers' bread-ration tokens, made from wood, plastered over and painted. Each one is in the shape of a particular kind of loaf, and bears a short incised inscription, difficult to translate. (1) A cylindrical loaf of the kind baked in pottery moulds, height 24.7 cm; the hieroglyphs refer to 75 loaves for a soldier. (2) A round flat loaf with raised centre, diameter 12.8 cm; the hieroglyphs refer to 90 loaves from 1 *hekat* of wheat. (3) An oval loaf with flat base, length 12.7 cm; the hieroglyphs refer to 60 ²/₃ loaves. From the late 12th Dynasty fortress of Uronarti in Nubia. After D. Dunham, *Uronarti, Shalfak, Mirgissa*, Boston, 1967, Pls XXVII, XXVIII, and pp. 34–5.

of procedure and calculation, and his procedures arose from an acceptance that a crucial part of the operation was virtually beyond his control.

Real ration lists show that the regular wage or ration was calculated in terms of so many loaves of bread and jugs of beer, with extras sometimes appearing, such as cakes or wine.[19] A standard daily basic wage consisted of ten loaves and a measure of beer that could fluctuate between a third of a jug to one or even two whole jugs. This was what was thought fit for an ordinary labourer. Ration lists also show that as one moved upwards through the ranks of officialdom the distributions increased by multiples of the basic ration. This was sometimes expressed by listing those of higher rank as if they were more than one person: perhaps five, ten or even twenty men. The Rhind Mathematical Papyrus helped the scribe cope with the consequences.

> Method of distributing 100 loaves amongst 10 men, if the skipper, the crew-leader and the doorkeeper [receive] double.
> Its procedure: you add up the people to receive supplies: thus 13.
> Divide the 100 loaves by 13. That makes $7 + \frac{2}{3} + \frac{1}{39}$ [i.e. $7\frac{9}{13}$].
> Then you say: [this] is the consumption of the 7 men, [while] the skipper, the crew-leader and the doorkeeper receive double.[20]

Thus the ten men with unequal shares are temporarily converted into thirteen fictitious 'recipients' with equal shares. The seven 'one-man' shares are each $7^9/_{13}$; the three 'two-man' shares for the three officials amount to twice that quantity, i.e. $15^5/_{13}$.

The Rhind Mathematical Papyrus also, however, envisaged more complicated cases of distribution where the scaling by rank was not done in simple multiples of one basic ration. '100 loaves for 5 men. $^1/_7$ of the rations for the three superiors goes to the two inferiors. What is the difference in the shares?' To answer this question (Rhind Problem 40), the author provided tabular calculations which show that he was really asking for an arithmetic progression of shares for the five men, each one $^1/_7$ smaller than the next. The answer is correctly found: $38^1/_3$, $29^1/_6$, 20, $10^2/_3 + ^1/_6$, and $1^1/_3$. The difference between any two is $9^1/_6$.

Documents about rations create a problem that tells us that we are dealing not just with a pragmatic earthy business of feeding people, but with an economic system of more ambitious scope having a greater notional or abstract content than at first sight seems to be the case.

If a basic minimum daily ration consisted of ten loaves, a senior official could be credited with anything up to 500 per day. This would have exceeded the most gargantuan of appetites. Was the extra to support his staff? Some texts make separate reference to staff payments and so help to rule this out. In any case, some of the ration lists relate to expeditions sent to mines and quarries in uncomfortable desert locations, such as Sinai and the Wadi Hammamat. These were hardly suited to taking along one's family or household, or to bouts of high living. But then there are the fractions to consider. The Rhind Mathematical Papyrus is not alone in considering awkward fractions of loaves and jugs of beer. The same occur in real lists. Equally arresting is the accounting system of a provincial Middle Kingdom temple, that of the god Wepwawet at Asyut.[21] Some staff were paid according to the number of 'temple days' allotted to them. A text explains:

> As for a temple day, it is $^1/_{360}$ part of a year. Now, you shall divide everything that enters this temple – bread, beer and meat – by way of the daily rate. That is, it is going to be $^1/_{360}$ of the bread, of the beer, and of everything that enters this temple for [any] one of these temple days which I have given you.

Each staff member was entitled to two temple days, except for the chief priest, who got four. The real entitlement was thus $^2/_{360}$ (or $^4/_{360}$ in the case of the chief priest) of every loaf and jug of beer that the temple received by way of its income. Part of the income was meat. The archive of another temple (at Kahun) deals with fractions of cattle![22]

Common sense tells us that we are not dealing with a system that distributed bread-crumbs and minced meat in finely weighed portions, and piled up uneaten surpluses around high officials. The system must have combined a distribution of real and of notional rations, the latter being, in effect, credit, in which a paper accumulation of undistributed ration allocation was exchangeable for something else. (Think of the modern system of frequent-flyer miles that are increasingly redeemable in a variety of services besides airline tickets, or the Time Dollar and other similar complementary currencies.)[23] The loaves and the jugs were measures of value, or units of account, as much as they stood for actual amounts of foodstuff in hand, waiting to be carried off and consumed. The *pesu*-system allowed the interchangeability of bread and beer to be calculated, as well as the keeping of a record of just how much wheat or barley lay behind them. The implication, however, is that a wider range of equivalents in value would have been needed, where, for example, the grain or bread equivalent of linen cloth was expressed. But it is here that the documentation runs out. Neither the Rhind Mathematical Papyrus nor administrative documents cover such a wider field of value exchanges. For the New Kingdom we have ample records of village barter transactions which display a broad range of values of commodities expressed in terms of *hekat*s of grain or weights of metal (mostly bronze; see Chapter 7). A feeling for relative values seems from this material to have been part of the basic mental equipment for living that Egyptians possessed from an early age. But at an official level the gap in the texts remains. Either we are missing some key element in the system, or the 'cashing' or redeeming of one's accumulated surplus of rations was done unofficially, by barter and out of the scope of normal record keeping.

The lack of standardized bread and beer strengths lets us down in another respect. We cannot jump immediately to the actual figures for the average wheat and barley allocations which lay behind the basic ration, and so answer the most essential question: how much cereal did the ancient Egyptians normally consume? How nutritious was the diet of those who dragged stones from quarries to pyramids? For convenience rations were normally expressed in simple numerical form, leaving it to the *pesu* system and the wooden tallies to satisfy any doubts or queries. There must, nevertheless, have been an average quantity that we can attempt to establish, or perhaps more realistically we can aim to set maximum and minimum figures.

It is possible to use the short inscriptions carved into the Uronarti tallies as a source. They are, unfortunately, cryptic and any results are therefore somewhat tentative. One study leads to the figure of two-thirds of a *hekat* of barley, and one *hekat* of wheat per soldier as a ten-day ration. How feasible is this in reality? Modern estimates of the size of the Egyptian *hekat* vary slightly. One reasonably reliable figure is 4.78 litres. One *hekat* of wheat is thus 0.00478 cubic metres. A cubic metre of wheat is reckoned to weigh 785 kilograms. One *hekat* of wheat should thus weigh around 3.75 kilograms. An equivalent amount of barley is reckoned to be lighter: 705 kilograms per cubic metre. Thus, two-thirds of a *hekat* of barley should amount to about 2.25 kilograms. When added together, 6 kilograms of grain per ten-day period is involved, or 0.6 kilograms per day. By the standards calculated for the Roman world this seems a somewhat meagre portion. According to another scholar, figures given by the Greek author Polybius, writing around 140 BC, imply for an infantryman, whether legionary or auxiliary, 0.94 kilograms of grain per day, although Roman records from Pselchis (modern Dakka in Nubia) can be interpreted to produce the smaller figure of 0.80 kilograms.[24] For both Egyptian and Roman societies there is another unknown factor: the amount and variety of dietary supplement to a grain ration. In the case of Egypt this was probably fairly small. The impression derived from many sources is that bread and beer from wheat and barley formed the staple diet.

The discussion can be taken at least one stage further by estimating caloric values.[25] One *hekat* of wheat represents about 8,100 calories, and barley about 9,720. One *hekat* of wheat and two-thirds of a *hekat* of barley thus would yield 14,580 calories for the ten-day period, or 1,458 per day. How realistic is this figure? A report on prison diet in Egypt published in 1917 gave the following energy values required in daily diets: 1,800 calories for subsistence, 2,200 for no work, 2,800 for light labour, and 3,200 for hard labour.[26] These figures derived from the regime laid down for prisoners in the Egyptian army.

They should be compared to modern medical opinion (for largely sedentary populations), that 1,750–1,950 calories suffice for men, and 1,200–1,500 for women (though commonly people's intake is higher). We may thus take, with some confidence, the figures from the Uronarti tallies as representing a minimum ration, and expect that in reality more was consumed by each man. If the tallies stand only for actual loaves we have to add the grain content of the separately issued beer and this might have brought the overall level into line with actual bodily requirements. But we should still accept that the pyramids were built on a modest health-food diet.

Apart from a general interest in ancient diet this discussion also serves a more specific archaeological enquiry concerning the capacities of ancient granaries and the number of people dependent on them that will surface in the next chapter.

Cereal administration was not confined to human foodstuff. The obliging Rhind Mathematical Papyrus (Problem 82b) includes the following:

> Amount of what a fatted goose eats:
> ten geese 1¼ *hekat*s [of flour made into bread]
> in ten days 12½
> in 40 days 50 *hekat*s
> which represents grain in double-hekats: 23½ + ¼ + ⅛ *hekat*s, and 4¼ + ⅙ *ro*
> (1 *ro* = ¹⁄₃₂₀ *hekat*).

The essence of this problem, somewhat cryptically laid out, is to calculate the volume difference between grain and flour. For this a tenth of two-thirds is subtracted – presumably a rule-of-thumb ratio – and the result halved to reduce it to double-*hekat*s. The answer is not quite correct, although the scribe has aimed at great exactitude by using fractions of *hekat*s.

Management and labour (and did slaves build the pyramids?)

A similarly intense scrutiny was applied to building projects, another major goal of administration. All concerned, whether officials and architects in charge, or the army of workers and craftsmen, were employed directly, and their work and their reward measured and scrutinized. A typical task was the precise measurement of materials to be moved and used, whether cut blocks of stone, sun-dried mud bricks, straw and earth for making bricks, rubble or sand. A conscientious scribe would measure (or write down the measurements called out by another) in the full standardized notation of Egyptian linear measure: cubits (20.6 inches or 523 millimetres), palms, fingerbreadths and fractions, as well as in halves, thirds and quarters of a cubit. He would then calculate the volume of material. The multiplication of fractions and subdivisions of a cubit involved considerable calculating skill, and the scribe may have referred to ready-made tables. From the volume he could calculate the number of labour-units that would be required, using standard ratios. In one example the daily labour norm for one man was to transport 10 cubic cubits. From these figures the scribe could estimate the rations that would be required and produce work figures that could later be compared with the actual work done (an example of the last stage might be present in the markings in Figure 64, p. 185). It has been pointed out that this reveals a disciplined approach towards the value of a working person's time that is more familiar in modern societies imbued with a positive work ethic.[27]

In this way the supply of the three essentials for major building projects – materials, labour and rations – could be constantly monitored. It was the scribe's pen as much as the overseer's lash or the engineer's ingenuity that built the pyramids.

Who did build the pyramids? Modern answers vary between slaves and seasonally employed labourers who perhaps felt a sense of fulfilment in participating in a national sacred task. The subject of slavery retains emotional content. The historical experience of black slavery in the Americas still causes outrage, and hidden forms of what is said to be slavery are from time to time identified around the world, amongst those employed in 'sweat shops', for example. Because overt slavery has been officially abolished it is easily condemned. Yet people tend not to see military conscription (otherwise known as national service or the draft) in the same light, even though it is marked by loss of liberty backed up by extreme punishments, by frequently harsh conditions, by separation from family and by only token payments. Slavery and conscription can be said to rest upon different concepts, upon outright ownership of the person as a piece of property in the former case, as distinct from a temporary claim to total service. Something of this distinction was present in ancient Egyptian terminology.[28] If we keep to the niceties of legal language then we must admit in the Egyptian case a lack of evidence that the large labour force for pyramid building consisted of people who were owned as pieces of property by the king and to whom a term translatable as 'slave' was applied. As actual experience, however, the two categories – of slavery and conscription – overlap. When we speak of slave labour camps in modern oppressive regimes, populated by citizens deprived indefinitely of their normal freedoms by the state and often worked to death, we are unlikely to be troubled by the thought that we are using the term 'slave' rather too loosely. We know what we mean. Conversely, if we say that the pyramids were built by people doing national service it does not seem nearly as bad as if we say that they were built by slaves. What we really want to know is whether the conditions of service were a lot harsher than those of normal life, and whether they were largely resented.

These are questions that are virtually impossible to answer, particularly if we demand quantification. Perhaps the clearest indication as to attitude is to be found in a religious text and practice which we first encounter perhaps a century after the end of the Old Kingdom. At this time a set of protective spells became available to those who could afford to have them painted on their coffins (hence the modern term Coffin Texts). One of them was unambiguously intended to enable a substitute statuette (called a *shabti*) 'to carry out work for their owner in the realm of the dead'. 'If N be detailed for the removal[?] of a block[?] to strange sites[?] of the desert plateau, to register the riparian lands, or to turn over new fields for the reigning king, "Here am I" shall you say to any messenger who may come for N, in place of him.'[29] The text and, as they later developed, the specially made statuettes proved to have enduring value and became a distinctive feature of Egyptian funerary religion. Fear of conscription, it seems, could pursue a person even of high rank beyond death. There is no mistaking the psychology of unwillingness, the sense of the inner self seeking to avoid by a trick sudden demands for labour which cannot be challenged. Perhaps 'trick' is too strong a word since the sending of 'substitutes' (primarily relatives) to fill the place of a conscripted person is documented from real-life situations.[30]

The likely picture for what was normal in ancient Egypt is that, by royal commands, the state from time to time cast its net over a larger labour force than was regularly available from the pool of those in part-time or full-time state employment. It was probably done through the tier of regional governors who could have drawn upon the hosts of obligations that inevitably pervade local societies. For its part, the state paid rations, so that those affected did not have their labour taken from them for nothing. But the postings were typically arduous: to the occasional army to serve abroad, or to support surges of activity at quarrying or construction sites, even the building of pyramids. There were those who tried to escape, and then the state revealed its punitive side. A key document from the late Middle Kingdom, a prison register, opens for us a little window on the fate of those who chose not to co-operate.[31] One typical entry reads:

> The daughter of Sa-anhur, Teti, under the Scribe of the Fields of the city of This: a woman. An order was issued to the central labour camp in year 31, third month of summer, day 9, to release her family from the courts, and at the same time to execute against her the law pertaining to one who runs away without performing his service. Present [check mark]. Statement by the Scribe of the Vizier, Dedu-amun: 'Carried out; case closed.'

This sounds very much as though her family had been held hostage until her arrest.

The mobilizing effects of bureaucracy when applied to a major project were impressive. Sadly we lack any part of the original documentation for major building works that have survived, such as the Giza pyramids. But our imagination is readily stimulated by records left scratched in the stone at ancient mines and quarries. For sheer scale we can turn to the same quarrying and mining records that have furnished us with detail on the method of payment. In the thirty-eighth regnal year of King Senusret I (1918 BC) an expedition went to the quarries in the Wadi Hammamat. It was under the leadership of a 'herald' called Ameny.[32] Under him were eighty officials, roughly 18,660 skilled and unskilled workers (who included thirty hunters and a contingent of soldiers), plus a train of millers, brewers and bakers (twenty of each). Amongst the officials were twenty 'mayors' of towns, presumably because it was their responsibility to supply most of the drafted or conscripted labour. Interestingly the whole enterprise was looked after by only eight scribes. A modern engineering estimate for the numbers who might have been needed for building the Great Pyramid at Giza has produced a similar figure: a maximum of 10,000, to whom should be added the labour for ramp construction and logistical support. Even if we allow for a higher tolerance of inefficiency and for time lost through mistakes, and double the figure, it will have represented less than 2 per cent of the estimated total population of Egypt at the time of pyramid construction.[33] When seen in this light, even the building of the Giza pyramids represents a level of conscription that could have been easily borne.

For the intensity of the control and scrutiny that the Middle Kingdom observed we can do no better than refer to a group of papyri that relate to various activities being carried out in a provincial part of Egypt, the area of the city of This, near Abydos.[34] No pyramid-building or quarrying expedition of epic magnitude was involved. Part of the archive relates to a carpentry shop attached to a royal boatyard, where every minor movement of planks and goat-hides was listed, and which received written instructions on matters great and small directly from the vizier based in the vicinity of Memphis. Another part deals with construction on a provincial temple, evidently an example of the type revealed by excavation, where mud brick rather than stone was the most common material. It is this text that provides the most striking evidence for detailed measurements of volumes of materials moved and conversion to work loads mentioned above. There is no reason to suppose that this provincial setting for so great an intensity of supervision was anything special. Rather it implies that this level was typical for the Middle Kingdom.

It is possible for an authority to order its people to do such-and-such a task and leave them to get on with it as best they can. Faced with incentives or punishments people can organize themselves quite effectively. Once you decide to take control of every detail of the operation, however, the burden of administration rapidly mounts and in the modern world easily gets out of hand. 'Less government' has become a modern political rallying-cry. The Egyptians, with clear (if ambitious) goals and no dissenting philosophies to divert their energies, got away with it. In part they did so also because the systems which kings and scribes used were more limited than at first sight appears to be the case. The friction or drag inherent within the systems of pre-modern societies can with hindsight appear as something of a blessing.

Bureaucracy is an attitude of mind, an aptitude that we encounter with most immediacy in original documents. It can easily appear to be a cosy self-contained world of order, particularly as the documents tend to be studied in isolation by experts in ancient language working in quiet studies or libraries and equipped with dictionaries and manuals of grammar. For the ancient scribe, however, the order belonged to his inner mental world. When he rested his pen and looked up from his sheet of papyrus the scenes that met his eyes may well have been a good deal less orderly. Indeed, the essence of the act of writing (and of drawing) is to reduce a complex and often chaotic reality to a comprehensible order.

Ancient documents lie at an interface of reality: the far side is available to us only through archaeology. This has already intruded in the description of baking and brewing. These messy and smoky processes were the reality behind the precisions of the Rhind Mathematical Papyrus. We can move even closer by examining a find of well preserved bakeries in a large establishment connected to the pyramids at Giza.[35] Figure 63 is a plan of one sample room, measuring roughly 5 by 2.5 metres. The free working space, however, is much less, around one metre in width. The left side (as one entered) was given over to preparation, with dough-mixing vats at the back. Current understanding of the Old Kingdom baking process sees the heavy bread-moulds used in pairs: the lower one containing the dough which will bake to become a heavy conical loaf, the upper one, heated separately in a stack on an open hearth, creating a miniature oven when inverted over the lower one. Just inside the door on the right stood a low hearth, presumably the place where the upper moulds were stacked for heating. Along the rest of the right side of the room ran two parallel rows of circular depressions where (there seems no reason to doubt) the paired moulds (now miniature ovens) had stood, able to produce just over twenty large loaves. The whole room, when first found, was buried in fine wood ash that reached the rim of the vats and to avoid which the bakers had built the hearth higher and higher. The accounting system, however, removed from the scribes the need to enter these dirty crowded places. All they needed to do was to stand outside and count the sacks of grain going in and the numbers of loaves being carried out. Figure 63 also illustrates an abiding characteristic of most archaeology, made more pointed by being associated with the Giza necropolis, home to the only surviving 'wonder' of the most popular list of seven compiled in Classical times, and the source for some of the finest and most sensitively carved statuary ever produced

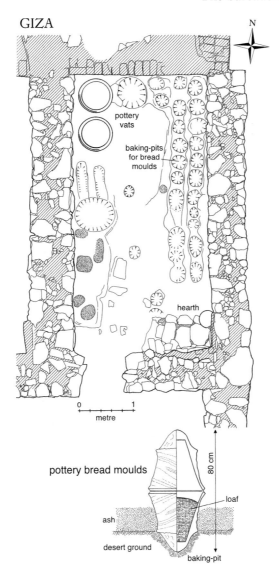

GIZA

N

pottery
vats

baking-pits
for bread
moulds

hearth

0   1
metre

pottery bread moulds

80 cm

loaf

ash

desert ground

baking-pit

Figure 63   A bakery from the large work camp of the 4th Dynasty at Giza. After M. Lehner, The Oriental Institute (Chicago), *News and Notes* 135 (Fall 1992), 8–9, Fig. 8; also (with modern reconstruction and experimental baking) D. Roberts, *National Geographic* 187, no. 1 (January 1995), 32–5. Shown as an inset is a reconstruction of how the bread-moulds were used, the upper mould, preheated, creating a temporary oven. The moulds are after *Aeragram* (Newsletter of the Ancient Egypt Research Associates) 3, no. 1 (1999), 12–13. The position of this bakery within the work camp is given in Figure 66, p. 189, labelled 'B'.

in Egypt. That characteristic is the utter lack of grandeur in the living- and working-conditions of most people of the past.

The best extant examples of scribes reaching out their hands to the rough surfaces of manual labour are to be found in some of the ancient quarries. Egyptian temples and quarries show that quarrymen and builders worked with blocks of stone that were generally of comparable sizes but, that said, still varied noticeably. Masons expended considerable effort to achieve close fits of blocks that were almost but not quite of the same size. Scribes wanted to know the rate at which stone was being extracted from the quarry. Since the blocks varied in size, the simple procedure of counting them would not do. Instead they could, as one option, mark the progress of each day or other work period by means of an annotated red line daubed along the final line of chisel cuts on the quarry face. This subsequently became the base line against which to measure the rate of progress for the next period.[36] When, say, a granite obelisk was needed, particularly close attention could be paid to monitoring the progress of the workmen. In one quarry at Aswan the fruits of their daily poundings of the granite with large balls of the hard stone dolerite were marked in paint, perhaps to ensure that no man received his rations or left the work until he had fulfilled his quota (Figure 64).[37]

It was possible to do things differently. Around 1350 BC, in the late 18th Dynasty, King Akhenaten embarked upon a scheme of religious change. One of the novelties of his reign was that the huge numbers of blocks of sandstone and limestone needed for his many buildings were all cut to the same handy size, chosen to be one cubit in length (c. 52 centimetres). Since Egyptian buildings were normally conceived as a series of cubit dimensions, planning in all its aspects was presumably made much easier. Some of the blocks were taken from fully managed quarries (one of them seemingly belonging to the king's mother, Queen Tiy). Much of the stone for the king's new city at El-Amarna, however, looks as though it came from unmanaged sources. The desert hilltops behind El-Amarna still preserve innumerable small surface quarries which look like the product of self-organization, in which many individuals (were they soldiers or citizens?), told to deliver a quota of blocks, have gone out in their own time and squatted down on a spare patch of stone desert and begun hacking (or conceivably 'employed' a substitute to do it for them). In making the delivery of stone blocks into a form of tax, the whole scribal business of control was made unnecessary.[38] Contrary to what one might have expected, the system of standardized blocks did not find general acceptance. After the end of Akhenaten's reign and the rejection of his ideas, the older style of labour-intensive stone-working reappeared.

The case of the El-Amarna quarries is an example where evidence from the ground modifies a picture derived from texts. It suggests that the ideal of bureaucratic control was not always followed through consistently and completely. Another possible example of compromise in the crucial area of rations will be pointed out in the next section, on the Giza work camps.

Building the pyramids

Although we lack the original written documentation on the building of the Giza pyramids, through the window of archaeology we can gain some idea of the physical complexities of the operation which bureaucracy had somehow to control. To do this we have, so to speak,

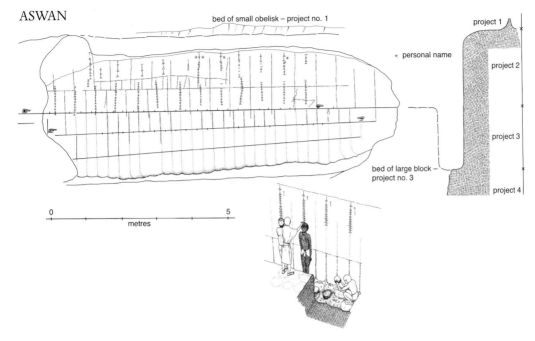

ASWAN

bed of small obelisk – project no. 1

project 1

* personal name

project 2

project 3

bed of large block – project no. 3

project 4

0   5
metres

Figure 64 Working practices recorded in red and black painted lines on the face of a granite quarry at Aswan, probably New Kingdom. The red lines are here rendered in grey. In two previous projects large granite blocks had been removed. The new project began with the cutting of a trench to separate the intended block from the parent rock, the vertically scalloped appearance preserving the method of removing the unwanted stone, by concentrated pounding with globular balls of hard stone (dolerite). The rock face left over from the previous project was smoothed so that it could be used to record the progress of the workmen, by means of vertical columns of red triangular marks, corresponding to each man's work position (a pair of the pounding scallops). Many of the intervals are about 7 cms in depth. Is this the amount of stone removed in one day? The variations between the lowest of the marks and the bottom of the trench suggest that progress was marked by the head height of each man (the last day probably going unrecorded). The record at the top suggests that some of the preliminary work was recorded every two working-periods (days?) for an unknown reason. Originally the name of each man seems to have been written beside each column of marks (the approximate position of the few that survived are marked by asterisks). Perhaps the payment of rations was dependent upon the removal of a certain amount of stone. The long straight vertical lines helped to keep the workmen evenly spaced. The long horizontal lines are probably part of a survey connected with the fashioning of the block to be removed. If this is a correct interpretation this piece of quarry face would represent the work of around fifteen men cutting the trench in under twenty days. After R. Engelbach, *The Aswân obelisk; with remarks on the ancient engineering*, Cairo, 1922, Pl. VI.

to stand back and not be overwhelmed by the pyramids themselves (Figure 65). We must try to see them in the context of their setting, the whole Giza plateau, as the outcome of a huge management operation, in which several interlocking lines of administration had to be pursued simultaneously, with the danger that a mistake in one could disrupt others and delay the whole gigantic project. To be successful this required a total managerial overview, the scope of which we can reconstruct using the range of archaeological observations from the site.[39]

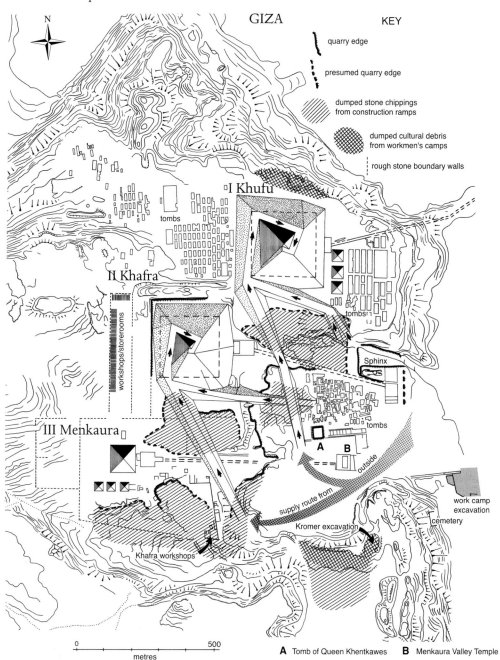

Figure 65 The archaeology of large-scale public works: the Giza pyramid plateau, showing quarries and construction debris, plus the hypothetical outlines of the partly 'spiral' construction ramps for the first and second pyramids. After M. Lehner, *AfO* 32 (1985), 136–58. For the large work camp towards the south-east corner see Figure 66, p. 189; for the Menkaura Valley Temple (B) see Figure 74, p. 208; for the Khentkawes town (A–B) see Figure 73, p. 206.

The Giza plateau was not a blank page on which the architects had a free hand to design and to lay out the buildings of their choice. One basic constraint was provided by the site's geology. Much of the surface of the plateau is the top of a bed of limestone (the Mokattam Formation) that has a general slope down to the south-east. It seems to have been the desire of the pyramid builders to keep to more or less the same level for each of the three major pyramids (of Kings Khufu, Khafra and Menkaura), and this could be met only by laying them out along a single line which is perpendicular to the direction of the slope and at the same time at an angle to the north–south trend of the river Nile. The limestone of the Mokattam Formation was also suited to providing much of the stone for the cores of the pyramids, although it was not fine enough for the outer casings. For each pyramid a convenient adjacent quarry was opened.

Convenience involved another major consideration. As the pyramid rose so the stones had to be taken to ever higher levels. Although scholars differ as to the details there is general agreement that much of the stone was raised by dragging it, loaded on to wooden sledges (see Figure 117, *bottom left*, p. 340), up huge ramps that had to be raised in phase with the construction work. Keeping the gradient to a minimum as well as minimizing its distance from the quarry was a further consideration of prime importance. Furthermore, the builders of the second and third pyramids had their limits of manoeuvre reduced by the works of their predecessors. Khufu had chosen an area at the far north-eastern end of the Mokattam Formation, immediately above a high escarpment, drawing stone from quarries on the south side, and filling up the ground to east and west with tombs for members of his court. His successors were obliged to move further to the south-west, so that no one was able to use the advantage of the natural slope of the ground by construct-ing their ramps down its line. All the ramps to some extent must have run up the slope. There was probably, however, a good reason for preferring this arrangement of ramps. Not all of the stone was quarried locally. Originally the pyramids were encased in a layer of fine limestone from quarries across the river, at Tura, supplemented in the cases of the pyramids of Khafra and Menkaura with granite from Aswan. The temples that accompa-nied the pyramids also required stone from outside, and there must have been, as well, a considerable demand for timber, which was, amongst other uses, laid across the tops of the ramps to provide a suitable surface for the sledges. Transport of heavy materials to the site must have been by boats on a canal or canals, requiring a docking area. The natural site for this is towards the south of the site, where the dip of the plateau leaves a depression. If the zone for receiving deliveries of building materials and preparing them for their places on the site was here, the alignments of the construction ramps would need to take this into consideration as well. Site management employing the skills of co-ordination and anticipa-tion was thus the real pinnacle of command in pyramid building, and it is not surprising to find that the task was performed by the most senior figures in the land, close to the king, to the extent of being, in the 4th Dynasty, normally a son of the king.[40]

The picture of managerial choices and constraints arises from two sources. One consists of direct observations. The locations of several of the quarries are apparent from modern excavations, and certain pieces of evidence point to the existence of an ancient basin towards the south end of the site. The other is the result of putting oneself in the position of the builders and looking for an economical solution within the framework provided by the archaeology. The alignments of the ramps, huge constructions in their own right, can be deduced only in this way since when the pyramids were finished the ramps were all cleared away, leaving no direct traces. The need for clear forward thinking and the demarcation of zones of activity to prevent them from spreading too far may have been one reason behind a pattern of rough stone walls which divides the Giza plateau in the areas of the pyramids of Khafra and Menkaura into large zones. They were left as permanent features and, with some additions, would have continued to define the ground that properly belonged to each pyramid.

The construction ramps were, as noted, major projects in themselves. Each one may have equalled two-thirds of the volume of its pyramid. At the end of the day they had to be disposed of. What were the ramps made of? Some later sources show that ramps could be built up from compartments constructed of mud brick and filled with sand. There is no sign at Giza, however, of huge dumps of mud brick. Instead several parts of the Giza plateau, especially the quarries and the low area to the south, were buried in stone chippings and dust, in vast quantities sufficient probably to account for the ramps. This provides another managerial responsibility: directing the quarrying and the necessary extra labour to put quarry debris and loose desert materials into the right position to create the appropriately graded ramp for the stage of pyramid construction reached, the ramp being a long and broadly based heap of loose material.

In recent years a great advance has been made in our knowledge of the archaeology of Giza through large-scale excavations centred on working- and living-areas. Three of these are currently known. As with the long walls which subdivided the Giza plateau, a common building material was rough stone and mud mortar; although in some places mud bricks were preferred.

1   The most informative of the three, and probably the heart of the whole Giza plateau construction community in the Old Kingdom, lay on sandy ground below the southern escarpment and beside the likely main ancient access route to the plateau. Much of it also lay outside, to the south, of the huge stone wall which bounded the pyramid area on the south. It is impossible to do justice in two paragraphs to the results of the large-scale excavations, begun in 1988, not least because of changes that the site underwent during its lifetime, although this seems to have been primarily confined to the 4th Dynasty. Overall it possesses a rectilinear plan but with significant deviations from the principal alignments which do not follow precise cardinal orientations (Figure 66).[41]

The largest part cleared so far (150 x 180 metres) is a portion of a sub-rectangular enclosure largely filled with long parallel chambers or galleries, each measuring about 4.5 x 31.5 metres, laid out in rows and served by straight narrow streets. The galleries were subdivided into bewildering clusters of rooms and spaces, constantly differing in detail from one chamber to another. Since much of the work at the Giza site would have been outdoor labouring, an *a priori* assumption arises that these tightly packed blocks are actually the living- or sleeping-quarters for some of the teams of labourers who could, of course, have occupied them seasonally. They are unlike what was to be found inside the provincial towns of the period (e.g. Figure 68, p. 196) and so perhaps represent an adaptation to the peculiar circumstances of a population temporarily separated from the normal concerns of property ownership and family provision. They also illustrate an Egyptian planners' fondness for breaking up large accommodation requirements – whether intended to house people, goods, or working facilities – into sets of

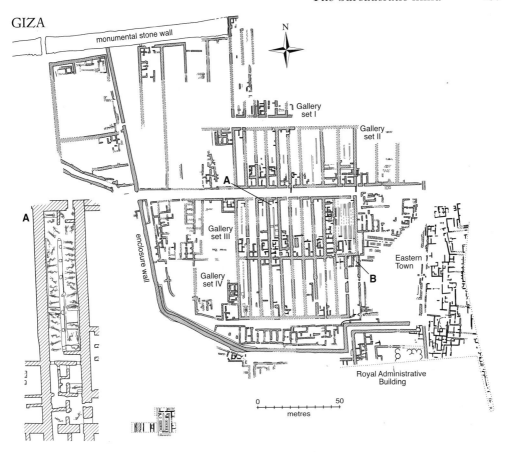

Figure 66 Overall site plan of the Giza work camp. The plan has been obtained through a combination of removing surface sand to reveal the tops of walls and full excavation of a selection of individual parts. One of the fully excavated long chambers is shown inset at a larger scale (A). The sleeping figures rendered in grey are intended to demonstrate that if this was an accommodation unit it could have housed between forty and fifty men. The position of the bakery shown in Figure 63, p. 183 is also marked (B). After M. Lehner, *The Millennium Project; report on season 2002*, Cambridge, Mass., 2002; M. Lehner, *JARCE* 39 (2002), 31, Fig. 2.

long parallel units. In these cases their length and degree of internal subdivision make it more likely that they were initially built without roofs, which were added to individual parts of the internal layouts. In a few of the chambers half or more of the front part contained column bases set into a narrow mud bench to support a more extensive roofed area. It has been experimentally demonstrated that each of the chambers could have slept up to fifty men, leading to an estimate of between 1,600 and 2,000 for the whole gallery complex that covers an area of around 2.5 hectares. This represents a population density of 640 to 800 persons per hectare, towards if not beyond the upper limit of known population densities from the past and present.[42] This is still only a fraction of a labour requirement of 10,000, but closer to the excavator's own estimate of only 4,000, and soundings suggest that what has been revealed by excavation is still only a fraction of the original site. There is a marked contrast between the relatively regular layout of the galleries and the Eastern Town. Only the western edge of this has been revealed. Although its building lines follow the same general orientation as the rest of the site, it is essentially a self-organized settlement of houses of varying sizes and layouts built around an irregular network of narrow 'streets'. It presumably accommodated a population differing in its circumstances from those of the galleries, perhaps because it was more permanently settled there.

A leading feature of the archaeology of this site is the widespread finding of pottery bread moulds and ash, as well as numerous 'bakeries' (one of them already illustrated in Figure 63). A similar ubiquity of evidence for baking is found at other and more conventional Old Kingdom settlements, implying that baking (and brewing) was a normal domestic skill, although we know that professional bakers, brewers and millers did exist (see the evidence from the Wadi Hammamat inscription, cited above, p. 181). At first sight this points to a divergence at Giza from the level of control described above and illustrates how the integration of texts and archaeology is often not straightforward. The natural interpretation of the site is that the work community was issued not with bread and beer but with raw cereal, and that each unit was left to prepare its own food (analogous to the situation at the much later workmen's/artists' village at Deir el-Medina, see p. 329). This would have represented a significant reduction in scribal work load and might suggest that, as circumstances varied, so it was indeed possible to vary the intensity of scribal control. On the other hand, we cannot exclude the possibility that those who lived in these barracks were under an obligation to bake and brew not only for themselves but also, under a quota system, for others as well, either their superiors or workers in more temporary accommodation. This kind of arrangement is well known from the New Kingdom (Chapter 7). If that were the case then the scribal system with its *pesu* ratio would have been needed.

2   A fine example of a block of long parallel units lies to the west of the Pyramid of Khafra, built against the western enclosure wall of this pyramid.

> Perpendicular walls extend like the teeth of a comb from the west wall of this enclosure which is 450 metres (1,476 feet) long, describing about 75 galleries, each 30 metres (98 feet) long and 3 metres (10 ft) wide. With another set leading from the north wall, there are nearly 100 galleries in all.[43]

The galleries had largely been cleaned out in antiquity, but such remains as have been discovered inside point to them having been workshops (for statuary amongst other crafts) rather than places of accommodation.

3   An area was excavated in 1971–2 to the south-east of the Pyramid of Menkaura (Figure 65).[44] It consists of a collection of small buildings, some of them for accommodation, on either side of a rubble wall that makes a series of sharp changes of direction. The full extent of the site is not known, for it continues unexcavated beneath the desert on both east and west. Across an open area were scattered a large number of rough blocks of alabaster, together with an unfinished alabaster column base. These help to identify this part of the camp as a masons' workshop. The site was relatively well preserved when found, because it had been buried beneath a vast dump of the

stone chippings that occur in various parts of the Giza plateau. Their late appearance on the scene – after the camp had been abandoned – is understandable if we see them as the remains of a pyramid construction ramp, removed after the end of building and dumped in the nearest convenient place.

Not all of the ancient dumps at Giza are of limestone chippings and archaeologically sterile. East and south of the Menkaura work camp lies a large bay in the line of the rock escarpment largely filled up. Although at first sight the filling appears to be natural, archaeological soundings have suggested otherwise. Petrie was the first to note that this was no natural patch of desert: 'The whole surface is covered for many feet deep with broken stone-chips from quarrying.'[45] Between 1971 and 1975 an Austrian expedition extensively probed the eastern edge, where it becomes the western slope of the prominent rock outcrop south of the Menkaura Valley Temple.[46] A substantial layered deposit of Old Kingdom domestic rubbish was revealed, which included pottery and other artefacts, but no structures. These two probings, and the record of the Menkaura work camp, are pointers to the possibility that the whole southern edge of the Giza plateau, which is its lowest part, is the site of a gigantic rubbish infilling consisting in part of ramp debris and in part of the dumped remains of building sites and work camps in addition to the ones, just summarized, that remain in place.

These largely hidden aspects of pyramid building, creating and maintaining the construction sites and then clearing them away, are no mean ones. From an administrative point of view it hardly mattered if the operation in hand involved highly skilled sculpting and engineering or the transportation of mountains of rubbish. The size of the Giza pyramids has, since ancient times, been a marvel, and people have speculated on the numbers of labourers needed and their conditions. But whilst it would be an exaggeration to say that in organizational terms the pyramids that we see are only the tip of an iceberg, we nevertheless have to recognize that administratively the actual piling up of stones into pyramidal shape was only one of several major and pressing tasks. If we had some of the ancient texts they would document the devices by which the huge administrative needs were met. But even then we would be unlikely to have the full picture. Looking at the less spectacular aspects of the archaeology of Giza is essential for understanding the total scope of the necessary administration. The study of ancient texts reveals to us only one aspect of ancient administration, the technical devices by which it was accomplished. Archaeology supplies an equally important part of the picture. In this particular case it also provides us with an interesting problem of evidence: the archaeology of what is no longer there.

Bureaucracy in the ancient world was an instrument of prosperity of a kind that has surfaced in modern economic debates, revolving around the question: public works entailing massive state employment: are they a good thing? Modern debates mix economics and ideology inextricably, and involve a degree of abstract knowledge and an ability to manipulate economies that is unique to our day. Nevertheless, even if we reject public expenditure as a modern route to prosperity, we must recognize that part of the backcloth of history is the fact that the central direction of resources committed to massive labour-intensive projects was the great engine of growth, creating many of the world's civilizations. For the ancient Egyptians we can reconstruct the system in a quite specific way. We can see that huge numbers of people received a basic ration – a minimum wage – and a not insignificant number did better still. The number of jobs (with ration entitlement) was artificially inflated by an early work-sharing device: the phyle system in which a person performed his duties for only a limited part of each year. The land and its farmers were obliged by the pressure of demand dictated from above to produce enough. The state had already become the great provider and it produced whatever it is that we wish to call Egyptian civilization. Welfare (as yet innocent of social ideology) arrived early in human history.

5
Model communities

Bureaucracy, although characteristically concerned with minutiae, cumulatively deals with large sections of society and to some degree shapes it. Nowadays this tends to be done in deliberate pursuit of social goals, and to be part of the processes of 'planning' and 'social engineering'. The modern landscape universally bears witness to this in the size, nature and distribution of towns and villages, as well as in the appearance of individual buildings. We should also expect to find counterparts in the archaeological record of ancient states. Although the balance between what the natural environment and human stubbornness allowed and what government dictated was much more weighted towards the former in ancient times, nevertheless it was a balance. We err if we treat ancient societies as having been passively moulded by nature.

The creation of settlements imposes order on the natural environment. From the way in which any society – ancient or modern – goes about it so it leaves its stamp, its signature on the ground. It is this which archaeologists most frequently encounter. The record that they make is inevitably shaped in the visual language of ground plans – a symbolic language of its own – frequently incapable of resolution into the terms of the builders' original intentions. Even in well-documented societies such as that of ancient Egypt it remains extremely difficult to determine the specific purpose for which individual rooms and sometimes whole buildings were made. But still this remains the most widespread testimony of one particular facet of the creative element in society: its capacity to structure its own environment, and beyond this, its power to create visions of how human society should look. Where people live – shanty town or garden city – is a statement not only about their own circumstances but also about their society more generally. To see the shapes of towns, ancient and modern, as microcosms of society gives us the most consistent basis there is for comparing societies across space and time. For whereas the survival of written records owes much to chance, and for some societies may amount to nothing at all, archaeology has a good world-wide record for the recovery of plans and other material information about the places where communities once lived. Moreover, as soon as we admit that the evidence in a particular case points to a clear and consistent ideal, then we are tacitly admitting the existence of an ideology – not necessarily one that has been formally conceived and expressed, as in the case of Egyptian kingship, but an implicit ideology of social ordering.

Our starting-point has to be the physical record supplied by the plans of ancient sites, but before we look at the spread of early Egyptian evidence we have to confront the difficult question of architectural aesthetics. Modern architects initially create their buildings as drawings and models on a small scale. The hoped-for harmony of the end-product can be seen at a glance and discussed in comfort. We do not know if the Egyptians, even when considering large temples, ever did more than make working sketches for use on the spot (Figure 67). What is likely to have been common is that planning and discussion were done directly on site at full scale. Ropes and pegs and simple sighting instruments took the place of scribal equipment, whilst the ground served instead of the papyrus sheet.[1] It may have been more laborious, but supply of labour was never a problem. The plan that first became really visible was the pattern of foundations in the ground.

In the process three elements came together. The first was the likely system of measuring over long distances, using a rope knotted at set intervals, as was used in land survey. When the ground was relatively flat and the buildings were intended to be rectangular a certain frequency of measurements tended to recur. The second element was the range of functions that each building was to house, expressed on the ground by a pattern of partition walls to create rooms and corridors. It was normal at this stage not to mark the positions of doorways. The third element was the natural sense of proportion and harmony which all of us have and use, for example, in arranging furniture in our living-rooms. The result was often a plan that looks as though it were the result of a much greater degree of premeditated planning based on a mathematical knowledge of the harmonies of natural proportion than was actually the case.[2]

Early town layouts and the 'village horizon'

For serious study all subjects require a system of classification. The study of towns is somewhat hampered in the English language by ambiguity in the common words available. The Latin *urbs* has given us the adjective 'urban' and the abstract noun 'urbanization' but not a concrete noun for the larger places where people live. Instead we use 'town' and 'city', somewhat arbitrarily distinguished. The ancient Egyptians, too, had a pair of words that are conventionally translated as 'town' and 'city' but their usage, too, offers a poor guide to drawing distinctions. I make this point because in absolute terms places that, in the earlier periods, functioned as towns could in actual size be more akin to what we would see as villages, whilst the leading administrative 'capital' of a province might not be much larger. This does not mean that ancient Egypt was under-urbanized. Rather it exemplifies the generally more modest scale of Egyptian society compared with what is normal experience in much of the present world, a scale commensurate with the modest size of the population. Archaeologists tend to fall back upon the neutral term 'settlement', but this often does not feel right when one is thinking of a place that, whilst it might have been quite small, was nevertheless the centre of local life and administration.

During the Old Kingdom (and sometimes before that) at many places towns came into existence. Commonly they were surrounded by a thick high brick wall, sometimes following a curving course, sometimes built in straight sections. The lack of conformity in what must have been the town's major building work – its enclosure wall – implies that they represent local initiatives rather than the result of royal decrees and central direction,

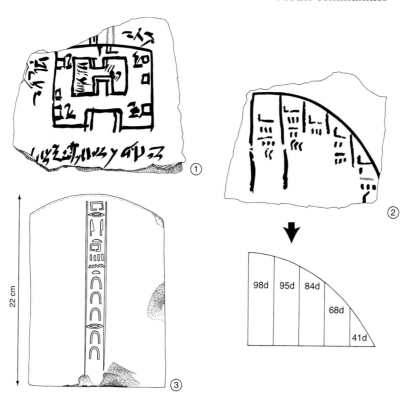

Figure 67   Practical scribal aids to building: (1) A quick sketch with overall dimensions may have
been all that was necessary to start the builders off, marking out the ground and digging the foundations. In this case the sketch is on a piece of broken pottery, and dates to the late 18th or early
19th Dynasty. Brief annotations, including measurements, are written in hieratic. The building was
evidently a way-station open at each end, containing an inner chamber also open at both ends, and
surrounded by a colonnade. The outside measurements were 27 cubits (about 14 m) each way; the
inner shrine was to be 14 by 6 cubits. Six columns are shown at the sides (labelled 'column' against
four of them), but this may not have been the exact number intended. Details were probably worked
out on the stonework as the building proceeded. Width 9.5 cm. British Museum 41228, from Deir
el-Bahari, after S.R.K. Glanville, *JEA* 16 (1930), 237–9. (2) A diagram sketched on a flake of limestone showing how to draw an even curve. At regular intervals (of one cubit each, though this is not
stated explicitly) one should draw a perpendicular line of a stated length. The lengths are given in
the cubit notation (here reduced for convenience to digits). When the points at the ends of the lines
are joined a curve is produced. From Sakkara, perhaps 3rd Dynasty and used in the building of the
curved top to the Southern Tomb of the Step Pyramid. Width 17.8 cm. Egyptian Museum, Cairo
JdE 50036. After S. Clarke and R. Engelbach, *Ancient Egyptian masonry*, Oxford, 1930, 52–3, Figs 53,
54. (3) Limestone tablet from Kahun, perhaps used to mark out the position of an intended group
of houses. The inscription reads something like: 'A four-house block – 30 x 20 (cubits)', i.e. about
15 x 10 m. After G.A. Wainwright, *ASAE* 25 (1925), 144–5, and plate; also H.G. Fischer, *CdE* 55,
no. 109–10 (1980), 13–16. Also C. Rossi, *Architecture and mathematics in ancient Egypt*, Cambridge, 2004,
101–22.

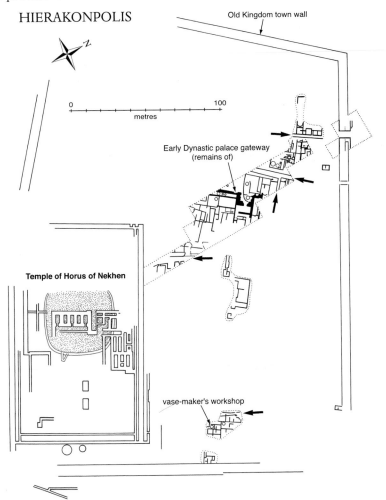

Figure 68 Urban layout with a degree of regularity dictated by a town wall: the Old Kingdom town of Hierakonpolis (see Figures 25, p. 80, 26, p. 82 and 41, p. 122). The arrows point to probable streets. After J.E. Quibell and F.W. Green, *Hierakonpolis* II, London, 1902, Pl. LXXIII; W. Fairservis, K.R. Weeks and M. Hoffman, *JARCE* 9 (1971–2), Figs 3, 9–15.

but whether true or not, perimeter walls played a significant part in shaping the internal layouts of individual towns. Buildings close to the town wall tended to align themselves by it, perhaps actually using it to prop up the whole structure. The alignment of adjacent streets could be similarly influenced. If the town wall were built as a series of straight sections then the interior would tend naturally to contain a degree of internal regularity. The clearest early example is Hierakonpolis (Figure 68).[3] The Old Kingdom wall enclosed an irregular area, but by means of a series of straight lengths. A broad diagonal swathe of the town has been excavated, together with a few isolated patches. Within these exposures we can see an obvious tendency for walls and the narrow streets to follow similar directions for some distances. At the south end the direction is set by the southern stretch of the enclosure wall. In the central area, however, it was set by an existing but by then ruined wall of an earlier palace (Figure 26, p. 82), which seems also to have been matched by the northern stretch of town wall. Similar house alignments taken from the nearest length of town wall can still be seen in exposed parts of the Old Kingdom/Middle Kingdom towns at Tell Edfu and Abydos.[4] Town walls require a judgement of how large the town will be. In these examples there is also an implication of prior site clearance that allowed the new houses to reflect the new wall alignments. This in turn points to a measure of local control or mutual agreement sufficient to bring about the remodelling of the whole community. At Hierakonpolis, as far as one can tell, the size of the future town was correctly assessed. At Tell Edfu (and at Elephantine, see below) the expansion that subsequently took place required the walling of additional adjacent areas.

The most thoroughly studied early town is Elephantine, the object of regular major excavations since 1969 (Figure 69). Allowance has to be made for Elephantine having been a frontier town and therefore requiring an additional measure of protection, even to supporting a garrison, yet it is possible still to interpret its history as an interaction between royal initiatives and local community interests.[5] A village had developed on the island in the Predynastic Period (in the Nagada IIc/d phase). In dynastic times it grew into a small walled town, its irregular shape reflecting the underlying granite island. The small exposures of the interior made by excavation reveal narrow irregular streets and buildings that were, for the most part, little more than huts, although a more substantial central building developed in the later Old Kingdom, tentatively identified as the residence or 'palace' of a senior official. Also in the Early Dynastic Period a more regular walled enclosure provided with rounded towers was inserted into the north-eastern corner. It has been interpreted as a fortress built under royal control, although again its interior has a strongly village-like character (rather like the interior of the Hierakonpolis palace compound, Figure 26, p. 82). One consequence of this intrusion was the confinement of the early temple to a marginal location in the town plan (compare Figure 39, p. 117). As discussed earlier (pp. 118–21), the temple itself is a fine exemplar of community religion, very occasionally made the object of royal patronage.

From a little later, some of the varied aspects of life at Elephantine are captured by one excavated neighbourhood of the Middle Kingdom defined by the buildings along a single street (Figure 70).[6] In even later centuries Elephantine came to be dominated by a colossal temple to the creator god Khnum, personified by a ram. Probings beneath the foundations have so far failed to find an Old Kingdom/Middle Kingdom predecessor, implying that, if it existed, it must have been small. The largest shrine of the Middle Kingdom found so far at Elephantine was built (or rebuilt) at the beginning of the 12th Dynasty by the local ruling family (its founder named Sarenput). It honoured not a conventional deity but a local 'saint', a governor called Hekaib who had lived in the 6th Dynasty and had been buried in the desert cemetery on the west bank of the Nile. Over the next three centuries (into the 13th Dynasty) members of the Sarenput family and others, including kings, added their own statues and tiny shrines, to create a saintly collective. Texts speak of Hekaib as a god who could benefit those who served him. Along the street facing it lay houses, what was apparently another shrine to an official named Sebekemsaf, and eventually a building perhaps with a corner tower which, to judge from the many storage units and from the finding of hundreds of mud seal impressions, was an administrative building from where

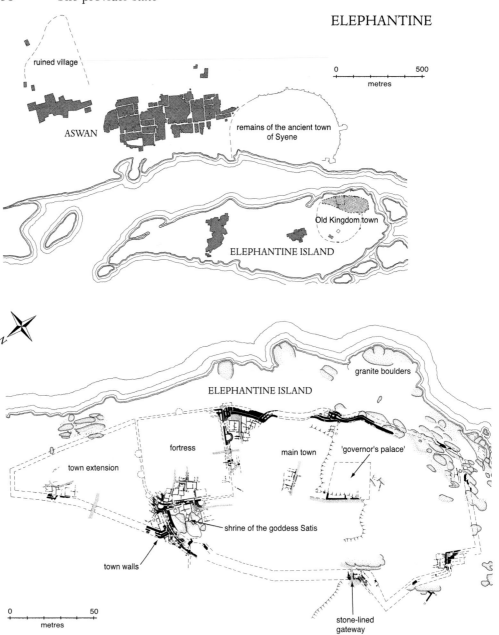

Figure 69 *Below.* The town and fortress at Elephantine, Early Dynastic Period and Old Kingdom. After W. Kaiser *et al.*, *MDAIK* 55 (1999), 234, Abb. 55. *Above.* Comparisons of settlement size over time at Elephantine and Aswan. The 'modern' settlements are those of 1798, see *Description de l'Égypte, Antiquités* 1, Pl. 31; see H. Jaritz, *MDAIK* 43 (1987), 68, Fig. 1; C. von Pilgrim, K.-C. Bruhn and A. Kelany, *MDAIK* 60 (2004), 119–48; also Bard, *Encyclopedia* (entries on Aswan and Elephantine, by E. Seidlmeyer and W. Kaiser).

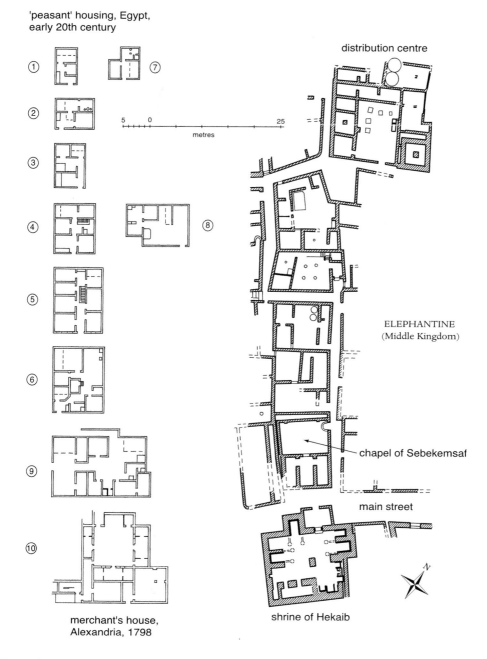

'peasant' housing, Egypt,
early 20th century

distribution centre

ELEPHANTINE
(Middle Kingdom)

chapel of Sebekemsaf

main street

shrine of Hekaib

merchant's house,
Alexandria, 1798

Figure 70 *Right*. A street in the town of Elephantine in the Middle Kingdom. Note how the shrine of Hekaib (a long-dead governor and now the local saint) blends with its surroundings. After *Elephantine; the ancient town. The official guidebook of the German Institute of Archaeology*, Cairo, 1998, 45, Abb. 9; see W. Kaiser *et al.*, *MDAIK* 55 (1999), 234, Abb. 56. *Left*. A series of plans of houses of peasants, from the landless – (1), (2) and (7) – to the prosperous (9), recorded in Egypt in the early part of the twentieth century AD, after J. Lozach and G. Hug, *L'Habitat rural en Égypte*, Cairo, 1930, 124–34. The merchant's house in Alexandria, *c.* 1798 AD, is from the *Description de l'Égypte, État moderne*, II. Pl. 91.6. All parts of Figure 70 are to the same scale.

rations were distributed. The homogeneity and human scale of the whole neighbourhood is notable. No part seeks to dominate.

Elephantine helps to define the scale and character of Egyptian society in its earlier phases. Alongside the detailed map of early Elephantine (Figure 69) I have inset at a smaller scale a map of the area that also shows the approximate outlines of settlements at two later periods. One is the Late Roman (Byzantine) and the other the early modern (specifically as mapped by Napoleon's expedition in 1798). After the Old Kingdom Elephantine continued to grow until it occupied about three times its former area, but a twin town on the east bank also began to develop in or after the New Kingdom. Under the name Syene (Aswan), it was to overshadow its predecessor. Eventually it reached about six times the area of the Old Kingdom original. The area of settlement recorded in 1798 AD is a little larger still even though it is generally thought that, at this time, Egypt's fortunes were at a low ebb. On Elephantine itself the twin modern villages roughly equal the size of the Old Kingdom town, yet the present state of knowledge provides no grounds for thinking that there was a town on the east bank in the Old Kingdom. The population seems to have lived primarily on the island. When island and mainland are taken together, there is thus an even bigger difference between the area of settlement of the Old Kingdom and that of early modern times. This is a commonplace observation for Egypt generally. Places of ancient settlement that we are entitled to call towns were often small even when compared to the villages of the early modern landscape, let alone modern towns. Why should this be so?

One direction in which to look is the size of houses and how far they might differ between those of the poor and the rich across the various periods. As a point of comparison I have added to Figure 70 specimen plans of houses of peasants from Egypt of the early twentieth century AD and a late eighteenth-century merchant's house. The comparison, though somewhat superficially based, does not suggest that the explanation lies here; for there is a rough comparability. I can only assume that the disparity in settlement size primarily reflects the overall size of Egypt's population in a landscape containing a roughly similar number of settlements. It is estimated that between the Old Kingdom and Roman times the population grew from just over one million to perhaps just under five, though the estimate for 1798 AD is around four.[7] This approximates to the order of magnitude by which the settlement sizes differ.

At the time of writing Egypt's population has grown to around seventy million. Although popular journalism emphasizes the 'timeless' quality of the present rural landscape of Egypt, it cannot be a good guide to what it was like in Pharaonic times generally, and more especially in the Old Kingdom. The valley landscape, richer in wildlife and far more lushly vegetated, would have seemed oddly deserted and lacking in mechanical noise by comparison with today. And although we are right to talk about 'urbanization' and to see towns as the normal home for a large proportion of ancient Egyptians, those towns, even when walled, were actually smaller in scale than many villages of modern Egypt. For a long time the Egyptian perception of what a town should look like was determined by a 'village horizon' which did not embrace significant 'public' architecture. An appreciation of urban grandeur developed slowly. The best-preserved city from Pharaonic Egypt, El-Amarna of the 18th Dynasty, lies only part way along that perceptual journey.

Societies do not necessarily maintain uniformity of scale across the built environment, however. Many that occupy an 'early' position on the timelines of archaeology proved able to direct a degree of organization and skill towards 'monuments' that seems, with hindsight, to be markedly out of proportion to the scale of their general way of life. The megalithic monuments of Europe and Malta, the statues of Easter Island, the large sculptured blocks and statues of the Anatolian society of Köbekli which was still at a hunter-gatherer stage, all are examples of a striving towards an exaggerated scale for the sacred which was not a measure for the rest of life.[8] So, too, for Egypt of the Early Dynastic Period and Old Kingdom, where the direction of extra effort was towards tombs, including pyramids, and the statues of kings and nobles which were often placed within them. Cemeteries, including that for Elephantine, seem to have absorbed more of the community's labour and ambition for social display than either the houses or shrines in their towns.

The later Old Kingdom also supplies an example of a new town built on virgin ground, in the Dakhla Oasis at the site of 'Ain Asil (Figure 71). This is the kind of circumstance where one most expects to see demonstrated the organizing powers of the state. At its centre was a well built mud-brick fortified town, its nucleus roughly 170 metres square and surrounded by a stout wall reinforced by semi-circular towers which also flanked one of the entrances.[9] Two later enclosures added to the sides almost doubled its area. There was, in addition, a population dispersed over the surrounding territory,[10] and the whole development was under the control of a line of 'governors of the oasis', who bore purely Egyptian names. They were buried in a cemetery about a kilometre from the town, beneath large mud-brick tombs provided with chapels and accompanied by fine grave-goods. As is known from places in the Nile valley (Hekaib on Elephantine is a good example), the cult of these deceased governors also had a prominent place in the local town itself. A group of excavated chapels to house their cult is so far the only representative of religious architecture identified inside the town. The size of the tombs and prominence of these chapels exemplify the priority that Egyptians at this time gave to buildings which marked social status through personal statue cults. The way of life of this colony, to judge from the architecture of town and cemetery, the pottery and other artefacts found, and the administrative framework that is visible from texts, seems to have been wholly Egyptian. There has to be a strong presumption that the governors, and perhaps many of the inhabitants, had in the beginning been sent out, or had volunteered to go out, from a home base in the Nile valley. The sense of exile was in this case not strong enough for them to seek repatriation and burial in Egypt proper.

Such of the order that we see in these early towns is likely to have arisen from immediate convenience, and it is misleading to apply to it the term 'planning'. It differs from the products of true urban planning in several ways. The latter tend to pursue predetermined alignments that ignore topography, to maintain common alignments over very long distances, and to display repeated modular building units, and signs of planning involvement in the internal layouts of buildings. The great uncertainty over who was responsible for initiatives in provincial town developments fogs the question of how far the Old Kingdom state had an interest in urban layout in the provinces. Fortunately there is another set of examples that does provide an answer of a kind.

Pyramid towns in the Old Kingdom

Organized life at pyramid sites did not end with the completion of the stone buildings and burial of the king. From Old Kingdom written sources we know of the existence of

AIN ASIL (DAKHLA OASIS)

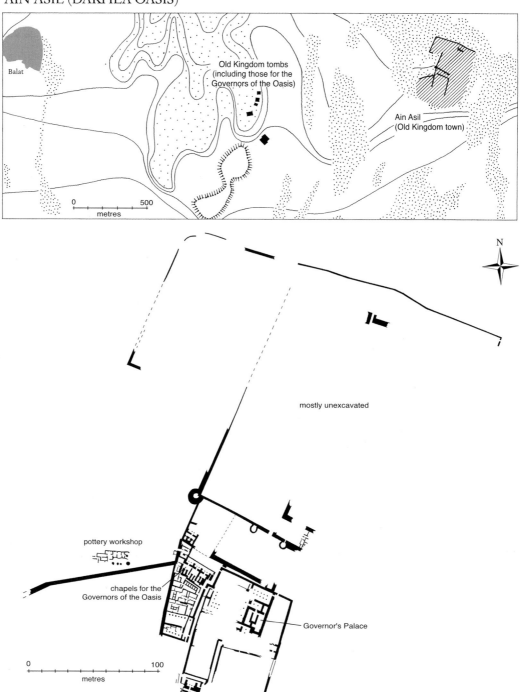

Balat

Old Kingdom tombs
(including those for the
Governors of the Oasis)

Ain Asil
(Old Kingdom town)

0   500
metres

N

mostly unexcavated

pottery workshop

chapels for the
Governors of the Oasis

Governor's Palace

0   100
metres

chapel of
Medu-nefer

'pyramid towns', looked after by a hierarchy of officials.[11] Altogether some forty-two different titles of officials have been recorded, though many are rare. Where these titles can be ranked, they tend to be headed by a senior priest, or by a 'director of the town'. The Neferirkara archive examined in the last chapter fills in the detail of how they were run. How were they represented on the ground?

The Neferirkara archive introduces us to a community busying itself in detailed daily bookkeeping exercises at one of the pyramids at Abusir. This is a good place to start looking. The most obvious traces of antiquity at Abusir were excavated first by a German expedition between 1902 and 1908 (Figure 72).[12] There had been, as usual, a mortuary temple built against the eastern face of the pyramid. It had consisted of the normal grouping of cult chambers, storerooms, colonnaded forecourt and entrance from the access causeway. It was a building finished cheaply, the forecourt and most of the storerooms being in brick with wooden columns. One unusual feature came to be added when the causeway was rerouted to serve the adjoining pyramid of King Neuserra: a formal columned entrance portico. This alteration coincided with the building of an inner enclosure wall of mud brick. The spaces between this wall and the stonework of the temple were filled with mud-brick buildings. Some of them appear to be houses. We can have little doubt that they belonged to the official community of priests and others looking after King Neferirkara's mortuary cult. We can recognize from the plan probably no more than nine separate 'houses'. They must be where the scribes and priests and others on duty – the serving phyle – resided whilst doing all the tasks so meticulously recorded in the papyri. As an example of a model community it falls into the 'out of sight, out of mind' category. The sole element of order was provided by the enclosure wall that fitted in with the pyramid's monumental exterior, and hid from the outside world the huddle of houses on the inside.

This 'town' could have accommodated only a small community, fewer, one would guess, than those who appear in the lists of the Neferirkara archive. Yet it must be remembered that temple personnel put in a month's work only periodically. The permanent homes of these people may have been elsewhere. Where we lack direct evidence altogether is in whether their permanent homes were in nearby villages that had grown up piecemeal, or whether the state had provided a complete planned town for them all, now situated beneath the fields.

The same site also dramatizes a problem faced by all states that foster grandiose building, namely, maintenance. By the end of the Old Kingdom Egypt possessed more than twenty pyramids with their associated temples, constructed with varying degrees of solidity (and not all of them finished). The Neferirkara temple was one of the less well-built examples. During the lifetime of its 'town' roofs became dangerous and the wooden columns weakened, no doubt from the attacks of termites that quickly turn their attentions to woodwork in desert locations. The priests' response (Figure 72.2) was to shore up the threatened

Figure 71 A late Old Kingdom colonial town: at ʿAin Asil, in the Dakhla Oasis. The map shows the relationship between the ancient town and its separately lying cemetery, some of the tombs containing rich burials. Balat is the nearest modern town. A more detailed plan of the excavated parts of the ancient town is given below. After A. Minault-Gout and P. Deleuze, *Balat II. Le mastaba d'Ima-Pépi. Tombeau d'un Gouverneur de l'Oasis à la fin de l'Ancien Empire*, Cairo, 1992, 8, Fig. 2 (map); M. Ziermann and C. Eder, *MDAIK* 57 (2001), 310, Abb. 1 (plan).

ABUSIR

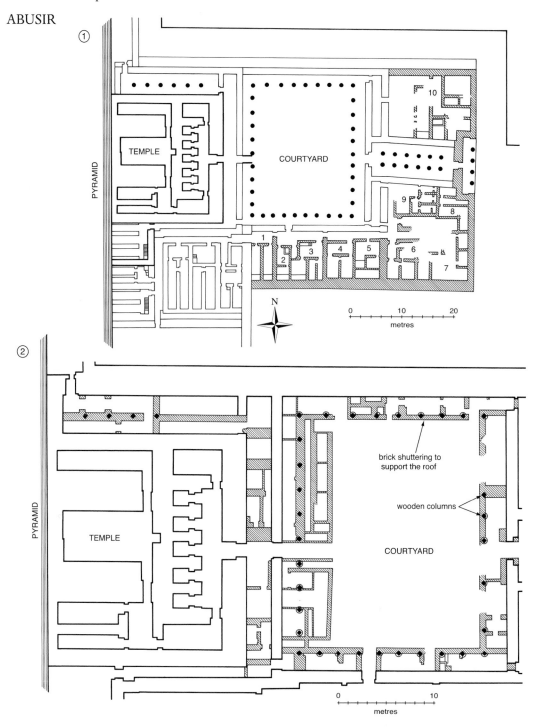

parts with brick walls and shuttering. It badly disfigured the building, completely obliterating the colonnade around the forecourt, but it presumably achieved its purpose.

From this, and from the even more cavalier treatment of Menkaura's Valley Temple by its priestly community to be described shortly, we may deduce that there was no general policy towards, or means of funding, the maintenance of the stock of historic buildings. At any one time a significant proportion of them would be derelict or shabby. We sometimes read of kings piously restoring particular temples, whilst Rameses II's eldest son, the priest Khaemwese, even took an interest in restoring a few of the ancient pyramid sites.[13] But this was a piecemeal process that cannot have kept pace with the decay. The principal improvement came with the New Kingdom, when a general policy was followed of replacing old temples in the towns with new ones of stone. But still the unequal fight against time did not go unnoticed. A poet of the period wrote, with respect to the tombs of famous wise men remembered for their teachings:

> Their portals and mansions have crumbled,
> Their mortuary-priests have vanished;
> Their tombstones are covered with dirt,
> Their graves are forgotten.
> Yet their name is pronounced over their books,
> Which they composed whilst they had being.[14]

Returning to the Old Kingdom pyramid towns: by the time of the 5th Dynasty pyramids at Abusir the peak of monumentality in pyramid building had already passed. Can we find more substantial traces at Giza?

The one part of the Giza necropolis where evidence for pyramid communities other than work camps has been found by excavation lies to the east of the third pyramid, of King Menkaura of the 4th Dynasty, towards the foot of the low desert plateau, where the cultivation begins to lap against it. As excavated, two separate parts seem to be involved, the one built into and around the Valley Temple of Menkaura's pyramid, the other adjoining the large tomb of Queen Khentkawes, one of the major figures of the 4th Dynasty. We will examine this latter one first (Figure 73).[15] The tomb of Queen Khentkawes was fashioned around a sculpted cube of rock, which provided a free-standing, rectangular podium. This had been raised higher by means of a large masonry construction. Near the south-west corner lay the pit for a wooden funerary boat. The mortuary temple had been cut into the eastern face of the rock podium. From in front of the entrance to the mortuary temple there extended a long narrow mud-brick compound, 150 metres from west to east. Along its south side ran a double street, and on the north a single one. A 2.5-metre-thick girdle

Figure 72 The decay of a monument and the archaeology of maintenance: the mortuary temple at the pyramid of King Neferirkara of the 5th Dynasty at Abusir. (1) Thicker lines of the temple represent stonework; the rest was built in brick. The hatched portion represents the pyramid 'town' built following the completion of the monument. Buildings 1 to 9 are presumably houses; the function of no. 10 is uncertain. (2) The same mortuary temple, a generation or more later. The hatched portions are brick supports and shutterings built by the priests to keep up the roof of the colonnade around the forecourt, and the roofs of the eastern and northern corridors of the temple. The columns had been of wood, and there was evidently a danger of the whole front of the temple collapsing. The extra shelter provided by the support walls was utilized where convenient for cooking-fires. After L. Borchardt, *Das Grabdenkmal des Königs Nefer-ir-ke-re'*, Leipzig, 1909, 56, Abb. 63, Bl. 10.

GIZA – tomb of Queen Khentkawes

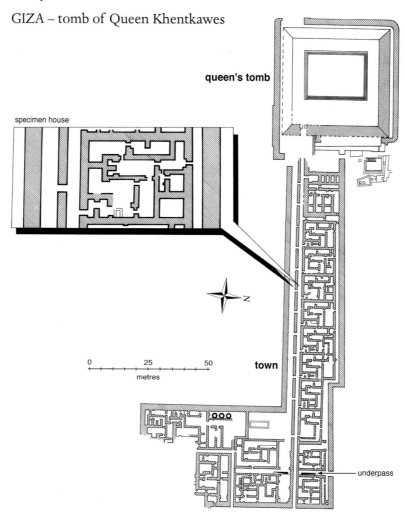

Figure 73 Early urban planning: the town intended to house the community supporting the cult of the deceased Queen Khentkawes at Giza, 4th Dynasty (see Figure 65A–B, p. 186, for location). After S. Hassan, *Excavations at Giza* IV *(1932–33)*, Cairo, 1943, Fig. 1.

wall marked the boundaries on these sides. To the east, an annexe ran southwards, measuring 80 by 40 metres, giving to the whole complex an L-shaped plan. Several entrances are visible in the girdle walls. The street running south passed actually beneath the main east–west street by means of a tunnel using a staircase on the north and a ramp on the south. The long northern wing contains a row of eleven separate buildings, most of which are probably houses. In several cases the same plan is repeated with minor modifications, perhaps brought about by changes introduced by occupants. In the centre are six such unit houses of similar plan, each measuring 12 by 15 metres. The house plans show a certain resemblance to those at other sites of the Old Kingdom as well as of the Middle Kingdom.

Within the interlocking rectangular rooms convenience of access seems often to be subordinated to privacy or security, leading to the use of corridors, anterooms and numerous turns, creating a minor labyrinth. In most of the houses a central room can be identified, which gives access usually to three other rooms. No signs existed that any of the roofs had been supported on columns. In two houses there were circular grain bins: a single one in the third house from the west; four in the sixth house from the west. The central room at the back (or south) served as the kitchen, determined by the presence of ovens and ashes.

The southern wing of the Khentkawes settlement contains at least four separate buildings that might have been for residence or administration. On the north side of an open space in the middle lay a group of four circular grain silos. This space was reached by means of a staircase on the west, reflecting the slope down from the desert. To the north of this court lay another, containing only a rectangular basin cut into the rock. Further excavation in the south and south-east of the town was prevented by the existence of a modern cemetery, but deep soundings revealed the presence of brick walls over a considerable area, but at depths of up to 6 metres below the modern ground level.

The reason for the L-shaped plan is not really clear, although it must be remembered that, according to the reconstruction of the overall ancient layout of the Giza plateau discussed in the last chapter, the quays and basins of the reception zone for building materials probably lay close by and provided a limit to eastward building. But the effect was to bring the southern extension almost into contact with another related and quite remarkable site: the Valley Temple of King Menkaura (Figure 74).[16] Menkaura's architects had planned that both his mortuary temple and his valley temple would be built in the prevailing megalithic tradition. The king probably died prematurely, however, and the building was completed in mud brick. At the pyramid temple itself up on the plateau, no trace has been found beside the pyramid of an accompanying settlement like that at Abusir, although the surrounding area has not been cleared to any great extent. We know that the mortuary temple was still in use late in the Old Kingdom from fragments of two inscriptions, probably decrees, bearing the name of King Merenra of the 6th Dynasty.

The Valley Temple had been completed in mud brick, and included a central courtyard surrounded by a wall decorated with niches in the panelled palace-façade style (Figure 74, Stage I). Outside the original front a formal addition in brick was made, which turned the entrance to the north, towards the space separating it from the town of Queen Khentkawes. It also faced a brick-paved roadway running in from the east. An entrance with two-columned portico led to a four-columned vestibule. This led in turn to a court crossed diagonally by a path of limestone slabs originally running into the Valley Temple building of Menkaura. Further corridors and spaces were laid out beyond, to the south. But over this area small dwellings were built, in places on accumulations of rubbish. Towards the south of these dwellings lay circular brick silos for storing grain.

Subsequent to the completion in brick of the Valley Temple proper, houses began to spread within the main courtyard. Circular granaries were constructed in some numbers, clustering towards the north side of the original court. From this point onwards most of the temple except for the sanctuary was allowed to decay. In places it was actually demolished to make further room for the expanding settlement, which gradually buried the lower parts of the temple. The plan shows walls constructed over the filled-in ruins, particularly on the south and south-west sides, where houses mounted the old enclosure wall. The excavators also found a good deal of temple equipment still in the original storerooms, buried

GIZA – Valley Temple of Menkaura

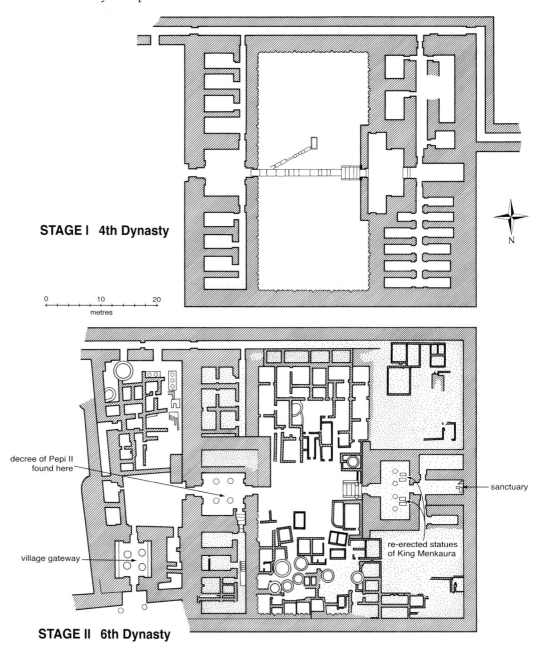

STAGE I   4th Dynasty

0   10   20
metres

decree of Pepi II
found here

sanctuary

re-erected statues
of King Menkaura

village gateway

STAGE II   6th Dynasty

in the dust and rubble. In this category were the 'slate' triads of the king and other figures which represent some of the finest work of Old Kingdom sculptors. The process of decay had been hastened by a flood from a sudden storm which had broken into the rear of the building. An attempt at renovation followed, but only on top of the debris. This recognized the existence of the settlement, and surrounded it with a new wall. A new gatehouse and sanctuary were also built over the sites of the old ones. Anyone approaching the sanctuary, therefore, still had to walk from the gatehouse between two groups of huts and silos.

The new sanctuary had a vestibule with four columns. These had been of wood on limestone bases. On the mud floor, four beautiful life-sized statues of Menkaura were set up, two on each side of the door to the inner chambers. The offering-place of the rebuilt sanctuary was found more or less intact. It consisted of an altar about 50 centimetres high, made from a worn slab of alabaster resting on two rough upright stones. A crude libation basin stood beside it. Nearby lay four unfinished diorite statuettes of the king, lying on their side. They may have actually stood on the altar and been the object of the offering-cult in this last phase of the temple's existence.

The date and circumstances of this rough-and-ready cult being carried on in a dingy chamber at the back of a tightly packed mud village (within a girdle wall and gateway which made it virtually into a fortified village) are clear from two sources. One is the associated archaeological material, which seems not to extend beyond the end of the Old Kingdom. The other is a decree of King Pepi II of the 6th Dynasty, found in the floor debris of the inner gateway. The text of the decree exempts the pyramid town from certain obligations, and appoints an official to it. It demonstrates that this site was officially regarded as part of the pyramid town at a date very close to the end of the Old Kingdom. After this time the site appears to have been abandoned and the cult of King Menkaura to have ceased entirely.

The whole history of this settlement reveals how great could be the gap between intention and practice, between the products of superlative craftsmanship and the way they were treated, and between the inner world of bureaucratic order and the rough reality outside. This was an application of the 'out of sight, out of mind' philosophy with a vengeance. The Khentkawes part seems to have remained free from this muddle, but the reason is probably that it was occupied for only a fairly short time.

Menkaura was not an unusual case. The Valley Temple of King Sneferu of the 4th Dynasty at Dahshur provides a further illustration (Figure 75).[17] Here we see the remains of a limestone temple with finely carved reliefs (including the personified offering-bearers of Figure 59, p. 00). It stood within a rectangular enclosure defined by a mud-brick wall, leaving a space on the south side of the temple, 15 by 48 metres. This was filled up with

Figure 74 The 'villagization' of a monument: the Valley Temple of the Pyramid of King Menkaura (Mycerinus) at Giza (see Figure 65, p. 186, for location). *Above*. Plan of the temple as finished after Menkaura's death (*c*. 2503 BC). Note the palace-façade decoration of the sides of the main court. The whole is a good example of formal, monumental architecture in mud brick. *Below*. The same building about three centuries later, in the time of King Pepi II. The royal decree on a stone tablet found in the entrance hall shows that the building was still the officially designated pyramid-town of Menkaura. As time had passed the priestly community had moved in and built its houses and granaries (the circular constructions) partly inside and partly on top of the remains of the temple. Its thick enclosure wall and twin massive gates made it, in effect, a fortified village. After G.A. Reisner, *Mycerinus*, Cambridge, Mass., 1931, Chapter III, Pls VIII, IX.

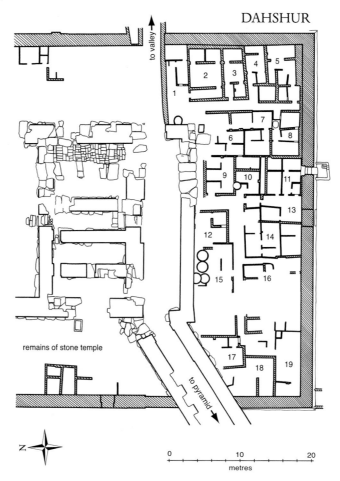

Figure 75 The Old Kingdom mortuary-cult 'town' attached to the Valley Temple of King Sneferu at Dahshur (see the reliefs, Figure 59, p. 167). Nos. 1–11, 13, 14 and 16 are probably houses, no. 15 contains a set of four granaries. After A. Fakhry, *The monuments of Sneferu at Dahshur* II.1, Cairo, 1961, Fig. 4.

the houses of the serving community, so creating another pyramid 'town'. Altogether some fifteen houses seem to have been present, offering accommodation for perhaps a hundred people if they were occupied by families.[18]

Bureaucracy begins by imposing order on defined areas of activity. The scope of control can grow, however, and become the prime factor in a community's existence. If this is harnessed to a tradition of architectural planning, the 'model town' comes into being. The available evidence suggests that in the Old Kingdom this connection was still in its infancy. Two ingredients were there in the form of the planned royal cemetery and the creation of new towns, particularly at the pyramids themselves. A kind of half-way stage is represented at the Giza work camps by the provision of the all-purpose corridor blocks which could be used as workshops or have houses fitted inside (Figure 66, p. 189); but these are set within a larger town whose individual buildings have arisen through innumerable piecemeal decisions. The Old Kingdom pyramid towns that were intended to be permanent – classic examples of communities deliberately planted by the state – reveal that the potential for careful planning was realized to only a limited degree, exemplified in the surviving evidence only by the town of Queen Khentkawes which turned out to have a short life. It was left to the Middle Kingdom to achieve integration.

Planning at its height: the Middle Kingdom town of Kahun

The name 'Kahun' was given in 1889 by Flinders Petrie to a large Middle Kingdom settlement in the vicinity of the modern town of El-Lahun, which stands close to the entrance to the Fayum depression (Figure 76).[19] It lies on the rising edge of the desert, and part has been lost to the lateral spreading of the cultivation since ancient times. The nature and purpose of the town are evident from its context. Beside it lay a temple, reduced to a slight ruin even by Petrie's day, and this, to judge from its position, was the Valley Temple to the pyramid of King Senusret II that stands just over a kilometre to the west. The town, following the same orientation as the pyramid, is clearly an unusually large example of a 'pyramid town', housing the priests and lay personnel responsible for the perpetual cult of the deceased king. Papyri found in the town confirm this, for they include part of the administrative archive of the mortuary cult. They also give us the ancient name of the town: Hetep-Senusret ('King Senusret is at peace'; in other contexts it appears to be called Sekhem-Senusret, 'King Senusret is strong').

The size of Kahun is, however, far greater than that of other known pyramid towns, although it has to be admitted that the basis for comparison is small. But on the general scale of ancient urbanism, too, Kahun stands out as an important town in its own right. Its functions may therefore have gone much further than simply housing the workmen who built the pyramid, and the priests and others who kept up the cult of the dead King Senusret II. A good many administrative papyri have come from Kahun, belonging to two main groups, each representing quite separate archives with noticeably few points of contact.[20] Only in part is this because they date from different periods within the Middle Kingdom. Much more is it because they reflect two different areas of organized life. One group, already mentioned, derives from the temple of the royal cult and is concerned with temple organization and temple personnel; the other comes from within the town and covers the life and business of a broader community involved not only with the priestly foundation but also with many unconnected areas of interest. A few documents actually deal with work located outside Kahun altogether, on a construction project of King Amenemhat III, possibly part of his own pyramid complex. The dragging of stone by gangs of men is the subject of several papyri, as is the farming and measuring of land belonging to the priests and to the temple estates. Whether Kahun also contained people who followed their own agricultural pursuits is not known. But perhaps we are starting to think along the wrong lines. A pyramid town of full urban dimensions and with a total inner administrative dependency may have been designed to match the king's ambitions rather than local economic needs.

The town was roughly square, its sides measuring 384 metres on the north and 335 metres on the west (12.86 hectares). The ground slopes gradually from the south-east

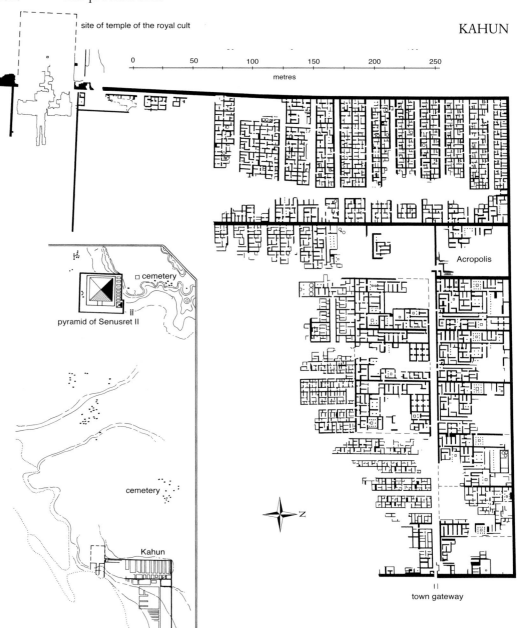

site of temple of the royal cult

KAHUN

cemetery

pyramid of Senusret II

Acropolis

cemetery

Kahun

town gateway

Figure 76   The type-site for orthogonal town planning in ancient Egypt: the Middle Kingdom town of Kahun, attached to the pyramid of Senusret II. After W.M.F. Petrie, *Illahun, Kahun and Gurob*, London, 1891, Pl. XIV; W.M.F. Petrie, G. Brunton and M.A. Murray, *Lahun* II, London, 1923, Pls II, XXXIII, XXXVIA.

corner up towards the north-west corner, the highest point being the so-called 'Acropolis'. A thick wall divides the main part of the town from a separate strip on the west. The reason for this division is not known. The surrounding walls show no trace of fortification. Only one gateway is preserved, that towards the north-east, measuring about two metres across. An isolated room just inside the gate may have housed a watchman, but no extra protection at the gateway is visible.

Within the walls the town displays a grid-iron or orthogonal plan which the builders adhered to far more strictly than had been the case with the Giza work camp. The north side of the main east–west street is subdivided into seven principal units, with three more on the south side. The westernmost stood on a natural eminence of rock that had been sculpted to form a platform with vertical sides rising above the town on east and south. Petrie called this the 'Acropolis'. The scant traces of walls on the summit imply that it was not dissimilar to the other large units. It was reached, however, by an impressive staircase cut into the rock. The other units seem to have been large houses (Figure 77). Most of them measured 42 by 60 metres.

As is usual with Egyptian buildings the focus of interest for these large houses is almost exclusively the interior. To judge from the plan, the exterior seems to have been a continuous blank façade of brickwork broken only by the door spaces. This would have created a stark effect if left entirely devoid of decoration of any kind. Fortunately, we have another source of evidence for what large Middle Kingdom houses actually looked like. These are more or less contemporary wooden models of houses buried in tombs, and particularly the ones from the tomb of Meketra at Thebes, which date to the early 12th Dynasty and provided the baking/brewing model illustrated in the last chapter (Figure 61.2, p. 173).[21] The outside of the two models of Meketra's house (Figure 77), as well as the inside wall facing the garden, has three rectangular panels. The central panel contains the main entrance to the house. It has two pivoting door-leaves, braced with horizontal struts, and secured by a central bolt. Above it is an ornate design based on the *djed*-hieroglyph, a simplified tree-trunk, used in the writing of the word 'stability', with two bunches of lotus flowers in the top centre. We cannot tell from the model if this upper part was a carved fanlight, or simply a painted moulding in the mud plaster of the façade. To the right of this on the outside wall is a side entrance, with single pivoting leaf and no surrounding decoration. To the left is another rectangular feature that seems to be a tall, latticed window with narrow openings which would admit air and a dim light, but could presumably be easily sealed during windy spells when much dust blows in the air. We can tentatively add these details to the sides of the Kahun main street and so enliven it a little.

The internal plan of the large Kahun houses is highly intricate.[22] The builder has strictly adhered to an unbroken rectangular outline that he has filled with a dense and complex arrangement of interlocking rectangular spaces, often using a labyrinthine solution to the problem of access. Rectangular modules are all-pervasive, and seem to fit the intensely structured and bureaucratic nature of the Middle Kingdom state as revealed from many sources.

From careful inspection of Petrie's plans we can recognize several basic subdivisions. The residential part – the house proper – seems to be the central group of rooms and courtyards. In the case of the houses on the north side of the street it was contrived that this group was also entered from the north, via a long passage which ran beside it to a garden court on the north side. A colonnade shaded this northern, inner façade of the

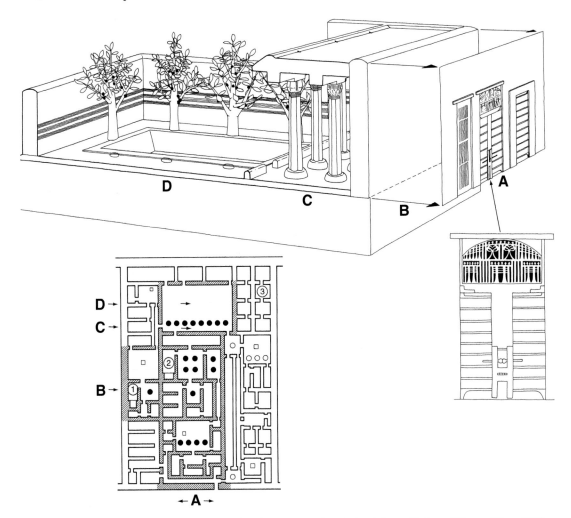

Figure 77 Large town houses: the plan is a composite derived from Kahun (Figure 76, p. 212). The core-house – the residential part – is cross-hatched. Two master bedrooms with bed alcoves can be recognized (nos. 1 and 2, see Figure 115, p. 328, for a New Kingdom example). The remainder of the building must be given over to storage (including a granary, no. 3), and workshops. The perspective drawing is derived from the 11th Dynasty house models from the tomb of Meketra at Thebes. The parts A to D correspond to the similarly labelled parts on the plan. 'A' is the façade to the street, 'B' is the core-house (reduced to the thickness of the wooden end panel in the model), 'C' is the portico, 'D' is the garden. After H.E. Winlock, *Models of daily life in ancient Egypt*, New York, 1955, Figs 9–12, 56–7.

house. With the houses on the south side of the street this inner court seems to have been more in the centre of the building. If one extracts this core-house plus its garden court and colonnade one has essentially what is represented in the Meketra house models: a house with formal entrances at back and front (reduced in these models to a single thickness of wood), adjacent to a walled garden, the inner façade of the house shaded by a columned portico. The Meketra models add further details which include the colour scheme (Figure 77): a central pool surrounded by trees, the garden and portico walls painted with a broad black dado, above which is a frieze of blue, yellow and white bands, topped by a wider white band. In the portico are two rows of four slender wooden columns, carved and painted, which rest on bases painted white to simulate limestone. The rear row of columns is carved in the form of a cluster of papyrus stalks, and the front row in the form of lotus buds bound together with bands of red and blue. The wooden architraves that they support are bespangled with stars, and the wooden ceiling between them is carved to represent palm trunks split in two, painted with stripes of green and red. The portico itself has a flat roof whose low front parapet is pierced by three rainspouts, painted white to indicate limestone.

Within the Kahun core-house a central reception room can be recognized, its roof supported on four columns. Beside it on the west is a small colonnaded court containing a stone tank set centrally in the floor. Petrie's plans also depict locations where the walls of a room were stepped back at the far end to create an alcove. Later evidence shows that alcoves like this were for beds in master bedrooms. If this holds true for Kahun, then one master bedroom was located within the central house core, but another was on the west, in what appears to be a residential annexe, with its own court. The possible purpose of this annexe will be returned to shortly.

On three sides, the core-house is surrounded by groups of chambers and little courts, comprising parts of an urban estate. For only one group can we identify its function directly from the plan. The group of square interconnecting rooms in the north-east with its courtyard in front is almost certainly a granary. Identical granaries occur in some of the Nubian forts dealt with later in this chapter. Their presence reflects the commodity-based nature of the Egyptian economy. The Meketra models include a fine granary evidently designed along the lines of those at Kahun. In this the entrance leads to a long vestibule, accommodating models of one doorkeeper, four seated scribes with document boxes, an overseer and his assistant, and three labourers who measure loose grain with a *hekat* measure before filling sacks. A door from the side of the vestibule leads to a room containing a staircase rising to a broad walk along the tops of three square interconnecting chambers where the grain is stored.

The combined capacity of the granaries in the large Kahun houses is very considerable. It is easy, from Petrie's plans, to measure the areas of the various storage chambers. For the height, some of the Nubian forts provide direct evidence: 3.4 metres. The Nubian granaries were, however, somewhat larger, so that for Kahun a reduced figure for filled height of 2.5 metres can be assumed. How much grain could they hold? Even more important: how many people could they support on the average rations calculated in the last chapter?

Table 1 summarizes the estimated capacities of the Kahun granaries. These seem to show that all the Kahun granaries together could hold sufficient grain for a population of 5,000 on maximum rations, and 9,000 on minimum rations, assuming five houses only on the north side with granaries. The latter figure of 9,000 is of the same order of magnitude

Table 1   The numbers of annual ration units storable in the granaries using minimum and maximum estimates of ration size

Site	Capacity of granary (cubic metres)	Minimum annual ration units	Maximum ration units
Kahun: N. house	337.50	1,164	675
Kahun: S. house	316.40	1,091	633
Kahun: all large houses	2,636.70	9,092	5,723

as the total population for Kahun that has been postulated on other grounds, namely between 8,500 and 10,000.[23] Even the lower figure implies that a significant proportion of the Kahun population was dependent on the large houses for rations. Moreover, as will be argued shortly, these population figures may themselves be too large.

The Kahun granaries are a key piece of evidence for regarding Kahun as a town not only created by administration but also maintained by administration, with much of the population dependent upon rations held in store by the chief officials. But why several large granaries instead of a single central one? The answer must lie in the social structure of Kahun, which will be looked into shortly.

What of the other parts within the Kahun large houses? The plans themselves and Petrie's notes have little more to tell us directly. But the range of activities that an important Middle Kingdom official might wish to see accommodated around him is provided again by some of the sets of tomb models. Here the Meketra group is particularly informative. We have already considered three so far: two almost identical ones of the main house, and the granary. There are five more building models. One of these is a cattle shed, a second is a butchery, a third is the combined bakery and brewery described in the last chapter (Figure 61.2, p. 173). The remaining models are a weaving shop and a carpentry shed.

Are all of these models together parts of a large house of the Kahun type? Here we need to jump forward in time, and in terms of the arrangement of chapters in this book, and bring in for comparison a typical dwelling for a high official from the New Kingdom city of El-Amarna (e.g. the houses of the general Ramose and the sculptor Thutmose in Figure 109, p. 312). Here we can recognize the various parts more easily. The dwelling consists not only of a residence but also of a granary, separate kitchen that might have an adjacent bakery-brewery, cattle-shed, other outbuildings which we know in some cases were used for craft production (including textiles), and frequently also a subsidiary house. Who lived in the latter is less certain. As a guess we might see it as intended for the eldest son who would gradually be taking over his father's responsibilities, but it must be admitted that other types of occupant can also be proposed: servants or a steward. All of these parts were arranged informally and rather loosely within a walled compound, with the house usually towards the centre. At El-Amarna, the hand of the planner was given only limited scope. In particular, it did not extend to laying out the residential areas, which seem to be the relaxed product of individual preferences within prescribed limits. However, if we try to imagine the ancient planner, faced with the task of laying out a compound containing the El-Amarna elements, we would find him quite likely producing a tightly organized scheme of interlocking rectangular rooms and spaces: the very kind we find at

Kahun. The large Kahun houses are best understood as planned and geometrically more elegant versions of the El-Amarna estates, containing a series of units that the Meketra models represent, for convenience, as single structures.

The contrast between El-Amarna and Kahun large houses tells us something important about the two different societies. At El-Amarna, household and services have been separately perceived, the services belonging to the perimeter of an enclosure in which the house stands as a central isolated feature. The variety of layout and size of compounds also reflects a society with a broad range of personal wealth and status. At Kahun, household and services have been indivisibly regarded as parts of a formally constituted unit. Nor is there much of a social gradient. As a model community it recognizes two main groups of people: owners of very big and owners of very small houses. The whole reflects the prevailing mentality of the Middle Kingdom, which tended towards an extreme structured view of society, partly reflected in an inclination to devise arithmetic calculations for every facet of economic life, and to seek to control human behaviour and property by means of a strict bureaucratic framework. El-Amarna reflects a subtly graded society, Kahun a society of distinct levels.

The Meketra models and the large Kahun houses give the impression that they were of only a single storey. Upper storeys are a perennial problem in archaeology where it is rare for walls to stand to sufficient height to provide a clear answer. Even the presence of a staircase is not proof since it could have led to no more than a flat roof. The problem recurs at El-Amarna where a likely solution in favour of more than one floor draws much of its support from artistic evidence. Some models of the Middle Kingdom also show a second storey (Figure 78). These belong to a category of baked clay 'soul houses' which combined house model with tray of model food-offerings for the dead. We do not yet have sufficient evidence to judge whether the prototypes stood in towns or were countryside villas.

A good part of the remainder of the interior of Kahun is occupied by small houses built in rows, frequently back to back. Somewhere in the region of 220 are present on Petrie's plan, a ratio of 1:20 with the large houses. Petrie's plan gives the impression that much more of the missing space in Kahun would have been filled by small rather than large houses, and to this unknown extent the ratio must be increased. The number of houses offers the safest guide to estimating the original population. Even if we assume that only half of the original houses are included in Petrie's plan, and allow, say, six persons per house, we reach a total population of just short of 3,000, well below the figure of up to 10,000 suggested on other grounds.[24]

The interior arrangements of rooms in the small houses vary considerably. To some extent this may reflect changes brought about by occupants in response to individual circumstances. They also show the same complex inner articulation of rooms as is present in the larger Kahun houses (an example is included in Figure 79). Characteristically an entrance passage leads to a room, which whilst not conspicuously large nevertheless acted as a pivotal point within the house, in that several doorways lead from it, frequently to ante-rooms rather than to terminal chambers. Anterooms sometimes deliberately lengthen journeys, placing security or privacy above convenience. In a few cases it looks as though two or more houses have been knocked together to form a larger house, and columns have been inserted. Examples lie in the west sector, eighth block from the north. In several houses circles are marked on Petrie's small-scale plan. Smaller ones seem usually to be

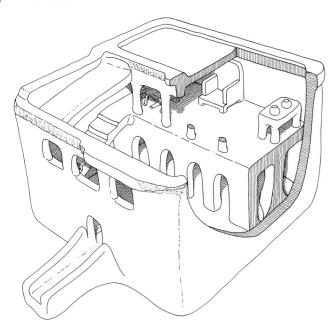

Figure 78 A pottery offering-tray modelled as a multi-storey house. (The modern term for these objects is 'soul house', and it was designed to have water poured over it which flows out through the front door.) Does the building represent a grander town house or a country villa? Note how the upper floor, reached by an external staircase with its own roof, is the more important, signalled by the presence of the formal seat accompanied by a table and also (this being an offering-tray) the carcase of a slaughtered ox (largely hidden from view in this drawing). The high enclosure wall around the court is itself pierced with windows at the front to ensure the maximum benefit to the upper floor from the breezes. The rounded arches of the lower arcade (which fronts a columned hall) could be either a rendering of actual brick arches on the real prototype or a consequence of making the model in slabs of wet clay. The model is in the Egyptian Museum, Cairo, and is illustrated in E. Baldwin Smith, *Egyptian architecture as cultural expression*, New York and London, 1938, 200, Pl. LXV.1. The drawing used here is a sketch only approximately scaled.

column bases, which according to Petrie supported octagonal wooden columns about 25 centimetres in diameter. In his brief published notes on the architecture Petrie himself describes granaries, circular brick structures measuring between 1.70 and 1.93 metres across, plastered inside and out. They seem mostly to have occurred singly, but one pair is present. In the western block of houses, from a total of about 150 houses, thirteen contain circles large enough to have been granaries. These would have augmented the grain storage capacity of the town, but their relative infrequency amongst the smaller houses points to significant differences in the wealth of the inhabitants of Kahun.

One further building inside Kahun deserves notice. It lies immediately south of the 'Acropolis'. It looks as though it stood in an open space. It may have been an administrative and storage building, but a temple is another possibility. We know from many references in papyri from Kahun that the town possessed its own temple, different from the mortuary temple of the pyramid. It was dedicated to the god 'Sepdu, Lord of the East', and possessed its own priesthood. To the south of this building is another which

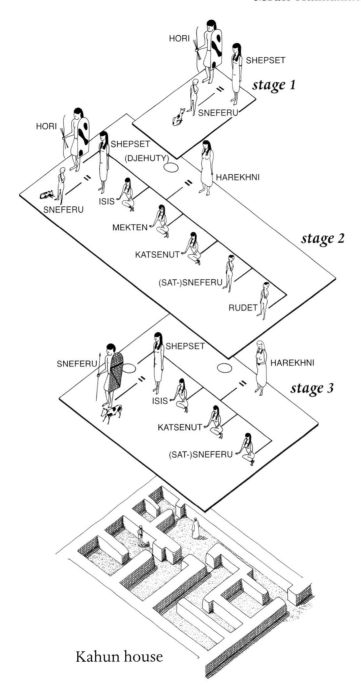

Figure 79 The changing size of a Kahun household, belonging to a soldier and his family. From a papyrus archive from the site. The timespan is not known but is probably fairly short. It is presumed that they lived in one of the ordinary houses, as illustrated.

does not resemble either the large or small residences and may, for this reason, have been administrative, whilst across the street to the east lay a court containing three medium-sized circular granaries.

Papyri found at Kahun deal with many aspects of the town's organization and again reveal the extent to which the scribal class felt that whatever they supervised needed to be documented in a manner that others could check. So the mortuary temple maintained a day-book into which letters to and from the mayor were copied, in one case an order that a piece of leather be given to a shoe-maker sent over from the mayor.[25] The papyri are a guide – albeit a very fragmentary one – to the kind of people whom we must put into the large and small houses if we wish to convert an archaeologist's plan into something more like its original living reality.

We can, without difficulty, identify a small number of important officials. The town had a 'mayor' (haty'a), the normal head of an ancient Egyptian town, who himself had a 'deputy'. It also possessed an 'office of the vizier', where legal proceedings took place and oaths were made, and where the vizier himself was sometimes present. We must exclude him as a permanent resident, however. He was a peripatetic figure, based at the capital. An office of the administrative subdivision called the 'area of the northern district' (wa'ret) was located somewhere, as also was an office for another senior government official, the 'reporter' (wehemu). In the latter, trials could take place. The town's population was caught in the system of labour conscription and so the town possessed a 'compound' where people could, if necessary, be held under restraint.[26] One text is a census-like household list that deals with a priest of the official mortuary cult of King Senusret II. His name was Khakaura-Sneferu. Of his own family one son and daughter are listed. But they are followed by groups of 'serfs' from various sources. These included the ones who evidently came with the office of priest, and numbered thirteen; a group of three given him by another official, and a group of unknown number (but a minimum of five) evidently inherited from the sister of his father. The most striking fact about these serfs is that most are female, and many are children of serfs. Just how extensive this list was is not known because the end of the papyrus is lost; but a document from the same period dealing with the serfs of an official at Thebes (probably the vizier Ankhu) listed originally ninety-five (see Chapter 1, p. 28), over half of them Asiatics, and with women outnumbering men by about 2:1. The men bear titles like 'domestic servant', 'field labourer', 'brewer', 'cook', 'tutor' or 'guardian', and 'sandal-maker'. Most of the women whose profession is listed are cloth-makers, but a 'hairdresser' and 'gardener' are also included. The Kahun list presumably belonged to one of the wealthier of the Kahun inhabitants, one of those who lived in the large residences in the north of the town. If we convert the Meketra models into the units of one of these residences, the 'serf' list presumably covers the figures who fill many of the models with industrious labour, though they need not have actually lived on the premises.

The dependence of many people upon the large residences is also to be read into the enormous provision for storing grain within each of them. A significant proportion of Kahun's population must have belonged to redistributive sub-centres in the form of the large residences. This in turn reflects a basic modular organization of society. Instead of all being dependent upon a single large granary with a single administration of rations, the population was broken down in this respect into several distinct groups. This team- or gang-organization of dependent populations seems to have been common in ancient Egypt. The temple phyle-groups encountered in the Neferirkara archive are one example, and Kahun, too, followed this model for the organization of the people who staffed the mortuary temple, whose names and ranks were duly entered into the day-book of the temple when their month-long period of service commenced.[27] Indeed, one might specu-late that the guild-like structure of the temple phyle is the very one around which life at Kahun was organized.

Apart from 'serfs' Kahun housed soldiers and their scribes, and temple personnel includ-ing doorkeepers and foreign singers and dancers of both sexes. Three more census lists have survived, found rolled up together. They list the members of the household of two soldiers, father (Hori) and son (Sneferu) over an unstated period of time (Figure 79).[28] The father's household consisted initially of himself, a wife and son (Sneferu); later they are joined by his mother, and five female relatives, who seem to be the householder's sisters, bringing the total to nine. When the son inherited, the final list was drawn up, and the household then consisted of just himself, his mother, his paternal grandmother and three of his father's sisters. It is tempting to regard this as the household of an occupant of one of the small houses. It reveals a second tier of dependence, within the small households, a tier that changed with individual family histories: early decease of wife, marriage of sister, and so on. The fluctuation in the size of the household, from three to nine to six, is within the range found in other sources.[29] Other papyri document the legal affairs of the Kahun inhabitants, as they disposed of property 'in town and country' and wrestled with prob-lems of debt, in all cases revealing that their dependence upon the state was only partial.

The variety apparent in Kahun society points to the central problem of all planning, in the past as now: matching reality to an abstract model of society.

> Officials of the modern state are, of necessity, at least one step – and often several
> steps – removed from the society they are charged with governing. They assess the
> life of their society by a series of typifications that are always some distance from
> the full reality these abstractions are meant to capture.[30]

Kahun was laid out by someone who saw only two social levels: top bureaucrats and others. In reality the latter was a diverse category with varied needs and expectations, exemplified by the changing size of the Hori–Sneferu household (Figure 79). The simple twofold division represented a social myth held by the elite. It made no serious attempt to cope with the social and economic differentials within the numerous body of people with an 'official' capacity of one lesser kind or another. After the Middle Kingdom the state gave up the idea of planning for communities other than small groups of workmen. The city of El-Amarna will illustrate this vividly.

Urban renewal and colonization

Kahun provides a classic example of the application of bureaucracy to community creation on the scale of a complete town of no mean size by ancient standards. Although the rest of the evidence from Middle Kingdom Egypt is very patchy, it is sufficient to suggest that Kahun illustrates a general preference for rigid large-scale layout of residential and admin-istrative quarters. Furthermore, from the spread of examples we can begin to conclude that the Middle Kingdom state embarked upon an extensive programme of remodelling

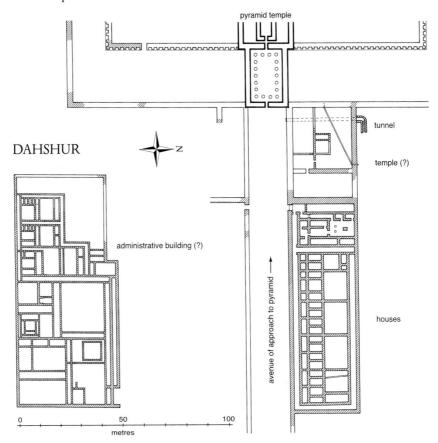

Figure 80   Foundations of the houses and ancillary buildings of the 'town' of the pyramid of Amenemhat III at Dahshur, showing orthogonal planning without a surrounding enclosure wall. After D. Arnold, *Der Pyramidenbezirk des Königs Amenemhet III in Dahschur*, I. *Die Pyramide*, Mainz, 1987, Taf. 36.

communities in this strictly regimented fashion. One example – of an integrated temple, storage, administrative and probably residential unit of the Middle Kingdom at Medamud – was briefly illustrated in Chapter 3 (Figure 46, p. 132). More sites will now be chosen to spread the picture further.

The first belongs to the Middle Kingdom mud-brick pyramid of King Amenemhat III at Dahshur (1831–1786 BC; Figure 80).[31] In function it must be comparable to Kahun, though the scale is smaller. Little more than the foundations have survived, frequently only up to a level below door thresholds, so that door positions are then not known. The buildings are aligned exactly with the pyramid, thus with the compass points as well, but unlike Kahun the group as a whole dispenses with an enclosure wall. Two main parts exist, on either side of the pyramid causeway. That on the south stands back from the causeway, and represents a building measuring about 50 by 100 metres. It displays the same nesting of rooms and larger units within a rectangular exterior as is present at Kahun, necessitating, as there, the use of long corridors. Note that one of the rooms in the central part displays the same thickening of walls towards the back (or south) as occurs at Kahun and in later times when it is taken as a sign of a major bedroom. The excavators also concluded from the pottery that the life of the building had been fairly short, perhaps no more than the reign of Amenemhat III itself. The amount of interior but evidently open space is much greater than usual in settlements of this kind. The excavators suggested, though very tentatively, a temporary centre for the organization of the pyramid construction work, and perhaps places where masons worked. If this were true it would offer an interesting contrast with the construction site of the Old Kingdom at Giza, described in the last chapter (Figure 66, p. 189), which represents a less thoroughgoing approach to planning a settlement.

Running beside the causeway on the north lay another block. It measures 33 by 137 metres, and seems to consist of a building with adjacent courtyard (both of uncertain purpose) at the west end, and then of several neighbouring houses with a room arrangement very similar to Kahun houses in its complex articulation. In size they fall mid-way between Kahun large and small houses.

The second example is even more closely comparable to Kahun but lay far from the pyramids in the heart of Upper Egypt, near the important religious site of Abydos. A small number of kings in the Middle and New Kingdoms went to the trouble and expense of creating special establishments to maintain a cult of themselves on ground sacred to the god Osiris whose own tomb was by this time thought to be located there. At a distance of 4 kilometres from the existing town of Abydos, where the temple of Osiris lay, King Senusret III (1870–1831 BC) constructed a huge replica tomb accompanied by a temple, and a full-scale town to go with it. Only the rear part has survived to be excavated (Figure 81), and consisted of perhaps sixteen large houses and one even larger (rather like one of the Kahun mansions) which belonged to the 'mayor' of the town, which was itself named after the king as 'Enduring are the places of Khakaura (Senusret III)'.[32] A case in somewhat different circumstances is that of Tell el-Dab'a, in the north-eastern Nile delta where the river floodplain peters out amidst low sand hills and, beyond them, lagoons and the Mediterranean coast. As the map shows (Figure 82), settlement began in the later Predynastic Period and was well advanced by the end of the Old Kingdom, reflecting both the proximity of the area to land- and sea-routes to the Near East, and probably the propensity of farming populations to colonize suitable land even when somewhat marginal. Early in the 12th Dynasty a planned town appeared in a place where so far nothing earlier has been detected.[33] Most of what has been revealed comprises streets of small unit houses, mostly arranged back to back and inside an enclosure wall. However, in the northeast corner one set of foundations points to a significantly larger building. Whereas Kahun seems to have maintained much of its plan intact for a long time, here, within a short time, modification to the neat original layout began as people converted the barracks-like dwellings into houses more amenable to personal circumstances. After an occupation estimated to have been no more than sixty years the whole settlement was abandoned. By this time it had become one part of a much larger area of settlement which developed into the leading city of the region (Avaris). Abandonment in this context might have been part of a peaceful process of redevelopment rather than the result of dramatic events.

One possible point of modern comparison concerns an institution that spread across the countryside of Egypt in the nineteenth century AD and is still commemorated in a host of village names: the *ezba*. This was a settlement provided by a landowner for his labourers.

ABYDOS SOUTH

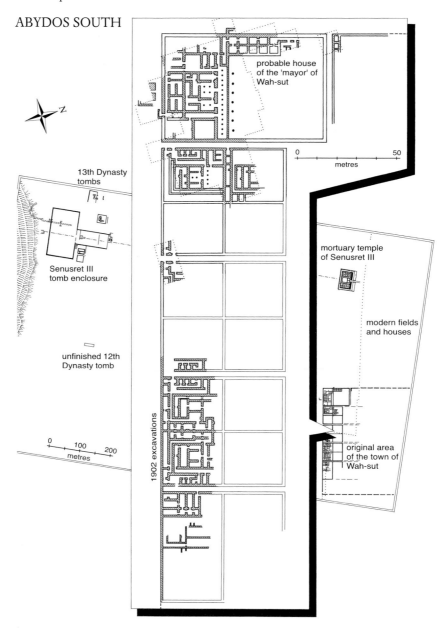

Figure 81   The model town of Wah-sut, built as part of Senusret III's tomb complex at South Abydos. After J. Wegner, *MDAIK* 57 (2001), 283–4, Figs 1, 2.

Some *ezba*s were perfect examples of rectilinear planning applied to the provision of tiny uniform dwellings within a walled compound, which bear a close resemblance to some ancient examples, especially that at Tell el-Dabʿa.[34] The parallel misses, however, the element of relative scale. *Ezba*s in modern Egypt remained small and rural. They were not towns; whereas by the scale of the times the planned Middle Kingdom settlements, including that of Tell el-Dabʿa, often were. They represent a more widely applied remodelling of society.

The final example from within Egypt is the city of Thebes. The most ancient city mound is nothing less than the ground on which the Karnak temple complex of the New Kingdom stands (Figure 97, p. 226). Indeed, it seems to have spread well beyond the limits of the later Karnak enclosure wall.

To date five excavations have contributed to the overall picture:

1   The most important was made in 1970–1 to the east of the Sacred Lake, behind the modern seating tiers for the Sound and Light Show at Karnak (Figure 83).[35] The edge of the lake is on the west. The wall with towers that divides the excavation is part of the 18th Dynasty temple enclosure wall. The walls to the east, however, are at a lower level, and run on beneath the wall and buildings on the west. They have a somewhat different orientation. Although only a fragment of plan is visible, it belongs to a settlement with buildings of markedly different degrees of solidity of construction. All, however, conform rigidly to a single grid plan. A 5-metre-thick enclosure wall crosses the site from west to east almost in the middle. On its south, and separated by a street, is a fragment of what seems to be another example of a large, rectangular, intricately planned building, with columns, for which the term 'palace' is probably not inappropriate. The edge of another smaller one lies at the northern edge of the excavation. If this section is at all typical, Middle Kingdom Thebes may have resembled a larger and internally more varied version of Kahun.

2   On the east side of the courtyard separating the 9th and 10th pylons, and immediately in front of the Jubilee Hall of Amenhetep II, a shallower excavation has brought to light house walls, circular grain silos and small storerooms, with pottery of the Middle Kingdom and Second Intermediate Period.[36]

3   To the east of the Karnak enclosure, and actually outside the 30th Dynasty enclosure wall, probes beneath the floor level of a badly damaged temple of Akhenaten have revealed town debris again of the Middle Kingdom and Second Intermediate Period. The evidence includes a length of 6-metre wide enclosure wall running true north–south (with this thickness we can conclude that it was probably the main city wall), and many surface finds of sherds of a distinctive kind of coarse domestic pottery with incised linear patterns. These are at home in Upper Egyptian town levels of the late Middle Kingdom and Second Intermediate Period; but are also part of 'pan-grave' culture (see Figure 12, p. 40).[37]

4   Again outside the 30th Dynasty wall, but this time on the north, the foundations of a stone building have been excavated which is aligned not to the main New Kingdom temple but to the general trend of the earlier walls exposed to the east of the sacred lake. The building itself is identified as a 'Treasury' of Tuthmosis I of the 18th Dynasty;[38] but test pits beneath the floor have encountered walls and pottery of the Second Intermediate Period, whilst outside the building similar earlier material occurs

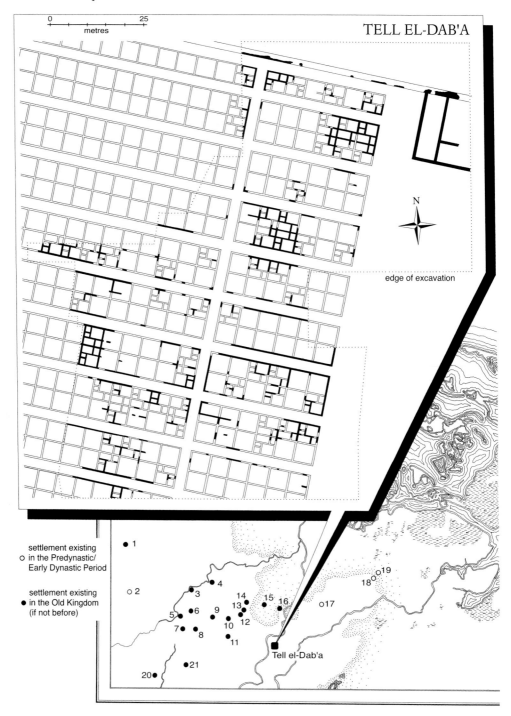

TELL EL-DAB'A

edge of excavation

settlement existing
○ in the Predynastic/
Early Dynastic Period

settlement existing
● in the Old Kingdom
(if not before)

at a level higher than the 'Treasury' floor. This suggests that the New Kingdom Treasury was built in a slight pit in the debris of the abandoned older city, and that the sides of the pit preserved the outlines of a plot of ground defined by the old city's general street alignment.

5   Middle Kingdom and Second Intermediate Period houses have been recovered beneath the New Kingdom ground level in the enclosure of the temple of the goddess Mut.[39]

These exposures derive from a city at least one kilometre in length. Only exposure no. 1 gives us an intelligible plan of any size, so that we cannot judge whether the whole of Thebes, or only a part of it, was turned into a giant version of Kahun at this time. We can suspect, however, that in the manner of some mediaeval European cities that retained outlines of the street-plans of their Classical predecessors, some of the New Kingdom and later alignments at Karnak reflect those of earlier times. Some of these are marked on Figure 83, but the true extent of this will only come from future excavations. We are already entitled, however, to consider Thebes as a major example of a Middle Kingdom planned city.

The limits that the drive for planning reached are represented by a stark scheme for human management at a particularly isolated site, at Kasr es-Sagha on the north-western edge of the Fayum.[40] Here a rectangular brick settlement was constructed, its sides aligned to the compass points (Figure 84). For once the context offers an explanation for its existence: it lay close to the end of a long paved road which led to basalt quarries in distant hills, and was probably close also to the then shoreline of the lake which, for a time in the Middle Kingdom, filled the Fayum depression. The settlement must have been there to house the men who worked the quarry and dragged the stone. It seems to have provided 150 identical rooms arranged in strictly regimented groups of five, but we have no way of knowing whether each room was for one occupant or for several. That it was possible to run such schemes without a model work camp of this kind is shown by, for example, the informal quarry settlement of the Old Kingdom at Umm es-Sawwan (Figure 111, p. 318).

Figure 82   Internal colonization: the earliest level at site F/I at the north-eastern delta site of Tell el-Dab'a, dating to the early 12th Dynasty. After E. Czerny, *Tell el-Dab'a IX. Eine Plansiedlung des frühen Mittleren Reiches.* Vienna, 1999, 18, Abb. 2. It is superimposed on a map of the area (the topography is that of the 1920s) showing sites which had already been settled by this time. The details derive from L. Krzyżaniak, 'Recent archaeological evidence on the earliest settlement in the eastern Nile Delta', in L. Krzyżaniak and M. Kobusiewicz, eds, *Late prehistory of the Nile Basin and the Sahara,* Poznan, 1989, 267–85; E.C.M. van den Brink, 'The Amsterdam University Survey Expedition to the Northeastern Nile Delta (1984–1986)', in E.C.M. van den Brink, ed., *The archaeology of the Nile Delta; problems and priorities*, Amsterdam, 1988, 65–110, esp. 65–76; also K. Kroeper and D. Wildung, *Minshat Abu Omar; Münchner Ostdelta-Expedition. Vorbericht 1978–1984*, Munich, 1985, 5, Abb. 1. The uneven distribution of settlements could, in part, be the result of the uneven intensity of modern archaeological survey.

Key to site numbers: 1 Tell el-Rub'a (Mendes); 2 Tell Samara; 3 Tell Umm el-Zaiyat; 4 Tell Geziret el-Faras; 5 Geziret Sangaha; 6 Tell el-Genidba; 7 Tell Abu Dawud; 8 Tilul Mohammed Abu Hasan; 9 Tell el-Marra; 10 Tell el-Akhdar; 11 Tell el-Dirdir; 12 Tell el-Abbasiya; 13 Tell el-Iswid (S); 14 Tell el-Iswid (N); 15 Tell Umm 'Agram; 16 Tell Ibrahim Awad; 17 El-Husseiniya (part of Nebesheh); 18 Minshat Abu Omar; 19 Tell el-Ginn; 20 Kufur Nigm; 21 Tell el-Khasna.

THEBES

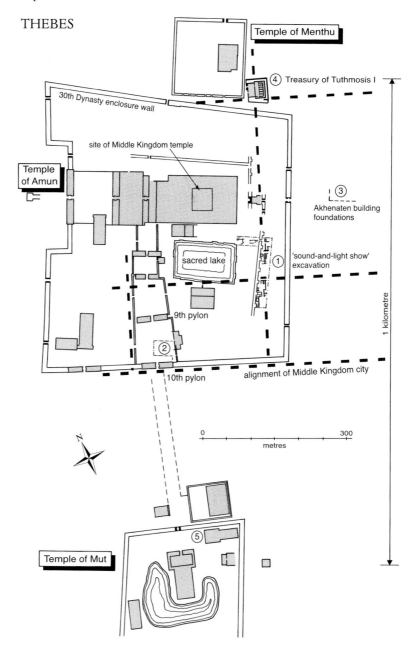

Figure 83 Planning at a prestige location: the ancient city of Thebes. *Left.* Outline plan of the New Kingdom temple complex showing principal exposures of the pre-New Kingdom city (nos. 1–5, see text for explanation). *Right.* Detail of exposure no. 1, part of the orthogonally planned Middle Kingdom city, after *Karnak* V *(1970–72)*, 26, Fig. 13.

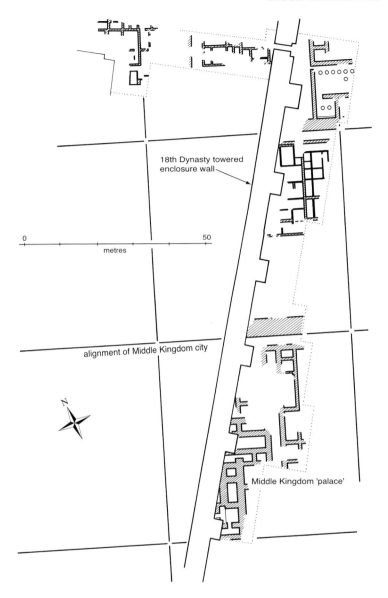

18th Dynasty towered
enclosure wall

0   50
          metres

alignment of Middle Kingdom city

Middle Kingdom 'palace'

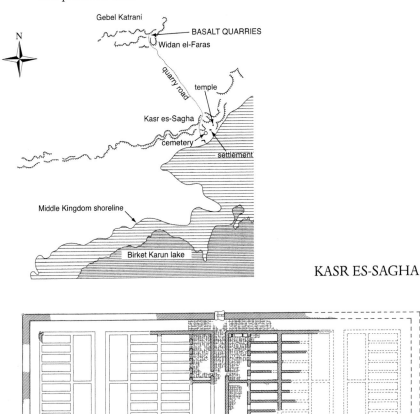

KASR ES-SAGHA

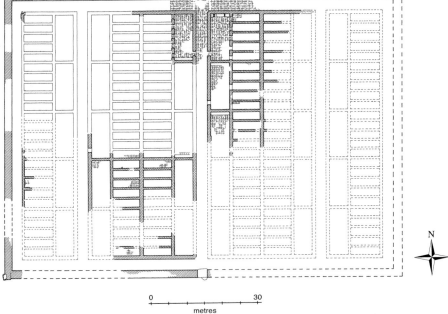

Figure 84 Planning applied to workmen's villages: the settlement at Kasr es-Sagha, serving the basalt quarries of the Gebel Katrani, northern Fayum. Contrast it with the Old Kingdom village at Umm es-Sawwan, Figure 111, p. 318. After J. Śliwa, *MDAIK* 48 (1992), 179, Abb. 1; also D. and Dorothea Arnold, *Der Tempel Qasr el-Sagha*, Mainz, 1979, 26, Abb. 14. The inset map, which also shows the greatly increased size of the Birket Karun lake in the Middle Kingdom, is after Arnold and Arnold, op. cit., 24, Abb. 13.

The Giza work camp (Figure 66, p. 189) seems to lie somewhere in between, where the state has provided a framework of walls but individual groups have been left to fill out the interiors, each according to a slightly different scheme.

This use of settlement creation (and the administration which would, in the Middle Kingdom, inevitably accompany it) as a means of asserting political control of land provides a suitable introduction to the major example of this from ancient Egypt: the Middle Kingdom in Nubia.

The Nubian forts

The experience gained in building pyramids, creating towns and dispatching quarry expeditions to distant regions found a new outlet in the Middle Kingdom: logistics for conquest. Important lessons had been learned. Valour, savagery and successful tactics on the battlefield were less certain if soldiers and commanders were not adequately provided for, and victory had little point if it could not be backed up by permanent control. Fighting in Nubia became only the sharp tip of a huge bureaucratic thrust. Empire-building now involved two very different sets of people, scribes and soldiers.

The Egyptian conquest of Nubia had begun in the 1st Dynasty.[41] In the Old Kingdom the Egyptians took the first steps towards settlement in Nubia. This reflected the attitude that was to become much more marked in later periods, that Nubia was a quasi-province of the Egyptian state. A fragment of an Old Kingdom town at Buhen North is the only site of this earliest phase known from excavation, but a few Old Kingdom sherds from Kubban further north may be a sign that Buhen was not alone at this time. Following the civil war of the First Intermediate Period, the reconquest of Lower Nubia seems to have got under way rapidly, in the reign of the victor of the civil war, King Nebhepetra Menthuhetep II (2055–2004 BC). A further campaign of conquest in year 29 of King Amenemhat I (1956 BC), first king of the 12th Dynasty, is recorded in a graffito actually within the heartland of Lower Nubia. The building policy which was well advanced in the reign of his successor, King Senusret I, is itself evidence of a massive kind that Lower Nubia had been thoroughly subdued. The powerfully bureaucratic attitude that seems to characterize the Middle Kingdom was now directed towards Lower Nubia, and to a renewed phase of settlement creation. This had produced, by the end of the 12th Dynasty, a line of forts and of fortified towns, regularly spaced along the 400 kilometres between the First Cataract and Semna at the head of the Second Cataract. Although these constructions reflect specialized local considerations, they also have much to tell us about the scale of Middle Kingdom administration and its determination to create a desired environment in the face of considerable difficulties.

The Nubian forts fall roughly into two groups, representing partly two different types of terrain and partly two major building phases. At some sites, moreover, forts built in the first phase saw several major modifications and enlargements, representing probably the initiatives of the local communities active during a period of more than two centuries.

The first group of forts may be termed the 'plains type'. They were constructed on the flat or shelving banks of the Nile north of the Second Cataract. They were the largest forts built in Nubia, and with their citadels and the even larger areas within an outer perimeter wall they could have accommodated many activities and housed a numerous human and animal population. The fort of Buhen towards the southern limit of this zone

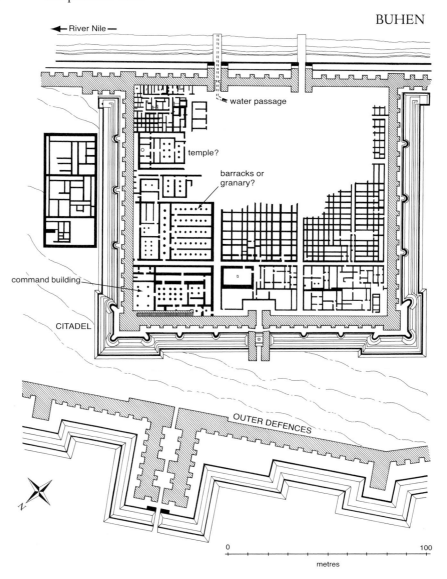

Figure 85 Planning in the service of the military: the Middle Kingdom fortress of Buhen in Nubia. The cellular pattern represents foundations; at ground level there would have been more doorways. After W.B. Emery, H.S. Smith and A. Millard, *The fortress of Buhen; the archaeological report*, London, 1979, Pl. 3.

provides the type site (Figure 85).[42] Inscriptions show that it was in existence by year 5 of King Senusret I (1951 BC). It lay on gently shelving desert adjoining the river directly, without significant cultivation in the vicinity. The indigenous population of both ancient and modern times was concentrated on the opposite and far more fertile riverbank. Two ancient concentric fortification lines enclosed an inner citadel and an outer area.

The citadel measured approximately 150 by 138 metres, and was defined by a mud-brick enclosure wall 5 metres thick, with external towers. One standing fragment has given an original height of between 8 and 9 metres. The river frontage was further protected by two spur walls that prolonged the eastern wall to north and south. Two gates gave access to the waterfront. Beneath the northern one ran a stone-lined passage intended to ensure a safe water supply in time of siege. A single massive gateway on the west, protected by two projecting parallel walls, provided access to the desert side. No direct traces were found of how the upper parts of the wall were shielded, but contemporary pictures of forts in the tombs at Beni Hasan show that crenellations were normal.

The base of the wall was protected not only by a ditch, but also by a narrow, brick-paved rampart with its own parapet wall (Figure 86.1). This was pierced by loopholes in groups of three, intended for the use of archers. At intervals, and at the corners, the rampart and lower parapet widened to form semi-circular towers, provided with a second set of loopholes. The preserved loopholes on the west pointed down into the ditch; but on the northern and perhaps southern sides an upper row pointed directly forwards. North and south sides differed also in that a special kneeling-step for archers, running along the inside base of each wall, was added as well. As for the ditch, it was dry, cut into the rock, and had average dimensions of 7.3 metres in width, and 3.1 metres in depth. A counter-scarp had been built up on the outer lip of the ditch to support a glacis.

The interior of the citadel seems to have been largely occupied by rectangular brick buildings arranged around a rectilinear or orthogonal grid of streets. All buildings, except the one of the north-west corner and some towards the north-east corner, were separated from the main wall by a continuous street. The buildings on the west and north had been relatively well preserved. But over the remainder destruction and erosion had reduced them to broken lengths of foundation walls. The excavator's plan of this part, in joining up many of these fragments into continuous lengths, creates an impression of a regular cellular design that is to a degree illusory. The walls were far more fragmentary than this and might have belonged to a more varied plan.

The building in the north-west corner seems to have been the garrison headquarters (the 'command building' of Figure 85). It was built directly against the main wall, and had its own staircase leading to the top. The building itself had possessed at least two storeys. At ground level it had contained pillared halls, and a colonnaded court with stone floor. A square stone tank was sunk into the floor of the main hall. This is a common feature of large Middle Kingdom buildings, and was noted in the large houses at Kahun. The pillars in these rooms had been of wood, octagonal and red-painted, standing on circular stone bases. Doorways had been framed with wooden jambs and lintels. Adjacent to this on the east stood a group of long columned halls that the excavator, W.B. Emery, conjectured was a barrack-block (for which support now comes from those found at Giza, Figure 66, p. 189), but could have served another purpose, perhaps storage. Further to the east lay a building that was identified as a temple. Its plan is suggestive, and it lay beneath the later 18th Dynasty temple of Queen Hatshepsut. No objects were found to bear this out, however, and during the Second Intermediate Period the building was re-used for domestic purposes. Yet texts from Buhen mention building work on a temple of Horus at this very time, implying that it lay separately.[43] Along the inside of the west wall of the citadel lay several buildings with layouts of interlocking rooms which exemplify Middle Kingdom domestic architectural practice. Over large parts of the remainder of the site a strict grid

Figure 86   The ingenious mind of the military engineer. (1) Reconstruction of the fortifications of the citadel at Buhen, see Figure 85, p. 232. (2) Wheeled siege-tower in use in the First Intermediate Period, from the tomb of Intef at Thebes. After D. Arnold and J. Settgast, *MDAIK* 20 (1965), Abb. 2, opposite p. 50.

of walls was laid out. Much of it most likely served as foundations for houses or workshops of modular design, perhaps comparable to back-to-back modular houses of a few rooms each found in some of the Second Cataract forts. One dense group of rectangular chambers lay in the north-east corner, touching the girdle wall directly. The preserved height here was sufficient to show that many must have been cellars entered from above, and some may have been for storing grain.

The outer line of fortifications enclosed an area measuring roughly 420 by 150 metres. The citadel lay within it. The outer defences ran as a series of rectangular salients, backed by a brick wall 5 to 5.5 metres thick, set with rectangular towers on the outside. The rock-cut ditch had an outer rampart with uninterrupted parapet, and was crossed by a rock causeway opposite the enormous gateway on the west side. The outer defences in this particular form may have been a creation of the late Middle Kingdom, for in places it was found that beneath them lay the remains of a much more lightly constructed brick parapet with rounded towers, perhaps a product of the early Middle Kingdom.

The space between the citadel and outer fortifications has never been fully examined, but it seems unlikely that it was ever built up to any great density. On the west side, the outer fortifications ran along a 2-metre-high escarpment. During the Middle Kingdom (probably the late Middle Kingdom) this had been utilized as a cemetery, running almost the full length of the enclosed ground. No traces of housing were found during its excavation, and so the entire western side of the outer enclosure might have remained open space. For the area south of the citadel we have very little information. But on the north an important construction was found almost immediately against the north wall of the citadel. It was so close, in fact, as to mask and render ineffective the whole northern side of the citadel fortifications. Only the foundations of this building survived, but they belong to a massive block, measuring 64.25 by 31.25 metres. Although some of the walls were preserved to a height of up to 1.5 metres, they showed no doorways, suggesting a basement or platform to support chambers at some height above the ground. In the early New Kingdom (or possibly during the Second Intermediate Period) this block was partly demolished, and the small temple of Horus built over. The internal divisions of this building make it a characteristic large pre-planned block of the Middle Kingdom.

The style and strength of the Buhen fortifications seem designed to thwart a fairly sophisticated type of siege. We know from pictorial evidence that by the beginning of the 12th Dynasty siege warfare using siege engines was known in Egypt, as is shown in a scene from the tomb of the seal-bearer and general Intef of the late 11th Dynasty at Thebes, where a wheeled siege tower is in use (Figure 86.2).[44] This poses the interesting question: might the Buhen citadel represent a form of urban fortification developed in Egypt during the civil wars of the First Intermediate Period, which was subsequently transferred to Nubia as an administrative act? Is the architecture itself, therefore, the product of a bureaucratic decision rather than of a local strategic assessment? Nothing comparable has so far been found in Egypt. This could be, however, because forts of this type were built separately from existing towns. This was the case at Elephantine where the old town, despite its strategic location, was not heavily fortified, but we know from texts that a fortress was constructed at a nearby site, now lost, which was called Senmet. Whatever the origin, the strength of the fortified frontier at Semna (described next), constructed late in the 12th Dynasty, suggests that the Egyptians took seriously the military threat from the tribal societies lying yet further to the south.[45]

The Second Cataract forts

The second group of forts resulted from an Egyptian annexation of the Second Cataract area in the reign of Senusret III (1870–1831 BC). Despite its name, the Second Cataract is not a single precipitous fall of water but a series of lesser obstructions in two groups, separated by about 35 kilometres of reasonably clear water. The northern end is marked by a dense group of rocky islands treacherous for navigation, the southern, at Semna, by a narrow rocky barrier through which the river gushes in several torrents. In both cases sailing was hazardous when the river was low, but at full flood the obstacles were sufficiently submerged to allow careful sailors safe passage. In the rugged and broken terrain each of the new forts took the form of an irregular polygonal figure designed to fit over an irregular natural prominence. Narrow ridges that ran up to the site were covered with spur walls to render them safe, and in most places the steep natural slopes made a ditch unnecessary. They show that, when occasion demanded, the rigidities of grid-iron planning could be sensibly abandoned.

A good example of this type of fort is Shalfak, on the west bank, on the edge of an escarpment overlooking the Nile (Figure 87).[46] The fortified area is relatively small, measuring 80 metres by 49 at the widest point. It was surrounded by a 5-metre-thick brick wall with external towers. The defended ground was, however, greatly increased by spur walls, that on the north running for 115 metres. On the north a small gateway led round the walls to a staircase descending the cliff to the water's edge. The main gateway was defended by a pair of projecting walls. The interior was completely built up except for narrow streets, which ran around the base of the main wall, and divided the principal blocks. Opposite the gateway lay the granary, well preserved and with a plan like those at Kahun, its grain chambers showing no sign of an external doorway. They must have been reached by ladder and roof entrances. Beside the east wall the command post can be recognized by its thick walls, which could have supported sufficient masonry to turn it into a tower. The other buildings presumably housed the garrison.

Shalfak was one of a number of forts built by King Senusret III which cluster around the southern part of the Second Cataract and form an obvious defensive grouping across the narrow Semna Gorge. An inscription of Senusret III from Semna confirms that this was indeed intended as a true frontier.

> Year 16, third month of winter: His Majesty made the southern boundary at Heh. 'I have made my boundary, having sailed further south than my fathers. I have increased what was bequeathed to me.'
>
> 'As for any son of mine who shall maintain this boundary which My Majesty has made, he is a son of mine who was born to My Majesty . . . But as for whoever shall abandon it, and who will not fight for it, he is no son of mine, and was not born to me.'
>
> 'My Majesty has had a statue of My Majesty set up on this boundary which My Majesty has made so that you might be inspired by it, and fight on behalf of it.'[47]

More will be said about this statue shortly.

At Semna a barrier of crystalline rocks crossed the Nile, leaving a gap of about 400 metres. On a rocky eminence at either end Senusret III sited a fortress: Semna, the larger,

SHALFAK

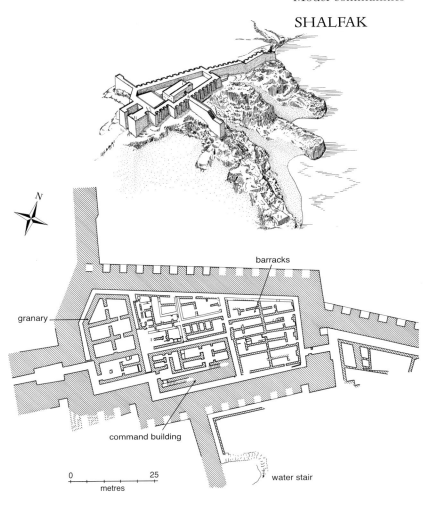

Figure 87 Imaginative adaptation of architecture to topography: the fortress of Shalfak in the Second Cataract area of Nubia, built by Senusret III of the 12th Dynasty on a high rocky outcrop above the river. Plan after G.A. Reisner, N.F. Wheeler and D. Dunham, *Second Cataract Forts* II. *Uronarti, Shalfak, Mirgissa*, Boston, 1967, Map X.

on the west, and Kumma on the east (Figure 88). Semna fort took an L-shaped plan, the western wing covering a piece of relatively flat ground.[48] The principal dimensions are about 130 metres from north to south, and the same from west to east. The girdle wall on the landward sides was protected by regularly spaced small towers, strengthened at greater intervals by larger projecting towers. The ground surrounding the wall was flattish, but still no outer rampart or parapet was thought necessary. Instead it was cleared for a distance of up to 29 metres, and beyond this, material was heaped up and covered with a stone pavement to form a glacis and counterscarp. At either end of the eastern wing the girdle wall was pierced by fortified gateways that allowed a road to pass entirely through the fort, crossing to the glacis by means of causeways. A narrow gate in the east wall gave

SEMNA

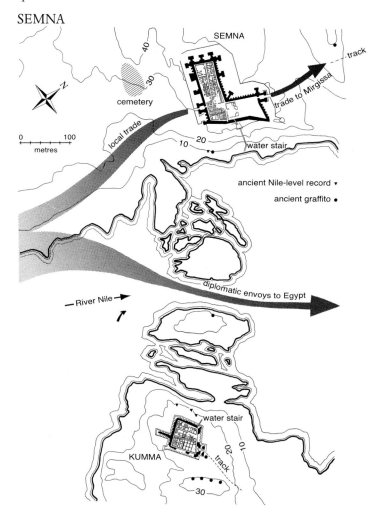

Figure 88   The southern frontier of Egyptian territory in the late Middle Kingdom. The fortress system at Semna not only provided military protection, it also regulated trade and diplomatic traffic northwards.

access to a stairway running down to the water's edge. This was protected by means of a substantial tunnel of dry-stone masonry.

The narrow streets within Semna were paved with irregular slabs of stone. They ran around the base of the girdle wall, and divided the interior into blocks. Unfortunately, we do not have the full plan of the inside. A certain amount had been lost or obscured by the 18th Dynasty stone temple built in the middle of the east wing, and a good part of the remainder has never been excavated. In the west wing the ground rose towards the west, and at the highest point in the fort a substantial building stood which was perhaps the command post. The walls were preserved to sufficient height to show the tell-tale marks of the ends of timber beams supporting the floor of an upper storey. Other buildings show the use of an initial modular layout and seem to have been houses, of two or three rooms. No granary has been identified.

The boundary inscription of Senusret III refers to a statue of the king present in the fort to inspire posterity to defend the frontier. The original statue has not been found. But in the reign of Tuthmosis III of the 18th Dynasty a small sandstone temple was built in the middle of the eastern wing. One of the statue cults within it was of King Senusret III, the founder of Semna. On the walls of the sanctuary were carved figures of the statue itself seated inside a portable boat shrine of standard New Kingdom design.[49]

Across the river from Semna lay Kumma, much smaller, and built over a steep rocky outcrop.[50] So steep were its sides that the walls had in some places to be built on stone embankments. The fort has an irregular quadrilateral outline, with projecting spur walls to cover lesser ridges. A water-gate with stairs lay at the northern corner. Inside was the usual arrangement of narrow streets, like those at Semna paved with irregular stone slabs. Amongst the individual buildings a granary is easily recognized.

The Semna defences included a third fort 1,500 metres to the south of Semna fort.[51] It lay in modern times on the southern edge of a plain of alluvium, but in ancient times it must have lain on the far side of a bay in the river bank, later silted up. It was small and square, measuring about 52 metres along each side. Its isolated position implies that it was a dependency of Semna, either a forward observation post, or a checkpoint for traffic coming in from the south. A further and striking defensive work was a 2.5-metre thick mud-brick wall, fortified by towers on high points, which ran beside the roadway which, on leaving the north gate at Semna, followed the river through the Second Cataract area.[52] It has been traced for a distance of no less than 4.5 kilometres and had actually begun to the south of Semna, skirting round the fort to the west to create a large protected zone. Possibly Semna South marked its real beginning. This wall brings home the seriousness of the threat felt by the Egyptians in the area, and the fact that land traffic played an important role in their strategy. It is also an early example of a linear territorial defensive work (of the Hadrian's Wall type), which has a probably contemporaneous counterpart at Aswan, protecting the land route around the First Cataract.[53]

The Second Cataract forts are striking examples of military architecture and illustrate an extension of the urban planning already encountered at Kahun and elsewhere. But in two further respects as well they illustrate Egyptian bureaucracy: the forts stood as centres for administered activity over an extensive open hinterland, and they provide a particularly vivid witness to the scale and importance of making provision for rations.

The Egyptian strategy in Nubia was not confined to static defence behind massive walls. A number of lookout posts were manned in the Second Cataract area. These are mostly known from groups of graffiti of the Middle Kingdom left at suitable points.[54] More explicit is a group of documents from a tomb at Thebes, dated to the reign of King Amenemhat III, which shows that the forts maintained contact with each other and with their base, probably Thebes itself, by means of regular written reports. Known as the Semna Despatches, they reveal that an active policy of desert surveillance was maintained (to which reference was made in Chapter 1, p. 26). This was done by sending out patrols to look for tracks and to bring in any wanderers for questioning. For this the Egyptians used desert inhabitants, the Medjay. The policy produced reports such as this: 'The patrol which set out to patrol the desert-edge … has returned and reported to me as follows: "We have found a track of 32 men and 3 donkeys".' Other despatches deal with trading with Nubians at the frontier fort of Semna itself. The fine detail in these letters, evidently written to be scrutinized at Thebes, is characteristic of the Egyptian urge to record happenings that might be of interest to a superior official, and nicely illustrates the bureaucratic framework of the Egyptian presence in Nubia.

The network of control that the Egyptians threw over the region extended to regulating contacts with the Nubian communities lying to the south, beyond the limits of direct Egyptian control. Semna has provided another formal inscription of Senusret III, already quoted in Chapter 1:

> The southern boundary which was created in the 8th year under the Majesty of King Senusret III to prevent any Nubian from passing it when faring northwards, whether on foot or by boat, as well as any cattle of the Nubians. An exception is a Nubian who shall come to barter at Iken, or one with an official message.[55]

Trade and diplomacy with the enemy were to be recognized and properly regulated.

For many years the location of Iken was disputed. It was settled by discoveries in the 1960s, which showed that Iken was the ancient name for the great fortress site of Mirgissa, lying 40 kilometres behind the fortified frontier area, at the northern end of the Second Cataract.[56] Below the main fort on a hill lay a settlement of stone huts and a few brick houses also protected within a massive wall. This might have served as the trading-post but from the available evidence this remains conjectural.

Many of the forts, including Mirgissa, possessed large well-built granaries. Since we can identify the granary buildings and measure them – and even find out what their original height was in some cases – we can also take the same tentative steps as at Kahun towards calculating how much grain they might have held, and what this tells us about the Nubian operation in general. Although there are many uncertainties in doing so we must bear in mind the Egyptian passion for measuring and calculating. No granary would have been built without it.[57] Table 2 lays out the capacities and, applying the minimum and maximum figures used above for Kahun, sets gross population figures. Even taking the lower figures the resulting populations are hugely excessive when compared to the size of garrison that has been postulated in the past. One excavator, G.A. Reisner, on intuitive grounds, estimated for Kumma a garrison of between fifty and 100 men, for Semna one of between 150 and 300, and for Uronarti one of between 100 and 200.

The activities of the Nubian forts are still only sketchily documented. The Medjay people who assisted the Egyptians in patrolling the desert were presumably paid partly in grain; some grain may been needed for the donkeys who must have formed an important element in transport; we also know that some of the forts engaged in trade in which bread and beer were given out by the Egyptians. If this last factor was a significant one, however, we might have expected the largest granary to have been at Mirgissa, which we know from Senusret III's boundary inscription quoted above to have been the officially designated trading-post for Nubians from the south, the place called Iken. This is not so.

The Nubian forts in the Second Cataract south of Mirgissa were built by Senusret III to defend a frontier newly established by him. However, the military measures undertaken at this time also involved campaigns into areas lying yet further to the south. Armies need rations, and although there would doubtless have been hopes of seizing defeated Nubians' grain stores, the Middle Kingdom administrative machine was not one to leave supplies

Table 2 The numbers of annual ration units storable in the granaries using minimum and maximum estimates of ration size

Site	Capacity of granary (cubic metres)	Minimum annual ration units	Maximum ration units
Shalfak	389.28	1,342	779
Uronarti (block VI only)	444.34	1,532	889
Uronarti (VI plus IV)	770.37	2,656	1,541
Mirgissa	1,063.69	3,668	2,127
Kumma	574.31	1,980	1,149
Askut	1,632.18	5,628	3,264
Semna	[1,000?]	[3,448?]	[2,000?]

and rations to chance. From the texts mentioned in the previous chapter we can well imagine the preparations: calculating the numbers of men, the length of time, the size of rations and thus the maximum size of the stores. We can only understand the size and location of the Second Cataract granaries if we see them as part of an integrated military strategy of defence and attack. The granaries belong to a carefully planned chain of supply. Their importance in military thinking is amply demonstrated by the island fortress of Askut, located well back from the Semna frontier and therefore the most secure of the group.[58] The granary occupies so much of the interior space as to suggest that the whole fortress was really a fortified grain store acting as an emergency or rear supply depot.

The care taken with all preparations is evident from two other excavated sites, where the 'ghosts' of two temporary Middle Kingdom palaces have been discovered. One is the 'Administrative Building' at Kor, the other is the 'Palace' on Uronarti island (Figure 89).[59] Both were occupied for only a brief period and were laid out with a ritual care for northerly orientation, ignoring the lie of the land. A tempting interpretation is that they were temporary residences thrown up for the king during his leadership of campaigns into the regions lying beyond the frontiers.

The archaeological evidence from Middle Kingdom Nubia projects into this military frontier region a massive application of Middle Kingdom administration. Behind the forts must lie a hidden mountain of scribal effort. We can only marvel at the excess of zeal and energy that the whole operation reveals.

The prescriptive society

The circumstances in which planned settlements were built in the Middle Kingdom varied greatly. The Nubian forts represent colonization of a limited sort on newly conquered territory. Tell el-Dab'a seems to have been a new town on the agricultural plain in an area already long settled; Kahun and Abydos South were on desert and attached to new religious foundations but also in areas with an existing town in the neighbourhood. At Thebes the planned town was an actual rebuilding of a major town with a long prior history. Apart from this last case, they raise questions about how they were populated which can at present be addressed only speculatively. They imply that the state had the means to identify sufficient social units (families), together with a corps of officials (including mayors),

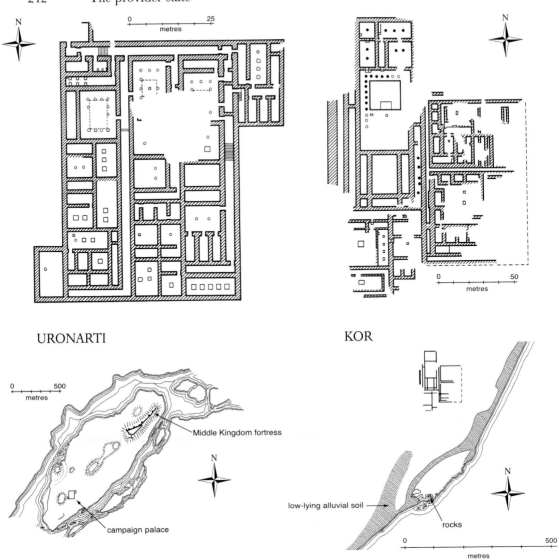

Figure 89 Two short-lived buildings in Nubia, carefully aligned to true north (see Figure 84, p. 230) against the natural trend of the ground, at Uronarti and Kor. Were they the king's temporary headquarters during major campaigns? After G.A. Reisner, N.F. Wheeler and D. Dunham, *Second Cataract Forts II: Uronarti, Shalfak, Mirgissa*, Boston, 1967, Maps II, VI, and J. Vercoutter, *Kush 3* (1955), Plan D, Pl. VI.

who were fully at its disposal and could be transplanted and given a secure and permanent economic base. Were there incentives or was it a form of punishment? Given that the
country had seen a period of civil war, are we looking at the result of a punitive policy
of forced resettlement of whole populations from other areas? This would help to cast the
Middle Kingdom as a time of grim centralization and of police-state control of the population, something which one might, by the uncertain process of empathy, read into the
faces of many of the statues of 12th Dynasty kings, which varied in expression between the
brutal and the careworn (though these features are most pronounced towards the end, in
the faces of Senusret III and Amenemhat III). Such an interpretation might apply to Tell
el-Dab'a but far less well to, say, Kahun and Abydos South, which were created later in
the Middle Kingdom.

What impact did these new places have upon the stock of existing towns, already some
centuries old? At Elephantine the answer seems to be, none at all (Figure 69, p. 198). No
new geometrically laid out town was built here in the Middle Kingdom, although we know
from texts that a fortress (at Senmet) was erected at this time not far away. Kahun and
Abydos South had older neighbours (El-Lahun and Abydos, respectively) but whilst they
remained in use into the New Kingdom, thus for several centuries, they were eventually
abandoned, leaving the existing nearby towns to continue as the local centres, although
we have no idea if they themselves had been redesigned. In fact, to date, the principal
evidence for the redesign of an existing place comes from Thebes (Figure 83, pp. 228–9).
It is, however, a key example. Because Thebes was so important, as the major city of the
south and probable home of the royal family, it directs us to the conclusion that grid-plan-
ning could have been an admired style. Rather than punishment, the geometric mud-brick
towns and forts of the Middle Kingdom could represent an attempt at remodelling society
that was seen as progressive in its day.

The history of town planning offers a paradox in value judgements. Today we regard
planning as a basic responsibility of civilized government; thus, a good thing. We are
therefore inclined to applaud it when it makes its appearance in antiquity. However,
ancient planning inclined towards a form – the grid-iron or orthogonal layout – that we
have come to regard as the very worst kind of planning, and much to be avoided. Modern
planners have returned to the roots of pre-modern community life and have attempted
to distil principles from unpremeditated 'organic' or self-organized communities, such as
mediaeval Italian hill villages. This being the case, we can choose to regard early grid-
iron plans as bureaucratic impositions and question whether they are really a civilized
virtue. Most modern city dwellers none the less, both poor and rich, live in fairly regimented flats and houses and seek individual expression and identity by other means. The
question is very much to the fore in considering the greatest city that has survived from
ancient Egypt: El-Amarna of the New Kingdom (Figure 109, p. 312). Most of this city was
built around a rejection of, or an indifference to, a social prescription and a geometric aesthetic. The organic harmonies and discords of personal decision-making prevail instead,
and reflect a mentality very different from that behind Kahun.

The paradox mirrors something more fundamental still. In the texts considered in the
last chapter and in the archaeological sites considered in this one, the Middle Kingdom
takes on a distinctive character: it was motivated by a vision – fragmentary and incomplete perhaps – of a bureaucratic Utopia, an unformulated ideology which acted as a
pattern in the making of decisions. We find it in an inclination to devise arithmetic devices

for regulating economic life, we see it in documents attempting a centralized control and direction of work and property, it lives at Kahun in a prescription for how a complete city should be arranged. It may seem crude in many respects, but it could have had a future. Better systems are built by improvements to older ones. But the resources of the state, and by this we mean in the end its human resources, proved unequal to the task. As the remaining chapters will show, the bureaucratic tendency of the Middle Kingdom made no further headway. The New Kingdom state, although successful for nearly five centuries in creating and distributing wealth and honours, was a less rigid system holding temporarily in check a great many individualistic ambitions.

Why did ancient Egypt fail to endure? The same answer applies as to all civilizations: too great and too prolonged a rejection of systematized life in favour of freedom of manoeuvre by ambitious individuals, and a general acquiescence in, or preference for, muddle, short-cuts, and, when it comes to built environment, the sense of familiarity and personal identity that arises from something with an element of personal idiosyncrasy which announces to its owner that, no matter how insignificant and irregular it might be, it is 'home'. If the work of Middle Kingdom Egypt – and of equivalent periods of bureaucratic dominance in ancient China, the Indus Valley, Mesopotamia and pre-Columbian Central and South America – had been pursued as a peaceful continuum, converting all who encountered it to enthusiastic support for order and the beauty of logical systems of government, then by now a Utopian world order might well have been achieved. But the anarchic love of disorder and of the rejection of authority is equally part of the human personality. History is a record of the struggle between the two polarities of the mind – order and disorder, acceptance and rebellion (as the ancient Egyptians themselves perceived). Both the rise and the fall of civilization are present in each one of us.

Part III
Intimations of our future

6
New Kingdom Egypt

The mature state

I live in a paradoxical world. It claims to be an age of reason and progress. Technology streaks ahead. Yet in people's minds there seem still to loom the essence and trappings of antique hierarchical power. Those who actually seek power find aspects of the ancient stage-managed style irresistible. They build monuments, they elevate symbols, they identify enemies to smite. We can argue that early societies, lacking a rational philosophical basis for government, needed, for the maintenance of unity and stability, leaders whose position was defined by theology and whose person was treated with the reverence and ceremonial of a god. The theological underpinning and the presentational devices had a real point. The divine ruler's authority was unique, beyond question, the threat of subdivision or duplication arising only in times of civil war. But humankind has moved on since the days of the Pharaohs. Between ourselves and ancient Egypt stretches a long and complex history of developing political thought and varieties of forms of government, in part based on philosophies that do not derive from religion. We know what some form of rational harmonious society might look like. Yet as the host society has changed, so the forms and trappings of rule by a divine leader have shown a remarkable capacity to adapt and to live on, often much loved. Rationality lures, atavism rules.

With the New Kingdom – the five centuries or so (1550 to 1069 BC) of the 18th to 20th Dynasties – we can see that Egypt was already well advanced along the path of complex accommodation between political reality and the myths of the state. We will find no evidence that people seriously considered alternative forms of government to direct rule by a divine king. What we can observe is, on the one hand, the evolution of a more pluralist society which destroyed the possibility of the state ever fully developing into a single hierarchy in which everyone knew and accepted their place; and, on the other, the adaptation of divine monarchy to the changing circumstances in ways that have proved to be indestructible. It is the purpose of this chapter (and parts of Chapter 7) to delineate the massive apparatus that articulated state myth and yet had the flexibility to accommodate a form of rule which was essentially political. All readers of this book will live under a similar compromise.

Outwardly the style of the New Kingdom was still in the tradition created in the earlier periods. It was, nevertheless, a different society from the one that had seen the building of the pyramids. The bureaucratic tendency advanced no further. Kings still wallowed in the exercise of personal power, but their state had to allow for a changed balance of internal forces, which had arisen principally through the emergence of institutions with a greater professional coherence. From their earliest stages states require the services of loyal agents who will offer advice and carry out the king's wishes, defend and even enlarge the realm by armed force, and look after the all-important practical aspects of ideology. Ministers, soldiers, priests: these three fundamental instruments of the state are identifiable in Egypt in the Old Kingdom. The first and the last also looked to a distinctive and prominent physical setting for their lives, palace and temple. The palace must early have become an institution, and by the 4th Dynasty so had the larger royal mortuary temples at the pyramids. But whereas in earlier periods the different sides to government appear to be facets of a single system, with the New Kingdom we can recognize their thoroughgoing institutionalization. To this we must add Egypt's unprecedented international position as an imperial power. And overall there were developing a polish and style that make the New Kingdom more like the states that have come and gone in the world ever since, down to recent times. We must reckon, too, with another force quietly and almost invisibly eating away at the prescriptive society: personal economic emancipation. This will form the basis of the next chapter. Ancient Egypt has a modern reputation for extreme cultural conservatism. But the New Kingdom demonstrates that this is itself something of a myth, brought about by confusion between form and substance. Circumstances had changed, and basic ideology and practices were adapting to them.

Temples and priesthood

Ideology needs architecture for its fullest expression. By its potential for a dwarfing scale architecture compels respect in the individual and becomes the dominating horizon for crowds. Together with its style and detailing it creates a mood. We will begin our survey of the New Kingdom with the temples, which now and in later periods also brought a kind of corporatism to Egypt. Subsequent to the New Kingdom they became the repositories of what was distinctive about ancient Egypt within a society that was otherwise changing greatly (see Chapter 8).[1]

If we look back to the Old and Middle Kingdoms, as far as we can tell, monumental architecture in the shape of the pyramids and their temples was kept to the periphery of the visible world: the edge of the western desert between the entrance to the Fayum and Abu Rawash, to the north of Giza. Local temples, built largely of mud brick, were scaled to fit within the dense vistas of modest brick-built towns and could be almost invisible, as in the case of the Hekaib shrine at Elephantine (Figure 70, p. 199). As an institution the local temple was an adjunct to the office of the head of the local community, so that the title 'chief priest' was frequently held by the local 'mayor'. In the New Kingdom the monumental scale and the preference for building in stone were brought into towns. This was the age of the Mature Formal temple, as outlined in Chapter 3. People in general began to live in the shadow of giant stone constructions that proclaimed the gentlemen's agreement between king and gods that power was exclusively theirs. New Kingdom Thebes epitomizes this, and will be illustrated later in this chapter.

For a fuller appreciation of the New Kingdom style in temples two particular factors

Figure 90 Religious processions in the New Kingdom centred on portable sacred barques (also Plate 5, p. 250). In this scene the barque is the major one for the image of Amun, having its own name 'Userhat'. It is shown at the mortuary temple of Seti I at West Thebes during the 'Beautiful Festival of the Valley'. The pylon of Seti's temple (identified faintly by painted cartouches, not shown in this drawing) is at the left side. The barque is carried by priests and accompanied by officials. (1) and (2) priests; (3) chief priests; (4) Ipiy, a sculptor from Deir el-Medina; (5) the vizier Paser; (6) the scribe of Deir el-Medina, Amenemipet. From a sculpted block from Deir el-Medina, reign of Rameses II, in the Egyptian Museum, Cairo 43591. After G. Foucart, *BIFAO* 24 (1954), Pl. XI (omitting texts); KRI (trans.) I, 333.

need to be pointed out. The first arose from the structural dualism of temple worship, accommodating a hidden and a revealed aspect (Chapter 3, p. 147). The New Kingdom saw great attention given to the latter, the portable religious image, of which the most familiar was the portable boat shrine. Sacred boats were not new. They seem from early times to have had an important symbolic and ritual role.[2] What the New Kingdom did was to lavish great attention on certain of them (especially the barge of Amun of Karnak called Userhat-Amun, 'Mighty of prow is Amun'), and to develop the smaller portable version. One 'Superintendent of Carpenters and Chief of Goldsmiths' called Nakht-djehuty, who lived in the reign of Rameses II and evidently specialized in making them, was repeatedly commissioned to make new ones for a variety of temples, probably up to a total of twenty-six.[3] Both the riverine and the portable boats were put at the centre of temple design and temple celebrations. The portable boat shrines were made of wood, but ornately gilded and decorated and equipped with a closed cabin (sometimes called a *seh-netjer*, 'Tent-shrine of the god', see p. 152) in which the image of the deity sat (Figure 90, and Plate 5). Long carrying-poles on each side or set laterally and up to five in number bore the shrine along on the shoulders of priests.[4]

The resting-places for boat shrines, or way-stations, have a distinctive plan: an oblong chamber with a doorway at each end and a central square stone pedestal on which the shrine rested (see Figure 91, p. 251). We should recall here the pedestals in early temples on which portable images were set, sheltered by a curved canopy of matting (see Chapter 3, and Figure 51, p. 145). Most New Kingdom temples were in fact built around the shrine

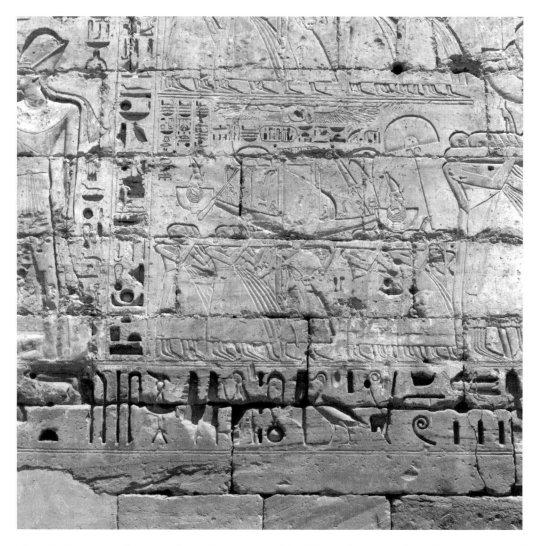

Plate 5 Large temples were places of constant activity. Here priests carry boat shrines, as part of the procession of the Festival of Amun. From the temple of Medinet Habu, reign of Rameses III, north-east wall of the second court.

Figure 91 The grand setting for religious processions provided by monumental architecture and colossal sculpture. The processional route linking the temple of Amun-Ra and the goddess Mut at Karnak, Thebes, see Figures 83, pp. 228–9, 97, p. 266. Two processional way-stations or resting-places for boat shrines are marked. Their stone pedestals for the boat shrines have long since vanished.

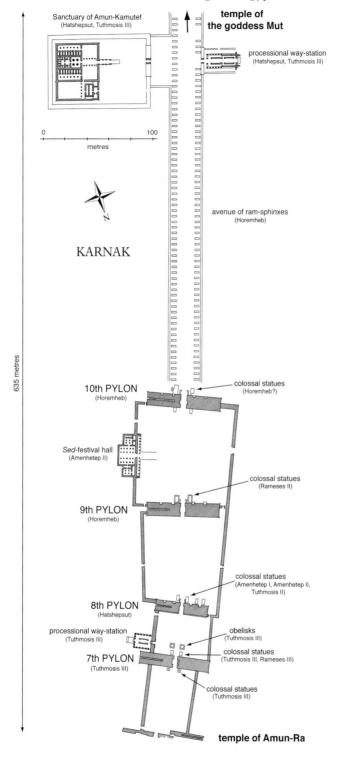

Sanctuary of Amun-Kamutef
(Hatshepsut, Tuthmosis III)

**temple of
the goddess Mut**

processional way-station
(Hatshepsut, Tuthmosis III)

0   100

metres

N

KARNAK

avenue of ram-sphinxes
(Horemheb)

635 metres

10th PYLON
(Horemheb)

colossal statues
(Horemheb?)

Sed-festival hall
(Amenhetep II)

colossal statues
(Rameses II)

9th PYLON
(Horemheb)

colossal statues
(Amenhetep I, Amenhetep II,
Tuthmosis II)

8th PYLON
(Hatshepsut)

processional way-station
(Tuthmosis III)

obelisks
(Tuthmosis III)

colossal statues
(Tuthmosis III, Rameses III)

7th PYLON
(Tuthmosis III)

colossal statues
(Tuthmosis III)

temple of Amun-Ra

of the sacred boat, and the plans of their interiors and the layouts of their exterior sacred precincts began from the desire to parade the boat shrine to the most dramatic advantage. Temples continued to contain fixed images of gods, but these now had second place. The elevation of the boat shrine to a position of eminence in temple religion matched the new monumental scale of local temples. Not only did they dominate the city physically, the processions of the boat shrines along prepared avenues brought a greatly enhanced degree of religious spectacle to the life of the city (Figure 91). The scale and professionalism of New Kingdom temple religion now held the populace more in thrall, replacing some of the older bureaucratic control with greater and more overt psychological manipulation. Then as now people love festive processions put on by the state, and feel more amicably disposed towards their rulers.

For the second factor we must turn to the external architecture of temples, how they looked to the world outside, a world that, for the most part, was excluded for ever from passing through the temple doors. The stone walls bearing scenes painted in hard bright colours on dazzling white backgrounds did not rise directly from streets or public spaces. Between the temple and the outside world lay a precinct filled with brick service buildings and perhaps lesser shrines, all surrounded by a massive wall of mud brick. It was by this wall that the temple made its most public statement. In the New Kingdom the enclosure walls of the larger temples were made to look like fortresses, with towers and battlements.[5] Part of the evidence comes from excavation. At Karnak the same excavation to the east of the sacred lake which revealed the planned Middle Kingdom town beneath (see Chapter 5, and Figure 83, p. 229) also uncovered a 200-metre-long stretch of the 18th Dynasty enclosure wall with square towers set at roughly 17-metre intervals. Other more complete examples are known from other sites. There is also, however, contemporary representational evidence. This is important because it depicts what the tops of the walls looked like, something that the excavation of foundations can never reveal. The most explicit source is a limestone libation tank of the 19th Dynasty from Memphis, which is modelled to show a wall with regularly spaced towers along all four sides and protecting the corners, and with a line of battlemented crenellations running all the way round the top (Figure 92).[6] The sides are inscribed with prayers to the god Ptah of Memphis, one of them reading: 'Praise to you at the great rampart; it is the place where prayer is heard.' To emphasize this a human ear has been carved at the top of each tower. There can be little doubt that this castellated structure represents the main enclosure wall of the New Kingdom temple of Ptah at Memphis, into the interior of which the public was not admitted. To the citizen of Memphis who made the model as part of a votive statue the temple was not a wondrous stone house of god, it was a citadel before which he could only stand and, in a small shrine beside or between the towers, appeal to the power of god to pass through the massive barriers that his fellow citizens had erected. The eastern temple at Karnak, mentioned below, is probably a more grandiose example of the same phenomenon.[7]

In later periods (see Chapter 8, pp. 351–60) the temple enclosure became in reality an urban citadel, containing the local community's principal assets and places of residence for its leaders, becoming in consequence a target for invading armies to attack. But in the New Kingdom the castellated appearance of temple walls must have been largely symbolic. In cases where the front pylon of the temple interrupted the wall and bore, as it normally did, giant scenes of the king vanquishing his foes in the presence of the gods, the towers and battlements on either side continued the mood. In scale, style and detailing the temple

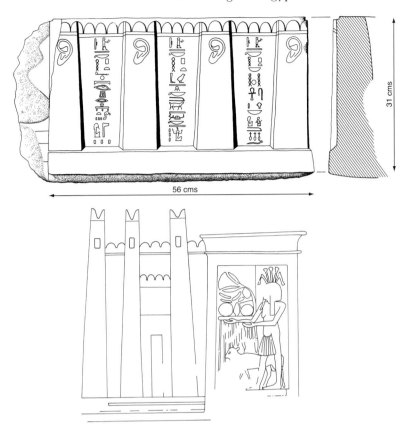

Figure 92   The forbidding appearance of large New Kingdom temples, surrounded by walls built to resemble fortresses. *Above.* Ancient model of the walls surrounding the temple of Ptah at Memphis, originally carved in the form of an offering-basin being presented by a kneeling statue. After J. Jacquet, *MDAIK* 16 (1958), 164, Fig. 1. *Below.* Portrayal of a temple wall and portal at Karnak, from a scene inside the temple of Khonsu at Karnak, reign of Herihor, transition to the 21st Dynasty, after The Epigraphic Survey, *The temple of Khonsu* I. *Scenes of King Herihor in the court*, Chicago, 1979, Pl. 53.

wall had, in a world now more militarily conscious than it had been, taken over the starkest image of coercion. Thus did the temple present to its community two contrasting faces: one of temporal might, the other, on feast days, of release through communal celebration. This did not prevent people from trying to establish a more personal contact with the great deity who dwelt within, as the Memphis shrine at the ramparts reveals.

So much that has survived from ancient Egypt is to do with religion that we might conclude that Egypt was a sacerdotal state. If we were unable to read hieroglyphs we might well deduce that Egypt was ruled by a high priest in view of the frequent occurrence of pictures of the king performing acts of piety towards figures of gods. We would not, in fact, be far wrong as long as we remember that modern English words like 'king' and 'priest' are not coloured in quite the way that they were in ancient times. But we would be wrong if we interpreted this as demonstrating that the state rested upon a greater degree of spirituality. Religion was the language in which weighty and important matters were couched.

Somewhere amidst the ranks of the priests whose names we know were the theologians responsible, for example, for the elaborate mythological texts and scenes which appear in the royal tombs, and who carefully copied and studied old sacred texts and read into them new interpretations. They are the ones, with an interest in theology, who would most resemble our image of a 'priest'. But they are hard to identify. As they appear in the sources that have survived, people with priestly titles look very much like the officials in other branches of the administration. Indeed, they might well possess a string of titles that cover a priestly role as well as others quite unconnected. The modern term 'priesthood', although convenient, misleads if it implies the existence of a class of people leading a particularly distinctive life. Much of the work in temples was either routine performance of well-established rituals or pure administration of commodities and personnel. The temples as institutions are of interest in a study of the New Kingdom state as much for their economic role as for their spiritual contribution, and for their part in bolstering the monarchy.

Egyptian temples were conceived, with some literalness, as a shelter for the divine images and a house for the gods who dwelt within them. The spiritual essence of gods (and of statues of kings and indeed of any person) required the sustenance that could be derived from food offerings placed regularly before them – offerings derived from productive sources owned by the temple. But this was not the only function of temple property. It also bestowed on the gods a status that corresponded to power and importance on a strictly material scale. The gods were given the status of landed nobility, which suited some of the Egyptians' concrete conceptions of divinity. Furthermore, we find the material enrichment of divine property a major theme in texts dealing with the duties of kingship.

The riches bestowed on the gods seem to have been drawn from the full diversity of Egyptian financial resources, both durable forms of wealth (precious substances as well as sacred vessels in valuable materials), and permanent sources of revenue. Foremost amongst the latter was cultivable grain land, not necessarily in the vicinity of the temple itself, but possibly several hundred kilometres distant, or even in the conquered territories of Nubia.[8] Although New Kingdom temples possessed their own labourers, often prisoners of war, much of temple land seems to have been farmed on a complex rented basis, with up to 30 per cent of the crop paid to the temple in rent.[9] One document late in the period, the Wilbour Papyrus, reveals a picture of temple land subdivided into an elaborate tapestry of holdings, some cultivated by temple agents, and others by people who cover almost the entire spectrum of Egyptian society, from small farmers cultivating on their own behalf, through priests and soldiers, to the vizier himself, these latter groups being clearly landlords employing labourers and so introducing a third party into the division of produce (Figure 93). The relatively high proportion of women is notable, as are the numbers of soldiers (including Sherden mercenaries, Figure 8, p. 32).[10] The implications of this for our understanding of the basis of middle-class life will be pursued in the next chapter. In another document, the Amiens Papyrus, we meet a fleet of twenty-one barges cruising slowly up the Nile and making repeated landings to collect the rents from smallholdings of this nature for transportation to temple granaries at Thebes (see Figure 95).[11]

Other forms of agricultural holding donated to temples included animal herds, fishing and fowling rights, flax fields to provide the raw material from which linen garments were

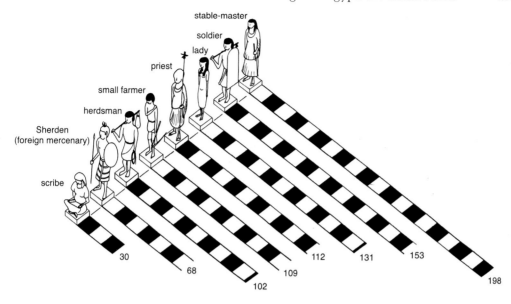

Figure 93 Temple business: categories of persons renting land in Middle Egypt in the 20th Dynasty (after the Wilbour Papyrus). Each square represents ten persons.

manufactured in temple workshops or under licence by private households, vegetable beds, vineyards and beehives. Animals, like crops grown from seed, multiply if tended properly, and it seems that, as with the land, it was common in the New Kingdom for people to look after livestock under a leasing arrangement with a temple. So a royal butler named Nefer-peret, who had fought in one of Tuthmosis III's Palestinian campaigns, was by a special decree of the king put in charge of four Palestinian cows, two Egyptian cows, one bull and a bronze bucket (presumably for carrying the milk).[12] His brother was to look after them and his son was to carry the bucket. The cattle were, however, to be 'offered' to the mortuary temple of Tuthmosis III, meaning that this temple was their real owner (the word 'offering' is not always to be taken literally). The decree made the arrangement heritable, so that Nefer-peret's heirs would go on looking after this little collection of livestock. It was also specifically excluded from the authority of the Overseer of Cattle, a mini-example of a well-documented area of ancient Egyptian law: protection from institutional poaching (which will be examined more in the next chapter). Thus Nefer-peret would go on tending his little herd, obliged to deliver to the king's mortuary temple a quota of offspring and of milk (which his son had to carry), and allowed to keep the rest for himself, secure in his legal protection from the official who was normally in charge of such arrangements.

Temples could be granted access to mineral resources. So the temple of Seti I at Abydos was granted rights at the gold mines in the eastern desert, a gang of workmen to bring the gold back to the temple, and a settlement with a well at the mines themselves.[13] The temple of Amun at Karnak seems to have had a similar arrangement for gold mining in this area, and another for acquiring galena, used for eye pigment and as a medicament, also from the eastern desert.[14] Direct gifts of precious stones and metals also appear as a regular expression of royal piety. It was to the temples, too, that the king turned to dispose of surplus or unwanted booty from foreign campaigns. The temples offered secure storage and administration and, perhaps even more important, a receipt in the form of texts and scenes displayed in the temple that recorded the gift as a great deed of pious generosity.

All of these various types of wealth, from beehives to boats, were designated by a common word for 'offerings'. What was actually presented to the god during the offering ceremonies must have been regarded merely as tokens.

In considering the economic role of temples we are faced with a classic example of the general problem which one culture (our own) has in categorizing another. Temple records were written as if each temple were an independent institution, and this can create the impression that they were independent sources of wealth and power. But if we take a more objective stance we can see that, shorn of theological nuance, temples comprised a major sector of 'the state' as we would see it, working in a symbiotic relationship with the palace. Thus a separate section of the Wilbour Papyrus is devoted to a special category of agricultural land, called *khato*-land, which belonged to Pharaoh but was administered by temples.[15]

The absence of demarcation between temples and other areas of administration becomes very prominent when we consider the example of the payment of the necropolis workers of Deir el-Medina at Thebes whose job it was to prepare the royal tomb in the Valley of Kings.[16] They were essentially employees of the king, and so it seems natural to find that their wages sometimes come from the 'Treasury of Pharaoh' and its overseers. However, late in the 20th Dynasty, apparently a time of economic difficulty at Thebes, we find grain from tax assessments on various temples, and from *khato*-land administered by them, taken to western Thebes for the necropolis workmen and stored in granaries under the charge of the mayor of western Thebes (another interesting use of mayors).[17] Somewhat earlier in the Dynasty we find the same official blamed for not having paid these workmen from the 'offerings' of the century-old mortuary temple of Rameses II (the Ramesseum). The demonstration by these men outside others of these temples suggests that they, too, regarded the mortuary temples as potential sources of payment, something largely confirmed by a few surviving pay records.[18] At other times these men were paid from the temple of Maat at Karnak, across the river.[19] And when things went wrong, the ultimate court of appeal was the vizier. The independence of temples as owners of wealth was probably very much a matter of theological nuance.

A second channel of expenditure was the temple overheads, principally the payment of staff in kind. By a ceremony called the 'Reversion of Offerings' the offerings actually presented to the god were first taken before any statues of lesser cults, and then finally divided amongst the priests and temple staff. The daily offering-list carved on the walls of the temple of Medinet Habu, for example, includes 5,500 loaves, fifty-four cakes, thirty-four dishes of sweets, 204 jars of beer, and an extensive array of other foods.[20] But temple stores were designed to handle even larger quantities and we have no way of knowing how many other people had entitlement to payments, although the Theban necropolis workmen from Deir el-Medina were amongst them. Did temples pay for their own aggrandizement and fabric maintenance? It is reasonable to think so. The building and enlargement of temples was another traditional duty of kings, but since temple income was initially bestowed by the king, the further use of this to pay for improvements would have remained within the spirit of the original bequest; and, in any case, his authority was presumably neces-sary for any major alteration in the disposal of temple income. By the Late Period it becomes clearer that temple building owed much to the initiative of the leaders of local communities. The system had an element of elasticity, too. Apart from a degree of *ad hoc* requisitioning by one institution from another (see Chapter 7), it was possible for one temple to rent lands from another temple and, as a result of occasional inventories and revisions of temple property, for parcels of land to be transferred from an old endowment to a new one which now seemed more worthy. Behind the florid language of piety lay a reassuring rationality.[21]

It seems clear from ancient written testimony as well as from the logic of the situation that temple economies produced a surplus of income over requirements. Some years were good to farmers, some years were bad. Temples expected in general to build up substan-tial reserves or buffer-stocks of grain and other commodities that they stored in massive warehouse-blocks (or magazines) within the temple enclosure. Several relatively complete layouts have survived, and these are supplemented by detailed contemporary pictures.[22] The best preserved archaeologically is the set of magazines attached to the Ramesseum, the mortuary temple of Rameses II (Figure 94 and Plate 6).[23]

To give the reader some idea of the immense concentration of cereal wealth that a major temple could store, the total capacity of the chambers most likely to have stored grain has been calculated, and is given in the caption to Figure 94. When converted to ancient Egyptian measures it amounts to 226,328 *khar* (or 'sacks'). On an average ration for a workmen's family of 66 *khar* per year of emmer and barley (attested in New Kingdom records from Deir el-Medina), the Ramesseum granaries, if ever filled to capacity, would have supported about 3,400 families for a year, i.e. 17,000 to 20,000 people, the population of a fair-sized ancient city, and a considerably greater population than the Memphis palace of Seti I discussed later in this chapter (p. 289). We can draw two general conclusions from this exercise. It is unlikely that at any one time the granary of more than one mortu-ary temple was fully in use; and, like the granaries at the Nubian forts discussed in the last chapter, storage capacity encompassed much more than the needs of an immediately resident and dependent population. The Pharaonic economy in times of internal stabil-ity operated at a level much higher than that of subsistence. Grain was wealth, and great stores of it were there for shipping around the country and even abroad for the realization of grandiose royal schemes. Major temples were the reserve banks of their day.

The ideal was excessive abundance, with granaries overflowing. There is no mention in ancient texts of a 'profit', but in practice that was what good harvests brought. For the larger temples also possessed their own merchant ships, not only in Egypt but also abroad. The temple of Seti I at Abydos, for example, was given a sea-going ship for foreign trade equipped with 'traders' by Rameses II.[24] 'Traders' seem to have been a regular component of temple staffs and presumably bore the responsibility for exchanging surplus produce – not only grain but other things such as linen – for goods for which the temple had a demand, which might be sesame oil or papyrus rolls.[25] Since everything in Egypt was exchangeable, a gradual accumulation of non-perishable goods, particularly metals, in the temple stores increased the temple's permanent reserves. The consequences of this are difficult to penetrate. But the institutional dominance of the country's economy and the capacity to build up massive reserves must have had a markedly steadying influence on the general economy, balancing out, for example, the effects of good and bad harvests and

Plate 6 Institutional wealth: some of the mud-brick granary chambers in the magazine-blocks attached to the Ramesseum, mortuary temple of Rameses II at western Thebes, looking north-east. The arched roofs belong to the original building.

so keeping prices reasonably stable through the year and from one year to another. Hence the parallel with modern reserve banks. When we come to consider the private sector in the next chapter this will emerge as a significant factor amidst the little evidence that we possess.

The wealth of the large temples and the authority of their gods lead to a key question. Did the managers – the priests – perceive the extent of their power? In particular, were the priests of Amun at Thebes a political threat to kings? To answer this we have to consider two further aspects of New Kingdom society: the relationship between the monarchy and the cult of Amun, and the power of other institutions, namely the palace and more particularly the army.

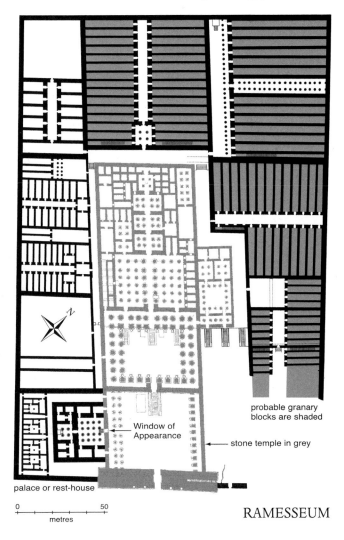

probable granary
blocks are shaded

Window of
Appearance

stone temple in grey

palace or rest-house

0   50
metres

RAMESSEUM

Figure 94 The Ramesseum, mortuary temple of Rameses II at West Thebes. The stone temple is rendered in grey; the surrounding brickwork in black. The latter includes a small palace or rest-house with a Window of Appearance (see Figure 100, p. 275), and a huge set of granary chambers (shaded). It has been assumed that all those blocks with staircases were granaries, the staircases enabling them to be filled through roof apertures. The total floor area is about 8,261 sq. m. The storechambers were tall and vaulted (Plate 6, p. 258) and it is reasonable to assume that grain was stored (perhaps in compartments) to a depth of 2 m. This would give a total capacity of 16,522 cu. m, or 16,522,000 litres, equivalent to about 226,328 *khar*. On an average annual ration for a working family of 66 *khar* of emmer and barley combined, the Ramesseum granary would have supported about 3,400 families, easily the population of a medium-sized city. After U. Hölscher, *The mortuary temple of Ramses III*, Part I, Chicago, 1941, Pl. 10, opp. p. 74.

MAGAZINE BLOCK AT AMARNA

3 tracts of land of this size were needed to fill the
Ramesseum granary at a 30% harvest-share

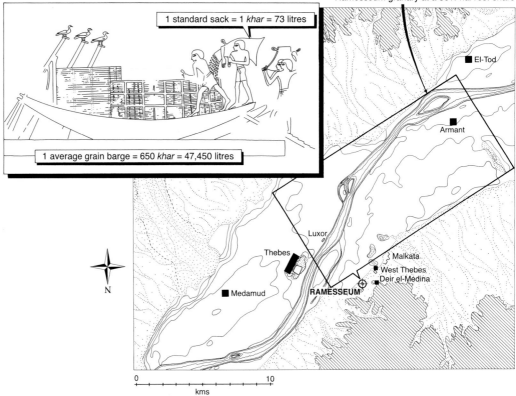

1 standard sack = 1 *khar* = 73 litres

1 average grain barge = 650 *khar* = 47,450 litres

Monarchy and the cult of Amun

The demands on kings were now considerable. They stood at the head of a large admin-istration that, in the case of the temples, now included substantial institutions of a semi-independent nature; theirs was the responsibility for leading armies into battle against the well-equipped forces of western Asia; and in them resided the dignity of an imperial state with far-reaching diplomatic ties. Respect for kings was essential if they were to hold the edifice of state together. Monarchy on its own, however, does not guarantee respect. Too much hangs on accidents of birth. It requires the backing of myth and the regular reinforcement of ceremony to put into perspective the shortcomings of individual kings. By myth and ceremony a king is not left to stand entirely by his own merits. The respect of his people focuses on the office. The New Kingdom put much effort into this, and nowhere more so than in the mutual absorption of king and Amun.

During the Old Kingdom the dogma emerged that the king was the son of Ra, the sun-god. From the mid-4th Dynasty onwards one of the king's two cartouche-names described his manifestation as just this: 'The Son of Ra, N' (where N was the personalized Ra-name of the king), as in the example, 'Enduring are the souls of Ra' (a translation of Menkaura, the name of the builder of the third pyramid at Giza). The importance of the royal dependence on the sun was proclaimed in stone in the form of the pyramids and, in the 5th Dynasty, by large solar temples attached to the pyramids. The Egyptians sometimes used the word 'son' metaphorically, to refer to a loyal and loving son-like status that a person, including a king, might hold vis-à-vis someone else. However, the 'son of Ra' claim was taken more literally. A late Middle Kingdom tale (Papyrus Westcar) set in past time, at the court of King Khufu, contains an account of how the future ultra-pious kings of the 5th Dynasty were borne from a sexual union between Ra and the wife of a priest of Ra.[26]

Having the sun as a supreme deity creates a difficulty. It is the most visible and obvious of sources of superhuman power. Yet its very visibility and fixed shape make it more dif-ficult to comprehend in personalized terms. A religion which has hymns and prayers and offerings assumes a human-like capacity on the part of the deity to receive them. The

Figure 95   The key to economic stability: buffer-stocks of grain. The long narrow storerooms – 'magazines' – in large temples such as the Ramesseum at West Thebes (Figure 94, p. 259, Plate 6, p. 258) were used to store a wide variety of commodities, as illustrated by the El-Amarna tomb scene (*top*, tomb of Meryra), which depicts part of a magazine block. However, it is highly likely that in any large magazine block most of the capacity was used to store cereal grain, as at the Ramesseum. We know (from the Amiens Papyrus) that the average capacity of a grain barge was 650 standard sacks, or *khar*. It would have taken about 350 boatloads of grain to fill the Ramesseum granary. Cereal yields varied according the quality of the land, between about 5 and 10 *khar* per *aroura* (2,735 sq. m). At the low but common yield of 5 *khar* from land which paid to the temple a 30 per cent harvest-rent, the Ramesseum would have been drawing on a tract of land equivalent to about 412 square km. To give readers some idea of what is involved, a piece of land about one third of this is marked on a map of the Theban area. In practice temple landholdings were split into large numbers of widely spaced fields. If one considers an extrapolation from the diagram to include the numer-ous lesser provincial temples it is easy to envisage just how much farmland was tied in some way to temple ownership or management. El-Amarna magazines after N. de G. Davies, *The rock tombs of El Amarna* I, London, 1903, Pl. XXXI; the boat-loading scene after B. Landström, *Ships of the Pharaohs*, London, 1970, 134, Fig. 393.

Egyptians instinctively appreciated this, and at an early date gave to most of the gods and goddesses of Egypt the form of a human body, though sometimes retaining as an emblem an animal head. One form of the sun-god, Ra-Horus of the Horizon (Ra-Horakhty), was a man with the falcon head of the god Horus. But in other contexts the sun's disk was left as a detached element, perhaps symbolically conveyed forwards by a scarab-beetle, itself a symbol of creation as the god Kheprer, or journeying in a solar barge above the head of a ram-headed god. When it came to the direct worship of the sun by hymns and the presentation of food-offerings, the air of mystery that is needed to cloak a somewhat artificial act was difficult to sustain. Sun temples were open to the sky, and the hymns were chanted and offerings presented from the top of an open platform. The sun provided a good poetic image for the king, but was far less suitable a model for his divine counterpart.

New Kingdom theologians overcame this. The supreme god who fathered the king and remained the ultimate basis of royal respect was given the form of a man. This was the god Amun. It was not an arbitrary choice, for Amun was an ancient god of Thebes, the home of the kings of the 18th Dynasty. The early history of Amun is not well documented, but it is clear that his pre-eminence in the New Kingdom was a result of deliberate theological emphasis.[27] Two characteristics, at least as old as the Middle Kingdom, gave Amun a particularly powerful image. With no modification to his human form he had become the sun-god, Amun-Ra, and was now the recipient (even under the simpler name Amun) of hymns addressed to the sun. He also took over the powerful ithyphallic image of Min of Coptos, a neighbouring city (see Figure 47, p. 138). In the New Kingdom his position was well expressed by a common epithet, 'Amun-Ra, King of the Gods'. At Thebes especially he was shown in the temples as the divine father-figure who looked after the king and presided over his victories, and this role extended to the mortuary cult now centred in new-style mortuary temples on the west bank of Thebes.

Amun also moved to the heart of the myth of the divine birth of the king, which now joined the repertoire of scenes on temple walls. Two complete examples have survived – in Queen Hatshepsut's mortuary temple at Deir el-Bahari, and in Amenhetep III's temple at Luxor – but fragments of others are known.[28] The crucial episode of the whole sequence is handled with great delicacy (Figure 96). The reigning monarch's mother is shown seated opposite the god Amun, who with one hand touches one of her hands, and with the other offers her the emblematic hieroglyph for 'life'. The protective goddesses Neith and Selket sit below on the marriage-bed, holding the couple aloft. The accompanying text is a little more explicit:

> Words spoken by Amun-Ra, Lord of Karnak, pre-eminent in his harem, when he had assumed the form of this her husband, King Menkheperura [Tuthmosis IV], given life. He found her as she slept within the innermost part of her palace. She awoke on account of the divine fragrance, and turned towards His Majesty. He went straightway to her, he was aroused by her. He allowed her to see him in his divine form, after he had come before her, so that she rejoiced at seeing his perfection. His love, it entered her body. The palace was flooded with the divine fragrance, and all his odours were those of the land of Punt.

After a brief speech of joy by the queen he declares: 'Amenhetep, prince of Thebes, is the name of this child which I have placed in your womb . . .' Subsequent scenes portray the

Figure 96 An immaculate conception: the god Amun (*upper right*) impregnates Queen Mutemwia (*upper left*) wife of Tuthmosis IV and mother of the future god-king Amenhetep III. Beneath them sit the goddesses Selket *(left)* and Neith *(right)*. A scene from the divine birth cycle at Luxor temple (see Figure 99, p. 271). After H. Brunner, *Die Geburt des Gottkönigs*, Wiesbaden, 1964, Taf. 4; E. Otto, *Egyptian art and the cults of Osiris and Amun*, London, 1968, Pl. 30 (redrawn by B. Garfi).

fashioning of the child and his spirit (*ka*) on a potter's wheel by the ram-headed creator-god Khnum, and the birth itself in the presence of numerous protector spirits.

Queen Hatshepsut's version goes on to illustrate how the power and authority of well-tailored mythical portrayals can replace reality. Historically she was the daughter of Tuthmosis I and wife of the next king Tuthmosis II, whom she outlived by more than twenty years. For the first few years of her widowhood she acted as regent for the young successor, her nephew Tuthmosis III, but then had herself proclaimed king, and ruled as the dominant partner. In her mortuary temple at Deir el-Bahari, western Thebes, she appears throughout as the rightful king, depicted and frequently referred to in texts as being of male gender. In this latter respect the conventions of kingship offered no choice. A fine set of scenes at Deir el-Bahari records the story of her origins. Early on occurs the divine birth sequence, in which she is from the beginning designated as king of Egypt. As the story unfolds it shifts gradually to the mortal world. She visits Lower Egypt with her real father, Tuthmosis I, and is taken in hand by all the gods of Egypt, who crown her and draw up her titulary. Now merging more closely into the material world her father presents her to the court and appoints her as his successor and co-regent:

> This is my daughter, Khnemet-Amun Hatshepsut, may she live. I designate her as my successor. She it is who shall be on this throne. Assuredly, it is she who shall sit on this heavenly throne. She shall issue decrees to the people from all departments of the palace. Assuredly, it is she who shall guide you. Obey her word, assemble you at her command . . . For she is your god, the daughter of a god.[29]

The people react with joy, the lector-priests compose her titulary, her name is set on buildings and on official seals, and finally her coronation takes place on New Year's Day. Other records of this situation – that Hatshepsut was the heir and successor of Tuthmosis I with no reference to either Tuthmosis II or III – have survived at Karnak. All of them describe on a monumental scale events that are specific, detailed, but, as far as we can see, wholly fictitious. Even the New Year's Day coronation date referred back to an ancient custom now obsolete.[30] Had accident deprived us of all sources for the period other than these, their detail and consistency would oblige us to accept their record as authentic history. Therein lies a warning.

This aspect of Hatshepsut's reign takes us back to Chapter 2 and the basic myth of the state: the uninterrupted sequence of legitimate kings ruling in a single line of succession descended from the gods. Hatshepsut's reign was simply made to conform to the ideal image. To dismiss the sources as propaganda misses the point, particularly if it is implied that they differ in purpose from documents of other reigns. The temples recorded for eternity and provided only a single formula for kingship into which earthly events had to be fitted with whatever degree of transformation was necessary. The record of Hatshepsut's reign was made consistent with an ancient, established pattern, and this was all that mattered.

Thebes: the ceremonial city

Thebes was not really, in the New Kingdom, Egypt's capital city in the sense that the court and the highest tiers of administration were centred there. This was the role of Memphis and, in the later New Kingdom, the eastern delta city of Per-Rameses (near the modern towns of Khatana and Kantir). The family of the 18th Dynasty kings had come from Thebes, and during the New Kingdom the Theban god Amun was given extraordinary prominence. This left the city with a special role in the state: a sacred city given over to religious festivals in which the cult of divine monarchy held a leading place. Poetry celebrated its symbolic primacy:

> Thebes is the pattern for every city. Water and earth were within her from the beginning of time. There came the sands to furnish land, to create her ground as a mound when the earth came into being. And so mankind also came into being within her, with the purpose of founding every city in her proper name. For all are called 'City' after the example of Thebes.[31]

Two comments are required: the basic image is that of the first primaeval mound emerging from the waters of chaos and on which the act of creation was first performed. Here the mound is identified as the site of Thebes. The second point is linguistic: Thebes was frequently called simply 'The City'.

The monumental heart of New Kingdom Thebes was the temple of Amun at Karnak.[32] This now stands within a huge enclosure surrounded by a massive brick wall of the 30th Dynasty. In places, particularly on the south, this wall must follow the line of the New Kingdom enclosure wall, but on the east it takes a course somewhat outside. Even so, in the New Kingdom the enclosure must have covered an area of at least 400 by 400 metres.

The temple as we now see it appears to be flush with the surrounding fields and with the modern town of Luxor. Excavations into the ground below (summarized in Chapter 5, see Figure 83, pp. 228–9) have revealed, however, that the New Kingdom temple was laid out at the expense of the earlier city of Thebes. This had grown by the late Middle Kingdom into an extensive city mound covering an area at least 1,000 by 500 metres and possibly a lot more. This puts it into a category of places that were quite large by ancient standards. A good part of it had been laid out to conform to a rigid grid plan, and within it lay palaces (known also from texts). During the 18th Dynasty the city was evacuated and levelled to provide a foundation platform for the new dominating stone temples. This probably occurred on a piecemeal basis, with some parts of the site, notably the 'Treasury' of Tuthmosis I and the southern part of the southward processional avenue (between pylons 8 and 10), aligned according to the prevailing street and plot pattern of the old city (Figure 83, pp. 228–9), whilst the rest of the temple took on an alignment perpendicular to the river which, apparently, the old Middle Kingdom temple had possessed as well.[33]

The residential part of Thebes must have been built anew, on open ground involving a fresh allocation of plot ownership. Being on new ground meant that it was at a lower level than the new temple now perched on the levelled top of the old city mound. This new city level must now be beneath the general level of the ground water. Modern excavations have encountered it in only small exposures. The location of one neighbourhood is given by an inscription on a giant obelisk quarried in the reign of Tuthmosis III and finally erected by Tuthmosis IV in a curious chapel built against the back, in other words, the eastern wall of the temple of Amun-Ra. This chapel was intended for people who had no right of access to the main temple. It was a 'place of the ear' for the god Amun, where the god could hear the prayers of the townspeople. It seems also to have contained a statue of 'Rameses who hears prayer', a revealing glimpse of the reality behind the cult of divine

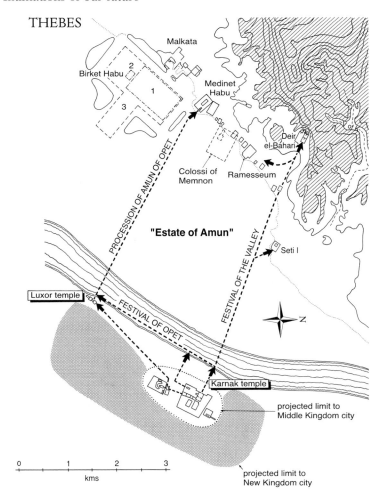

Figure 97 Map of Thebes, the 'Estate of Amun', in the New Kingdom, showing main temples and processional routes. The rectangles marked along the western desert edge are royal mortuary temples. 'V of K'= Valley of Kings. For Malkata and the Birket Habu see Figure 101, p. 278, and Plate 8, p. 279. The numbered parts of the Birket Habu are: (1) Hypothetical first basin; (2) Palace for the first *Sed*-festival; (3) Probable second basin, defined by earth mounds.

kings.[34] The obelisk inscription states that it was set up in 'The Upper Gateway of Karnak, opposite Thebes'.[35] The implication is that it faced towards the city lying over to the east. We should imagine, however, a city covering a much larger area than before, reflecting the more expansive atmosphere of the New Kingdom (Figure 97). The short-lived city of El-Amarna spread its main built-up part over an area about 5 kilometres (3 miles) long by a kilometre wide.

There is evidence at other sites to show that what happened to Thebes in the New Kingdom was not unusual. The period seems to have been characterized by urban renewal. For the Middle Kingdom we can speak of urbanization as a policy of the state, achieved by

laying out planned settlements which in their rigid grid-plans reflected an intense bureaucratic control of society. Urban renewal in the New Kingdom displays far less of this, and
may have arisen as a consequence of the redevelopment of key sites within towns as temple
precincts. Provincial temple building on a grand scale became a priority of state expenditure in the New Kingdom for the first time; the rebuilding of towns and cities, in a more
open style which reflected the changed nature of Egyptian society, was a by-product which
became generally desirable in itself.

The main part of the temple of Karnak was constructed during the 18th Dynasty, surrounding on four sides the old Middle Kingdom temple that had an alignment at variance
with the main axis of the planned Middle Kingdom quarter of the city and faced directly
towards the river. Egyptian temples of the 18th Dynasty display considerable variation and
originality in design, and this is particularly true at Karnak. The layout is unique, both
in its internal complexity and in the small allocation of open space. The central element
was a shrine, open at both ends, which contained the portable barque by which the image
of Amun could be carried outside the temple on important festivals. The present granite
shrine is a very late replacement (by the Macedonian king Philip Arrhidaeus) of the New
Kingdom original. In the reign of Tuthmosis III the main temple building was enlarged
by about 50 per cent through the addition at the rear of a stone building that has come to
be known as the 'Festival Hall' of Tuthmosis III, a building evidently designed for the celebration of varied theological aspects of kingship (the rituals of the *Sed*-festival included).[36]

Somewhere in the grounds of Karnak temple lay a royal palace.[37] Its position changed
during the New Kingdom as the temple was enlarged. It must have been built of mud
brick for nothing has been found either of foundations or of loose stone blocks. But we are
sure of its existence from references in inscriptions. In the case of Queen Hatshepsut they
are sufficiently explicit to suggest an actual location: in front of the 18th Dynasty temple
façade, on the north side. References to a palace at Karnak continue through the New
Kingdom, even though by the mid-18th Dynasty kings were no longer residing at Thebes.
The texts themselves make it clear, however, that this was no ordinary domestic palace,
but a ceremonial building used, for example, during a royal coronation. The king visited
Thebes as the divine son of Amun. Wherever he was accommodated took on the character
of a sacred building.

The Hatshepsut texts also reveal the political value of the Amun cult at Karnak. On
various festivals the portable barque containing the god's image was carried out of the
main temple, borne on poles resting on the shoulders of priests. This could be made the
opportunity for Amun to perform a 'miracle'. Some movement from the heavy wooden
barque would be communicated to the shoulders of the bearers, and magnified so that a
distinct deviation from the prescribed course occurred, and sometimes a dipping forwards
of the shrine. The texts also claim that speeches were communicated from the god, but by
what means is unclear. In this way Hatshepsut was publicly picked out by Amun and the
miracle interpreted as being a divine choice of the next monarch.[38] Subsequently Tuthmosis III claimed that by a similar miracle at Karnak he also had been chosen by Amun.[39]

How should we react to claims of this kind? Should we be cynical and say that it was
all made up afterwards for propaganda reasons? Should we be more broad-minded and
consider that chosen people in a state of excitement might actually hear voices, or voice
openly the urgings of their conscience? Or was there a device by which the god's voice was
made to speak? The question is made more acute by a case where a king (Tuthmosis III

again) claims that in the important cord-stretching ceremony during the foundation rituals preparatory to building a new temple at Karnak (his 'Festival Hall'), 'the majesty of this revered god [i.e. Amun] desired to do the extending of the line himself'.[40] How much deeply felt religious experience as against cynical use of stereotyped religious phraseology we think was present will depend very much upon the individual reader's own state of mind. It is not something that scholarly research can properly answer. What we can say is that statements of this kind make an ideological point, stressing the particular importance of the event in question. The reader is informed that the choice of the next king or the laying out of a temple (or the various other acts sanctioned by Amun's oracle) has the greatest authority that mind and vocabulary can convey. They demonstrate the legitimizing role of Amun and the use of the Karnak temple precinct as the proper arena for it.

A striking illustration of how Karnak lay at the heart of the ideology of the New Kingdom state is to be seen in the reign of King Akhenaten, who carried through a fundamental, though short-lived, reform of the theology of the state and the imagery of kingship in the late 18th Dynasty (Figure 98). This involved the total rejection of Amun, and the creation of temples to the visible sun (the Aten) built along novel lines (with open courts rather than enclosed sanctuaries) and with novel decoration (the many-rayed sun-disc the only divine image allowed). Akhenaten began his programme at Karnak itself, with the construction of several of the new temples and a palace, and the celebration of a grand *Sed*-festival.[41] By choosing to begin at Karnak he was proclaiming as powerfully as he could that the new style of kingship and state theology, which amounted to a new deal struck between king and god, emanated from the established seat of authority in such matters. At the same time, of course, he was admitting the continued importance of the old home of Amun, but within a short time he was to change that, too, by creating a new city for his sun cult at El-Amarna, half way between Thebes and Memphis (pp. 284–8).

The parading of the divine image was a basic part of temple life in ancient Egypt, Thebes in particular. We know this from the architectural design of Karnak, as much as from the scenes and inscriptions on the temple walls. From the New Kingdom onwards almost as much attention and resources were directed towards laying out processional routes as to the temples themselves. Processional routes were, ideally, paved with stone, lined on both sides with sphinxes or similar statues, and punctuated at intervals by way-stations: small formal shrines or temples set perpendicularly to the route and designed to accommodate a portable boat shrine on a square stone pedestal. They, too, were called 'tent-shrines of the god' (*seh-netjer*). The physical demands of reverently carrying a heavy wooden boat shrine may perhaps have dictated the intervals between way-stations if not the actual practice itself. At Karnak one such route ran from the front of the temple westwards towards the river, ending in a stone quay above a basin at the head of a canal. In the 19th Dynasty this was shortened by the building on its line of the Great Hypostyle Hall and the 2nd Pylon, which became the new front to the temple. A second processional route was laid out in the 18th Dynasty to run southwards from the then temple front (Figure 91). It was given a particularly handsome and impressive appearance. By the time of Horemheb it consisted of four pylons separating as many courts, with obelisks, flagpoles and colossal royal statues in front of the pylon towers, and a way-station and royal jubilee hall built into the courtyard sides. Beyond the last pylon (no. 10 in the Karnak series) the route continued for a further 350 metres, lined with ram-headed sphinxes of the reign of Horemheb and flanked with two way-stations, until it reached a completely separate temple, belonging

Figure 98 Kingship according to the reformation of Akhenaten: an official picture of the Royal Family relaxing at home beneath the rays of the sun (the Aten), the sole god whom they recognized. Compare the flowing urgent style with that of Figure 96 (p. 263). The picture was itself an object of private veneration for it came probably from a chapel in the grounds of a private house at Akhenaten's new city of El-Amarna. He sits on the left, holding the eldest daughter and heiress Meritaten; his queen Nefertiti sits opposite, with the second daughter Meketaten (soon to die) on her lap, and cradling the third daughter Ankhsenpa-aten (later the wife of Tutankhamun) in her arms. Limestone. Height 32 cm. Berlin Museum 14145.

to the goddess Mut who, in the New Kingdom, was held to be Amun's consort. A third avenue, lined subsequent to the New Kingdom with re-used stone rams of Amenhetep III's reign, ran on an almost parallel course from the temple of Khonsu, who, as the son of Amun and Mut, completed the Theban holy family. The present building dates to the 20th Dynasty. This avenue is thought also to have ended in a quay above a basin connected to the Nile.[42] Close by lay the beginning of another processional route that ran southwards for a distance of 3 kilometres, finally ending in front of the temple of Luxor. The sphinxes that now line this route date only to the 30th Dynasty, but a source from Hatshepsut's reign shows that the route must have been marked in some way in the New Kingdom.

The festivals of Thebes were many, and the larger ones involved the temples in considerable extra expenditure in food 'offerings', which, by the 'Reversion of Offerings', were distributed as extra rations to the temple personnel and others involved in the festivals. As examples we can quote a damaged text of Tuthmosis III from his Festival Hall at Karnak that listed fifty-four feast days each year,[43] which compares with the sixty listed at Medinet Habu in the time of Rameses III.[44] For the quantities of offerings the Calendar of Feasts and Offerings at Medinet Habu gives us as a minimum basis for some of the regular monthly feasts eighty-four loaves of bread and fifteen jars of beer, but rising steeply for more favoured feasts to 3,694 loaves, 410 cakes and 905 jars of beer in the case of the Feast of the god Seker.

The processions of images of the holy family of Thebes and of other sanctified beings (including statues of kings of olden times) setting forth from the huge brightly painted temples, and making their slow progress along formally arranged avenues with carefully stage-managed halts at intermediate way-stations, and the occasional excitement of a 'miracle': all this brought to the city as a whole spectacle and munificence which regularly reinforced the physical and economic dominance of the temples. And for the greatest of the festivals the king came to Thebes in person to be at the centre, and to absorb some of the power that the occasion generated.

This most important of festivals was the Festival of Opet.[45] It came round every year, in the second month of the season of Inundation. In the mid-18th Dynasty it lasted for eleven days. By the end of the reign of Rameses III in the 20th it had been lengthened to no less than twenty-seven days. At that time at Medinet Habu the festival was celebrated by the distribution of 11,341 loaves, 85 cakes, and 385 jars of beer. The core of the festival was an unusually long procession of images of the holy family of Thebes. The route lay between Karnak itself and the temple of Luxor (Figure 97, p. 266). In the time of Hatshepsut the outward journey was made by land, using the newly built southward extension of courts and pylons at Karnak, pausing at six way-stations, whilst the return journey was by river. By the late 18th Dynasty both the outward and the return journeys were being made by river. Each of the deities travelled in a separate barge, towed by smaller boats and by gangs of men on the bank, who could include high court officials, hauling on ropes. It was one of the occasions when the public could present pleas to the gods before their portable barques, and before colossal *ka*-statues of the king (see below for the meaning of *ka*). Detailed scenes of the processions, depicting also the soldiers, dancers and musicians who followed the progress of the barges from the bank, were carved on the walls of Luxor temple, the destination of the festival.

The present Luxor temple is largely the work of Amenhetep III and Rameses II. In facing towards Karnak rather than towards the adjacent river it proclaims its dependence upon Karnak. Indeed, the temple seems to have existed primarily to create a suitably monumental setting for the rites in which the annual Opet festival culminated (Figure 99).[46] These rites addressed the fundamental problem which sublime authority inevitably creates: how to reconcile the humanity of the current ruler with the divinity of his office.

We have already examined the process by which divinity was first infused into a mortal child destined to become king. It was explained in a rather literal way, as brought about by a sexual union between his mother and the god Amun who had temporarily assumed the form of his father. One set of scenes illustrating this occur in the inner part of Luxor temple (Figure 96, p. 263). However, the nature of that divine essence was also separately

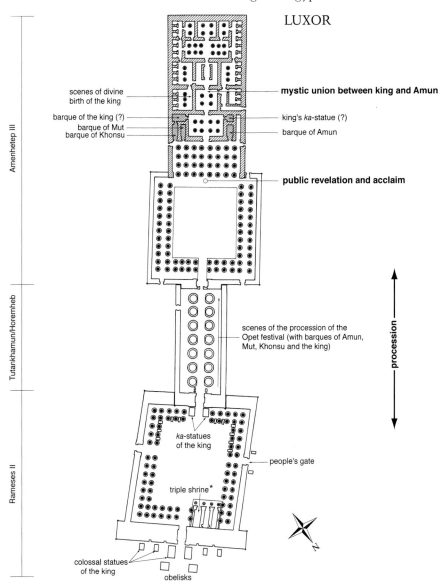

LUXOR

scenes of divine birth of the king

barque of the king (?)
barque of Mut
barque of Khonsu

mystic union between king and Amun

king's *ka*-statue (?)

barque of Amun

public revelation and acclaim

← procession →

scenes of the procession of the Opet festival (with barques of Amun, Mut, Khonsu and the king)

ka-statues of the king

people's gate

triple shrine *

colossal statues of the king

obelisks

Amenhetep III

Tutankhamun/Horemheb

Rameses II

Figure 99 Luxor temple: centre of the mystic relationship between king and the god Amun, and focus of the Opet festival. The cross-hatched part at the rear is the earliest, and remained the sacred precinct in which the mysterious union between king and god took place each year. '*': the triple shrine in the outer court, originally a way-station from the time of Queen Hatshepsut, contained more *ka*-statues of kings, and was a place for prayers and petitions by the people, hoping for an oracular response. The temple served as a place of coronation for at least one king, Horemheb.

identified: it was the royal *ka*. All persons had a *ka*, fashioned at their birth from the invisible continuum of life-force and destined to exist forever. But, just as living kings belonged to the restricted uppermost band of the social hierarchy, so the *ka* of the king was part of the divine essence shared by gods and by the royal ancestors. Each new royal *ka*, created at the moment of the future king's conception (and depicted thus in the scenes of the king's divine birth), represented the next encapsulation of divine power in the sequence that stretched back through the long line of ancestral kings to the period when the gods had ruled in person. The indestructible royal *ka* existed in parallel to the life of the living king, its earthly manifestation, and gave the king his legitimacy. It was, of course, only an idea. But like all important religious ideas it was given a greater semblance of reality through the performance of ritual. Luxor temple was the focus of that ritual, its decoration giving great prominence to the king's *ka*. The procession of the Opet Festival took the king to the temple. Leaving the crowds outside he entered and proceeded in the company of priests to the enclosed chambers at the back. There, in a charged incense-laden atmosphere and the mystic presence of the god Amun (and his ithyphallic manifestation Amun-Min), the king and his *ka* were merged, and the king's person transformed. When the king reappeared, he did so miraculously transformed into a divine being, 'Foremost of all the living *Ka*s'. His reappearance in public freshly transfigured was the real climax, the moment of cheering which implied that the miracle had worked and had been accepted as having worked. Luxor temple was, in the words of its original builder (Amenhetep III), 'his place of justification, in which he is rejuvenated; the palace from which he sets out in joy at the moment of his Appearance, his transformations visible to all'. Luxor temple provided for the king the essential setting for the interplay between the hidden and revealed aspects of a divinity that other temples did for images of the gods.

The annual festival centred on the presence of the king in person. By the mid-18th Dynasty kings were no longer residing at Thebes. They lived for the most part in the north of Egypt, particularly in the palaces at Memphis. The royal participation every year in the Opet festival thus came to involve a state progress upstream that spread the public acclamation further, and grew into an institution in itself. The job of feeding the court during the many overnight stops there and back fell to the mayors of provincial towns, and by the late 18th Dynasty this had become a burden that required a royal edict to correct (see p. 306).

The merging of the king with the god Amun and all his pageants had the important consequence of drawing a line between politics and myth. The royal succession could go badly wrong, some could even plot to kill the king and replace him with another (as happened with Rameses III). But behind visible reality lay an immensely weighty edifice of myth, festival and grand architectural setting that could absorb the petty vagaries of history and smooth out the irregularities. It guaranteed the continuity of proper rule that was so important an element in the Egyptians' thinking. In particular it could convert usurpers (or new blood, depending on one's point of reference) into models of legitimacy and tradition. Horemheb is a prime example. The 18th Dynasty ended with the royal line petering out in the aftermath of the Amarna Period (the reign of Akhenaten and his short-lived successors). The throne passed to an army officer, the general Horemheb, who had risen to prominence in the reign of Tutankhamun. By lineage he apparently was not royal. He was part of the court at Memphis, and during this time saw to the completion of a handsome tomb for himself and his family in the court cemetery at Sakkara. His elevation to the kingship is recorded in formal texts. These go so far as to recognize the early part of his life when he was 'supreme chief of the land' and an adviser to the king. When, through the machinations of court politics, and the leverage that his leadership of the army bestowed, he became king himself, his coronation was carried out at Karnak and Luxor as part of the Festival of Opet of that year. As the texts describe it the whole coronation ceremony was integrated with the Opet festival so that the great Karnak–Luxor procession became a celebratory parade for the newly validated king.[47]

The Theban city of the dead

Karnak, Luxor and the city of Thebes proper lay on the east bank of the Nile. Across the river on the west bank the New Kingdom witnessed the large-scale development of a city of the dead. From the beginning of the 18th Dynasty kings abandoned the building of pyramids in the Memphite area. They put their tombs at Thebes, and their successors continued to do so until the very end of the 20th Dynasty. But now the nature of the royal tomb was very different. The new-style burial place was a catacomb dug into the desert hills in the Valley of the Kings, its security dependent mainly upon the careful policing of the area. It lay quite separate from the all-important offering-cult that was now housed in a temple lying separately beside the alluvial plain. The change involved a fundamental revision of the symbolism of the royal tomb, affecting the relationship between king and supreme deity. In the new tombs the king's body and statue cult were no longer subsumed into a gigantic image of the sun-cult, the pyramid. The only gesture now made to the cult of the visible sun was an open court containing a platform and stairs built into the back of the new mortuary temples. Instead, the new temples proclaimed the centrality and supremacy of Amun.

Although we are accustomed to speak of these temples as being royal mortuary temples, they were in reality temples dedicated to a specific form of the god Amun with whom the king became fused both in death, through the presence of his images within their own shrines, and in life during his visits to the temple.[48] At Deir el-Bahari there was Amun 'Holy of Holies', at the Ramesseum (mortuary temple of Rameses II), Amun 'within United-with-Thebes' (the ancient name for the Ramesseum), and at Medinet Habu, Amun 'of United-with-Eternity' (the ancient name for Medinet Habu). Each of the mortuary temples was really an Amun temple in which the form of a particular king had taken up residence. This is very apparent from the architecture of the better preserved ones. Those of the 19th and 20th Dynasties (of Seti I, Rameses II and Rameses III) reserved the rear central chambers, the holiest part of the temple, for the cult of Amun, not only in a permanent image but, most importantly, in a portable boat shrine kept within a pillared hall with central pedestal. For the 18th Dynasty only the temple of Hatshepsut preserves sufficient of its masonry, and here, behind the centre of the upper terrace, a rock-hewn sanctuary housed the image of Amun. The king who had commissioned the temple naturally had a prominent part in the temple cult, to the extent that, to judge from texts preserved at Medinet Habu, his spirit was thought to merge with that of the local form of Amun.[49] The mortuary temples catered for other aspects of ideology, too. As just noted, the old cult of the visible sun was given an open court on the north side equipped with a stone platform reached by steps, a construction which the Egyptians rather oddly called a 'sunshade', and from the top of which solar hymns were declaimed. A room or suite of rooms to the south of the Amun sanctuary accommodated the cult of historical continuity, in the form of the king's father and sometimes his ancestors as well.[50] Yet another portable boat shrine stood here.

The network of Amun's connections to the west bank of Thebes was expressed through more processions. Once a year, roughly five months before the Opet festival, the 'Festival of the Valley' took place.[51] In this the images of Amun, Mut and Khonsu, the holy family of Thebes, were brought from Karnak and ferried over the river. Once across they continued their journey either by road or canal to Deir el-Bahari, site of the ancient mortuary temple and tomb of King Menthuhetep II of the 11th Dynasty (Figure 57, p. 157) and of the recent mortuary temple of Queen Hatshepsut. Deir el-Bahari lies almost exactly opposite to Karnak so that the whole journey could have been accomplished along a single line. However, as the New Kingdom progressed the route was extended so that the portable barques with their statues could rest overnight in the mortuary temple of the reigning king. On the next day the procession returned to Karnak. Although it was a much shorter festival than that of Opet it was highly regarded and was the occasion for families with relatives or ancestors buried in the Theban hills to make their own journey to the family tomb, to have a meal there, and to stay overnight.

A lesser but more frequent connection between east and west banks was maintained at a small temple built (or rebuilt) at the southern end of the Theban necropolis in the time of Tuthmosis III (1479–1425 BC), beside the space which later would be occupied by Rameses III's mortuary temple of Medinet Habu (Figure 122, p. 352).[52] The shape of the temple was standard for its day, but its innocuous form disguised the fact that it was regarded as embodying yet another of the primaeval mounds on which creation had first taken place. It was 'The Genuine Mound of the West', a name which probably also conveyed the notion that original creation and the rebirth of the dead in the western desert cemetery were linked. Inscriptions from the 21st Dynasty reveal that every ten days (the normal length of a working 'week' in ancient Egypt) the image of Amun of Opet (Luxor) was brought across to visit this temple, and it is likely from inscriptions at Luxor itself that this custom extends back to at least the time of Rameses II.

When the routes of these processions – the Festivals of Opet and of the Valley and the regular trip to Medinet Habu – are marked on a map they form a pattern: a processional perimeter to Thebes (Figure 97, p. 266). To see the Theban temples on east and west as parts of a master-scheme is not just modern fancy. Certain brief texts, particularly names specifying certain buildings or building parts, reveal a distinct parallelism in Egyptian thinking between the mortuary temples on the west and Karnak and Luxor on the east, a parallelism that the processions of boat shrines articulated.[53] The master-scheme, the unitary overview of the sacred places of Thebes, is summed up in the simple fact that all of them belonged to the 'Estate of Amun'. This was what the processional perimeter really defined. Its realization on the ground, however, also reveals the limits of New Kingdom area planning. There was no attempt to build on the legacy of the Middle Kingdom by extending the overall planning of a settlement to the premeditated arrangement of a huge religious complex of temples and tombs. Individual Theban temples impress us with their carefully symmetrical layouts. But their particular locations seem to have depended largely on local factors of sanctity or convenience, giving rise to an *ad hoc* landscape of religious architecture. This was where the processional avenues made their contribution, binding the disparate parts together and creating a semblance of unity.

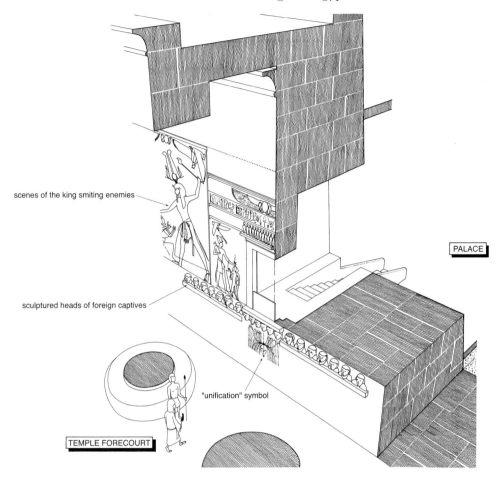

scenes of the king smiting enemies

PALACE

sculptured heads of foreign captives

"unification" symbol

TEMPLE FORECOURT

Figure 100   Theatrical setting for the 'appearance' of the king: the symbol-laden ornamental palace balcony, the 'Window of Appearance' of Pharaoh. This slightly restored version is from the first palace at Rameses III's mortuary temple, Medinet Habu, West Thebes, after U. Hölscher, *The mortuary temple of Ramses III*, Part I, Chicago, 1941, chapter II. See Plate 7, p. 276, for a photograph of the remains of the palace, and Figure 122, Phase I, p. 352, for a location plan.

Just as Karnak and Luxor provided an important ceremonial opportunity for the king, so also did the mortuary temples on the west bank. From the time of Horemheb onwards each contained a small palace situated near the front of the temple (Figure 94, p. 259, Plate 7; also Figure 122, p. 352).[54] It offered limited but evidently adequate accommodation for the king and his entourage during parts of his normally infrequent visits to Thebes. The best-known example, at Medinet Habu, has two entrances to the inner part of the palace and each is graced with a scene of the king making an entrance, in the one case 'to see his father Amun in his feast at the beginning of Opet', and in the other 'to cause his father Amun to appear in the Feast of the Valley'.[55] The mortuary temple palace was always on the south side, and where it faced into the temple forecourt or towards the avenue leading into the temple it possessed a formal balcony, the 'Window of Appearance' (Figure 100).[56]

Plate 7   Part of the small palace attached to the south side of the mortuary temple of Rameses III at Medinet Habu. The walls are partly restored.

This was the setting for a reward ceremony that, in view of the Theban festival programme, would have occurred no more than once or twice a year. A cushion was laid on the sill of the window itself, courtiers and high officials were led before it, and rewards and honours bestowed on them. This Theban reward ceremony was only a local version of a general gift-giving ceremony that later New Kingdom Pharaohs indulged in. The Edict of Horemheb describes in glowing terms how the army unit temporarily serving its ten-day period of guard-duty in the palace was given special extra rations at a reward ceremony performed at the Window of Appearance.[57]

Amenhetep III's Sed-*festivals*

The Egyptians had a genius for adapting old styles to new requirements. New Kingdom Thebes was the product of a society that had changed significantly since the great age of pyramid building. But in the appeal to traditions the Egyptians found legitimacy for novelties.

As was discussed in the earlier chapters, some of the first intelligible monuments to kingship to have survived concerned the celebration of the earthly power and vigour of kings, the *Sed*-festival. In the New Kingdom it was still as prestigious an occasion as ever; but typically, although they would never openly admit to it in formal texts, the Egyptians invented new forms of pageantry and adapted the symbolism to the changed environment. The best-known case is the set of three *Sed*-festivals celebrated by King Amenhetep III (1390–1352 BC) in the twenty-ninth/thirtieth, thirty-fourth and thirty-seventh years of his reign.[58] The choice of these particular years was not wholly a personal matter. The *Sed*-festival had come to be, perhaps always had been, a celebration of thirty years of reign in the first instance. But thereafter, kings were free to hold repeats at frequent intervals. Amenhetep III's jubilees are of special interest because of the survival of the actual site where at least the first two were celebrated. It now bears the name Malkata, and lies on the west bank of Thebes, to the south of the line of mortuary temples and the Theban processional perimeter (Figure 101).[59] In being a kind of festival showground created for great pageants of kingship it offers a vivid and somewhat unconventional example from archaeology of the profligacy in the use of resources characteristic of despotic states at the height of their powers.

The classic *Sed*-festival was, as pointed out in Chapter 2 (pp. 103–7), itself an amalgamation of two separate rituals, the *Sed*-festival proper and the ceremony of territorial claim. Early royal funerary architecture, best exemplified by the Step Pyramid at Sakkara, created a setting for both festivals in which one crucial part was a large arena where the king would run a sacred course. At Malkata this part was transformed into a water ceremony. A huge artificial basin was dug where the floodplain met the desert, designed in the shape of a modern letter 'T'. This was the common shape for small tanks and pools containing pure ritual water. By the end of the king's reign the Malkata basin had been enlarged to the extent that the main part measured 2 kilometres long by 1 kilometre wide. The earth dug out from this stupendous hole in the ground was partly spread out to make an artificial terrace on which the king's mortuary temple and part of the adjacent palace stood, and was partly heaped up into rows of artificial hills. Remnants of this early example of landscaping still survive (Plate 8). A contemporary Theban tomb, belonging to a high court official called Kheruef, has left a brief and very stylized description of this principal event from the king's first jubilee:

> The glorious appearance of the king at the great double doors in his palace, 'The House of Rejoicing'; ushering in the officials, the king's friends, the chamberlain, the men of the gateway, the king's acquaintances, the crew of the barge, the castellans, and the king's dignitaries. Rewards were given out in the form of 'Gold of Praise', and ducks and fish of gold, and they received ribbons of green linen, each person being made to stand according to his rank. They were fed with food as part of the king's breakfast: bread, beer, oxen and fowl. They were directed to the lake of His Majesty to row in the king's barge. They grasped the towropes of the Evening Barge and the prow rope of the Morning Barge, and they towed the barges at the great place. They stopped at the steps of the throne.
>
> It was His Majesty who did this in accordance with the writings of old. [Yet] past generations of people since the time of the ancestors had never celebrated such jubilee-rites.[60]

The Evening and Morning Barges carried divine statues, and were so called because they were supposed to be imitations of the heavenly barges in which the sun-god made his daily journey. Elaborate river processions had become part of the tradition of celebration at

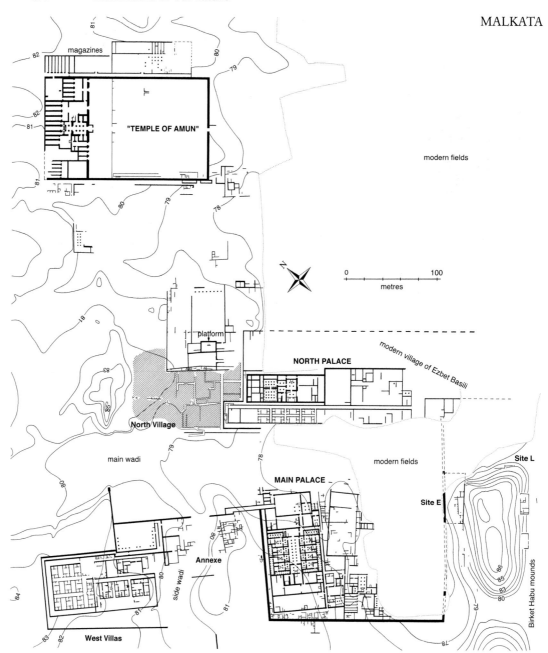

Figure 101 A setting for pageantry: Amenhetep III's constructions at Malkata, West Thebes, probable site of the celebrations of the king's first and second *Sed*-festivals. The map has been built up from a variety of sources, including aerial photographs, and notes and measurements made during a survey of the site for the University Museum of Pennsylvania. It includes the results of excavations carried out in 1973, and details from the plans in P. Lacovara, *The New Kingdom royal city*, New York, 1997.

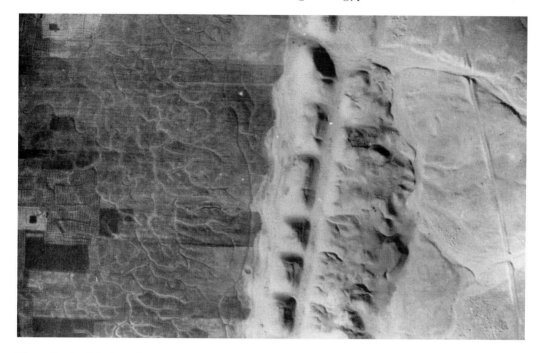

Plate 8 Aerial view of part of ancient Egypt's largest earthwork: landscaped mounds of spoil from the digging of Amenhetep III's ceremonial lake at the Birket Habu site, Malkata.

Thebes, and now provided the model for the *Sed*-festival. The last piece of the text catches the Egyptian approach well: it was novel, an invention of the day, yet in accord with people's feeling for tradition.

The ability to invent with sound historical taste is illustrated by another of Kheruef's scenes of Amenhetep's *Sed*-festivals. In this the king is shown ceremonially raising into an upright position a carved pole called a *Djed*-pillar.[61] The pillar had the form of a hieroglyph that wrote a word which meant something like 'stability', and the act of raising it belonged to the range of symbols and ceremonies which encouraged orderliness in society. More specifically, by this time it was regarded as a symbol of resurrection and was thus associated with Osiris, god of the dead. Amenhetep III's master of ceremonies evidently felt it to be entirely fitting to add the *Djed*-pillar ceremony to the jubilee festival, although historically there was probably no connection. The interchangeability of ritual and associated ideas made it relatively easy to invent new combinations by stirring the pot of tradition. However, scenes of the festival in Amenhetep's own temples (as distinct from those in Kheruef's tomb) appear to be far more traditional and to shy away from the novelties.[62]

The texts mention a palace. Another scene in Kheruef's tomb shows king and queen emerging from it.[63] This first appearance at the palace door on jubilee day, clad in the special jubilee costume, was another vital moment imbued with great significance. It was also truly traditional, since at the Step Pyramid this moment of first emergence from the palace seems to be commemorated. It was not the regular royal palace, however. Malkata was a site specially developed for this festival. So beside the ceremonial lake a special palace was built, of mud brick, its walls brightly painted with scenes and colourful designs. The food and drink for the celebrations were delivered to it in pottery amphorae whose tall mud stoppers bore the impressions of wooden stamps that recorded the great occasion. The festival day arrived, the amphorae were opened by having their tops expertly knocked off in one piece, the celebrations took place, and then the palace was closed for the last time. Within a short time work resumed on the lake, to enlarge it in time for the next jubilee. The palace stood in the way, so it was demolished and its rubble, mixed up with all the broken amphorae, was carried across to the desert and dumped there. This mixture of bricks, painted wall plaster and broken empties was partially excavated in 1973.

For the next jubilee, four years later, a new ceremonial palace was built, again of mud brick. This one was left standing. The ruins, still with hundreds of fragments of leftover amphorae from the king's jubilee meal, were excavated in 1916. The plan of the building resembles a temple, complete with a small hypostyle hall and group of sanctuaries, and this likeness was made explicit by stamped bricks used in the construction which refer to 'The Temple of Amun in the House of Rejoicing'. This last element in the name, it will be recalled, occurred in the Kheruef text quoted above. On such an august occasion the distinction between king and god, and the architecture that went with each, became quite arbitrary, just as at Luxor temple, which was built primarily as a setting for an annual royal ritual. It also emphasizes how, even in the ancient *Sed*-festival rites that had no historical connection with either Thebes or its gods, Amun had been inserted to play the dominant role.

The royal family, the court, the servants who fed them and the workers who kept them supplied with whatever was necessary – including glass vessels and glazed trinkets – were housed for the duration of the celebration in a large central complex of palaces, villas and huts. The main palace contained the king's bedchamber and bathroom behind a formal arrangement of halls that included several suites for individual members of the royal family. Much of this building was painted with scenes from nature. Not far away a natural elevation of the desert formed the base of a brick dais facing a courtyard where perhaps the king could receive the more important visitors to his feast.

A pageant on water, distribution of gifts and a special meal, the erection of festival buildings and the assembling of dignitaries and foreign envoys and representatives: here are the ingredients for the archetypal state jamboree. Nor was it necessary to wait for a king blessed with longevity to reach his thirtieth year. The Festivals of Opet and of the Valley were almost as grand.

The integration of king and temple cult of Amun enveloped the person of the king in an elaborate cocoon of mystery and pageant. It successfully blurred the difficulty that people might have in reconciling the divine and earthly aspects of a ruler who was also the head of a series of powerful institutions. For a brief time, however, it looked as though this compromise was only an intermediate stage in the evolution of a charismatic monarchy that sought the same level of adulation, but now directly focused on the king without the obscuring veil of religious mystery. This brief time was the reign of King Akhenaten, late in the 18th Dynasty (Figure 98, p. 269). Although Akhenaten's twin visions of a monarchy worshipped for itself, and of a theology that was so simple as to release the king from the shrouds of mystery, failed to convince his contemporaries and died with him, it offered a glimpse of a future that is still with us. Akhenaten's kingship provides an unintended caricature of all modern leaders who indulge in the trappings of charismatic display. The

Egyptians themselves did not like what they saw. It evidently offended their sense of good taste. After his death they returned to intellectual compromise and wrapped again the nakedness of monarchy in the shrouds of high theology.

Secular powers

Akhenaten's reign of seventeen years without the support of the traditional priesthood and all the colourful shows that they could provide, and the failure of this new style after his death which can by no means be described as a vengeful triumph of the priesthood, brings into focus two further institutions within New Kingdom society: the palace and the army.

In terms of bricks and mortar the word 'palace' is useful for any distinctive building in which a king or important royal relative stayed.[64] The Egyptian kings travelled inside their country quite extensively. If the journey was not on a regular route temporary accommodation could be in a tented encampment, as was used by Akhenaten on his first prospecting visit to El-Amarna.[65] But for scheduled journeys where something was built to provide accommodation, be it only for an overnight stop, it would of necessity have a certain degree of formality (with a throne room, for example) that attracts the modern word 'palace' when the remains are excavated. There were probably at any one time in ancient Egypt a very large number of 'palaces', ranging from overnight lodges or rest-houses which could be quite small to great sprawling complexes at major cities which a Pharaoh might have thought of as 'home'. (Figures 117, *top*, p. 340, and 118, p. 342, illustrate 'palaces' of the Middle Kingdom that might not have properly belonged to kings at all.) When one adds to this the fact that from their unique position kings can build palaces stamped with an individuality lying outside the norms of the architecture of the day, reflecting considerations that may amount to whimsy, it is hardly surprising to find that the excavated New Kingdom palaces do not fit into the kind of standard pattern that one can recognize in temples and tombs.

Most journeys within Egypt used the river extensively. The small overnight palaces on royal routes were therefore sometimes called 'The mooring-places of Pharaoh'. The term 'rest-house' perhaps renders the sense best into English.[66] River travel did not necessarily cramp the king's style: one model letter commanding preparations for the king's arrival at the riverine rest-houses shows that a force of chariotry was expected to be with him.[67] Provisioning the rest-houses exposed an administrative problem: how to cater for the occasional and not necessarily regular excesses of a brief royal passage. A partial solution lay in allocating to them farmland so that a permanent income maintained a small staff and could be stored in granaries ready for the direct feeding of the king's party and presumably for use in barter to purchase the extras which the farm did not produce itself. A group of 'mooring-places of Pharaoh' in Middle Egypt are known from the Wilbour Papyrus, a massive document on land-rents.[68] One lay near the harem-palace of Medinet el-Ghurab, another was at the city of Hardai on the Nile. This one owned 401 *arouras* of land (about 110 hectares). It is hard to imagine, however, that such a simple device solved the problem. Some kings were more extravagant than others, or might travel with a harem of excessive demands (remembering that the harem was a semi-independent institution with its own officials). The model letter of command to a local official in charge of some royal rest-houses is notable for the range of its list of demanded commodities. Being a model letter we can suspect an element of vocabulary practice, but New Kingdom Pharaohs were not modest in their tastes. This is the point at which the only solution for the hard-pressed official in charge was to go out and to commandeer extra supplies from other institutions and risk the appalling penalties laid down in royal decrees intended to protect individual institutions (such as the Nauri Decree, described in the next chapter, pp. 306–8).

A good compromise was simply to make the mayor of the local town responsible. An excessive use of this device was corrected in the Horemheb Edict (see the next chapter, p. 306). Ancient Egyptian mayors are an interesting group. In earlier periods they had been all-powerful locally, commonly holding the office of chief priest in the town's temple as well. To some extent they lay outside the regular bureaucratic systems, and did not possess a hierarchy of their own officials. Their power must have lain in the respect and influence they commanded by virtue of local landownership and family ties and a network of patronage and obligation. Although they had no bureaucracy of their own theirs was normally the responsibility for seeing that local taxes were collected and delivered to the vizier, the king's chief representative. They presumably acted as a buffer between the external demands of the state and the wellbeing of the local community of which they were the symbolic head. For making up a shortfall in supplies for a sudden royal arrival who better to lean on but the local mayor? Another example of mayoral responsibility for keeping the palace in food will be cited shortly.

What did these royal rest-houses look like? A fair guide is probably to be found in the small palaces attached to the west-bank mortuary temples at Thebes, adding in a magazine and some kitchens and small houses for servants and caretakers (Plate 7, p. 276, Figures 94, p. 259, and 100, p. 275). The model letter just cited refers several times to the existence of a special window at the 'mooring-place', which we should probably take as a 'Window of Appearance'. The fact that this was a standard feature of the west-bank mortuary-temple palaces strengthens the case for using them as a model for this type of provincial royal rest-house. One example of a rest-house, used apparently as a hunting-lodge, has actually been discovered and excavated, but never properly published. It dates to the time of Tutankhamun and lay close to the Great Sphinx at Giza (Figure 102). Why here? By the New Kingdom the Great Sphinx – originally a statue of Khafra, the king who built the second pyramid at Giza – had been re-identified as a statue of the sun-god Horemakhet. Kings and private individuals rendered acts of piety to it. Amenhetep II built a special little brick temple not far from it. The site had an added attraction, too. The large stele in Amenhetep II's temple records how, when still a prince, he had exercised his chariot over the nearby desert. His son, the later Tuthmosis IV, went hunting for game, including lions, over the same ground. Just to the south of the Sphinx and incorporating the ruins of the ancient Valley Temple of Khafra, 18th Dynasty kings maintained a small palace. Tragically, it was destroyed by early archaeologists too interested in Old Kingdom monuments, with very little record being made.[69] A plan of part of it suggests that it consisted of a group of buildings that resembled the larger houses at El-Amarna (see Figure 109, p. 312). One of them contained an inscribed stone door frame bearing the

Figure 102 A royal rest-house at a sacred site. By the 18th Dynasty, the body of the Great Sphinx at Giza (then 1,000 years old and evidently neglected) had been buried by sand, which had also mounded up over the two contemporary stone temples in front. The Sphinx was now designated as an image of the sun-god Horemakhet (Horus on the Horizon). Amenhetep II built a small brick

THE GIZA SPHINX IN THE NEW KINGDOM

SPHINX

presumed edge of 18th Dynasty
pit in drift sand

site of building of Tutankhamun

stele of Tuthmosis IV

TEMPLE OF
AMENHETEP II

outline of Khafra valley temple
(buried in sand)

outline of Old Kingdom
sphinx temple (buried in sand)

18th Dynasty house
or small palace

N

0   50

metres

shrine facing the Sphinx's face, and following a dream whilst resting in its shadow, Tuthmosis IV cleared the sand from around the statue's base and commemorated this with a granite stela erected between the statue's front legs. The royal interest was not, however, wholly spiritual. Texts show that the desert area behind, around the pyramids, was being used by kings to exercise their chariots and practise archery (in the same way that the area today is a centre for horse-riding). A royal rest-house was also constructed here, around the flat-topped mound of sand in which the Valley Temple of Khafra (the original creator of the Sphinx) lay buried. The whole complex, itself buried by sand and even later buildings, survived in reasonably good condition until modern times, when it was mostly destroyed with little record being taken by archaeologists obsessed with finding sculpture and Old Kingdom stonework. After U. Hölscher, *Das Grabdenkmal des Königs Chephren*, Leipzig, 1912, Bl. XV; Selim Hassan, *The Great Sphinx and its secrets*, Cairo, 1953; H. Ricke, *Der Harmachistempel des Chefren in Giseh* (Beiträge zur Ägyptischen Bauforschung und Altertumskunde 10) Wiesbaden, 1970; and conversations with M. Lehner. See also J. van Dijk and M. Eaton-Krauss, *MDAIK* 42 (1986), 39–41.

cartouches of Tutankhamun later usurped by Rameses II. Several wine-jar stoppers were recovered. One description of a 1907 excavation may refer to a brick enclosure wall with square external towers at regular intervals.

The archaeology of New Kingdom palaces is best illustrated at Akhenaten's new city of El-Amarna (Figure 103). Although the city was laid out on a relatively flat and unencumbered stretch of desert, the degree of forward planning was not great, and was largely confined to a group of royal buildings which were strung along a straight avenue, the so-called Royal Road, which connected a northern outlier (the North City) to the Central City. The former contained a substantial building, the North Riverside Palace which was probably the principal royal residence, private, well protected with a fortified wall, and separate from the rest of the city.[70] Part of the outer wall, pierced by a large gateway, is still a prominent feature. Between the wall and the palace proper were service buildings that could well have included a barracks for the king's bodyguard, but sadly the palace itself has been lost through river-bank erosion. Across the road lay a group of houses, some of them the largest in the whole city and presumably for some of the courtiers closest to the king. The North City was closed to the north by a large administrative building terraced up into the lower slopes of the cliff, and containing a huge warehouse block for commodities, part of it perhaps a granary. This implies that the North City and the king's private residence were self-sufficient in food, with a supply independent of the sources that sustained the rest of the city. The whole site, because of the overshadowing cliff, has an atmosphere very different from the rest of the city, and was evidently as attractive a place to Akhenaten as it remains to visitors today.

The Royal Road began here, and then struck southwards across low open ground towards the Central City. This, we may presume, was the route for the royal chariot drive, a favourite subject of the scenes in the tombs of Akhenaten's courtiers and officials. Perhaps he was trying to replace with military dash and public adulation of himself the stately, colourful and noisy carrying of the divine images of old. If so we again catch a whiff of the world to come. King, queen, daughters, retainers in their chariots, the bodyguards running along in stooping posture (Figure 104): we can recognize the basis of the scene re-enacted today in capital cities and on state occasions the world over. The presidential limousine, the royal landau, motorcycle outriders, presidential advisers and security guards, all are parts of a public performance acted out over the subsequent millennia as rulers and leaders have responded to the urge for public acclaim.

On its way south, the Royal Road passed an isolated building facing the river, the North Palace.[71] When excavated in the 1920s it was found to be a self-contained royal residence, with formal reception halls, a domestic suite with bedroom and bathroom, an open-air solar temple, and gardens and courts where the walls were painted with bright scenes from nature, and where animals were kept. The many fragments of inscriptions recovered show that the person for whom the North Palace was finally intended was the eldest princess and heiress, Meritaten. It may have become, when she came of age during her father's reign, her main residence. In its basic purpose – providing a quite separate palace for a major queen and her household – it conforms to the type of harem-palace documented both from texts and from the site of Medinet el-Ghurab (see p. 288), and in its formality it can be compared with, for example, the surviving fragment of the Palace of Merenptah at Memphis.

The Royal Road ran to its terminus within a group of temples, palaces and buildings for the support of the court that in modern times has been called The Central City.[72]

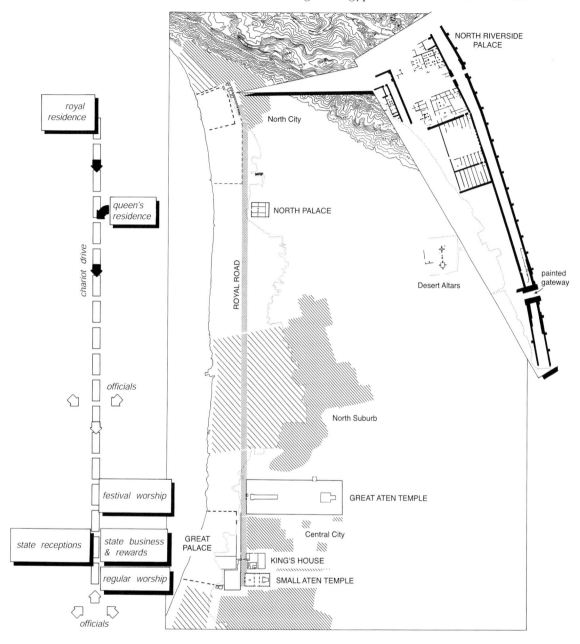

Figure 103 Diagram of the principal structural element at El-Amarna, the royal processional route.

Along the entire western side and probably covering all the ground to the waterfront lay the Great Palace. This included an intimate area of pleasant courts and halls, brightly painted (see Figure 105, p. 290 for a fragment of painted pavement) and having features in common with the North Palace. But the heart of the building was an enormous court-yard surrounded by large statues of Akhenaten, and a complex of halls and smaller courts and monuments arranged very formally along processional routes. These parts were con-structed of stone, and since, after the city was abandoned, the stonework was systematically removed, it is now difficult to be sure how these parts appeared. Whatever the details were, however, the whole served to provide the king with a sumptuous semi-religious setting which advertised his new religion and art and in which formal receptions and cer-

Figure 104 The royal chariot drive. *Upper register.* Akhenaten and Nefertiti in a chariot leave one of the Aten temples (represented as a pylon entrance with flag-poles). They head towards a fortified building set between what look like fences, probably the North Riverside Palace (Figure 103, p. 285), flanked by a running bodyguard headed by the 'Chief of Police of Akhetaten, Mahu'. *Lower register.* The royal couple drive along a road marked by what looks like the same fence, again accompanied by Mahu and his bodyguard. From the tomb of Mahu, after N. de G. Davies, *The rock tombs of El Amarna* IV, London, 1906, Pls XX–XXII.

emonies could be held, including those perhaps for the most important envoys from foreign courts who would return to their masters with tales of wonder at the extravagance and innovation of the new ruler. At the southern end of the Great Palace was an extraordinary addition, a hall built for Akhenaten's immediate successor, Smenkhkara, containing 544 brick columns, and with walls encrusted with glazed tiles. A bridge of brick across the Royal Road linked the Great Palace with a small residence, the King's House. This is a representative of the smaller palaces – the rest-houses or 'mooring-places of Pharaoh' – discussed earlier. In one or more of the palaces the king, accompanied by his family, appeared ceremonially at a special window, the 'Window of Appearance', there to reward loyal officials and to announce their promotions to higher offices.

The dispersal of buildings where the royal family could spend time extended well beyond the limits of the city proper. Perhaps other royal residence cities, too, had their equivalents, set amongst the lush countryside on the floodplain of the Nile. The location of El-Amarna offered somewhat uncompromising settings for such places, on rather bleak windswept areas of desert. The most ornate was called Maru-Aten. Within two large enclosures the builders did their best to recreate the parkland and marshes of the floodplain, planting shrubs and trees and lining with mud a large shallow basin to create a central water feature. Dispersed around the edges were small pavilions and rest-houses, of decorated stone and brick, where the cult of the sun could be celebrated and where the royal owner could find some peace and leisure. Several others were built and all, as far as the slight documentation tells us, belonged to royal women.[73] The overall picture from El-Amarna is that the royal family – in which, apart from the king, women were more prominent than men – arranged their lives across many widely spread buildings with each one sometimes visiting with an entourage a place which was set aside for them alone. In these buildings, which varied considerably in size and layout, the categories 'palace' and 'temple' readily merge.

Outside El-Amarna the excavated evidence is less rich than one might have hoped. We know from texts that large residential palaces existed at Memphis and, from the reign of Rameses II onwards, at Per-Rameses (near the modern towns of Khatana and Kantir) in the eastern delta. So far the Per-Rameses palaces are represented by lengths of massive brick wall and the disembodied remains of a glazed throne dais. Memphis has fared a little better. A fine reception hall belonging to King Merenptah, with the proportions and dignity of a temple, was excavated in the early twentieth century.[74] The clearest picture we have of the extent of a real residential palace outside El-Amarna comes from Malkata (Figure 101, p. 278), put up to accommodate Amenhetep III's huge entourage when it moved up to Thebes for his jubilee festivals.

One motive in the siting of some palaces seems to have been to create a retreat, away from the pressures of the full court and its administrators. One such retreat palace, or rather set of two palaces with accompanying villages, was built by the early 18th Dynasty kings in the desert at Ballas, just 22 kilometres north of Thebes.[75] Another is the palace at Medinet el-Ghurab, on the desert edge close to the entrance to the Fayum.[76] Built by Tuthmosis III it remained in use through the Amarna Period and beyond. It is a particularly interesting palace because it housed the senior royal ladies, with their own officials and servants and staff of weavers. It was a harem-palace where the occupants could live a secluded private life, and also bring up some of the royal children. At least one important Ramesside prince was buried there.[77] The hot atmosphere of personal scheming and political intrigue that such a place could engender need not be left only to the imagination. The greatest Pharaoh of the 20th Dynasty, Rameses III, vanquisher of foreign hosts, including the 'Sea Peoples', fell victim to a plot hatched in one of them. We know this from a surviving summary of verdicts from the trial of the conspirators.[78] Thirty-one men were implicated, together with six of their wives. All except four were executed or allowed to take their own life. The plot centred, however, on the women of the harem, and one named Teye, whose son the conspirators evidently hoped to make king. Although the son was amongst those found guilty the harem women themselves seem to have been left alone. Who the male conspirators were is revealing: eleven were officials of the harem itself, twelve were officials or courtiers with other titles, only five were military men, and there was one solitary priest. One of the soldiers, a captain of bowmen of Nubia, was involved because his sister who was in the harem had written to him urging him to start an uprising.

Provisioning the royal household involved not only getting supplies to a travelling pocket of gross consumption but also supporting permanent communities at the larger palaces that served as home bases. One of these was at Memphis. We have an important set of documents from the administration of the Memphis palace bread supply in the time of Seti I (1294–1279 BC).[79] States one heading: 'Receiving wheat from the granary of Pharaoh in Memphis, in order to make it into loaves in the bakery which is under the authority of the mayor of Memphis, Neferhetep, to be sent over to the storehouse of Pharaoh.' There follow lists of daily amounts of between 100 and 190 sacks (about 7,300 and 13,000 litres). A complementary list picks up the trail: 'Receiving the bread of the bakery which is under the authority of the mayor of Memphis, Neferhetep, at the storehouse of Pharaoh.' The quantities, received every few days, were usually between 2,000 and 5,000 small loaves. Note the way that the mayor of Memphis had been made responsible for the difficult part – the running of the actual bakehouse, a labour-intensive place where the system of keeping tabs on the flow of commodities was very vulnerable as grain was turned into flour and then made into loaves. This was separately documented in these papyri. We learn that 3.5 sacks of flour make 168 standard loaves, or 602 small loaves, with separate notations for weight and for losses of weight during the baking process. A sack of flour seems to be the product of about two sacks of grain, but no one is allowed to take an average ration for granted. Measurement took place at every step and the discrepancies were noted. Milling was traditionally a woman's job, and there is one brief entry illustrating this: on one day three women, representing a group of twenty-six, collected 10.5 sacks of grain and turned it into 7.5 sacks of flour. The rate of issue of wheat would have amounted to some 50,000 sacks each year, which would have required a granary about one-quarter of the size of that at the Ramesseum, although we also have to allow for a separate and substantial amount of cereal used for brewing beer. But since the wheat was for immediate baking we must also accept the existence of a substantial dependent population, running into many hundreds, if not the low thousands.

The palace was much more than just architecture and provisions. Decisions of state and matters of dynastic succession must have been far more prominent in the minds of those who lived there, and what they concluded and did provides historians with the raw material for their profession. The harem conspiracy of Rameses III's time is a case in point. The area that most consistently illustrates the political realism with which business at court was conducted is foreign affairs. The New Kingdom saw a great change in Egypt's international position. Conquest and empire moved to the forefront of real policies as well as of ideology. The result was an empire that took in much of the northern Sudan and, to the north-east, Palestine and parts of Syria. The reality of significant conquest boosted the portrayal of the king as mighty conqueror, something done with much vigour and total lack of embarrassment on temple walls and in many other contexts (Figure 105). Success in battle, however, also led to deadly political gamesmanship with powerful enemies even further afield, whom Pharaoh could never hope to conquer. A study of New Kingdom foreign relations becomes the most important window open to us for observing the existence, at the highest level, of political acumen coping pragmatically with difficult real situations far removed from the cosmic tramplings of kings as depicted simultaneously in Egyptian art.

The prime source is a cache of clay tablets from a government office in the centre

of Akhenaten's capital, El-Amarna, written in cuneiform script employing local forms of the Akkadian language.[80] The bulk of the tablets are letters from western Asiatic courts, and copies of letters sent from the Egyptian court in return. In political terms the letters fall into two main groups which immediately delimit the real sphere of Egyptian power abroad. One is correspondence between Egypt and other states of great-power status where the mutual mode of address is 'brother'. These are the states of Babylonia, Assyria, Mitanni, Hatti (Kingdom of the Hittites) and Alashiya (Cyprus). The content is mainly personal, but might include a political element, as with the King of Alashiya's advice not to align with the kings of Hatti and Babylon (EA 35). With the letters went exchanges of presents, a practice taken very seriously and about which kings were most sensitive in balancing what they gave against what they received. Arranged diplomatic marriages were one such delicate area.[81]

The second group of letters concerns the city-states of Palestine and Syria, their princes and their resident Egyptian officials. They address Pharaoh as 'my lord'. Those closer to Egypt had little prospect of an improved alternative, but the Syrian princes were in a position to make choices of major importance for themselves. Their aims have been summarized as: preservation of their own local autonomy, extension of their own rule over neighbours, maintenance towards the Egyptians of a show of loyalty to secure men and money, and either opposition or submission to the Hittite king according to circumstances.[82] Their letters tend to have the form of a long introductory protestation of absolute loyalty couched in obsequious language:

> This is the message of a slave to his master after he had heard what the kind messenger of the king [said] to his servant upon arriving here, and [felt] the sweet fragrance that came out of the mouth of Your Majesty towards his servant.

Thus Abimilki, Prince of Tyre (EA 147). In such cases the direct political message tends to be reserved for a brief final sentence or two, although some writers, notably Rib-addi of Byblos, could sustain loquacious pleas for support for much of their letters. A constant element is denunciation of a neighbouring prince on grounds of disloyalty to the king of Egypt. Since the accusations at times extended to the murder of one prince by another (e.g. EA 89, also 73, 75, 81, 140), these were not necessarily to be dismissed as inventions.

The obvious conclusion to be drawn from this material is that, although no trace has survived of anything like an objective comment on an international situation, behind the

Figure 105 Imperial images. *Above.* God's blessing for Pharaoh's conquests. Rameses II smites a Semitic victim, whilst god, in the form of Atum Lord of Tju (= Tjeku, a local place), offers him a sickle-sword to legitimize the act. From a temple at Tell el-Retaba, eastern delta (marked on the map, Figure 13, p. 43). After W.M.F. Petrie, *Hyksos and Israelite Cities*, London, 1906, Pls XXIX, XXX. *Below.* Pharaoh Akhenaten tramples his enemies, within the security of his palace. *Right.* A section of painted pavement from the Great Palace at El-Amarna, depicting two themes – a rectangular pool surrounded by vegetation (B), and a central path of bound foreign captives alternating with groups of three bows, symbolic of the king's enemies in general (A). After W.M.F. Petrie, *Tell el Amarna*, London, 1894, Pl. II. *Left.* Outline plan of part of the Great Palace showing the context of the painted pavement, and how the painted pathway continued. As the king strode from hall to hall he crushed his enemies underfoot. After J.D.S. Pendlebury, *The City of Akhenaten* III, London, 1951, Pl. XIIIA, and comments on p. 40. F. Weatherhead, *JEA* 78 (1992), 182, Fig. 1 restores the layout of the pathways a little differently.

façade of total military supremacy Egypt's foreign relations were politically based, required careful interpretation and judgement, and involved discussion of situations in terms of human motives. For this one may assume that the Egyptians were well equipped. In the first place they tended to write letters to their superiors in a not dissimilar exaggerated style. Second, the giving of judgements in Egypt (something which was not confined to a class of professional judges but was probably a basic attribute of holding a significant office) although it might well involve reference back to documentary archives, was essentially a matter of resolving conflicting testimonies and assessing human motives. People who could pronounce judgement in a convoluted case of disputed land ownership going back over several generations had the right frame of mind for reading between the lines of diplomatic letters.[83]

The letters, however, had another and more insidious dimension. They created a mental world of their own, into which all the correspondents were drawn. For the king of Egypt, more or less at the end of the letter-writing line in geographical terms, it was a world of maybe fifty members, each one a ruler or occasionally another member of a ruler's family. The members rarely if ever met. They wrote to each other with long intervals in the correspondence, but there were enough of them to sustain at the Egyptian court (and doubtless in many courts elsewhere) a permanent office and secretariat to deal with them. As they read letters and dictated replies they must have formed in their minds shadowy images of one another which were frequently very wrong in detail, but which captured the essence of the situation: that they were all players on a political stage and had a broadly similar motivation. Although they usually wrote to gain a specific end, their letters also represented moves in a game where the stakes were measured in prestige and dignity. In this artificially constructed world of long-distance communication a king might blush or rage at thoughts of what had been said about him in a distant court that he would never see and could not punish, thoughts conjured up by the words of a letter of clay and the tales of the envoy who brought it. The Egyptian battle scenes on temple walls reduced international conflict to a level of absolute simplicity. Backed by the gods Pharaoh smote helpless and impotent foes with impunity. The letters, however, drew the same Pharaoh into a world of international vanity in which the price of acceptance as a star player was exposure to competition. Here he was no longer a god.

The multicultural court

At first sight, the consequences at home of participation in the rounds of warfare and diplomacy in the Near East were slight. New Kingdom palaces as they have survived seem to be quintessentially Egyptian, with their halls of columns shaped like papyrus stems and their paintings of marsh life beside the Nile or of Pharaoh in his chariot. If we wish to imagine them with people then the scenes of court life of the time direct us to a refined and elegant Egyptianness of style. Other kinds of evidence, however, although generally less obvious, point towards a more complex picture. They suggest that in possessions, dress, language and other aspects of culture, court life actually followed a more international style and was perhaps not quite as one might first imagine it to have been.

In Chapter 1 we saw how, in the New Kingdom especially, Egypt became home to numerous people of foreign origin who, from the evidence at our disposal, seem easily to vanish from our gaze through the adoption of Egyptian culture. Amongst the exiles were foreign princesses accepted in marriage for reasons of diplomacy. Tuthmosis IV had married a daughter (her name not preserved) of the king of Mitanni (Artatama). Amenhetep III had done the same, twice over, marrying first Gilukhepa, daughter of Shuttarna II, and then her niece Tadukhepa, daughter of Tushratta, both successive kings of the same Mitanni. There are also records of marriages to two daughters of Babylonian kings, and to the daughter of the ruler of an important state (Arzawa) in south-east Anatolia. Akhenaten followed with marriage to another Babylonian princess. Rameses II married two daughters of the Hittite king, and one each of the kings of Babylon and of a client state in Syria, Zulapi.[84]

For their subsequent lives in Egypt we must rely primarily upon circumstantial evidence. The marriages simultaneously brought to the Egyptian court costly dowries and attendants. A tribute list of Tuthmosis III mentions for his twenty-fourth year the 'daughter of a prince together with her ornaments of gold and lapis lazuli of her land, and the retainers belonging to her, male and female slaves, thirty of them'. When Gilukhepa arrived as Amenhetep III's latest bride she brought with her 317 ladies-in-waiting. As for the dowries, we are fortunate in possessing, on two large clay tablets, a detailed itemized list of what was sent by Tadukhepa's father to accompany his daughter when she set out some years later to be a further bride to Amenhetep III. It is a treasure-list of the kind that historical romances imagine: earrings, finger-rings, ornamental dress-pins and necklaces of gold set with precious stones, bunches of grapes and pomegranates of gold, combs of silver, drinking-horns from aurochs overlaid with gold, a plaque depicting 'Deluge Monsters' in gold and silver, multi-coloured textiles, boxes of special woods also overlaid with gold and silver. With the princess came two principal ladies-in-waiting and at least 270 female and thirty male attendants, and the gifts included jewellery for them as well, a useful reminder that the court was relatively densely populated with people of whom rich attire was expected.[85]

If we try to imagine what the dowry would have looked like, it would be a collection of treasures of rich materials and of stunning craftsmanship that, had it survived to fill museum cases, would probably have been more at home in the national museums of Syria or Iraq, or perhaps Turkey. Partly because it might not have been appropriate to include such material amongst the furnishings of tombs, and partly through past successes by tomb robbers, almost nothing of this kind has actually survived from Egypt. But the implication is that somewhere in the rather bland storerooms of palaces at El-Amarna and elsewhere there would have been wooden chests of these rich exotica, and doubtless individual pieces were to be found scattered through the living-quarters and worn by their owners on suitable occasions; worn not necessarily with the white linen that was the traditional dress of the Egyptians, but with garments and textile wraps of bright colours such as those in specified Near Eastern styles, using red and blue-purple which were amongst Tushratta's wedding gifts.[86]

The cultural mix at court extended beyond clothing and jewellery. Some of the El-Amarna cuneiform clay tablets were not letters at all, but carried literary texts, derived not from Egypt but from the Near East. One (EA 356; Figure 106) contained part of the myth of Adapa and the South Wind, Adapa being a Mesopotamian culture hero from the city of Eridu and son of the god Ea. In the tale, whilst on a fishing trip in the sea, he breaks the wing of the south wind but, with his father's advice, visits heaven and is offered the chance of redemption. When read in translation the whole style and cultural associations

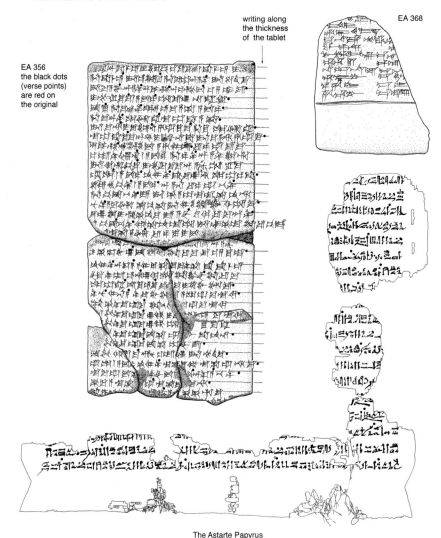

The Astarte Papyrus

Figure 106 A different view of the outside world: a source of myth and literature. *Top left.* El-Amarna tablet EA 356, verso, contains part of the myth of Adapa and the South Wind, the lines of cuneiform script pointed with red dots in Egyptian style. Height 17.5 cm. *Top right.* El-Amarna tablet EA 368, verso, a fragment of a vocabulary which transcribes ancient Egyptian words into the cuneiform script in the left column and gives their equivalent meaning in Akkadian in the right. Height 6.5 cm. After S. Izre'el, *The Amarna scholarly tablets*, Groningen, 1997, Pls XXII, XL. *Below and right.* Fragments of a papyrus roll containing, in the Egyptian hieratic script, the story of the appeasement of the angry sea by the goddess Astarte. After A.H. Gardiner, 'The Astarte Papyrus', in S.R.K. Glanville, ed., *Studies presented to F.Ll. Griffith*, London and Oxford, 1932, Pl. 9, opp. p. 76.

of the story seem very un-Egyptian.[87] Details of script and language show that the writer came from the Mesopotamian heartland, from Babylonia; but, together with two other El-Amarna literary tablets, it is unique in having red dots added at intervals along the lines of writing. This appears to be a distinctively Egyptian practice that helped to give expression when reading aloud. Moreover, the language and style of writing of these literary tablets differ from those used by the scribes who wrote the cuneiform letters that form the bulk of the El-Amarna collection. This implies that the literary texts were not scribal practice pieces but were read aloud to an understanding audience for the sake of their cultural interest. Is this what the Babylonian princesses of Amenhetep III and Akhenaten listened to?

Study of the finer points of the language and writing of these tablets has also suggested that scribes (dare we call them 'scholars'?) from other faraway centres left their mark on the Egyptian court school at El-Amarna: from the Hittite capital of Hattusas (modern Boghazköy), where Akkadian was studied by people whose native language was a form of Indo-European, and probably from Ugarit in Syria. Two more of the El-Amarna tablets are parts of an epic that tells of an expedition of Sargon, king of Akkad, to Anatolia, in which Hurrian influence has been detected.

The evidence adds up to the likelihood that a scribal 'school' (an international centre of learning in the making?) was run in or near the 'Records Office' at El-Amarna, and that it was for the benefit not only of Egyptians but of students from the Near East as well. There are practice pieces for learning the trade of letter-writing but also aids to a more confident knowledge of cultural background (such as a list of names of Near Eastern gods, EA 374). One of the pieces of evidence is part of a vocabulary tablet (EA 368; Figure 106). On the left on one side is a column of Egyptian words written out in the cuneiform syllabary, which incidentally gives us a more reliable guide to how the words were pronounced than is normally to be derived from hieroglyphs. In the right-hand column cuneiform signs have been used to write the Akkadian equivalents. The last seven lines preserve the entries: 'The house, The door, The bolt, The door-posts, The chair, The bed, [Offering]-table'. These are not words that one would need often, if at all, in writing diplomatic letters. They look more like words of everyday speech. Moreover, the form of the list points to it having been for an Akkadian native speaker who was learning colloquial Egyptian. It seems to be the ancient equivalent of a page from a phrase book.

This tablet was not found anywhere near the 'Records Office'. It was found in a private house (O49.23) some way from the centre of the city. Does this mean that an Akkadian speaker from somewhere in the Near East – Babylon itself perhaps? – actually stayed in this house for a while? And if so, was he there as the guest of an Egyptian family or was the house available for rent? Although the New Kingdom is generally better documented than other periods, we simply do not know enough to be able to answer such questions. It is not unique in this respect. Another of the tablets (EA 359) is a fragment of the epic of Sargon of Akkad mentioned above, which was found in house O47.2. A third tablet (EA 379), a fragment of a sign list which might, therefore, have been useful to someone learning Akkadian, was found in house N47.3. In this case the learner could have been an Egyptian.

The cosmopolitan pooling of literary knowledge and imagination shows up, too, on the Egyptian side. The clearest example survives only as small fragments of what had once been a long papyrus, written in a clear hand shortly after the end of the Amarna Period, in the vernacular idiom of the day (Late Egyptian) though the place where it was found is not known (Figure 106, *bottom*). The setting is one familiar from other Egyptian tales: a disturbance to the essentially domestic life of the gods and goddesses, who here include the creator god Ptah and the great company of gods, the Ennead. What makes the tale distinctive is that the disturbance in their lives is caused by the Sea (*yamm*), who is described as ruler of the earth and sky, and has the power to cover the earth and the mountains unless his demands for tribute are met. An intermediary is sought, namely the goddess Astarte (of Near Eastern origin), who is given the role of 'daughter of Ptah' and is summoned by the (Egyptian) goddess Renut who sends birds to awaken her. The ending is lost.[88]

Although our dominant image of Egypt is of an oasis-like country fed by the Nile but isolated by the desert, where the Nile delta meets the Mediterranean actually represents a minimum 300 kilometres of coastline. Although journeys to the Near East by sea were dangerous (sometimes from piracy), so, too, were journeys by land. Even at the times of greatest Egyptian military assertion, northern Sinai and Palestine were home to Bedouin peoples who were not part of the world of treaties, trade, agricultural towns and local government to which both Egypt and much of the Near East belonged. Particularly from the New Kingdom onwards a proportion of the Egyptian scribal class would have taken the sea route and thus have had experience of sea travel. It seems fitting that the entry of the sea into the range of tales that, for most Egyptians, probably defined their mythology was in one that also gave a prominent part to the goddess Astarte. She, along with Baal and a few other Near Eastern divinities, was adopted into the Egyptian pantheon in the New Kingdom. By this time the Egyptians had started to replace their traditional term for the sea, 'the great green', with an imported Semitic word, *yamm*, and it is as Yamm that the Sea, now personified as a god, appears in the story. That same personification was present in the mythology of the Near East. He appears, as Prince Yamm, in fragments of a mythological tale preserved on clay tablets found at the port city of Ugarit, and is vanquished after a lengthy contest with the god Baal, son of El, the head of the pantheon.[89]

Given that the El-Amarna tablets reveal at least a limited circulation of Near Eastern literature at the Egyptian court it is easy to understand how the story of the Astarte Papyrus could have been composed and written down in good Egyptian by a scribe who could seamlessly weave into his tale elements from both cultural worlds. From this perspective it seems less strange that the kings of Mitanni should send on a temporary goodwill visit, on two separate occasions, a statue of Shaushka of Nineveh (the Hurrian version of the goddess Ishtar, of whom Astarte of Palestine was another regional form) to the court of Amenhetep III, perhaps to bless the marriages of the Mitannian princesses to the king. Once arrived in Egypt, the goddess 'dwelt there and they honoured her' until it was time to send her back.[90]

Most people reading this book will have some liking for ancient Egypt and will attempt to imagine it as it is defined by its most familiar sources. But for the king and his courtiers at this time, Egyptian traditions were all too familiar. What evidently took their fancy, in promoting a cultivated if perhaps superficial style of living, were the tastes of the wide world of western Asia. In their daily lives they were prepared to sacrifice cultural integrity just as easily as they were prepared to ignore traditional strictures about keeping foreign peoples at bay. An appreciation of this is important for understanding what was to happen in the centres of power during the centuries that came after the New Kingdom, a theme pursued in Chapter 8.

Soldiers and priests

The empire brought to Egypt an enhanced militarism. In earlier periods civil wars had been fought and territories conquered, particularly in Nubia. A striking level of specialist military architecture for the defence of towns had been developed (Chapter 5). But all the evidence suggests that the fighting was done by militias raised for a specific campaign, sometimes stiffened by Nubian desert warriors (Medjay people). Battlefield weaponry remained strangely crude – clubs and flint spears even in the Middle Kingdom. All this changed in the New Kingdom. Faced with the need to battle against the well-equipped armies of western Asia the Egyptians borrowed technology and tactics, and seem for the first time to have established a standing army of long-serving soldiers and officers.[91] Armies have a clear and straightforward purpose and much of what can be said about them takes the form of a catalogue of weapons, a listing of ranks and units, and a chronicle of particular fights. The army of the New Kingdom was no exception. From our point of view a much more interesting concern is this: all institutions have a place in the state, are part of the system by which power is wielded at home. Where did the Egyptian army fit into the government of the New Kingdom?

Because of the nature of the Egyptian administration – basically an extended cluster of centres of activity potentially in rivalry with one another – it is by no means clear that members of one 'profession' felt themselves to be part of a group with a common interest and thus, potentially at least, possessed of political power. Even the priesthood was probably no exception; the army, however, may well have been. We can call the New Kingdom army professional not merely on the grounds of general business-like appearance. It took in young recruits and put them into training camps, and campaigns and garrison duty were fairly regular. Army units were stationed within Egypt. The Horemheb Edict, for example, speaks of two corps of the army, one in the south and one in the north. Its soldiers had the chance to be in the palace to guard the king personally. The Edict also reaffirms a custom of employing as the king's bodyguard a group of soldiers from the provinces that was changed every ten days (the Egyptian 'week'), the changeover marked by the distribution of special extra rations at the Window of Appearance. For veterans there is evidence from the 18th Dynasty as well as from the late 20th that they were settled with grants of land.[92] By the very nature of its life the New Kingdom army was a body of men, an institution, with its own sense of identity arising from its separateness from normal life. This separateness was heightened as the New Kingdom progressed by the increasing practice of recruiting or impressing foreigners, from Libya and from the countries of the eastern Mediterranean. They, too, enjoyed grants of land in Egypt (Figure 8, p. 32). Many of them would also have been in a position of close proximity to the king, sufficiently so to observe what he was like as a real person.

In considering the role of the army – institutionalized armed force – we have to ask ourselves a very basic question: who really were the kings of Egypt? Where did they come from? The Egyptians themselves put up a great and very effective screen around this question. The elaborate array of pageant, ritual, myth, insignia and sycophantic language that surrounded kings from coronation to death and beyond represented in total an overwhelming intellectual and behavioural assault on society to the effect that the reigning king's position was unquestionable and unassailable. Granted that within the confines of the court the question of which royal male would succeed next offered opportunities for scheming, for long periods the royal succession remained within a single family, a dynasty. Even when dynasties changed the newcomer might seek legitimacy by marrying a woman from the ousted royal house. But dynasties did change. The origins of the newcomers, except when foreign, are almost invariably hard for us to trace simply from a general lack of evidence. Sometimes they seem to have been already prominent at court, sometimes they arose from the provinces. What we have to accept is that they saw the office of king for what it really was: a goal for an ambitious man to grasp at a time when the great screen of divine kingship was temporarily lowered and made it seem practicable. Usurpers and founders of new lines were not summoned from a state of innocence by priests or by mysterious voices or supernatural signs. They responded to crude ambition. Before the New Kingdom there appears not to have been a professional standing army. But if militarism was less a factor in previous periods, so also was people's experience of it. It simply means that intimidation could be achieved by less. The 11th Dynasty, and the historical prominence of Thebes, arose from victory in a civil war. The background to the change from the 11th to the 12th is not very clear, but the successful usurper, Amenemhat I, himself fell victim to assassination. And if we go back to the very beginning of Egyptian history the sources show that kingship arose from a period of internal warfare, which reappeared at the end of the 2nd Dynasty. The screen of divine kingship maintained kings and dynasties in power for long periods of political stability, but ultimately kingship was the outcome of force.

The New Kingdom developed from the defeat of foreign armies. To the new militarism in society the portrayal of kingship responded with a greatly reinforced image of military leadership. Some kings developed a taste for the battlefield and for annual campaigns. But whereas in the past armed force could be mustered in the service of ambition, now the armed force was there all the time, dispersed through the provinces both at home and abroad. It became the source of ambition itself. This came to maturity at the end of the 18th Dynasty. In the Amarna Period, so we have to imagine, the religious changes of Akhenaten alienated the priests of the old cults, especially those of Amun, whose very existence Akhenaten tried to destroy. But in the aftermath the group whose representative became king – in the person of the general, Horemheb – was the army. In succession to him the throne passed to a military family from the eastern delta who founded the Ramesside line of kings.[93]

Before they became kings, Horemheb and Rameses I carried a title that seems to mean 'heir apparent'.[94] By whom was it bestowed? It implies prior agreement as to how the succession would proceed and, furthermore, that amongst the ranks of senior figures who are known to us only by names and titles were some who could form an authoritative council that could make such a decision. Were they mainly civilians (senior priests, treasurers and so on) who recognized where real power lay and whose job it was to bestow legitimacy on it, or was there something like a military council? One of the specified duties of the vizier was to receive an 'army council' prior to giving it instructions.[95] Was this the body, presided over by the vizier, that chose Horemheb and then Rameses I? Our inability to penetrate the workings of the state severely limits what we can write about the political history of ancient Egypt. An army council, even though almost invisible to us, might be the key to much that happened in Egypt in the New Kingdom.

Yet militarism was evidently not characteristic of educated Egyptian society as a whole. Outside the stylized portrayals of kingly victories, the celebration of valorous deeds on the battlefield is conspicuous by its absence both in literature and in the art of private tombs. These provided space for a man to record his successes, but refined taste none the less excluded combat and bloodshed. Literature and art left warriors voiceless.[96] As far as we can tell, no Egyptian equivalent to the *Iliad* was written down to stir the blood of listeners at home. Moreover, the army and the empire in the end depended on the civil administration, from whose ranks also came politically powerful individuals. At school, through the texts that served as models for copying, young scribes were taught a disdain for all professions other than their own. This extended to military careers, and scorn was poured on the soldier and on the chariot officer and on service abroad. These texts evince no positive side other than selfishness – being a scribe 'saves you from toil, it protects you from all manner of labour'[97] – but simply in preferring power through orderly administration to glory through action and adventure people who had accepted this ethos must have been a source of counter-arguments to those of the military. The creation of colonies in Nubia modelled on Egyptian temple-towns of the New Kingdom extended Egyptian-style administration over one complete sector of the Empire, leaving western Asia to provide the main scope for military shows, though even here, as the Amarna Letters imply, identifying the enemy was itself a task for home-based officials.

We can see the shadowy outline of two opposed interest groups in the New Kingdom: army and civil scribes, the latter with well-placed representatives amongst the courtiers. The harem conspiracy in the time of Rameses III involved many of these, and the leaders had sought the support of the army (though not of a priesthood). This conspiracy was 'political' in the narrow sense that those involved plotted and acted in accord with a pragmatic evaluation of risks and rewards.

Where does this leave the priesthood? In the case of the most important office, that of high priest of Amun at Karnak, we can follow its fortunes through most of the New Kingdom.[98] For the 18th Dynasty and the 19th into the reign of Rameses II each high priest was a royal appointment drawn from the ranks of officialdom (two, Ptahmes and Paser had been viziers) or from people with a background of temple service, though not necessarily at Karnak or even Thebes. The later 19th and the 20th Dynasties were, however, largely spanned by two families (with a marriage connection) who managed to monopolize the office and many lesser ones in the Amun cult at Karnak, forming veritable dynasties of priests. Their power base, however, was civilian: the dignity of high office, the family connections, the patronage at their disposal. In the last resort they themselves were only tolerated. They fail the ultimate test: families of priests from civil backgrounds did not provide future kings. The break between the two families coincided with civil unrest connected with the dynastic dispute that led to the coming of the 20th Dynasty (at the centre of which was the Chancellor Bey, probably an Asiatic at court who was also known as the 'Chief of the troops of the Great King, the King of Egypt').[99] For a time in the early 20th Dynasty the office of high priest was held by one Bakenkhonsu, son of a man who had been in charge of the military garrison which by now the estate of Amun at Thebes maintained. But the full extent of the dependence of civilian power on the military came only at the end. The penultimate high priest of the second family, Amenhetep, was actually ejected from his office for eight or nine months during a veritable civil war in Upper Egypt in which the viceroy of Kush at the head of a Nubian army was involved. This man established himself at Thebes and, for a short time, put himself in charge of the grain deliveries to the Estate of Amun (an act which seems to have stabilized previously erratic grain prices).[100] When the dynasty ended the office of high priest was taken over by a military commander, Herihor, who is likely to have been of Libyan origin (see p. 45–6). The ensuing three centuries were a time of private armies. The Thebaid became a semi-autonomous province governed by the high priest of Amun who was both commander of an army and frequently a prince of the reigning house in the north of Egypt, the same fusion of religion and secular power as was embodied in kingship.

It was a triumph not so much of either army or priesthood but of political realism. Herein lies an important lesson. Religious awe was not a basis of power in itself. Its images of power were an illusion unless they articulated the political determination of people who, either by birthright or by ambition, felt the urge to rule. They would not have put it so crudely themselves. For one thing, there was no ready vocabulary of politics and cynicism. But if they accepted the pious language and concepts they also bent the images in their direction and projected themselves into their centre. A powerful civilian priesthood was tolerated by the real men of power only so long as it did not get in their way.

I began the chapter by saying that one can argue that early societies actually needed the symbols and ceremonies of a political power merged with religion as a means of maintaining political cohesion. This is the argument of functional necessity. In the modern world, however, this pattern of behaviour as it survives does not fully coincide with the exercise of power. Although my own country, Britain, retains a monarchy that is the head of the state religion, pageantry and ceremony are not fully a symbolic articulation of political power. Much of this resides with people around whom pomp is subdued, whilst at the same time the glamour and the extravagant formalized behaviour, including the crowd adulation at staged 'appearances', has spread, perhaps largely transferred itself, to celebrities who are outside the political process. Circus and power overlap but each has an independent existence. Things seem to have changed a great deal since antiquity. But have they really?

The audience at which the pomp of Pharaohs was directed commenced with the court, spread to lesser officials, and probably included by the New Kingdom at least token groups of the people at large. But the notion of collective power was hardly born. The audience was for the most part politically neutral. People complained of unjustified tax demands, and demonstrated when rations failed to arrive, but they did not form political parties or revolutionary mobs. The pageantry was not buying off a real threat. Those who most represented a threat to the king were individuals closest to him, on the 'inside' of the pomp, who probably helped to organize it and were thus least impressed by it.

We are right to look for essential communications on ideas of rule within court pageantry, couched in the understood terms of the day, for the terms themselves may have had little existence independent of the celebration itself, and the preparations for it. Could we claim, for example, that the *Sed*-festival existed independently of its celebration (or anticipated celebration)? The means of communication was itself ideology. Pageantry and ceremonial were a reciprocal therapy, an 'in-touch' form of expression which all concerned found satisfying to indulge in, including the theoreticians – presumably priests – who devised the meaning, and for whom, without the performance, there would have been no meaning. Not only was the audience embraced by it, so also were the key performers. Modern society, in making pageantry and ceremonial more democratic and offering it as well to celebrities of sport and entertainment, usefully reveals that pomp and adulation serve a collective social need that is independent of political power. In the ancient world the merging of roles tends to obscure this, but it must still have been true. Who ruled, who rose in favour and who fell, what wars were fought, what taxes raised, what new edicts were issued: the exercise of real power, behind the screens, was irrelevant to the pomp and the ceremonial.

7
The birth of economic man

It is possible to compile a 'Who's Who' of ancient Egypt for certain periods. The New Kingdom is one of them. If we look at the result, one very clear fact will emerge: no one who was prominent and successful claimed to be so on a basis independent of the state. Everyone was an 'official'. You could rise from a humble background to be the most powerful man in the land next to the king, but only because the king recognized your merits, one of them being loyalty. We will find no self-made men of trade or of manufacture, no merchants or moneylenders, no one who boasted of 'profit'. At least, that is what the inscriptions, the ideal autobiographies carved in tombs, tell us. As a consequence, on the basis of the formal written and pictorial evidence, we can conclude that the effective part of Egyptian society consisted only of institutions.

As always, however, we must be on our guard against confusing myth with structure. It is equally true to say that ancient Egypt possessed no politicians, in the sense in which that word is used now, that is, to refer to people who make it their business to articulate and to struggle for the interests of one particular group. But the Egyptians were not politically innocent. Within the framework of the loyal hierarchy of officialdom ambitious individuals pushed themselves forwards and plotted to undermine those who stood in their way. The politics of self-interest most definitely existed, contained within the single system of administration. It was a later world, more given to abstract thought and less internally cohesive, that provided the political schemer with the 'cause' and the special-interest group, and thus the opportunity to reveal politics as an independent subject and calling.

Economics offers a roughly similar picture. No one thought 'economics' or pursued it as an independent goal, yet should we conclude that the Egyptians were economically naïve? The matter is clouded by the existence of a body of broad theory which encompasses both ancient and 'primitive' societies, and which tends to claim just this economic innocence. Characteristic of this approach is a careful and self-conscious distancing of the historian from the modern economic world. It urges us not take for granted, for example, the basic experience of valuing our transactions in terms of profit and loss. The reason given is that the economic systems of the ancient past were significantly different from those of the present. We can construct models of how they worked only from the ancient sources themselves, from a judicious use of ethnographic literature, and from certain points of reference that seem to be generally valid for economies in early complex societies. We must be alert, according to this view, to the dangers of implanting into the past the motivations and the means of the economies that we ourselves are familiar with. This is a valuable, indeed essential discipline, yet if left here it runs the risk of unnecessarily isolating the past and impoverishing the discussion. In particular it depicts ancient systems as static entities devoid of mechanisms of adjustment to changing circumstances.[1]

Furthermore, if the contrast between present and past is so crucial, it is important to have an informed basis of just what does constitute 'the present'. Herein lies another source of weakness. In discussions of this kind the economic systems of the present are made synonymous with 'market economies', the product of mercantilist thinking and practice of recent centuries that had its beginnings in the west. This is a false basis from which to begin. At the level of individual states the modern world contains no examples, nor has it ever, of an economic system based fully on market forces. Even for those politicians who most desire this, it remains an unattainable goal. All macroeconomic systems represent a balance, a compromise, an uneasy truce between two forces: the urge of the state to provide itself with a secure base for its own existence and its plans, and the fragmented pressure of private demand.

At one end of the spectrum we have those states that, for reasons of ideology (or sometimes the exigencies of war), institute a wholly administered economy. The former Soviet-bloc countries offered the most obvious examples for a good part of the twentieth century. They used modern means to achieve something now familiar from studying ancient systems: 'redistribution' (a word which, in archaeology, has come to mean widespread centralized collection of produce which is subsequently disbursed on a similarly large scale). Within systems of this kind economic transactions are intended to achieve egalitarian social goals and are thus 'embedded' within a political ideology which aims to engineer a particular set of social and economic relationships (socialism in these cases). For such a system to work as its creators intend, it must be sufficiently sensitive in its prediction of personal demands and circumstances, and flexible in its response with the supply of goods and services so that all people are content. All modern systems fail to meet the immensity of the task, and where failure occurs a market solution arises, although the modern world misleadingly renames a normal market response within a controlled economy a 'black market' and takes steps to suppress it. The 'black market' simply fills the interstices within a megalithic system.

Then there are those states dedicated to market freedom. This philosophy is in its application, however, invariably restricted. It flourishes most obviously in the manufacturing and retailing of consumer products. Modern states of this kind nevertheless retain huge administered sectors: civil service, armed forces, defence procurement, farm price support, unemployment benefit, social insurance schemes, and control of the banking system within which the free market operates. Modern market-sector states are large employers and (through welfare schemes) supporters of people, and large purchasers of many things, including money, yet are themselves not commercial organizations ruled by the maximization of profit and minimization of loss. At anything other than the local scale the self-regulating, price-fixing market responsive wholly to supply and demand is an illusion. Modern market mechanisms remain embedded within and draw for part of their performance on the administered state sector, not least the state's almost invariable control of the banking system, levels of taxation and supply of money, a sector which is in turn embedded within broader notional considerations such as 'national interest', 'party political agendas', 'social and moral responsibility', and so on. The threshold that 'privatization' dares not cross is the issuing of currency free from regulation, so that 'forgery' or 'counterfeiting' becomes simply a market opportunity. Free-market economics applies to the manufacture of cane furniture but not to the printing of paper money. The severity of the penalties for the latter is an indication of the extent to which a notional free market in commodities is in the end controlled by governments and is not therefore free. It is this threshold that, more than any other, separates the modern from the ancient world. And from this perspective ancient economies based on commodities came closer to the ideal of the free market than do modern economies based on money, the viability of which depends much upon manipulation and confidence (a particular kind of belief). More will be said on this at the end of the chapter.

What has this to do with the study of the ancient past? All modern macroeconomic systems, despite huge differences in philosophy and practice, represent different mixes of the same two basic ingredients: state ambition on the one hand, and private demand for more than an egalitarian share-out of the state's resources on the other. Whether we focus on states devoted to free enterprise that may wish to withdraw from final economic control, or those with an entirely contrary philosophy, we find in reality that they merely shift the boundaries between the two zones. We are thus entitled to ask of past systems: do they, too, represent a mix of their own within a universal and inescapable macroeconomic structure created when the first states emerged, allowing for the possibility that, like the modern 'black market', some aspects may appear in a different guise?

No doubt attaches itself to one side of the ancient mix: that directed by institutional administration, of the redistributive kind. This is not the case, however, with the other side: the satisfaction of individual demand, where the emphasis in modern studies is often to minimize its economic power. If, as we are encouraged to do with ancient states such as Egypt, we regard the administered economy as overwhelmingly dominant, we have to accept that one of two conditions was present: either the system itself was able constantly to assess every individual's real needs and satisfy them, or the needs of very large sections of the population remained not so much static as passive, offering a mirror-image of fluctuations within the state system, that is, when the state had less to give out, people resigned themselves to receiving less. For the first condition, had it ever existed it would have to be regarded as one of the lost arts of antiquity, since it would represent a level of economic management that eludes the grasp of all modern governments. For the second, however, we have to consider both the nature of ancient demand and the extent to which ancient systems were static.

The state sector: its power and its failings

The administered, redistributive side to the Egyptian economy is too well known to require much explanation. Several papyri or groups of papyri document specific instances in considerable detail for the various periods,[2] and to these major sources we can add a host of minor ones. Chapters 4 and 6 covered some of the relevant ground. We can utilize archaeological evidence, including huge granaries, witnesses to the scale of the state's maintenance of buffer-stocks of grain, which evened out fluctuations in supply brought about by varying harvest yields over the years.[3] To illustrate their magnitude, in the last chapter attention was directed towards one particular example: at the Ramesseum (Figure 94, p. 259). Their passive economic weight should not be underestimated. Economic performance is a cyclic affair, and in the modern world state control of key sectors acts to bridge the gap between the inevitable peaks and troughs. We understand far too little of pure economic interactions in the ancient world to be able to model the changing economic climate which we must recognize was a major and ever-present factor, but in the case of Egypt we can be sure of one cyclic element: that of the volume of Nile waters. The annual inundation, the key to agriculture, not only varied from year to year, but was also subject to broader climatic cycles which, over a period of time, would have had inexorable consequences on the agrarian economy. The intervention of the state (palace and temples) would have had a powerful cushioning effect.

It was not a monolithic system. As we have seen, alongside the palace and its various centres of administrative authority there was a complex network of quasi-autonomous pious foundations or religious institutions where the focus of attention was the cult of statues of gods and kings, the latter including those belonging to the royal tombs and their associated temples.[4] All of these institutions were, to varying degrees, collectors of revenue, storing part and distributing part as rations or wages. The number of people who benefited seems sometimes to have been deliberately multiplied through the phyle system, which shared out temple duties (and benefits) on a part-time basis.[5] As we have seen, it was the Middle Kingdom that seems to have progressed furthest down this particular road.

An important general point arises here. It is legitimate to regard ancient societies as 'systems'. Their component parts and lines of interaction can be identified and laid out diagrammatically like a modern management flow-chart.[6] It is a valuable perspective, but it carries a semantic pitfall. We may identify systems in the workings of ancient societies, but they need not have been at all systematic, for the latter word implies a prominent degree of reason and order. The workings of the Egyptian administration at its various periods are reasonably apparent, but they seem not to be the product of an abstract concept of administration elegantly applied across a broad spectrum of activities. Far from it. The system ran in channels of authority. Within any one channel the procedures could be remarkably effective (though not efficient) in achieving a given target of the kind: quarry, transport and erect a colossus of a particular size. This is where bureaucratic talents flourished. But we will look in vain for evidence of conscious integration of the individual parts into a general scheme of management. The workings of the Egyptian administration are another example of self-organization, of a system evolving its coherence through innumerable local adjustments to circumstances, the 'checks and balances' process which prevents societies, for most of the time, from straying far from a common path.

One document from the New Kingdom brings out very clearly the way that ancient government consisted of an accumulation of individual institutional arrangements of very restricted scope. This is the Edict of Horemheb (*c.* 1320 BC).[7] When the Edict was issued the Amarna Period had just ended, and the military leader Horemheb had become king. It might be anticipated that this would be a time of reorganization throughout the country, and of the reassertion of royal power of a traditional form. But the first part of the Edict is a collection of individual royal decrees directed against specific cases of wrongful or excessive collection of revenues by various groups of persons responsible to the king. They give the distinct impression of being responses to individual petitions of complaint rather than of being the result of a considered exercise in overhauling the administration generally. In so doing they imply that there was no codified system of revenue collection as we might understand it. In its place there was a range of individual practices sanctified by tradition. One group of officials did this, another did that. In one case the tradition was of recent memory. A separately mentioned authority in the Edict is the royal harem which had its own revenue-raising powers. Every year the king and some of his household travelled upstream to Thebes for the Festival of Opet. The job of feeding them *en route* had been passed on, in the time of Tuthmosis III, to the mayors of local towns. The officials of the queen and of the royal harem had turned this into a predatory affair which the Edict now tried to correct. It is tempting to imagine an irascible queen making up for the boredom of a long journey away from the comforts of her own palace by preying on hapless provincial mayors, and thereby creating a little administrative tradition. But to think in this way is to reveal an uncomfortable truth about academic scholarship: it takes on life only when it breathes in the vapours of historical fiction.

Because ancient Egypt was for long periods successful as a complex society we have to accept none the less that some kind of overall economic balancing act prevailed. Part of the process lay in what was, in effect, a massive delegation of short-term management through the pious foundations. We have already, in the last chapter, commented on the symbiotic relationship between temples and palaces. Their status as religious centres embedded within the overall ideology of the state, and their internal bureaucracies gave them the authority and means to function effectively but not divisively. In the longer term, however, they were subject to a process of piecemeal adjustment in which older and less prestigious foundations lost their benefactions to new foundations.[8] The notion that cults were founded for eternity was a myth that did not hinder state interference. In revenue and expenditure terms the sum of their activities plus a general level of royal expenditure on court life, on large and thus long-term building programmes, and on the military, represented a general 'budget' or balance-sheet for the country. Complaints from below of insufficient resources would have signalled to senior officials a degree of imbalance, which they could then have sought to correct. This is how self-organization works.

The basic level of royal expenditure was maintained partly through the income of lands and other productive resources directly owned, partly through revenue-raising powers bestowed on particular officials of particular institutions, and partly through a country-wide tax levy. From time to time this was recalculated, presumably in response to perceived shortfalls in revenue.[9] The one detailed record we have of a general tax levied on provincial towns and districts for the benefit of the king (through his vizier) is the taxation scene in the tomb of Rekhmira at Thebes (Figure 107).[10] This source implies, however, that the amounts raised in this way were very modest. Yet particular circumstances regularly created extra if short-lived demands. The procedure then was simply to pass them down the administrative channels. Ideally such a demand would be accompanied by an order to release some of the state's buffer-stocks from the magazines of a convenient institution to cover the demand. In practice, however, this did not always work. An *ad hoc* solution was expected, and this could be found either by a peremptory local demand on whomsoever was vulnerable, or by raiding the resources of another area of administration.

The ill-feeling generated by the tangle of individual systems of revenue collection, by which institutions and groups of officials quite literally lived off the land, is illustrated by a second document from the New Kingdom, the Nauri Decree of Seti I.[11] It belongs to

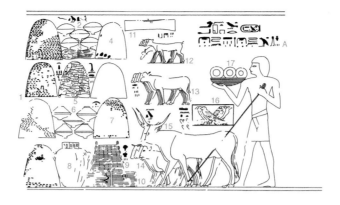

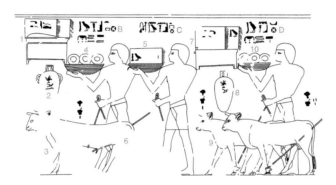

Figure 107 Paying in kind: local taxation in a cashless economy, illustrated by a portion of the revenue scene from the tomb of the vizier Rekhmira at Thebes, mid-18th Dynasty. Not all commodities can be identified. *Top.* (A) Taxes delivered by the 'mayor of [the town] of Huwet-weret-Amenemhat' (somewhere to the south of Abydos). (1) four heaps of barley; (2) cakes; (3) rope; (4) *dôm* nuts; (5) cakes; (6) spices (?); (7) carob beans; (8) honey (?); (9) sacks; (10) reed mats; (11) grass mats; (12) six goats; (13) five calves; (14) four head of cattle; (15) two head of long-horned cattle; (16) 500 pigeons; (17) two gold, one silver ring-ingots. *Bottom.* (B) 'The recorder of the town of Wah-sut' (Abydos South, see Figure 81, p. 224), and (C) 'The scribe of the recorder of the town of Wah-sut'. (1) two lengths of linen cloth in a chest; (2) honey; (3) one head of cattle; (4) three gold ring-ingots; (5) one linen garment; (6) one head of cattle; (D) 'The recorder of Abydos'; (7) one length of cloth and one garment in a chest; (8) honey; (9) one head of cattle; (10) two gold, one silver ring-ingots. After N. de G. Davies *The tomb of Rekh-mi-rēʿ at Thebes*, New York, 1943, Pl. XXXIV; P.E. Newberry, *The life of Rekhmara*, London, 1900, Pl. VI.

the reign of one of the 'great' kings, so lifting it above the charge that it reveals a good system going wrong under a bad king. One of the leading pious works of Seti I was the building of a sumptuously decorated and equipped temple for Amun and Osiris at the holy city of Abydos. As was customary he donated sufficient land and other sources of income to make the temple a permanently wealthy institution. Some of the land lay far away in the conquered territories of the Sudan. The purpose of the decree was to protect the new donations from other official institutions whose agents might arrive at some distant farm or cattle station and demand payment of a tax. For such officials the punishments were fierce: heavy fines, beatings and mutilations. Every year, too, a flotilla of ships set off from the Nubian lands on the long journey downstream not only to replenish the huge storerooms attached to the temple with the year's Nubian harvest, but also to bring exotic trade goods purchased through barter by 'traders' employed by the temple. On its long journey downstream the flotilla passed Egyptian fortresses whose real job it was to protect Egyptian life and property. One must have lain near Nauri, a lonely, isolated place:

> As for any commander of the [local] fortress, and scribe of the fortress, any inspector belonging to the fortress who shall board a boat belonging to the Temple and shall take gold, [ivory, ebony?], leopard and other animal skins, giraffes' tails, giraffes' hides, etc., any goods of Kush which are brought as revenue to the Temple, punishment shall be meted out to him in the form of one hundred blows, and he shall be fined on behalf of the Temple in terms of the value of the goods at the rate of eighty to one.[12]

The remoteness and isolation of Nauri does not, in itself, make the decree an exception. The full text makes it clear that the Nauri version was only one copy of a decree that applied to the open farmlands of Nubia where Egyptian colonial towns had been built and a full Egyptian-style administration functioned. Nor is the decree itself unique for its period. Others are known from other reigns, including one of Rameses III from Elephantine and others from the Ramesside period from Armant and Hermopolis.[13] Indeed, the tradition of decrees to protect individual institutions from the exactions of others goes back to the Old Kingdom.[14]

Government in ancient Egypt was by royal decree, the system of administration was the sum of those decrees, and the resulting overlaps and confusions of responsibility were tackled by fresh decrees in response to specific complaints. This cycle of decision – petition of complaint – redress was a basic part of bureaucratic life, to the extent that collections of model letters used in the training of scribes often contained a model letter or petition of complaint.[15] The universal picture of the rapacious tax-collector and the suffering peasant is joined in ancient Egypt by the picture of the predatory official victimizing his colleague.

The state sector of the Egyptian economy existed to satisfy institutional demands, and must have had very limited flexibility. For it also to have satisfied most private demand, that demand must have been of low intensity. We need to look next, therefore, at the real pattern of private demand.

The power of private demand

When we turn to the record of archaeology, especially that from cemeteries, it is very clear that during the latter part of the Predynastic Period Egyptian society entered that crucial stage of social and psychological development which is still with us: conspicuous consumption. The creation of large and striking private tombs and the accumulation of burial goods affected the whole of Egypt geographically, and created an aspiration that penetrated deeply into society. Conspicuous consumption is not incompatible with the redistributive economy. Social obligation brings the two together: the king rewards his great men, many of them having provincial connections. They in turn pass on bounty to poorer relatives and dependants. Everyone is satisfied (or unable to articulate their dissatisfaction in economic terms), and in death takes their place in a cemetery which likewise reflects the social and economic order: local leaders in centrally placed handsome tombs surrounded by myriad smaller tombs of lesser folk (Naga ed-Deir and Beni Hasan providing fine examples from the Old and Middle Kingdoms respectively).[16] We can, if we are sufficiently selective, make Egypt into a model of the redistributive economy.

At a political level (i.e. in the wish to exercise power), however, the Old Kingdom shows that the ideal of consensus is an illusion. Provincial governors (nomarchs) appear, and when, at the end of the 6th Dynasty, occasion allowed, the more ambitious amongst them strove by any means to carve out larger territories for themselves, leading in some cases to civil war.[17] (I will say more about this in Chapter 8.) The politics of self-interest were well and truly alive. The sense of social obligation was not lost, the classic example being Ankhtify the nomarch of Hierakonpolis who, having taken over the neighbouring nome of Edfu early in the First Intermediate Period, found himself distributing famine relief over a huge territory. Ankhtify, having seized lands, was, for a short time, in effect ruling a miniature state.[18]

Famine relief is a special case of obligation. Would Ankhtify have also headed an administration capable of satisfying normal demands? We lack the archaeological evidence from contemporary cemeteries in his own area that would enable us to see for ourselves how people in his territory fared. Further north, however, in Middle Egypt we have a particularly well documented cemetery record for this and the preceding periods. This is the work of the archaeologist Guy Brunton in the Qau/El-Badari/Matmar/Mostagedda areas.[19] In the First Intermediate Period this belonged to the frontier zone between the warring dynasties of Herakleopolis and Thebes, although the role of the local nome administrator is nowhere made clear in the surviving sources. The period is particularly well represented by burials. Their grave goods show no sign of general impoverishment. Brunton addressed himself particularly to this point:

> In the cemeteries at Qau and Badari the tombs with the most objects are precisely those of the vii–viiith dyn. period. Here we find the greatest profusion of beads and amulets; no diminution in the number of alabaster vases, and all the alabaster head-rests; the greatest number of mirrors of any period; and the least number of simple shallow graves. The workmanship of the glaze amulets may show great delicacy; the carnelian legs are the best of their kind; and the animal-backed seal-amulets are cut with skill and care.[20]

Brunton then showed that more gold beads and amulets occurred in this period as well. It is unreasonable to argue that this was mostly material robbed from earlier graves because much of it is in styles peculiar to the period. Nor were these graves clustered around large centrally placed tombs of leaders and providers. They occur in a series of small cemeteries spread out along the edge of the desert as if representing the burials of a wide scatter of villages. It strains credulity to suppose that these people were passive recipients of a state redistributive system, which was, by its nature, of limited flexibility.

The anonymous people of Qau and Badari accumulated possessions during a time of change that, in its magnitude, was unusual in the course of Pharaonic history. But although ancient economies never experienced the prolonged volatility of modern times it is a mistake to think of them as static. Overall, between say 2100 and 1500 BC, the boundaries of state power ebbed and flowed in two cycles of great magnitude (the first two 'Intermediate Periods'). And at the best of times, when famines and civil war were no more, the state system still had to adjust to change, particularly demands made by ambitious kings. New temples, new fleets of ships, the re-equipping of the army for fresh campaigns: these could create sudden demands both for the redirection of existing resources and for additional revenue. Any economic system that we propose for ancient Egypt has to be able to account for the apparently successful adjustments which local communities made to changes of different magnitudes within a relatively crude state system of economic direction.

As modern societies have found, 'consuming' is good for economic growth. The act of consumption often though not inevitably involves destruction: the food is eaten and then burnt off as energy, the car is driven but is later crushed. Both need to be constantly replaced and this is good for farmers and car manufacturers. Consumerism ought to work just as well, however, if the goods once purchased were placed directly into a hole in the ground. What one needs is a set of beliefs to make it seem worth while. Providing for the eternal existence of the dead is just such a set of beliefs. Whether burial goods in ancient Egypt were purpose-made and purchased for that end alone, or whether a person set things aside during life, or left it to heirs to select from what was available, the effect was the same: theoretically a bottomless hole into which a proportion of the country's goods were cast, creating a constant demand for replacement – theoretically, because tomb robbery constantly brought some of it back in a clandestine recycling. In the case of the most favoured officials the royal resources might well assist at least in providing the labour for cutting and decorating the tomb itself. This is claimed in inscriptions.[21] But for the majority, the cost of burial was a private matter. Private responsibility for a good burial was enshrined within the law: '"Let the possessions be given to him who buries", says the law of Pharaoh.' So declares one New Kingdom party in a case of disputed inheritance. This document, with others, shows that the normal pattern of inheritance of property was subject to the proviso that the whole inheritance would go to whomsoever undertook to have the actual burial carried out.[22] A potential heir would disinherit himself or herself by ignoring this. The practice and the kind of costs involved for non-officials are illustrated by the case of the man Huy (from Deir el-Medina), buried by his wife Iy. She apparently inherits from him since she orders a coffin and pays for it with a house originally belonging to her husband. In relative terms this was a heavy expense involving the sale of a house, although the hope of inheritance must have made the weight of obligation easier to bear.

A good burial, however, was only part of the economic pressure in private demand. A prospering official might seek to build a new house for himself. This is promised in New Kingdom school texts,[23] but we also have a real letter on the subject written by a provincial mayor (possibly of Armant) of the 18th Dynasty called Menthuhetep to a friendly and, as a deputy to a 'chief of works', a usefully placed official at Thebes, a 'scribe' called Ahmose. The subject matter is instructions on the early stages of building a new house for Menthuhetep, a house which, to judge from its dimensions, was to be an impressive one. Here we probably have a case of a provincial dignitary setting up a second house in a royal city, in this instance Thebes, and clearly paying for it himself. For at the end of the letter he adds: 'have the price of the land for the house given to its owner, and make sure

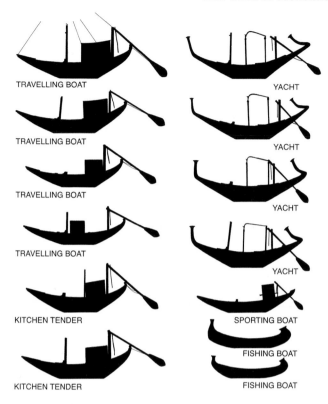

TRAVELLING BOAT

TRAVELLING BOAT

TRAVELLING BOAT

TRAVELLING BOAT

KITCHEN TENDER

KITCHEN TENDER

YACHT

YACHT

YACHT

YACHT

SPORTING BOAT

FISHING BOAT

FISHING BOAT

Figure 108   Affluence: the chancellor Meketra's river fleet. Silhouettes of the wooden boat models from his tomb at Thebes, early 12th Dynasty, after H.E. Winlock, *Models of daily life in ancient Egypt*, New York, 1955, Figs 70–82.

he is happy with it. See to it that when I come he doesn't have words with me' (Papyrus B.M.10102).[24]

Then there were the goods that daughters and sons needed to acquire to create the joint properties which formed the basis of a marriage contract; there were pious outlays at shrines, possible gifts or bribes for advancement, and the general competitive display of wealth engendered by the existence of an ostentatious and lavish court. Apart from the property and goods which the excavation of settlements and cemeteries reveals, other sources tell us that officials maintained fleets of Nile boats (Figure 108),[25] and, in the New Kingdom, horses and chariots as well. People were surrounded by reasons to accumulate wealth, which might arise quite suddenly.

The effects of a relatively free play of competitive acquisition unconnected with burial customs can be seen in the extensive private residential neighbourhoods of the New Kingdom city of El-Amarna (Figure 109, and see further below, pp. 326–30), where wealth and status were advertised by a finely graded array of house sizes and architectural status symbols. The houses of rich and poor are distinguished more by size than by design, although larger houses did possess features, such as an entrance porch, which denoted status by themselves. If we take the size of a person's house as even a rough-and-ready

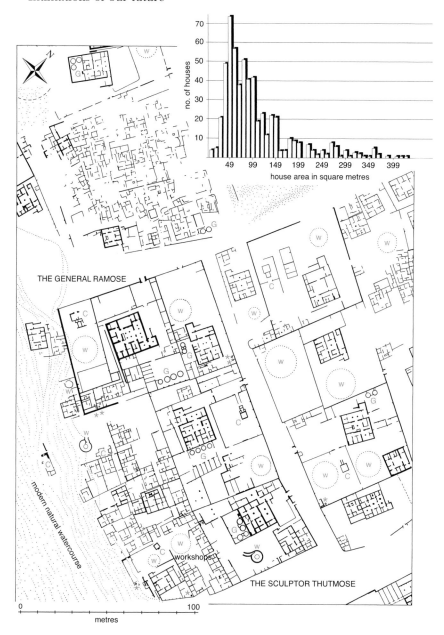

Figure 109 Plan of a characteristic part of a residential area at El-Amarna, in the Main City. The famous painted bust of Queen Nefertiti was found in the house of a sculptor, whose name may have been Thutmose. The letters on the plan are: 'W': well; 'C': chapel; 'G': granary. The '*' indicates the probable presence of a pottery kiln. Figure 115, p. 328 is based on part of this map. *Inset.* Bar-chart showing the frequencies of houses of varying sizes within the Main City at El-Amarna. House sizes are given in steps of 10 sq. m. The regularity of the curve of distribution is striking. After Piers Crocker, unpublished dissertation, University of Cambridge, and see *JEA* 71 (1985), 52–65.

measure of his status, the spread of house sizes provides a general profile of the kind of society we are dealing with.[26] An easy way to view the whole mass of data is in tabular form (Figure 109, *inset*). Although there are some jumps and gaps the overall pattern of the data fits a single curve in which, beyond a point of very basic housing, ever-larger houses grow steadily rarer. There are no obvious breaks or plateaux. The fine grading of house sizes implies an absence of bottlenecks in the movement, up and down the scale of relative wealth, which people are always subject to, even if slowly. Remembering that this was a time of great national prosperity, we might note that the gulf between rich and poor in this respect was not as great as we might expect. The rich and powerful lived in large houses, not in palaces. This points to the one great exception in what appears to be an economic system finely tuned to individual ambition and circumstances: the gulf was between the king and everyone else. If added to Figure 109 *inset*, royal palaces would be way off the edge of the page.

It is occasionally possible to find in ancient texts a degree of reservation on acquisitiveness: 'A cup of water quenches thirst, a mouthful of herbs fortifies the heart' is the ascetic advice of the sage to the vizier Kagemni.[27] At the other extreme, however, were those who made the best of whatever chances for enrichment came their way. The late New Kingdom provides some spectacular documentation (in the form of an archive of papyri dealing with investigations and trials) concerning the promise of instant enrichment through theft.[28] Nothing was sacred: temple grain supplies were siphoned off, tombs were robbed, temple equipment and fittings were plundered. Although tomb robbery attracted people of mainly lowly status, less arduous forms of theft and dishonesty drew in officials as well, including temple priests. Indeed, the scale of the thefts often required official participation. Apart from depicting the seamier side to the crumbling fabric of late New Kingdom society and also the processes of law when they were eventually invoked, the papyri illustrate in a highly coloured way motives and means in the contemporary economy. They dramatize the existence of a crude urge for self-enrichment, which in more orderly circumstances would have been sublimated by participation in the market-place, selling goods, renting or leasing land, making loans bearing interest, all of them practices explicitly documented. They also reveal the fate of the stolen goods as they re-enter the economy of the living, and in so doing add usefully to our restricted knowledge of the economic behaviour of the time.

The thieves generally, even when of lowly status, were town or village dwellers and householders, many apparently living in the medium-sized town of Maiunehes which lay in and around the mortuary temple of Rameses III (Medinet Habu; see Chapter 8, and Figure 122, p. 352). Much of what they stole they simply kept as part of the household property. Apart from gold and silver the lists of recovered goods include a fair quantity of linen pieces and garments, vases of oil, coffin trimmings and pieces of wood. Copper and bronze in any form was much favoured. A set of copper carrying-rings prized off a wooden chest was the haul from one temple theft (Papyrus B.M.10402). One list of recovered goods consists almost entirely of these metals. Sometimes the item is specified – 'a wash-bowl of bronze equal to 20 *deben*' – but mostly a figure of how many *deben* were involved is given, and the amounts could be quite small: 'The lady Aref of the Necropolis, wife of the workman Hori: 1; the lady Takiri of the Necropolis: 1' (Papyrus B.M.10053, recto 2.18–19). One *deben* was only half the price of a pair of sandals.

In the end, however, material wealth was the means of purchase. The wife of one of the thieves confesses: 'I took my husband's share and put it aside in my storeroom, then I took one *deben* of silver from it and used it to buy grain' (Papyrus B.M.10052, 6.6–7). Another wife, smarter (or perhaps more honest), when asked how she bought servants if not by stolen silver, replied: 'I bought them in exchange for garden produce' (Papyrus B.M.10052, 10.14–15). Though her words may sound naive she clearly hoped to be believed and was, in effect, basing her case on being able to grow cash crops on a significant scale, a most important point in itself. An equally positive defence was given by another wife when asked to explain the origin of a quantity of silver: 'I got it in exchange for barley in the year of the hyenas, when there was a famine' (Papyrus B.M.10052, 11.5–8). Here the claim is based on scarcity driving up the price of a basic commodity, a classic supply–demand relationship. A more elaborate case is provided by the confession of another priest and temple gardener Ker on the subject of stripping gold foil from off the temple doors:

> We went yet again to the door-jambs . . . and we brought away 5 *kite* of gold. We bought corn with it in Thebes and divided it up . . . Now after some days Peminu our superior quarrelled with us saying: 'You have given me nothing.' So we went again to the door-jambs and brought 5 *kite* of gold from them, and exchanged it for an ox and gave it to Peminu.
>
> (Papyrus B.M.10053, verso 3.10–13)

This case is particularly interesting: Peminu preferred good farm livestock to a suspicious quantity of gold foil.

Many more examples can be quoted to illustrate the variety of purchases. 'Charge concerning the shrine of cedar, both the image and the timber, which the scribe of the royal records Setekhmes stole. He sold it in Thebes and received its price' (Papyrus B.M.10053, verso 5.5). The overseer of the field of the temple of Amun, Akhenmenu gives '1 *deben* of silver and 5 *kite* of gold in exchange for land' (Papyrus B.M.10052, 2.19). The scribe Amenhetep called Seret, of the temple of Amun, gives '2 *deben* [of silver] in exchange for land, for 40 *deben* of copper, and for 10 *khar* of barley' (Papyrus B.M.10052, 2.22). The servant Shedbeg disposes of quite a list of commodities 'in payment for the slave Degay' (Papyrus B.M. 10052, 2.23–5). Another confesses: 'I gave 5 *kite* of silver to the incense-roaster Penementenakht of the temple of Amun in exchange for 10 *hin* of honey' (Papyrus B.M.10052, 2a.1; cf. lines 4–14). The confession of the herdsman Bukhaaf begins: 'The lady Nesmut came to where I was and said to me: "Some men have found something that can be sold for bread. Let's go so that you can eat it with them"' (Papyrus B.M.10052, 1.8–10). We can recognize Theban slang here: 'bread' must mean 'fine goods', or something similar.

Sometimes the loot was needed to buy services, in the form of protection: 'Now when we were arrested, the district scribe Khaemipet came to me . . . and I gave him the 4 *kite* of gold which had fallen to my lot' (Papyrus B.M.10054). And in another case: 'But the scribe of the royal records, Setekhmes, had overheard and threatened us saying: "I am going to report it to the chief priest of Amun." So we brought 3 *kite* of gold and gave it to the scribe of the royal records, Setekhmes' (Papyrus B.M.10053, verso 3.13–14). Some disposals were probably to settle obligations or to gain favours:

> Charge concerning the 4 boards of cedar belonging to the 'Floor of Silver' of King Usermaatra-Setepenra [Rameses II], the great god, which the scribe Sedi

gave to the lady Teherer, wife of the god's father Hori: he gave them to the carpenter Ahauty of the funerary chapel of Hui, and he made them into an inner coffin for her.

(Papyrus B.M.10053, verso 4.15–17)

Perhaps the most intriguing entry from the economic point of view is a list of gold and silver 'recovered from the thieving workmen of the Necropolis, which they were found to have given to the traders of every establishment' (Papyrus B.M.10068, recto 4.1–18). Fourteen traders are listed, attached both to temples and to private households. It was the job of a 'trader' to maintain the supply–demand balance of an employer by trading surplus or unwanted commodities for whatever was required. These thieves, who would not have been in a position to have 'traders' in their own employ, were therefore latching on to a professional system for converting their loot into other commodities, doubtless for a fat commission. As urban dwellers in Maiunehes they had channels of communication with a wider world.

The rotten state of society at the end of the New Kingdom was cured, if only temporarily, by the imposition of military rule. The legal papyri of the time are not necessarily a guide to the state of affairs earlier in the period (though one cannot be wholly sure). They are relevant because they provide verbatim testimony to attitudes to material wealth and to the easy and natural recourse that people had to a free market in goods, slaves, livestock, food and even land. It would be foolish to claim that the opportunities for exchange, the markets themselves, were created by the dishonesty of the day. In more orderly times people still received windfalls – from inheritance, gifts from the state – and had a similar range of choices in what they did with them, hoarding them at home or exchanging them for other things. The late New Kingdom robberies released a surge of wealth into society from, as it were, the bottom. The 18th Dynasty had done the same, from spoils of battle, but from the top and according to an administered system.

One discovery, at El-Amarna, does actually reveal that concentrations of liquid wealth were in circulation in this earlier time. In a small open space beside a public well in the North Suburb a pottery jar had been buried, containing twenty-three bars of gold and a quantity of silver fragments and roughly made rings, as well as a silver figurine of a Hittite god (Figure 110).[29] The gold bars had been made simply by pouring melted-down gold into grooves scooped by the finger in sand. The total weight of the gold was 3,375.36 grammes, equivalent in ancient terms to 37 *deben*. The total weight of the silver came to at least 1,085.85 grammes, or 12 *deben*. This represents a fair amount of wealth, though not a staggering sum. The most successful of the recorded late New Kingdom tomb robberies, in the tomb of the 17th Dynasty king Sebekemsaf, netted the thieves 160 *deben* of gold. But some idea of its purchasing power can be obtained from the ratios of gold to silver (5:3 later becoming 2:1), and of silver to copper (1:100). Thus the silver could have been used to purchase, say, ten or twelve head of cattle. The archaeologist who made the El-Amarna find assumed that it was part of a thief's loot, and in view of the odd place in which it was found this still seems credible, although there are other possibilities. Stock from a jeweller's workshop has also been suggested.[30] Yet we cannot be sure that the only remarkable thing about the find is simply that someone had failed to recover it. There is an uncanny parallel in a letter from a slightly later period (and unconnected with El-Amarna) in which the writer gives instructions as to where, in the pigsty beside the house, a mass of bronzework

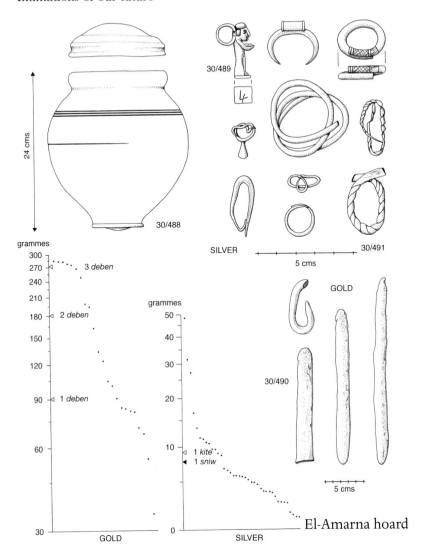

Figure 110   Part of a hoard of gold and silver buried in a pottery jar in a suburb of El-Amarna. The silver is made up partly of finished items (including the Hittite figurine, no. 30/489), and partly of coils and irregular pieces, some cut from vessels; the gold in crude bars. As the weight tables show, there is little to suggest that pieces of standard weight (proto-coins) were desired. Rather, with the coils, scraps and bars, pieces were cut off to meet a specific demand, their weight (and thus value) determined by weighing (as in Figures 113, p. 321, and 114, upper, p. 325). After H. Frankfort and J.D.S. Pendlebury, *The City of Akhenaten* II, London, 1933, 59–61, Pl. XLIII, and original record cards.

was buried and, alongside it, a pottery jar containing a hoard of gold and silver items. Secret burial around one's house might have been not uncommon.[31] Whatever the origin of the El-Amarna hoard, it illustrates easily convertible wealth poised on the point of re-entering the economy at a private level.

The satisfaction of private demand for finished goods required an availability of raw materials. Official inscriptions are often taken to imply that a royal monopoly existed on those raw materials that lay outside the Nile floodplain. Inscriptions at mines and quarries do, indeed, reveal a scale of operation that only a state could undertake.[32] But these need not have been the norm. Take 'alabaster' (more properly called travertine), for example. One prime source was the desert to the east of the Assiut–Minia area in Middle Egypt, the area that includes the Hatnub quarries.[33] Hatnub was one target for large expeditions despatched by kings. It can, however, easily be visited by donkey in a single day (the journey time is about three hours in each direction). If a group of people took with them a supply of water and food for a few days, some baskets and simple tools, they could bring back a sizeable load of small lumps of alabaster suitable for vase-making, perhaps using pieces left behind by the major expeditions. There was, for example, no shortage of small pieces of alabaster for the vase-makers of Middle Egypt in the First Intermediate Period, who produced a distinctive range of small elegant vessels that are common in the tombs of that period. Simple operations of this kind could leave few traces behind them. A further indication that written sources are not a full guide to the procurement of raw materials is that certain substances are excluded altogether. We have no records of expeditions to quarry the soft rock that was the basis for the marl clays widely used in pottery manufacture,[34] and the same is true for natron and for gypsum. These operations had no need for military-style expeditions. They could be accomplished by small groups of hardy labourers camping and working in a primitive manner (such as at the Fayum gypsum quarries, Figure 111).[35] By invoking a simple mode of supply we can easily explain the continued availability of raw materials during times of internal weakness.

In the Graeco-Roman Period natron was, with some other commodities, the subject of state monopoly. Monopoly is a word that is sometimes used for the Pharaonic Period as well.[36] Its earlier existence is, however, a matter of inference rather than of documentation, and does not accord with the general picture of people's attitudes in Pharaonic Egypt. The political stability and cultural coherence of ancient Egypt over long periods of time are part of its abiding image. They must reflect a broad acceptance of the ideas and ideals that originated within the court. But beneath this bland law-abiding exterior lurked a predatory instinct directed towards property rather than persons. Institutionalized vigilance pursued elaborate schemes of checking, and threatened fearsome punishments. When it slipped, dishonesty quickly flourished. In this atmosphere no monopoly could have relied upon a tacit acceptance of its validity. It, too, would have required enforcement by decrees and punishments. Within the corpus of administrative documents we will look in vain for such references.

Even with foreign trade we should be cautious in using the term 'monopoly'.[37] It is not, for example, the natural interpretation to place on the famous scene in the tomb of the nomarch Khnumhetep III at Beni Hasan which shows the arrival of a small Palestinian group from Moab bringing a quantity of eye paint (*msdmt*) with them (Figure 112).[38] Although one of Khnumhetep's titles, 'administrator of the eastern desert', suggests some formally recognized responsibility for the adjacent desert area, the general intention of the

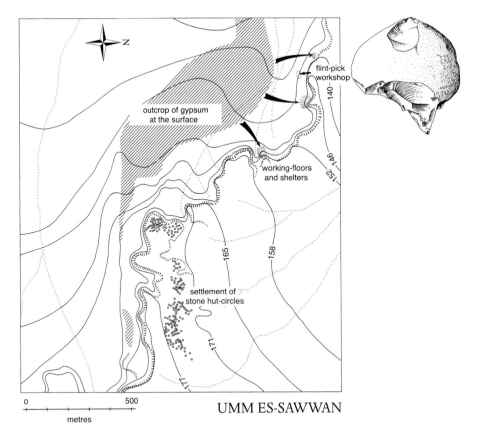

Figure 111 Low-level exploitation of a mineral resource: the gypsum quarries of Umm es-Sawwan (north Fayum) of the early Old Kingdom. The seasonal encampment of about 200 circular stone shelters occupies the top of a ridge along the edge of an escarpment overlooking a broad surface outcrop of gypsum on the desert plain below. The gypsum was dug out, using crude flint picks, in part as lumps for the making of vessels, and in part as powder to be used as mortar. The workshops for the vessels were in more sheltered places against the escarpment face. The flint picks were made on the spot, from flint nodules brought in from outside. Other types of flint tools were used in the vase-making. The informal nature of the settlement should be contrasted with the planned Middle Kingdom workmen's village at Kasr es-Sagha, Figure 84, p. 230. After G. Caton-Thompson and E.W. Gardner, *The desert Fayum*, London, 1934, Pl. LVIII.

scene is clear enough. The Palestinian group represents just one part of the broad range of products of Khnumhetep's 'estate', which included game hunted in the desert as well as agricultural produce from the Nile floodplain. Indeed, the Palestinians are introduced by a 'chief of the huntsmen'. Here again we have a means of low-level satisfaction of local demand for products which were out of the direct reach of industrious valley dwellers: small trading groups from further afield making their way along the desert wadi-systems to provincial points of contact within the Nile valley. One tomb scene does not make a pattern, but it does point to a possibility which can only be denied by having recourse to the dogmatic statement: 'foreign trade was a royal monopoly', a statement which can be

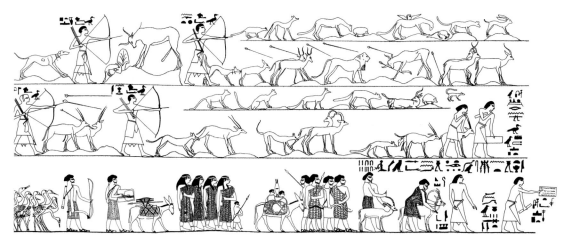

Figure 112 Produce of the eastern desert received by the nobleman appointed to control it, the nomarch of the Oryx Nome and 'Overseer of the Eastern Deserts' in the 12th Dynasty, Khnumhetep. The produce is mainly in the form of hunted game, but also (*bottom register*) includes a Palestinian trading party bringing eye pigment, who are introduced by an Egyptian official, 'Chief huntsman, Khety', a title which illuminates the status of the Palestinian group in Egyptian eyes. From tomb no. 3 at Beni Hasan, after P.E. Newberry, *Beni Hasan* I, London, 1893, Pls XXX, XXXI.

given no direct support. The availability of raw materials and imported finished goods in ancient Egypt is potentially a further exemplar of where the balance lay from period to period between state and the private domain.

Economics without money

The methods of small-scale economic transaction are well known for the New Kingdom, particularly from the wealth of data from the workmen's village of Deir el-Medina (Plate 9).[39] Acquiring and disposing of goods was done by barter, but not just by an impulsive gesture of the kind: I'll swap you a pig for two pairs of sandals. Everything had a value, expressed in various units that coincided with quantities of certain commodities: weights of silver and copper/bronze (often the *deben* and the *kite*), and units of capacity of grain and sesame oil (the *khar* and *oipe* for the former, the *hin* for the latter; Figure 113). Metals were themselves used in exchanges but not as coinage. The nearest step on the road to money is to be found in the stone weights which, when used in the pans of scale balances, checked the weights and thus the values of metals, precious and otherwise. One group of the thieves of Thebes scrupulously kept in a house a stone weight which they had used in dividing up the spoil from one tomb (Papyrus B.M.10052, 3.8–13; cf. 5.20). Prices varied from occasion to occasion, and the ratios of commodity values changed (e.g. that of silver to bronze declined late in the New Kingdom at Thebes from 1:100 to 1:60, perhaps because of the flood of silver from the spate of robberies). In a typical transaction one of the guards at the Theban necropolis buys an ox from a workman, and pays for it with a

Plate 9   The setting of village life: part of the village of necropolis workmen and artists at Deir el-Medina, western Thebes, late New Kingdom. The photograph is taken looking north-west down the central line of one house, no. III.NE. More houses continue beyond a transverse road, and in the background are terraces which originally supported tomb chapels. The walls are partly restored.

jar of fat worth 30 *deben*, 2 linen pieces worth 10 *deben*, scraps of copper/bronze weighing (and thus worth) 5 *deben*, and 10 *hin* of vegetable oil worth 5 *deben*.[40] The total is 50 *deben* (of copper), and the little receipt calls the total 'silver', which word was used colloquially to mean something very close to the modern word 'money'. This system of values also covered the price of labour and of raw materials. Stringing a wooden bed cost 1 *khar* of grain, actually making it cost about 5 *khar*, decorating it cost 1.5 *khar*, whilst the wood might cost 3 *deben*. With a *khar* of grain approximately equal to two *deben*, the total is about

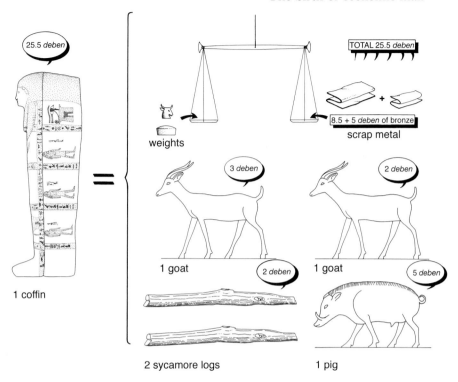

Figure 113 Buying and selling by barter-exchange, illustrated by an example from Deir el-Medina, 20th Dynasty. On one side of the exchange is a coffin, notionally valued at 25½ *deben* of bronze. The buyer has to make up a set of commodities of equal value, and does so partly with other items with notional values in bronze *deben* (two goats, a pig and two logs of wood, perhaps raw material for coffin-making), and partly with actual bronze items or scraps where the *deben* value was obtained by direct weighing on scales (as in Figure 114, p. 325), using small stone or bronze weights sometimes carved in animal shapes. The example is from Ostracon Deir el-Medina 73, verso, from J.J. Janssen, *Commodity prices from the Ramessid Period*, Leiden, 1975, 10.

18 *deben*. To buy a ready-made bed would cost between 12 and 25 *deben*, which is a rational reflection of the labour plus material costs.[41]

Did the state play any role in the fixing of prices? We can be sure that it did not explicitly regulate them. There is no direct evidence for kings or other officials ever doing this, and the study of the prices themselves, although it throws up broad regularities, also reveals too many variations. Prices fixed themselves. However, from the very fact that, at least during periods of strong centralized administration, the institutions were heavily involved in paying wages and collecting, storing and releasing commodities held as buffer-stocks, we can deduce that general levels were implicitly maintained. This is, however, a general framework within which all modern economic systems work no matter how active their 'free' market sector.

The fixing of prices for raw materials and other commodities, from grain to servant girls, takes us to the heart of the difficulties in coming to terms with ancient economies. Some people are tempted to draw a contrast between how this might have been done in ancient times and what is regarded as the modern solution to fixing prices: by means of a free market in which the relationship between supply and demand does it automatically. This modern process seems to attract an unnecessary degree of mystique. The rise of consumerism has so vastly increased the number of transactions in society that they come to reflect arithmetic regularities, something further enhanced by the speed with which information is transmitted. These regularities are often, misleadingly, called economic 'laws'. In the street-market selling home-made jams, bankrupt stock and second-hand books, however, the abstract constructions of modern economics begin to dissolve. Although a rare second-hand book sold at auction can illustrate, through competitive bidding, a fixing of price by demand greatly exceeding supply, seemingly unimportant books are priced at what the seller thinks intuitively is a general value, but which in individual cases the buyer may regard as an amazing bargain, although other buyers might not agree.

The very personal concept of 'value' – do I think that something is worth a particular price? – provides an overall limitation on all marketing, the supply and demand relationship acting within it with an intensity that varies with circumstances. It is a relationship that basically reflects a general human preference for buying cheaply, coupled with thresholds of resistance against prices which seem to be high as measured against an intuitive appreciation of the 'value' of a thing. How values are formed is ultimately a psychological question outside the scope of economics altogether, which exists as a modern rigorous discipline only because, given sufficient examples of any phenomenon, statistical regularities are bound to occur.

When we consider ancient societies, since the level of trading and speed of communication must have been far less than in modern times, statistical regularities which appear to be 'laws' in economics, if they existed at all, are bound to have lain within wide margins of variation. A more irregular and unpredictable pattern of prices is what one should expect if prices were freely fixed. Such a pattern is not evidence against marketing and exchange of goods by people motivated towards coming out of a deal with a sense of having done well, given that, if they know each other already, friendship or obligation may have tempered the vigour with which they pursued their deal.

The price data from ancient Egypt are more or less neutral as a source of evidence on how they themselves were fixed. Thus in the case of the price of a pair of sandals: over nearly 150 years they remained within a range of 1 to 2 *deben*, occasionally 3.[42] It is likely that 'tradition' played a part here, people becoming accustomed over the years always to paying roughly the same amount. This does not, however, exclude an underlying rationale. We can also say that, lacking modern machinery for mass production, the price of a pair of sandals reflected a floor price of subsistence for the sandal-maker. Prices were held at this level by the resistance of the buyer, who, if faced with a high price, could hobble far enough away on his worn-out sandals to buy from another sandal-maker at the usual price. 'Tradition' might itself represent an equilibrium of supply and demand.

A particularly interesting set of prices is that for grain (wheat and barley), a commodity generally prone to volatile price movements and thus the object of huge intervention schemes in modern 'free-market' economies. Intervention in the form of massive storage capacity creating buffer-stocks was standard in ancient Egypt, too, both at the institutional level and within the economies of private estates whether in times of peace and plenty (e.g. the El-Amarna estates, pp. 327–9) or in times of famine and unrest (e.g. Ankhtify, p. 309). This was a passive intervention that did not extend to official attempts to regulate prices.

The New Kingdom price data show many prices of between 1 and 2 *deben* per *khar*, which presumably reflected a fair return for all those involved in farming, although the margin of difference was no small one where large consignments of grain were involved. But the buyer's resistance threshold could be much lower, driven there by the prospect of hunger. In the economy of western Thebes in the late 20th Dynasty prices show great volatility, ranging from some near-normal to far higher levels, reaching, during the reigns of Rameses VII–IX, 8 and even 12 *deben*. This was not a case of general 'inflation' of the kind so familiar from the modern world, since other prices fail to display a similar trajectory, and there is no evidence for alterations in the units of measurement themselves. One clue is the famine reference quoted above: the woman who claimed to have sold barley for silver 'in the year of the hyena, when there was a famine'. Unfortunately the source fails to say what quantities were involved, but the way that she phrases her reply implies that a barley/silver exchange made during that famine was a distinctive transaction, and a high price is the natural interpretation. Actual prices from around this time (the first part of the reign of Rameses XI) show a common doubling of the traditional maximum price, thus 1 *khar* equal to 4 *deben*. We can also look to the repeated complaints of food shortages by the Deir el-Medina community from the reign of Rameses III onwards to explain the fluctuations of the grain prices in later Ramesside times, though a cause-and-effect connection has to remain circumstantial.[43]

The evidence we have been considering points inescapably to people being autonomous economic individuals; constrained within a system, of course, but none the less alert for opportunities. Another such person, living much earlier, towards the beginning of the 12th Dynasty, was Hekanakht, a farmer apparently from near Memphis or the Fayum.[44] On trips away from home he wrote testy letters back to his family. These display a strong urge to maximize family income by means of shrewd deals with neighbours and others, with no reference at all to an outside system or authority.

> He was able to pay rent for his lands in advance, could, in addition, lend substantial amounts of grain and had at his disposal copper, oil, and cloth woven from the flax raised on his farm, all of which could be used to make purchases. He cultivated more than was needed for the immediate requirements of his household, and had substantial capital reserves.[45]

He also possessed a herd of thirty-five cattle. Towards members of his household he displayed an obligation of a strict kind, issuing everyone including his mother with a monthly ration, and so repeating on a tiny scale the precise system of ration distribution so familiar from administrative texts. But to the outside world the relationship was one of calculated gain. He displays the mentality of one who survives by shrewd personal dealing rather than of one whose fortunes depend upon his position within a system of social obligation and of administered support. He urges one of his household, for example, to retain one bull in a herd about to be sent out because a chance of a particularly good sale had arisen: 'his price has increased by half'.[46]

Egyptians like Hekanakht lived economics rather than thought it. Having no word that we can translate as 'profit' they could not strive for it as an abstract measure of success in trading or making things. But this did not hinder them from distinguishing a good from a bad price, and should not hinder us from crediting them with an adequate business sense.

The Deir el-Medina records of transaction are devoid of locale, as are, in general, the confessions of the Theban thieves. Some transactions must have arisen because buyer and seller, in the same village, knew each other. This might apply when manufacturing was involved. If you wanted to obtain a new footstool you presumably knew where a carpenter lived, and the transaction took place at a house, either his or yours depending on your relative status. But would informal and personal contacts suffice entirely to match demand with supply? Were there markets in which sellers spread their wares in recognized market-places? One of the accused women in the robbery papyri sets a telling scene: 'Now I happened to be sitting hungry [begging?] under the sycamore-fig trees, and the men happened to be trading copper as we were sitting hungry' (Papyrus B.M.10403, 3.5–7). Where the sycamore-fig trees were in terms of the topography of western Thebes we do not know. But some markets at Thebes were on the river bank.[47] This we know from tomb paintings. There are no texts to explain these pictures, no hieroglyphic comments filling spaces around the figures. Our understanding of them depends on correctly interpreting the mime that the artist has used to convey the meaning. One of them comes from the tomb of a Deir el-Medina sculptor named Ipy, who looked forward in the next world to the life of the scribal ideal (Figure 114, *below*).[48] The centre of the scene is a river boat bringing the annual grain harvest to the private granary, as well as bundles of papyrus and what are probably bundles of fodder. As the unloading takes place some of the sacks of grain, as well as the green-stuff, are sold. The buyers are simultaneously sellers: women who sit with a single basket of produce in front of them. In return for grain they sell fish, loaves and vegetables. Behind a seller of bread a shelter has been erected shading two jars of drink. The logic of the picture is that this also is a saleable commodity.[49] The scene complements well the testimony of some of the robbery papyri: the role taken by many women in buying and selling for the household, including cash crops.[50]

The second scene, although similar in design, depicts transactions at a significantly different level. It comes from the tomb of Kenamun, an 18th Dynasty mayor of Thebes who was also in charge of the granaries of Karnak temple (Figure 114, *top*).[51] The subject is the arrival at Thebes of a fleet of sea-going ships from Syria and the Aegean. They unload their cargo and, in a further portion of the scene, present their goods to Kenamun himself. Herein lies the first ambiguity. Is Kenamun, who as mayor would have been a leading and wealthy citizen, receiving the goods for himself, acting out the line in the school text where the scribe's ship 'has returned from Syria laden with all manner of good things'? Or is he receiving goods destined for, say, the temple treasuries? As with Ipy's painting, *en route* to their destination some of the goods are sold, presumably on the river bank. The buyers are, inevitably, sellers also, but no longer housewives with a single basket of foodstuff. Two of the three traders are men, and all three sit beneath shelters, offering a range of goods: sandals, lengths of cloth (some with fringes), bread and other food, and what may be metal fish-hooks. One transaction is shown: a Syrian proffers a stoppered jar of wine. The male traders hold little scale balances in their hands. These are occasionally found in excavation (two came from one small house in the North Suburb at El-Amarna),[52] and are sometimes depicted in use in more detail. One (perhaps their main) purpose was to weigh metal against stone weights of known values on the *deben* scale. The implication of their appearance in this scene is that metals were part of the transaction, with the foreigners perhaps carrying their own sets of weights as a safeguard against being cheated. The Egyptian traders look much more professional than the housewives in the tomb of Ipy. But who were

Figure 114 Scenes of barter-exchange in New Kingdom tombs. *Above.* Traders in booths make deals with Syrians unloading their wares at the river bank, from the tomb of Kenamun at Thebes, after N. de G. Davies and R.O. Faulkner, *JEA* 33 (1947), Pl. VIII. *Below.* Workers unloading a grain barge use sacks of grain to buy fish and vegetables from village women, from the tomb of Ipy, after N. de G. Davies, *Two Ramesside tombs at Thebes*, New York, 1927, Pl. XXX.

they really? This is a crucial area of ambiguity. Were they 'traders' as the Egyptians used the word, that is, commercial agents for officials? Or were they trading for themselves? If we knew the answer we would have an important piece of knowledge for the Egyptian economy of the period. For in the latter case they would have been, in effect, shopkeepers, living from buying and selling and thus from the profit between transactions. But even without this knowledge we must admit that these scenes do not illustrate *ad hoc* exchanges between neighbours in a village. They display the kind of purposeful behaviour on the part of the sellers which belongs to proper markets in which buyers are not necessarily from the same community at all, and thus not necessarily much influenced by social obligation: the very kind of mechanism that is required for an economic model which allows greater scope to private enterprise.

These New Kingdom scenes have a long history behind them, with important predecessors in several Old Kingdom tombs, which have received much discussion.[53] Like their later counterparts, however, they are to be explained as much from how we perceive the general economic framework as from any specific details within the scenes themselves, which remain, on their own, ambiguous. There is one social change to notice: in the Old Kingdom scenes the sellers are normally men. There is also one unusually explicit accompanying text: in a sale of cloth the statement is made: 'xx cubits of cloth in exchange for 6 *shat*'. Although the exact nature of the *shat* at this time is not known, it must be a unit of absolute value similar to the New Kingdom units of copper, grain, oil and so on.[54]

Deir el-Medina, the source for so much of our evidence about economic life in ancient Egypt, was an atypical community, in two respects. Though a small village it was in contact with senior officials and wealthy clients and thus with affluent living, which rubbed off on the villagers' own expectations; and its basic needs were supplied as rations by the state. This latter circumstance, however, only adds interest to the evidence for private enterprise on the part of the villagers: exchanging goods with each other and with outsiders, manufacturing beds, selling their specific skills as artists in the making of statues and coffins, hiring or lending donkeys for exorbitant interest or rental, and generally directing part of their lives towards accumulating wealth, part of which ended up in their well-appointed burials.[55] The villagers show in their lives that the state, even when in the position of supplier of needs, could do so only in a rough-and-ready way, through regular grain rations and a few other perks, leaving the detail of individual demand to local and private transactions, in other words to a market.

Economics in a city

Although hugely informative through its unique body of texts, Deir el-Medina was only a village, albeit one of special character. For a balanced view across the full range of society we need to look at the economics of a major city, and in particular the role of the administrative class, that tier of families which effectively ran the country and were, after the royal family, the main consumers. The best place to study this is Akhenaten's short-lived city of Akhetaten (the modern Tell El-Amarna). We have to approach it, however, somewhat differently from Deir el-Medina. There is no large set of texts to guide us. We have to make the archaeology serve instead, and also use inferences drawn from other Egyptian sources. We looked briefly in Chapter 6 at the royal buildings, which provide the stage on which the daily life of king and court was played out. It is now time to turn to the places where the rest of the people lived.

Most of them lived in two large housing areas north and south of the Central City.[56] The Middle Kingdom had seen the growth of a tradition in Egypt of simple grid planning, applied to the streets and houses of settlements up to the scale of full-size towns. But in the New Kingdom the idea of total planning lost its attraction. We have already seen this, in effect, at Thebes, in the contrast between the rigid symmetrical planning of individual temples, and their casual interrelationships that were disguised by linking processional routes. In El-Amarna, outside the corridor of royal buildings, planning petered out altogether. Instead of a grand unitary design we find a few broad but far from straight streets running more or less parallel to the Nile to join the suburbs to the centre, while narrower streets cross at right angles. The overwhelming impression is of a series of joined villages. The individual house plots interlock in complex patterns, creating distinctive neighbourhoods (Figures 109, p. 312; and 115). Sometimes groups of larger or smaller houses occur together, but they are often intimately mixed. Within them rich and poor lived side by side. There was little concept of prime location, other than frontage to one of the main north–south thoroughfares. Exceptionally in the North City a group of unusually large houses lay adjacent to the main palace (the North Riverside Palace), and from this we can guess that they housed people with a particularly close relationship to the king. But otherwise proximity to the Central City or to the Royal Road seems to have held little if any attraction. Thus one of the king's most senior officials, the vizier Nakht, lived almost as far away from the king as he could. The house of the high priest Panehsy (one of the favoured few with a large tomb in the northern group of rock tombs as well as an official residence beside the Great Aten Temple) lay in the Main City well back from the Royal Road; another priest Pawah lived in a large house in the middle of the Main City. Business in the Central City and with the king meant commuting, by chariot. This is also faithfully recorded in the tomb scenes.

The ideal house stood within its own grounds, surrounded by a wall which could reach at least 3 metres in height, its main entrance marked by a pair of low projecting walls which guided chariots in at right angles, and so prevented the projecting ends of the axles from catching the door posts.[57] The loose arrangement of elements in the compounds stands in marked contrast to their carefully prearranged place in the formal Middle Kingdom layouts discussed in Chapter 5 and exemplified at Kahun. Many details of usage are still not clear but the general outline is tolerably so. The list of basic elements is:

- granaries: up to a certain individual capacity they were tall circular constructions of brick, in diameter about 2.5 metres on average, and with domed tops. The principal grains were wheat and barley, and they were poured in at the top and withdrawn through a trap-door at the bottom. Over a certain size, however, they were replaced by long vaulted rooms of the kind that form the basis of 'magazines'. Then, since other commodities were stored in them as well, it becomes much more hazardous to estimate stored grain capacity;
- animal byres: generally identified as sheds with roof supported on several square brick pillars; sometimes stone tethering-posts and built mangers occur;
- a well;
- a garden presumably for both vegetables and flowers, planted with trees;

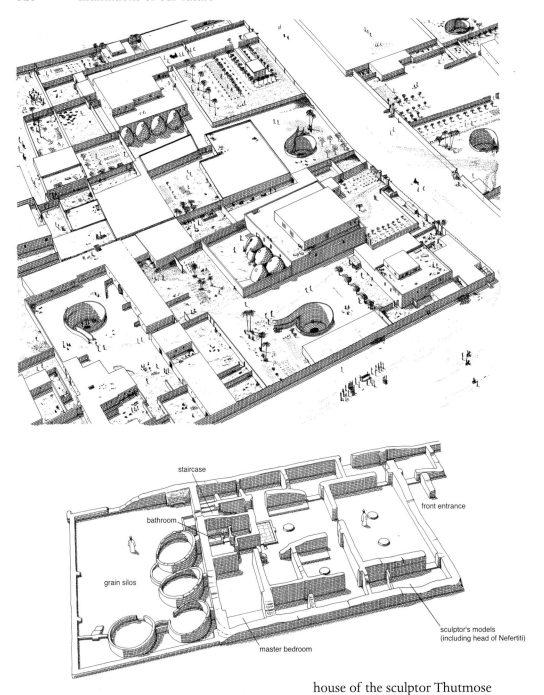

house of the sculptor Thutmose

Figure 115   Perspective reconstruction of part of the area of Figure 109, p. 312. The house of Thutmose is shown in the condition in which it was found when excavated in 1914.

- kitchens: they often lay at the southern end, downwind of the prevailing north wind, which reduced nuisance from smoke (except to neighbours). They were simple affairs: small groups of circular clay ovens used primarily for baking bread. When cooked meals were prepared an open fireplace was used, again outside the house, with cooking probably done in bronze or copper basins;
- sheds and enclosures of uncertain purpose, though in some cases they could have been used for craft activities. Sculptors, whose debris archaeologists can easily identify, are one group whose workshops were in and beside their house compounds;
- a shrine, which only the houses of the richest possessed (and not all of them). It stood in its own formal grounds with ornamental lake and separate pylon entrance to the street;[58]
- separate accommodation, including a porter's lodge at the gate, but most importantly a completely separate house. It remains a mystery who occupied this house: a steward, a married son, servants?

The larger houses look like little farms, and in so doing both reflect the commodity-based nature of the Egyptian economy, and at the same time make an important contribution to the debate about private economics in New Kingdom Egypt. We can estimate that the capacity of an average grain silo not filled in its entirety was about 9,500 litres, equivalent in ancient terms to about 125 *khar* of emmer-wheat. At the Theban necropolis workmen's village of Deir el-Medina a skilled artisan's annual wage for his family included a maximum of 48 *khar* of emmer, whilst the foreman received 66. For guards and porters the annual rate was 24 and 12. The payments in barley seem to have been about a third of that. Thus two or three of these silos, a not uncommon number in the El-Amarna house compounds, would appear just to suffice for a family with a purchasing power somewhat larger than a Deir el-Medina foreman. However, the Deir el-Medina householders did not have large silos to store their grain in. They were paid monthly and evidently consumed most of it, either as food or as a medium of exchange. They did not accumulate grain balances. To be able to do that was a significant mark of status. The groups of silos at El-Amarna thus indicate two possibilities (as alternatives or present together): either storage of an annual harvest, or a monthly receipt of ration payments far in excess of basic rations.

To form a better judgement of what lies behind the silos we must turn to outside data, and consider certain aspects of the agrarian economy and landscape of the New Kingdom, beginning with the extent and nature of private land-holding. Hereditary possession of land was possible. A text known as the Inscription of Mes introduces us to a parcel of land granted by King Ahmose at the beginning of the 18th Dynasty to an 'officer of ships' as a reward for military service (Chapter 6, note 83). About three centuries later, in the reign of Rameses II, we find the same land still in the hands of the same family, descendants of the original hero, now squabbling over its division into lots, and appealing to a duplicate set of government land records, kept by the treasury and by the department of the granary, wherein was recorded the history of ownership. A papyrus of the time of Rameses IX (Papyrus Valençay I) is even more explicit in drawing a distinction between *khato*-lands of Pharaoh and privately owned land whose taxes were paid independently to the treasury.[59] We must add to this the evidence for the widespread leasing of temple lands, with hints that this might have been a hereditary practice. Put the evidence together, and we have the outline for the private sector of a complex pattern of land-holding in which a 'farm' was not a single discrete parcel of agricultural land, but a whole series of scattered plots held in more than one way: either owned outright, or rented from a temple or from some other landowner.

And the 'farmers'? They were none other than people with official titles who, for a position of respect and comfortable living, needed the income of a small estate. The school exercise texts make this very clear. In addition to the model letters they contain pieces that dwell on the benefits accruing to the successful literate man. They cast his lot not as a constant round of important duties in official surroundings but as a life of bucolic ease in one's villa, surrounded by the produce of a well-stocked and well-managed farm.

> You go down to your ship of fir-wood manned from bow to stern. You reach your beautiful villa, the one you have built for yourself. Your mouth is full of wine and beer, of bread, meat and cakes. Oxen are slaughtered and wine is opened, and melodious singing is before you. Your chief anointer anoints [you] with ointment of gum. Your manager of cultivated lands bears garlands. Your chief fowler brings ducks, your fisherman brings fish. Your ship has returned from Syria laden with all manner of good things. Your byre is full of calves, your weavers flourish. You are established whilst [your] enemy is fallen, and the one who spoke against you is no more.[60]

The emphasis on the self-made aspect of the official is notable. No hint here of the good life being handed down from the king in return for loyal service. This is also, of course, the ideal portrayed in many tomb pictures of the New Kingdom and earlier periods. Officials of whatever kind looked forward to an eternal life that featured prominently the pleasures of watching with serenity happy peasants working the fields of the estate.[61]

A more exact picture of who was taking responsibility for farming the land comes from the Wilbour Papyrus, a register of measurement and revenue assessment for certain categories of agricultural land in a stretch of some 150 kilometres in Middle Egypt in year 4 of Rameses V (1143 BC), thus towards the very end of the New Kingdom (Chapter 6, note 10). It is possible to extract from the figures a profile of the categories of persons who were renting fields from the temples (Figure 93, p. 255). This has some surprising features, the high proportion of women being one. The numbers of soldiers (including Sherden mercenaries, Figure 8, p. 32) might be a local peculiarity, though it well reflects the practice of settling army veterans on the land.

The silos and stockyards in the little farm centres at El-Amarna are therefore likely to have stored the produce of the lands owned or managed by officials of various callings, including priests and military officers. Their interest in producing did not end with farm produce. Within and around many of the houses at El-Amarna we also find much evidence for manufacture. A number of sculptors' workshops have been discovered, one of them belonging to the sculptor Thutmose who had owned the famous bust of Queen Nefertiti. Other workshops in the residential areas (one seemingly at Thutmose's house) made pottery and the little glazed (faience) rings and other ornaments widely worn at this time, whilst the spinning and weaving of textile lengths seems to have been almost standard.[62] Written evidence for the New Kingdom suggests that householders had contractual relationships with institutions (primarily temples) to make cloth, part of which they would surrender, just as if it were a portion of the harvest, and another part of which they would keep either

Plate 10   A poor-man's industry: a pig-pen at the workmen's village, El-Amarna. It is one from Building 300, looking north. The scale is 1 m long. By courtesy The Egypt Exploration Society.

for home use or as a medium of exchange when purchasing other things.[63] An interesting extension of private initiative to people below the level of the more senior officials has been the discovery of a pig farm at an isolated outlier at El-Amarna, the so-called Workmen's Village.[64] The animals had been born and raised in sets of specially constructed pens (Plate 10). They had been fed on grain, and most of the litters had been slaughtered in their first or second year. The butchering, salting and packing of meat in pottery jars had been done in special areas coated hygienically with white gypsum. The whole complex represents a well-organized operation that so far has no parallel in the main city, nor, for that matter, at Deir el-Medina. It implies that it was more than a sideline run by some of the villagers for the food requirements of their own community; rather that it also served to supplement income by sales into the main city.

The brief life of El-Amarna illustrates that its location was not one naturally to attract a population. It did not lie where different communities might meet to exchange goods and news. It was created to serve the dream of a king who claimed to have been guided to the location by his god. Once the court and its supporting population had taken up residence, however, El-Amarna necessarily became a major inland port, receiving a share of the produce of Egypt, tribute from the empire and trade goods from an even wider area. Pictures in the rock tombs and the denuded outlines of buildings close to where the archaeological site meets the modern fields point to the existence of a large area dedicated to storage, of goods and livestock, originally situated between the waterfront and the main private residential area of the city.[65] It is likely to have been the main channel into the city for necessities and luxuries, where they remained for a time waiting to be distributed.

The lives of officials, the group most exposed to competitive pressures, are the crucial area of contact between state system and private need. Although in receipt of rations and other rewards from the state, the households of these people were often organized, so it would seem, to bring in an income well in excess of subsistence. What did they do with the excess, men and women who were too busy or proud to haggle over the price of a donkey with a ragged neighbour, but who nevertheless had wealth stored in plenty in and around their houses? The answer is provided by a class of persons already encountered, tied up in dealings with the robbers of western Thebes. They are the men with the title *shuty*, a word best translated as 'trader'.[66] They appear always in the employ of someone else, either a temple or an official, and must have been commercial agents, to whom was delegated the job of buying what was needed in exchange for accumulated wealth. The employer overlap between temple and private household is itself revealing as to the essentially common nature of the economic basis of both. Both accumulated farm produce and manufactured goods (with linen cloth prominent in the case of households) from regular income but were not wholly self-sufficient and needed to purchase from suppliers of one kind or another. In the robbery papyrus referred to earlier (Papyrus B.M.10068, recto 4.1–18) gold and silver had been recovered from fourteen 'traders of every establishment'. No fewer than seven of them (two of them brothers) belonged to the household of a high-ranking soldier, a chief of Hittite troops called Amennefer; two belonged to the daughter of another officer, a lady called Isis who was also a temple singer; two more belonged each to military officers; and the remaining three belonged to temples, and were responsible to a named priest. Elsewhere in this group of papyri a group of eight traders appears from the town of Mer-wer, at the entrance to the Fayum. This was where one of the principal harem-palaces for royal ladies was situated (at the archaeological site of Medinet el-Ghurab), and this could have provided a suitably safe outlet for stolen treasure.

The status of traders varied. They could be rich enough to own their own slave, or poor enough to be at the same time a slave to their employer. Their contacts enabled them to do business for themselves on the side: not only receiving stolen goods but also, in a satirical school text, lending grain to the poor peasant who is unable to discharge his debt even by offering his wife to them.[67] The picture that is painted by a variety of texts is that the 'trader' – the commercial agent, the arranger of deals – was a ubiquitous figure of New Kingdom Egypt. To find the right markets they plied the Nile in boats: 'The traders fare downstream and upstream, as busy as bees [lit. copper] carrying goods from town to town, and supplying wants' (Papyrus Lansing, 4.8–4.9). Their journeys took them abroad, even to Syria, if we follow the logic of the description of the ideal life of the official quoted earlier (p. 330).[68] This long-distance aspect to trading emphasizes the point made in connection with the tomb scenes of marketing: there can have been little if any sense of social obligation between trader and customer.

Internal mobility provides, in fact, a weighty argument against the view that personal economic transactions were so often cosy reciprocal exchanges between relations and neighbours as to form the only serious alternative to redistribution. Two aspects are particularly telling. One was the provincial origin (and continuing links) of some officials who based themselves in a royal city. When the mayor Menthuhetep moved into his new house at Thebes (see p. 310), built on land purchased from a stranger, those with whom he came to do business would not have belonged to his own social nexus, and there would have been no grounds for the idea of 'reciprocation' to skew prices demanded and prices paid. The other was the well-documented long-distance internal trading initiated by large institutions and conducted through their 'traders', as just outlined. The implication of a range of sources is that internal riverine movement of goods was a major factor in the life and economy of Egypt, probably at times overshadowing the local movement of produce at village level. The fact of 'internal cosmopolitanism' invalidates too great a reliance on case studies of modern peasant communities to provide the social and economic models for ancient Egypt. To do so is to accept too parochial a horizon and to ignore the power of the river Nile, not only to sustain life, but also to provide a channel of communication.

The status of the trader was a lowly one. No one who had made a success of his life used the word as a title. For this reason we should not translate it as 'merchant'. It is here that the ancient and modern worlds divide on economics. Trading was akin in status to making sandals. Rich people enjoyed the benefits of trading but did not pursue it as an occupation, whilst the idea that the activity could bring wealth and position on its own terms was literally unthinkable to all concerned. There were no merchant princes just as there were no princes of sandal-makers. Officials – 'scribes' – maintained the monopoly of power, prestige and wealth. It was not a conspiracy. The attitudes were held, so one imagines, unthinkingly.

The economic system of ancient Egypt is tolerably clear, if we allow logic to create the framework in which textual and archaeological evidence can be set. The beginning of understanding is an acceptance that ancient Egypt was, by the standards of the ancient world, a rich country. In stable times it had wealth in plenty stored and in circulation, offering to all the prospect or the dream of a life far above subsistence level. This created the phenomenon of private demand: powerful and widely spread from the late Predynastic Period onwards. When the state was strong and well organized many people gained much from its redistributive mechanisms, which must, in these same times, have acted as a general control over the whole economy simply on account of their magnitude. But for those demands which could not be met by state hand-outs (and this would amount to virtually everything in times of weak government) marketing provided the answer: both local face-to-face dealings sometimes skewed by social obligation, and wider ranging exchanges involving employed intermediaries – 'traders'. Social values obscured the reality of the process, leaving a blind-spot over the concept of profit. But any ancient Egyptian who could argue over a price was a representative of 'economic man'.

This provides us with a far more challenging role for economic history within ancient Egypt. The descriptive approach to the Egyptian economy defines two spheres – peasant exchanges and state redistribution – and leaves neither with a dynamic that fits it for a role in history. But, as we have seen, this approach fails to account both for the manifest integration of materially ambitious officials within the system, and the equally evident capacity for adjustment which the system as a whole possessed. These we can accommodate by accepting the existence of a relatively dynamic private sector. We can therefore say that one of the principal themes of political history – the ebb and flow of centralized power vis-à-vis provincial assertion – must have had its economic counterpart, in the expansion and contraction of the private sector, partially manifested in local and regional marketing. Here we have a truly dynamic theme couched in economic terms, and thus the basis for real economic history.

The attempt to identify ancient economies as a special type of economic system containing special modes of transaction and interrelationships may be a useful means of grouping sources and focusing attention, but it also leads to arguments about nothing. Within the single framework of macroeconomics, which embraces all states that have ever existed, the goal of research is to identify the ways in which the two forces – institutional and private – satisfied their interests, in terms of both the means employed and the disguises in which they were clad. It is likewise misleading to view ancient economies as a stage in an evolutionary process. For there is sufficient variety of economic system in the modern world to make the choice of evolutionary line an arbitrary one. Rather they should be seen as further variations of a single theme, different solutions to a common problem: how do large communities, inevitably made up of competing interests, remain in existence for long?

There is an interesting twist to this question, which can help us to understand the resilience of ancient Egypt, its capacity to rebuild itself into a successful prosperous country after the reverses of civil war or invasion. Money in the modern world is not tied to specific commodities but is based in part upon faith. It mostly circulates endlessly, and the amounts increase as the years pass, although to some extent this is countered by depreciation in value. In the course of circulation it tends to gravitate towards the more successful economies (which pay higher interest), exacerbating the gap between the richer and the poorer. Part of ancient Egypt's wealth took the form of metals (gold, silver and bronze), just as is the case with modern states, whose gold reserves are one measure of economic health. Another and important part took the form of perishable commodities (primarily grain). Where the Egyptian economy was so different from ours was in the use (though not exclusively) of grain and other items as a major part of personal and institutional wealth and as a means of exchange. Perishable commodities have a short life. They cannot be banked for long and become savings. They cannot earn interest or be directed elsewhere as investments, but must be put into circulation after which they will vanish. They have storage costs, and the effort required to transport them for any distance encourages local consumption. People in ancient Egypt were indeed 'consumers' in a very literal way. If one adds to this the huge social prestige of having land to work and overflowing granaries, it was hard to be a miser. The rich individual and the rich institution were obliged by necessity and by social convention to spend locally, and in so doing to support the local community.

The system was not, in truth, designed to do this out of altruism. It was a happy consequence because no serious alternative had yet been developed. It could have been a key factor in the success of the ancient Egyptian way of life, one of the marked characteristics of which was how the provincial regions continued to thrive. They were not impoverished at the expense of an over-large capital city. Local institutions – the nomarchs and their estates and then the large temples – were centres of commodity production, storage and consumption. The difficulties of getting a significant portion of this to flow out of the region are likely to have encouraged local prosperity.

In the face of modern capitalism's tendency to create huge inequalities and to suffer chronic instabilities a radical view has been advanced which advocates a return to a some-what artificial version of the ancient economic style which is intended to bring greater stability to the international currency system and to give better support to local communities.[69] It draws upon a history of modern local experiments, often done in times of crisis, in creating local currencies tied to local goods and services which are designed to be spent rapidly and locally because they depreciate in value steadily, by having negative interest applied to them. Misers become losers. The proposal envisages the creation of a global reference currency tied to a standard basket of commodities and services selected because they are particularly important for international trade. As an example, one unit might equal one tenth of a barrel of oil, one bushel of wheat, two pounds of copper or one hundredth of an ounce of gold. The costs of storage would be borne directly by the currency as a sustainability or negative-interest fee, to discourage hoarding. The ancient Egyptian economy is actually a classic example of such a system at work, and so provides historical depth for the idea. By variations on it much of the world survived and developed for thousands of years.

8
Moving on

So far I have tried to develop a picture of ancient Egypt that most people will find familiar, a society running like the ideal model of a large corporation. At the top, in a normally unassailable position, ruled the king. Below him extended a chain of management in the form of paid officials, and finally there were the managed, the ordinary people, who were mostly agriculturalists, 'peasants', and who, from time to time, laboured on royal projects. But it is now time to consider a motif, sometimes only indistinctly visible, which is woven into the history of any complex non-democratic society that seems to have solved the problems of identity and legitimacy. With a hereditary ruler at the top, what do others do who are not in the line of succession yet are driven by ambition? People who, had they lived during a period of state formation, might have become kings themselves?

Even in traditional societies such people do not necessarily acquiesce. One path to follow is that of treason, seeking to replace the king either by a palace coup or by raising a revolt and risking civil war. The other is to follow a deflected path of compromised ambition, though the risk remains of wanting too much and thereby of provoking retribution. An extreme example of what is possible is provided by mediaeval Japan. Its divine emperor received elaborate shows of respect but wielded only limited power. This was primarily dispensed by a warrior class headed by a hereditary warlord, the *shogun*. In mediaeval Europe deflection was less overtly turned into an institution, but kings, who claimed some degree of divine sanction for their power, none the less engaged in endless political manoeuvrings with their troublesome lords. Something along these lines is a theme in ancient Egyptian history running parallel to the more familiar one of the deeds of kings, but our understanding of it is still at an early stage.

The never-ending game

Let us go back for a moment to the process of state formation, the subject of Chapter 2. It appears to be a historical tale that has an end and is satisfying for that. In the metaphor of competitive gaming one player won all, and, at the beginning of the dynastic sequence, initiated a line of kings who were invested with the trappings of divine authority and who, in theory at least, were alone able to maintain down the centuries a legitimacy to rule that was beyond challenge. We have, in the last two chapters, been looking at their heirs – the kings of the New Kingdom – of more than fifteen centuries later. But, as also pointed out in Chapter 2, in real life the game never actually ends. It goes on as a largely subterranean stream of history, coming fully into the light only when the state retracts its powers.

In the case of Egypt, provincial concentrations of wealth and power proved collectively to be a pronounced and persistent aspect of society. As explained in the previous chapter, the commodity-based economic system fostered this. Perhaps part of the success of ancient Egypt in maintaining itself for so long lay in a productive tension between, on the one hand, the claims of universal power on behalf of the king, couched in a style which was synonymous with all that was civilized and, on the other, the pragmatic limits to that power which were set by deeply rooted traditions of wealth and authority maintained by provincial families. Such families, like the royal houses themselves, rose and fell. Manifestations of their existence have survived unevenly distributed across the landscape of the Nile valley and across time. It is, as always, a difficult judgement to make as to what extent the survival of any particular collection of evidence is accidental and to what extent it reflects real variations in local fortunes, how they advanced and faded at different times. My impression is that, when Egyptian history is looked at in blocks of time (groups of reigns), only the 4th Dynasty in the Old Kingdom and the 18th and perhaps 19th Dynasties in the New Kingdom achieved a system in which ambitions were, by and large, integrated. At other times either kings were obliged to compromise or the unitary system of rule broke down and Egyptian society switched to an alternative mode of lesser territories and of local rule that could extend to claims to kingship.

These latter times are primarily the 'Intermediate Periods'. In some ways the term 'intermediate' is justified (it is certainly convenient), but it does make it harder to see that the periods in question were also normal, but normal in a different way. In the first millennium BC (much of it the 'Late Period') the distinction between 'Intermediate Period' and its converse (for which there is no proper term) to a great extent dissolves. The Late Period, like the Intermediate Periods, forces the topic of social and political complexity on to our agenda and is to be welcomed for that. It leads on to the question: what is the history of ancient Egypt really about? Should its subject matter primarily be kings and the rise and fall of dynasties? Certainly the relaunching of the Egyptian state at the beginning of the 18th Dynasty reveals the great scope that kings had to be catalysts for change and growth through fostering a stable system. Or should the history of ancient Egypt concentrate more on the fortunes of provincial regions and their leading families? Therein lay much of the continuity and stability that made ancient Egypt what it was. From this perspective most of the kings were playbeings accorded vast politeness but successful only in so far as they filled their ceremonial role and maintained a balance amongst the ambitious.

Snapshots of local power

I have chosen to illustrate this side to ancient Egypt, prior to the Late Period itself, through a series of five vignettes. Each represents a relatively short interval of time, more or less that of someone in the prime of life. I have arranged them chronologically. To begin with they involve a return to the earlier periods, but they also take us beyond the end of the

New Kingdom and serve to introduce the Late Period itself. They should be seen as fragments of a narrative of power dispersal much of which remains to be written.

1 The tomb of the ruler of Dara: the First Intermediate Period at a glance[1]

The map in the lower right of Figure 116 shows a section of the Nile valley in Middle Egypt. Several ancient towns are known to have lain in the area although not all have been located. During the Old and Middle Kingdoms it was common for power and wealth to be expressed through tomb display. Several cemeteries on the edge of the desert in this area exemplify this. Mostly they are rock-cut chapels with carved or painted wall scenes (as at Deir el-Bersha, see below, Figure 117). At Dara, however, local aristocrats and their followers constructed huge brick tombs for themselves. The largest tomb equals or surpasses in area many royal pyramids of the Old Kingdom. Although it has sloping sides it looked, when finished, probably like an artificial mound, with rounded corners, rather than a pyramid. In Figure 116, for comparison, a section of the royal cemetery at Sakkara is shown, drawn to the same scale. The tomb of King Shepseskaf of the 4th Dynasty was also not a pyramid but a plain rectangle of stone. The small pyramid tomb of King Ibi of the '8th' Dynasty (Figure 116, *top right*) illustrates the more limited resources which kings of the First Intermediate Period had at their disposal, although Ibi had access to quarrymen and masons in a way that the ruler of Dara evidently did not. In so far as monuments signify status, the ruler of Dara was a near-equal to the king at Memphis, yet even so he chose a tomb design which was not in imitation of a royal pyamid.

Who was the owner of the Dara tomb who sought to rival what kings could build? The finding nearby of a piece of stone vessel bearing the name of a King Khui might indicate that the owner actually claimed to be a king, perhaps in the years immediately following the end of the 6th Dynasty. But where was his residence: at a country estate near Dara itself, or in an existing town, either Asyut or Cusae? A chapter of local history is blank, apart from what little we can say about the tombs themselves.

2 Djehutyhetep's colossus[2]

The ruler of Dara seems to have flourished in his provincial home at a time when kingship was weak. But that was not a prerequisite for a grandiose style of living. In the same area of the Nile valley but during the first part of the Middle Kingdom many tombs were cut into the cliffs for local governors, who variously used the old title 'nomarch' or that of 'mayor' and were often chief priest of the city temple as well. One such was Khnumhetep III of Beni Hasan (pp. 317–19, Figure 112). Another was the nomarch, mayor and chief priest of Hermopolis, Djehutyhetep (Figure 117). A scene in his tomb at Deir el-Bersha (Figure 117, *below*) shows lines of men dragging from the quarries a statue of alabaster, which is stated to be thirteen cubits (6.8 metres) high and is identified as being of Djehutyhetep himself. It also shows the statue's destination: a building represented by its most impressive and characteristic part, its monumental stone doorframe, complete with its decoration. This bears pictures of Djehutyhetep (including, as an inset, a scene from one of the side faces) and his name and titles; also the name of the doorway (or of the building itself): 'Enduring of love is Djehutyhetep in the Hare nome.' The people of the nome, including the soldiery, rejoice 'when they see their master and their master's son in the

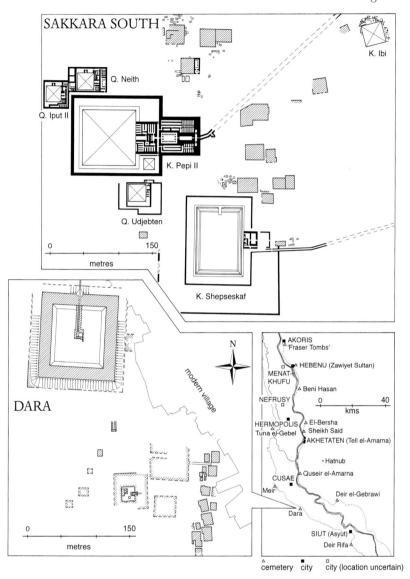

Figure 116 Size of tomb and relative power: plans of tombs at Sakkara South and Dara in Middle Egypt drawn to the same scale. The large tomb at Dara is close in time to the end of the Old Kingdom and thus to the reign of Pepi II. Dara after R. Weill, *Dara. Campagnes de 1946–1948*, Cairo, 1958, Pl. I; J. Vercoutter, *CdE* 27 (53), (1952), 98–111, Fig. 7. Sakkara South after G. Jéquier, *Tombeaux de particuliers contemporains de Pepi II*, Cairo, 1929, Frontis.; G. Jéquier, *La pyramide d'Aba*, Cairo, 1935, Pl. I.

TELL BASTA
(BUBASTIS)

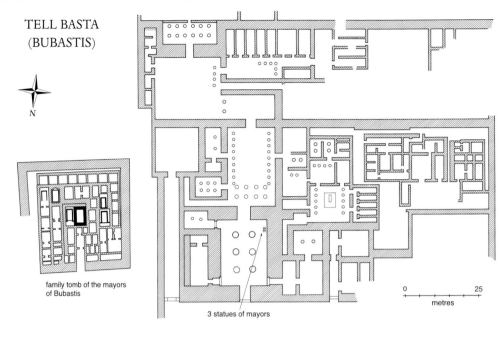

family tomb of the mayors
of Bubastis

3 statues of mayors

0   25
metres

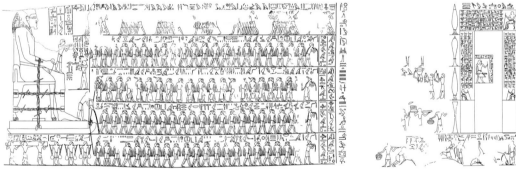

EL-BERSHA

Figure 117   The grand lifestyle of Middle Kingdom mayors and nomarchs. *Below.* Scene in the tomb of Djehutyhetep at Deir el-Bersha which shows the transportation of a colossal alabaster statue of Djehutyhetep from a quarry to the portal of his palace in the city of Hermopolis (*shown on the right*). Around the portal are scenes of rejoicing: the slaughter of cattle (*below*) and the carrying of food for a feast (*left*). After P.E. Newberry, *El Bersheh* I, London, 1895, Pls XII–XIX. *Above.* A mud-brick 'palace' at Tell Basta (Bubastis) in the Nile delta. After C.C. van Siclen, 'Remarks on the Middle Kingdom palace at Tell Basta', in M. Bietak, ed., *Haus und Palast im alten Ägypten*, Vienna, 1996, 239–46, and Fig. 1; C.C. van Siclen, 'The mayors of Basta in the Middle Kingdom', in S. Schoske, ed., *Akten des vierten Internationalen Ägyptologen-Kongresses: München 1985*, Band 4 (Studien zur Altägyptischen Kultur, Beihefte 4), Hamburg, 1991, 188, Abb. 1

favour of the king, making his monument'. Expressions of loyalty to the king have their place, but the real focus of interest is the nomarch and what he accomplishes.

3 Tell Basta: a grand mayoral residence[3]

What kind of place would have lain behind Djehutyhetep's handsome portal? Excavations at his home city of Hermopolis (modern El-Ashmunein) have reached only small and not very informative parts of levels as early as the time of Djehutyhetep so we have no direct evidence as to what his residence looked like. The mayoral house at Abydos South (Figure 81) covers much ground but does not look as though it was designed for display. We can find something of the grandeur we are looking for at the delta city of Tell Basta (Bubastis, Figure 117, *above*) and its Middle Kingdom 'palace'. Within a walled enclosure, measuring around 115 x 93 metres, lay another example of a single planned and intricately arranged complex of mud-brick rooms and courts, with frequent colonnades and columned roof supports. Three broad divisions can be recognized. The main (public?) entrance appears to have been on the north, through a deep columned portal into a court that also gave access to storerooms. Beyond, a single doorway led to a deep colonnaded court at the end of which, and with a slight shift of axis, lay the principal (audience?) hall, 15 x 20 metres in size. To judge from the size of column bases and the thickness of the walls it had reached a greater height than the rest. What were presumably the private residences of the owners filled a large extension on the west. The whole complex is roughly three times the size of one of the Kahun large residences. How it compared with a major royal palace of the same period we do not know since none has yet been identified.

Amongst the finds were pieces from a fine limestone doorframe that celebrated the jubilee (*sed-*)festival of King Amenemhat III. It must have been added late in the life of the building and might have been a mark of loyalty rather than a sign of who primarily laid claim to the building. Who did that is revealed close by. On the east side stood a large square brick mausoleum that contained many burial chambers arranged within a cellular plan. Originally it would seem that chapels for the cult of their owners had been laid out above, forming a second storey. At least six of the tombs had belonged to mayors of Tell Basta, some of them simultaneously chief priest, whose careers spanned much of the Middle Kingdom. Small statues of three of them stood in the palace's great hall. As a consequence the interpretation has been put forward that the palace was actually the residence of the mayors themselves, an identification that matches the pretensions of Djehutyhetep at Deir el-Bersha.

We have only fragments of the overall layout of Tell Basta at this time. We know where the main temple was (dedicated to the cat goddess Bastet) but know nothing of its appearance at this time. And as for the town itself in the Middle Kingdom, did it lie alongside and have the appearance of a Kahun or Tell el-Dab'a?

4 Tell el-Dab'a: the onset of the Second Intermediate Period[4]

Further to the north-east, 40 kilometres down the same ancient branch of the Nile, another 'palace' has been discovered of the late Middle Kingdom, at the site of Tell el-Dab'a (Figure 118). It is a key piece of evidence in a local history of further political evolution. It was built over the site of the earlier planned town previously described

TELL EL-DAB'A

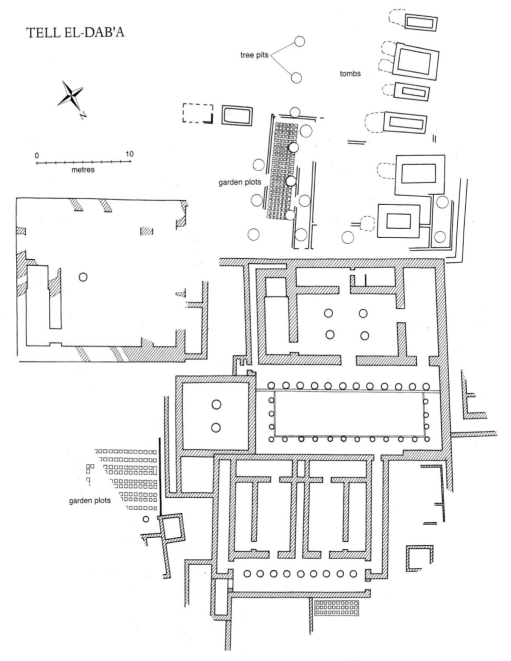

tree pits

tombs

garden plots

0   metres   10

garden plots

Figure 118 A 'palace' of the late Middle Kingdom at Tell el-Dab'a. For an independent ruler or for a grand governor? After M. Bietak, *Avaris: the capital of the Hyksos: recent excavations at Tell el-Dab'a*, London, 1996, 23, Fig. 18.

(p. 223 and Figure 82, p. 226) though with other building levels in between. In plan it is an assembly of several separately conceived units laid out on a common rectilinear basis, no one unit being particularly large. Around it lay areas of garden, recognizable from the gridded cubit-plots of soil so characteristic of ancient Egypt (compare Figure 2, p. 12). As at Tell Basta, several tombs, probably surmounted originally by chapels at ground level, lay alongside, though far more modest in scale. The life of the palace spanned no more than a generation, after which the ground was given over to smaller houses.

The identity of the owners of this complex is intriguing if uncertain, and is closely tied to reconstructions of the history of the delta at this time. These involve two particular factors. One is that there is sufficient archaeological evidence to conclude that at this time a significant part of the population of Tell el-Dab'a (as well as of the region to the east) was Palestinian (Figure 13, p. 43 is an illustration of one of their tombs). The second is that, at some point after the end of the 12th Dynasty, at least one separate mini-state developed in the eastern delta, eventually becoming the core of the Palestinian kingdom of the Hyksos. But when exactly? And how are the two factors related? By one interpretation (advanced by the excavator) it took place later than the period of the palace, which was occupied by officials who, although Palestinian in origin, were acting for the 13th Dynasty kings of Egypt, supervising trade with Palestine and Syria. By another interpretation the fragmentation of the delta began earlier, and the palace was for a time the centre of this new mini-kingdom, its rulers and hence its occupants a line of Palestinian kings (the 14th of Manetho's Dynasties) who were antecedent to the Hyksos proper.[5] Although both views are presented by their authors with much confidence, the underlying evidence lacks the precision that is needed to come to a clear decision. In truth the scale and design of the building – big and elaborate enough to be seen as a palace yet not actually huge – seems compatible with both interpretations. Granted that in neither case is the exposure total, the Tell el-Dab'a palace is actually much smaller than that of the Tell Basta mayors, and probably more comparable to the mayoral house at Abydos South.

In times of prosperity and high kingship the palace could be a world away from the houses even of the highest officials. This much is dramatically clear from the palaces of Akhenaten at El-Amarna. At other times, however, convergence set in and, in terms of architectural setting at least, the step up from high officialdom to royalty vanished. The distinction between who was and who was not a king might not always have been so great. This is neatly illustrated by the next and final vignette.

5 The Piankhy stela: the year of the five Pharaohs

Well past the end of the New Kingdom, around 730 BC, the Sudanese king Piankhy, already in control of Thebes and southern Egypt, embarked upon a campaign into the north of Egypt which brought him a measure of success. A triumphal stela records the campaign and the political situation that he found, providing a unique picture of political subdivision (Figure 119).[6] On the top panel Piankhy (his figure largely defaced, no. 6), shown as a full Pharaoh with a set of cartouches, stands in the middle facing to the right, the god Amun-Ra and goddess Mut behind him. In front of him four kings, their names written in cartouches, make their submission to him: Nemlut (no. 7, of Hermopolis), Osorkon (no. 8, of Bubastis), Iuput (no. 9, of Leontopolis) and Peftja-awybastet (no. 10, of Herakleopolis). Behind Piankhy five other rulers, who did not claim to be kings,

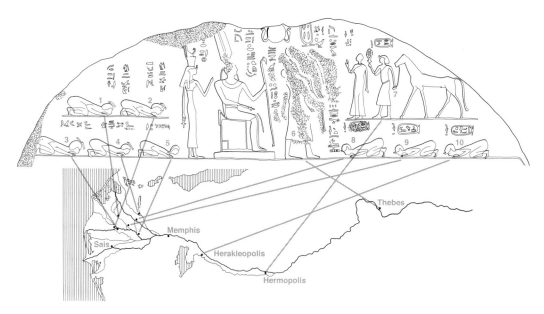

Figure 119   The victorious king Piankhy (or Piye) greets the rulers of Egypt. The top panel of his stela in the Egyptian Museum, Cairo. The figures are to be identified as follows: (1) Great chief of the Me(shwesh) (and mayor of Mendes) Djedamun-iufankh; (2) Great chief of the Me(shwesh) Akanosh of Sebennytos; (3) The mayor (of Busiris) Pamay; (4) The mayor (of Per-seped) (and chief of the Meshwesh) Patjenef; (5) Prince Petisis (of Athribis/Heliopolis); (6) Piankhy himself; (7) King Nemlut (of Hermopolis), leading his horse and preceded by his wife; (8) King Osorkon (IV, of the 22nd Dynasty, of Bubastis/Tanis); (9) King Iuput (II of the 23rd Dynasty, of Leontopolis); (10) King Peftja-awybastet (of Herakleopolis). After N.-C. Grimal, *La Stèle triomphale de Pi(ʿankh)y au Musée du Caire JE 48862 et 47086–47089*, Cairo, 1981, Pl. V.

also prostrate themselves. The first are two Libyan tribal leaders: the great chief of the Me(shwesh), Djedamun-iufankh (no. 1, of Mendes), and the great chief of the Me(shwesh), Akanosh (no. 2, of Sebennytos). There follow the mayor Pamay (no. 3, of Busiris), the mayor Patjenef (no. 4, of Per-Seped), and the prince Petisis (no. 5, of Athribis). The names of their cities are listed elsewhere in the text. Their territories contained other towns and cities as well. One figure missing from the scene is Piankhy's principal antagonist, Tefnakht, another Libyan leader, who controlled the western delta (from Sais) and who did not submit to him. Although he seems more powerful than the others Piankhy does not call him a king, but gives him the simple title 'Prince of the West'.

Some of these people are independently documented from statues and other inscribed pieces. King Nemlut of Hermopolis, however, is not and so is a worrying figure. Had Piankhy's campaign not been recorded in this way, or had the stela not survived, we would not know of Nemlut's existence. As it is we do not know if he alone of his family claimed kingship or if he was last in a family line, an otherwise 'lost dynasty'. No tombs or palace for this family have been discovered despite the survival of the main cemetery for Hermopolis on the nearest stretch of desert, at Tuna el-Gebel.

In circumstances like these what did it mean to be Pharaoh? Indeed, why did others such as the prince of Athribis, Petisis, not give themselves cartouches and call themselves king also? Although the value of kingship must have been less than at times when it was a unique office, it was evidently not open to all to claim it. The most likely reason is that some families had an ancestral claim, a forebear who had been king, whilst others did not, and that a sense of good taste or decorum mostly discouraged mere power seekers from claiming an ultimately divine descent. It is necessary to say 'mostly' because at least two of the five kings on Piankhy's stela were of Libyan descent (see Figure 14, p. 45) and Piankhy himself was Sudanese!

Winners and losers

It is now time to look more closely at the periods which followed the end of the New Kingdom. Although I have sought not to emphasize it, within much of the text of this book so far there is a degree of narrative, a journey, a progression as the scale and complexity of Egyptian society increased. A chapter on the New Kingdom entitled 'The mature state' implies that previous periods merited this description less. But history continues on its way. Where does a judgement of this kind leave us when we look beyond to what came afterwards?

The answer takes us back to a point made at the beginning. Modern historians see the nation-state as a modern western development. But people find it natural to write about ancient Egypt as if it had existed as a nation-state from around 3000 BC onwards. Why the discrepancy? The answer is to be found in the last third of ancient Egypt's existence when, its cultural colours still flying, Egypt began to take on a more complex identity – or rather set of identities – a process by which it slowly became a local branch of trans-regional cultures and empires. It becomes ever harder after the New Kingdom to answer the question: who were the Egyptians?

Egypt in the first millennium BC is conventionally divided into three historical periods: the Third Intermediate, the Late, and the Ptolemaic/Roman. A first encounter can readily bring on a feeling of being swamped by a narrative of seizures of power, from within and more especially from without. The highlights easily assume the character of newspaper headlines:

Libyan warlord takes control of all Egypt (Sheshonk I, 945 BC)
Sudanese strong-man's daring bid to end disunity (Piankhy's invasion of the north, 730 BC)
Assyrians loot holy city of Thebes (Ashurbanipal, 660 BC)
Persian army overwhelms Pharaoh's troops. Greeks fight on both sides (Cambyses, 525 BC)
Macedonia's idol greeted as liberator (Alexander the Great, taking over from the Persians, 332 BC)

The urge to identify with the fortunes of one group (usually the Egyptians) and to write history as a record of winners and losers in these terms is powerful and hard to avoid. Personalizing the record is part of the process. Did the Persian conqueror of Egypt, Cambyses, really go mad (as the Greek historian Herodotus claimed[7]) or was he the victim of Greek smear stories?

With the exception of the start of formal Libyan rule (as the 22nd Dynasty) in the Third Intermediate Period, these great events are barely recorded in sources from within Egypt (as would also be the case if it is accepted – as mentioned in Chapter 1, p. 44 – that Egyptian armies also suffered major defeats at the hands of the Libyans in the years after the reign of Rameses III). Often virtually all that we know comes from Assyrian annals and from the Greek historians. It illustrates the colossal loss of historical documentation that has taken place, as well as the fact that historical narrative was not a favoured Egyptian genre. But it also helps to put political history in its place. Losing battles, even if it sweeps in new leaders from outside and redirects commodity surpluses to a foreign court, does not necessarily damage the infrastructure or curb the energies of groups within that society. Societies are often far more robust and also more complex than a football-match philosophy of history encourages one to imagine. The Late Period in Egypt is no Dark Age. It shows all the signs of prosperity appropriate to the ancient world: temple building, superlative sculpture, the raising of armies, the administration of land. Together the evidence illustrates the capacity of a society to survive and adapt to great changes in political leadership, often violently wrought. Indeed, for evaluating the nature of society and culture in these times, the details of political history are something of a distraction. Moreover, Egypt was not only a very wealthy country, able to supply surpluses to the coffers of foreign rulers. Its culture possessed a prestige sufficiently great for the proudest of conquerors to enjoy the association. Egypt was a prize to be taken and then nurtured. From the broad-brush perspective that we have to adopt for ancient history, we can judge the results to have been generally favourable.

Business as usual

An example of 'business as usual' in the face of what, to us (perpetually engulfed as we are in political journalism), seem momentous changes, is provided by the records of Menthuemhat, mayor of Thebes and virtual governor of Upper Egypt in the later 600s BC (Figure 120). His great-grandfather and grandfather had been vizier, his father had been mayor of Thebes. He is known from many 'monuments' (mainly statues of himself), a modern study of which has filled a thick volume.[8] An inscription in a crypt chapel at Karnak records his responsibility for a long schedule of building works and repairs to temples, and also to the 'purifying' of temples. It was at this time that the kings of Assyria and the kings of Napata in the Sudan vied with each other for control of Egypt. Around 630 BC, as a punishment for resistance to his attempted rule, an army of the Assyrian king Ashurbanipal sacked Thebes.[9] The Assyrian annals record quantities of plunder taken back to Assyria, including a pair of large bronze obelisks. The annals are a rare contemporary outsider's view of conditions in Egypt. They inform us that Esarhaddon, Ashurbanipal's father, had appointed (or reappointed) twenty 'kings, governors and regents' in Egypt. There follows a list of twenty names and places, with Menthuemhat in last place as 'king of Thebes'. Another name is that of Necho of the western delta city of Sais. Necho has to be singled out because, in the complex circumstances surrounding the collapse of both the Assyrian and Napatan attempts at rule, his son Psammetichus became the next Pharaoh of Egypt, the first of the 26th Dynasty. We last meet Menthuemhat heading a list of donors to a fund intended to provide an income for the daughter of Psammetichus,

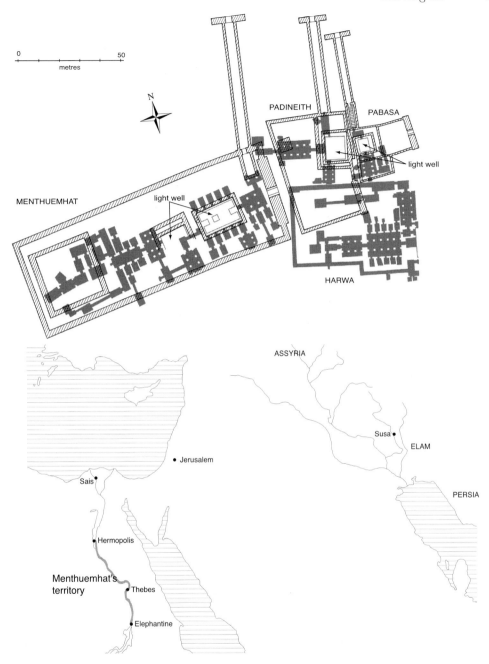

Figure 120 A king in all but name: Menthuemhat, 'mayor' of Thebes and effective ruler of southern Egypt under the regimes of the Kushite 25th Dynasty, the Assyrians, and the early 26th Dynasty. The map shows the area of his authority. The plan includes his tomb and those of some other members of his ruling echelon. The tomb plan is after D. Eigner, *Die monumentalen Grabbauten der Spätzeit in der thebanischen Nekropole*, Vienna, 1984, Abb. 67, opp. p. 96, Plan I.

the lady Nitokris, following her appointment to the prestigious Theban priestess office of 'God's Wife of Amun'.[10] Menthuemhat had survived another change of dynasty.

Behind the restrained and decorous and ultimately superficial façade which is all that survives we know nothing of Menthuemhat's personal and inner life, how he dealt with people and what his feelings were; although we can note that whilst the Assyrians labelled him a 'king' he seems never to have used the title himself. We can only see him exemplifying a process: the exercise of personal authority and patronage within a society that, although under intense strain, remained receptive to the balm of traditional culture and forms of respect. The survival of so much of ancient Thebes has been kind to Menthuemhat. Through the much greater losses to archaeology further north we know little or nothing – beyond their names – about many of his nineteen colleagues of similar status recognized by the Assyrians and listed in their annals. But the group as a whole, and Menthuemhat as an individual, are a further continuation of the long tradition of prominent regional figures around a few of whom the first section of this chapter was written and upon whom the continuing integrity of the Egyptian state depended in large measure.

A second example of local continuity, which illustrates the superficiality of historical narrative when transferred to community undertakings, is the building of the temple of Hibis in the Kharga Oasis (Figure 121). By the first millennium BC the population of Kharga must have been heavily Egyptianized. The oasis had, for example, been used as a place of banishment for enemies of the ruling families during the 21st Dynasty. It was the largest of the oases and became the site of a major stone temple in Egyptian style, dedicated to Amun-Ra and built at the ancient town of Hibis. Its history of construction implies the existence of an infrastructure, not necessarily very large, which was capable of sustaining the project over two centuries.[11] The decoration of the main part bears in many places the name of a king, whose second cartouche, if one is not prepared for it, is at first sight puzzling. It is in fact a rendering into Egyptian hieroglyphic of the name of the Persian emperor Darijava(l)ush, whom the Greeks knew as Darius. The 27th Dynasty, scrupulously recorded in his Greek-language text by Manetho, is nothing but the line of the most famous of the Persian great kings who had conquered most of the Near East, Egypt included, and were intent upon expansion into south-east Europe, principally Greece and the Ukraine (ancient Scythia).[12] Darius' foreign origin has not perturbed the priests responsible for the decoration at the temple of Hibis. He becomes the epitome of the legitimate Pharaoh, as in the scene beside the front doorway (Figure 121, *left*), where he is shown as a royal child, suckled by the goddess Mut.

> Words spoken by Mut, the eye of Ra, Lady of Hibis, for she speaks to her beloved son, the son of Ra, Darius, living forever, in order that you might be suckled, placing him as a royal child, in order to take for yourself the throne of Geb, forever and ever.[13]

As is often the case, however, what appears to be simple turns out on closer inspection to be not so straightforward. A sharper-eyed re-examination of the reliefs in the temple has revealed that many of the cartouches of Darius have been added at a mature stage to a building whose beginning is not recorded. Some of the decoration had apparently been done during the one-year reign of Psammetichus III of the previous 26th Dynasty, but several decades of construction are likely to have preceded this.

HIBIS (KHARGA OASIS)

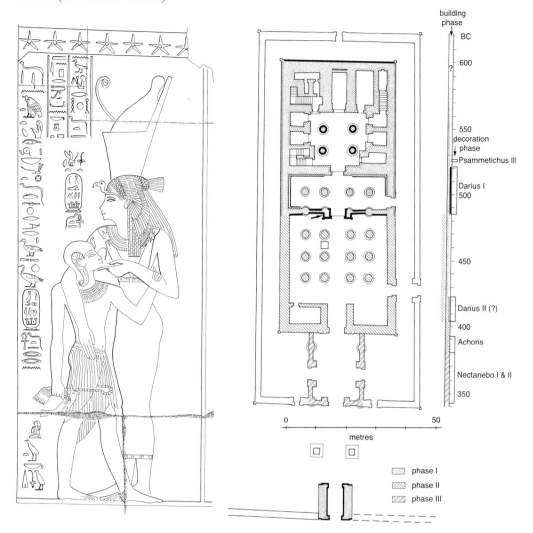

Figure 121 The temple of Hibis in the Kharga Oasis. Was it built through a discontinuous succession of royal initiatives or as an ongoing community project? The plan of the temple is after H.E. Winlock, *The Temple of Hibis in El Khārgeh Oasis* I, New York, 1941, Pls XXX, XXXII, with additions by E. Cruz-Uribe, *VA* 3 (1987), 229, Fig. 12. The temple scene on the left shows the Persian king Darius being suckled by the goddess Mut. The arrow on the plan (at the middle doorway) marks the position of the scene. After N. de G. Davies, *The Temple of Hibis in El Khārgeh Oasis* III. *The decoration*, New York, 1953, Pl. 39.

A few kings identify themselves as great initiators of building programmes. Amen-hetep III and Rameses II of the New Kingdom are the most obvious. In many other instances, however, we can suspect that a temple owed its inception and its prosecution over many years to the leaders of the local community, often men who combined civil and priestly authority. A decorated stone temple must have brought prestige as well as employ-ment, and perhaps added revenue from pious donations obtained through petitioning the king. A case in point is Peftuaneith, a high official probably from the north of Egypt, who, having gained the agreement of King Amasis of the 26th Dynasty, took the credit himself for a range of pious initiatives at Abydos, including building and increasing revenues.[14]

The temple of Hibis was clearly intended from the beginning to be roughly the size that we see it now. It is likely that no design was drawn up which went beyond specify-ing overall dimensions in cubits, but that was the moment for those involved to reveal the scale of their ambition. Perhaps at the outset the reigning king was approached for approval and for material assistance. But in then saying that one particular king built this part and another that part, all that one may be doing is marking the points along a fairly continuous history of building; points at which a particular portion, with all or most of its decoration completed, reached the stage when it was time to insert the current royal name. It is not necessary to assume that building and decoration proceeded at the same rate. For the laying out and sculpting of the decoration it was probably necessary to bring in outsiders, especially when, as with this temple, some of the scenes were unusual and complex. Such people were probably in short supply. Figure 121 shows that if the sequence of royal names in the decoration is taken as a precise guide to progress in construction, a very uneven rate was achieved, with far more time spent on building the rear half than the front half. It is equally possible, however, that the building of the front half was well advanced by the time that the decoration of the rear was at last finished. Many of the cartouches had been left empty at first, and several of those of Darius had been inserted only in paint. One can only speculate that the promise of a visit by a major figure of state created an incentive to complete the decoration of at least part of the temple. Perhaps the local community petitioned for this as a way of demonstrating loyalty to the new regime.

At a more everyday level the need to maintain the continuities of life is exemplified by papyrus documents that, amongst other subjects, record transactions in land and cattle. They show that the age-old practice of establishing pious foundations by private individu-als remained a common part of the fabric of life. One group of documents, dealing with transfers of individual cows and bulls (which continued to maintain their high values), spans what in historical terms is the dramatic change of national fortunes between the 26th (Saite) and 30th Dynasties, a period of some two centuries (588–364 BC) which includes the 27th (Persian) Dynasty. The transfers, sometimes with complex arrangements, reflect the secure continuities of the provincial economy, and followed 'a unified and well-formulated system which was able to deal with all circumstances involving obligations and contracts'. The documents are virtually interchangeable in terms of their dates of compo-sition, something illustrated by the way that a minor improvement in the reading of one word (actually recognition of the name Darius) has moved one of the documents by fifty years without any sense of the circumstantial context having been violated.[15]

Temple enclosure or urban citadel?

One means by which the continuities and discontinuities of life can be observed is through the study of settlements over long periods of time. In Egypt that is actually quite difficult, a consequence of the savaging of ancient town sites by industrial-scale fertilizer digging in the nineteenth and early twentieth centuries. None the less, the evidence does accumulate and a picture is emerging for the millennium after the New Kingdom of a distinctive style of town, the nature of which is easily misunderstood.

A good place to begin, because it was better preserved than most, is the town of Djeme, on the west bank of Thebes (Figure 122).[16] The settlement began as nothing less than the mortuary temple of Rameses III of the 20th Dynasty, now known as Medinet Habu. Around the temple ran a mock-fortification that also enclosed the huge magazines and a small palace. Built concentrically outside was a far more massive enclosure wall, and the intervening space was filled with rows of houses for the temple community. This was a New Kingdom equivalent of Kahun (Figure 76, p. 212), the contrasts between them serving as a telling comment on the differences between Middle and New Kingdom societies (and one might also compare the pyramid settlements illustrated in Figures 72–5, pp. 204–10). By the late New Kingdom this settlement had become the administrative centre for the western half of Thebes. The Paser family, who supplied the mayors of Thebes in the 20th Dynasty and also various officers in the Amun priesthood, had a row of decorated tomb chapels situated just outside, a sign that they probably had a residence in the temple enclosure. Between the late 20th and the early 21st Dynasties the palace was rebuilt with more rooms being added, and this then served as a residence for a succession of priestly administrators.[17] What fate befell the great temple of Rameses III? Much of its masonry survived into Roman and then Christian times, and this alone suggests that parts of the temple remained in use, presumably for the cult of the local form of Amun. Various of the chambers of the rear part, which had been originally intended to house sacred images and equipment and which included the sanctuary, had had the paving stones taken up, a space dug out underneath, and then the paving replaced. The spaces were used either for human burials, in some cases of priestesses of Amun (one of them 25th Dynasty in date), or for the burial of votive statuettes of gods. This is an interesting development in temple usage and strengthens the idea that the temple was still a sacred as well as a secure place. It was, however, the earlier and smaller temple in one corner of the enclosure (a terminus for one of the major Theban processional festivals, see p. 274) which continued to attract pious acts of building, presumably because it offered a less intimidating scale to work with. Small additions continued to be made into the Roman Period.

The neat brick layout of magazines and houses from the time of Rameses III, however, did not last beyond the New Kingdom. It fell victim to the process already illustrated at some of the pyramid towns of the Old Kingdom: that of piecemeal rebuilding which replaced the straight lines of the original scheme with a sea of houses and yards separated by winding alleys. The original excavators saw this as a decline in fortunes, accompanied by deliberate destructions brought on by attackers, but a more likely reading of the evidence is that this is a classic case of the triumph of self-organization. Reflecting perhaps the more uncertain times, Medinet Habu also came to illustrate the preference after the New Kingdom for siting the tombs of important people inside temple enclosures. A portion of the housing area was cleared to make way for a precinct in one corner, and this became

MEDINET HABU

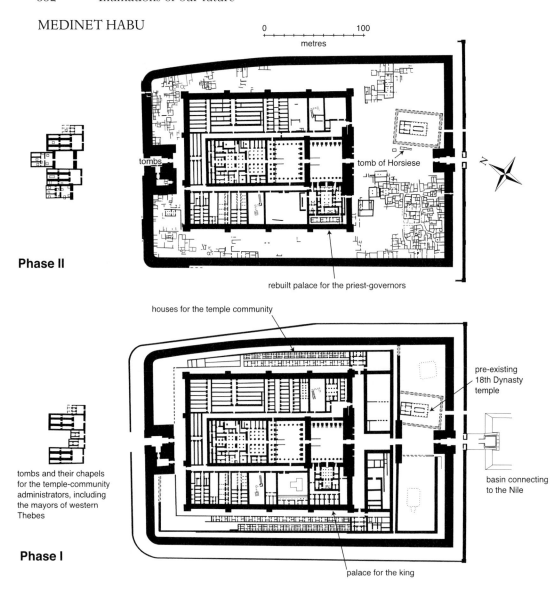

Phase II

Phase I

the site for a short row of small mortuary temples covering tomb chambers, a portion of which is still to be seen. They belonged to the God's Wives of Amun, highly placed female relatives of the king who held this office for just over two centuries, from between near the end of the Libyan 22nd Dynasty to the Persian conquest (for the façade of one, see Figure 54.2, p. 151). Other tombs in the area have fared much worse, but the burial chamber of one can be identified as having belonged to Horsiese, one of the high priests of Amun in the 22nd Dynasty and also a member of Egypt's (Libyan) royal family. It is a reasonable inference that the people buried in these various tombs lived in the adjacent settlement, the God's Wives perhaps the last residents of the palace beside the temple.

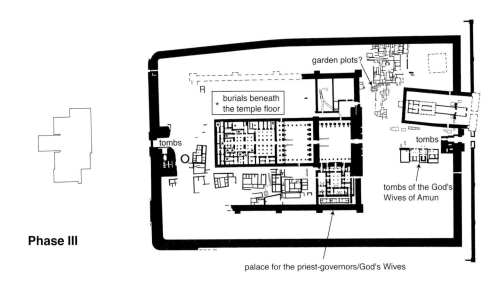

Phase III

palace for the priest-governors/God's Wives

Figure 122   Medinet Habu. Imposed order versus self-organization. Three phases in the development of the temple enclosure at Medinet Habu. Phase I is the initial layout of the time of Rameses III (died *c.* 1153 BC); phases II and III are parts of a continuum of development that continued after the death of Rameses III for at least five centuries. After U. Hölscher, *The Excavation of Medinet Habu* I. *General views and plans*, Chicago 1934.

The period of the 25th/26th Dynasty, in which period lived Menthuemhat, seems to have been one of particular prosperity at Thebes. Huge tombs of the leading families (including Menthuemhat's, Figure 120, p. 347), some as big as conventional temples though using much mud brick, were built some way to the north of Medinet Habu. Their owners probably lived across the river, at Karnak. It is to this time at Medinet Habu that must date a rebuilding of the town. Instead of an interlocking village sprawl the new houses, which were laid out further back from the cemetery, were discrete rectangular blocks, separated from their neighbours and looking like closely set architectural islands. Their walls, at around a metre in thickness and built with curving bedding planes for the bricks,

TELL EL-NEBESHA

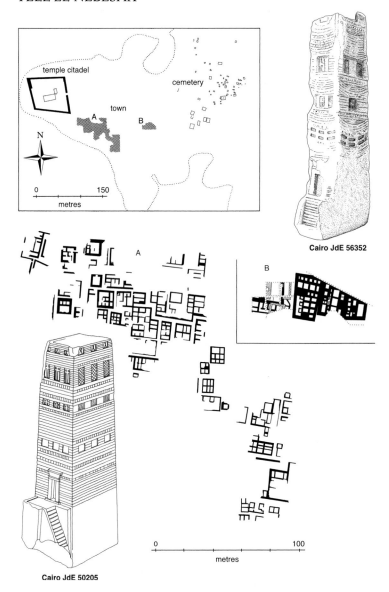

Cairo JdE 56352

Cairo JdE 50205

Figure 123   The outlines of a delta city: Tell el-Nebesha. The small-scale plan shows the general division of the city into large zones for the unwalled town and the cemetery, with the walled temple citadel standing at the edge. The plans of two excavated areas of the city, A and B, are given below. There is no detailed plan for the temple citadel. After W.M.F. Petrie, *Nebesheh (Am) and Defenneh (Tahpanhes)*, London, 1888, Pls XV, XVII; I.A. Mustafa, 'A preliminary report on the excavation of the E.A.O. at Tell el-Fara'on – "Imet", season 1985–1986', in E.C.M. van den Brink, ed., *The archaeology of the Nile Delta; problems and priorities*, Amsterdam, 1988, 148–9, Figs 2, 3. *Inset top right and bottom left.* Two limestone models of tower houses, 'Graeco-Roman' in date, in the Egyptian Museum, Cairo. Both have been designed so that the 'ground floor' could become a basement. The example (*top right*) was built with curving courses of brickwork. After R. Engelbach, *ASAE* 31 (1931), 129, Fig. 3; Pl. III.

were substantial enough to have supported two or more upper storeys, and the best preserved had a staircase in a corner. These are houses probably designed so that the main
living-quarters were upstairs, and belong to a house type frequently encountered over the
next centuries until well into the Roman Period (see below). At this point there is a major
break in the continuity of evidence and the next phase is Roman. The condition of the
site, however, leaves it unclear whether this represents a major abandonment, a levelling
down of the site prior to the Roman rebuilding, or inadequate evidence from which to
draw a full chronological picture. It is worth pointing out that there is no sign of a second
'town' enclosure beside Medinet Habu. If and when houses were built outside (as they definitely were in Roman times) they were not surrounded by their own wall. The history and
character of Medinet Habu over the centuries should be kept in mind as a possible, indeed
likely, guide to understanding the numerous 'temple' enclosures of the Late and subsequent
periods that have not been so well preserved.

Many late temple enclosures lie in the delta but the buildings within them have generally been reduced to their foundations. One of the broadest exposures has been at Tell
el-Nebesha (Tell el-Fara'on) in the eastern delta, where, in 1886, Petrie worked at the same
time that local labourers were digging out much of the archaeological site as cheap fertilizer
for the fields (Figure 123; Figure 127, p. 362 marks the location).[18] The site, which covers
an area of around 80 hectares, had three parts. One is the temple enclosure surrounded
by a massive wall. Close by lay the town. A plan of part of it shows it composed of isolated
squarish house foundations built with thick walls capable of supporting a tower-like building, each separated narrowly from its neighbours and aligned in roughly common directions
to create short lengths of straight street which none the less did not follow the same line for
long. The third part is the cemetery, which occupied another large portion of the site. As
we will see, this is essentially the plan of another early Petrie discovery of the same period,
the city of Naukratis (Figure 129, p. 368); a similar division of the ground, on a larger scale,
is emerging at Tanis.[19] An initial reading of this evidence is that temple, town and cemetery
were distinct zones, the main effort of walling safeguarding only the sacred precinct.

The fashion for putting up large blocky buildings of mud bricks often laid in concave
beds seems to have been widespread. In many cases what they leave behind in the ground
is a particularly impenetrable form of archaeology. Their thick walls cover much ground,
which tends to defeat the usually modest scale of modern excavations. They were built
with unusually deep foundations to support floors raised well above the level of the adjacent ground and streets, and everything above the foundations has usually been eroded or
destroyed. In the absence of conventional floor deposits there is little scope for understanding what went on in the buildings either from the ground plan or from associated finds.[20]
More often than not even the positions of doorways are unmarked. Such foundation platforms have been found in the towns outside the temple enclosures, as at Tell el-Nebesha
and Naukratis (Figures 123, 127), and in a sector of Memphis.[21] But others have been
found inside the temple enclosures, sometimes occupying a good deal of the space (e.g. at
Tanis, Tell el-Maskhuta, Mendes, Tell el-Balamun; Figure 124).[22] At the last named site
one corner of the temple enclosure was occupied by the compartmented foundations of
a large square building that the excavators have identified as a fort, perhaps of the 26th
Dynasty. Although the identification is not absolutely secure it seems to be a good working
hypothesis, and the building has a close parallel in one which is located on one side of the
large temple enclosure at Naukratis (Figure 129, *bottom centre*, 'citadel'). It would seem, in

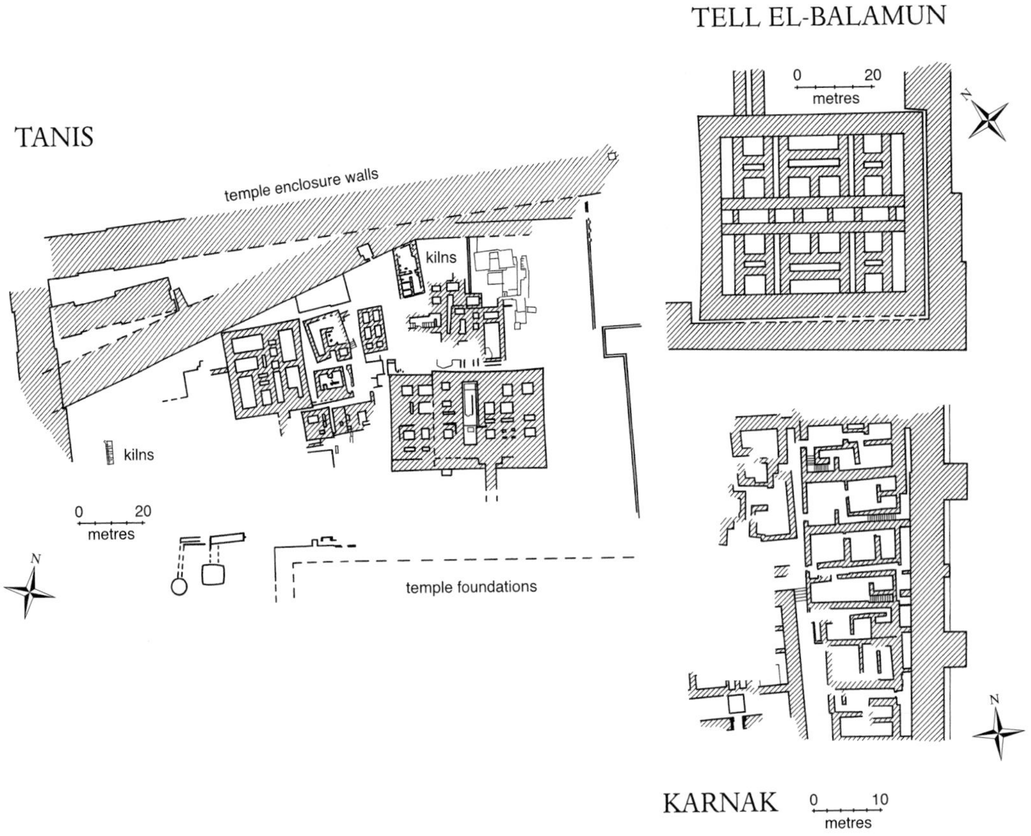

Figure 124 Interior buildings inside temple enclosures. At Tanis the illustrated sector is filled with the foundations of towered buildings and with industrial premises. At Tell el-Balamun one corner of the enclosure was filled with a towered building thought to have been a fortress. At Karnak the ground inside the old New Kingdom enclosure wall was densely built up with houses which seem to have been left alone despite a stated policy of cleaning secular buildings from the 'domain of Amun'. After P. Brissaud and C. Zivie-Coche, eds, *Tanis; travaux récents sur le tell Sân el-Hagar* 2, Paris, 2000, 59, Fig. 3 (Tanis); A.J. Spencer, *Excavations at Tell el-Balamun 1991–1994*, London, 1996, Pl. 27 (Tell el-Balamun); P. Anus and R. Saʿad, *Kêmi* 21 (1971), Fig. 5 (Karnak), following p. 220.

fact, that foundation platforms of this kind were used for a range of building types, namely, the temples themselves, fortresses, houses and probably administrative and storage buildings (the latter including granaries). Some of them could have been, for the ancient world, quite high. A few models of houses probably of this kind show up to four storeys, with the lowest externally accessible floor, the first, reached by a lengthy flight of steps (Figure 123, *insets*).[23] They were built to last, and whether intentional or not, successfully countered the gradual accumulation of rubbish in the streets. This could build up to several metres so that what began as a closed-off ground floor became an underground cellar lit by narrow slit windows angled steeply upwards.

The enclosure walls that normally surrounded the temple were massively thick and often built in separate sections some of which had their brick courses laid in concave beds.[24] I

Figure 125 *Above.* The Assyrian army attacks an Egyptian citadel. A portion of a relief slab from the palace of Ashurbanipal at Nineveh (*c.* 660 BC). After H.R. Hall, *Babylonian and Assyrian sculpture in the British Museum*, Paris and Brussels, 1928, Pl. XL. At the bottom a column of Assyrian soldiers walks away in triumph, brandishing as trophies severed heads and (in a lower portion not reproduced here) leading into captivity Egyptian and Kushite prisoners. *Below.* A reconstruction of a portion of the 30th Dynasty enclosure wall at Karnak. The battlements and curving wall tops are taken from the still preserved top of the Ptolemaic enclosure wall at Deir el-Medina. After J.-C. Golvin and El-S. Hegazy, *Cahiers de Karnak, IX 1993*, Paris, 1993, 155, Figs 3–6.

cited evidence in Chapter 6 that shows that the larger temple enclosure walls of the New Kingdom were given the appearance of fortresses through the addition of battlemented tops (Figure 92, p. 253). An example of the Ptolemaic period, at Deir el-Medina, still preserves some of its original top, and that also is crenellated even though the enclosure and its temple were quite small.[25] We can use this as a model for restoring a battlemented appearance to other similar enclosure walls of the first millennium BC (Figure 125).

Because these huge walls usually surrounded the principal local temple we are accustomed to call them temple enclosure walls. This creates an anomaly in the evidence. It is to be expected that the troubles that loom so large in the historical record had some effect on the appearance of towns and the character of their life. The most obvious sign to look for is urban fortification. For the 21st Dynasty a number of fortified settlements in Middle and Upper Egypt have been identified, although there is little confirmatory detail.[26] An impressive fortress of the Persian period has been discovered at Tell el-Herr in the far north-eastern delta.[27] What is noticeable is that at towns in the delta, the part of Egypt most open to invasion from Asia, there is little evidence for the building of even plain boundary walls around towns (as distinct from around the temples). No trace has been found at Tell el-Nebesha, for example, or at Naukratis. But this cannot be the full picture. Piankhy's record of fighting the northern coalition early in the 25th Dynasty makes frequent reference to walls with battlements and gates which could be countered with siege towers/battering rams and the erection of earthen ramps, although Piankhy himself preferred the tactic of direct storming. Within the circuit of the walls lay treasuries and granaries and, in the case of Hermopolis, the palace of the local king Nemlut together with its stables for horses. Contemporary impressions of the appearance of such places are contained in a relief from the palace of Ashurbanipal at Nineveh from about a century later which shows the Assyrian army attacking an unidentified Egyptian fortified enclosure, and much later from a Roman mosaic pavement (Figures 125, 126).[28] Little is known from excavation of the appearance of the places that Piankhy attacked. Two of them, Tehna and El-Hiba in Middle Egypt, are both situated on desert directly beside the Nile in naturally defensive locations, and it looks as though the small temples and the towns occupied the same walled space over a very long period, although the El-Hiba enclosure also contained a separate citadel at one end.[29]

There is, indeed, one simple way of explaining why it is that temple enclosure walls of the first millennium BC have often survived as a feature of the landscape into recent times whilst separate town enclosure walls have not. This is that the term 'temple enclosure wall' is itself misleading if it is taken to mark a separation between the sacred and the secular. These huge enclosures, which represent a considerable expenditure of resources, were really the community's citadel, the equivalent on Egypt's flat land of an acropolis, and contained its most precious assets. These began with the temples but extended to the main storerooms, the residence (dare we call it the palace?) of its leader (be he a 'mayor', chief priest or local king like Nemlut of Hermopolis) and of other prominent citizens, and presumably of the local garrison, too, with its stables. All of these different buildings would have stood on the same kind of large blocky foundations. The huge platform beside the main temple at Tanis could as easily have been for a palace for the kings of the 21st and 22nd Dynasties as for another temple.[30] A few of the richest and most powerful people also sometimes chose to site their tombs here too, in the case of Tanis the royal family. As part-building site for long periods and beset rather haphazardly with tall and rather severe brick buildings, these enclosures would not have been neat, tidy and refreshing places. At Tanis bronze foundries and pottery kilns lay inside the same enclosure as the temple and royal tombs, and one of the uppermost levels has preserved an area of streets and houses of the Ptolemaic Period.[31] They could even be places of fear. Another temple enclosure, El-Hiba, is the setting for a criminal drama, part of a real family history preserved in a long papyrus. Two young men go to the temple to claim a payment of wheat. On arrival they are attacked by ruffians who, hired by the priests, have hidden their staves in the grain. When the two flee into the sanctuary they are murdered and their bodies hidden in a chamber (a crypt?) in the stone part of the building.[32]

Figure 126 The closest thing to an ancient photograph of an Egyptian temple. Part of the Roman Palestrina mosaic which depicts elements of the Egyptian landscape as it was under Roman rule. The restoration lines are based upon the way that the mosaic has itself been restored. Note the crenellated enclosure wall (1) and the many tall tower houses (especially 2 and 3) that seem to form part of the enclosure wall. They have curving courses of masonry and resemble the models of houses included in Figure 123, p. 354. After G. Gullini, *I mosaici di Palestrina*, Rome, 1956, Tav. XX, which separates the surviving ancient areas from subsequent restorations. H. Whitehouse, *The Dal Pozzo copies of the Palestrina mosaic*, Oxford 1976, 17, 18, 46, 47, Figs 11a, 11b; H. Whitehouse, *The Paper Museum of Cassiano dal Pozzo, Series A, Part 1: Ancient mosaics and wallpaintings*, London 2001, 108–9 publishes the seventeenth-century copies made when the scene was more complete. Convenient is A.K. Bowman, *Egypt after the Pharaohs; 332 BC–AD 642*, London, 1986, 184, Fig. 112.

The remainder of a town's population at most places, often the greater part, lived in a tightly packed unwalled area outside, but perhaps saw the great enclosure as a place of refuge at a time of emergency. It would be valuable to seek archaeological evidence for social and economic distinctions between those who lived inside and those who lived outside the enclosure wall, but as yet the serious study of these sites has barely begun. Unusually at El-Kab, in a sparsely populated part of southern Egypt, at least half of the huge enclosure (where the great walls were provided with internal ramps to the top) seems to have been left empty and so could have provided refuge for a scattered population or for passing caravans from Nubia or nomadic herdsmen from the eastern desert.

We will shortly be looking at the remarkable autobiographical text of a senior Egyptian figure, Udjahor-resenet, who served under the Persian king Cambyses. One of his achievements was to obtain royal permission to 'expel all the foreigners [who] dwelled in the temple of Neith, to demolish all their houses and all their unclean things which were in this temple'.[33] If, as was clearly the case at Medinet Habu (and at Tell el-Balamun), secular buildings were regularly built within temple enclosures, it is likely that the offending houses here had actually strayed inside the sacred stone building itself or perhaps had been built as lean-tos against the stone walls or even on the roof. Indeed, Udjahor-resenet as a member of the governing class and a senior priest as well quite likely had his own residence inside the temple enclosure, for reasons explored below. The text is not unique. Earlier the high priest of Amun at Karnak, Menkheperra of the 21st Dynasty, had recorded how he had removed the houses of Egyptian people installed in the court of the 'domain of Amun'. Since excavation has revealed that houses lay at this time inside the main temple enclosure and remained there for a long time afterwards (Figure 124) we can infer that Menkheperra's target was localized at the stone temples proper.[34] Shortly prior to the conquest of Egypt by Alexander, another priest, Djedher, this time at the delta city of Athribis, told a similar tale. Again the target was the houses of soldiers, this time said more explicitly to be inside the temple enclosure wall, but the tone is more generous: the owners were given land outside the enclosure and there they rebuilt their houses so that they were better than before.[35]

The history of Medinet Habu after the end of the New Kingdom is of the ebb and flow of secular buildings. Something of this kind is visible at Tell el-Balamun, where intrusive houses of the Third Intermediate Period were cleared away for temple building in the 22nd Dynasty, yet in the Persian period kilns were situated over the ruins of another of the temples. In the 30th Dynasty widespread reconstruction took place again. It was perhaps only the occasional intervention of individuals sensitive to the demarcation between the secular and the sacred that prevented the great stone temples from being invaded by people hungry for opportunities to create a secure home. When they were foreign soldiers it might have taken especially strong resolve to dislodge them. This cyclic process, which we would do better to regard as a normal feature of society rather than the occasional aberration, creates an explicit research agenda for excavation within temple enclosures.

In parts of the world where the inhabited landscape is uneven, times of trouble encourage some, usually the rulers, to retreat to fortified strongholds on high places. In Greece and the Aegean it produced the 'acropolis'. This was so even at Athens until a Delphic oracle in 510 BC ordered that it should remain forever the province of the gods, unoccupied by humans. The case that I am advancing here is that in the first millennium BC Egypt's temple enclosures served the same purpose. The thickness of the battlemented walls and the platforms of its interior buildings, probably linked by raised street levels, created for many towns and cities an artificial acropolis. Here the community's main assets – spiritual and temporal – were protected.

Temple enclosures in the New Kingdom and the private residential areas of the city of El-Amarna provide abundant evidence, easy to interpret, that buildings for the storage of commodities (more especially the bulk storage of cereal grain) lay close at hand to the temples and to the houses of the private individuals who owned them. The same clarity of exposition – here is a house or temple and here beside it is the owner's granary – does not recur in the Late Period. Perhaps there was already a greater move towards storing wealth in the form of metals. Yet these were troubled times, when attacks might have to be faced and a protected yet accessible store of grain would be essential. The straightforward solution is to accept that some of the buildings were actually places of storage, probably largely for grain.[36] Even so, the storage capacity seems small by comparison with the huge magazine blocks of the New Kingdom. Something has changed in the way that temple economies were managed, but what that was remains elusive.

Under new management

If we set warfare on one side, measured by administrative stability and the long-term continuation of patronage expressed in architecture and art, the Late Period was as successful as the Middle Kingdom, which lasted for roughly the same period, namely four centuries (if we include the 13th Dynasty within the latter). The military leaders might lose the battles but the country managed well. We might, however, allow ourselves the thought that in a complex system such as that represented by ancient Egyptian society, dramatic changes of rule by exceptionally capable outsiders could reverse the tendency of such a system when fully stable to drift towards stagnation. Some of the conquerors and usurpers could have had a positive energizing influence.

I can think of no clearer example of external vision and energy brought to bear on Egypt and expressed in a great public work than the digging of a fresh-water canal to link the Nile to the Red Sea at the head of the Gulf of Suez.[37] There are sufficient sources to suggest a previous history of complete or partial success in this undertaking, possibly extending back to the New Kingdom. But the finalization of the scheme, perhaps in the form of a rerouting and re-engineering, was done under Darius. In contrast to what we see at the temple of Hibis, where Darius takes his place as just the current Pharaoh, the new regime took the opportunity to proclaim the existence of a new world order. The archaeology of this great project is poorly documented and unfortunately has to rely upon investigations done in the nineteenth and early twentieth centuries (in connection with the creation of the Suez Canal and its towns). The approximate line of the canal is known, as is the fact that at intervals it was marked by free-standing granite stelae (Figure 127). These were carved on both sides, though which side faced the canal and was therefore given the greater prominence we do not know. One side bore Egyptian designs and hieroglyphic texts that austerely avoid depictions of Darius or leading deities. Beneath a winged sun-disc two figures that symbolize Upper and Lower Egypt bind together the heraldic plants of the north and south in the ancient gesture of peaceful unification (see Figure 20, p. 70). Below comes a row of kneeling figures surmounting the names of subject nations, which extend from Persia itself to Armenia and include, on one of the stelae, Egypt, Libya, Nubia as well as Oman and India. The main hieroglyphic text, now very fragmentary, contained a wordier version of the historical narrative better preserved on the other side.

The other side bears a design of compelling interest. A winged disc of somewhat non-Egyptian appearance hovers beneath a curving Egyptian hieroglyphic sign for the sky, flanked at the edges of the stela by a pair of Egyptian ceremonial staves, copying the design of the other side. Beneath the disc stand two crowned figures draped in a robe and with one arm raised, clearly kings who are not traditional Pharaohs. Between them is the name of Darius in a cartouche, but the script is cuneiform, not hieroglyphic. In horizontal lines below follows a text also in cuneiform script and given in three languages: Old Persian (an Indo-European language), Elamite and Akkadian. It opens with an uncompromising statement of creed:

A great god is Ahuramazda, who created yonder heaven, who created this earth, who created man, who created happiness for man, who made Darius king . . .

I am a Persian, from Persia I seized Egypt. I gave orders to dig this canal from a river by name the Nile which flows in Egypt, to the sea which goes from Persia.

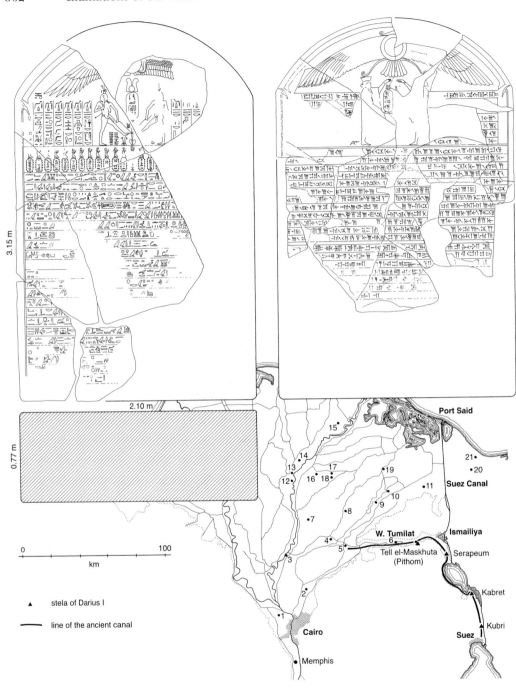

3.15 m

2.10 m

0.77 m

0   100

km

▲   stela of Darius I

——   line of the ancient canal

Port Said

15

14

13
12   16 18   17
      19
      10   11
   8   9   Suez Canal
7

4   5   W. Tumilat   Ismailiya
6
Tell el-Maskhuta   Serapeum
(Pithom)

3

Kabret

2
Kubri

1

Cairo   Suez

Memphis

21
20

Afterwards this canal was dug thus as I had ordered, and ships went from Egypt through this canal to Persia thus as was my desire.[38]

The surviving stelae come from the eastern stretch of the canal, some way from the Nile delta. It is unlikely that we will ever know what marked the point where it diverged from the Nile at its western end, wherever that point was. But it is a fair guess that the opportunity was taken by the new government to make a larger and bolder statement than would have been represented by just another stela. By a temple, perhaps? But then, what would its decoration and cult have been like, given the determination of Darius or his agents to introduce Persian iconography to at least a limited extent into northern Egypt? Darius would have been at least nominally a believer in the prophet Zoroaster who had expounded on a world in conflict between justice and falsehood, presided over by the supreme deity Ahuramazda, a structure of thought with a strong parallel in Egyptian theology. Yet the stelae themselves, like many other sources for the Persian (Achaemenid) empire, also reveal an acceptance of other cults and mythologies, to a much greater extent than was tolerated in later centuries when Zoroastrianism developed into an uncompromising monotheism. There is a close parallel in this with the contemporary Jewish colony at Elephantine, to be described shortly.

During the New Kingdom, as we have seen in Chapter 6, the Egyptian court was an outpost of a cosmopolitan multicultural world which embraced the Near East yet barely impinged upon the manifestations of culture in Egypt that are now most visible to us. Without the chance survival of the Amarna Letters we would barely recognize it. Now, eight and a half centuries later, we find that the process had developed further. By this time the universal language (the *lingua franca*) of the Near East was no longer versions of the Akkadian language written in cuneiform (as with the Amarna Letters themselves), but had become Aramaic. A chance find at an unknown site in Egypt has given us a diplomatic mailbag from the Persian empire, complete with its letters (the writing-material leather and originally numbering around eighteen or nineteen).[39] They were mostly written by the Persian prince and governor of Egypt, Arsham, whilst he was out of the country,

Figure 127   A composite drawing of the granite stelae erected by Darius I along the line of the canal linking the Nile to the Red Sea. That on the left is the hieroglyphic side, based on the fragments from Tell el-Maskhuta; that on the right is the cuneiform side, based on the fragments from Kabret. The dimensions of the stelae were around 3.15 m high, 2.10 m wide, and 77 cm thick. After G. Posener, *La Première domination perse en Égypte*, Cairo, 1936, Pl. IV, and J. Menant, *RdT* 9 (1887), 145, Figure.

Numbered ancient place names:

1 Letopolis (Ausim)
2 Leontopolis (Tell el-Yahudiya)
3 Athribis (Tell Atrib)
4 Bubastis (Tell Basta)
5 Per-Sopdu (Saft el-Henna)
6 Tell el-Retaba
7 Leontopolis (Tell Mukdam)
8 Pharbaithos (Hurbeit)
9 Per-Rameses (Kantir)
10 Imet (Tell el-Nebesha)
11 Daphnae (Tell Dafana)
12 Busiris (Abusir)
13 Sebennytos (Samanud)
14 Iseum (Behbeit el-Hager)
15 Tell el-Balamun
16 Hermopolis Parva (el-Bakliya)
17 Mendes (Tell el-Rub'a)
18 Thmuis (Tell el-Timai)
19 Tanis (San el-Hager)
20 Tell el-Herr
21 Pelusium (Tell el-Farama)

possibly back home in Susa in Elam (the present-day region of western Iran not far from the frontier with Iraq, see map, Figure 120, p. 347). He possessed estates in Egypt, presumably sequestrated following the Persian conquest. Seven of the letters are addressed to Arsham's steward or agent, a man who, to judge from his name, Nehtihur (Nakht-her, 'Strong is Horus'), was Egyptian. Other Egyptians are also in positions of responsibility. The subject matter is primarily property: transferred, stolen, yielding rent, and including runaway slaves or army deserters (from Cilicia in the south-east of modern Turkey). There are several references to an uprising but on what scale is not clear. It might sound like a rough world, but Nehtihur had travelled (by horse) with ten servants at least as far as Syria, carrying an official letter from Arsham to cover his maintenance from local officers of the Persian empire. It is another case of business as usual, but now conducted in Aramaic. Its main purpose was the same as ever, namely, the extraction of revenue. What about those wonderful administrative devices that we met in Chapter 4? Did Nehtihur's scribes still perform miracles of precision with baking ratios and notional work units? We do not know. Equivalent texts from these later periods have not survived.

A second example of the multicultural society comes from Elephantine. Over the centuries since the Old Kingdom (see Figure 69, p. 198) the ground level of the town had gradually risen as people rebuilt their houses upon the old foundations and rubbish accumulated in open spaces. Diggings into this mass of stacked walls in the late nineteenth and early twentieth centuries AD, by local people and then by archaeologists, brought to light three archives of papyrus also dated to the time of Persian rule and also written in Aramaic (Figure 128).[40] The writers this time were a colony of Jewish soldiers and their families. We know of the colony only from the papyri and from some ostraca (texts written on pieces of broken pottery) most of which deal with property and finance and other personal matters. Like most immigrants to Egypt then and earlier, these people are not recognizable from archaeological material. Indeed, it has proved to be difficult to isolate to which of the many building levels the papyri and hence the colony belong. Without the texts we would not be aware of their existence, even though we know (from the texts) that they had managed to build a temple of their own, dedicated to their god Yehu (an early form of Yahweh, i.e. Jehovah of the Old Testament). As reconstructed from the texts the colony occupied, though not exclusively, a tight cluster of houses in two streets beside their temple in an area of about 60 metres square, which perhaps supplies a scale for other immigrant communities in Egypt. A list of donations to the temple comprised 111 names, more than thirty of which were female.

Despite intermarriage the colony retained its ethnic distinctiveness primarily through the cult of Yehu, the observance of special festivals (similar to those known from the later accounts of the Old Testament and including the Passover) and its own recognition that Jerusalem was the seat of religious authority. Yet just as the Zoroastrianism of the period accepted the existence of the deities of other cultures, so this community recognized both Egyptian and Aramaean deities. This is apparent from the oaths they swore, from blessings in letters, and from the donation list just mentioned which divided the proceeds amongst three deities, Yehu, Eshembethel and Anathbethel. The Jewish group was itself part of a larger Aramaean community based in the locality. A different set of papyrus letters acquaints us with a non-Jewish Aramaean part living in the town of Syene (Aswan) across the river. They, too, had their own shrines, dedicated to the divinities Nabu, Banit, Bethel and the 'Queen of Heaven' (Malkat-Shmayin, probably an epithet of the goddess

ELEPHANTINE

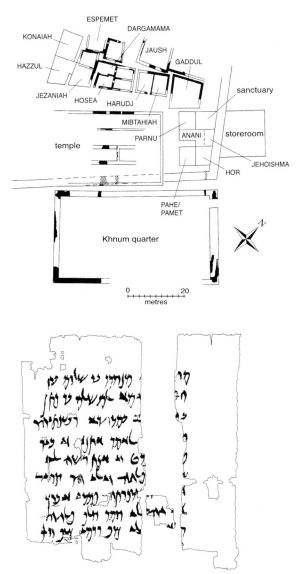

Figure 128 The Aramaic community at Elephantine. *Above.* The plan is of houses which date to the appropriate period and are probably those of the community. The property owners are reconstructed from details contained within the Aramaic documents. After G. Dreyer *et al.*, *MDAIK* 58 (2002), 195, Abb. 12. *Below.* The piece of papyrus bears an oath written in Aramaic, and dates to the end of the fifth century BC. A translation is: 'Oa[th which] Menahem ben Shallum ben Ho[shaiah?] swore to Meshullam ben Nathan by H[erem?] the [god] in the place of prostration and by (the god) Anathyahu and [swore to him] saying: "The female donkey which is in the possession of Pa[misi ben Pe]met a[bout whi]ch you sued me, [with the words] 'Half of it belongs to me', I [am] entitled [to tr]ansfer it to Pamisi. Your father did no[t] give me a male donkey in exchange for half of it nor [did he give] me money or the equivalent of money in exchange for [half of it]."' After B. Porten, *Archives from Elephantine*, Berkeley and Los Angeles, 1968, 154, 317–18, Pl. 10.

Anath). The Jewish temple attracted the hostility of the staff of the neighbouring temple of the Egyptian god Khnum, who seem to have wanted to extend their own temple at its expense. They persuaded the Egyptian element in the garrison to wreck it though no casualties are mentioned. In response the community appealed to various Persian and Jewish authorities in Judah and Samaria for help in rebuilding, and after delays it seems that at least a limited shrine was re-established.

It is within this multicultural (including multilingual) world that we should set the life of an Egyptian who has left us a short but unusually revealing autobiographical text, Udjahor-resenet, a high official from a priestly family of the city of Sais in the western delta. Under the last two kings of the 26th Dynasty, whose home city was Sais, Udjahor-resenet had commanded the royal navy and must have experienced the total defeat of the Egyptian forces (in 525 BC) by the Persians under their king, Cambyses. In such circumstances individuals have a choice: to rebel (and rebellion against foreign rule was already a tradition in Egypt), or to collaborate, not only for personal gain but in the hopes of softening the effects of defeat. Udjahor-resenet chose the latter and recorded the consequences on a stone shrine which he dedicated to a temple to the goddess Neith, at Sais.

> The Great Chief of all foreign lands, Cambyses, came to Egypt, and the foreign peoples of every foreign land were with him. When he had conquered this land in its entirety, they established themselves in it, and he was Great Ruler of Egypt and Great Chief of all foreign lands.
>
> His majesty assigned to me the office of chief physician. He made me live at his side as companion and administrator of the palace. I composed his titulary, to wit his name as King of Upper and Lower Egypt, Mesutira [i.e. his first cartouche].
>
> I informed his majesty of the greatness of Sais, that is the seat of Neith-the-Great, the mother who bore Ra and inaugurated birth when birth had not yet been.[41]

Cambyses visited Sais and ordered the renovation of the temple. In the reign of his successor, Darius, Udjahor-resenet journeyed to Elam and returned with a further commission to restore the 'House of Life', the name for the centres of learning which were attached to temples in Egypt and which must have been repositories of traditional knowledge and the sources of inspiration for cultural renewal. It is hard to avoid the conclusion that Udjahor-resenet would have been bilingual (as we must presume Nehtihur was), and would have conversed with the kings and philosophers of the Persian court in Aramaic. Was there a meeting of minds, on the one side expressing the mobile kaleidoscopic universe of Egyptian mythology (and thereby explaining it in terms that outsiders would understand, something that Egyptian texts never do), and on the other side the revelations of Zoroastrianism?

Absorbing the Greeks

Of Udjahor-resenet's home city of Sais, the centre and burial place of the kings of the 26th Dynasty and the site of a major temple, of the goddess Neith, very little indeed has survived.[42] At a distance of 16 kilometres (10 miles) to the west lies the archaeological site that, since the late nineteenth century, has been known as Naukratis. It was then a large mound in which lay buried the remains of a major town, our knowledge of which is still a fundamental reference point for the history and culture of Egypt at this time. In the 1880s, during travels in the Nile delta, Flinders Petrie came across it at the moment that a local project was under way to dig the site out completely as a source of cheap fertilizer. Gaining an official permit to conduct archaeological explorations, and as the site disappeared before his eyes, Petrie mapped the lines of such walls as he could distinguish amidst the damp, salt-encrusted chaos, and supplemented his investigation with limited diggings of his own.[43] His rescued plan (and the site barely exists any more) suggests a town of medium size composed largely of houses with the familiar thick rectangular blocky foundations probably rising for some height and creating a street plan which, whilst not a grid, consisted of straight lengths at somewhat varying angles (Figure 129). In this respect it was probably fairly typical of Egyptian towns of the time. Like other such places there is no trace of an enclosing wall. Despite its seeming Egyptianness in layout, however, Petrie was able to identify without difficulty that a number of enclosures had contained Greek temples, though only fragments of their stone architecture survived. Clear identifications for some came from votive Greek pots inscribed with Greek dedications. They point to temples for the goddesses Aphrodite and Hera, for Apollo and for the Dioscuri (the twin gods Castor and Pollux). A mass of Greek pottery from the excavations has been intensively studied, both for the range of its dates (back as far as 620 BC, equivalent in Egypt to the early 26th Dynasty) and for knowledge of from where it had been imported (Corinth, Sparta, Rhodes, Chios, Samos, Lesbos and Athens itself). At the same time, many Egyptian-style artefacts, including pottery, were present and even manufactured on the spot. And although even by Petrie's day not much of it survived, the city acquired, after the conquest of Egypt by Alexander the Great, a temple to the Egyptian god Amun. This had been constructed on a grand scale, and was the one part of Naukratis which had been surrounded with a massive wall. Also within the enclosure was a particularly large example of blocky brick foundations that might have been for a stronghold or fortified store.

On its own, the archaeological evidence would probably be easily sufficient to point to the presence of a Greek immigrant population, even though the city plan and most of its buildings were not 'Classical' in the accepted sense. We might draw a comparison with the archaeological evidence for a Palestinian presence in the eastern delta (especially at Tell el-Dab'a/Avaris) in the Second Intermediate Period. But what gives to Naukratis an added significance is that it provides an archaeological anchor for the most extensive written commentary on the affairs of Egypt at this time, lengthy portions of the *History* of the Greek historian Herodotus of Halicarnassos, who lived between the approximate dates of 490 and 425 BC and visited Egypt, journeying as far south as Elephantine.

Herodotus sought as much to entertain as to inform. As one who publicized his own work by reading extracts aloud, from the steps of the temple of Zeus at Olympia at the height of the panhellenic games, colourful anecdote and ripe story were important ingredients, and especially those chosen to entertain or flatter his countrymen. In the history of the objective study of human society he represents a milestone (there is absolutely nothing like his narrative from ancient Egypt before his day). Yet we have come a long way since then, and have developed altogether more demanding expectations in the pursuit of knowledge. Much of what he wrote now reads like dinner-table stories and newspaper gossip. But since there is often no other source for what he has to say, the modern reader should hold his statements in that same delicious and ironically suspended (so one

NAUKRATIS

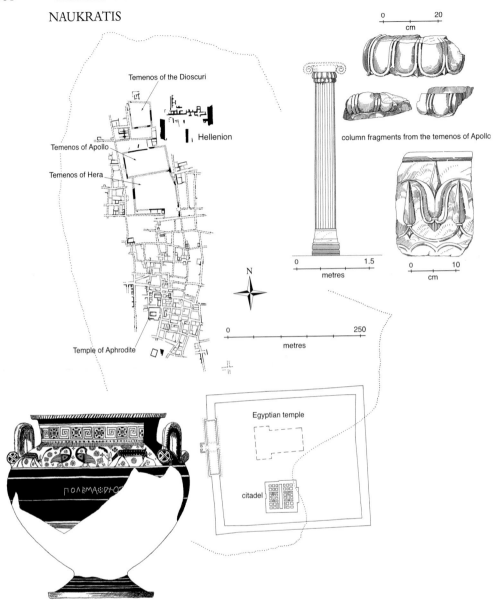

Figure 129 Naukratis. In part from the appalling conditions in which Petrie worked it is hard to be sure to which part of its history his city plan belongs. Did it keep its plan for several centuries? The large enclosure in the south can now be judged to have been a very late addition, a monumental temple complete with large enclosure built probably by the early Ptolemies and dedicated to the Egyptian god Amun. It was presumably fully in Egyptian style. It contains its own citadel. Main plan after W.M.F. Petrie, *Naukratis* I, London, 1886, Pls XLI–XLIII, with an addition (north-east corner) from D.G. Hogarth, H.L. Lorimer and C.C. Edgar, *JHS* 25 (1905), 113, Fig. 1. The Classical architectural fragments (*top right*) and the vase dedicated to Apollo by Polemarchos (*bottom left*) are reproduced from Petrie, op. cit., Pls III, IV.

hopes) category as: 'It must be true I read it in the tabloids'.[44] In his anecdotes rulers everywhere, in Egypt, in Greece, in Persia, transcend their cultures and act out their convoluted personal stories with a cheerful superficiality of motive: greed, lust, wronged honour. It is a very different voice from that of the Egyptian scribal tradition which otherwise supplies our historical sources, and which, in formal solemn language, maintained respect for traditional cultural forms, especially those surrounding divine kingship.

Herodotus' *History* contains by far the earliest eyewitness account of life in ancient Egypt written by an outsider for the benefit of his own people and should be treasured for that. He had something to say about Naukratis. He states that King Amasis (of the Saite 26th Dynasty, 570–526 BC) had given Naukratis as a favour to the Greeks 'as a commercial headquarters for any who wished to settle in the country', and went on to mention Greek temples built by the joint efforts of various Greek city-states, more or less the very ones discovered by Petrie. Naukratis is actually one of a large number of places around the eastern and central Mediterranean where, from a convergence of archaeology and ancient written (usually Greek) testimony, we can with reasonable certainty conclude that substantial Greek communities established themselves in the eighth and seventh centuries BC, often as colonies amongst less developed societies. It is the only site in Egypt, however, where the evidence is so clear. Quantities of imported Greek pottery have been excavated at other sites (e.g. Tell Defenna/Daphnae in the far north-east delta, and at Memphis), but on its own pottery is no evidence for the identity of those who used it, pottery being a common object of trade.

Herodotus told his readers and listeners of more extensive Greek involvement in Egypt, not as merchants or colonists, but as soldiers. It began in a suitably legendary way, when bronze-armoured 'sea-raiders from Ionia and Caria were forced by bad weather to land on the Egyptian coast'. Seen by some Egyptians as an answer to a prophecy they helped Psammetichus of Sais become king of Egypt (as first king of the 26th Dynasty) and were rewarded with grants of land. 'They were the first foreigners to live in Egypt, and after their original settlement there, the Greeks began regular intercourse with the Egyptians, so that we have accurate knowledge of Egyptian history from the time of Psammetichus onward.' (It was a nice conceit, the thought that they, the Greeks, had 'discovered' Egypt.)[45] In fact, they were probably part of a much older tradition of sea raiding from the west and north which targeted the rich lands of the eastern Mediterranean.[46]

Later, so he tells us, Greek soldiers played a major role in a civil war between two contenders for the throne, Apries and Amasis. The latter had a force of 30,000 Ionians and Carians who 'gave a good account of themselves but were greatly outnumbered and defeated'. Despite this, the victor, Amasis, 'favoured the Greeks and granted them a number of privileges, of which the chief was the gift of Naukratis' described above. Amasis relocated the descendants of the original soldiers from their lands in the delta to Memphis so that they could 'protect him from his own people', he married a Greek woman from the Libyan coastal colony of Cyrene, and participated in the same kind of courteous long-distance gift-giving so familiar from the world of the Amarna Letters, except that now the recipients were Greeks rather than Near Eastern rulers:

> Amasis further showed his goodwill to Greece by sending presents to be dedicated in Greek temples; to Cyrene he sent a gold-plated statue of Athene and a painting of himself; to the temple of Athene at Lindos [Rhodes], two statues in stone

and a remarkable linen corslet; and to the goddess Hera in Samos two likenesses of himself, in wood, which until my own time stood behind the doors in the great temple.[47]

In his description of a similar corslet – 'of linen, embroidered with gold thread and "tree-wool" [silk or cotton?], [which] had a number of figures of animals woven into the fabric' – which Amasis sent to Sparta we have another example of the costly garments which also featured in the gift-exchanges of the Amarna Letters.[48] When the temple at Delphi burnt down 'and the Delphians went round from city to city asking for contributions, Egypt was by no means least in giving assistance. Amasis gave them a thousand talents of alum, and the Greeks who had settled in Egypt, twenty *minae*'.[49]

Armies of occupation

Herodotus gives a brief analysis of the composition of Egyptian society, as he saw it. 'The Egyptians are divided into seven classes named after their occupations: priests, warriors, cowherds, swineherds, tradesmen, interpreters, and pilots.'[50] Other and later Classical authors who categorized Egyptian society agreed on the priests and the warriors but differed with the rest, presumably because the subdivisions of the mass of the people were more opaque. He has much to say on the warrior-class (*machimoi*): how they formed two separate groups and were spread in lesser groups through the districts of the country; and how they had certain privileges (shared with the priests), namely grants of land held free of tax, and an entitlement to food rations. He gives a total for both warrior groups of 410,000. As a factual statement it would amount to one tenth of Egypt's estimated total population, but perhaps he was trying to say simply 'a great many'.

A dispersed army, settled with land in the provinces, recruited in part from foreigners, and prominent in people's perception of society is just what we find when we look back to Ramesside Egypt. In the testimony preserved on Papyrus Harris I, Rameses III is made to give an address to his people, categorized as 'the dignitaries, the leaders of the land, the infantry, chariotry, Sherden, ordinary troops, and every citizen of the land of Egypt'. He talks of his reorganization of society into 'numerous groups: butlers of the palace, great chiefs, infantry and chariotry, Sherden and Kehek, and retainers'. Not even the priests are singled out. They and the herdsmen and craftsmen are subsumed into a more general category.[51]

What role did these warriors or soldiers have within Egypt? It is the fate of many current societies to live under the control of ubiquitous and very visible armed force, a situation in which the distinction between 'police' and 'army of occupation' becomes academic. Keeping local order with whatever degree of force is needed merges with the defence of the realm against outside enemies. It is an unpleasant reality that people learn to live with. Is that what we have here, a society living under a veritable army of occupation, answerable to a king who had been, since the fall of the 18th Dynasty, a military man and, after the end of the New Kingdom, was often of foreign origin? If, none the less, we were to line up all the numerous non-royal statues of the first millennium BC – and hundreds of them have survived – we would not see a parade of generals. A few would have a military title (such as an army commander Psamtek from Sais[52]), but most would identify themselves as priests or holders of what appear to be civil titles. Such a line of statues would represent Egypt's governing class. Each one's career varied somewhat, its progress marked by the addition of yet another office and its stipend, and so their titles represent endless permutations of a broad set, some of them revivals of ancient titles created during the Old Kingdom. One will look in vain for clear groupings and subdivisions. Udjahor-resenet, it will be remembered, whilst a physician and senior priest under the Persian kings, had also been a commander of the navy under the previous 26th Dynasty, of Egyptian kings. Buried within a long string of priestly titles on the statue of Horkheb of the 22nd Dynasty is the fact that he also held the office of 'commander of the army of the estate of Amun'.[53] The control of army units by the civil governing class was a tradition reaching back to the Old Kingdom. The prestige of chariotry seems to have given career officers a more prominent role in the New Kingdom (and one such family became the kings of the 19th Dynasty), but that trend did not advance further. This is the governing class whose base and probable location of residence was the urban citadel that we see as the temple enclosure.

The bag of letters of the Persian governor Arsham mentioned above illustrates the system in action. Three of Arsham's 'officers' are Egyptians and they are clearly administrators, doubtless the kind of persons who would commission statues of themselves for the local temple, complete with sets of normal Egyptian titles which would most likely tell us that they were 'priests'. The military detachments with their commanders are under their overall charge, to be used as occasion demanded. The destruction of the temple of Yehu at Elephantine was done by Egyptian soldiers at the instigation of the priests of Khnum. Outside the governing class, however, the tradition of making permanent hieroglyphic memorials was dead. The Late Period has not left us the equivalents of the crude Gebelein tombstones of Nubian soldiers from the First Intermediate Period (Figure 6, *right*, p. 27). The men who now inspected the weapons, shouted the orders and perhaps meted out the beatings to people who became a nuisance were no longer interested in memorializing themselves, and for many of them Egyptian would not have been their first language. Yet the statement of Herodotus, which is in line with late New Kingdom evidence, implies that they were a numerous and prominent part of Egyptian society. Were they there just to keep order and defend the ruler's interests or did they also offer a pool of labour readily available for other tasks, especially the building work on all of those temple citadels that dotted the flat alluvial plains? For a section of society that contemporaries saw as important it is surprising how little we know of them. Perhaps more than ever, our picture of Egypt is as seen through the governing class, who enhanced their position by keeping to a style which everyone else had abandoned. In Chapter 3 (p. 135) I made the claim that, 'for about a third of its history, Pharaonic Egypt was a country of two cultures'. Perhaps this is an over-bold assessment in terms of scale. But if one adds to the picture the Late Period, it looks more like an understatement both in scale and duration.

In touch with the past

In a world of mixed identities, the past (as recalled and imagined) is especially important as an anchor. For the Greeks a key component was knowing one's city and its history. If you lived at Naukratis you knew whether you were an Ionian from Chios or a Dorian from

Halicarnassos, and also that the largest of the temples, the Hellenion, belonged to you and not to someone from Samos, who would have a separate temple at Naukratis, sacred to Hera. The Aramaean-Jewish colony at Elephantine recognized at least a spiritual home in Jerusalem. For Egyptians of the Late Period the past was more locally situated and very visible. They, too, put much emphasis upon local city and local god. Udjahor-resenet illustrates this in respect of his home city of Sais. The flow of business and the minor turbulences of family affairs were often conducted in the shadows (real and metaphorical) of the local temple, which remained the foundation of local identity, preserving a link with a distinctive past.

The temple of Hibis at the Kharga Oasis is probably representative of a renewed enthusiasm by the governing class to connect more closely with the traditional past, something that was widespread through Egypt from the 25th Dynasty onwards. It maintained its appeal for a remarkably long time, passing through a further phase of renewal that began in the 30th Dynasty and reached its peak under the Ptolemies. Some Egyptians sought to refresh their understanding of their own culture by studying and copying old forms, often of the Old Kingdom. A straightforward example is a sandstone stela, 3 metres high, which once stood in or near the temple of Ptah at Memphis. It bears the name of King Amasis of the 26th Dynasty (570–526 BC), and is a decree of an age-old type that protected the lands and other revenues of the temple.[54] More particularly it is based on a standard format of the Old Kingdom and employs the vocabulary and grammar of that far-off time (though with numerous places where Middle or New Kingdom writings have been used instead, creating a sense of inconsistency in the modern mind which the Egyptian scribes evidently did not appreciate). For a second example, involving artists, we can turn to the case of a high official called Ibi. In the seventh century BC (reign of Psammetichus I of the 26th Dynasty) he commissioned the decoration of his tomb at Thebes. He had discovered that a man of the same name had made a tomb long before (sixteen centuries, in fact), at the end of the Old Kingdom, in the necropolis of Deir el-Gebrawi in Middle Egypt (see map, Figure 116, p. 339). Ibi must then have sent an artist to copy some of the themes, many of them scenes of craftsmen at work. These reappear in the later Ibi's tomb, though worked into fresh compositions rather than as precise copies (Figure 130).[55] A similar case from the royal sphere, though from more than a generation before, concerns a royal scene of victory over Libyans.[56] It occurs on the southern outer wall of a temple built by the 25th Dynasty king Taharka (690–664 BC) at Kawa in the Sudan. Depicted as a sphinx, he tramples his enemies. A group of Libyans stands to one side, beseeching mercy, their names recorded in hieroglyphs. Below them are shown their flocks. Exactly the same names occur in a similar (but not wholly identical) scene of Libyan conquest carved on the wall of the pyramid temple of Pepi II at Sakkara from sixteen hundred years before. Even this, however, is not the original. It is in turn based on a scene in the pyramid temple of Sahura, older by three further centuries. Whether this is the original or was itself based on a yet earlier predecessor we cannot tell. The Kawa scene is not an exact copy of either, nor is Pepi II's an exact copy of Sahura's. It looks as though artists maintained collections of copies of bits of scene that interested them. This would have helped to keep them true to the proper style of their country's art. When composing new scenes they turned to these for inspiration or for a telling detail, using the knowledge so gained but spurning to reproduce them exactly.

Given the Egyptians' general preference for maintaining cultural traditions across the

Tomb of Ibi at Deir el-Gebrawi (*c.* 2200 BC)

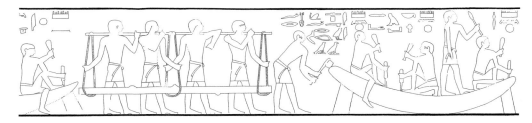

Tomb of Ibi at Western Thebes (*c.* 630 BC)

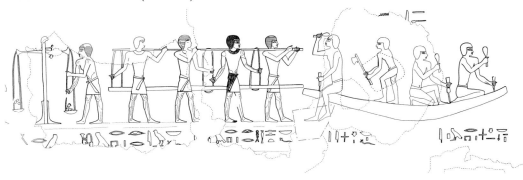

Figure 130   Deference to the past: tombs of the two men Ibi. *Above.* Scene in the tomb of Ibi, 6th Dynasty (twenty-second century BC), at Deir el-Gebrawi. *Below.* Scene in the tomb of Ibi, 26th Dynasty (seventh century BC), at Thebes. The same elements reappear but not as exact copies. After N. de G. Davies, *The rock tombs of Deir el-Gebrâwi* I, London, 1902, Pls XIII–XVI; K. Kuhlmann and W. Schenkel, *Das Grab des Ibi; Theben Nr. 36*, Mainz, 1983, Taf. 30.

centuries, the potential impact of going back to the past in this way must have been rather limited. The examples represent details in compositions that were traditional in any case. They seem to be, however, manifestations of a more profound and widely held interest in moving closer to the past, or at least to a past which was imagined to have existed.

Sacred animals

Some of the most visited temples in Egypt today were built after the conquest of Egypt by Alexander the Great in 332 BC, in the time of his Greek-speaking successors, the dynasty of fifteen kings each called Ptolemy. Those temples are dedicated to quintessentially ancient Egyptian deities: Horus at Edfu, Hathor at Dendera, Sebek and Horus at Kom Ombo, Khnum at Esna. Each of these deities can be identified in texts more than two thousand years earlier, and Horus at least on carvings from the end of the Predynastic Period (e.g. Figure 28.2, p. 85). They all had one thing in common. Their images were based upon animals: a falcon for Horus, a cow for Hathor, a crocodile for Sebek and a ram for Khnum. To varying degrees these images had been humanized, to the extent that at Dendera Hathor's cow image was represented only by cow's ears on a human female face, whilst at Kom Ombo Horus appears in a distinct separate form, Horwer ('Horus the Elder', the Greek form being Haroeris), wholly human.

Why certain animals were sacred provokes modern answers which are guesses at the obvious: the crocodile (Sebek) because of its size and ferocious attacking habits, the ram (Khnum, a creator god) because of its procreative power, the jackal (Anubis associated with the dead and embalming) because cemeteries are likely to have been a favourite haunt, and so on. The species of scarab beetle which lays its eggs in large balls of muddy dung was taken as a metaphor of creation (and also of how the ball of the sun might travel across the sky) and became a god whose name, Kheprer, is clearly derived from the verb *kheper*, 'to come into existence'. Its name seems to be its epithet. The historical process by which certain animals became divine must actually owe much to accidents of local tradition. This becomes apparent when one considers those animals that did *not* become sacred. Take the owl, for instance. It was prominent as a hieroglyph and appears on a Predynastic 'slate' palette as if a naming element for a place (Figure 33, p. 96). In other cultures (for example, that of ancient Athens where it was the bird of the goddess Athene) the owl has been seen as having magical properties. Yet in Egypt there was no owl god or goddess, owls had no special place in myth, and do not appear amongst the species of the early votive deposits described in Chapter 3. The hare, easily taken as a symbol of swiftness, in Egypt was used to write the important verb 'to be'. It is easy to imagine how it could have become a god of continuing existence, but nothing of the kind developed, although the fifteenth province of Upper Egypt was called the 'hare nome'. The hedgehog early entered the list of creatures that had special properties. Its image could ward off dangers on boats, for example (note the hedgehog-boat figurines, Figures 40.1, 44.2, pp. 119, 127). It failed, however, to progress to the full status of a divinity.[57] Further down the scale, a range of other creatures were seen as possessing special properties and so featured in healing prescriptions in medical texts but remained within that 'folk' domain. One should imagine the Egyptian pantheon as the outcome of a long-running process of selection through innumerable personal acts and occasional more weighty decisions that together favoured one candidate for inclusion in the canon of supported deities over many others. If minor circumstances at different times and places had been different, the Egyptian pantheon would itself have had a different composition, though the nature of the underlying religious system would probably have been the same.

Until the end of the New Kingdom hardly any of the animal deities were represented on earth, as far as we can tell, by individual living creatures held to be divine in themselves. There was no line of sacred falcons, rams, and so on. We know of two exceptions, both of them bulls, the Apis bull of Memphis, and the Mnevis bull of Heliopolis. The former is first recorded in the 1st Dynasty.[58] Yet despite this antiquity the burial of sacred Apis bulls on the Sakkara plateau (in a complex known as the Serapeum) seems to have begun only in the 18th Dynasty, but then continued in a more or less unbroken line for thirteen centuries, between the reigns of Amenhetep III and Ptolemy VIII (1390–116 BC). To begin with, each bull was buried in a separate tomb, the burial chamber reached by a short ramp cut into the rock and having a small chapel above ground. In the reign of Rameses II a common catacomb was started that could be extended with new chambers as time passed, the whole served by a single chapel. A second catacomb on a grander scale was begun in the 26th Dynasty and was thereafter maintained until the end of the cult, becoming another record of continuity in the face of political change. Still to be seen are the huge granite sarcophagi of sacred Apis bulls which died in the reigns of Amasis of the 26th Dynasty, of the Persian king Cambyses, and of Khababash, apparently an Egyptian who for a time gained control of at least part of the country during the second period of Persian rule. Above ground a major temple complex developed reached by an avenue of sphinxes stretching across the Sakkara plateau and down to the floodplain.[59]

Initially the evidence we have concerns royal patronage rather than national popularity. This is reflected throughout the later history of other animal cults in their close links with the theology of kingship and with the cult of the king. Around the Apis cult developed a prestigious and well-staffed institution whose history is, to some extent, reflected in stelae of personal commemoration discovered inside the Serapeum. If we consult the standard listing of them from the main discovery they are sparse in the three centuries of the later New Kingdom (the total is fourteen), increase to 135 in the 360 years of the Third Intermediate Period, peak at 330 in the 380 years of the Late Period, and drop to a mere ten under the Ptolemies.[60] The period of Persian rule straddles the peak and many are specifically dated to that era. The majority of people commemorating themselves are priests and priestesses, but high officials with more secular offices appear, too, thus members of the same governing class discussed earlier.

Success bred diversification, and another tradition was invented, apparently in the 26th Dynasty, namely, burials with public cult for the mothers of the Apis bulls (identified with the goddess Isis), in a separate section of Sakkara called the Iseum.[61] The Apis bull and its mother were, in their lifetimes, exclusively divine. No mass burial of common cattle herds developed at Sakkara (although cattle were interred at other sites – e.g. El-Khawalid and Tuna el-Gebel in Middle Egypt, Kom el-Hisn and Kom el-Adami in the delta – where there is no evidence that a named sacred bull or cow was worshipped). None the less, other parts of Sakkara saw the development of mass burials of mummified smaller animals, sometimes in extensive catacombs. Some (dogs, cats, ibises, baboons and falcons) were historically associated with specific deities, though these lacked, as far as our knowledge goes, earlier associations with Memphis and Sakkara. Cult centres above ground developed for some of them: for Isis, for Anubis, for Bastet, for Thoth. For other species (gazelle, antelope, shrews) it is hard to find a divine counterpart. At Sakkara the limited dating evidence suggests that these catacombs developed in the 30th Dynasty and Ptolemaic Period, although the evidence from the site of Tuna el-Gebel (see below) suggests that there such faunal enrichment was already taking place in the 26th.

Animal cemeteries of diverse species are a distinctive late feature of Egyptian society. They were numerous. The standard work of reference catalogues 120 different localities, from Mediq in Lower Nubia to Alexandria, some of them embracing several separate catacombs or other places of burial, sometimes re-used tombs from earlier periods (Figure 131).[62] There must have been many more, since some of the finds are of modest collections of bones not associated with a known cult centre and probably therefore the result of piety at village level. The cemeteries as a whole cover a period of many centuries, and some of them originally contained truly vast numbers of individual burials, as illustrated by the startling case of 'a single shipment of cat remains, weighing about nineteen tons and thought to have contained some 180,000 mummified cats, which was sent to England to be processed to make fertilizer towards the end of the [nineteenth] century'.[63] It is important to seek variations in practice over time and from place to place. These cemeteries have, however, suffered from robbery, from inattentive excavation and from

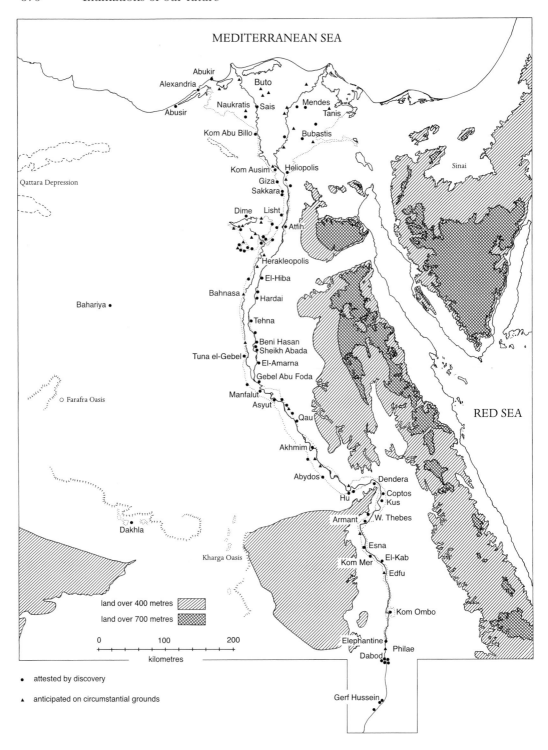

MEDITERRANEAN SEA

Abukir

Alexandria   Buto

Abusir   Naukratis   Sais   Mendes
                                           Tanis

Kom Abu Billo   Bubastis

Sinai

Qattara Depression

Kom Ausim   Heliopolis
            Giza
            Sakkara

Dime   Lisht
               Atfih

Herakleopolis

Bahariya   Bahnasa   El-Hiba
                            Hardai

                  Tehna

                  Beni Hasan
                  Sheikh Abada
Tuna el-Gebel   El-Amarna
                  Gebel Abu Foda

Farafra Oasis   Manfalut
                  Asyut
                       Qau

                  Akhmim

Dakhla

Abydos   Dendera
                       Coptos
Kharga Oasis   Hu   Kus

            Armant   W. Thebes

                  Esna
            Kom Mer   El-Kab
                      Edfu

RED SEA

land over 400 metres

land over 700 metres   Kom Ombo

0   100   200

kilometres   Elephantine   Philae
                     Dabod

•   attested by discovery

▲   anticipated on circumstantial grounds

                     Gerf Hussein

a general neglect to a very great extent. It is particularly difficult to give dates to many of the sites and to their individual parts other than within very broad limits. Only in relatively recent years have surviving portions at some places started to be the subject of detailed multi-disciplinary research.

Separate location is one of their characteristics. Given the practice that had developed, albeit on a limited scale, of siting the tombs of the royal family and of other selected women and men inside the precincts of temples/urban citadels the option must have been there to develop a sacred animal necropolis in another portion of the enclosures. Although there are a few exceptions (e.g. Karnak) this was not normally the case (for example, there appears not to have been an animal cemetery in the Medinet Habu enclosure).[64] Two explanations come to mind. One is that the congested interiors of most enclosures would not have offered sufficient space; the other is perhaps the popularity of the cults, drawing in crowds of ordinary people. Instead most animal cemeteries had their own temples, which sometimes accommodated a cult of the king, but laid claim to their own quite separate stretches of ground. In the river valley this seems almost always to have been at the edge of the desert. In the delta the desert was mostly far away, so as with cemeteries for humans the cemeteries for animals and the associated cult buildings lay in areas of uncultivated ground that formed part of the broad zone of urban use.

The factors at work in the selection of which animals were buried and where, in so far as we can detect them, provide an insight into the Egyptian mind. In part we can see a logical scheme based on ancient cult geography where there is a strong likelihood and sometimes clear written statement that high-level official initiative was responsible. These are cases such as the rams of Khnum at Elephantine, the cats of Bastet at Bubastis, dogs at Cynopolis, lions at Leontopolis, crocodiles of Sebek at Kom Ombo and the Fayum. But local practice also seems to have responded strongly to local and presumably more popular preferences. This was both geographically and faunally eclectic. Mummified cats were buried not only at Bubastis, but at over twenty other sites stretching as far south as Armant. Conversely, some animal deities were largely if not wholly excluded. The hippopotamus, representative of Taweret, a protectress of childbirth, was one. There seems to have been no line of sacred frogs, symbol of the goddess of magic Hekate, although frogs have occasionally been reported from animal cemeteries.[65] Faunal variety is well illustrated at Tuna el-Gebel, the desert-edge cemetery for the city of Hermopolis, centre of the cult of the god Thoth, to whom the ibis and the baboon were sacred. Selected baboons were given individual names, were kept in a special pen at the temple of Osiris-Baboon, and were eventually mummified and buried in the catacombs, having been properly deified through having the ritual of the 'opening of the mouth' performed over them. There is as yet no trace at Tuna of a New Kingdom phase (although at the temple of Thoth in Hermopolis a pair of colossal baboon statues in quartzite were carved and erected in the reign of Amenhetep III). The earliest evidence comes from the 26th Dynasty, with the cutting of underground galleries in the soft desert strata for the burial

Figure 131 Distribution map of animal cemeteries. The concentration in the Fayum reflects the prosperity of the area in Ptolemaic and Roman Periods and illustrates the popularity of animal cults amongst these communities. The delta is probably under-represented by actual finds, on account of the more rapid destruction of ancient sites in recent times. After D. Kessler, *Die Heiligen Tiere und der König*, Teil I, Wiesbaden, 1989, Abb. 1.

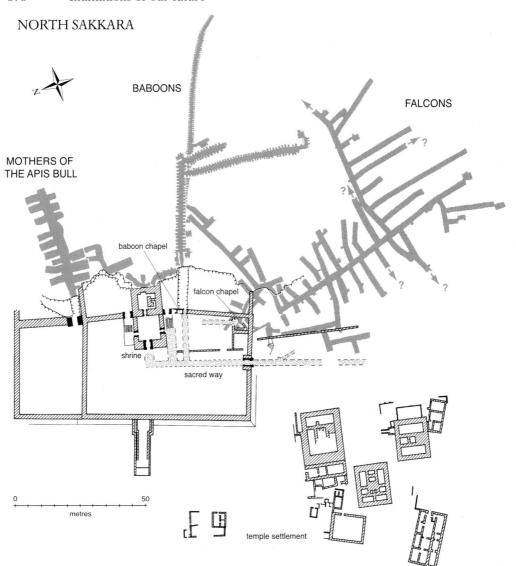

NORTH SAKKARA

BABOONS

FALCONS

MOTHERS OF
THE APIS BULL

baboon chapel

falcon chapel

shrine

sacred way

0   50

metres

temple settlement

Figure 132 Sacred Animal Necropolis at North Sakkara. After H.S. Smith, *A visit to ancient Egypt; life at Memphis and Saqqara (c. 500–30 BC)*, Warminster, 1974, 40, Fig. 9; 33, Fig. 7; 44, Fig. 10; G.T. Martin, *The Sacred Animal Necropolis at North Saqqâra; the southern dependencies of the main temple complex*, London, 1981, Pl. 1A; E.A. Hastings, *The sculpture from The Sacred Animal Necropolis at North Saqqâra 1964–76*, London, 1997, xxv, Plan 2.

of ibises in some numbers. This was the time when the large Apis galleries at Sakkara were begun (see Figure 132).

Baboons and ibises, however, were only the iconic leaders in the field at Tuna el-Gebel. Identifications embrace a 'wide variety of buried sacred birds and animals, ranging from ibises and 37 other different kinds of birds, to baboons, other monkeys, cats, dogs, crocodiles, shrews, snakes, rats and even pigs'. In the case of the ibises, after death, either naturally or through sacrifice, 'even the tiniest remains of these sacred animals were collected, including parts of eggs, nest material or single feathers'. Carcasses had apparently been buried first for a natural defleshing process to clean the bones.[66]

The inclusion of a broader range of species than is to be expected from our modern reading of the zoological identifications of the ancient cult animals cannot realistically be put down to carelessness or lack of scruple on the part of those who, at the time, ran the cult centres. It is too pervasive. A case where going beyond taxonomic exactitude is obviously deliberate is provided by 'baboons'. These were animals that were not indigenous to ancient Egypt in historic times. Tuna el-Gebel is not the only site where other monkeys supplement them. A study of a group of 169 individuals from 'baboon' galleries at Sakkara has shown that whilst the majority were, indeed, baboons (though of the 'olive' or 'Anubis' kind not the traditional 'sacred' hamadryas type), a significant minority (twenty-one) were macaques and two were guenons. Macaques, in being tail-less, are visibly distinct from baboons. They also have a different habitat, north-west Africa, and it has been suggested that their presence at Sakkara is a result of a fairly short-lived export trade from Carthage to Egypt in the Ptolemaic Period. This might have helped to supplement an insufficient supply of the hamadryas baboons.[67] Was this inexactitude in selecting sacred animals a late degradation of an earlier more discriminating practice? Seemingly not. At Tuna el-Gebel a single Saite or Persian linen bundle, thus one from a relatively early phase, 'could contain a wide variety of parts of sacred animals, including ibis bones, ranging from a single broken fragment to a more complete skeleton mixed with a few bones of other fauna (falcons, pelicans, cats, dogs, shrews, fishes), bird eggs, single feathers and even single human bones'.[68]

Objects that people deem to be suitable and worthy for religious donation vary enormously in their properties and, viewed across time and cultural boundaries, are quite unpredictable. For the formal temple cult of ancient Egypt secular commodities served very well: bread, beer, tracts of land, bronze vessels, and so on. The donor's action and the formal words that went with it were sufficient, so it seems, to put the gift or offering into the category of something special. But phases come, and unpredictably so, when the ordinary is not enough. What is brought into the devotional sphere then has to possess an intrinsic character that is out of the ordinary. In the case of the votive material from the early shrines dealt with in Chapter 3, that special character came from the shape, often a figurine or sometimes an oddly shaped stone. With the animal cemeteries we are looking at a category whose special character was that it had formerly been alive and had also belonged to a creature thought to possess some special property. Although the usage was somewhat different, a similar aura evidently surrounded the fragments of human saints gathered and venerated as relics in Christendom from the early centuries AD onwards.

It is tempting to see the animal cults of ancient Egypt as a precursor to modern environmental respect. The case of cats is a good illustration of how dubious this view is. Although they famously appear in tomb pictures of household scenes, cats seem to have been regarded not as endearing pets but as essentially hunting animals, and members of a feline group whose cruel power required to be placated. The tale of the sun-god Ra using the feline goddess Sekhmet as his instrument of vengeance against mankind captures this view. Subsequent to the New Kingdom the cult of the goddess Bastet, whose form was that of a female cat, attracted greater attention. Close examination of some mummified specimens has revealed that they died through strangulation or having their necks broken, and that they were sometimes little more than kittens. The huge numbers buried at some places clearly show that they were bred on something like an industrial scale simply for early killing.[69] At Bubastis itself they were partially cremated, and as early as the Third Intermediate Period the burnt remains of cat bones were being sealed in small bronze caskets bearing an image of a cat.

The ancient written evidence concerning animal cults not surprisingly belongs primarily to their organization at an official level, and illustrates a degree of regional if not national co-ordination. It tells us, for example, that individual ibises, mummified and interred in sarcophagi or pots, were sent to Hermopolis/Tuna el-Gebel from distant places, including Elephantine and Ptolemais (in the Fayum). The principal study of this material has consequently drawn the conclusion that the animal cults of the last five centuries BC were primarily official in their inspiration and support, and essentially an aspect of the cult of the (frequently largely absent) ruler.[70] The colossal numbers of buried specimens at some places, however, have for others conjured up a picture of crowds of pilgrims otherwise unconnected with the priesthood visiting the holy sites and either purchasing on the spot or bringing with them animal mummies to add to quantities that, in time, would run into millions.[71] The idea of popular participation is supported by the existence of small provincial cemeteries, lacking traces of an adjacent shrine, which must have belonged to local villages which presumably lay outside the official sphere altogether.[72] In the case of the larger centres at least, visitors sought in return to benefit from a kind of personal guidance service. One path of guidance was through 'incubation', by sleeping in a designated place in the hopes of receiving dreams that a dream-interpreter would unravel. Or the gods would communicate 'utterances' which similarly required interpretation. Something in the behaviour of baboons – their chattering? – was one source, as we know from a record of a baboon imported to Sakkara for the purpose of giving oracles.[73]

One way of explaining the intensity of animal cults is to regard them as an assertion by Egyptians of the distinctiveness of their culture in an increasingly pluralist world. Perhaps in the end it was, since it does seem to have been a return to what the Egyptians seem to have thought (not necessarily correctly) were the roots of their religion. But one must be careful not to draw a battle-line and to place animal cults and an Egyptian nationalism on one side and foreign culture and rulers on the other. The late animal cults were intimately bound up with the cult of the ruler, and were maintained throughout the country as a major expenditure of both the state and the local community. Royal patronage remained strong whether or not the ruling house came from within Egypt or was the result of conquest from outside. This is evident at the Serapeum, an extension of the capital Memphis, where official patronage seems to have peaked under Persian rule. The chief priest of one of the leading centres of animal cults, Petosiris of Hermopolis, living at the time of the conquest of Alexander the Great, had the walls of the outer hall of his handsome tomb chapel at Tuna el-Gebel, which was built as a scaled-down replica of a temple, decorated with scenes of life where the subject matter was traditional but the dress and method of portraying the human figures was Greek.[74] This runs contrary to the notion that cultural form was a nationalist statement. Even at Naukratis itself there is some evidence for animal burials.[75] Religious belief is subject to the same unpredictable nonlinear processes of development amongst the myriad acts and thoughts of a people – here probably hundreds of thousands of them – as produce other kinds of change in society, and the more strongly outlined actions that make history. The late animal cults were not caused by any one historical circumstance but, once tentatively started (when and where we do not know), were more successful than existing ways of expressing piety, and simply 'caught on'.

They go to the heart of how we evaluate the last phase of ancient Egyptian culture. They help to form the mood, if you like, in which we bid farewell to Egypt of the Pharaohs. There are two broad approaches to religion. One judges, the other observes. The former sees the history of religion as a movement towards enlightenment of a certain kind, to be defined by rationality or perhaps by a belief in monotheism. Late Period religion and especially the animal cults score badly on this scale. The vehicle of progress towards a spirituality more easily recognizable in the west, which people like to discern in the New Kingdom, appears to have gone into reverse, attracting unfavourable modern judgements on the animal cults in which the word 'superstition' often occurs. This is not simply a case of modern evaluation alienated from its ancient context. A double layer of disapproval is involved. Eventually the whole nature of indigenous Egyptian religion came under assault from the Christian church in Egypt. 'Pagans' were persecuted and their holy places destroyed, the animal cemeteries and their temples included.

By contrast, modern westernized views of living religions which lie outside the great 'faiths', including those of African societies which have not converted to Islam or Christianity, have generally grown more tolerant and even sympathetic. Such indigenous religions are now more likely to be accepted as valid experience, to be observed and interpreted in an open-minded spirit of exploration, rather than vilified or ridiculed. The late animal cults of Egypt have barely benefited from this enlightenment. Yet why should they not?

Bidding farewell

There is no intrinsic reason why the religion and language of ancient Egypt, which lay at the heart of ancient Egyptianness, should not have survived to the present day, although had this happened it is inevitable that they would both have changed in the process. Indeed, change was well under way in religious belief in the last centuries of ancient Egyptian culture. The example I have chosen to illustrate this starts at the temple of Seti I at Abydos, built around 1250 BC. It housed a major shrine to Osiris and others to Amun-Ra, Seti I himself, Ptah, Ra-Horakhty, Isis, Horus, Nefertem and Ptah-seker. Huge in scale, labyrinthine in plan, decorated according to outstanding levels of craftsmanship (see Figure 18, p. 63), it seems to have remained unaltered yet still functioning into the third century AD. It contains several hundred graffiti in Greek, Cypriote, Carian, Phoenician and Aramaic, starting in the sixth century BC. The modern visitor to the temple enters it from the original front courtyards but, to judge from the distribution of the graffiti, by that time one walked around to the back of the temple, perhaps because the original front had become buried in sand. There one was faced with two doorways, one opening to a staircase leading down into a series of rooms and corridors and ultimately into the original sanctuaries and columned halls, and the other directly into a small undecorated chamber.[76] Mostly the graffiti record the names of visitors. Some mention the god Serapis, a form of Osiris which in the north had taken on Classical imagery and become popular, but a few (around twenty) mention the god Bes. The most revealing is on a wall inside the small room.

> Here slept and saw dreams Harpokras of holy Panias [a place in Palestine], a priest, dear descendant of Kopreias the priest, for Bes whose voice is all. And his gratitude is not small.[77]

This tells us that one of the attractions of the temple was that it was a place for 'incubation', the practice of dream interpretation mentioned above.

Bes had a striking appearance: a bandy-legged dwarf, with thick beard, wild hair and tongue stuck out, wearing a lion's skin and beating a broad flat drum. He stood outside the Egyptian pantheon, his appearance the very antithesis of the traditional repose of Egyptian gods. He represented noisy intervention and release from constraint, a turbulence that anyone feeling the need of protection could harness. He had appeared in the decoration of houses in the New Kingdom, and in some contexts he was associated with childbirth, but in these later centuries his cult was growing in status. An outpost, built during the Ptolemaic Period, was discovered at Sakkara in the early days of Egyptian archaeology. On the edge of the desert escarpment a huge mud-brick enclosure wall was erected to surround a temple, now completely destroyed, and its ancillary buildings. Beside the entrance a group of rooms had been built against the inside face of the wall and had thereby been protected (Figure 133).[78] The walls were a mixture of mud brick and limestone fragments, and on several of them figures of Bes, between 1 and 1.5 metres high, had been modelled in clay and painted. Flanking several of them were smaller figures of nude women. Beneath one set lay a broad mud platform, perhaps for sleeping on. Amongst the debris were around thirty limestone figurines of Bes, generally playing a drum, and provided with an overlarge penis. Several unfinished specimens suggest that they were made on the spot. On the parallel supplied by Abydos, incubation is one of the likely activities of this little cult centre.

The cult of Bes was now part of a religion that was in the process of evolving and transforming itself into something different and of interest to a wider non-Egyptian world. His cult and the whole practice of dream interpretation could so easily have had a long future in the eclectic world of the Roman empire and beyond. In a Europe in which (so we might imagine) Christianity did not triumph dream interpretation might have grown into a system of whole-person healing, whilst some of the gods and goddesses from Egypt and the surrounding areas (Isis, Serapis, Bes, Mithras, the drowned and beautiful youth Antinous[79]) gradually attracted layer upon layer of interpretation which took them ever further from their roots and made them seem essentially European. We know a little of why, in the case of Bes, this did not happen. A later Roman historian (Ammianus Marcellinus) records how, in AD 359, the Christian emperor Constantine II, ruling from Constantinople, was told of letters being sent to the oracle of Bes in Upper Egypt asking questions about his life. Angry and fearful of a plot he ordered the oracle to be suppressed (although it survived, since it was attacked again in the fifth century by a local Christian hero of Abydos, St Moses).[80] The process of culture extinction was under way.

The last known hieroglyphic inscription (at the temple of Philae) is dated to AD 394.[81]

SAKKARA

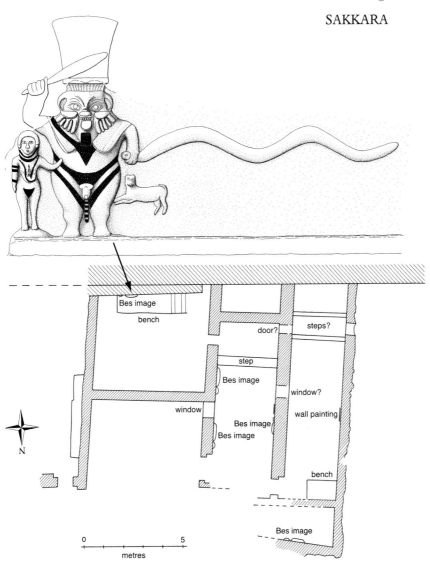

Figure 133 Bes at Sakkara. After J. Quibell, *Excavations at Saqqara (1905–06)*, Cairo, 1907, 12–14, Frontis., Pls I–VI, XXVI–XXIX.

This was not the end of the Egyptian language, however. It continued to be spoken and written for some centuries, alongside the successive languages of government, first Greek and then Arabic. The written form of Egyptian, known as Coptic, replaced the indigenous cursive demotic script with an alphabet mostly derived from Greek and became the means by which Christian writings were disseminated. There is a view that language is a window into the minds of those who use it and that particularities of perception are embedded in grammar and vocabulary. Be that as it may, it does not stand in the way of changes in ways of thinking. When people's views of the world alter, so does their language. Although the surest way to discover what ancient Egyptian sounded like is to learn Coptic, a translation into Coptic of the Old Testament Book of Ruth, for example, is no guide at all to ancient Egyptian thinking. Just supposing that Coptic had survived as a spoken vernacular language, perhaps in the villages of Middle Egypt where Christianity has retained its strongest hold, it would be a delusion to imagine that, on hearing it, one was in touch with the voice of ancient Egypt. Christian doctrinal purity long ago ironed out of Coptic all those aspects of ancient Egyptian thought that we find most interesting and characteristic of the time of the Pharaohs. Coptic does show that ancient Egyptian language had the capacity to adapt and the potential to become a modern language. Instead, through local competition and in no longer being a language of government it became one of many victims of the process of language extinction that continues to gather pace in the modern world.

If language proved to be too malleable to preserve it, what did happen to ancient Egyptian thought? For a time, under the Ptolemies and into the Roman empire, what we recognize as ancient Egyptian culture retained its integrity and coherence through the perpetuation of that aristocratic ruling class who were based in and around the temples and their urban citadels and who managed for quite a time to elicit official patronage. The buildings themselves continued to be enlarged and embellished into the third century AD. They ensured the continuation of ancient rituals and festivals, they housed libraries of texts and the priests who maintained the knowledge of how to interpret them, directly and indirectly they supported artists and craftsmen who kept alive the style and symbols of the old religion which still found expression in the furnishings of traditional burials. But they were swimming against the tide.[82]

The Roman empire, far more than that of the Persians, worked towards integration and an idea of what an empire should be. Scholarly opinion holds that temple wealth was seriously reduced and brought under the centralized control of Roman civil authority, although this cannot be quantified, and some degree of central control had been in place at least as far back as the New Kingdom. Perhaps more significantly, Roman rule offered opportunities for power and rewards, and a culture of rule and prestige that was not directly derived from Egypt. There was much to lure away the old ruling class which otherwise faced the prospect of being left on the margins of progress.

A far more profound enticement proved to be Christianity. Why should this be so? When in a reflective mood people seem to have two main concerns. One is who they are as individuals in an uncertain world. The other concerns the nature of the universe in which they exist. One is personal, the other academic. The most satisfying answers to the first essentially have the form of therapies centred on the self. They give the individual a sense of importance and tell him what to do to retain the favour of a god. The monotheism of the Near East which emerged with the later phase of Judaism and developed further with Christianity and Islam focused intensely on this, in a style which encouraged passion and built on the human urge to find a personal place within a group identity, made more visible by the division between believers and non-believers. Religion became a weapon and therefore a more effective channel for the dispersal of energy. By contrast, in ancient Egypt the broad area of thought and behaviour that we lump together as 'religion' certainly provided for this therapeutic need but very diffusely and as a matter of secondary importance to the main interest of the speculative elite. They directed their thoughts towards the nature of the medium which existence itself occupied and invented a complex universe centred on the power of the sun but peopled by beings who seem to represent forces of creation and disturbance. Humanity and its cares were incidental and were thus excluded. In this respect their approach represents a major step in rationality, a low rung on the ladder of the history of the philosophy of science. With hindsight we can see that they had wholly inadequate concepts with which to pursue their investigations, but they were at least facing in the right direction.

In that it excluded the bulk of the population and that passion was its antithesis, a huge pool of potential human energy remained weakly directed. Something similar seems to have been the case throughout the ancient Near East. From the final centuries of the last millennium BC and the early centuries AD there have survived written sources that document a widespread and urgent personal enquiry into how the individual rather than a class of professional thinkers fitted into an uncertain world and how that individual should wrestle with the forces of good and evil. In a way it was an expression of democracy, people seeking a system of belief that had more in it for them: the narcissistic 'me'-culture. It proved to be and has remained an almost perfect vehicle for perversity and turmoil and hence for human energy dispersal. Amongst the early victims were the versions of ancient Egyptian culture that were in the process of being transformed into something of interest to a wider world.

Epilogue

One way of approaching Cairo from the south, which I do often when returning from fieldwork at El-Amarna in Middle Egypt, is to take the western desert road that avoids much of the valley and so makes for a quicker journey. At the end the road swings eastwards and follows a side valley down towards the city past the pyramids of Giza, the upper parts of which are visible from the right-hand car window rising above the edge of the low escarpment from behind a tangle of power lines. I have seen a picture postcard of this valley from the 1920s or 1930s, pyramids in the background, showing the desert floor filled with lines of white tents from the British army of occupation. Now in their place comes the current edge of greater Cairo, villas, businesses and a huge private residential development for the affluent called Dreamland, complete with grassy golf course and shopping mall. The road sweeps on and rises on stilts, curving its way between low blocks of apartments whose builders have taken no trouble to plaster over the raw concrete frames and the infilling walls of brick. From their roofs a myriad satellite dishes crane expectantly towards a magic point in the sky. On and on they stretch and are as good an introduction as any to the awesome scale and density of Cairo's modern population. At twenty million it is almost twenty times the estimated size of the population of the entire country that built the Giza pyramids.

Modern Egypt has been an inescapable if episodic part of my life for forty years. Over that time I have struggled to come to terms with what I see, an Egypt emerging from the tunnel of time two thousand years after the point at which my own specialist studies reach their end. Egyptology barely extends into the Roman-Christian-Byzantine era, and certainly not into the long and complex centuries of Arab-Islamic rule that are the prelude to modern Egypt. Nevertheless I know roughly what happened. The conventional narrative sees Egyptian fortunes, after a glorious flourishing of culture in the Middle Ages, reaching a low point in the centuries of Ottoman rule prior to Napoleon's invasion in 1798. Since then Egypt has striven to catch up with the developed world. But since progress in many countries, including my own, has been more rapid, Egypt seems perpetually to be poor.

But not stagnant. I sat recently in the cab of an elderly pickup truck in the street at the centre of one of the modern villages (Et-Till) that lies beside El-Amarna whilst the driver purchased breakfast from a nearby shop. I had first come to this spot twenty-five years before. Barely a year has passed since then without my revisiting it. When I first came none of the El-Amarna villages had electricity, nor were there vehicle ferries. The only mechanical transport consisted of a handful of dilapidated tractors from the agricultural co-operative that were called into service from time to time to haul tumbril-like trailers carrying tourists out to the tombs. For the rebuilding of the expedition house which I undertook at that time the iron roofing-girders came across the river on a felucca with a large sail, and made the final stage of their journey slung along the sides of camels. Now, sitting in Et-Till, I notice how there are no longer houses of sun-dried mud bricks to be seen. One by one they have been rebuilt in red brick, concrete and stone. They are taller, more spacious and certainly more hygienic. They have plumbing and television aerials. Most are connected to underground cess pits. Motor vehicles, mostly pickup trucks, constantly pass through the narrow awkwardly angled streets. These streets may be unpaved and the overall picture untidy, but a very definite increase in living-standards has taken place, year by year, imperceptible but cumulative all the same.

This has happened not through accidentally acquired natural resources nor by clever economic manipulation from above. It has come about through the efforts of individuals who daily struggle to improve their situation in the face of countless obstacles, remaining stoical, often unreasonably cheerful. They themselves are better dressed and better educated. Food is plentiful. The younger children now routinely learn at school basic computing skills, sometimes to the amused mystification of their parents. It would be wrong to think that the people who lived in the ancient city of El-Amarna three and a half thousand years before, at the height of ancient Egypt's prosperity, had a better standard of living. Modern Egypt's progress does indeed proceed at a slower pace than the most prosperous countries take for granted, but it is inexorable, brick upon brick. The continuing high birth rate, often seen by outsiders as alarming, ensures into the future that more and more individuals will be adding their own layers of bricks, will be deploying their ingenuity to find a niche for themselves, and generally increasing the local supply of human energy which has already left the Egypt of the Pharaohs far, far behind. Although outsiders might not at first see it, modern Egypt, quite apart from the millionaires of Dreamland, is incomparably richer than it was in ancient times.

Through five thousand years Egypt has shown an impressive capacity to adapt, to absorb the outside world, to find outlets for the turbulent energy that populations build up, and yet at the same time, to remain itself. We are right to admire the distinctiveness of the culture of ancient Egypt. But we should not allow it to detract from this more long-lasting achievement that is worthy of great respect in itself. It encourages me to feel, on behalf of the Egyptians, an optimism that I know they themselves generally do not share.[1] At the very least I wish them luck.

Notes

Introduction

1   Even ant colonies are not quite what they seem. Shortly before completing the manuscript I read a report on recent research which reveals that social insects, bees and ants alike, are latently anarchic but are for the most part held in check by policing strategies which are genetically controlled: L. Spinney, 'Anarchy in the hive!' *New Scientist*, 15 January 2005, 42–5.

2   E.C. Köhler, 'On the origins of Memphis – the new excavations in the Early Dynastic necropolis at Helwan', in S. Hendrickx, R.F. Friedman, K.M. Ciałowicz and M. Chłodnicki, eds, *Egypt at its origins; studies in memory of Barbara Adams*, Leuven, Paris and Dudley, Ma., 2004, 295–315, esp. pp. 301, 308, Figs. 2, 7.

1 Who were the ancient Egyptians?

1   'Contributors to recent literature on the nation and nationalism locate the origin of the "nation", in the sense implied by the term "nation-state", in modern European history': C.B. Keely, *International Migration Review* 30 (1996), 1046–66, p. 1047, with references.

2   Cf. D.M. Master, *JNES* 60 (2001), 117–31, esp. pp. 127–30.

3   B. Anderson, *Imagined communities; reflections on the origin and spread of nationalism*. Revised edition, London and New York, 1991, 6.

4   I.M. Lewis, *Social anthropology in perspective; the relevance of social anthropology*, Harmondsworth, 1976, 1981, 357.

5   *AEL* I, 222–35; J.L. Foster, *Ancient Egyptian literature; an anthology*, Austin, Tex., 2001, 124–48; R.B. Parkinson, *The Tale of Sinuhe and other ancient Egyptian poems, 1940–1640 BC*, Oxford, 1997, 21–53. Although Sinuhe's crisis arose whilst he was on a military expedition with his king, his position was probably that of a high-ranking personal companion to the king. S. Morschauser, *JARCE* 37 (2000), 187–98 makes Sinuhe into something more like a mediaeval European man-at-arms but this seems to me contrary to the ethos which Sinuhe (or his author) embraced. For the subject as a whole, see A. Leahy, 'Ethnic diversity in ancient Egypt', in J.M. Sasson, ed., *Civilizations of the ancient Near East* I, New York, 1995, 225–34; T. Wilkinson, 'Reality versus ideology: the evidence for "Asiatics" in Predynastic and Early Dynastic Egypt', in E.C.M. van den Brink and T.E. Levy, eds, *Egypt and the Levant; interrelations from the 4th through the early 3rd millennium BCE*, London and New York, 2002, 514–20.

6   Abd el-Mohsen Bakir, *The Cairo Calendar: no. 86637*, Cairo, 1966, 25, rt. xv.9–10; *Lexikon* I, 76–8.

7   *AEL* II, 197–9. The 'Destruction of Mankind' is part of a longer text, described in E. Hornung, *The ancient Egyptian books of the afterlife*, Ithaca, N.Y., and London, 1999, 148–51.

8   Hatshepsut's temple at Deir el-Bahari: *Urk.* IV: 345.14; E. Blumenthal, I. Müller and W.F. Reineke, *Urkunden der 18. Dynastie, Übersetzung zu den Heften 5–16*, Berlin, 1984, 25.

9   W.M.F. Petrie, *Ancient Egypt* 1917, 57–61, p. 58.

10 Instruction to Merikara, *c.* 2050 BC; AEL I, 104. In general, see T. von der Way, *Göttergericht und 'heiliger' Krieg im Alten Ägypten; die Inschriften des Merenptah zum Libyerkrieg des Jahres 5*, Heidelberg, 1992.

11 Boundary stela of Senusret III, *c.* 1864 BC; *AEL* I, 119; R.B. Parkinson, *Voices from ancient Egypt; an anthology of Middle Kingdom writings*, London, 1991, 45.

12 A.J. Peden, *Egyptian historical inscriptions of the Twentieth Dynasty*, Jonsered, 1994, 49.

13 Herodotus, *Histories*, Book II, 39; A.B. Lloyd, *Herodotus Book II. Commentary 1–98*, Leiden, 1976, 183–4.

14 Genesis 43.32; cf. 46.34; D.B. Redford, *A study of the biblical story of Joseph (Genesis 37–50)*, Leiden, 1970, 235.

15 M. Abd el-Maksoud, *Tell Heboua (1981–1991): enquête archéologique sur la Deuxième Période Intermédiaire et la nouvel empire à l'extrémité orientale du Delta*, Paris, 1998; D. Valbelle and M. Abd el-Maksoud, 'La frontière orientale du Delta depuis le bronze moyen jusqu'au bronze récent', in *L'Acrobate au taureau; les découvertes de Tell el-Dabʿa (Égypte) et l'archéologie de la Méditerranée orientale (1800–1400 av. J.-C.)*, Paris, 1999, 85–98. More generally J.K. Hoffmeier and M. Abd el-Maksoud, *JEA* 89 (2003), 169–97.

16 S.T. Smith, *JARCE* 28 (1991), 107–32, p. 126; *Askut in Nubia; the economics and ideology of Egyptian imperialism in the second millenium BC*, London and New York, 1995, 40.

17 T.A.H. Wilkinson, *Royal annals of ancient Egypt: the Palermo Stone and its associated fragments*, London and New York, 2000, 141. The pretentious ancient phrasing is not necessarily a guide to scale. If the former was the enclosure wall around the settlement at Buhen it was quite modest and appears to have lacked the characteristics of a fortification. For the Buhen plan, see W.B. Emery, *Kush* 11 (1963), 116–20.

18 L. Habachi, *BIFAO* 80 (1980), 13–30; S. Snape, 'Walls, wells and wandering merchants: Egyptian control of Marmarica in the Late Bronze Age', in C.J. Eyre, ed., *Proceedings of the Seventh International Congress of Egyptologists, Cambridge 3–9 September 1995*, Leuven, 1998, 1081–4; *EA* 11 (1997), 23–4.

19 P.C. Smither, *JEA* 31 (1945), 3–10; Parkinson, *Voices from ancient Egypt*, 93–5; see further pp. 239–40.

20 R.A. Caminos, *Late-Egyptian miscellanies*, London, 1954, 293.

21 Weni: *AEL* I, 19–20. The 'friendly Nubians' appear in the Dahshur Decree of Pepi I, H. Goedicke, *Königliche Dokumente aus dem Alten Reich*, Wiesbaden, 1967, 56, 62–3.

22 H.G. Fischer, *Kush* 9 (1961), 44–80; M. Bietak, 'Zu den Nubischen Bogenschützen aus Assiut. Ein Beitrag zur Geschichte der Ersten Zwischenzeit', in *Mélanges Gamal Eddin Mokhtar* I, Cairo, 1985, 87–97. For Kubbaniya see H. Junker, *Bericht über die Grabungen der Akademie der Wissenschaften in Wien auf den Friedhöfen von El-Kubanieh-Nord, Winter 1910–1911*, Vienna, 1920. The Hierakonpolis find is reported in *EA* 19, 2001, 30; and in *Sudan and Nubia* 5 (2001), 29–38. Gebelein: Bard, *Encyclopedia* 338–40. Pan-grave sherds from Thebes are published by D. Redford, S. Orel, S. Redford and S. Shubert, *JARCE* 28 (1991), 75–106, pp. 99–103.

23 J. Malek, *EA* 2 (1992), 18. A preliminary translation is H. Altenmüller and A.M. Moussa, *SAK* 18 (1991), 1–48; H. Goedicke, *RdE* 42 (1991), 89–94. In general, G. Posener, *Syria* 34 (1957), 145–63; P.-M. Chevereau, *RdE* 42 (1991), 43–88.

24 W.C. Hayes, *A papyrus of the late Middle Kingdom in the Brooklyn Museum*, Brooklyn, N.Y., 1955, 87–109, 148–9; S. Quirke, *The administration of Egypt in the late Middle Kingdom; the hieratic documents*, New Malden, 1990, 148–9.

25 U. Luft, in S. Quirke, ed., *Lahun studies*, Reigate, 1998, 29–30.

26 KRI (trans.) II, 67.

27 Rhetorical Stela of Rameses III from Deir el-Medina, KRI V, 90–1; Peden, *Egyptian historical inscriptions of the Twentieth Dynasty*, 64–5.

28 Tuthmosis IV: W.M.F. Petrie, *Six temples at Thebes*, 1896, London, 1897, Pl. I; H.M. Stewart, *Egyptian stelae, reliefs and paintings from the Petrie Collection*, Part I, Warminster, 1976, 4, Pl. 3.1; Amenhetep III: *Urk.* IV, 1649.12; B.G. Davies, *Egyptian historical records of the later Eighteenth Dynasty*, fasc. IV, Warminster, 1992, 2 translates 'served by the towns of the Levant'; Hittite field: *Urk.* IV, 2109.16; Davies, op. cit., fasc. VI, Warminster, 1995, 65.

29 P. Harris I: 77.5–6; Peden, *Egyptian historical inscriptions of the Twentieth Dynasty*, 217; P. Grandet, *Le papyrus Harris I (BM 9999)*, Cairo, 1994, I, 337.

30 P. Harris I: 10.15; 31.8; 51a.9; 10.8; Grandet, *Le papyrus Harris I*, I, 236, 266, 292, 235.

31 B.G. Davies, *Egyptian historical inscriptions of the Nineteenth Dynasty*, Jonsered, 1997, 165.

32 *ANET*, 247 provides a translation of the text. K.W. Butzer, *Early hydraulic civilization in Egypt*, Chicago, 1976, 80–7 attempts a population estimate.

33 Wilkinson, *Royal annals*, 141–2.

34 C.J. Eyre, 'Work and the organisation of work in the New Kingdom', in M.A. Powell, *Labor in the ancient Near East*, New Haven, Conn., 1987, 167–221, pp. 188–90; J. Janssen, *JEOL* 17 (1964), 141–7; W.C. Hayes, *JEA* 46 (1960), 29–52, pp. 44–5.

35 The exact numbers are 51, 181, 513, 702, 522, 197, 65 and 295, see W. Helck, *Die Beziehungen Ägyptens zu Vorderasien im 3. und 2. Jahrtausend v.Chr.* second edition, Wiesbaden, 1971, 347.

36 W.L. Moran, *The Amarna Letters*, Baltimore, Md., 1992, letter no. EA 288; other examples are EA 17, EA 19, EA 44, EA 268, EA 301, EA 309, RA 31.

37 P. Harris I: 31.8; Grandet, *Le papyrus Harris I*, I, 266.

38 N. de G. Davies, *The Tomb of Rekh-mi-rē˓ at Thebes*, New York, 1943, 29, Pls XXI–XXIII.

39 W.L. Westermann, *The slave systems of Greek and Roman antiquity*, Philadelphia, Pa., 1955. A key witness is Thucydides I.29.5; 98.2; II.67.4; III.50.1; 68.2; IV.48.4; V.32.1; 116.4; VI.62.3–4; VII.87.3–4; also Xenophon, *Hellenika*, II.2.3–23.

40 Both are quotes from the Rhetorical Stela of Rameses III (Deir el-Medina): Peden, *Egyptian historical inscriptions of the Twentieth Dynasty*, 65.

41 The land-register is Papyrus Wilbour. Convenient summary discussions are D. O'Connor, 'The geography of settlement in ancient Egypt', in P.J. Ucko, R. Tringham, and G.W. Dimbleby, eds, *Man, settlement and urbanism*, London, 1972, 681–98, esp. pp. 690–5; M.D. Adams, 'A textual window on the settlement system in ancient Egypt', in J. Lustig, ed., *Anthropology and Egyptology: a developing dialogue*, Sheffield, 1997, 90–105. The legal document is translated by A.H. Gardiner, *JEA* 26 (1940), 23–9. Also A.J. Spalinger, *War in ancient Egypt*, Malden, Ma., Oxford and Carlton, Victoria, Australia, 2005, 264–5, 274–5.

42 *AEL* II, 77; Davies, *Egyptian historical inscriptions of the Nineteenth Dynasty*, 185.

43 Peden, *Egyptian historical inscriptions of the Twentieth Dynasty*, 219–21. The word translated here as 'foreigners' is derived from the common word for 'other' but, by this time, was used in a way which also embraced the sense of 'outsiders', 'aliens', see Caminos, *Late-Egyptian miscellanies*, 350. In a popular Ramesside school practice text, P. Anastasi I, an imaginary foreign expedition of 5,000 soldiers consists of 1,900 'men' (i.e. Egyptians), 520 Sherden, 1,600 Kehek, 100 Meshwesh and 880 Nubians, see E. Wente, *Letters from ancient Egypt*, Atlanta, Ga., 1990, 106.

44 P Bologna 1086: Wente, *Letters*, 125; KRI (trans.) IV, 65.

45 A.H. Gardiner, *JEA* 26 (1940), 23–9; C.J. Eyre, *JEA* 78 (1992), 207–21. On slavery in Egypt see A.M. Bakir, *Slavery in Pharaonic Egypt*, Cairo, 1952.

46 *Urk.* IV, 690.4–5; Helck, *Die Beziehungen Ägyptens*, 350.

47 Owner of Theban tomb 343, R. Mond and W.B. Emery, *LAAA* 14 (1927), 13–34, esp. pp. 28–9.

48 Helck, *Die Beziehungen Ägyptens*, 353, no. 5.

49 A.R. Schulman, *CdE* 65 (1990), 12–20.

50 W.K. Simpson, *Heka-nefer and the Dynastic material from Toshka and Arminna*, New Haven, Conn.,

and Philadelphia, Pa., 1963. A background study is T. Säve-Söderbergh, 'Teh-Khet, the cultural and sociopolitical structure of a Nubian princedom in Tuthmoside times', in W.V. Davies, ed., *Egypt and Africa: Nubia from Prehistory to Islam*, London, 1991, 186–94.

51 Reports of excavations at a Third Intermediate Period elite cemetery inside the city of Ehnasya el-Medina (Herakleopolis), an important centre of Libyan takeover, give no hint of anything other than a purely Egyptian style; e.g. M. del Carmen Pérez Die, *EA* 6 (1995), 23–5.

52 W.M.F. Petrie, *Diospolis Parva; the cemeteries of Abadiyeh and Hu 1898–9*, London, 1901, chapter XI; J. Bourriau, 'Nubians in Egypt during the Second Intermediate Period: an interpretation based on the Egyptian ceramic evidence', in Dorothea Arnold, ed., *Studien zur altägyptischen Keramik*, Mainz, 1981, 25–41; K. Sadr, *Archéologie de Nil Moyen* 2 (1987), 265–91. J. Bourriau, 'The Second Intermediate Period (*c.* 1650–1550 BC)', in I. Shaw, ed., *The Oxford History of Ancient Egypt*, Oxford, 2000, 203 suggests that slight differences in two cemeteries from opposite sides of the river at the border area in Middle Egypt between the Hyksos and the Thebans show that the two groups were serving the rival kings (i.e. Apophis and Kamose).

53 W.V. Davies, *EA* 23 (2003), 3–6; *Sudan and Nubia* 7 (2003), 52–4. The prominent family of mayors and other leading citizens of El-Kab at this time and on into the New Kingdom were themselves descended from foreigners, perhaps an earlier generation of Medjay who had settled, adopted Egyptian culture and changed allegiance. The evidence comes from some of their names, including one who was called 'Medjay-man'.

54 For the Hyksos the starting-point should be the account of Hyksos rule by Manetho: W.G. Waddell, *Manetho*, Cambridge, Mass., and London, 1940, 77–91. *ANET*, 230–2 provides translations of two other key texts (the tale of Apophis and Sekenenra; the Speos Artemidos inscription). The best account of Avaris and the culture of the time is M. Bietak, *Avaris: the capital of the Hyksos: recent excavations at Tell el-Dabʿa*, London, 1996. On the Hyksos themselves see E.D. Oren, ed., *The Hyksos: new historical and archaeological perspectives*, Philadelphia, Pa., 1997 (which also contains translations of the main sources), and the revisionist interpretations of K.S.B. Ryholt, *The political situation in Egypt during the Second Intermediate Period c. 1800–1550 BC*, Copenhagen, 1997.

55 The revealing text of Kamose's pair of stelae is translated in L. Habachi, *The second stela of Kamose, and his struggle against the Hyksos ruler and his capital*, Glückstadt, 1972, and in *ANET* 232–3, 554–5.

56 Plutarch, *Life of Antony*, 27.3.4; S. Walker and P. Higgs, eds, *Cleopatra of Egypt, from history to myth*, London, 2001, 23, 130.

57 Davies, *Egyptian historical inscriptions of the Nineteenth Dynasty*, 151–88; Peden, *Egyptian historical inscriptions of the Twentieth Dynasty*, 7–22, 37–62, 215–17.

58 For the presence of Libyans in the Theban area in the late 20th dynasty see J. Černý, 'Egypt: from the death of Ramesses III to the end of the Twenty-first Dynasty', in I.E.S. Edwards, C.J. Gadd, N.G.L. Hammond and E. Sollberger, eds, *The Cambridge Ancient History*, third edition, Vol. II, Part 2, Cambridge, 1975, chapter XXXV, specifically pp. 616–19.

59 Pasenhor: K.A. Kitchen, *The Third Intermediate Period in Egypt (1100–650 BC)*, third edition, Warminster, 1995, 105–6, 488, Table 19; M. Malinine, G. Posener and J. Vercoutter, *Catalogue des stèles du Sérapéum de Memphis* I, Paris, 1968, no. 31, 30–1, Pl. 10.

60 For background: A. Leahy, ed., *Libya and Egypt c. 1300–750 BC*, London, 1990; S. Snape, 'The emergence of Libya on the horizon of Egypt', in D. O'Connor and S. Quirke, eds, *Mysterious lands*, London, 2003, 93–106. Herihor's sons: The Epigraphic Survey, *The Temple of Khonsu*, 1. *Scenes of King Herihor in the court*, Chicago, 1979, 11–13, Pl. 26; Kitchen, *The Third Intermediate Period*, 540–1.

61 Standard manuals are T.D Stewart, *Essentials of forensic anthropology; especially as developed in the United States*, Springfield, Ill., 1979, chapter 11; D.H. Ubelaker, *Human skeletal remains*, second edition, (Manuals on Archeology 2), Washington, D.C. 1989. I thank Corinne Duhig for these references.

62 A.M. Roth, 'Building bridges to Afrocentrism: a letter to my Egyptological colleagues.' *NARCE* 167 (Sept 1995); 168 (Dec. 1995). Several thoughtful papers on different aspects of this theme will be found in D. O'Connor and A. Reid, eds, *Ancient Egypt in Africa*, London, 2003.

63 D.E. Derry, *JEA* 42 (1956): 80–5, a paper by an anatomist who had studied key sets of skulls from the period; (W.M.) F. Petrie, *The making of Egypt*, London, 1939, whose opinions are reviewed in B.G. Trigger, *Beyond history: the methods of prehistory*, New York, 1968, 76–86.

64 Differences with Nubian and Egyptian populations of Neolithic and historic times have been taken to show further effects of local small-scale evolution probably in part induced by the change to a settled farming way of life which developed along the Nile valley around 5500 BC. See A.H. Goodman, 'Diet and Post Mesolithic craniofacial and dental evolution in Sudanese Nubia', in A.R. David, ed., *Science in Egyptology*, Manchester, 1986, 201–10.

65 As illustrated by the charts of the same sets of skulls, one chart based on the use of ten measurements and the other based on the use of seven, in F.W. Rösing, *Qubbet el Hawa und Elephantine; zur Bevölkerungsgeschichte von Ägypten*, Stuttgart and New York, 1990, 192–200, Abb. 128–31.

66 A good modern treatment of the origins of human groups in Africa is M.M. Lahr, *The evolution of modern human diversity; a study of cranial variation*, Cambridge, 1996, especially chapter 11. More popular accounts of the peopling of Africa are J. Hiernaux, *The people of Africa*, London, 1974; J. Diamond, *Guns, germs and steel; a short history of everybody for the last 13,000 years*, London, 1997, chapter 19.

67 F. Wendorf, 'Site 117: a Nubian Final Paleolithic graveyard near Jebel Sahaba, Sudan', in F. Wendorf, ed., *The prehistory of Nubia* II, Dallas, Tex., 1968, 954–95; J.E. Anderson, 'Late Paleolithic skeletal remains from Nubia', in ibid., 996–1040. F. Wendorf and R. Schild, *The Wadi Kubbaniya skeleton: a Late Paleolothic burial from southern Egypt* (The Prehistory of Wadi Kubbaniya I), Dallas, Tex., 1986; also Lahr, *The evolution of modern human diversity*, 283.

68 Rösing, *Qubbet el Hawa und Elephantine*.

69 I am grateful to Robert McCaa, Professor of History at the University of Minneapolis, for guidance in this matter.

70 Butzer, *Early hydraulic civilization*, 80–7.

71 Implicit in S. Keita, *American Journal of Physical Anthropology* 87 (1992), 245–54, though his study is based only on 1st Dynasty skulls from Abydos. It is also the conclusion of an analysis of mitochondrial DNA samples taken from 224 living inhabitants of Egypt, Nubia and the Sudan, see M. Krings, A.H. Salem, K. Bauer, H. Geisert, A.K. Malek, L. Chaix, C. Simon, D. Welsby, A. Di Rienzo, G. Utermann, A. Sajantila, S. Pääbo and M. Stoneking, *American Journal of Human Genetics* 64 (1999), 1166–76.

72 Rösing, *Qubbet el Hawa und Elephantine*.

73 P. Smith, 'The palaeo-biological evidence for admixture between populations in the southern Levant and Egypt in the fourth to third millennia BCE', in E.C.M. van den Brink and T.E. Levy, eds, *Egypt and the Levant; interrelations from the 4th through the early 3rd millennium BCE*, London and New York, 2002, 118–28.

74 E.-M. Winkler and H. Wilfing, *Tell el-Dab'a* VI, Vienna, 1991.

75 D.E. Derry, *JEA* 42 (1956), 80–5; the quotation is from p. 81.

76 S. Keita, *American Journal of Physical Anthropology* 87 (1992), 245–54; S. Keita, *American Journal of Physical Anthropology* 83 (1990), 35–48. Non-metric studies are those of A.C. and R.J. Berry, and P.J. Ucko, *Man* NS 2 (1967), 551–68; A.C. Berry and R.J. Berry, *Journal of Human Evolution* 1 (1972), 199–208.

77 O.P. Nielsen, *Human remains; metrical and non-metrical anatomical variations* (The Scandinavian Joint Expedition to Sudanese Nubia 9), Stockholm, 1970; T. Säve-Söderbergh and L. Troy, *New Kingdom Pharaonic sites; the finds and the sites* (The Scandinavian Joint Expedition to Sudanese Nubia 5), 1991, 7–10.

78 For CRANID see R.V.S. Wright, *Archaeology in Oceania* 27 (1992), 128–34; also *New Scientist*

2331, 23 February 2002, 34–7. The original excavation report is W.M.F. Petrie, *Gizeh and Rifeh*, London, 1907, 29, Pls XXXI–XXXVIIA. The few inscribed objects and the adjacent decorated tomb of Thary are included in PM III.1, second edition, Oxford, 1974, 296–7. Petrie's indications as to where the cemetery lay are vague, but include the statement (p. 29) that one tomb was close to a large 2nd Dynasty mastaba (tomb superstructure) on the top of the ridge, the remains of which are still visible.

79 J. Prag and R. Neave, *Making faces; using forensic and archaeological evidence*, London, 1997, chapter 3; E. Doxiadis, *The mysterious Fayum portraits; faces from ancient Egypt*, London, 1995; S. Walker and M. Bierbrier, *Ancient faces; mummy portraits from Roman Egypt*, London, 1997.

80 See various papers in W.V. Davies and R. Walker, eds, *Biological anthropology and the study of ancient Egypt*, London, 1993, including S. Pääbo and A. Di Renzo, 'A molecular approach to the study of Egyptian history', pp. 86–90.

2 The intellectual foundations of the early state

1 In general, see D.B. Redford, *Pharaonic king-lists, annals and day-books: a contribution to the study of the Egyptian sense of history*, Mississauga, Ontario, 1986.

2 Now in the Louvre, E13481 bis. See PM II.2, 111–12; also D. Wildung, *GM* 9 (1974), 41–8; D. Wildung, *MDAIK* 25 (1969), 212–19.

3 Now in the Cairo Museum, CG34516. See PM III.2, 2.2, 666; D. Wildung, *Die Rolle Ägyptischer Könige im Bewusstsein ihrer Nachwelt* I, Berlin, 1969, Taf. I; Sir A.H. Gardiner, *Egypt of the Pharaohs*, Oxford, 1961, 49, Fig. 8.

4 G. Posener, *Littérature et politique dans l'Égypte de la XIIe dynastie*, Paris, 1956, 1–3; D. Arnold, *Der Tempel des Königs Mentuhotep von Deir el-Bahari* I, Mainz, 1974, 92–5; Gardiner, *Egypt of the Pharaohs*, 127.

5 T.A.H. Wilkinson, *Royal annals of ancient Egypt: the Palermo Stone and its associated fragments*, London and New York, 2000. The possibility that has been voiced that the Palermo Stone is itself a late copy of earlier documents, perhaps made in the first millennium BC, has been lessened by the discovery of a similar basalt slab inscribed with detailed royal annals of the 6th Dynasty re-used not long afterwards for making the lid of a queen's sarcophagus, see M. Baud and V. Dobrev, *BIFAO* 95 (1995), 23–92.

6 Sir A.H. Gardiner, *The royal canon of Turin*, Oxford, 1959. J. Málek, *JEA* 68 (1982), 93–106, provides a provocative analysis of the text and the way in which texts of this kind could have given rise to Manetho's dynasties. Further improvements in placing the fragments and in understanding the format are K.S.B. Ryholt, *The political situation in Egypt during the Second Intermediate Period c. 1800–1550 BC*, Copenhagen, 1997, 9–33 (pp. 29–30 are a critique of Málek); *ZÄS* 127 (2000), 87–100.

7 Ryholt, *Political situation*, 24–5, logically places several small fragments here which then gives us a list of demi-gods and legendary heroes who include 'He who possesses noble women', and 'The follower Meni great of height'.

8 B. Gunn, *JEA* 12 (1926), 250–1; Posener, *Littérature et politique*, 31–3; Wildung, *Die Rolle Ägyptischer Könige*, 104–52.

9 BAR IV, 228, §471; KRI VI, 19.12–13; A.J. Peden, *The reign of Ramesses IV*, Warminster, 1994, 93.

10 E.g. *AEL* I, 215–22.

11 Herodotus II.124–7; W.G. Waddell, *Manetho*, Cambridge, Mass., 1948, 47, 49.

12 G. Posener, *RdE* 11 (1957), 119–37; *Lexikon* V, 957; R.B. Parkinson, *Voices from ancient Egypt; an anthology of Middle Kingdom writings*, London, 1991, 54–6.

13 *AEL* I, 149–63.

14 *ANET*, 12.

15 The tale is preserved in Papyrus Chester Beatty I, in the British Museum, written in the reign

of Rameses V, 1147–1143 BC. See A.H. Gardiner, *The Library of A. Chester Beatty. Description of a hieratic papyrus with a mythological story, love-songs, and other miscellaneous texts*, London, 1931. There are small fragments of a Middle Kingdom version, Parkinson, *Voices from ancient Egypt*, 120–1. For the private library in which it was found see A.G. McDowell, *Village life in ancient Egypt; laundry lists and love songs*, Oxford and New York, 1999, 134–5.

16 Waddell, *Manetho*, 61, 63.

17 *AEL* I, 139–45; R.B. Parkinson, *Poetry and culture in Middle Kingdom Egypt; a dark side to perfection*, London and New York, 2002, 200–4.

18 See chapter 1, note 54.

19 BAR I, 332–7; R. Anthes, *Festschrift zum 150 jährigen Bestehen des Berliner Ägyptischen Museums*, Berlin, 1974, 15–49.

20 H.G. Evers, *Staat aus dem Stein*, Munich, 1929; C. Aldred, *Metropolitan Museum Journal* 3 (1970), 27–50; J. Bourriau, *Pharaohs and mortals; Egyptian art in the Middle Kingdom*, Cambridge, 1988; B. Fay, *The Louvre sphinx and the royal sculpture from the reign of Amenemhat II*, Mainz, 1996.

21 *AEL* I, 51–7; III, 4–5; F. Junge, *MDAIK* 29 (1973), 195–204; T. Hare, *ReMembering Osiris*, Stanford, Ca., 1999, 169–84.

22 J.-E. Gautier and G. Jéquier, *Mémoire sur les fouilles de Licht*, Cairo, 1902, 30–8; good photographs of two of the throne sides are in K. Lange and M. Hirmer, *Egypt: architecture, sculpture, painting in three thousand years*, third edition, London, 1961, 86, 87.

23 On Seth see H. te Velde, *Seth, god of confusion*, Leiden, 1967.

24 A.H. Gardiner, *Ancient Egyptian onomastica*, London, 1947.

25 Chapter 15, Papyrus of Ani, as quoted by A. Piankoff, *The Litany of Re*, New York, 1964, 46. R.O. Faulkner, *The ancient Egyptian Book of the Dead*, London, 1985, 40, translates differently. Another good example built around the name of Osiris is 'Osiris-Apis-Atum-Horus in one, the Great God', cited in H. Frankfort, *Kingship and the gods*, Chicago, 1948, 146, 196; S. Morenz, *Egyptian religion*, London, 1973, 143. Pages 139–46 deal with the general phenomenon of individuality/plurality in Egyptian divine names, as does E. Hornung, *Conceptions of god in ancient Egypt: the one and the many*, London, 1983, chapter 3.

26 Morenz, *Egyptian religion*, 145.

27 T.G. Allen, *The Book of the Dead or Going Forth by Day*, Chicago, 1974, 118–20. A similar invoking of the manifold forms of Ra (seventy-five in all) is contained within the Litany of Ra, see Piankoff, *The Litany of Re*. Pages 3–9 discuss the phenomenon of name plurality in other religions, including Islam.

28 *AEL* I, 52–3; Frankfort, *Kingship and the gods*, chapter 2; Hare, *ReMembering Osiris*.

29 Useful discussions here are J. Gwyn Griffiths, *The conflict of Horus and Seth*, Liverpool, 1960, 130–46; B.G. Trigger, *Beyond history: the methods of prehistory*, New York, 1968, chapter 6, 'Predynastic Egypt'.

30 T.A.H. Wilkinson, *State formation in Egypt; chronology and society*, Oxford, 1996; *MDAIK* 56 (2000), 377–95. K.A. Bard, *From farmers to Pharaohs; mortuary evidence for theories of complex society in Egypt*, Sheffield, 1994; 'The emergence of the Egyptian state (c. 3200–2686 BC)', in I. Shaw, ed., *The Oxford history of ancient Egypt*, Oxford, 2000, 61–88; B. Midant-Reynes, *The prehistory of Egypt*, Oxford, 2000, 231–50.

31 At least, I find it hard to imagine. According to the 'circumscription theory', which has been applied to Egypt, small societies peacefully grew and extended their territory by spreading into unclaimed land. When the limits of claim were reached, conflict ensued. See K.A. Bard and R.L. Carneiro, 'Patterns of predynastic settlement location, social evolution, and the circumscription theory', *Cahiers de recherches de l'Institut de Papyrologie et d'Égyptologie de Lille* 11 (1989), 15–23. I see the urge to compete arising within people's minds as part of the very process of claiming land for farming and settlement irrespective of how much potentially additional land there is. Greater weight always deserves to be given to consciousness and the interactions of individuals as parts of systems than to single external causes. Nor should we assume that

violence was the inevitable outcome. The ancient Egyptian view was as much about judgement and reconciliation as about physical conflict. The 'circumscription theory' is in the tradition of 'social Darwinism' and was given a crude airing by A. Hitler, see N. Gregor, *How to read Hitler*, London, 2005, 36–44. Recent discussions are B. Andelković, 'The Upper Egyptian commonwealth: a crucial phase of the state formation process', in S. Hendrickx, R.F. Friedman, K.M. Ciałowicz and M.Chłodnicki, eds, *Egypt at its origins; studies in memory of Barbara Adams*, Leuven, Paris and Dudley, Ma., 2004, 535–46; M. Campagno, 'In the beginning was the war. Conflict and the emergence of the Egyptian state', in ibid., 689–703.

32   For the somewhat enigmatic Mesopotamian connection see H. Frankfort, *The birth of civilization in the Near East*, London, 1951, 100–12; *AJSL* 58 (1941), 329–58; H.J. Kantor, *JNES* 1 (1942), 174–213; *JNES* 11 (1952), 239–50; 'The relative chronology of Egypt and its foreign correlations before the First Intermediate Period', in R.W. Ehrich, ed., *Chronologies in Old World Archaeology*, third edition, Chicago and London, 1992, I, 3–21; II, 2–43; H.S. Smith, 'The making of Egypt: a review of the influence of Susa and Sumer on Upper Egypt and Lower Nubia in the 4th millennium B.C', in R. Friedman and B. Adams, eds, *Followers of Horus; studies dedicated to Michael Allen Hoffman*, Oxford, 1992, 235–46; B. Teissier, *Iran (Journal of Persian Studies)* 25 (1987), 27–53; J.A. Hill, *Cylinder seal glyptic in Predynastic Egypt and neighboring regions*, Oxford, 2004.

33   C. Renfrew, *The emergence of civilisation; the Cyclades and the Aegean in the third millennium BC*, London, 1972, 15–44 contains a clear portrayal of the concept of positive feedback applied to the early developing societies of the Aegean. In a growing field of research within diverse subject areas the idea of 'game' is translated into computer-based simulations of interactions (the nature of which are precisely identified), which move onwards from quantified starting-conditions. Examples are provided in T.A. Kohler and G.J. Gumerman, eds, *Dynamics in human and primate societies; agent-based modeling of social and spatial processes*, New York and Oxford, 2000.

34   K.V. Flannery, *CAJ* 9 (1999), 3–21 reviews theories of state formation in the light of five historically documented case studies in which named individuals have played a transforming role, invariably one that was excessively violent.

35   W.M.F. Petrie and J.E. Quibell, *Naqada and Ballas*, London, 1896; W. Kaiser, *MDAIK* 17 (1961), 14–18; B.J. Kemp, *JEA* 59 (1973), 36–43; W. Davis, *MDAIK* 39 (1983), 17–28; *Lexikon* IV, 343–7.

36   J.E. Quibell, *Hierakonpolis* I, London, 1900; J.E. Quibell and F.W. Green, *Hierakonpolis* II, London 1902; B. Adams, *Ancient Nekhen; Garstang in the City of Hierakonpolis*, New Malden, 1995. Chapter II, pp. 21–80, summarizes the key results from what has become an extensive and complex bibliography; M.A. Hoffman, *The Predynastic of Hierakonpolis*, Cairo and Macomb, Ill., 1982.

37   Quibell and Green, *Hierakonpolis* II, 20–2, Pls LXXV–LXXIX; [F.W. Green], *The prehistoric wall-painting in Egypt* [London, British School of Egyptian Archaeology, 1953]; H. Case and J.C. Payne, *JEA* 48 (1962), 5–18; J.C. Payne, *JEA* 59 (1973), 31–5; B.J. Kemp, *JEA* 59 (1973), 36–43. The other elite cemetery is published in B. Adams, *Excavations in the Locality 6 cemetery at Hierakonpolis 1979–1985*, Oxford, 2000; 'Elite graves at Hierakonpolis', in J. Spencer, ed., *Aspects of early Egypt*, London, 1996, 1–15; A. Figueiredo, 'Locality HK6 at Hierakonpolis: results of the 2000 field season', in Hendrickx *et al.*, *Egypt at its origins*, 1–23.

38   W.A. Fairservis, K.R. Weeks and M. Hoffman, *JARCE* 9 (1971–2), 7–68; W.A. Fairservis, *The Hierakonpolis Project, season January to May 1981. Excavation on the Kom el Gemuwia*, Vassar College, Poughkeepsie, N.Y., 1986.

39   R. Engelbach, *ZÄS* 65 (1930), 115–16; A.H. Gardiner, *JEA* 30 (1944), 47, Pl. VI.4. In historic times one of these forms had its own name, Anty, as if it were a separate divinity.

40   A.H. Gardiner, *JEA* 30 (1944), 23–60 discusses in some detail the problems of Behdet and related matters.

41   N. Moeller, *EA* 23 (2003), 7–9; *CAJ* 14 (2004), 261–5; B.J. Kemp, *Antiquity* 51 (1977), 185–200;

M. Bietak, 'Urban archaeology and the "town problem" in ancient Egypt', in K. Weeks, ed., *Egyptology and the social sciences*, Cairo, 1979, 97–144, esp. 110–14.

42 S. Hendrickx, 'The Late Predynastic cemetery at Elkab (Upper Egypt)', in L. Krzyżaniak and M. Kobusiewicz, eds, *Origin and early development of food-producing cultures in north-eastern Africa*, Poznań, 1984, 225–30.

43 D.A. Faltings, 'The chronological frame and social structure of Buto in the fourth millennium BCE', in E.C.M. van den Brink and T.E. Levy, eds, *Egypt and the Levant; interrelations from the 4th through the early 3rd millennium BCE*, London and New York, 2002, 165–70.

44 E.C.M. van den Brink, 'A transitional Late Predynastic-Early Dynastic settlement site in the northeastern Nile Delta, Egypt.' *MDAIK* 45 (1989): 55–108; several of the papers in E.C.M. van den Brink, ed., *The Nile Delta in transition: 4th–3rd millennium BC*, Tel Aviv, 1992; M. Chłodnicki, 'Tell el-Farkha and explorations of the central *kom* 1987–2002', in Hendrickx *et al.*, *Egypt at its origins*, 357–70; K.M. Ciałowicz, 'Tell el-Farkha 2001–2002. Excavations at the western *kom*', in ibid., 371–88. Another important site is the Neolithic village of Merimda Beni Salama on the south-western edge of the delta: J. Eiwanger, *Merimde-Benisalâme* I, II, III, Mainz, 1984, 1988, 1992. A good summary of older fieldwork at Merimda and other northern localities remains W.C. Hayes, *Most ancient Egypt*, Chicago, 1965, chapter 3, 91–146.

45 K. Kroeper and D. Wildung, *Minshat Abu Omar. Ein vor- und frühgeschichtlicher Friedhof im Nildelta* I, II, Mainz, 1994, 2000. Middle Egypt remains something of a blank on the distribution map, but this may well be a consequence of a much greater lateral spreading of Nile alluvium in Middle Egypt since ancient times. Modern fields have buried the key desert-edge sites that contribute so much to our knowledge of Predynastic culture further south, and the kind of survey on the floodplain that has brought rapid gains in knowledge in the delta has not yet been attempted in this part of Egypt.

46 I. Rizkana and J. Seeher, *Maadi III. The non-lithic small finds and the structural remains of the Predynastic settlement*, Mainz, 1989; J. Golden, 'The origins of the metals trade in the eastern Mediterranean: social organization of production in the early copper industries', in van den Brink and Levy, *Egypt and the Levant*, 225–38; U. Hartung, 'Rescue excavations in the Predynastic settlement of Maadi', in Hendrickx *et al.*, *Egypt at its origins*, 337–56.

47 Thucydides I.10.

48 *Lexikon* I, 28–41; Bard, *Encyclopedia*, 93–114.

49 G. Dreyer, *Umm el-Qaab* I. *Das prädynastische Königsgrab U-j und seine frühen Schriftzeugnisse*, Mainz, 1998. The sceptre is object no. 200.

50 Manetho claimed that the first two dynasties were from the city of This, but this might reflect the same connection with the Abydos cemetery that we make. Hierakonpolis was a place of no importance by his time and he makes no mention of it. The city of This and its god Onuris had no position of special significance in the later symbolic geography of Egypt.

51 Wildung, *Die Rolle Ägyptischer Könige*, 4–21; *Lexikon* IV, 46–8. For the Early Dynastic kings, the later lists used alternative names to the Horus names familiar to us from Early Dynastic sources, and there remains a technical problem in equating the two sets for the very first group of kings. Mud seal impressions of the 1st Dynasty from the Umm el-Qaʿab which list successive kings feature the *men*-hieroglyph prominently but not as a royal name Menes, see G. Dreyer, *MDAIK* 43 (1987), 33–43; T.A.H. Wilkinson, *Early Dynastic Egypt*, London and New York, 1999, 62–3, Fig. 3.1.

52 Waddell, *Manetho*, 26–33.

53 For the Narmer year-label, see G. Dreyer, U. Hartung, T. Hikade, E.C. Köhler, V. Müller and F. Pumpenmeier, *MDAIK* 54 (1998), 77–167, 139, Abb. 29; Wilkinson, *Early Dynastic Egypt*, 218–19, Fig. 6.7.

54 T.A.H. Wilkinson, *Royal annals of ancient Egypt*, 85–9, and the general section 60–81, presents the Palermo Stone evidence in some detail, and with appropriate scepticism as to how literally we should take it.

55 The same is true for a single individual of roughly the same period buried at Kubaniya near Aswan: F. Wendorf and R. Schild, *The Wadi Kubbaniya skeleton: a Late Paleolithic burial from southern Egypt*, Dallas, Tex., 1986.

56 J. Vandier, *Manuel d'archéologie égyptienne* I.1. *La préhistoire*, Paris, 1952, chapters X, XI; J. Capart, *Primitive art in Ancient Egypt*, London, 1905; H. Asselberghs, *Chaos en beheersing*, Leiden, 1961; H. Kantor, 'Ägypten', in M.J. Mellink and J. Filip, eds, *Frühe Stufen der Kunst* (Propyläen Kunstgeschichte 13), Berlin, 1974, 227–56; W.M.F. Petrie, *Ceremonial slate palettes and corpus of Proto-dynastic pottery*, London, 1953; W.M. Davis, *Masking the blow; the scene of representation in Late Prehistoric Egyptian art*, Berkeley, Ca., 1992; E.C. Köhler, 'History or ideology? New reflections on the Narmer Palette and the nature of foreign relations in Pre- and Early Dynastic Egypt', in van den Brink and Levy, *Egypt and the Levant*, 499–513.

57 *Lexikon* II, 146–8 ('Feindsymbolik'); VI, 1009–12 ('Vernichtungsritualen'); 1051–4 ('Vogelfang'); M. Alliot, *RdE* 5 (1946), 57–118; H.W. Fairman, 'The kingship rituals of Egypt', in S.H. Hooke, ed., *Myth, ritual and kingship*, Oxford, 1958, 74–104: pp. 89–91; a scene of this kind also occurs in Hatshepsut's temple at Deir el-Bahari in a context which strongly implies a symbolic reference to triumph over hostile forces, E. Naville, *The temple of Deir el Bahari* VI, London, 1908, 8, Pl. CLXIII.

58 B. Williams and T.J. Logan, *JNES* 46 (1987), 245–85, argue that the 'voyage' in tomb 100 is an early portrayal of the royal jubilee (*sed-*)festival, but this barely explains the full range of imagery.

59 W. Kaiser, *ZÄS* 91 (1964), 113–14, Abb. 7; *MDAIK* 38 (1982), 262–9, Abb. 14.

60 The earliest evidence for the pairing of Horus and Seth is almost as ancient, from the reign of King Djer of the 1st Dynasty. In a queen's title 'She who sees Horus and Seth' the king is presented as an embodiment of the two gods (A.H. Gardiner, *JEA* 30 (1944), 59, note).

61 W. Kaiser and G. Dreyer, *MDAIK* 38 (1982), 242–5 discuss the importance of unusually large and well-appointed graves as evidence for the existence of political elites, and draw attention to Petrie's Abadiya cemetery. B. Williams, *Excavations between Abu Simbel and the Sudan frontier, Part 1: the A-group royal cemetery at Qustul: Cemetery L*, Chicago, 1986, publishes an elite cemetery from Lower Nubia (Qustul). For a parallel process taking place in southern Palestine vis-à-vis Egypt, see E. Kansa and T.E. Levy, 'Ceramics, identity, and the role of the state: the view from Naḥal Tillah', in van den Brink and Levy, *Egypt and the Levant*, 190–212.

62 The basic earlier excavation reports are W.M.F. Petrie, *The royal tombs of the First Dynasty* I, London, 1900, and *The royal tombs of the earliest dynasties* II, London, 1901. A thorough re-examination is still in progress, see regular reports by G. Dreyer in *MDAIK* from 1982 onwards, and Dreyer, *Umm el-Qaab* I.

63 The original investigation is reported in E.R. Ayrton, C.T. Currelly and A.E.P. Weigall, *Abydos* III, London, 1904, chapter I. A re-examination of the whole area, reported in D. O'Connor, *JARCE* 26 (1989), 51–86, has established that probably each king of the 1st Dynasty had built an equivalent. The claim that a brick-covered rectangular mound had stood at the centre of the interior space, developed in D.B. O'Connor, 'The status of early Egyptian temples: an alternative theory', in Friedman and Adams, *The followers of Horus*, 83–98, has not been substantiated; see D. O'Connor, 'Pyramid origins: a new theory', in E. Ehrenberg, ed., *Leaving no stones unturned; essays on the ancient Near East and Egypt in honor of Donald P. Hansen*, Winona Lake, Ind., 2002, 169–82, esp. 181–2. The presence of enigmatic large basins is reported in *EA* 19, 2001, 32.

64 Documentation is conveniently summarized in W.B. Emery, *Archaic Egypt*, Harmondsworth, 1961, and discussed by B.J. Kemp, 'Architektur der Frühzeit', in C. Vandersleyen, ed., *Das alte Ägypten* (Propyläen Kunstgeschichte 15), Berlin, 1975, 99–112. Good examples of later funerary architecture which preserve the style of decoration are J.E. Quibell, *The tomb of Hesy*, Cairo, 1913, Pls VIII, IX; L. Borchardt, *Das Grabdenkmal des Königs Ne-user-reʿ*, Leipzig, 1907, Bl. 24; S. Hassan, *Excavations at Giza 1929–1930*, Oxford, 1932, Pls LXI–LXV.

65 The basic publications are C.M. Firth and J.E. Quibell, *The Step Pyramid*, Cairo, 1935; J.-Ph. Lauer, *La pyramide à degrés*, Cairo, 1936. A valuable and detailed summary is J.-Ph. Lauer, *Histoire monumentale des pyramides d'Égypte* I, Cairo, 1962. Some remarkable architectural drawings of the timber and matting architecture prototypes are in H. Ricke, *Bemerkungen zur ägyptischen Baukunst des alten Reiches* I, Zurich, 1944.

66 Unless the stone-built enclosure to the west, the Gisr el-Mudir, is of the 2nd Dynasty, see I. Mathieson, E. Bettles, J. Clarke, C. Duhig, S. Ikram, L. Maguire, S. Quie and A. Tavares, *JEA* 83 (1997), 17–53; J. van Wetering, 'The royal cemetery of the Early Dynastic Period at Saqqara and the Second Dynasty royal tombs', in Hendrickx *et al.*, *Egypt at its origins*, 1055–80, esp. pp. 1069–71.

67 *Lexikon* VI, 873–5 ('Urhügel'); M. Lehner, *The complete pyramids*, London, 1997, 74–5; R. Stadelmann, 'Origins and development of the funerary complex of Djoser', in P. Der Manuelian, ed., *Studies in honor of William Kelly Simpson*, Boston, 1996, II, 787–800. The subject is also considered from an external perspective by C. Scarre, 'The meaning of death: funerary beliefs and the prehistorian', in C. Renfrew and E.B.W. Zubrow, eds, *The ancient mind; elements of cognitive archaeology*, Cambridge, 1994, 74–82, specifically pp. 77–9.

68 Firth and Quibell, *The Step Pyramid*, Pls 15–17, p. 104. J.-Ph. Lauer, *Monuments et Mémoires* (Fondation Eugène Piot) 49 (1957), 1–15; F.D. Friedman, *JARCE* 32 (1995), 1–42; 'Notions of cosmos in the Step Pyramid Complex', in Der Manuelian, *Studies in honor of William Kelly Simpson*, I, 337–51.

69 A.J. Spencer, *JEA* 64 (1978), 52–5.

70 Whether the enigmatic structure at locality 29A at Hierakonpolis has any connection with royal usage of this kind is debatable, see below, p. 148.

71 Frankfort, *Kingship and the gods*, chapter 6; *Lexikon* V, 782–90; Fairman, 'The kingship rituals of Egypt', 83–5; C.J. Bleeker, *Egyptian festivals: enactments of religious renewal*, Leiden, 1967, chapter V; E. Hornung and E. Staehelin, *Studien zum Sedfest*, Geneva, 1974. A.M. Blackman, *Studia Aegyptiaca* I (Analecta Orientalia 17, 1938), 4–9 has interesting comments on one 1st Dynasty depiction.

72 The most explicit early reference occurs on the Palermo Stone in a 1st Dynasty entry (probably for King Den). It shows the double throne dais and accompanies it with the legend: 'Appearance of the King of Upper Egypt, Appearance of the King of Lower Egypt: *Sed*-festival'. See Wilkinson, *Royal annals of ancient Egypt*, 107–8.

3 The dynamics of culture

1 M.C. Jedrej, *Ingessana; the religious institutions of a people of the Sudan–Ethiopian Borderland*, Leiden, New York and Cologne, 1995, chapter 11, 99–115, the quote being from p. 100.

2 Examples of Predynastic villages with distinct huts are Hemmamiya: G. Brunton and G. Caton-Thompson, *The Badarian civilisation and Predynastic remains near Badari*, London, 1928, 82–8, Pl. LXIII; and Merimda Bemi Salama: H. Junker, 'Vorbericht über die fünfte von der Akademie der Wissenschaften in Wien und dem Egyptiska Museet in Stockholm unternommene Grabung auf der neolithischen Siedlung Merimde-Benisalâme vom 13. Februar bis 26. März 1934', *Akademie der Wissenschaften in Wien, Sitzung der philos.-hist. Klasse* vom 25. April, Jahrg. 1934, Nr. X, 118–32: 122, Abb. 1. The Nubian C-group village at Aniba is another potential example: G. Steindorff, *Aniba, Erster Band*, Glückstadt and Hamburg, 1935, 202–15.

3 D. Zahan, *The religion, spirituality, and thought of traditional Africa*, Chicago and London, 1970, 19.

4 C. Renfrew, *The archaeology of cult. The Sanctuary at Phylakopi*. London, 1985, 11–26; C. Renfrew and P. Bahn, *Archaeology; theories, methods and practice*, London, 1991, 358–60. Criticism of this approach is offered by T. Insoll, *Archaeology, ritual, religion*, London and New York, 2004, 92, but this dismissal is in turn open to question, see the review by A. Stevens in *PalArch online journal* (dated 1 January 2005): http://www.palarch.nl/non_scientific/archive.htm.

5   Preliminary reports by G. Dreyer, *MDAIK* 31 (1975), 51–8; 32 (1976), 75–87; 33 (1977), 68–83; and one final report, G. Dreyer, *Elephantine* VIII. *Der Tempel der Satet; die Funde der Frühzeit und des Alten Reiches*, Mainz, 1986. A convenient summary of the early development of the town in general is *Elephantine; the ancient town. Official guidebook of the German Institute of Archaeology, Cairo*, Cairo, 1998.

6   The existence of a tradition that avoided direct images is well attested in the Near East. Judaism is its most famous example but apparently was not unique. See T.N.D. Mettinger, *No graven image? Israelite aniconism in its ancient Near Eastern context*, Stockholm, 1995; T.J. Lewis, *JAOS* 118 (1998), 36–53.

7   Dreyer, *MDAIK* 32 (1976), 78–80.

8   The significance of this object is pointed out in S.J. Seidlmayer, 'Town and state in the early Old Kingdom: a view from Elephantine', in J. Spencer, ed., *Aspects of early Egypt*, London, 1996, 108–27, p. 115. It should not be taken for granted that it came from within the Satet shrine.

9   Both figure in the scenes beneath the Step Pyramid at Sakkara, for example (see Figures 36 and 37, pp. 104 and 106). Baboon and scorpion images were still included amongst the temple furniture of the pyramid of King Neferirkara of the 5th Dynasty at Abusir, see P. Posener-Kriéger, *Les archives du temple funéraire de Néferirkarê-Kakaï (Les Papyrus d'Abousir). Traduction et commentaire*, Cairo, 1976, 87–98.

10 J.E. Quibell, *Hierakonpolis* I, London, 1900; J.E. Quibell and F.W. Green, *Hierakonpolis* II, London, 1902; B. Adams, *Ancient Hierakonpolis*, with Supplement, Warminster, 1974; W.A Fair-servis, *The Hierakonpolis Project, Season January to March 1978. Excavation of the temple area on the Kom el Gemuwia*, Vassar College, Poughkeepsie, N.Y., 1983; W.A. Fairservis, *Excavation of the archaic remains east of the niched gate, season of 1981*, Vassar College, Poughkeepsie, N.Y., 1986; B. Adams, *Ancient Nekhen; Garstang in the City of Hierakonpolis*, New Malden, 1995; Dreyer, *Elephantine* VIII. *Der Tempel der Satet*, 37–46.

11 D.B. O'Connor, 'The status of early Egyptian temples: an alternative theory', in R. Friedman and B. Adams, eds, *The followers of Horus; studies dedicated to Michael Allen Hoffman 1944–1990*, Oxford, 1992, 83–98, has argued that the large enclosure wall around the Hierakonpolis temple is to be dated not, as the original excavator (F.W. Green) thought, to the 18th Dynasty, but to the Early Dynastic Period. Green's view still has much to commend it. Although brick sizes are usually a poor guide to dating, the one chronological marker that does seem to work is that Early Dynastic bricks are relatively small. Green cites dimensions from the west side that are significantly larger than the early norm (Quibell and Green, *Hierakonpolis* II, 23). His carefully drawn sections (Pl. LXXII) also locate the base of these walls, on both east and west sides, at more than 1 metre above the ground on which key early structures stood, amongst them the stone revetment. O'Connor cites in support of his case a section-drawing from the re-excavation of W.A. Fairservis which, in terms of its relative levels, generally corresponds with Green's (by Fairservis's time the lower part of the early revetment was beneath the water-table and unreachable). In this drawing the top 25 centimetres of a deeper stratum (no. 5) of the Old Kingdom, which also buried an earlier wall, rests against the side of the enclosure wall and so, technically, makes the latter earlier. The section is, however, a schematic one that lacks the finesse of fine stratigraphic detail (including foundation trenches, which can be quite narrow). Level 5 as a single undivided deposit does not make stratigraphic sense: there must have been a division within it to correspond to the two superimposed walls. Fairservis himself accepted the 18th Dynasty date, and also included in his list of finds a piece of rim from a decorated faience bowl of a type to be expected in the Middle or New Kingdoms which he found beneath the base of the wall. In truth, the available records from both excavations are not capable of supporting close argumentation. On balance, I find the case for an early date for the large enclosure wall to be a lot weaker than the case for a later date.

12 See D. Arnold, *Der Tempel Qasr el-Sagha*, Mainz, 1979, 22–3, where a Middle Kingdom date for the Hierakonpolis building is preferred.

13 The date of this image is not easily discernable from its style. One scholar has argued for a New Kingdom date, U. Rössler-Köhler, *MDAIK* 34 (1978), 117–25. The archaeological context, however, makes a Middle Kingdom or earlier date more likely.

14 Photographs taken at the time are B.J. Kemp, 'Architektur der Frühzeit', in C. Vandersleyen, ed., *Das alte Ägypten* (Propyläen Kunstgeschichte 15), Berlin, 1975, 99–112, 104, Abb. 1; B. Adams, *Ancient Nekhen*, 60, Fig. 21. The Fairservis re-examination of the area failed to find it again, leading to scepticism that it had ever existed in the form recorded by drawings in Quibell and Green's publication. The photographs show that the drawings are a faithful rendering. A rise in the water-table prevented the Fairservis expedition from reaching the lower part. The upper part must have been robbed of its stone in the intervening years.

15 Quibell and Green, *Hierakonpolis* II, 10, 51, Pls LXVII, LXXII; B. Adams, *Ancient Hierakonpolis, Supplement*, 28–9. The *benben*-stone of Heliopolis had a similar form and perhaps supplied a model, see later in this chapter.

16 Quibell, *Hierakonpolis* I, 6, Pl. II; Quibell and Green, *Hierakonpolis* II, Pl. LXXII; R. Engelbach, *JEA* 20 (1934), 183–4; B. Adams, *Ancient Hierakonpolis, Supplement*, 17.

17 Quibell and Green, *Hierakonpolis* II, 53, Pl. LXXII; Adams, *Ancient Hierakonpolis, Supplement*, frontispiece.

18 One guess is a timber-and-matting shrine of the kind called a *per-wer* ('great house') by the Egyptians, visualized in M. Lehner, *The complete pyramids*, London, 1997, 72–3.

19 W.M.F. Petrie, *Abydos* I, II, London, 1902, 1903; B.J. Kemp, *MDAIK* 23 (1968), 138–55; *GM* 8 (1973), 23–5; *Antiquity* 51 (1977), 186–9; Dreyer, *Elephantine* VIII. *Der Tempel der Satet*, 47–58. For the town which filled another area of the same enclosure, see M.D. Adams, 'The Abydos settlement site project: investigation of a major provincial town in the Old Kingdom and First Intermediate Period', in C.J. Eyre, ed., *Proceedings of the Seventh International Congress of Egyptologists, Cambridge, 3–9 September 1995*, Leuven, 1998, 19–30.

20 Sir R. Mond and O.H. Myers, *Temples of Armant*, London 1940, 29, and the section drawing on Pl. II.

21 A.J. Spencer, *Catalogue of Egyptian antiquities in the British Museum* V, *Early Dynastic objects*, London, 1980, 67, Pl. 55, no. 483.

22 A small factory which actually made these figurines and which dates to the Old Kingdom and possibly into the Middle Kingdom has been found beside the ancient town of Abydos. See M.D. Adams, 'The Abydos settlement', 28.

23 Petrie, *Abydos* II, 7–8, Pl. L.

24 The urban character of much of the enclosure is best illustrated by the excavations reported in M.D. Adams, 'The Abydos settlement'.

25 D. Eigner, 'A temple of the early Middle Kingdom at Tell Ibrahim Awad', in E.C.M. van den Brink, ed., *The Nile Delta in transition: 4th–3rd millennium BC*, Tel Aviv, 1992, 69–77; W.M. van Haarlem, *EA* 18 (2001), 33–5; *EA* 20 (2002), 16–17.

26 A similar plan can be seen, for example, in the building in the south-east corner of the Medamud enclosure, Figure 46, p. 132.

27 W.M. van Haarlem, *JEA* 82 (1996), 197–8; *MDAIK* 54 (1998), 183–5.

28 Dreyer, *Elephantine* VIII. *Der Tempel der Satet*, 54–8. The single most important group is published by H.W. Müller, *Ägyptische Kunstwerke, Kleinfunde und Glas in der Sammlung E. und M. Kofler-Truniger, Luzern*, Berlin, 1964. A further note on date and provenance is provided by W. Needler, *Predynastic and Archaic Egypt in The Brooklyn Museum*, Brooklyn, N.Y., 1984, 261. A further group of early votive figurines has been discovered at the site of Tell el-Farkha in the eastern Nile delta. K.M. Ciałowicz, 'Tell el-Farkha 2001–2002. Excavations at the western *kom*', in S. Hendrickx, R.F. Friedman, K.M. Ciałowicz and M. Chłodnicki, eds, *Egypt at its origins; studies in memory of Barbara Adams*, Leuven, Paris and Dudley, Ma., 2004, 371–88, esp. pp. 384–7.

29 W.M.F. Petrie, *Koptos*, London, 1896; B.J. Kemp, A. Boyce and J. Harrell, *CAJ* 10 (2000),

211–42; B. Williams, *JARCE* 25 (1988), 35–59; L. Baqué-Manzano, *BIFAO* 102 (2002), 17–61.

30   B. Adams, *Sculptured pottery from Koptos in the Petrie Collection*, Warminster, 1986. In view of the circumstances of finding, no clear date can be given to this material, although Petrie claims that Old Kingdom pottery lay in the vicinity. A similar piece was amongst the material found by Petrie at Abydos, see S.P. Harvey, 'A decorated protodynastic cult stand from Abydos', in P. Der Manuelian, ed., *Studies in honor of William Kelly Simpson*, Boston, 1996, I, 361–78. Note the suggested date from a time before the 1st Dynasty.

31   B. Adams and R. Jaeschke, *The Koptos lions* (The Milwaukee Public Museum, Contributions in Anthropology and History 3), January 1984.

32   Modern and ancient references to the hill are collected in W.C. Hayes, *JEA* 32 (1946), 9, note 5.

33   C. Robichon and A. Varille, *CdE* 14, no. 27 (1939), 82–7; D. Arnold, 'Architektur des Mittleren Reiches', in Vandersleyen, *Das alte Ägypten*, 161–3, Abb. 36; D. Arnold, *Der Tempel des Königs Mentuhotep von Deir el-Bahari* I: *Architektur und Deutung*, Mainz, 1974, 76–8; R.H. Wilkinson *The complete temples of ancient Egypt*, London, 2000, 22.

34   C. Robichon and A. Varille, *Description sommaire du temple primitif de Médamoud*, Cairo, 1940; see also the comments by Arnold, *Der Tempel des Königs Mentuhotep*, 76–8.

35   (London 1905), an English translation of a French-language edition published in Brussels in 1904.

36   K. Sethe, *JEA* 1 (1914), 233–6; D. Wildung, *Die Rolle Ägyptischer Könige im Bewusstsein ihrer Nachwelt* I, Berlin, 1969, 52, note 3. Many references are on the Palermo Stone, T.A.H. Wilkinson, *Royal annals of ancient Egypt: the Palermo Stone and its associated fragments*, London and New York 2000.

37   On the history of writing and literacy in ancient Egypt, see J. Baines, *Man* 18 (1983), 572–99; *Antiquity* 63 (1989), 471–82; J.D. Ray, *World Archaeology* 17 (1986), 307–16; P. Wilson, *Sacred signs; hieroglyphs in ancient Egypt*, Oxford, 2003.

38   The most detailed and scholarly of introductions is H. Schäfer (translated and edited by J. Baines), *Principles of Egyptian art*, Oxford, 1974. Others are W. Davis, *The canonical tradition in ancient Egyptian art*, Cambridge, 1989; G. Robins, *Proportion and style in ancient Egyptian art*, Austin, Tex., 1994; G. Robins, *The art of ancient Egypt*, London, 1997.

39   J. Vandier, *Mo'alla; la tombe d'Ankhtifi et la tombe de Sébekhotep*, Cairo, 1950.

40   *Lexikon* IV, 136–140; A. McFarlane, *The god Min to the end of the Old Kingdom*, Sydney, 1995.

41   For this last aspect see R. Germer, *SAK* 8 (1980), 85–7; M. Defossez, *SAK* 12 (1985), 1–4.

42   G. Jéquier, *Le monument funéraire de Pepi II* II, Cairo, 1938, Pls 12, 14; H. Goedicke, *Königliche Dokumente aus dem Alten Reich*, Wiesbaden, 1967, 43, Abb. 4.

43   Petrie, *Abydos* I, 4, Pl. III, no. 48. See also the entry on the Palermo Stone, Wilkinson, *Royal annals*, 138, Fig. 1.

44   J. Baines, *Orientalia* 39 (1970), 389–404; *Lexikon* I, 694–5.

45   J.D.S. Pendlebury, *The City of Akhenaten III*, London, 1951, Pl. IX; N. de G. Davies, *The rock tombs of El Amarna* I, London, 1903, Pls XI, XXXIII; II, London, 1905, Pl. XIX; III, London 1905, Pl. XXX.

46   *Lexikon* I, 680; LD II, Bl. 119.

47   Pyramid Texts, Utterance no. 600. R.O. Faulkner, *The ancient Egyptian Pyramid Texts*, Oxford, 1969, 246; *ANET*, 3.

48   *Lexikon* I, 31.

49   The best general treatment of ancient Egyptian pottery is J. Bourriau, *Umm el-Ga'ab. Pottery from the Nile Valley before the Arab Conquest*, Cambridge, 1981. It is profusely illustrated.

50   A.L. Kelley, *NSSEA* 4, no. 2 (1973), 5–8; R.M. Boehmer, *Archäologischer Anzeiger* 1974, 4, 495–514. Also B. Williams, 'Aspects of sealing and glyptic in Egypt before the New Kingdom', in M. Gibson and R.D. Biggs, eds, *Seals and sealing in the ancient Near East*, Malibu, Ca., 1977, 135–40; J.A. Hill, *Cylinder seal glyptic in Predynastic Egypt and neighbouring regions*, Oxford, 2004.

51 H.G. Fischer, *Metropolitan Museum Journal* 6 (1972), 5–16. Large numbers are published by P. Kaplony, *Die Inschriften der ägyptischen Frühzeit*, Wiesbaden, 1963; and for more, running through the Old Kingdom, P. Kaplony, *Die Rollsiegel des Alten Reichs* II, Brussels, 1981. A convenient selection is in W.M.F. Petrie, *Scarabs and cylinders with names*, London, 1917, Pls I–VII. Dreyer, *Elephantine* VIII. *Der Tempel der Satet*, 94–5, 151, Taf. 57, nos. 449–51 are three faience tablets with similar designs from the Elephantine shrine deposits.

52 W.A. Ward, *JEA* 56 (1970), 65–80.

53 N. Jenkins, *The boat beneath the pyramid; King Cheops' royal ship*, London 1980; P. Lipke, *The royal ship of Cheops*, Oxford, 1984; B. Landström, *Ships of the Pharaohs; 4000 years of Egyptian shipbuilding*, London, 1970, 26–34.

54 G.A. Reisner, *A history of the Giza necropolis II. The tomb of Hetep-heres the mother of Cheops*, Cambridge, Mass., 1955, 23–7, Pl. 5.

55 E.g. N. de G. Davies, *The rock tombs of Sheikh Said*, London, 1901, Pl. XV.

56 Conveniently collected in A. Badawy, *Le Dessin architectural chez les anciens égyptiens*, Cairo, 1948, chapters I and II. Also K.P. Kuhlmann, 'Serif-style architecture and the design of the archaic Egyptian palace ("Königszelt")', in M. Bietak, ed., *Haus und Palast im alten Ägypten/House and palace in ancient Egypt*, Vienna, 1996, 117–37.

57 W.M.F. Petrie, *Abydos* II, London, 1903, Pl. VII, nos. 131, 132; Pl. XI, no. 243; Müller, *Ägyptische Kunstwerke*, A29a–c, A31; Dreyer, *Elephantine* VIII. *Der Tempel der Satet*, 64–5; W. Kaiser, *MDAIK* 39 (1983), 275–8.

58 One should recall the panelled dais in the courtyard of the Early Dynastic palace at Hierakonpolis, Figure 26, p. 82. Some much later representations add this panelling to the sides of the carrying frame (see W. Kaiser, *MDAIK* 39 (1983), 264–5, Abb. 1, 2), but this could well be the kind of decoration derived from the association of ideas that the Egyptians were so fond of.

59 A detailed discussion is provided by W. Kaiser, *MDAIK* 39 (1983), 261–96; also Dreyer, *Elephantine* VIII. *Der Tempel der Satet*, 64–5. The human face with cow's ears which later became a symbol of the goddess Hathor was, in early times, a female divinity called Bat, see H.G. Fischer, *JARCE* 1 (1962), 7–24; *JARCE* 2 (1963), 50–1; *Lexikon* I, 630–2.

60 G. Legrain, *BIFAO* 13 (1917), 1–76.

61 P. Spencer, *The Egyptian temple: a lexicographical study*, London, 1984, 125–30.

62 The remains of the early shrines at Abydos and Hierakonpolis are too incomplete for comparison. At Medamud the provision of two domains is evident in the earliest shrine, but the brick benches in the outer area do not look entirely suitable to be pedestals for the support of canopies for the revealed image.

63 See especially H.G. Fischer, *JARCE* 1 (1962), 12, and note 39.

64 R. Friedman, 'The ceremonial centre at Hierakonpolis Locality HK29A', in J. Spencer, ed., *Aspects of early Egypt*, London, 1996, 16–35; D.L. Holmes, 'Chipped stone-working craftsmen, Hierakonpolis and the rise of civilization in Egypt', in Friedman and Adams, *The followers of Horus*, 37–44. A subsequent further excavation is reported in *Nekhen News* 15, Fall 2003, 4–5.

65 P. Spencer, *The Egyptian temple*, 114–19.

66 A good and representative set of photographs of Edfu temple is in J.-L. de Cenival, *Living architecture: Egyptian*, London, 1964, 147–59. An informative summary of the history and religious activity of the temple is H.W. Fairman, 'Worship and festivals in an Egyptian temple', *Bulletin of the John Rylands Library* 37 (1954), 165–203. Also R.H. Wilkinson, *The complete temples of ancient Egypt*, 204–7.

67 E.A.E. Reymond, *The mythical origin of the Egyptian temple*, Manchester, 1969; C. Rossi, *Architecture and mathematics in ancient Egypt*, Cambridge, 2004, 161–73.

68 E. Naville, *The XIth Dynasty temple of Deir el-Bahari* II, London, 1910, 14–19, Pls XXIII, XXIV.

69 Arnold, *Der Tempel des Königs Mentuhotep*, 28–32, 76–8.

70 R. Stadelmann, *Die ägyptischen Pyramiden: Vom Ziegelbau zum Weltwunder*, Mainz 1985, 229, Abb. 74.

71 *AEL* I, 115–18.

72 E.S. Bogoslovsky, *ŽÄS* 107 (1980), 89–116; C.A. Keller, *JARCE* 21 (1984), 119–29.

73 *Lexikon* III, 145–8; D. Wildung, *Imhotep und Amenhotep – Gottwerdung im alten Ägypten*, Berlin, 1977; *Egyptian saints: deification in pharaonic Egypt*, New York, 1977.

74 *AEL* I, 6–7, 58–61; Wildung, *Die Rolle Ägyptischer Könige*, 102–3; *Lexikon* III, 290, 980–2.

4 The bureaucratic mind

1 Both passages are in Papyrus Chester Beatty IV, see A.H. Gardiner, *Hieratic papyri in the British Museum. Third series: Chester Beatty Gift*, London, 1935, 41. The first passage also occurs in Papyrus Anastasi II and Papyrus Sallier I, see R.A. Caminos, *Late-Egyptian miscellanies*, London, 1954, 51, 317.

2 P. Posener-Kriéger and J.L. de Cenival, *Hieratic papyri in the British Museum. Fifth series: The Abu Sir Papyri*, London, 1968; P. Posener-Kriéger, *Les Archives du temple funéraire de Néferirkarê-Kakaï (Les papyrus d'Abousir)*, Cairo, 1976.

3 A. Fakhry, *The monuments of Sneferu at Dahshur* II. *The Valley Temple, Part I: the temple reliefs*, Cairo, 1961. A detailed study of all Old Kingdom sources of this kind is H. Jacquet-Gordon, *Les Noms des domaines funéraires sous l'Ancien Empire Égyptien*, Cairo, 1962.

4 Posener-Kriéger, *Les Archives*, 565–74; A.M. Roth, *Egyptian phyles in the Old Kingdom; the evolution of a system of social organization*, Chicago, 1991. Note her thought-provoking hypothesis that phyles had originated in prehistoric times as 'totemic clans' and perhaps still retained even in the Old Kingdom something of the nature and status of a guild; also M. Lehner, *The complete pyramids*, London, 1997, 224–5, 233–5.

5 Posener-Kriéger and de Cenival, *Hieratic papyri*, Pl. XXXI; Posener-Kriéger, *Les Archives*, 429–39.

6 On Egyptian mathematics see T.E. Peet, *The Rhind Mathematical Papyrus*, London, 1923; R.J. Gillings, *Mathematics in the time of the Pharaohs*, Cambridge, Mass., and London, 1972; O. Gillain, *La Science égyptienne: l'arithmétique au Moyen Empire*, Brussels, 1927; G. Robins and C. Shute, *The Rhind Mathematical Papyrus*, London, 1987.

7 Favourable comments by the mathematics community surface from time to time, e.g. J. Newman, *The world of mathematics*, New York, 1956, Vol. 1, 169–78; letter in *New Scientist*, 1 December 2001, 101.

8 They actually still exist and attract serious interest, see the end of chapter 7.

9 Rhind Mathematical Papyrus Problem 42.

10 D. Samuel, 'Baking and brewing', in P.T. Nicholson and I. Shaw, eds, *Ancient Egyptian materials and technology*, Cambridge, 2000, 537–76.

11 H.E. Winlock, *Models of daily life in ancient Egypt*, New York, 1955, 27–9, 88, Pls 22, 23, 64, 65.

12 Samuel, 'Baking and brewing', 561, Figs. 22.12, 22.13a.

13 H. Jacquet-Gordon, 'A tentative typology of Egyptian bread moulds', in Dorothea Arnold, ed., *Studien zur altägyptischen Keramik*, Mainz, 1981, 11–24.

14 Peet, *Rhind Mathematical Papyrus*, 112–13; Gillings, *Mathematics*, 128–36.

15 Rhind Mathematical Papyrus Problem 75.

16 But not always, e.g. F.Ll. Griffith, *Hieratic papyri from Kahun and Gurob*, London, 1898, 65, Pl. XXVIa.

17 Experimentally verified at El-Amarna in 1987, see P.T. Nicholson, 'Experimental determination of the purpose of a "box oven"', in B.J. Kemp, ed., *Amarna Reports* V, London, 1989, 241–52.

18 D. Dunham, *Uronarti, Shalfak, Mirgissa*, Boston, 1967, 34–5, Pls XXVII, XXVIII; W.K. Simpson, *JEA* 59 (1973), 220–2; J.P. Allen, *The Heqanakht Papyri*, New York, 2002, 148.

19 Excellent treatments are D. Mueller, *JNES* 34 (1975), 249–63; A. Imhausen, *Historia Mathematica* 30 (2003), 3–16.

20 Rhind Mathematical Papyrus Problem 65, also translated by Imhausen, *Historia Mathematica*, 10.

21 G.A. Reisner, *JEA* 5 (1918), 79–98; A.J. Spalinger, *JAOS* 105 (1985), 7–20.

22 Griffith, *Hieratic papyri*, 45–6, Pls XVI, XVII.

23 An example made much of by B. Lietaer, *The future of money: a new way to create wealth, work, and a wiser world*, London, 2001, cf. the end of chapter 7 of this book.

24 Uronarti tallies: W.K. Simpson, *JEA* 59 (1973), 220–2; see B.J. Kemp, *ZÄS* 113 (1986), 120–36; Polybius: A.P. Gentry, *Roman military stone-built granaries in Britain* (British Archaeological Reports 32), Oxford 1976, 23–4.

25 On this subject and many related issues of land yields, see K. Baer, *JARCE* 1 (1962), 25–45, esp. p. 42. Allen, *Heqanakht Papyri*, 146, 258 follows R.L. Miller, *JESHO* 34 (1991), 257–69, esp. p. 258 in preferring higher caloric values, of 13,340 for wheat and 12,180 for barley.

26 Cited in Kemp, *ZÄS* 113 (1986), 120–36, p. 132; cf. P. Garnsey, *Food and society in Classical antiquity*, Cambridge, 1999, 19–20.

27 W.K. Simpson, *Papyrus Reisner* I, Boston, 1963, 83–5; *Papyrus Reisner* III, Boston, 1969, 13–15. G.E. Kadish, 'Observations on time and work-discipline in ancient Egypt', in P. Der Manuelian, ed., *Studies in honor of William Kelly Simpson*, Boston, 1996, II, 439–49 discusses the rather strict work ethic that these texts reveal.

28 The most comprehensive study remains A.M. Bakir, *Slavery in Pharaonic Egypt*, Cairo, 1952.

29 R.O. Faulkner, *The Ancient Egyptian Coffin Texts*, II, Warminster, 1977, 106–7, Spell 472; H.D. Schneider, *Shabtis: an introduction to the history of ancient Egyptian funerary statuettes*, Leiden, 1977, I, 53–5.

30 S. Quirke, *RdE* 39 (1988), 83–106, esp. 87–90.

31 W.C. Hayes, *A papyrus of the late Middle Kingdom in the Brooklyn Museum*, Brooklyn, N.Y. 1955. The quotation is from p. 64; also translated in R.B. Parkinson, *Voices from ancient Egypt; an anthology of Middle Kingdom writings*, London, 1991, 85, 99–101.

32 G. Goyon, *Nouvelles inscriptions rupestres du Wadi Hammamat*, Paris, 1957, 17–20, 81–5, no. 61; D. Mueller, *JNES* 34 (1975), 256.

33 S.K. Weir, *CAJ* 6 (1996), 150–63; Lehner, *The complete pyramids*, London, 1997, 224–5; *Aeragram*, 7, 1 (spring 2004), 12–13 prefers a lower figure of 4,000 for the labour of cutting and setting the stones.

34 Simpson, *Papyrus Reisner* II.

35 Lehner, *The complete pyramids*, 236–7; M. Lehner, 'Excavations at Giza 1988–1991. The location and importance of the Pyramid Settlement', The Oriental Institute (Chicago), *News and Notes* 135 (Fall 1992), 4–9; D. Roberts, 'Rediscovering Egypt's bread-baking technology', *National Geographic* 187, no. 1 (January 1995), 32–5.

36 S. Nishimoto, S. Yoshimura and J. Kondo, 'Hieratic inscriptions from the quarry at Qurna: an interim report', *British Museum Studies in Ancient Egypt and Sudan* 1 (2002), 20–31 = http://www.thebritishmuseum.ac.uk/egyptian/bmsaes/issue1/nishimoto.html; T. Endo, 'On the daily amount of excavation for the construction of the rock-cut tombs during the New Kingdom period of ancient Egypt', in S. Huerta, ed., *Proceedings of the First International Congress on Construction History, Madrid, 20th–24th January 2003*, Madrid, 2003, II, 812–15.

37 R. Engelbach, *The Aswân obelisk; with remarks on the ancient engineering*, Cairo, 1922, 17–21, Pl. VI.

38 These observations are based upon an unpublished study by the author, plus J. Harrell, *EA* 19 (2001), 36–8.

39 What follows is essentially a summary of the work of the American archaeologist Mark Lehner, for which see *AfO* 32 (1985), 136–58; *MDAIK* 41 (1985), 109–43; *The complete pyramids*, London 1997. I myself have learnt much from long discussions with him on the pyramid plateau itself. Also Z. Hawass, 'The workmen's community at Giza', in M. Bietak, ed., *Haus und Palast im alten Ägypten/House and palace in ancient Egypt*, Vienna, 1996, 53–71.

40 N. Strudwick, *The administration of Egypt in the Old Kingdom: the highest titles and their holders,*

London, 1985, 237–50 covers the duties of the 'overseer of works', and his prime role in managing work-forces employed in a variety of tasks.

41   Reports are available in the series *Aeragram* (Newsletter of the Ancient Egypt Research Associates); also M. Lehner, *JARCE* 39 (2002), 27–74.

42   R. Fletcher, *The limits of settlement growth; a theoretical outline*, Cambridge, 1995, 74, Fig. 4.3; 79, Fig. 4.6. For Lehner's much lower estimate of 4,000 for the labour needed to cut and set the stones of the Great Pyramid see note 33.

43   Lehner, *The complete pyramids*, 238; a full account is N.J. Conard and M. Lehner, *JARCE* 38 (2001), 21–60; also W.M.F. Petrie, *The pyramids and temples of Gizeh*, London, 1885, 34.

44   Abdel-Aziz Saleh, *MDAIK* 30 (1974), 131–54; Lehner, *The complete pyramids*, 239.

45   W.M.F. Petrie, *Gizeh and Rifeh*, London, 1907, 9.

46   K. Kromer, *Siedlungsfunde aus dem frühen Alten Reich in Giseh*, Vienna, 1978. A clarifying review is by K.W. Butzer, *JNES* 41 (1982), 140–1.

5 Model communities

1   C. Rossi, *Architecture and mathematics in ancient Egypt*, Cambridge, 2004; D. Arnold, *Building in Egypt; pharaonic stone masonry*, New York and London, 1991; S. Clarke and R. Engelbach, *Ancient Egyptian masonry*, London, 1930.

2   This is the approach of A. Badawy, *Ancient Egyptian architectural design: a study of the harmonic system*, Berkeley and Los Angeles, Ca., 1965. See the discussion in Rossi, *Architecture and mathematics*, 32–56.

3   To be appreciated by comparing the plans in J.E. Quibell and F.W. Green, *Hierakonpolis* II, London, 1902, Pl. LXXIII with the results of the 1967 and later American excavations, particularly W.A. Fairservis, K.R. Weeks and M. Hoffman, *JARCE* 9 (1971–1972), 7–68, esp. pp. 14–21 and accompanying plans and sections.

4   Still scarcely published. Some information is in B.J. Kemp, *Antiquity* 5 (1977), 185–200, and for Tell Edfu, N. Moeller, *EA* 23 (2003), 7–9; *CAJ* 14 (2004), 262–3. For a part of Abydos see M.D. Adams, 'The Abydos settlement site project: investigation of a major provincial town in the Old Kingdom and First Intermediate Period', in C.J. Eyre, ed., *Proceedings of the Seventh International Congress of Egyptologists, Cambridge 3–9 September 1995*, Leuven, 1998, 19–30.

5   S.J. Seidlmayer, 'Town and state in the Early Old Kingdom: a view from Elephantine', in J. Spencer, ed., *Aspects of early Egypt*, London, 1996, 108–27; W. Kaiser, F. Arnold, M. Bommas, T. Hikade, F. Hoffmann, H. Jaritz, P. Kopp, W. Niederberger, J.-P. Paetznick, B. von Pilgrim, C. von Pilgrim, D. Raue, T. Rzeuska, S. Schaten, A. Seiler, L. Stalder and M. Ziermann, *MDAIK* 55 (1999), 63–236; *Elephantine; the ancient town. Official guidebook of the German Institute of Archaeology, Cairo*, Cairo, 1998.

6   In addition to *Elephantine; the ancient town*, 44–6, see L. Habachi, *Elephantine IV. The sanctuary of Heqaib*, Mainz, 1985; D. Franke, *Das Heiligtum des Heqaib auf Elephantine: Geschichte eines Provinzheiligtums im Mittleren Reich*, Heidelberg, 1994.

7   On population estimates for Egypt over the ages, see K.W. Butzer, *Early hydraulic civilization in Egypt*, Chicago, 1976, 81–92; J.C. Russell, *JARCE* 5 (1966), 69–82; J. A. McCarthy, *Middle Eastern Studies* 12, 3 (October 1976), 1–39; D. Panzac, *Asian and African Studies* (Haifa) 21 (1987), 11–32. There is growing evidence from archaeology that settlements in the Old Kingdom were considerably more numerous than previously thought, and that Butzer's estimate should be increased. Should we double it?

8   For Köbekli (or Göbekli Tepe) see, for example, M. Beile-Bohn, C. Gerber, M. Morsch and K. Schmidt, *Istanbuler Mitteilungen* 48 (1998), 5–78; S. Mithen, *After the ice; a global human history, 20,000–5000 BC*, London, 2003, 65–7, 89–90.

9   G. Soukiassian, M. Wuttmann and D. Schaad, *BIFAO* 90 (1990), 347–58; G. Soukiassian, *EA* 11 (1997), 15–17; G. Soukiassian, M. Wuttmann and L. Pantalacci, *Balat VI. Le Palais des gou-*

verneurs de l'époque de Pépy II. Les sanctuaries de ka et leurs dépendances, Cairo, 2002; A. Minault-Gout and P. Deleuze, *Balat II. Le Mastaba d'Ima-Pépi. Tombeau d'un gouverneur de l'oasis à la fin de l'Ancien Empire*, Cairo, 1992.

10   A.J. Mills, 'Pharaonic Egyptians in the Dakhleh Oasis', in C.S. Churcher and A.J. Mills, eds, *Reports from the survey of the Dakhleh Oasis 1977–1987*, Oxford, 1999, 171–8; 'Another Old Kingdom site in the Dakhleh Oasis', in R. Friedman, ed., *Egypt and Nubia; gifts of the desert*, London, 2002, 74–8; O.E. Kaper and H. Willems, 'Policing the desert: Old Kingdom activity around the Dakhleh Oasis', in ibid., 79–90.

11   W. Helck, *MDAIK* 15 (1957), 91–111; K. Baer, *Rank and title in the Old Kingdom*, Chicago, 1960, 247–73.

12   L. Borchardt, *Das Grabdenkmal des Königs Nefer-ir-ke-Re*, Leipzig, 1909.

13   K.A. Kitchen, *Pharaoh Triumphant: the life and times of Ramesses II, King of Egypt*, Warminster, 1982, 103–9; Farouk Gomaà, *Chaemwese Sohn Ramses' II. und Hoherpriester von Memphis*, Wiesbaden, 1973.

14   Papyrus Chester Beatty IV = P. British Museum 10684, *AEL* II, 175–8.

15   Selim Hassan, *Excavations at Gîza IV. 1932–1933*, Cairo, 1943, 1–62; F. Arnold, *MDAIK* 54 (1998), 1–18. An overview of the evidence for pyramid towns is provided by R. Bussmann, *MDAIK* 60 (2004), 17–39.

16   Primarily G.A. Reisner, *Mycerinus*, Cambridge, Mass., 1931, chapter III; Selim Hassan, *Excavations at Gîza*, adds a further part of the plan.

17   Ahmed Fakhry, *The monuments of Sneferu at Dahshur I. The Bent Pyramid*, Cairo, 1959, 114–17; vol. II, part II. *The Finds*, Cairo, 1961, contains a record of the pottery, largely Old Kingdom in date.

18   What is probably the remains of a much larger town has been located beneath the fields to the east of the pyramid: N. Alexanian and S. Seidlmayer, *EA* 20 (2002), 3–5; N. Alexanian and S.J. Seidlmayer, *MDAIK* 58 (2002), 1–28.

19   W.M.F. Petrie, *Kahun, Gurob, and Hawara*, London, 1890, chapter III; *Illahun, Kahun and Gurob*, London, 1891, chapters II and III; W.M.F. Petrie, G. Brunton and M.A. Murray, *Lahun* II, London, 1923, chapter XIII; A.R. David, *The pyramid builders of ancient Egypt*, London, 1986; S. Quirke, ed., *Lahun studies*, Reigate, 1998.

20   The group discovered by Petrie is fully published in F.Ll. Griffith, *Hieratic papyri from Kahun and Gurob*, London, 1898; many valuable comments on both groups are in U. Luft, 'Toponyms at Lahun', in S. Quirke, *Lahun studies*, 1–41.

21   H.E. Winlock, *Models of daily life in ancient Egypt*, Cambridge, Mass., 1955. For the date, see Dorothea Arnold, *Metropolitan Museum of Art Journal* 26 (1991), 5–48.

22   M. Bietak, 'Zum Raumprogramm ägyptischer Wohnhäuser des Mittleren und des Neuen Reiches', in M. Bietak, ed., *Haus und Palast im alten Ägypten/House and palace in ancient Egypt*, Vienna, 1996, 23–43.

23   A. Badawy, *JARCE* 6 (1967), 103–9.

24   With an area of 12.86 hectares an upper population limit of around 7,000 is fairly assured from comparative data, see R. Fletcher, *The limits of settlement growth; a theoretical outline*, Cambridge, 1995, 74, Fig. 4.3; 79, Fig. 4.6.

25   Luft, *Toponyms*, 15–16.

26   S. Quirke, *RdE* 39 (1988), 83–106, esp. 87–90.

27   Luft, *Toponyms*, 27–8.

28   Griffith, *Hieratic papyri*, 19–24; also the discussion by D. Valbelle, 'Eléments sur la démographie et le paysage urbains, d'après les papyrus documentaires d'époque pharaonique', *Cahier de Recherches de l'Institut de Papyrologie et d'Égyptologie de Lille* 7 (1985), 75–87.

29   The farmer Hekanakht arranged rations for a household of fourteen but this included the dependants of some of the relatives as well as servants, and they might as a whole have been accommodated in more than one house. R.B. Parkinson, *Voices from ancient Egypt; an anthology of*

Middle Kingdom writings, London, 1991, 106; E.F. Wente, *Letters from ancient Egypt*, Atlanta, Ga., 1990, 61; J.P. Allen, *The Heqanakht Papyri*, New York, 2002, 16–17, 107–17. House lists from Deir el-Medina suggest between one and five persons per house. A.G. McDowell, *Village life in ancient Egypt; laundry lists and love songs*, Oxford, 1999, 51–2; D. Valbelle, *'Les ouvriers de la tombe'; Deir el-Médineh à l'époque ramesside*, Cairo, 1985, 57–8, 243–4. The widow Naunakht of the same place had eight children, but some of them were 'workmen' and must have had their own houses: J. Černý, *JEA* 31 (1945), 29–53.

30 J.C. Scott, *Seeing like a state; how certain schemes to improve the human condition have failed*, New York and London, 1998, 76, from a chapter entitled 'Cities, people, and language'.

31 D. Arnold and R. Stadelmann, *MDAIK* 33 (1977), 15–18, Abb. 2; D. Arnold, *MDAIK* 36 (1980), 15–17, Abb. 1; Dorothea Arnold, *MDAIK* 38 (1982), 25–65.

32 J. Wegner, *JARCE* 35 (1998), 1–44; J. Wegner, *MDAIK* 57 (2001), 281–308. The town appears in the tax list of the vizier Rekhmira, Figure 107, p. 307.

33 M. Bietak, *Avaris: capital of the Hyksos: recent excavations at Tell el-Dabʿa*, London, 1996; E. Czerny, *Tell el-Dabʿa* IX. *Eine Plansiedlung des frühen Mittleren Reiches*, Vienna, 1999.

34 A brief illustrated account of *ezba*s can be found in J. Lozach and G. Hug, *L'Habitat rural en Égypte*, Cairo, 1930, 49–52. The authors comment upon the demoralizing effect of the uniformity of those built like barracks, and the attempts by a few enlightened landowners to do better by providing larger individual houses, more widely spaced.

35 J. Lauffray, Ramadan Saʿad and S. Sauneron, *Karnak* V, Cairo, 1975, 26–30, with plan on Fig. 13; J. Lauffray, *Karnak* VI, Cairo, 1980, 44–52; F. Debono, *Karnak* VII, Paris 1982, 377–83; J. Lauffray, *Karnak d'Egypte*, Paris, 1979, 197–209.

36 M. Azim, *Karnak* VI, 153–65.

37 D.B. Redford, *Akhenaten, the heretic king*, Princeton, N.J., 1984, 95–8.

38 J. Jacquet, *Le Trésor de Thoutmosis Ier: étude architecturale*, Cairo, 1983.

39 R. Fazzini and W. Peck, *NARCE* 120 (Winter 1982), 44.

40 J. Śliwa, *MDAIK* 48 (1992), 177–91.

41 Good general histories of ancient Nubia and of Egyptian involvement are W.Y. Adams, *Nubia: corridor to Africa*, London, 1977; B.G. Trigger, *Nubia under the Pharaohs*, London, 1976. The subject is related to more theoretical studies of imperialism in S.T. Smith, *Askut in Nubia; the economics and ideology of Egyptian imperialism in the second millennium BC*, London and New York, 1995.

42 W.B. Emery, H.S. Smith and A. Millard, *The fortress of Buhen: the archaeological report*, London, 1979.

43 H.S. Smith, *The fortress of Buhen; the inscriptions*, London, 1976, 76–8, suggests that the brick temple rebuilt by Amenhetep I outside the citadel was perhaps the building referred to. Buhen also seems to have possessed a mound shrine during the Middle Kingdom, and this also is a candidate for the first Horus temple, see B.J. Kemp, *CAJ* 5 (1995), 45; 43, Fig. 5.

44 D. Arnold and J. Settgast, *MDAIK* 20 (1965), Abb. 2, opposite p. 50.

45 On the difficulties of a modern strategic assessment of these fortresses, see K. Spence, *CAJ* 14 (2004), 267–9.

46 G.A. Reisner and D. Dunham, *Kush* 8 (1960), 16, Plan 2; G.A. Reisner, N.F. Wheeler and D. Dunham, *Uronarti, Shalfak, Mirgissa* (Second Cataract Forts II), Boston, 1967, Section II.

47 *AEL* I, 118–20.

48 G.A. Reisner, D. Dunham and J.M.A. Janssen, *Semna, Kumma* (Second Cataract Forts I), Boston, 1960, Section I.

49 Ibid., Pls 17, 22.

50 Ibid., Section II.

51 J. Vercoutter, *Kush* 14 (1966), 125–32.

52 A.J. Mills, *Kush* 15 (1967), 206, Pl. XXXVIIIb.

53 Marked on the map in J. de Morgan, U. Bouriant, G. Legrain, G. Jéquier and A. Barsanti,

Catalogue des monuments et inscriptions de l'Égypte antique, Series I, Vol. 1, Vienna, 1894, 65; for recent investigations see H. Jaritz, *MDAIK* 43 (1987), 67–74; *MDAIK* 49 (1993), 107–32.

54 W.Y. Adams and H.Å. Nordström, *Kush* 11 (1963), 23; Adams, *Nubia: corridor to Africa*, 183.
55 Ibid., 185.
56 J. Vercoutter, *RdE* 16 (1964), 179–91; *Mirgissa* I, Paris, 1970, 187–9.
57 B.J. Kemp, *ZÄS* 113 (1986), 120–36; Smith, *Askut in Nubia*, 43–7; *JARCE* 28 (1991), 107–32.
58 Smith, *Askut in Nubia*.
59 Kor: J. Vercoutter, *Kush* 3 (1955), 4–19; H.S. Smith, *Kush* 14 (1966), 187–243; Uronarti: Reisner, Wheeler and Dunham, *Uronarti*, 22–31, Pls XV–XIX, Map VI.

6 New Kingdom Egypt: the mature state

1 General discussions of the role of the temple in the society of the New Kingdom and later are J.J. Janssen, 'The role of the temple in the Egyptian economy during the New Kingdom', in E. Lipiński, ed., *State and temple economy in the ancient Near East* II, Leuven, 1979, 505–15; B.J. Kemp, 'Temple and town in ancient Egypt', in P.J. Ucko, R. Tringham and G.W. Dimbleby, eds, *Man, settlement and urbanism*, London, 1972, 657–80; J.H. Johnson, 'The role of the Egyptian priesthood in Ptolemaic Egypt', in L.H. Lesko, ed., *Egyptological studies in honor of Richard A. Parker*, Hanover, N.H., and London, 1986, 70–84.

2 *Lexikon* I, 619–25: 'Barke'.

3 K.A. Kitchen, *JEA* 60 (1974), 168–74; *Pharaoh triumphant: the life and times of Ramesses II, king of Egypt*, Warminster, 1982, 172.

4 G. Legrain, *BIFAO* 13 (1917), 1–76 is still a valuable documentary source on the transport of sacred boat shrines in the New Kingdom and later.

5 B.J. Kemp, 'Fortified towns in Nubia', in Ucko, Tringham and Dimbleby, *Man, settlement and urbanism*, 651–6.

6 J. Jacquet and H. Wall-Gordon, *MDAIK* 16 (1958), 161–75; R. Anthes, *Mit Rahineh 1956*, Philadelphia, Pa., 1965, 72–5, Pls 24–5.

7 See note 34. Another example, at the gate of the temple of Soleb in Nubia, is documented in *Kush* 9 (1961), 186, Fig. 3.

8 E.g. the temple of Khnum at Elephantine, which owned lands somewhere in the north of Egypt, and the temple of Seti I at Abydos, which owned a range of productive resources in Nubia, as the Nauri Decree reveals, see A.J. Peden, *The reign of Ramesses IV*, Warminster, 1994, 69–72, 109–16 for the former; B.G. Davies, *Egyptian historical inscriptions of the Nineteenth Dynasty*, Jonsered, 1997, 277–308 for the latter.

9 K. Baer, *JARCE* 1 (1962), 25–45 provides a good introductory discussion of sources and interpretations relevant to landholding in ancient Egypt. Fundamental for the economy is D.A. Warburton, *State and economy in ancient Egypt; fiscal vocabulary of the New Kingdom*, Freibourg and Göttingen, 1997. Pages 165–9 deal with the Wilbour Papyrus, the main source for landholdings.

10 A.H. Gardiner and R.O. Faulkner, *The Wilbour Papyrus* I–IV, Brooklyn, N.Y., 1941–52; D. O'Connor, 'The geography of settlement in ancient Egypt', in Ucko, Tringham, and Dimbleby, *Man, settlement and urbanism*, London, 1972, 681–98, esp. pp. 690–5; M.D. Adams, 'A textual window on the settlement system in ancient Egypt', in J. Lustig, ed., *Anthropology and Egyptology: a developing dialogue*, Sheffield, 1997, 90–105.

11 A.H. Gardiner, *JEA* 27 (1941), 37–56; J.J. Janssen, *Grain transport in the Ramesside Period*, London, 2004.

12 Discussed in J.-M. Kruchten, *Le Décret d'Horemheb*, Brussels, 1981, 92–3.

13 S. Schott, *Kanais. Der Tempel Sethos I. im Wadi Mia*, Göttingen, 1961, 143–59; *AEL* II, 52–7; B. Davies, *Egyptian historical inscriptions of the Nineteenth Dynasty*, 205–20; KRI (trans.), I, 56–60.

14 W. Helck, *JARCE* 6 (1967), 135–51. The galena mines have been located, and a small and very

crudely built shrine excavated: G. Castel, J.-F. Gout and G. Soukiassian, *ASAE* 70 (1984–5), 99–105; G. Castel and G. Soukiassian, *BIFAO* 85 (1985), 285–93.

15 Warburton, *State and economy in ancient Egypt*, 168–9.

16 J.J. Janssen, *Commodity prices from the Ramessid Period*, Leiden, 1975, 455–9.

17 A.H. Gardiner, *JEA* 27 (1941), 22–37.

18 A.G. McDowell, *Village life in ancient Egypt; laundry lists and love songs*, Oxford, 1999, 231–8; W.F. Edgerton, *JNES* 10 (1951), 137–145, p. 144; P. Vernus, *Affairs and scandals in ancient Egypt*, Ithaca, N.Y., and London, 2003, 50–69; S. Häggman, *Directing Deir el-Medina; the external administration of the necropolis*, Uppsala, 2002, 160–74.

19 T.E. Peet, *The great tomb-robberies of the Twentieth Egyptian Dynasty*, Oxford, 1930, 12, note 1; Häggman, *Directing Deir el-Medina*, 121–2.

20 H.H. Nelson and U. Hölscher, *Work in Western Thebes 1931–33* (Oriental Institute Communications 18), Chicago, 1934, 46–51. A good illustration of how the 'Reversion of Offerings' worked and temple wealth circulated is provided by texts connected with a cult of Amenhetep III at Memphis, see R.G. Morkot, *JNES* 49 (1990), 323–37. It appears amidst the ration disputes at Deir el-Medina, Vernus, *Affairs and scandals in ancient Egypt*, 63–4.

21 J.J. Janssen, *Late Ramesside letters and communications*, London, 1991, 44–6 illustrates a case where lands from the endowment for the cult of Amenhetep III and Queen Tiy, although they had kept their identity to the end of the New Kingdom, had somewhere along the way been added to the estates of the temple of Mut, and one portion was in the process of being transferred again to an estate of the God's Wife of Amun.

22 Pictures of temple magazines and granaries are A. Badawy, *A history of Egyptian architecture: The Empire (the New Kingdom)*, Berkeley and Los Angeles, Ca., 1968, 128–47; N. de G. Davies, *Bulletin of the Metropolitan Museum of Art*, November 1929, Section II supplement, 41–9.

23 U. Hölscher, *The mortuary temple of Ramses III* I, Chicago, 1941, 71–82.

24 BAR III, 113, §274.

25 J.J. Janssen, *Two ancient Egyptian ship's logs*, Leiden, 1961, esp. 101–2; also chapter 7 below.

26 *AEL* I, 215–22.

27 *Lexikon* I, 237–48: 'Amun'; D. Arnold, *Der Tempel des Königs Mentuhotep von Deir el-Bahari* I. *Architektur und Deutung*, Mainz, 1974, 78–80; F. Daumas, *BIFAO* 65 (1967), 201–14.

28 H. Brunner, *Die Geburt des Gottkönigs*, Wiesbaden, 1964. The most easily accessible set of scenes is that of Hatshepsut at Deir el-Bahari, E. Naville, *The Temple of Deir el Bahari* II, London 1896, Pls 47–55. The Amenhetep III texts are translated in W.J. Murnane, *Texts from the Amarna Period in Egypt*, Atlanta, Ga., 1995, 22–7.

29 Naville, *The temple of Deir el-Bahari* III, 1898, Pl. LXI. An account of Hatshepsut's reign is J. Tyldesley, *Hatchepsut, the female Pharaoh*, London, 1996.

30 On Coronation Days in the New Kingdom, see A.H. Gardiner, *JEA* 31 (1945), 25–8; *Lexikon* VI, 532–3.

31 Papyrus Leiden I.350. A.H. Gardiner, *ZÄS* 42 (1905), 12–42, esp. 20–2; C.F. Nims, *Thebes of the Pharaohs: pattern for every city*, London, 1965, 69; B.J. Kemp, *CAJ* 10 (2000), 335–46, p. 339.

32 For Thebes in general see Nims, *Thebes*. Descriptions of Karnak appear in guide books and books on Egyptian architecture, but more detailed treatments are: P. Barguet, *Le Temple d'Amon-Rê à Karnak: essai d'exégèse*, Cairo, 1962; J. Lauffray, *Karnak d'Égypte: domaine du divin*, Paris, 1979.

33 L. Gabolde, 'Les temples primitifs d'Amon-Rê à Karnak, leur emplacement et leurs vestiges; une hypothèse', in H. Guksch and D. Polz, eds, *Stationen; Beiträge zur Kulturgeschichte Ägyptens, Rainer Stadelmann gewidmet*, Mainz, 1998, 181–96.

34 Barguet, *Le Temple d'Amon Rê*, 219–42; C.F. Nims, 'The Eastern Temple at Karnak', in *Beiträge zur ägyptischen Bauforschung und Altertumskunde* 12 (Festschrift Ricke), Wiesbaden, 1971, 107–111; L. Habachi, *Features of the deification of Ramesses II*, Glückstadt, 1969, 20.

35 J. Yoyotte, *Kemi* 14 (1957), 81–91.

36 Barguet, *Le temple d'Amon-Rê*, chapter IV, and pp. 283–99; J. Lauffray, *Kêmi* 19 (1969), 179–218; F. Daumas, *Karnak* VI, Cairo, 1980, 261–84; G. Haeny, *Basilikale Anlagen in der aegyptischen Baukunst des Neuen Reiches*, Wiesbaden, 1970, 7–17, 81–93; Lauffray, *Karnak d'Égypte*, 125–31; G. Björkman, *Kings at Karnak*, Uppsala, 1971, 84–90; G.A. Gaballa and K.A. Kitchen, *Orientalia* 38 (1969), 1–76, esp. 27–8.

37 M. Gitton, *BIFAO* 74 (1974), 63–73; D.B. Redford, *JARCE* 10 (1973), 87–90; R.W. Smith and D.B. Redford, *The Akhenaten Temple Project* I, Warminster,1976, chapter 9.

38 On oracles in ancient Egypt, see J. Černý, 'Egyptian oracles', in R.A. Parker, *A Saite oracle papyrus from Thebes in The Brooklyn Museum*, Providence, R.I., 1962, 35–48; *Lexikon* IV, 600–6; A.G. McDowell, *Jurisdiction in the workmen's community of Deir el-Medîna*, Leiden, 1990. The Hatshepsut text: P. Lacau and H. Chevrier, *Une chapelle d'Hatshepsout à Karnak* I, Cairo, 1977, 92–153; J. Yoyotte, *Kêmi* 18 (1968), 85–91; M. Gitton, *BIFAO* 74 (1974), 63–73. One Deir el-Medina text is fairly explicit in showing that the voice of an oracle was that of a scribe reading aloud from one of two prepared texts which the god's statue had somehow chosen, McDowell, op. cit., 110.

39 *Urk. IV*, 157–62.

40 *Urk. IV*, 837.3; see G. Björkman, *Kings at Karnak*, Uppsala, 1971, 86–7.

41 D.B. Redford, *Akhenaten, the heretic king*, Princeton, N.J., 1984, chapter 7.

42 F. Laroche-Traunecker, *Karnak* VII, Cairo, 1982, 313–38, esp. p. 315.

43 A.H. Gardiner, *JEA* 38 (1952), 20–3; B. Cumming, *Egyptian historical records of the later Eighteenth Dynasty* I, Warminster, 1982, 12.

44 Nelson and Hölscher, *Work in Western Thebes 1931–33*, 24–5.

45 W. Wolf, *Das schöne Fest von Opet*, Leipzig, 1931; *Lexikon* IV, 574–9; The Epigraphic Survey, *Reliefs and Inscriptions at Luxor Temple* 1. *The Festival Procession of Opet in the Colonnade Hall*, Chicago, 1994; R.H. Wilkinson, *The complete temples of ancient Egypt*, London, 2000, 95–8.

46 L. Bell, *JNES* 44 (1985), 251–94.

47 Murnane, *Texts from the Amarna Period*, 230–4; R. Hari, *Horemheb et la reine Moutnedjemet*, Geneva, 1964, 208–16.

48 H.H. Nelson, *JNES* 1 (1942), 127–55.

49 Ibid., 151–5.

50 R. Stadelmann, *MDAIK* 25 (1969), 159–78; B. Lesko, *AJA* 73 (1969), 453–8.

51 G. Foucart, *BIFAO* 24 (1924), 1–209; S. Schott, *Das schöne Fest vom Wüstentale*, Wiesbaden, 1952; Kitchen, *Pharaoh triumphant*, 169; Wilkinson, *The complete temples of ancient Egypt*.

52 W. Murnane, *United with eternity: a concise guide to the monuments of Medinet Habu*, Chicago and Cairo, 1980, 76–7; *Lexikon* III, 1256–8.

53 R. Stadelmann, *MDAIK* 34 (1978), 171–80.

54 R. Stadelmann, *MDAIK* 29 (1973), 221–42. It seems unnecessarily complicated to regard these palaces as only symbolic, housing not the living king during his lifetime but a statue. The latter is the view of R. Stadelmann, 'Temple palace and residential palace', in M. Bietak, ed., *Haus und Palast im alten Ägypten/House and palace in ancient Egypt*, Vienna, 1996, 225–30. The second palace at Medinet Habu was probably built in the late 20th/early 21st Dynasty to act as a priestly residence, see chapter 8, below, pp. 351–3.

55 Murnane, *United with eternity*, 70.

56 Stadelmann, *MDAIK* 29 (1973); B.J. Kemp, *JEA* 62 (1976), 81–99.

57 Kruchten, *Le Décret d'Horemheb*, 162–77, 199–200; 'Rétribution de l'armée d'après le décret d'Horemheb', in *L'égyptologie en 1979: axes prioritaires de recherches* II, Paris, 1982, 144–8; Murnane, *Texts from the Amarna Period*, 239–40.

58 The source material is conveniently listed in E. Hornung and E. Staehelin, *Studien zum Sedfest*, Geneva, 1974, 33–6. See also W.J. Murnane, *MDAIK* 37 (1981), 369–76.

59 W. Stevenson Smith, *The art and architecture of ancient Egypt*, third edition, New Haven, Conn., and London, 1998, chapter 15; W.C. Hayes, *JNES* 10 (1951), 35–56, 82–111, 156–83, 231–42;

B.J. Kemp and D.B. O'Connor, *International Journal of Nautical Archaeology* 3 (1974), 101–36; Waseda University, Architectural Research Mission for the Study of Ancient Egyptian Architecture, *Studies on the Palace of Malqata: Investigations at the Palace of Malqata, 1985–1988*, Tokyo, 1993.

60 The Epigraphic Survey, *The tomb of Kheruef*, Chicago, 1980, Pl. 28, p. 43. It is interesting to note that the earliest depiction of a *Sed*-festival element – the king seated on a high throne beneath a tent – occurs on one of the boats in the Hierakonpolis Painted Tomb, see Figure 25, p. 80. However, we cannot be sure that a *Sed*-festival is meant. In depictions of the Early Dynastic Period and at the Step Pyramid boat imagery is absent.

61 *The tomb of Kheruef*, Pls 56, 57, pp. 59–61.

62 The most important comparative source would have been the king's mortuary temple, of which little now survives. The *Sed*-festival fragments are published in G. Haeny, *Untersuchungen im Totentempel Amenophis' III*, Wiesbaden, 1981, Taf. 40–2. The Soleb temple scenes, LD III, Bl. 83, 84, also contain no reflection of the Kheruef scenes, although the ritual door-knocking is also a new element in the repertoire.

63 *The tomb of Kheruef*, Pls 42, 43, pp. 49–51.

64 A good general review of New Kingdom palaces is in Stevenson Smith, *The art and architecture of ancient Egypt*, chapters 15 and 17; much of the evidence is also included in P. Lacovara, *The New Kingdom royal city*, New York, 1997.

65 As mentioned on the king's boundary stelae, Murnane, *Texts from the Amarna Period*, 83. For a discussion of royal tenting, see B.J. Kemp, *JEA* 63 (1977), 77–8.

66 A.H. Gardiner, ed., *The Wilbour Papyrus* II, Brooklyn, N.Y., and Oxford, 1948, 18; Kruchten, *Le Décret d'Horemheb*, 111–12.

67 R.A. Caminos, *Late-Egyptian miscellanies*, London, 1954, 198–201.

68 Gardiner, *The Wilbour Papyrus* II, 18; W. Helck, *Materialien zur Wirtschaftsgeschichte des Neuen Reiches*, Wiesbaden, 1960–4, II (235).

69 U. Hölscher, *Das Grabdenkmal des Königs Chephren*, Leipzig, 1912, 81–3, 86–7, Bl. XV, Abb. 75; Ahmed Bey Kamal, *ASAE* 10 (1910), 116–17. See also the aerial photograph in H. Ricke, *Der Harmachistempel des Chephren in Giseh* (Beiträge zur ägyptischen Bauforschung und Altertumskunde 10) Wiesbaden, 1970, Frontispiz. A staircase probably belonging to this palace is illustrated in Taf. 3, see p. xii.

70 For preliminary reports, see J.D.S. Pendlebury, *JEA* 17 (1931), 240–3; *JEA* 18 (1932), 143–5; T. Whittemore, *JEA* 12 (1926), 3–12; M. Jones, *JEA* 69 (1983), 15–21; B.J. Kemp and S. Garfi, *A survey of the ancient city of El-'Amarna*, London, 1993, 39–42, Sheet 1.

71 F.G. Newton, *JEA* 10 (1924), 294–8; T. Whittemore, *JEA* 12 (1926), 3–12; H. Frankfort, ed., *The mural painting of El-'Amarneh*, London, 1929, chapter III; K. Spence, *EA* 15 (1999) 14–16.

72 The Central City is published in J.D.S. Pendlebury, *The City of Akhenaten* III, London, 1951; Kemp and Garfi, *A survey of the ancient city of El-'Amarna*, 50–65, Sheets 4 and 5.

73 Maru-Aten: T.E. Peet and C.L. Woolley, *The City of Akhenaten* I, London, 1923, 109–24; A. Badawy, *JEA* 42 (1956), 58–64. For these buildings as a group: B.J. Kemp, 'Outlying temples at El-Amarna', in B.J. Kemp, ed., *Amarna Reports* VI, London, 1995, 411–62.

74 A convenient plan is Badawy, *A history of Egyptian architecture*, 53, Fig. 29; see also D.G. Jeffreys, *The Survey of Memphis* I, London, 1985, 15, 19–20, Fig. 63. A fuzzy outline plan of large parts of Per-Rameses has been recovered by a magnetometer survey, see E. Pusch, *EA* 14 (1999): 13–15.

75 Stevenson Smith, *The art and architecture of ancient Egypt*, 159–61; P. Lacovara, *NARCE* 113 (Winter 1980), 3–11; 129 (Spring 1985), 17–29; 'The Hearst Excavations at Deir el-Ballas: the Eighteenth Dynasty town', in W.K. Simpson and W.M. Davis, eds, *Studies in ancient Egypt, the Aegean and the Sudan: essays in honor of Dows Dunham*, Boston, 1981, 120–4; P. Lacovara, *Deir el-Ballas; preliminary report on the Deir el-Ballas expedition, 1980–1986*, Winona Lake, Ind., 1990; Lacovara, *The New Kingdom Royal City*.

76 B.J. Kemp, *ZÄS* 105 (1978), 122–33.

77 D. Polz, *MDAIK* 42 (1986), 145–66; S. Ikram and A. Dodson, *The mummy in ancient Egypt; equipping the dead for eternity*, London, 1998, 216, 225.

78 A. de Buck, *JEA* 23 (1937), 152–64; also *ANET*, 214–16; A.J. Peden, *Egyptian historical inscriptions of the Twentieth Dynasty*, Jonsered, 1994, 195–210. Y. Koenig, *BIFAO* 101 (2001), 293–314 argues that the apparent trial summary is actually a protection text for the deceased king against acts of the deceased conspirators in the afterlife.

79 W. Spiegelberg, *Rechnungen aus der Zeit Setis I*, Strasbourg, 1896; Helck, *Materialien zur Wirtschaftsgeschichte*, IV, (633)–(41); KRI (trans.), I, 207–30.

80 W.L. Moran, *The Amarna Letters*, Baltimore, Md., 1992 provides a complete translation. A selection is also translated in *ANET*, 483–90; A.L. Oppenheim, *Letters from Mesopotamia*, Chicago 1967, chapter 6. For discussions of the mentality of those who wrote them and the extent to which they grasped a broader political dimension, see R. Cohen and R. Westbrook, eds, *Amarna diplomacy; the beginnings of international relations*, Baltimore, Md., and London, 2000. The rationale of ancient imperialism is not that easy to reconstruct, as is evident from exchange of views by B. Kemp and S.T. Smith in *CAJ* 7 (1997), 123–37, 301–7.

81 A.R. Schulman, *JNES* 38 (1979), 177–93.

82 K.A. Kitchen, *Suppiluliuma and the Amarna Pharaohs*, Liverpool, 1962, 14. A detailed reconstruction of the politics is included in W.J. Murnane, *The road to Kadesh: a historical interpretation of the battle reliefs of King Sety I at Karnak*, Chicago, 1985.

83 The classic case is that of the Inscription of Mes, summarized in Kitchen, *Pharaoh triumphant*, 128–9, and translated in G.A. Gaballa, *The Memphite Tomb-chapel of Mose*, Warminster, 1977, 22–3.

84 See note 81.

85 Moran, *The Amarna Letters*, 51–61 (EA 22), 72–84 (EA 25).

86 Ibid., EA 22.

87 This less familiar aspect of the El-Amarna 'letters' is covered in depth by S. Izreʿel, *The Amarna scholarly tablets*, Groningen, 1997; S. Izreʿel, *Adapa and the South Wind; language has the power of life and death*, Winona Lake, Ind., 2001.

88 A.H. Gardiner, 'The Astarte Papyrus', in S.R.K. Glanville, ed., *Studies presented to F.Ll. Griffith*, London and Oxford, 1932, 74–85; *ANET*, 17–18; P. Collombert and L. Coulon, *BIFAO* 100 (2000), 193–42.

89 *ANET* 129–31; *Lexikon* I, 509–11.

90 EA 23: Moran, *The Amarna Letters*, 61–2.

91 A.J. Spalinger, *War in ancient Egypt: the New Kingdom*, Oxford, 2005; I. Shaw, *Egyptian warfare and weapons*, Princes Risborough, 1991; 'Egyptians, Hyksos and military hardware: causes, effects or catalysts?' in A.J. Shortland, ed., *The social context of technological change; Egypt and the Near East, 1650–1550 BC*, Oxford, 2001, 59–71; A.R. Schulman, *Military rank, title and organization in the Egyptian New Kingdom*, Berlin, 1964; Y. Yadin, *The art of warfare in Biblical lands*, London, 1963 provides a good illustrated summary of Egyptian military technology of the period.

92 Kruchten, *Le Décret d'Horemheb*, 82–95, 164–77; *Lexikon* IV, 135, 'Militärkolonie'; D.B. O'Connor, 'The geography of settlement in ancient Egypt', in Ucko, Tringham and Dimbleby, eds, *Man, settlement and urbanism*, 695. The land at the heart of the dispute in the Inscription of Mes (note 83) provides another example.

93 The military background to the Amarna Period is discussed by A.R. Schulman, *JARCE* 3 (1964), 51–69. On Horemheb's origins, see Schulman, *JARCE* 4 (1965), 55–68, esp. pp. 58–61. Subsequently Horemheb came to be regarded as the inaugurator of a new era, see A.K. Phillips, *Orientalia* 46 (1977), 116–21. For the origins of the 19th Dynasty, see Kitchen, *Pharaoh triumphant*, 15–18; E. Cruz-Uribe, *JNES* 37 (1978), 237–44. A. Kadry, 'The social status and education of military scribes in Egypt during the 18th Dynasty.' *Oikumene* (Budapest) 5 (1986), 155–62 is also valuable.

94 Schulman, *JARCE* 4 (1965), 55–68.

95 G.P.F. Van den Boorn, *The duties of the vizier; civil administration in the early New Kingdom*, London, 1988, 218–28; T.G.H. James, *Pharaoh's people; scenes from life in imperial Egypt*, London, 1984, 66.

96 In a fragmentary tale about the capture of the Palestinian city of Joppa by 'the strong arm of Pharaoh', the capture is actually done by a stratagem that enabled Egyptian soldiers to be smuggled inside; see *ANET*, 22–3.

97 Caminos, *Late-Egyptian miscellanies*, 51, 317.

98 *Lexikon* II, 1241–9; the classic source remains G. Lefebvre, *Histoire des grands prêtres d'Amon de Karnak*, Paris, 1920.

99 D.B. Redford, 'Egypt and Western Asia in the Late New Kingdom: an overview', in E.D. Oren, ed., *The Sea Peoples and their world: a reassessment*, Philadelphia, Pa., 2000, 1–20, esp. pp. 5–6; I. Singer, 'New evidence on the end of the Hittite Empire', in ibid., 21–33, esp. p. 24.

100 C. Aldred, 'More light on the Ramesside Tomb Robberies', in J. Ruffle, G.A. Gaballa and K.A. Kitchen, eds, *Glimpses of ancient Egypt; studies in honour of H.W. Fairman*, Warminster, 1979, 92–9.

7 The birth of economic man

1 An important influence has been that of the economic historian Karl Polanyi; see D.A. Warburton, *State and economy in ancient Egypt; fiscal vocabulary of the New Kingdom*, Freibourg and Göttingen, 1997. S. Quirke, *ZÄS* 118 (1991), 141–9 discusses the issues in terms of the more impenetrable society of the Middle Kingdom.

2 E.g. the Abusir Papyri for the Old Kingdom: P. Posener-Kriéger, *Les archives du temple funéraire de Néferirkarê-Kakaï*, Cairo, 1976; P. Posener-Kriéger, 'Les papyrus d'Abousir et l'économie des temples funéraires de l'Ancien Empire', in E. Lipiński, ed., *State and temple economy in the ancient Near East* I, Leuven, 1979, 133–51; and a subsequently discovered group, P. Posener-Kriéger, *Mélanges Gamal Eddin Mokhtar*, Cairo, 1985, 195–210; *JSSEA* 13 (1983), 51–7; for the Middle Kingdom the Lahun/Kahun Papyri: *ZÄS* 37 (1899), 89–103; F.Ll. Griffith, *Hieratic papyri from Kahun and Gurob*, London, 1898; and Papyrus Bulaq 18: *ZÄS* 57 (1922), 51–68; A.J. Spalinger, *SAK* 12 (1985), 179–241; for the New Kingdom the Memphite palace accounts from the reign of Seti I: W. Spiegelberg, *Rechnungen aus der Zeit Setis I*, Strasbourg, 1896; KRI (trans.), I, 207–30; J.J. Janssen, *Grain transport in the Ramesside Period*, London, 2004; M. Megally, *Le Papyrus hiératique comptable E.3226 du Louvre*, Cairo 1971; *Recherches sur l'économie, l'administration et la comptabilité égyptiennes à la XVIIIe dynastie d'après le papyrus E.3226 du Louvre*, Cairo, 1977; J.J. Janssen, *SAK* 3 (1975), 166–70.

3 A. Badawy, *A history of Egyptian architecture: the empire (the New Kingdom)*, Berkeley and Los Angeles 1968, 119–23, 128–47; B.J. Kemp, *ZÄS* 113 (1986), 120–36.

4 See B.G. Trigger, B.J. Kemp, D. O'Connor and A.B. Lloyd, *Ancient Egypt: a social history*, Cambridge, 1983, 85ff.; B.J. Kemp, 'Temple and town in ancient Egypt', in P.J. Ucko, R. Tringham and G.W. Dimbleby, eds, *Man, settlement and urbanism*, London, 1972, 657–80; J.J. Janssen, *SAK* 3 (1975), 180–2; 'The role of the temple in the Egyptian economy during the New Kingdom', in Lipiński, *State and temple economy*, II, 505–15; H. Goedicke, 'Cult-temple and "state" during the Old Kingdom in Egypt', in ibid. I, 113–31; J.H. Johnson, 'The role of the Egyptian priesthood in Ptolemaic Egypt', in L.H. Lesko, ed., *Egyptological studies in honor of R.A. Parker*, Hanover, N.H., and London, 1986, 70–84.

5 A.M. Roth, *Egyptian phyles in the Old Kingdom; the evolution of a system of social organization*, Chicago, 1991; *Lexikon* IV, 1044: 'Phyle'; P. Posener-Kriéger, *Les Archives*, II, 565–74.

6 As is done for temple organization in D. Kessler, *Die heiligen Tiere und der König*, Teil I, Wiesbaden, 1989, 49, Abb. 2; 288, Abb. 30.

7 J.-M. Kruchten, *Le Décret d'Horemheb*, Brussels, 1981; W.J. Murnane, *Texts from the Amarna Period in Egypt*, Atlanta, Ga., 1995, 235–40. It has also been pointed out that 'The Duties of the

Vizier' text known from several New Kingdom tombs, whilst it has an internal logic of association which enables it to achieve its purpose of profiling the importance of the vizier, lacks the
systematic presentation of the vizier's duties that we ourselves tend to expect of such a text. See
G.P.F. Van den Boorn, *Orientalia* N.S. 51 (1982), 369–81.

8   B.J. Kemp, *CAJ* 5 (1995), 25–54, p. 37.
9   E.g. the autobiography of Weni, *AEL* I, 21; A.A.M.A. Amer, *RdE* 36 (1985), 18–20.
10 N. de G. Davies, *The tomb of Rekh-mi-rē' at Thebes*, New York, 1943, 32–6, 103–6, Pls XXIX–
    XXXV.
11 F.Ll. Griffith, *JEA* 13 (1927), 193–206; B.G. Davies, *Egyptian historical inscriptions of the Nineteenth
    Dynasty*, Jonsered, 1997, 277–308.
12 Ibid., 301.
13 Elephantine: *JEA* 13 (1927), 207–8; Armant: R. Mond and O.H. Myers, *Temples of Armant*,
    London, 1941, 161; Hermopolis: *MDIAAK* 8 (1939), 161–4.
14 H. Goedicke, *Königliche Dokumente aus dem Alten Reich*, Wiesbaden, 1967.
15 E.g. R.A. Caminos, *Late-Egyptian miscellanies*, London, 1954, 17–20, 273–5, 280–93, 325–8,
    454–64.
16 Beni Hasan: J. Garstang, *The burial customs of ancient Egypt*, London, 1907, esp. Pls III, IV; Naga
    ed-Deir: G.A. Reisner, *A provincial cemetery of the Pyramid Age: Naga-ed-Dêr*, Part III, Oxford, 1932;
    D.B. O'Connor, *World Archaeology* 6 (1974), 22–3.
17 Serious political intrigue amongst these locally powerful men is hinted at in the 6th Dynasty
    letter from Elephantine published by P. Smither, *JEA* 28 (1942), 16–19. For the politics of the
    First Intermediate Period, see F. Gomaà, *Ägypten während der Ersten Zwischenzeit*, Wiesbaden,
    1980.
18 For Ankhtify, see J. Vandier, *Moʿalla: la tombe d'Ankhtifi et la tombe de Sébekhotep*, Cairo, 1950;
    W. Schenkel, *Memphis, Herakleopolis, Theben*, Wiesbaden, 1965, 45–57; Gomaà, *Ägypten*, 38–9;
    similar claims by other men of the time are conveniently translated in *AEL* I, 87–90.
19 G. Brunton, *Qau and Badari* I, II, London, 1927, 1928; *Mostagedda*, London, 1937; *Matmar*,
    London, 1948; O'Connor, *World Archaeology* 6 (1974), 24–7; J.S. Seidlmayer, *Gräberfelder aus dem
    Übergang vom Alten zum Mittleren Reich; Studien zur Archäologie der Ersten Zwischenzeit*, Heidelberg,
    1990.
20 Brunton, *Qau and Badari* I, 76.
21 W. Helck, *MDAIK* 14 (1956), 63–75; 24. W. Helck, *Wirtschaftsgeschichte des Alten Ägypten im 3. und
    2. Jahrtausend vor Chr.*, Leiden, 1975, chapter 8. These sources also boast of private provision of
    the same.
22 J.J. Janssen and P.W. Pestman, *JESHO* 11 (1968), 137–70.
23 Caminos, *Late-Egyptian miscellanies*.
24 S.R.K. Glanville, *JEA* 14 (1928), 294–312; T.G.H. James, *Pharaoh's people; scenes from life in
    imperial Egypt*, London, 1984, 172–5; E.F. Wente, *Letters from ancient Egypt*, Atlanta, Ga., 1990,
    90–1, no. 113.
25 H.E. Winlock, *Models of daily life in ancient Egypt*, New York, 1955, Section IV.
26 B.J. Kemp, *World Archaeology* 9 (1977), 123–39; P. Crocker, *JEA* 71 (1985), 52–65; C. Tietze,
    ZÄS 112 (1985), 48–84; 'Amarna, Wohn- und Lebensverhältnisse in einer ägyptischen Stadt',
    in M. Bietak, ed., *Haus und Palast im alten Ägypten / House and palace in ancient Egypt*, Vienna, 1996,
    231–7.
27 *AEL* I, 60.
28 T.E. Peet, *The great tomb-robberies of the Twentieth Egyptian Dynasty*, Oxford, 1930.
29 H. Frankfort and J.D.S. Pendlebury, *The City of Akhenaten* II, London, 1933, 59–61, Pl. XLIII.
    For the Hittite figurine, and a discussion of the circumstances of the find and its significance,
    see M. Bell, *AJA* 90 (1986), 145–51.
30 James, *Pharaoh's people*, 186, and Pl. 11 (top).
31 Wente, *Letters from ancient Egypt*, 146, no. 196.

32 R. Müller-Wollermann, *JESHO* 28 (1985), 121–68, esp. 163–4.

33 P.T. Nicholson and I. Shaw, eds, *Ancient Egyptian materials and technology*, Cambridge, 2000, 59–60; I.M.E. Shaw, 'A survey at Hatnub', in B.J. Kemp, *Amarna Reports* III, London, 1986, chapter 10.

34 Nicholson and Shaw, eds, op. cit., 121–47. See also the suggestive diagram of the sources of raw materials needed for the basic Egyptian industry of faience manufacture in A.J. Shortland, *Vitreous materials at Amarna. The production of glass and faience in 18th Dynasty Egypt*, Oxford, 2000, 145, Fig. 5.15.

35 G. Caton-Thompson and E.W. Gardner, *The desert Fayum*, London, 1934, chapters XXIII–XXVI.

36 *Lexikon* IV, 197–8, 358; cf. J.J. Janssen, *SAK* 3 (1975), 127–85, esp. p. 163; Warburton, *State and economy in ancient Egypt*, 67, quoting Assmann on art and craftsmanship.

37 On foreign trade discussed from an archaeological background see R.S. Merrillees, *The Cypriote Bronze Age pottery found in Egypt*, Lund, 1968, 173f., also 194; B.J. Kemp and R.S. Merrillees, *Minoan pottery in second millennium Egypt*, Mainz, 1980, 276 ff.

38 P.E. Newberry, *Beni Hasan* I, London, 1893, 69, Pls XXX, XXXI, XXVIII, XXXVIII; J.R. Harris, *Lexicographical studies in ancient Egyptian minerals*, Berlin, 1961, 174–6; W. Helck, *Die Beziehung Ägyptens zu Vorderasien im 3. und 2. Jahrtausend v.Chr.*, second edition, Wiesbaden, 1971, 41–2; H. Goedicke, *JARCE* 21 (1984), 203–10; S.H. Aufrère, 'The deserts and the Fifteenth and Sixteenth Upper Egyptian nomes during the Middle Kingdom', in R. Friedman, ed., *Egypt and Nubia; gifts of the desert*, London, 2002, 207–14.

39 J.J. Janssen, *Commodity prices from the Ramessid Period*, Leiden, 1975; James, *Pharaoh's people*, chapter 9. For the stone weights, see D. Valbelle, *Catalogue des poids à inscriptions hiératiques de Deir el-Médineh. Nos. 5001–5423*, Cairo, 1977; M. Cour-Marty, *RdE* 36 (1985), 189–200.

40 Janssen, *Commodity prices*, 9.

41 Ibid., 180–4.

42 Ibid., 292–8.

43 Ibid., chapter 2. Hunger is given as the main reason for some of the Ramesside strikes at Deir el-Medina, P. Vernus, *Affairs and scandals in ancient Egypt*, Ithaca, N.Y., and London, 2003, 63–5; C.J. Eyre, 'A "strike" text from the Theban necropolis', in J. Ruffle, G.A. Gaballa and K.A. Kitchen, eds, *Orbis Aegyptiorum Speculum: glimpses of ancient Egypt: studies in honour of H.W. Fairman*, Warminster, 1979, 80–91. For Libyan raiders as another cause of Theban disruption, see K.A. Kitchen, *RdE* 36 (1985), 177–9.

44 J.P. Allen, *The Heqanakht Papyri*, New York, 2002; K. Baer, *JAOS* 83 (1963), 1–19; James, *Pharaoh's people*, 113–14, 242–7; U. Luft, *Oikumene* (Budapest) 5 (1986), 150–3; Wente, *Letters from ancient Egypt*, 58–63; R.B. Parkinson, *Voices from ancient Egypt; an anthology of Middle Kingdom writings*, London, 1991, 101–7; J. Ray, *Reflections of Osiris; lives from ancient Egypt*, London, 2001, 23–39. For a general approach, C.J. Eyre, 'Peasants and "modern" leasing strategies in ancient Egypt.' *JESHO* 40 (1997), 367–90.

45 K. Baer, *JAOS* 83 (1963), 12; cf. U. Luft, *Oikumene* (Budapest) 5 (1986), 150; Allen, *Heqanakht Papyri*, 179–89.

46 Baer, *JAOS* 83 (1963), 19; Allen, *Heqanakht Papyri*, 19 translates differently.

47 Whether the well-known 'bank' (*mryt*) of Western Thebes where trading and other activities took place was really by the river, or a different kind of place using the word 'bank' metaphorically remains to be determined. See J. Černý, *A community of workmen at Thebes in the Ramesside Period*, Cairo, 1973, 94–7 for the basic references; R. Ventura, *Living in a city of the dead; a selection of topographical and administrative terms in the documents of the Theban necropolis*, Freiburg and Göttingen, 1986, 79–82; A.G. McDowell, *Jurisdiction in the workmen's community of Deir el-Medina*, Leiden, 1990, 220–2.

48 N. de G. Davies, *Two Ramesside tombs at Thebes*, New York, 1927, Pl. XXX; James, *Pharaoh's people*, 250–2, Fig. 25.

49 The jar on the left is fitted with a right-angled drinking tube, particularly used with beer, cf. James, *Pharaoh's people*, 252.

50 C.J. Eyre, 'The market women of Pharaonic Egypt', in N. Grimal and B. Menu, eds, *Le commerce en Égypte ancienne*, Cairo, 1998, 173–91.

51 N. de G. Davies and R.O. Faulkner, *JEA* 33 (1947), 40–6; James, *Pharaoh's people*, 253–6, Fig. 26.

52 Frankfort and Pendlebury, *The City of Akhenaten* II, 19, Pl. XXXIII.3 (House U36.41).

53 A. Moussa and H. Altenmüller, *Das Grab des Nianchchnum und Chnumhotep*, Mainz, 1977, 84–5, Taf. 24, Abb. 10; Müller-Wollermann, *JESHO* 28 (1985), 138ff.; James, *Pharaoh's people*, 254–8, Fig. 27; see also S.I. Hodjash and O.D. Berlev, *Altorientalische Forschungen* 7 (1980), 31–49.

54 For Old Kingdom cattle prices expressed in terms of vases of oil, see B. Vachala, *ZÄS* 114 (1987), 91–5.

55 J.J. Janssen, *OMRO* 58 (1977), 221–32; Janssen, *Commodity prices*, 533–8; E.S. Bogoslovsky, *ZÄS* 107 (1980), 89–116.

56 The various excavators' plans are unified in B.J. Kemp and S. Garfi, *A survey of the ancient city of El-ʿAmarna*, London, 1993.

57 L. Borchardt and H. Ricke, *Die Wohnhäuser in Tell el-Amarna*, Berlin, 1980; S. Lloyd, *JEA* 19 (1933), 1–7; I.M.E. Shaw, *CAJ* 2 (1992), 147–66; D. Arnold, *The royal women of Amarna; images of beauty from ancient Egypt*, New York, 1996, 41–83.

58 S. Ikram, *JEA* 75 (1989), 89–101.

59 A.H. Gardiner, *RdE* 6 (1951), 115–24; Warburton, *State and economy in ancient Egypt*, 136–7.

60 Papyrus Anastasi IV: R.A. Caminos, *Late-Egyptian miscellanies*, London, 1954, 137–8.

61 James, *Pharaoh's people*, chapter 4 covers well the rural ideal that lay so deeply within Egyptian consciousness.

62 For Thutmose see Borchardt and Ricke, *Die Wohnhäuser*, 87–100, Plan 27; R. Hanke, *MDOG* 110 (1978), 43–8; Arnold, *The royal women of Amarna*; for glass and glazing, Shortland, *Vitreous materials at Amarna*; for textiles, B.J. Kemp and G. Vogelsang-Eastwood, *The ancient textile industry of Amarna*, London, 2001, chapter 11. For glazed objects made at Thutmose's workshop see Shortland, op. cit., 171, Fig. 7.15.

63 Kemp and Vogelsang-Eastwood, *The ancient textile industry*, chapter 11 discuss quotas.

64 B.J. Kemp, *Amarna Reports* I–IV, London, 1984–1987.

65 N. de G. Davies, *The rock tombs of El Amarna* I, London 1903, Pls XXV, XXIX, XXXI; V, London 1908, Pl. V; B.J. Kemp, *JEA* 86 (2000), 14–16.

66 J.J. Janssen, *Two ancient Egyptian ship's logs*, Leiden, 1961, 101–4; James, *Pharaoh's people*, 247–8.

67 Papyrus Lansing 6.9–7.1 = Caminos, *Late-Egyptian miscellanies*, 390; cf. Janssen, *Two ancient Egyptian ship's logs*, 103.

68 Caminos, op. cit., 138; also the trader returning from Syria in ibid., 16 = Papyrus Bologna 1094, 5.5–5.6.

69 B. Lietaer, *The future of money: a new way to create wealth, work, and a wiser world*, London, 2001. One inspiration is the writings of Silvio Gessell (1862–1930) on whom even J.M. Keynes looked with favour (pp. 252–3).

8 Moving on

1 Dara: R. Weill, *Dara. Campagnes de 1946–1948*, Cairo, 1958; J. Vercoutter, *CdE* 27 (53) (1952), 98–111; S.J. Seidlmayer, *Gräberfelder aus dem Übergang vom Alten zum Mittleren Reich*, Heidelberg, 1990, 351–2, 403–5. Sakkara South: G. Jéquier, *Tombeaux de particuliers contemporains de Pepi II*, Cairo, 1929; *La pyramide d'Aba*, Cairo, 1935.

2 P.E. Newberry, *El Bersheh* I *(The Tomb of Tehuti-hetep)*, London, 1895, 16–26, Pls XII–XIX.

3 C.C. van Siclen, 'The Mayors of Basta in the Middle Kingdom', in S. Schoske, ed., *Akten des vierten internationalen ägyptologen Kongresses München 1985*, Band 4, Hamburg, 1991, 187–94;

C.C. van Siclen, 'Remarks on the Middle Kingdom palace at Tell Basta', in M Bietak, ed., *Haus und Palast im alten Ägypten/House and palace in ancient Egypt*, Vienna, 1996, 239–46. Several large granite columns have been recovered from the nearby temple and a Middle Kingdom date has been suggested for their manufacture although they bear the names of much later kings. Granite columns are probably not suited to limestone column bases and so they are probably not from the palace; but neither is their pre-New Kingdom date secure. See D. Arnold, 'Hypostyle halls of the Old and Middle Kingdom?', in P. Der Manuelian, ed., *Studies in honor of William Kelly Simpson*, Boston, 1996, I, 39–54.

4   M. Bietak, *Avaris: the capital of the Hyksos: recent excavations at Tell el-Dabʿa*, London, 1996, 21–30.

5   K.S.B. Ryholt, *The political situation in Egypt during the Second Intermediate Period c. 1800–1550 BC*, Copenhagen, 1997, 103–5.

6   N.-C. Grimal, *La stèle triomphale de Pi(ʿankh)y au Musée du Caire JE 48862 et 47086–47089*, Cairo, 1981; *AEL* III, 66–84; A. Spalinger, *SAK* 7 (1979), 273–301. The habit of naming this king Piy rather than Piankhy might not be well founded, see C. Rilly, *BIFAO* 101 (2001), 351–68.

7   Book III, 33–9.

8   J. Leclant, *Montouemhat quatrième prophète d'Amon, prince de la ville*, Cairo, 1961. For the tomb decoration see E.R. Russmann, *JARCE* 31 (1994), 1–19.

9   The relevant parts of the Assyrian annals are translated in *ANET*, 289–301. See also A.J. Spalinger, *JAOS* 94 (1974), 316–28; *Orientalia* 43 (1974), 295–326.

10   R.A. Caminos, *JEA* 50 (1964), 71–101; P. Der Manuelian, *Living in the past; studies in archaism of the Egyptian Twenty-sixth Dynasty*, London and New York, 1994, 297–321.

11   H.E. Winlock, *The Temple of Hibis in El Khārgeh Oasis*, I, New York, 1941; E. Cruz-Uribe, *JARCE* 23 (1986), 157–66; *VA* 3 (1987), 215–30; D. Arnold, *Temples of the last Pharaohs*, New York and Oxford, 1999, 77–9, 103, 113–15, 134.

12   Convenient summaries of the growth and extent of the Persian empire are J. Boardman, N.G.L. Hammond, D.M. Lewis and M. Ostwald, eds, *The Cambridge Ancient History*, second edition, Vol. IV, Cambridge, 1988, 234–53, by A. Fol and N.G.L. Hammond; A. Kuhrt, *The ancient Near East c. 3000–330 BC*, London and New York, 1995, II, chapter 13.

13   N. de G. Davies, *The Temple of Hibis in El Khārgeh Oasis* III. *The decoration*, New York, 1953, Pl. 39; E. Cruz-Uribe, *Hibis Temple Project* I, San Antonio, Tex., 1988, 145.

14   *AEL* III, 33–6.

15   E. Cruz-Uribe, *Saite and Persian demotic cattle documents; a study in legal forms and principles in ancient Egypt*, Chico, Ca., 1985. The quotation is on p. 99, and the redating is remarked upon on p. 126. On continuity in temple economies see E. Cruz-Uribe, *JEA* 66 (1980), 120–6.

16   U. Hölscher, *The excavation of Medinet Habu*, I–V, Chicago, 1934–54, esp. Vol. V, *Post-Ramessid remains*. The detail plans are published in Vol. I, *General plans and views*. The separately coloured phases in this handsome volume are somewhat arbitrary divisions within a more continuous process of alteration and rebuilding in which much of the brickwork of earlier phases was destroyed. There is some scope for recombining the various wall fragments into different groupings. Hölscher, pp. 1–2, summarizes the tragic history of earlier excavation in which much of the interior of the enclosure was handed over to local diggers of *sebakh* working under licence from the government antiquities organization.

17   In the original reports the second palace is also dated to the reign of Rameses III. The evidence of the name of the high priest Rameses-nakht on a threshold and, more especially, the name of the high priest Panedjem I on doorways of the second palace imply rather that the rebuilding had nothing to do with Rameses III but was a conversion and an improvement to serve a new generation of priestly governors of western Thebes. See R. Stadelmann, 'Royal palaces of the late New Kingdom in Thebes', in B.M. Bryan and D. Lorton, eds, *Essays in Egyptology in honor of Hans Goedicke*, San Antonio, Tex., 1994, 309–16. The standing brickwork of the second palace was unfortunately destroyed to its foundations, unrecorded, by an earlier 1912 excavation of T.M. Davis. A convenient summary of the Paser family is *Lexikon* IV, 912: 'Paser'.

18 W.M.F. Petrie, *Nebesheh (Am) and Defenneh (Tahpanhes)*, London, 1888; I.A. Mustafa, 'A preliminary report on the excavation of the E.A.O. at Tell el-Fara'on – "Imet", season 1985–1986', in E.C.M. van den Brink, ed., *The archaeology of the Nile Delta; problems and priorities*, Amsterdam, 1988, 141–9.

19 P. Brissaud, *EA* 16 (2000), 9–11; P. Brissaud and C. Zivie-Coche, eds, *Tanis; travaux récents sur le tell Sân el-Hagar* 2, Paris, 2000, 12–13, Figs. 1–3.

20 The claim at Tell el-Maskhuta that wooden floors were inserted (and that the building was a storeroom) is probably a mistaken interpretation of the ends of wooden beams which were routinely inserted within large walls to reduce the risk of cracking; see J.S. Holladay, *Cities of the Delta* III: *Tell el-Maskhuta*, Malibu, Ca., 1982, 30, Fig. 43. The foundations in question could have been for a temple.

21 D.G. Jeffreys, *The Survey of Memphis* I, London, 1985; W.M.F. Petrie, *Memphis* I, London, 1909, 11, Pl. XXVII; B.J. Kemp, *MDAIK* 33 (1977), 101–8.

22 Tanis: P. Brissaud and C. Zivie-Coche, eds, *Tanis* 1, Paris, 1998, 16, Pl. II; 2 (2000), 59, Fig. 3; Mendes: K.L. Wilson, *Cities of the Delta* II: *Mendes*, Malibu, Ca., 1982; Tell el-Balamun: A.J. Spencer, *EA* 7 (1995), 9–11; *Excavations at Tell el-Balamun 1991–1994*, London, 1996; *Excavations at Tell el-Balamun 1995–1998*, London, 1999.

23 R. Engelbach, *ASAE* 31 (1931), 126–31, pp. 129–31; N. Davies, *Metropolitan Museum Studies* 1 (1929), 233–55, p. 250, Fig. 14.

24 B.J. Kemp, 'Soil (including mud-brick architecture)', in P.T. Nicholson and I. Shaw, eds, *Ancient Egyptian materials and technology*, Cambridge, 2000, 78–103.

25 J.-C. Golvin and El-S. Hegazy, *Cahiers de Karnak* IX (1993), 145–60.

26 K.A. Kitchen, *The Third Intermediate Period in Egypt (1100–650 BC)*, third edition, Warminster, 1995, 268–70, Fig. 1; P. Lacovara, S. Quirke and P.V. Podzorski, 'A Third Intermediate Period fortress at El-Ahaiwah.' *Cahiers de Recherches de l'Institut de Papyrologie et d'Égyptologie de Lille* 11 (1989), 59–68.

27 D. Valbelle, *EA* 18 (2001), 12–14.

28 H.R. Hall, *Babylonian and Assyrian sculpture in the British Museum*, Paris and Brussels, 1928, 44, Pl. XL; mosaic pavement: G. Gullini, *I mosaici di Palestrina*. Rome 1956, Tav. XX; H. Whitehouse, *The Dal Pozzo copies of the Palestrina mosaic*, Oxford, 1976, 17, 18, 46, 47, Figs. 11a, 11b; H. Whitehouse, *The Paper Museum of Cassiano dal Pozzo, Series A, Part 1: Ancient mosaics and wall-paintings*, London, 2001, 108–9; P.J.P. Meyboom, *The Nile Mosaic of Palestrina; early evidence of Egyptian religion in Italy*, Leiden, 1995, 53–5, Fig. 18; A.K. Bowman, *Egypt after the Pharaohs; 332 BC–AD 642*, London, 1986, 184, Fig. 112.

29 Tehna: H. Kawanishi, *Akoris. Report of excavations at Akoris in Middle Egypt 1981–1992*, Kyoto, 1995. El-Hiba: A. Kamal, *ASAE* 2 (1901), 84–91.

30 Brissaud and Zivie-Coche, *Tanis* 2, 59, Fig. 3.

31 P. Brissaud, ed., *Cahiers de Tanis* I, Paris, 1987, 35, Fig. 20.

32 An episode in the Petition of Petiese (Papyrus Rylands IX), translated in F.Ll. Griffith, *Catalogue of the demotic papyri in the John Rylands Library*, Manchester and London, 1909, III, 60–112, and retold in J. Ray, *Reflections of Osiris; lives from ancient Egypt*, London, 2001, chapter 6; and S. Sauneron, *The priests of ancient Egypt*, Ithaca, N.Y., and London, 2000, 17–22.

33 *AEL* III, 38.

34 P. Barguet, *Le Temple d'Amon-Rê à Karnak – essai d'exégèse*, Cairo, 1962, 37; P. Anus and R. Sa'ad, *Kêmi* 21 (1971), 217–38.

35 G. Daressy, *ASAE* 18 (1918), 113–58: p. 148; E. Jelínková-Reymond, *Les Inscriptions de la statue guérisseuse de Djed-her-le Sauveur*, Cairo, 1956.

36 Some barrel-vaulted storage chambers, to which access could be gained only from a roof aperture, were amongst the Late Period buildings at Medinet Habu, and the suggestion was made by the excavator that they had been used for storing grain, Hölscher, *The excavation of Medinet Habu* V, 16, Pl. 24D. They were, however, very small.

37   The most useful treatments are C. Bourdon, *Anciens canaux, anciens sites et ports de Suez*, Cairo, 1925; C.A. Redmount, *JNES* 54 (1995) 127–35. G. Posener, *La Première domination perse en Égypte*, Cairo, 1936, 48–87, 180–9 publishes the Egyptian side of the stelae; for the 'Persian' side, see R.G. Kent, *Old Persian; grammar, texts, lexikon*, second edition, New Haven, Conn., 1953, 111, 147; also F.H. Weissbach, *Die Keilinschriften der Achämeniden*, Leipzig 1911, xxi–xxii, 102–5.

38   Kent, *Old Persian*, 147; Weissbach, *Die Keilinschriften*, 103, 105.

39   G.R. Driver, *Aramaic documents of the fifth century BC*, second edition, Oxford, 1957. On the relationship between demotic and Aramaic for official documents see, e.g. Posener, *La Première domination perse*, 189, n. 3.

40   Translations: A. Cowley, *Aramaic papyri of the fifth century BC*, Oxford, 1923; P. Grelot, *Documents araméens d'Égypte*, Paris, 1972. A detailed study of the community is B. Porten, *Archives from Elephantine*, Berkeley and Los Angeles, Ca., 1968. Also B.A. Ayad, *JNES* 56 (1997), 37–50. The recent archaeological re-investigation of the area is G. Dreyer, H.-W. Fischer-Elfert, C. Heiz, A. Klammt, M. Krutzsch, C. von Pilgrim, D. Raue, S. Schönenberger and C. Ubertini, *MDAIK* 58 (2002), 157–225, esp. 192–7.

41   A convenient translation of the text is *AEL* III, 36–41. See also A.B. Lloyd, *JEA* 68 (1982), 166–80; J. Baines, 'On the composition and inscriptions of the Vatican statue of Udjahorresne', in Der Manuelian, *Studies in honor of William Kelly Simpson*, I, 83–92.

42   It is currently the focus of an archaeological survey: P. Wilson, *EA* 12 (1998), 3–6; 18 (2001), 3–5.

43   W.M.F. Petrie, *Naukratis* I, II, London, 1886, 1888; B. Muhs, *JARCE* 31 (1994), 99–113.

44   A full translation of *Herodotus, The histories* by A. de Sélincourt, revised by J. Marincola, is published in the Penguin Classics Series, Harmondsworth, 1954. A detailed study of Book II, where most of the Egyptian observations are to be found, is the three-volume set by A.B. Lloyd, *Herodotus Book II. Introduction*, Leiden, 1975; *Herodotus Book II. Commentary 1–98*, Leiden, 1976; *Herodotus Book II. Commentary 99–182*, Leiden, 1988. We owe the story of Herodotus at Olympia to the Roman historian Lucian. A convenient presentation is R. Drees, *Olympia: gods, artists and athletes*, London, 1968, 62–3. In general: J. Boardman, *The Greeks overseas*, Harmondsworth, 1964, chapter 4, 'The Greeks in Egypt'.

45   Book II, 154.4.

46   It is possible to see the 'Sea Peoples' in this light, as persuasively argued by R. Drews, *JNES* 59 (2000), 161–90. Also E.H. Cline and D. O'Connor, 'The mystery of the "Sea Peoples"', in D. O'Connor and S. Quirke, eds, *Mysterious lands*, London, 2003, 107–38.

47   Book II, 182; Lloyd, *Commentary 99–182*, 235–41. His near-contemporary Thucydides, Book I, 104–10, mentions in passing a force of 200 Athenian and allied ships which had entered the Nile delta and for a while held most of Memphis and were 'masters of Egypt' during a revolt against Persian rule.

48   Book III, 47.

49   Book II, 180. Lloyd, *Commentary 99–182*, 233 calculates the weight of the alum as 26.196 metric tons, which presumably the Delphians would have sold, using the proceeds for the temple building.

50   Book II, 182; Lloyd, *Commentary 99–182*, 182–91.

51   A.J. Peden, *Egyptian historical inscriptions of the Twentieth Dynasty*, Jonsered, 1994, 212–15; A.J. Spalinger, *War in ancient Egypt*, Malden, Ma., Oxford and Carlton, Victoria, Australia, 2005, 264–77.

52   An interesting exception is K. Jansen-Winkeln, 'Ein Kaufmann aus Naukratis.' *ZÄS* 124 (1997), 108–15. From his extolling of his wealth, the owner of this statue was evidently a merchant, but revealingly from the trading city of Naukratis.

53   Cairo 42231: G. Legrain, *Catalogue général des antiquités égyptiennes du Musée du Caire. Statues et statuettes de rois et de particuliers*, Cairo 1914, III, 75–8.

54   B. Gunn, *ASAE* 27 (1927), 211–37; Der Manuelian, *Living in the past*, 373–80.

55 N. de G. Davies, *The rock tombs of Deir el-Gebrâwi* I, London, 1902, 36–40, Pls XIII–XVI, XXIV; K. Kuhlmann and W. Schenkel, *Das Grab des Ibi; Theben Nr. 36*, Mainz, 1983, 89–90, Taf. 30.

56 L. Borchardt, *Das Grabdenkmal des Königs Sahu-reʿ* II: *die Wandbilder*, Leipzig, 1913, Bl. 1; G. Jéquier. *Le Monument funéraire de Pepi II 2: Le temple*, Cairo, 1938, Pl. 9; M.F.L. Macadam, *The temples of Kawa* II, Oxford, 1955, Pl. IX. The three are illustrated together in B. Kemp, *CAJ* 1 (1991), 242, Fig. 2.

57 The place of the hedgehog and other mammals in ancient Egypt is summarized in D.J. Osborn and J. Osbornová, *The mammals of ancient Egypt*, Warminster, 1998. The place of animals in the belief systems of Predynastic Egypt is being clarified by archaeology, see W. van Neer, V. Linseele and R. Friedman, 'Animal burials and food offerings at the elite cemetery HK6 of Hierakonpolis', in S. Hendrickx, R.F. Friedman, K.M. Ciałowicz and M.Chłodnicki, eds, *Egypt at its origins; studies in memory of Barbara Adams*, Leuven, Paris and Dudley, Ma., 2004, 67–130; D.V. Flores, 'Funerary sacrifices of animals in the Egyptian Predynastic Period', in ibid., 731–63.

58 An authoritative study of animal cults with distribution maps and lists of species is D. Kessler, *Die Heiligen Tiere und der König*, Teil I, Wiesbaden, 1989. It has provided much of the information in the following paragraphs.

59 A. Mariette, *Le Sérapeum de Memphis*, Paris, 1882. Plan (1) at the end marks the course of the avenue.

60 PM, second edition, III, 2, Oxford, 2003, 780–815.

61 H.S. Smith, *RdE* 24 (1972), 176–87.

62 Kessler, *Die Heiligen Tiere*, 17–43.

63 The quotation is from J. Malek, *The cat in ancient Egypt*, London, 1993, 129.

64 For Karnak, see Kessler, *Die Heiligen Tiere*, 193. Kessler (pp. 193, 249) has also envisaged that Medinet Habu was at the centre of a range of animal cemeteries, including a local Serapeum, but supporting evidence is hard to find.

65 A single hippopotamus mummy from Thebes was reported in the nineteenth century, see Kessler, *Die Heiligen Tiere*, 172. According to Herodotus II.71 the hippopotamus was venerated in the town of Papremis near the delta apex but no burials are known. The frogs are from Thebes and from Manfalut, Kessler, op. cit., 20–1, no. 18; 22, 38, no. 35; 169–70.

66 D. Kessler and Abd el-Halim Nur el-Din, *EA* 20 (Spring 2002), 36–8.

67 J. Goudsmit and D. Brandon-Jones, *JEA* 85 (1999), 45–53; *JEA* 86 (2000), 111–19.

68 Kessler and Nur el-Din, *EA* 20 (Spring 2002), 36–8 at p. 38.

69 A radiograph is also in Malek, *The cat*, 131, Fig. 106.

70 This is the main theme of Kessler, *Die Heiligen Tiere*.

71 Most vividly H.S. Smith, *A visit to ancient Egypt; life at Memphis and Saqqara (c. 500–30 BC)*, Warminster, 1974.

72 For example, the dogs which appear to have been buried in the ruins of Akhenaten's city at El-Amarna, for which the main source is J.G. Wilkinson, *Manners and customs of the ancient Egyptians*, London, 1837, Pl. VI, opposite p. 106; also B.J. Kemp and S. Garfi, *A survey of the ancient city of El-ʿAmarna*, London, 1993, 12–15, Figs 2, 3. The bones still lie in small fragments on Pendlebury's dumps at the same site. Many dog bones probably from a similar context were found mixed with disturbed debris in excavations south of the Great Palace carried out in 1999.

73 Ray, *Reflections of Osiris*, chapter 8, 'People of the Serapeum'; *The Archive of Hor*, London, 1976, 130–6. For the Sakkara baboon imported as an oracle see J. Goudsmit and D. Brandon-Jones, op. cit. 2000, 115.

74 G. Lefebvre, *Le tombeau de Petosiris*, Cairo, 1923–4.

75 Kessler, *Die Heiligen Tiere*, 27, 41, no. 94.

76 P. Perdrizet and G. Lefebvre, *Les Graffites grecs du Memnonion d'Abydos*, Nancy, 1919; M. Lidzbarski, *Ephemeris für semitische Epigraphik* III, Giesen, 1915, 93–116, Pls VII–XI; I. Rutherford,

'Pilgrimage in Greco-Roman Egypt: new perspectives on graffiti from the Memnonion at Abydos', in R. Matthews and C. Roemer, eds, *Ancient perspectives on Egypt*, London, 2003, 171–89. Parallels with other cult centres of the time lead one to suspect that somewhere close by – perhaps actually above or in front of the Seti temple, which lies in a hollow easily filled with wind-blown sand – there had once lain a religious complex of the Ptolemaic/Roman Period, probably constructed largely of mud brick. Texts of the time also show that a garrison was stationed somewhere at Abydos, though this could have been at the urban citadel on the site of the ancient town of Abydos lying further to the north. Another function of this now lost complex was to serve the various cemeteries of sacred animals which were scattered across the desert to the rear.

77   Rutherford, *Pilgrimage*, 180; Perdrizet and Lefebvre, *Les Graffites*, 94, no. 528.

78   J.E. Quibell, *Excavations at Saqqara (1905–06)*, Cairo, 1907, 12–14, Frontis., Pls I–VI, XXVI–XXX. Note that by the time the general photographs of the site were taken, Quibell had already removed the plaster sculptures, evidently intending them for the Cairo Museum. The site is included in H.S. Smith and D.G. Jeffreys, *JEA* 64 (1978), 10–21. Interpretations are discussed by G. Pinch, *Votive offerings to Hathor*, Oxford, 1993, 240–1.

79   H. Meyer, *Antinoos: die archäologischen Denkmäler unter Einbeziehung des numismatischen und epigraphischen Materials sowie der literarischen Nachrichten: ein Beitrag zur Kunst- und Kulturgeschichte der hadrianisch-frühantoninischen Zeit*, Munich 1991; R. Lambert, *Beloved and god; the story of Hadrian and Antinous*, London, 1984.

80   W. Till, *Koptische Heiligen- und Martyrerlegenden* II, Rome 1936, 46–81.

81   Even later (*c.* AD 450) and in the same temple is an inscription written in demotic (a very cursive way of writing ancient Egyptian).

82   For Roman Egypt see Bowman, *Egypt after the Pharaohs*; N. Lewis, *Life in Egypt under Roman rule*, Oxford, 1983; D. Frankfurter, *Religion in Roman Egypt: assimilation and resistance*, Princeton, N.J., 1998.

Epilogue

1   A very readable inside view of contemporary Egypt is Galal Amin, *Whatever happened to the Egyptians? Changes in Egyptian society from 1950 to the present*, Cairo and New York, 2000. His judgement is not all bad, but woven into his text is a lament on the rise of materialism and the decline of the virtues of an older patrician society. Many readers could probably write similarly of their own country. I certainly could of mine.

Index